P9-BYM-333

INSIGHT GUIDES

Spain

DISCOVERY CHANNEL

APA PUBLICATIONS
Part of the Langenscheidt Publishing Group
L

Spain

ABOUT THIS BOOK

Editorial
Project Editor
Helen Partington
Managing Editor
Dorothy Stannard
Editorial Director
Brian Bell

Distribution

UK & Ireland
GeoCenter International Ltd
Meridian House, Churchill Way West
Basingstoke, Hampshire RG21 6YR
Fax: (44) 1256 817988

United States
Langenscheidt Publishers, Inc.
36–36 33rd Street 4th Floor
Long Island City, New York 11106
Fax: (1) 718 784 0640

Australia
Universal Publishers
1 Waterloo Road,
Macquarie Park, NSW 2113
Fax: (61) 2 9888 9074

New Zealand
Hema Maps New Zealand Ltd (HNZ)
Unit D, 24 Ra ORA Drive,
East Tamaki, Auckland
Fax: (64) 9 273 6479

Worldwide
**Apa Publications GmbH & Co.
Verlag KG (Singapore branch)**
38 Joo Koon Road, Singapore 628990
Tel: (65) 6865 1600. Fax: (65) 6861 6438

Printing
Insight Print Services (Pte) Ltd
38 Joo Koon Road, Singapore 628990
Tel: (65) 6865 1600. Fax: (65) 6861 6438

©2007 Apa Publications GmbH & Co.
Verlag KG (Singapore branch)
All Rights Reserved
First Edition 1983
Seventh Edition (Revised 2007)

CONTACTING THE EDITORS
We would appreciate it if readers
would alert us to errors or out-
dated information by writing to:
**Insight Guides, P.O. Box 7910,
London SE1 1WE, England.
Fax: (44 20) 7403 0290.
insight@apaguide.co.uk**

NO part of this book may be reproduced,
stored in a retrieval system or transmitted
in any form or means electronic, mechanical, photocopying, recording or otherwise, without prior written permission of
Apa Publications. Brief text quotations
with use of photographs are exempted
for book review purposes only. Information has been obtained from sources
believed to be reliable, but its accuracy
and completeness, and the opinions
based thereon, are not guaranteed.

www.insightguides.com
In North America:
www.insighttravelguides.com

The first Insight Guide pioneered the use of creative full-colour photography in travel guides in 1970. Since then, we have expanded our range to cater for our readers' need not only for reliable and practical information about their chosen des-tination, but also for a real under-standing of the history, people, culture and workings of that destina-tion. Now, when the internet can supply inexhaustible (but not always reliable) facts, our books marry text and pictures to provide those much more elusive qualities: knowl-edge and discernment.

To achieve this, they rely heavily on the combined authority of locally based writers and photographers.

How to use this book

Insight Guide: Spain is structured both to convey an understanding of Spain and its people and to guide readers through its important places of interest:

◆ To understand the country, you need to know about its past. The book's **Features** sec-tion, with a yellow bar, covers the country's his-tory and culture in a series of lively and infor-mative essays.

◆ The **Places** section, with a blue bar, provides a guide to the sights. Places of special interest are coordinated by number with full-colour maps.
◆ The **Travel Tips** section, with a red bar, provides a handy reference for information on travel, hotels, restaurants, etc.

The contributors
The task of coordinating the original team which put together this book fell to **Helen Partington**, assisted by **Liz Clasen** and produced by **Kathleen Wheaton.**

Other contributors to the previous editions include **David Baird, Lisa Beebe, Gil Carbajal, Francisco Conde, Robert Crowe, Andrew Eames, Lucinda Evans, Natalia Far- rán, Muriel Feiner- Graves, Julian Gray, Lindsay Hunt, Ruth MacKay, Vega McVeagh, Eric Robbins** and **John Smith**.

The essay on Spanish painting was reworked by **Caroline Bugler,** while **Ian Chilvers** wrote the feature on Antoni Gaudí.

The **Places** chapters were revised by a team of writers who are based in Spain. **Vicky Hayward** updated the chapters describing Extremadura and Galicia. She also translated the essay on flamenco by **Joaquín San Juan** and updated the **History** chapters along with the late **Mark Little**, who also wrote the feature on gardens, and updated the chapters on the regions known as "Green Spain", along with Seville, Córdoba, Granada and the Andalusian Heartland.

George Semler updated the chapters on Catalonia, Cantabria and Asturias, Aragón, Navarre and the Basque Country. He also wrote and updated the sections on Castilla-La Mancha and Rioja.

Judy Thomson concentrated on Barcelona and revised the story on the Guggenheim Museum (originally written by Roger Williams), while **Nick Inman** updated the chapter on Valencia, having written the story on Spain's festivals.

Pam Barrett brought the Canary Islands fully up to date, and Insight Guides' in-house editor **Tom Le Bas** revised the material on the Balearic Islands.

This updated edition builds on the first and was coordinated and edited by **Sylvia Suddes** in the London office. Thanks also go to to **Penny Phenix** for indexing.

Map Legend

▬ ▪ ▬ ▪	International Boundary
▬ ▬ ▬ ▬	Regional Boundary
⊖	Border Crossing
▬ ▪ ▬ ▪	National Park/Reserve
▬ ▬ ▬ ▬	Ferry Route
Ⓜ	Metro
✈ ✈	Airport: International/ Regional
🚌	Bus Station
🅿	Parking
❶	Tourist Information
✉	Post Office
✝ † ☩	Church/Ruins
†	Monastery
☾	Mosque
✡	Synagogue
🏰 🏯	Castle/Ruins
∴	Archaeological Site
∩	Cave
🗿	Statue/Monument
★	Place of Interest

The main places of interest in the Places section are coordinated by number with a full-colour map (e.g. ❶), and a symbol at the top of every right-hand page tells you where to find the map.

Insight Guide
Spain

CONTENTS

The magical
Alhambra,
Granada

Travel Tips

Insight on ...

Information panels

Places

BIENVENIDO

Spain's remarkable light and stimulating vitality are omnipresent: all else is rich diversity

Spain. To the ancient Greeks, it was the land where Hercules' golden apples grew; to the Arabs, it was the ground floor of heaven; to writers such as George Orwell and Ernest Hemingway, it was an arena where history skittered between heroic feats and tragedy, and bullfighters flirted with death in the work of an afternoon. Few other places so dramatically stimulate the imagination.

Yet despite the steady traffic to and from its coastal resorts, Spain has remained in the eyes of outsiders a mysterious, half-mythical country. Some of the best-known Spaniards are fictional characters: Don Juan, Don Quixote and Carmen. Fiestas and flamenco are alluring not only for their flamboyance but for their undeniable exoticism, with influences from outside Europe.

Spain's long stretches of isolation from the rest of Europe began with her peninsular geography and were underscored by history: 700 years of Moorish occupation were followed by a powerful empire that colonised the New World, the failure of which led via civil war to the oppressive regime of General Franco. But as the traveller who sets out across Spain will discover, hundreds of years of solitude have created a country that is anything but homogeneous. Spaniards have traditionally spoken of their land as *Las Españas*: a notion of plurality embracing four languages and around seven dialects and climates ranging from the subtropical south, sweet with its pomegranates and hibiscus, to the emerald north, with its gorse and heather and plunging fjords.

Your trip will have a couple of constants. One is light: the sunshine northern Europeans flock to bask in, the burnished red-gold that suffuses whole cities, the lunar contrasts of sun and shadow, the light El Greco, Velázquez and Picasso saw and painted by. The other is a tremendous vitality, ubiquitous as the light, which is observed in cafes and strolling Sunday evening crowds, in haughty urbanites and exuberant fiesta crowds, or in the dignified courtesy of a stranger on a country road, who offers to share his lunch with you and enquires after your family.

Of all the Spains you encounter on your Spanish sojourn, surely the most striking and intoxicating is the "new Spain" of post-Francoism: ever more confident democracy, ambitious member of the European Union, a Spain that in just three decades has become an outrageous artist, uncensored journalist, idealistic politician, stage for world events and voracious consumer and producer of news and culture. This Spain is joyfully dispelling a few of the darker old myths, and has given an optimistic glow to the landscapes that await you.   ❑

PRECEDING PAGES: the Picos de Europa massif; olive plantations near Olvera; windmills at Consuegra; Cadaqués, Spain's most easterly resort, the Costa Brava. **LEFT:** a mime artist plays to the tourist crowd, Palma de Mallorca.

Decisive Dates

11th–5th century BC Phoenicians and Greeks land; they establish trading centres and colonies. Invading Celts intermingle with indigenous Iberians.
3rd and 1st century BC Carthaginians conquer southeast Spain. The capture of Sagunto by the Carthaginian general Hannibal leads to the Second Punic War (218–201BC). Rome triumphs and begins its 200-year conquest of Spain (Hispania).
1st century AD Christianity spreads in Spain.
409 Vandals and Barbarians invade from north.
414 Visigoths conquer Swabians and Vandals and

establish a monarchy. They rule Spain as a Christian nation for three centuries, with Toledo as their capital. In 589 Roman Catholicism is adopted as Spain's state religion.
711 Battle of Guadalete: the Muslims invade and conquer the kingdom. They succeed in capturing most of Spain in two years.
722 Battle of Covadonga won by Christians.
756 Córdoba Caliphate established.
1085 Toledo recaptured by Christians.

THE CATHOLIC MONARCHS (1474–1516)
1474 Isabel, wife of Fernando of Aragón, succeeds Henry IV of Castile.
1478 The Inquisition introduced by papal bull.

1479 Fernando becomes King of Aragon; Christian Spain is united under one crown.
1483 Torquemada appointed Grand Inquisitor.
1492 The fall of Granada, the last Muslim stronghold, completes the Reconquest of Spain from Muslims. Expulsion of all Jews who refuse to be baptised. Christopher Columbus "discovers" the New World.
1496 Juana, daughter of Isabel and Fernando, marries Philip, the son of Emperor Maximilian of Austria.
1499 4,000 Muslims baptised at Toledo by order of the Catholic monarchs Fernando and Isabel.
1504 Death of Isabel; Fernando rules in the name of Juana La Loca (Jane the mad) and later as regent for his child grandson Carlos.

HABSBURG RULE 1516–1700
1516 Death of Fernando: his grandson becomes Charles I of Spain; in 1519 he is elected Holy Roman Emperor Charles V, on the death of Maximilian of Austria.
1519 Cortés lands in Mexico.
1521–56 Charles wages war five times against the French; prevents advances of Francois I.
1532 Pizarro lands in Peru.
1556 Felipe II succeeds to the throne.
1561 Capital moved from Toledo to Madrid, which becomes focus for artistic excellence.
1571 Battle of Lepanto against the Turks gives Spain control over the Mediterranean.
1588 Defeat of the Spanish Armada by English destroys Spain as a sea power.
1598 Felipe II dies. He leaves a huge kingdom which, despite wealth from the New World, is debt-crippled after 70 years of war and massive building projects such as the Escorial.
17th century Golden age of art and literature continues under Felipe III, Felipe IV and Charles II, but Spain declines economically and politically.
1609 Expulsion of the Muslims *(moriscos)*.
1618–48 Thirty Years War. Treaty of Westphalia recognises the independence of the Netherlands.
1659 Treaty of the Pyrenees ends war with France. Felipe IV's daughter promised in marriage to Louis XIV.
1667–97 Further wars against France.

BOURBON RULE AND THE WAR OF INDEPENDENCE
1700 Carlos II dies without heir. He wills the crown to Philip of Anjou; this offends Emperor Leopold who supports the claim of his son, Archduke Charles.
1702–14 War of Spanish Succession brings the Bourbon Felipe V to the throne.
1750–88 Carlos III rules; an enlightened despot.
1788 Carlos IV ascends throne; a weakling, he allows

his wife María Luisa and her favourite, Godoy, to rule.

1793 Louis XIV dies; Spain and France at war.

1804 Napoleon is crowned Emperor; Franco-Spanish *rapprochement*.

1805 Spain helps France in war against England. Battle of Trafalgar ends Spanish naval power.

1808 French occupation of Spain. Napoleon arrests Carlos IV and his son Fernando VII and declares King his own brother, Joseph. The Madrid rising heralds the start of the War of Independence (Peninsular War).

1811 Venezuela declares independence, and is followed by other South American republics.

1814 Ferdinand, freed by Napoleon, returns to Spanish throne and reigns as absolute monarch.

19TH-CENTURY: DISPUTES AND DISTURBANCES

1820 Liberal revolt at Cádiz.

1833 Death of Fernando VII. His brother Don Carlos disputes the right to the throne of Fernando's daughter Isabel II, leading to the First Carlist War (1833–39).

1847–49 Second Carlist War.

1872–76 Third Carlist War.

1873 First Spanish Republic declared.

1874 Alphonso XII, son of Isabel, accedes throne. The Bourbon restoration heralds peace.

1898 Cuban independence at end of Spanish-American War; end of Spanish overseas empire.

MONARCHY IN CRISIS, THE REPUBLIC AND CIVIL WAR

1914–18 Spain is neutral during World War I, but faces growing discontent and strikes at home.

1923 General Primo de Rivera sets up dictatorship with the king's agreement. Order restored; opposition increases among working classes.

1930 Primo de Rivera goes into exile; replaced by General Berenguer.

1931 Republicans seize power in Catalonia. Republic proclaimed; some regions granted provincial autonomy.

1933 The Falange group, opposed to regional separation founded by José Antonio Primo de Rivera; right-wing opposition grows; military plot against regime.

1934 Catalonia proclaims its autonomy. Insurrection in the province of Asturias is brutally suppressed.

1936 Popular Front wins elections. General Franco leads rebellion from Morocco. Civil War swiftly follows.

THE FRANCO YEARS

1938 Franco becomes head of Nationalist Government.

PRECEDING PAGES: 16th-century map of Iberia.

LEFT: Fernando and Isabel adorn Salamanca University.

RIGHT: detail from a 19th-century painting of Madrid's bullring by Mañuel Castellano.

1939 Nationalist victory in Civil War.

1941 Franco supports Germany in WWII.

1953 Spain agrees to US bases in exchange for US$226 million of aid.

1955 Spain admitted to United Nations.

1969 Juan Carlos proclaimed heir to throne.

DEMOCRACY, REFORM, MODERNISATION

1975 Franco dies. Juan Carlos becomes king and a democratic state is established.

1982 Socialists sweep into power in elections.

1986 Spain joins NATO and the EU.

1992 Expo '92 in Seville, Olympics in Barcelona.

1996 Conservatives win elections. José María Aznar

becomes Prime Minister following deal with Catalan and Basque nationalists who hold balance of power.

1999 ETA's year-long truce ends. Violence resumes.

2000 Partido Popular (PP) win landslide second term.

2002 Euro replaces Peseta. Oil-spill on NW coastline.

2003 Basque separatist party, Batasuna, banned.

2004 Ten bombs rip through trains in Madrid, killing 191 – an Islamic group is blamed. The General Election is won by Socialists (PSOE), who had been against Spain's involvement in the Iraq war. A Moroccan man is charged with Madrid train bombings.

2005 Car bomb in Madrid injures 40 – ETA blamed. Spain grants amnesty for undocumented immigrants. Referendum approves the EU constitution. Government offers peace talks with ETA if the group disarms. ❑

IBERIA: BEGINNINGS

From the earliest times, foreign invaders came to Spain from beyond the Pyrenees and across the sea. Under the Phoenicians and the Greeks trading flourished

The land now covered by Spain and Portugal is a portion of the former Hercynian continent, which broke apart at Gibraltar sometime before the last Ice Age. Today the southern tip of the peninsula is 13 km (8 miles) from North Africa, but stands somewhat aloof from the main mass of Europe, jutting out into the Atlantic as far west as Ireland, and separated from the rest of the continent by the Pyrenees, whose average height of 1,500 metres (5,000 ft) exceeds that of the Alps.

Among western European countries Spain is second only to France in size, or equal to an area slightly larger than California. Most of her 40 million people live in a few densely populated cities, and her long reaches of unfarmed, uninhabited terrain enhance a sense of vastness and solitude. Traditionally in Spain people have tended to speak of Europe as if it were somewhere else.

Mountain barriers and few rivers

Within this self-contained fragment of land, two geographical facts have helped to shape Spain's history: the presence of mountains and the absence of rivers.

After Switzerland, Spain is Europe's most mountainous country: the average altitude of the peninsula is around 600 metres (2,000 ft). Mountains serve as a barrier to both Atlantic and Mediterranean air currents, dividing Spain into distinct climatic regions. To the north, in the shadow of the Pyrenees, are the wettest provinces; the eastern and southern coasts have a Mediterranean climate; the *meseta,* Spain's vast dry central plateau, suffers searing summer heat and long, bitterly cold winters.

The peninsula was named Iberia – Land of Rivers – by tribes who crossed over from North Africa. To those desert people, Spanish rivers must have looked impressive, although centuries later only two – the Ebro and the Guadalquivir – are still reliably full enough to be useful in

LEFT: shepherds tending their flocks in Aragón.
RIGHT: dolmen near Roses, Costa Brava.

navigation and irrigation. Muslims who settled along the banks of the Guadalquivir praised it to heaven, causing the French author Alexandre Dumas to write indignantly, in 1846: "French writers, never having seen it at all, believed the Arabs. True, Spanish writers could have revealed the less picturesque truth, but since it

is the only river in their country large enough to take a boat, why should they decry it? When we got there we found that between the flat and uninteresting banks rolled a mass, not of water but of liquid mud with the colour and consistency, if not the taste, of milk chocolate."

Chopped up by high, jagged mountains and lacking any unifying waterways, it was perhaps hardly surprising that Spain developed as a handful of linguistic and cultural shards; a land "without a backbone", in the words of philosopher Ortega y Gasset.

However, while Iberia's landscape encouraged internal fragmentation and isolation, her position at the mouth of the Mediterranean made her a natural destination for a succession of migrants, colonisers and traders.

Continental drifters

Until the late 1990s, it was thought that Neanderthal Man arrived in Spain about half a million years ago, following herds of European elephants as they migrated west and south. But remarkable recent finds give new insights into cannibalism and occupations such as toolmaking: fossilised pollen and plants, as well as bone fragments dated *circa* 1.6–1.4 million years BC, unearthed at Atapuerca (Burgos) and Orce (Granada), may cause the existing chronology of climate

and 5,000 years ago, they are similar to African paintings of the era, and presage the powerful influence that continent would have over Spanish culture for the next several thousand years.

Great waves of immigration occurred around 3000 BC, when the Iberians crossed the Strait of Gibraltar and the Ligurians descended the Pyrenees from Italy. In 900 BC, the Celts moved into Spain from France and Britain – then, as now, fleeing the northern winters and seeking the sun.

Celt-Iberians

The word Celt-Iberian, a generic term used to describe all of these groups, does not mean that

changes, the first hominid settlement in Europe and human evolution to be radically rewritten.

Of the abundant prehistoric remains in Spain, the most remarkable are the caves of Altamira on the northern Atlantic coast. There, Stone Age artists painted bison, stags, horses and wild boars some 14,000 years ago. Bones of the depicted animals found on the floor of the caves imply that the paintings served a ritual purpose to ensure good hunting. But their vividness and baffling technical perfection have made them the first chapter in the history of Spanish art. Other cave paintings, showing lively stick figures using bows and arrows, have been found near Valencia. Painted between 10,000

they intermingled much. Territory occupied mainly by the Celts included Asturias, Galicia and Portugal, and the northwestern corner of the peninsula, where numerous forts, or *castros*, have been unearthed. In general, the Celts were known as violent, rustic shepherds who made good mercenaries. Their many and varied contributions to succeeding civilisations on the peninsula included iron implements and trousers.

The Iberians flourished in the south. They lived in walled cities, cremated their dead before burying the ashes, and began exploiting the rich copper deposits around Almería. These people have been characterised as peaceful farmers, who were much more receptive to foreigners and foreign ways than their inland neighbours.

However, the 1st-century Greek geographer Strabo found common traits among all the isolated bands living on the peninsula: hospitality, grand manners, arrogance, indifference to privation and hatred of outside interference in their community affairs. Over the centuries, historians have continued to hold up Strabo's description as a good thumbnail sketch of the Spanish temperament; it still holds good today.

> **NEW TECHNOLOGY**
>
> Greek colonisers introduced the potter's wheel as well as high artistic ideals. Sophisticated Greek ceramic vases were an inspiration to native craftsmen.

El Dorado

The Iberian skill in metallurgy attracted the attention of trading peoples from all over the eastern Mediterranean; it is thought that early Spanish metalwork such as the treasure at Villena (Alicante) taught the world to perceive gold as valuable. In 1100 BC, Phoenician traders discovered Spain's mineral wealth and set up ports of call along the coast, notably at Gadir (Cádiz), which soon became their most prosperous city. The Phoenicians brought the art of fish-salting, the Punic alphabet and music from Tyre to Spain; they left Cádiz so laden that their ships' barrels and anchors were said to be of solid silver.

Another seafaring nation anxious for trade, the Greeks, chanced upon Spain when a Greek ship was carried by a storm to Tartessos, a city that stood somewhere near Málaga. At the time, Tartessos had scarcely been touched by Phoenicians, and the Greeks returned home "with a profit greater than any Greeks before their day", according to one contemporary chronicler. They began to colonise Iberia in the 7th century BC, at Empúries (Girona) and Mainake in the south.

The Greeks made their own contributions to the culture of the already cosmopolitan coast, including wine and a stirring passion for bulls, and had a strong influence on art. The Lady of Elche *(see page 245)*, a haughty stone statue of an Iberian princess carved by an unknown artist 2,500 years ago, is Spain's beloved example of

---

LEFT: Iberian metalwork taught the world to perceive gold as valuable.
RIGHT: the style of dress of the Lady of Elche blends Iberian and Greek styles.

the fusion of Greek and native Iberian style.

Cádiz became a melting pot of Greeks, Phoenicians and native Iberians, and by the 6th century BC the city had acquired a reputation as a rich and sinful place, with tall (three-storey) buildings, millionaires and castanet-clicking dancers. Tartessos, according to the Greeks, was so refined that its laws were written in verse.

Spain eventually worked her way into Greek mythology: the golden apples of the Hesperides

were said to grow there, and it was one of the labours of Hercules to gather them.

Some historians have identified Tartessos as the Tarshish of the Bible, the fabulous source of "gold and silver, ivory, apes and peacocks", where Jonah was headed when he was swallowed by the whale. A case has also been made for placing the lost Atlantis in the vicinity of Cádiz.

The Romans knew the peninsula as Hispania, which is rooted in a Semitic word meaning "remote, hidden". This western land loomed large in the Mediterranean imagination, and before long it became a target of conquest as well as trade. ❑

ROMANS AND VISIGOTHS

Spain became the most advanced of the Roman Empire's provinces. After 300 years of Visigoth rule as a Christian nation, it was conquered by the Muslims

The future of the Iberian peninsula was to be decided by Carthage and Rome as these two great powers jockeyed for military and economic supremacy in the western Mediterranean. Defeated by the Romans in 241 BC during the First Punic War and then driven out of the island of Sicily, the Carthaginians bided their time in their North African base rebuilding their armies and preparing for war.

The battle for the peninsula

Carthage made its move into Spain under Hamilcar Barca. With a vastly superior army, Hamilcar took over most of Andalusia, burning Tartessos to the ground in the process. He then proceeded up the Valencian coast, defeating those Iberian settlements foolish enough to oppose him.

To bolster the Carthaginian war machine, native Iberians were either drafted into the army or were forced to work as slaves in the gold and silver mines. Hamilcar set about fortifying Carthage's coastal settlements on the peninsula: Barcelona is named after Hamilcar Barca; the second Carthaginian city became Carthago Novo, today's Cartagena.

After Hamilcar's death, his son Hannibal, steeped in his father's hatred of the Romans, led his 60,000-man army out of Carthago Novo and headed northwards to the Pyrenees. As he took his troops up the coast, he made alliances with groups of Celts and Iberians who contributed money and manpower to his army. With his now legendary band of war elephants, Hannibal crossed into France, headed over the treacherous Alps, and swept down towards Rome from the north. In 216 BC he confronted and routed a far larger Roman army at Cannae.

But total victory was to elude Hannibal; for the next 13 years his troops moved up and down Italy, never able to defeat the Romans

once and for all. The Romans captured his brother-in-law, Hasdrubal, and in a morale-crushing gesture tossed his head into Hannibal's camp. Hannibal stayed on in Italy for four more years and was finally forced to return to North Africa in 203 BC. A year later, he was soundly defeated in battle near Carthage.

During this period Rome also had to contend with the Carthaginian base on the Iberian peninsula. In 218 BC, Publius Scipio had landed at Empúries with an expeditionary force. For several years he fought the Carthaginians and finally, in 209 BC, he captured Carthago Novo. But there were more furious battles before Scipio's army overran Gadir (Cádiz) in 206 BC, banishing Carthage for ever.

The Roman conquest

It took the Romans only seven years to subdue Gaul, but the conquest of Hispania (Spain) dragged on for nearly two centuries. The Spanish wars depleted the Roman treasury and

LEFT: statue of a Roman woman. Roman occupation of Spain lasted some seven centuries.
RIGHT: Roman mosaic in Segóbriga, showing the days of the week.

forced the army to adopt conscription, because nobody wanted to fight in Spain. The Phoenicians and the Greeks, who came to the peninsula as traders, had found the natives to be courteous, but the invading Carthaginians and Romans encountered ferocious warriors. The Romans in Spain also had the disadvantage of overextended communications. The countryside over which they marched was hot and bleak, with little water or fodder.

The natives, on the other hand, accustomed to the harsh climate and to deprivation, defended their territory desperately. However, Celto-Iberian patriotism did not extend beyond city walls, and tribes often betrayed each other to the Romans. The Iberian lack of unity slowed Rome's conquest, since each Roman victory was simply a triumph over an isolated area.

The last stage of the Roman conquest was the Cantabrian War (29–19 BC). Seven Roman legions were forced to participate, and Augustus himself was called in to lead the final campaign in the Cantabrian Mountains. So defiant were the Cantabrians that they continued to struggle against their conquerors even after their leaders had been nailed on crosses by the Romans. Rome finally established a *Pax Romana* in 19 BC, under the reign of Augustus.

THE STUFF OF LEGEND

It took the Romans 200 years to conquer Spain, largely because of the fierce opposition they met from the native people. The most dramatic resistance was by Numancia, a city of 4,000 inhabitants situated in Soria Province. It took a 60,000-strong Roman army several years to subdue the town and, in the final siege, the few citizens who had not perished through disease or cannabalism hurled themselves into the flames of their burning homes rather than submit to Roman domination.

This battle took on symbolic value, and was invoked centuries later to spur Spaniards to defend their home against invaders.

Life under the Romans

During the rule of Caesar, Latin became the unifying language on the Iberian peninsula and Roman law and customs were quickly adopted. As the Carthaginians had discovered much earlier, Hispania was rich in mineral wealth and provided Rome with a seemingly endless supply of gold and silver. Also rich in livestock and agricultural goods, particularly fruit and vegetables, it became one of the wealthiest, and thus most exploited, provinces of the empire.

The extension of citizenship proved decisive in the Romanisation of Spain. At first, only colonists of Roman or Italian origin were granted citizenship. Though full citizenship was not granted to all Celto-Iberians until the Edict of Vespasian (AD 74), initial attempts to include the native population in the greater Roman Empire went a long way to establish at least the appearance of cultural cohesiveness on the peninsula.

Along with language and customs came religion: Christianity entered Spain in the 1st century AD, during the reign of Nero. It is generally believed that St Paul visited Spain – possibly Aragón – around AD 63–67, and St James, one of Christ's disciples, is said to have preached the gospel in Spain. The Roman resistance to Christianity, however, led to the per-

Constantine's reign (AD 325), but it was only under Theodosius I (AD 379–395) – who was born in Spain – that Christianity became the one accepted religion in the Roman Empire.

The influence of Roman civilisation on the peninsula was enormous, particularly in the fields of construction and architecture. Roman aqueducts, bridges, roads and walls are still in use throughout Spain. Segovia's two-tiered aqueduct is among the most perfect structures of its kind. Tarragona, just south of Barcelona, still has a three-tiered aqueduct, circus vaults and an amphitheatre, all in mint condition. The well-preserved Roman theatre in Mérida is still

secution, torture and the eventual martyrdom of many Spaniards.

Early church history in Spain is full of tales of tortured bodies redeemed by eventual sainthood. The hymns of Prudentius (AD 348–405) bring to light the tortures – no details spared – that these early Christian martyrs endured.

Yet despite persecution, Christian communities began to flourish on the peninsula. Spain was predominantly Christian by the time of

used for staging classical dramas. Carmona has a Roman cemetery, Cartagena a theatre and the remains of mausoleums can be found in Fabara, Jumilla, Tarragona and elsewhere.

In literature and philosophy, the Roman occupation gave rise to Spain's Silver Age. Notable figures born in Spain include the Cordoban philosopher Seneca, whose Stoical ideals have had a marked effect on the Spanish character; the agriculturalist Columela; the historian and poet Lucan; the poet Martial; and Quintilian, the master rhetorician who later became the teacher of Pliny and Tacitus. These men were all trained in the Latin schools of rhetoric and spent most of their lives in Rome

LEFT: Mérida's Roman theatre is used today to stage classical productions.
ABOVE: detail on a Roman sarcophagus in the Alcázar museum in Córdoba.

penning works for Italian audiences. Only in the later work of Martial, after he had left Rome – escaping "the togas stinking of purple dye and the conversation of haughty widows" – and retired to his native Aragón, do we find verses that reflect the Spanish landscape.

Vandalism

By the 5th century, the Roman empire was in decline throughout southern Europe. The Visigoths, a warlike Germanic race under the leadership of Alaric, crossed the Alps in 401 and nine years later sacked Rome. Tribes of Seubians, Vandals and Alans swept across the Pyrenees

into Spain, and proved too numerous for the private armies of Spanish landowners. Notoriously barbaric and ruthless (the word "vandalism" can be traced to the Vandals), the warriors looted and killed as they went, effectively ending five centuries of prosperous Roman rule.

The occupation of Hispania by these Germanic tribes was almost complete by 415. Alliances were forged and power shared, until the Visigoths invaded from Gaul and established their own dynasty on the peninsula. Oddly enough, these barbarian invaders had at one time been Romanised – after having served the Romans as allies and mercenaries – so this new conquest initially brought about few changes. The

Visigoths established military rule yet permitted local culture with separate political and administrative structures, laws and religion. In theory the Hispano-Romans had their own sovereigns, and their lives proceeded so independently that marriage with Visigoths was not allowed until the reign of Leovigild (568–584).

King Leovigild did more than any other Visigothic king to unite the peninsula. Militarily, he subjugated the Basques in the north, conquered the Seubians who had managed to keep an independent kingdom in Galicia, and recovered Baetica (later to become Andalusia) from Byzantine control. He allowed Latin to become

EARLY ANTI-SEMITISM

Blame for the numerous plots that threatened the Visigothic monarchy often fell upon the Jews, who had emigrated to Hispania primarily during the reign of Hadrian (AD 117–138).

Under Roman rule, Jews had been permitted to move about freely, and they were widely recognised as industrious and intelligent.

Under the Visigoths Jews enjoyed the same freedom until the election of King Sisebut in 613. Sisebut drafted the first anti-Semitic legislation in Spain, under which Jews were compelled by royal edict to be baptised or banished. Thousands suffered the first alternative; those who refused conversion – and remained on the peninsula – were tortured and had their property confiscated.

By 693, unconverted Jews were denied access to the marketplace and were forbidden to trade with Christians. It was no wonder that the Jews of Hispania were among the natives who rallied to the Muslims when they launched their invasion from North Africa in 711.

the dominant tongue on the peninsula, and for the first time permitted Visigoths and Hispano-Romans to marry. By stressing cultural, geographical and linguistic unity, Leovigild provided Hispania with a sense of national destiny, quite independent from Rome.

Leovigild failed, however, in his attempt to convert the Hispano-Romans to Arianism, a form of natural Christianity that refuted the concept of the Trinity and subordinated the Son to the Father. He was liberal enough to allow his son Hermenegild to marry a Christian, but when Hermenegild converted to Christianity and rose up against him, Leovigild sought his revenge. He plundered churches, exacted huge sums of money from wealthy Christians, and sent many who opposed him to their deaths.

But the door had been opened. When Leovigild died, his son Recared converted to Christianity and became Spain's first Christian king. With the religious issue resolved, Hispano-Romans developed a new, strong loyalty to the Visigothic monarchy. Recared's conversion symbolised the victory of Hispano-Roman civilisation over the barbarians, and signalled the start of a new alliance between church and state on the peninsula that would last, with few interruptions, into the modern age.

Drawing on Roman precedents, the Visigoths

Decline and fall

When King Witizia assumed the throne in 702, he hoped to side-step the tradition of the elective monarchy and leave the crown to his son Akhila; those nobles who opposed him were beaten and punished. But when Witizia died in 710, Akhila was in the north and Roderic, the Duke of Baetica, was acclaimed king instead by the southern Visigoths.

Witizia's family appealed to the Muslims in North Africa for help. Fired by his zeal for the new religion of Mohammed, Tarik ibn Ziyad, the governor of Tangier, agreed to join in the battle. His force of 12,000 men, the majority

introduced a codified law and a workable tax system. But while they spoke Latin and emulated Roman laws, administration, customs and dress, they clung tenaciously to their belief in an elective monarchy. Visigothic society was an assembly of warriors who cherished the right to elect their king and permitted ambitious nobles to aspire to the throne. Smooth transitions to the throne were rare; in the first 300 years of Visigothic rule there were more than 30 kings, many of whom met bloody deaths.

LEFT: jewel-studded Visigothic crown in beaten gold.
ABOVE: Visigothic stone carving in the 7th-century church of Quintanilla de la Viñas, near Burgos.

of them Berbers, was ferried across the Strait of Gibraltar into southern Spain. King Roderic was routed in the Battle of Guadalete and perished by drowning.

The year was 711 and the Visigoths were without a king; they retreated to Mérida, where they put up a desperate last stand in vain. Tarik should have returned home to North Africa victorious, but he was driven by two overriding desires; to carry his religion into the land of the unconverted and to seize King Solomon's legendary treasure, purported to be in Toledo. The Muslims swept through Spain and by the year 714 they had established control over almost all parts of the peninsula. ❑

MUSLIM SPAIN

The Muslim presence in Spain (al-Andalus) gave rise to a brilliant civilisation.
After almost eight centuries, the last bastion fell in the Reconquest

The Muslim invasion ended the cultural, linguistic and religious unity that the Visigoths had tried to achieve on the peninsula. Yet Muslim values did not flourish exclusively during the years of their occupation of Spain (711–1492).

While Muslims took Seville, Mérida, Toledo and Zaragoza, Visigothic nobles regrouped in the mountains of Asturias. In the same region where 700 years earlier hardy mountaineers had held off Roman legions for 10 years, Pelayo's small Christian force confronted a more powerful invading army. Though fired up by their zeal for the new religion of Mohammed, the Muslims could not prise Pelayo's men from their mountain stronghold and the Christians achieved victory at Covadonga in 722. This triumph marked the start of the *Reconquista* – the Reconquest of Spain – and assumed symbolic proportions; the Christians regarded the victory as proof that God had not abandoned his people after all.

Islam sweeps north

However, the Muslims, intent on conquering all of Europe, were undeterred by Covadonga. They continued over the Pyrenees into France, until they were stopped at the Battle of Poitiers in 732 by French troops led by Charles Martel, "Charles the Hammer". This stunning defeat forced the Muslims to look southwards again and to begin the difficult task of ruling over the land and the people they had recently conquered.

Unlike the Romans, who established a link with a strong centralised government outside the peninsula, the Muslim invaders were only nominally the political and spiritual subjects of the Caliphate of Damascus, a distant overlord. The conquerors fought each other for power and control, dividing up the booty.

These early years of Muslim rule were

LEFT: *A Spanish King* by Alonso Cano portrays an archetypal medieval monarch.
RIGHT: under Islamic rule painting was encouraged as a courtly skill.

characterised by rebellions and frequent infighting among the individual kingdoms. Moreover, Spain became the nesting ground for new converts to Islam coming over from North Africa. The Berbers, for example, came from Mauritania and, after a generation of being treated like second-class citizens by the Arab

nobles, rose up against them. After years of internecine fighting, a new Muslim governor redivided the conquered lands. The Berbers were given territory in the Duero River valley but, after years of famine, many returned to North Africa.

Meanwhile Pelayo, followed by his son Favila, set about creating a powerful Christian kingdom in the north. Later, under King Alfonso I (739–757), the Asturians occupied Galicia to the west and Cantabria to the east; under Alfonso II, they moved their capital to Oviedo, where the Asturians tried to restore the institutions of the Visigothic monarchy.

In the meantime, the Basques, usually intent

on maintaining independence, were willing to form alliances with fellow Christians. Such manoeuvrings had one aim: to expel the Muslims and restore Christianity. When Charlemagne took control of Pamplona and Catalonia late in the 8th century, he set up the Spanish March, a buffer zone to keep Muslims out. They had no choice but to build their base in the south, in the area now known as Andalusia.

The emirate

In 756, Abd-al-Rahman I, an Umayyad prince, came to power in Córdoba and established an emirate aligned with, but independent of, the

main seat of power in Damascus. He proclaimed himself Emir of *al-Andalus* (the Muslim name for Spain), and his ascendancy marked the dawning of the most important and advanced civilisation of the Middle Ages.

Córdoba was at the heart of this Golden Age; it became one of the largest, wealthiest and most cultured cities in the world. At its height in the mid-10th century, Córdoba's population had swelled to more than 300,000 and there were well over 800 mosques to serve the religious needs of the predominantly Islamic population. As the Muslims performed daily ablutions *(wudu)* as part of their religious obligations, some 700 public baths dotted the city.

The caliphs of Córdoba supported all aspects of learning. During the reign of al-Hakem II (961–976), the city library was established and soon held 250,000 volumes. Greek texts, which the Arabs had come across in their triumphant march across the Middle East, were also introduced to Europe. The works of Aristotle, Euclid, Hippocrates, Plato and Ptolemy were translated and commented upon by such noted Arabic philosophers as Avicenna and Averroës.

Poets, too, were highly regarded. They also served a political function similar to that of television commentators today. The bloodthirsty al-Mansur was reputedly surrounded by 30 to 40 poets when he marched off to battle. Poetry was written in Castilian, Galician and Hebrew, but the most powerful verse was written in Arabic: with its fondness for metaphor this poetry would influence 15th-century Spanish lyrics and, in the 20th century, the sensuous *casidas* and *gacelas* of García Lorca.

Arabic influence

More than 4,000 words of Arabic origin are still in use in modern Spanish. Foods introduced by the Muslims – *azúcar* (sugar), *berenjena* (aubergine), *naranja* (orange) and *sandía* (watermelon) – make up the daily diets of most Spaniards. Also, words connected with administration, irrigation, mathematics, architecture and medicine can be traced back to Arabic.

Many phrases still in use in Spain have their roots in Arabic culture, especially those that express courtesy – *Esta es su casa* (This is your house) and *Buen provecho* (Enjoy your meal) – and the role of God in everyday life – *si Dios quiere* (if God wills it), and the word *ojalá,* from the Arabic *wa shá' a-l-lah* (may God will it).

Córdoba also became the scientific capital of Europe during the Middle Ages. The introduction of Arabic numerals into Spain – far less cumbersome than their Roman counterparts – spurred great advances in mathematics; the Arabs are thought to have invented algebra as well as spherical trigonometry. Astronomers and astrologers were numerous, and there was a significant following for the occult sciences.

New industries flourished in Córdoba. The royal factory of carpets was known throughout Spain, and Córdoba's many wonderful silk weavers increased its fame as a place where fine garments could be bought. Glass and ceramics factories were built, and the old heavy

PALACES AND POOLS

As they were a desert people and because the Koran required daily ablutions, the Arabs were extremely fond of water. In addition to their numerous public baths, the Muslims incorporated fountains and pools into their palaces and villas. This can be best appreciated in Granada's Alhambra – the Red Palace – and its neighbouring Generalife, which served as the summer residence of the caliphs. Built in the 14th and 15th centuries, towards the end of the Islamic occupation, both these structures combine water and greenery to establish a mood of elegance and relaxed splendour.

Islamic architecture

But the Muslims left their most indelible stamp upon Spain with their architecture. The solid Romanesque churches of earlier centuries were far surpassed by constructions that were lighter, airier and more colourful. The cupola, the horseshoe arch and the slenderest of columns, often of jasper, onyx and marble, were all introduced by the Muslims and can best be appreciated by visiting Córdoba's *Mezquita* or mosque. As the Koran forbade the representation of human figures, Muslim artists used geometric patterns that often incorporated the graceful letters of the Arabic alphabet.

metal tableware was replaced by glass or glazed pottery. Spaniards journeyed to Córdoba to examine the latest designs by its renowned leatherworkers and silversmiths. Islamic physicians were highly prized for their ability to diagnose illnesses and for their surgical skills. They used anaesthetics, and are known to have performed complicated and delicate surgeries such as cataract removal and trepanning to reduce pressure on the brain.

LEFT: Alfonso the Wise (1252–84) encouraged scholars to master Arab culture and translate Greek texts.
ABOVE: fresco from Galicia showing the Muslims and Christians at war.

The Jews in Spain

The story of the Islamic occupation would be incomplete without including the illustrious, and eventually tragic, role played by the Jews during this renaissance of culture. Savagely persecuted by the Visigoths, the Jews were held in high esteem by Muslim invaders for their role in bringing the invasion about. Generally speaking, they were protected by both kings and nobles for whom they worked in administrative posts. Jews were valued as merchants, ambassadors and emissaries and were taken into the confidence of Muslim and Christian rulers when their own people could not be trusted. Abd-al-Rahman III's minister of finance was a Jew, as was the vizier of the king of Granada in the 11th century.

Because of their honesty, many Jews were used as tax collectors, igniting the hatred of the labouring classes. With the arrival of the Almoravids and the Almohads, fanatical converts to Islam who came from North Africa, the Jews were either expelled to Christian lands or murdered.

EL CID (1043–99)

Rodrigo Díaz de Vivar of Burgos battled Christian and Muslim tyrants alike. A man of courage, he was dubbed El Cid from the Arab *Sidi* (Lord). The poem *El Cantar del Mío Cid* immortalised him as a hero of the Reconquest.

Jews fared well especially under the Caliphate of Córdoba. Maimonides, the great Jewish

philosopher and author of the *Guide to the Perplexed*, was born in Córdoba and lived there until forced to flee to Egypt during the Almohad invasion. The Talmudic School of Córdoba attracted Jewish thinkers from all over Europe.

Jews were also held in high esteem in the Christian kingdoms; they held positions as royal treasurers and physicians, and the Catholic Monarchs came to depend upon their Jewish subjects for financial and medical advice. Alfonso X (1252–84), the "Wise King" of Castile and the founder of the University of Salamanca, created a school of translation in Toledo where Christian, Jewish and Islamic scholars worked together. The Bible, the Talmud, the Cabala and the Koran were all translated into Spanish at the king's behest.

Soon, however, the effect of the Crusades, which fanned hatred throughout Europe, was felt in Spain. When outbreaks of plague in 1348 and 1391 resulted in the deaths of hundreds of Christians, Jews were singled out as the cause. Zealous friars stirred up a wave of anti-Semitism which led to the burning of Jewish ghettos and the murder of their inhabitants. In the 14th century, the Valladolid *Ordenamientos* deprived Jewish communities of their financial and juridical autonomy. Expulsion and the Inquisition were yet to come, under Isabel and Fernando.

Reconquest

The Reconquest of Spain, which spanned 750 years, was both a battle against an invader, and a war against Islam, seen as a heretical religion that did not recognise Christ as the Messiah.

In the later 9th century, Alfonso II (866–911), taking advantage of Muslim infighting, began to colonise the Duero River valley, now abandoned by the retreating Berbers. To the east, he built many fortresses to repel Islamic attacks. These Asturians saw themselves as the heirs of Visigothic power and tradition, responsible for wrenching power from the Muslims.

But when García I moved the Asturian capital from Oviedo to León in 914, the unified Muslims – under the rule of the caliphs of Córdoba – wreaked great destruction upon the Christians.

Al-Mansur came to power in Córdoba in 976 and, to distract the Muslims from his own misrule, led what became almost yearly raids into the five kingdoms of Christian Spain: Asturias, León, Navarre, Aragón and Catalonia. In 985 he burned Barcelona, and its inhabitants were killed or enslaved; three years later, he plundered Burgos and León. In Santiago de Compostela he destroyed the cathedral, holiest of Christian shrines, and had its bells and doors carried by Christian slaves to Córdoba where they were used to make lamps and the ceiling for the *Mezquita*.

When al-Mansur died in battle in 1002, the Christian states counter-attacked. Count Ramón Borrell of Barcelona led troops southwards where they joined rebellious Muslims. However, progress was slow: Córdoba was finally sacked in 1010, ending its pre-eminence in *al-Andalus*. Meanwhile, Sancho III became the King of Navarre (1000–35); by alliance and warfare, he came to rule over Aragón, Castile, Ribagorza, Sobrarbe and the city of León.

Civil wars and the division of territories into splinter states called *taifas* further undermined Islamic power on the peninsula. The Christian kings played one Muslim ruler off against another. By weakening them in this way, the Castilians were able to retake Toledo, widely acknowledged as the capital of Spain, in 1085.

strength, the Muslim kings sought aid from Morocco. Help came from the Almoravids – "those vowed to God" – a group of Saharan people who had recently converted to Islam and had conquered much of West Africa.

Under the leadership of Yusuf, the Almoravids brought camels and African guards to carry their weapons. In time, they captured Badajoz, Lisbon, Guadalajara and Zaragoza. Though they were repelled at the gates of Barcelona and held at bay in Toledo, the Almoravids remained in control of their territories for 50 years. By the middle of the 12th century, however, the power of the Almoravids was collaps-

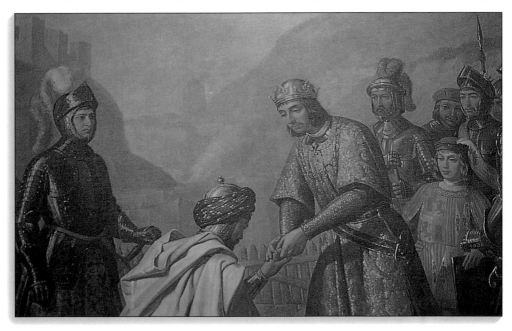

ing and the Christians regained most of Andalusia. But then, in 1195, the Almohads, a Berber group from Morocco's Atlas Mountains, invaded Spain. They defeated and killed the Christian king of Castile at Alarcón and drove thousands of *Mozárabes* (Christians living on Islamic lands) and Jews out of Andalusia.

This marked the fall of the first Muslim city and allowed the Christian forces to advance south. Meanwhile, the Aragonese won Zaragoza and the Catalans retook Lérida and Tarragona. When the King of Aragón's daughter married Count Ramón Berenguer of Barcelona in 1151, Catalonia and Aragón were united under one ruler.

Holy wars

But the Muslims were not going to relinquish Spain easily. To counter the growing Christian

In response, Pope Innocent III called for a Crusade and many Christian kingdoms in Europe sent contingents of knights to wage war against the "infidel". A furious battle ensued at Las Navas de Tolosa in 1212. Alfonso VIII of Castile united troops from Navarre, Aragón and Portugal against the forces of Miramolin, the Almohad leader. Not only did the Christians

LEFT: statue of El Cid in his home town of Burgos.
ABOVE: the Muslims admit defeat before the Catholic monarchs. Granada was the last kingdom to fall.

achieve victory, but they were now poised for attacks on northern Andalusia.

The subjugation of Muslim Spain was to follow quickly. Jaime I, the "Conqueror King", defeated Valencia and the Balearic Islands. Meanwhile, Fernando III, "the Saint", united Castile and León, thus merging their forces for further attacks. Córdoba surrendered to his troops in 1235, followed by Valencia in 1238. Many other Muslim territories futilely resisted the Christian advance. In 1246, Fernando III laid siege to Jaén, which fell after months of battle. After a siege lasting over 16 months, Seville surrendered in 1248. Many of its houses were burned, vineyards destroyed, orchards set ablaze; the mosque in Seville was pulverised and only its minaret, the Giralda, was left.

With these Christian victories, Islamic domination in Spain was vastly reduced. By the end of the 13th century, only the provinces of Granada and Málaga and parts of Cádiz and Almería were still in Muslim hands. A Muslim state under Christian protection was set up in Granada; refugees from the rest of Spain settled there under the rule of the Nasrid Dynasty.

Yet, because of partisan politics and feuding, the reunification of Spain was delayed by 150 years. The kings of Spain contested the throne in repeated bloody encounters. Pedro I, "The Cruel", ruled from 1350 to 1369 leaving a trail of blood including the murder of family members.

Fernando and Isabel

Early in the 15th century, the Aragonese took control of Catalonia and Valencia, and the House of Castile assumed charge of Murcia and Almería. Union between these two powerful

kingdoms came about in 1474 when Fernando of Aragón married Queen Isabel of Castile. But this was a union of crowns, not kingdoms, for each region maintained its own leadership, government, traditions and rules of succession.

From 1483 to 1497 the *Cortes*, the assembly of nobles in court, did not convene, and the "Catholic Monarchs", Fernando and Isabel, put an end to feudalism and established an absolute monarchy. They took over the nobles' privileges and created a new upper middle class.

The Inquisition

In order to achieve Catholic unity, in 1478 Fernando and Isabel obtained a papal bull from Sixtus IV to set up the Sacred Office of the Holy Inquisition, a court at which alleged *conversos,* "false converts" to Catholicism, would be tried. Thousands were condemned and imprisoned or killed; others fled the country.

Converted Jews could stay only if their conversion was total. Many had posts both in the government and even in the Church itself. In 1483, all Jews were ordered to leave Andalusia and Fernando demanded their expulsion from Zaragoza, but both instructions were largely ignored.

In the meantime, the troops of the Catholic Monarchs were laying siege to Granada. Ironically, Fernando and Isabel once more sought lands from wealthy Jews to finance the final phase of the *Reconquista.* On 2 January 1492, after 11 years of battle, the Muslim King Boabdil personally surrendered the keys of Granada to Fernando and Isabel.

Within two months of capturing Granada, the Catholic Monarchs, on the advice of Tomás de Torquemada, the first Inquisitor-General and son of a *converso* family, ordered the expulsion of all Jews who refused to be baptised. Some 170,000 Jews were expelled. They went to North Africa, Greece or Turkey. Many of these Sephardic Jews still use their Castilian language, known as *Ladino*, today.

Over 300,000 *conversos* remained in Spain. They were treated badly and were required to show the solidity of their new faith. But the Golden Century of Spain would not have been possible without them. ❑

THE SPANISH INQUISITION

Set up by Fernando and Isabel in 1480, the Inquisition was intended to unite all Spain under Catholicism. Authorised by a papal bull, it was a court, presided over by the Inquisitor General, in which suspected *conversos*, false converts to Catholicism from Jewish and Muslim faiths, were tried. The Inquisition accepted denunciations and used torture to obtain confessions. Defendants were not informed of the charges against them, were denied counsel, and were not allowed to cross-examine hostile witnesses. Those found guilty faced imprisonment, beheading, hanging or burning at the stake. The court, later directed against Protestant heretics, lasted until the 19th century.

RIGHT: enforcing the sentences of the Inquisition: *The Burning of Heretics* by Pedro Berruguete shows St Dominic seated beneath the canopy.

THE EXPANDING EMPIRE

Freed from the Muslim yoke, Spain looked abroad. Colonial expansion made it briefly, under the Habsburg kings, the greatest power on earth

Towards the end of the 15th century Portugal was the world maritime power, aggressively exploring the Atlantic coast of Africa and establishing colonies on the Azores and the Cape Verde Islands.

In 1485 Christopher Columbus, a Genoese navigator who had been in the service of Portuguese captains, approached the Catholic Monarchs Fernando and Isabel and asked for financial support to find the shortest westward route to India. He offered them new territories, abundant riches and more souls for God.

Columbus was held off for nearly seven years, but once Granada had been conquered, Spain began to concentrate its resources on overseas exploration.

Spain discovers America

On 12 October 1492, about 70 days after setting sail from Spain, Columbus and his crew landed on the island of San Salvador in the Bahamas. He claimed the new lands, which he mistook for India, for the Spanish Crown. The Papal Bull of 1494 ceded much of the New World to Spain, thereby encouraging Fernando and Isabel to finance other expeditions. In time, Spain would conquer huge empires in the Americas, notably in Peru and Mexico.

The Spaniards were driven by two equally powerful desires: to obtain gold, power and land in the Americas; and to convert and "educate" the American Indians. As Castilian money had financed the voyages, the Crown insisted that it had the right to control all trade with the colonies and that the *quinto real* – the royal fifth – of all monies should revert to the Crown.

On the spiritual side, the Spaniards regarded themselves as missionaries bringing Christianity to distant lands, and subjugating barbaric natives who practised human sacrifice; what was before a barren landscape, would become the site of

towns, cathedrals, universities. Along the way, several successful Amerindian empires were destroyed by germs as well as gunpowder and their vast mineral wealth usurped in order to finance wars in Europe thousands of miles away.

When Isabel died in 1504, her daughter Juana became Queen of Castile. After the

sudden death in 1506 of her husband Philip, the Archduke of Austria, she became depressed and was widely judged to be mad – thus her nickname *Juana la Loca* – and her father, Fernando took charge of Castile.

Fernando's rule was characterised by a number of struggles in which he tried to consolidate power under the Spanish Crown. Aragón held Sicily and Sardinia but, when the French intervened in Italy, Fernando went to battle; victorious, he annexed the Kingdom of Naples in 1504 and established Spain as a powerful challenger to French designs on the continent. In 1512, he annexed the Kingdom of Navarre, south of the Pyrenees, to Castile.

LEFT: *Las Meninas* by Velázquez, arguably his greatest painting.
RIGHT: the "invincible" Spanish Armada (detail), destroyed in 1588.

By shrewdly marrying off his children – Catalina to Henry VIII of England, Juana to Philip, the son of Maximilian, Emperor of Austria and Duke of Burgundy, and María to King Manuel of Portugal – Fernando had strengthened Spain's position with several of its European rivals.

The Habsburgs

When Fernando died in 1516, the crown devolved on his grandson Charles, the son of Juana and Philip. The heir to the Habsburg lands in Austria and southern Germany, Charles was unattractive, inexperienced and spoke no Spanish. Spain was apprehensive about being

ing of the *comuneros* or commoners; led by the town of Toledo, the *comuneros* wanted to dethrone Charles and replace him with *Juana la Loca*. They also declared that only Castilians should have administrative posts, and that the Cortes (parliament), not the king, had the right to declare war. The nobles vacillated, but when they finally aligned themselves with the court, the army crushed the rebels at the Battle of Villalar in 1521. The *comunero* leaders were executed. The power of the monarchy was restored and, in gratitude for the support of the nobles, Charles V rescinded some of his tax levies.

Charles V's rule coincided with the opening

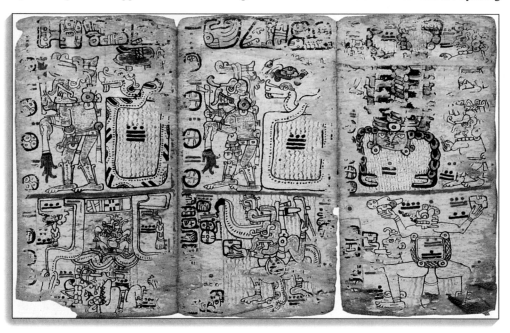

ruled by a foreigner. His arrival at Santander in 1517 and his first gestures did not quell fears. The Spanish nobility, especially, resented the King's reliance on his Flemish advisers and his unwillingness to consult with them. One unpopular decision was to appoint his own nephew to the rich prestigious Archbishopric of Toledo. To make matters worse, Charles tried to levy new taxes on both the church and nobility, as well as raise the *alcabala* or sales tax.

When his grandfather Emperor Maximilian died in 1519, Charles was elected Holy Roman Emperor as Charles V. But as he set sail for Germany, the Castilians, feeling overtaxed and ignored, rebelled. This was the infamous upris-

up of the Americas. During his reign, Hernán Cortés conquered the Aztecs and Francisco Pizarro defeated the Incas in Peru; after raiding the treasuries, both conquerors opened huge gold and silver mines in Mexico, Bolivia and Peru. Seville was placed at the centre of the burgeoning metal trade and in a few years the city doubled in size.

Debt and heretics

With peace at home and gold flowing across the Atlantic, Spain – now the most powerful country in Europe – became involved in several long and expensive wars abroad. As Charles V defended southern Italy from Turkish incursions, he became embroiled in combat with the Ottoman Empire. He also waged four wars with France, and by the end of his reign he had gone to war with almost every European nation.

Spain was forced to use the gold and silver of the Americas as collateral to secure loans from foreign bankers to finance the wars. As prices shot up, the Crown levied higher taxes and set up price controls. But as the nobles had invested much of their newly acquired wealth in land, jewellery and decorative objects rather than in industry or agriculture, Spain remained economically weak and uncompetitive. It sank deeper into debt while its European rivals developed their industries.

Another of Charles V's struggles was with the Protestant movement. As the ideas of Martin Luther took root in Germany, Switzerland and England, the Pope appealed to Charles to put an end to a heresy which claimed that "the Pope could not release souls from Purgatory on payment of a fee" and which allowed Christians to communicate directly with God without intermediaries. Charles responded by giving support to Catholic military groups, including St Ignatius Loyola's "Society of Jesus", which fought for the Papacy. In Spain itself there was a Counter Reformation in which certain books were prohibited and the popular humanist ideas of Erasmus were considered heretical.

In 1556 Charles V abdicated, retiring to the monastery of Yuste in Extremadura. His brother Ferdinand was given most of the Habsburg Empire though he left his Spanish possessions, Flanders and parts of Italy to his son, Felipe II.

Unlike his extrovert father, Felipe was withdrawn, sickly, almost bookish in his imperial pursuits. He dedicated over a decade to building the palace, monastery, retreat and church of El Escorial near Madrid.

Felipe II

As his kingdom was more limited than that of his father, Felipe II generally pursued issues pertinent only to Spain and Catholicism. When the Calvinists rebelled in Holland, he had their leader beheaded and many of his followers slaughtered, thus cementing his reputation as a

LEFT: fragment of the Mayan Codex.
RIGHT: conquistador Hernán Cortés.

ROYAL FANATIC

King Felipe II once said he would prefer not to rule rather than to reign over a nation of heretics.

religious fanatic and a merciless king. He even had his own son arrested and accused of treason and heresy, and ordered the Primate of Spain be deposed for having voiced his admiration for Erasmus. Felipe's cruelty was immortalised both in Schiller's *Don Carlos* and Goethe's *Egmont*.

By the 1560s Spain was, despite a surface opulence, in dire financial straits. Its industries were floundering, foreign wars were depleting her treasury and English pirates began hijacking Spanish ships returning with much-needed gold from the Americas.

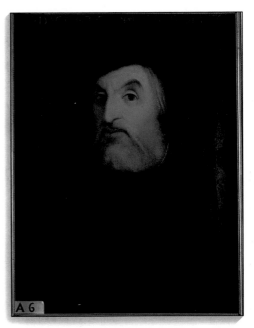

By 1575 Felipe II owed so much money to foreign banks that he was forced to suspend his debt payments.

But Felipe's aggressive religious principles dominated his economic considerations. He made the Inquisition hunt out the *moriscos*, Spaniards of Islamic ancestry, many of whom had converted to Christianity during Queen Isabel's rule but were still suspected of adhering to the Muslim faith. Spain's best farmers took refuge in the stony mountains of Andalusia until it was safe to return to their lands.

To encounter the Turks who from time to time had menaced the Spanish coastline, Felipe II formed a league with Pope Pius V, Malta and

Venice. Under the command of Felipe's brother, John of Austria, the alliance defeated – at great financial cost – the Turks in 1571 at the Bay of Lepanto, near Corinth.

Spain sinks

In Felipe II's struggle with England, however, economics and religion fused: he prepared the Spanish Armada not only because Queen Elizabeth protected the pirates who attacked Spanish galleons, but also because she persecuted English Catholics and had imprisoned his cousin Mary Stuart. But when the "Invincible Armada" confronted the more manoeuvrable

English fleet led by Sir Francis Drake in 1588, Spain lost thousands of sailors and more than half its ships. Defeat led Felipe into a long period of indecision and introspection: had God abandoned the Catholics? What was certain was that Elizabeth's victory established English maritime supremacy for decades to come.

Spain was ruled during the 17th century by the last three Habsburg kings. When Felipe III became king in 1598, his kingdom included Spain, Portugal, Flanders, much of central and southern Italy, the Americas from California to Cape Horn and the Philippines. But he was indifferent towards his responsibilities, and left the affairs of state to the Duke of Lerma, who used his position to increase his wealth and to appoint relatives to important administrative posts. In 1609 he advised Felipe III to expel the *moriscos* on religious grounds, but also to break the power of the Valencian nobles. Half a million *moriscos* were forced out, many of whom were among Spain's best farmers.

With silver production down, agriculture in disarray and corruption rife, Spain was drawn into conflict with Holland, France and England during the Thirty Years' War. Felipe IV became king in 1621 and political/military reversals during his reign brought the Empire to the verge of collapse. When in 1640 he tried to get the Catalans to pay for the maintenance of Castilian troops, they sought help from the King of France; Felipe backed down, and was forced to grant the Catalans nominal independence.

Later that same year the Duke of Braganza proclaimed himself King of Portugal, which signalled that kingdom's final independence. Separatist movements were also underway in

THE GOLDEN AGE OF SPANISH LITERATURE

Under the Habsburg kings Spain enjoyed its greatest literary flowering. Heralding this golden age was *La Celestina* (1499) by Fernando de Rojas. Written as a play, its sense of time, plot and character development is as modern as Celestina herself, a go-between for illicit lovers.

The poet Garcilaso de la Vega, whose pastoral *Églogues* were published in 1543, revolutionised Spanish poetry with Italian verse forms. Fray Luís de León, imprisoned for five years accused of practising Judaism, wrote mostly prose, but also lyric poetry of great elegance. St Teresa of Ávila wrote with a simplicity and clarity unusual in her time, while the poetry of her disciple, the ascetic St John of the

Cross (1542–91), is deeply mystic or lyrically ecstatic. The baroque poets Luís de Gongora (1561–1625) and Francisco de Quevedo (1580–1645) had contrasting styles: Gongora lush and ornate, Quevedo dry, acerbic, pessimistic.

Of the playwrights, Lope de Vega (1562–1635), founder of Spain's National Theatre, wrote some 1,500 plays (mostly popular comedies), poetry and novels; Calderón de la Barca (1600–81) is known for his philosophical dramas.

The crowning achievement of the age is the novel *Don Quijote* by Miguel de Cervantes. An instant bestseller when published in 1605, the story of a deluded idealist battling with flawed reality still has a universal appeal.

Andalusia and Naples. The French defeated the Spanish at Rocroi in 1643, and the Peace of Westphalia (1648) marked the end of Spain's role as Europe's supreme military power.

Military defeats were not the only cause of Spain's demise. Spain failed to use gold and silver from the Americas to build strong industries at home: wool sheared in Spain was sold cheaply to Europe's northern countries, where it was converted into cloth, then resold on the peninsula at exorbitant prices.

Once the *moriscos* were expelled, the best lands were given over to sheep and cattle grazing; farm goods had to be imported. The

A regency ruled until Carlos II took the throne at 15. War with France continued for most of his rule and he was forced to surrender valuable territories in the Peace of Nimega (1678) and Ratisbonne (1684).

Carlos died without an heir and left his crown to Philip of Anjou, the grandson of Louis XIV, in the vain hope that he might keep Spain intact from further French incursions.

The Bourbons

Lacking in experience, the newly crowned Felipe V, the first Bourbon, relied on French advisers. Austria, alarmed by the prospect of

church and the nobility were exempted from paying taxes, and so the poorest of merchants and peasants were obliged to support the state. The *escudo*, once accepted as currency throughout Europe, tumbled in value and Spain was unable to secure foreign loans. As a result, the vast armies of the Empire were underfed and underpaid, and morale sank.

Felipe IV died in 1665. He left an economy in shambles, deeply in debt, to his only son Carlos, a five-year-old who had yet to be weaned.

LEFT: King Felipe V painted by Hyacinth Rigaud.
ABOVE: a public spectacle in the Plaza Mayor, Madrid, around 1700.

French hegemony in Europe, declared war on France; Catalonia, Valencia and the Balearic Islands saw an opportunity to oppose Felipe V and accepted Charles, the Archduke of Austria and a Habsburg, as their ruler,

This War of the Spanish Succession lasted 13 years and, for the first time since the Reconquest, a foreign enemy marched across Castile. The Treaty of Utrecht (1713) recognised Felipe V as the King of Spain, but exacted a heavy toll on the old Spanish empire; Flanders and all of Spain's Italian possessions were lost, and Gibraltar was ceded to the British.

The ruling Bourbons embarked on a plan to unify Spain; by diminishing the role of the church, they hoped to strengthen the power of the state. By the middle of the 18th century, Spain's economy had stabilised; its army and navy had been reconstructed, and new industries, primarily in Catalonia, began to develop.

The Frenchification of Spain, both in customs and thought, was launched. The ruling kings adopted French mannerisms and clothes, believed in the Age of Enlightenment and introduced a more liberal church service. Carlos III (1759–88) was a devout Catholic but, more than that, a believer in an absolute monarchy: at his behest, church burials were forbidden, and the Inquisitor-General was expelled for drafting

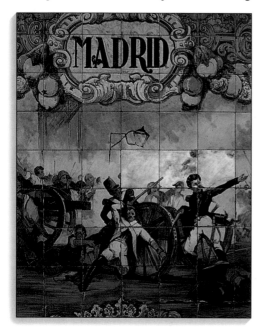

a bill without the king's authority. In 1766 he ousted the reactionary Jesuit Order from Spain because of what he perceived as their political intrigues. Unfortunately for the Bourbons, the Spanish masses were deeply conservative and suspicious of any attempt to liberalise life.

Spain truly revived under Carlos III. When he first came to Madrid, he was shocked by the squalor of the Spanish capital. During his reign, work on the Royal Palace was completed and the Prado Museum, originally intended as a science museum, was built. He also built new canals, roads and highways. A steady rise in prices brought economic growth and prosperity. When Louis XVI was guillotined in 1793,

the Spanish king Carlos IV – a nephew of the beheaded French monarch – grew frightened of the growing liberalism on his northern border and declared war on the French. Years of war followed: Spain lost.

Napoleon

Carlos IV was a weak-minded and weak-willed ruler. His queen María Luisa and her favourite, Godoy – a common soldier who rose to become Prime Minister – actually ran the state. After Napoleon gained control in France, he turned his eyes towards Spain. On the pretext of going to occupy Portugal, Napoleon brought his imperial army into Spain and lured the royal family to Bayonne for a meeting. By exploiting the intense factionalism among the Spanish royal family, Napoleon was able to broker an agreement: Carlos abdicated, his son Fernando was banned from Spain and Napoleon gave the crown to his own brother Joseph Bonaparte.

On 2 May 1808, the Spanish peasantry rose up spontaneously in protest; any Frenchman on the Madrid streets became a target. The crack French troops responded swiftly and brutally. Francisco Goya's *The Third of May, 1808* captures in blazing colours the execution of a group of *madrileños* who resisted. Regional uprisings followed, and France found it increasingly difficult to govern Spain. The War of Independence (also known as the Peninsular War) dragged on until Napoleon was defeated in 1814 by Wellington.

During these years of war, the liberal Spanish Cortes (parliament) gathered in Cádiz to draft a constitution. In 1812 it was approved, abolishing the Inquisition, censorship and serfdom, and declaring that henceforth the king had to abide by whatever the Cortes decided.

Looking backwards

Despite this, however, Fernando VII took over the throne and was pronounced absolute monarch. He refused to pledge allegiance to the constitution, re-established the Inquisition, stifled free speech and allowed the Jesuits to return. Seeing no hope for accommodation with his despotic regime, the Spanish provinces in the Americas rebelled and established independence.

Fernando VII turned his back on the three major movements of the 18th century – the Enlightenment, the French Revolution and the Industrial Revolution – and kept Spain apart from the rest of Europe, brooding over its imperial glories and deep religious soul.

When in old age Fernando VII repealed the Salic law limiting royal succession to male heirs in favour of Isabel II, his daughter by his fourth wife, María Cristina, a woman of liberal background, a far-right religious group that was known as the *Apostólicos* rebelled in protest. The conservatives decided to join them and threw their support behind Don Carlos, the king's brother.

The Carlist Wars were actually civil wars

TURNING POINT

Spanish sea power came to an end when Admiral Lord Nelson defeated the Franco-Spanish fleet off Cape Trafalgar in 1805.

water supply, dozens of nuns were slaughtered.

This internecine struggle continued until Alfonso XII, the son of Isabel II, assumed the throne in 1874, after a brief republic. By signing the Sandhurst Manifesto Alfonso tried to unite all Spaniards: "Whatever happens I shall not fail to be a good Spaniard, nor, like all my forefathers, a good Catholic, nor, as a man of this century, truly liberal."

Liberals and conservatives put down their weapons in favour of political debate and manoeuvring. Both sides agreed to adhere to

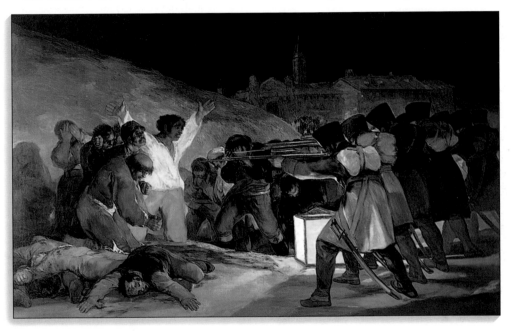

between liberals who believed in constitutional government without church domination and conservatives who favoured an alliance between church and state. The liberals were most powerful in the urban areas while the conservative Carlists drew their strength from the countryside, particularly in the northern provinces. The clergy supported the Carlists, thereby stoking anticlerical fires: when it was rumoured that clerics had poisoned Madrid's

LEFT: stormy days of the Napoleonic era.
ABOVE: Goya's famous painting *El Tres de Mayo, 1808* immortalises the *madrileños* who rose up against Napoleon.

the principle of "the peaceful rotation of the parties". The now united troops were sent off to Cuba and the Philippines where the native populations were demanding independence.

Prosperity and progress

Spain's population grew, its standard of living rose and there were great advances in transport and communications. For the first time in centuries, agriculture was revitalised. In 1890, under liberal leadership, universal suffrage with a limited electorate became law and, with the secularisation of education, schools began to improve. At the end of the century, Spain found herself hesitantly joining the rest of Europe. ❑

THE CIVIL WAR AND THE FRANCO REGIME

A period of instability and polarisation of Spanish politics led to a brief republic, the horrors of civil war and 40 years of dictatorship

The Civil War in the United States inspired an insurrection in Cuba by those seeking the abolition of slavery on the island and independence from Spain. The rebellion failed, but Cuba won a nominal degree of autonomy. In 1895, the Cuban poet and patriot José Martí resumed the struggle for independence and, after his death, the rebellion quickly spread.

Early in 1898 the United States sent the battleship *Maine* to Cuba to protect American interests; whether because of a mine or some mechanical malfunction, the ship exploded in Havana harbour. Public passion in the United States was aroused; believing that Spain had sunk the ship, President McKinley called for an armistice and the immediate release of all imprisoned rebels. Spain refused.

A series of naval battles followed in which Spain was hopelessly outmatched. The US Navy attacked Spanish ships in the Philippines and, in August, Manila surrendered. The Treaty of Paris, signed in December, granted Cuba its independence, ceded Puerto Rico to the United States as indemnity and passed the Philippines to the US for the sum of $20 million.

The end of an empire

This defeat marked the end of all Spanish pretentions to being an international power. In response, a group of writers and intellectuals, including Miguel de Unamuno, Antonio Machado and Ramón Marin del Valle Inclan – the "Generation of '98" – declared that Spain should abandon dreams of world supremacy in favour of a new, modern course. They stressed the need to revitalise the country's agriculture, reform tax structure and extend free public education to all.

PRECEDING PAGES: Picasso's *Guernica* depicts the saturation bombing of a Basque village by German planes in the Civil War.
LEFT: soldiers in war-torn Madrid.
RIGHT: King Alfonso XIII with Eduardo Dato.

It was during this period after the Spanish-American War – referred to as *El Desastre* (The Disaster) – that labour became unionised and radicalised, primarily in the industrial areas of Catalonia. Anarchism, which had attracted a

modest following during the 1870s when Bakunin's ideas were introduced, resurfaced more militantly, and in 1902 an anarchist union was formed in Barcelona, which proposed general strikes.

When the liberal leader Sagasta died in 1903, both liberals and conservatives, whose leader Cánovas had been assassinated in 1897, were in disarray. The army, comprising mostly Castilian liberals opposed to the absolutist tendencies of the conservatives, was seen by all Spaniards as the traditional upholder of the existing order. But its defeat by the US in 1898 made it vulnerable to criticism, mainly by the Socialist Party and Catalan autonomists.

The people rise up

When the Spanish army found itself under siege in Morocco in 1909, Catalan reservists were called to report for duty by the ruling conservative regime. The Catalans, however, saw no need to risk their lives by clashing with Berber tribesmen. A general strike was called in Catalonia and during this so-called "Tragic Week", 200 churches and more than 30 convents were razed by the strikers and, in retaliation, the army shot dozens of strikers and passers-by.

The whole of Spain was temporarily placed under martial law. When a popular Catalan

anarchist was unjustly accused and summarily executed for his role in sparking the strikes, mass demonstrations followed. The conservatives were toppled, and the liberal José Canalejas came to power.

Being a liberal in those days simply meant that one believed in parliamentary government, not full democracy. By giving the Catalans regional control in education and over public works projects, Canalejas sought to block the growing strength of the anarchists. He went further by letting the Socialists be part of Spain's municipal governments, and he tried to woo the Far Left by attempting to limit the number of clergy. But when the railway workers went on

strike in 1912 he broke the strike militarily, arousing the hatred of many workers. Later that year he was assassinated by an anarchist.

When World War I began, Spain declared its neutrality. It was an expedient move; by continuing to trade with Allied and Axis powers alike, Spain eliminated its national debt and increased its gold reserves.

In 1917 the part-anarchist, part-socialist labour unions called for the first nationwide strike to protest against price increases and Alfonso XIII's appointment of conservatives to the cabinet. The strikes began in Barcelona and Madrid, but soon spread to Bilbao, Seville and Valencia. The economy ground to a halt. The army crushed the strike, killing hundreds of workers and imprisoning the strike leaders.

When the wartime industrial boom came to a sudden end, thousands of workers were left without employment. With the success of the Russian Revolution fresh in their minds, the anarchists resumed their struggle in the streets. Military law was once more imposed in Barcelona.

Popular feeling against the army was strong. To make things worse, some 15,000 soldiers were killed in Morocco in another attempt to subdue the Muslims. An inquiry into the army's conduct in Morocco brought down the government and García Prieto, an old monarchist who had become liberalised, came to power.

Terrorism against the church and the army intensified – the Cardinal-Archbishop of Zaragoza was assassinated – but the government refused to cede to the army's wishes for a sterner crackdown on protesters. In September 1923 the garrison in Barcelona revolted. It was followed by other rebellions throughout the country, and the civilian government collapsed. With the blessing of Alfonso XIII, Miguel Primo de Rivera, the Captain-General of Barcelona, took control of Spain.

Dictatorship

Primo de Rivera immediately suspended the 1876 Constitution and ended parliamentary rule by closing the Cortes. He made plans to restore the army, the church and the monarchy, the traditional forces of order. He placed the press under strict military censorship, rescinded Catalonia's nominal autonomy and, by favouring the socialists within the trade union movement, neutralised the power of the anarchists.

In 1926 Spain signed a treaty of friendship with Italy. Following Mussolini's example, Primo de Rivera set up management and worker councils to resolve labour disputes and to draw up collective contracts. A period of economic expansion followed in which new railways and roads were built. But this led to huge budget deficits that became all the more critical because of the world depression of 1929. Moreover, Primo de Rivera began meddling in the army's traditional system of promotion and as a result lost

SWISS ROLE

By staying neutral during World War I, for a few short years Spain became a kind of Switzerland where international and financial issues were resolved.

The Second Republic

The elections of April 1931 were crucial. The leftist parties won overwhelming majorities and King Alfonso XIII was forced to leave Spain without formally abdicating. The Second Republic was proclaimed on 14 April, and liberal constitutionalists were installed in power. The monarchy had been overthrown without shedding one drop of blood. Briefly, it seemed as if much of Spain – industrialists, intellectuals and workers – had united for the first time.

much support. Popular feeling against the dictatorship mounted, anarchism resurfaced and there were battles between workers and the police.

In 1930 Primo de Rivera failed to rally the Captains-General behind him: under pressure, Alfonso XIII asked for his resignation. General Berenguer assumed power, but his attempts to return to a rotational constitutional system failed. Berenguer eased censorship, reopened the universities and permitted strikes.

LEFT: satirical cartoon of "Bomb City", Barcelona.
ABOVE: snapshot (wrongly dated) taken after an unplanned *corrida* in Madrid's Gran Via.

Yet the constitutionalists were caught in the middle between a Far Right that clung to its privileges and memories of past glories and the growing anarchist unions that were opposed to any form of government. When elections were held for parliament, in June 1931, the socialists and anarchists were swept into power. Six months later a new constitution was drafted, in which Spain became a "democratic republic of workers of all classes". In one fell swoop Spain ceased to be a Catholic country in which the church was subsidised by the state. War was renounced as an instrument of national policy, civil marriages and divorces were to be permitted without church sanction and state-supported education was secularised. Spain had made a complete about-face.

Manuel Azaña came to power and set about expelling the Jesuits – always considered a fifth column by the Left for their allegiance to the Pope – and confiscating their property.

Other liberal measures were adopted. The Agrarian Reform Act of 1932 expropriated large estates and compensated their owners by giving them government bonds: these lands were either redistributed to the rural peasantry or reorganised on a socialist/collectivist model. Certain Spanish provinces, including Catalonia and Galicia, were granted semi-autonomy.

army; a month later more than 1,400 Asturians had been killed and several thousands injured.

When elections were held in 1936, the Left garnered the majority of the vote; though the Right was almost equal in power, the Centre had crumbled. A new wave of church burnings, coupled with new seizures of land by the peasants, followed the elections. Assassinations by the Right and the Left became the daily fare.

The Spanish Civil War

On 18 July 1936, the rightist revolt was launched: the army, supported by the National Socialist parties of Italy and Germany, decided

In the 1933 elections, the Right – monarchists, Catholics, and José Primo de Rivera's newly formed Falange Party – achieved a small plurality. A centrist coalition was formed, but it discovered that Spain was now almost irreconcilably split between an organised but divided leftist camp and a rapidly growing Falange Party modelled on the fascist parties of Italy and Germany. The ruling Centre had to contend with the Basques and Catalans who still sought independence, and peasants and anarchists incensed by the government's decision to halt the expropriation of large estates.

The government was further weakened when striking miners in Oviedo rose up against the

HEROES AND EXILES

The few heroes of the Civil War were the intellectuals who defended the Second Republic. The Andalusian poet Federico García Lorca was shot by the fascists in 1936 for simply signing a document in support of the Republic. Many writers were killed or imprisoned, but most – including Rafael Alberti, Jorge Guillén and Luis Cernuda – were exiled. Picasso's horrifying *Guernica,* inspired by the German bombing of a small Basque town, mobilised artists against Franco. The composer Manuel de Falla died in exile, heartbroken by the Civil War, and the Catalan cellist Pablo Casals refused to perform in Spain as long as Franco lived.

to seize power and put an end to the Second Republic. The Spanish Civil War had begun.

While the Republicans established their base of support in the urban areas of Madrid and Barcelona and in the provinces of Catalonia, Murcia and Valencia, the Nationalists – as the rebels proudly called themselves – led by General Francisco Franco, moved in from Morocco. They established their control in rural areas and in the more conservative provinces of Andalusia, Old and New Castile and Galicia. As the army, police and the civil guard sided with the Nationalists, the Republicans had to improvise a fighting force by arming the workers.

arms embargo and in essence abandoned an ally and a legally elected government.

While the Allies pussyfooted, Germany, Italy and Salazar's Portugal poured arms and munitions into the Nationalist forces. By early 1937 Germany and Italy had recognised the Franco regime, Italian troops had taken part in the capture of Málaga and German and Italian ships were patrolling Spain's Mediterranean coast.

The Republicans, meanwhile, delivered their gold reserves over to Russia to pay for arms and support. In many countries of the world there were calls for volunteers to form International Brigades in defence of the Republic.

Franco, the former Captain-General of the Canaries, internationalised the conflict: only days after the rebellion began, Italian warplanes were in Morocco and Italian forces had secured the Balearic Islands. The French and the British responded by setting up a Non-Intervention Committee with Italy and Germany that feebly attempted to limit the flow of arms into Spain and thereby contain the conflict. The United States, for its part, also decided to respect the

FAR LEFT: central Madrid under blitz attack in 1937.
LEFT: the bombing of Barcelona port in the Civil War by Italian aircraft loyal to Franco.
ABOVE: refugees flee to France, September 1936.

Franco's *Reconquista*

The Republicans, who saw themselves as opposing fascism in Europe, were at a disadvantage from the start. In terms of military hardware, they were outnumbered by more than ten to one. Furthermore, they were not united; some of the fiercest struggles were between the communists, who wanted to establish disciplined cadres, and the anarchists, whose militias were loosely organised guerrilla forces where decisions were made communally. The anarchists gained control in Aragón and Valencia where they set up skeletal governments, burned churches and killed the hated clergy, and collectivised the local factories.

But on the battlefield, the Republicans could never do more than hold off the furious Nationalist charges. The most striking Republican victory was in 1938 when they occupied Teruel. Had the Republicans been more united and had they received real support from abroad, the result might have been different.

The Nationalists, on the other hand, were well-disciplined and well-armed troops. They were led by experienced generals and had all the necessary material from abroad. Moreover, the Nationalists

WHERE IS HE NOW?

Franco lies in the Valley of the Fallen, a mausoleum near Madrid with a 135-metre (450-ft) cross, built by Republican prisoners in memory of the half-million people who died in the civil war.

the Axis powers could not be denied. Franco did not want an exhausted Spain, dependent on supplies from other countries, involved once more in war. So when Hitler refused to accede to Franco's demand that Morocco, Tunisia and Algeria be handed over to him, he adopted a course of non-intervention. He did not give German troops permission to pass through Spain in order to attack the British at Gibraltar and, perhaps unbeknown to Hitler, he allowed thousands of Jews safe passage into

seemed to be on a Holy Crusade to crush the infidels. The death knell for the Republicans sounded early in 1939 when Franco's forces, after weeks of siege, entered Barcelona. The remaining 250,000 Republicans withdrew, most of them crossing into France.

By 1 April, Franco had entered Madrid and the Civil War was over. In the following months thousands of Republican sympathisers were killed in mass executions and millions of others were brought in for questioning and jailed.

World War II

Franco attempted to maintain Spain's neutrality during World War II, but his indebtedness to

North Africa as they fled from the Nazis in occupied France.

Yet Spain's sympathies were unmistakable. When Germany attacked Russia in 1941, Franco sent a 17,000-man volunteer division to fight alongside the Germans.

The Franco era

When World War II drew to a close, the Allies, angered by Franco's role of professed neutrality and responsive to the clamours of thousands of Republican exiles living within their borders, blocked Spain's entrance into the United Nations and NATO and excluded it from the Marshall Plan. Spain, the only fascist country left in Europe, was isolated by an economic blockade, but survived thanks to huge shipments of meat and grain from Perón's Argentina.

In 1947 a referendum was held and the Spaniards, given no other option, voted to establish a Catholic kingdom with the knowledge that Franco would be head of state for life and would choose a successor of royal blood. Domestically, Franco stifled all dissent and ruled, supported by the church and the army, with an iron hand.

But in 1953 two important agreements were signed that signalled world *rapprochement* with Spain. As the Truman administration was worried about Soviet designs on Europe and North Africa, Spain's wartime role was cast aside and the United States signed a treaty giving the administration bases on the peninsula in exchange for $226 million in aid. The second agreement was a concordat signed with the Pope. Roman Catholicism was recognised as the sole religion of Spain, the church was given state financial support and the right to control education, church property was exempted from taxation and all appointments of prelates were to be agreed by the Pope and Franco. The Franco regime had been legitimised.

In 1955 Spain was admitted to the United Nations and its isolation ended. Its economy began to improve due, in large part, to the increase in tourism. As tourist dollars began to reach Spain, Franco earmarked the money for the revitalisation of industry. He also started a huge public works programme that expanded highways, built hydroelectric plants and brought cheap water to the dry central plains.

In the social sphere, social security was extended to cover all workers, free medical care was offered to those Spaniards unable to pay for it, and subsidised housing was given to the poor. Education was liberalised, and thousands of Spaniards now had the chance to attend university. A powerful upper middle class of executives, managers and technocrats developed. With a million Spaniards working abroad and sending money home, Spain was prospering.

Financial progress brought about a degree of liberalisation. Perhaps to gain access into the European Common Market, Spain passed the

Religious Liberty Act in 1967, which loosened the grip of the Catholic Church on all worship; and the Press Act of 1968, which made some effort to restrict press censorship. In 1969, Juan Carlos, the grandson of Alfonso XIII, was proclaimed heir to the throne. When Franco either retired or died, Juan Carlos would become king.

Forty years of Franco

Nearly 40 years of rule under Franco were characterised by order at the expense of freedom. Any protest against the severe restrictions on speech, press and assembly was met sternly. Moreover, the desire of both Basques and

Catalans to establish linguistic, cultural and financial autonomy through protest, and at times violence, was rapidly crushed.

Most artists and intellectuals within Spain were forced to take an obscurist path. While many writers wrote religious poems and sonnets in the style of Garcilaso de la Vega, others, including Blas de Otero and Dámaso Alonso, expressed thoughts and emotions in print that most Spaniards were afraid even to whisper.

Franco's regime, until his death in 1975, was empowered by the army, the Church and the Falange Party. But as Spain's standard of living rose, a new, more liberal bourgeoisie not haunted by memories of the Civil War came of age. ❑

LEFT: in a new political climate, General Franco and his wife welcome President Eisenhower to Madrid.
RIGHT: headlines announce the death of Franco.

DEMOCRACY AND AUTONOMY

*Spain has made remarkable strides forward since Franco's demise,
pushing ahead unprecedented political and social reform*

In 1980, five years after Franco's death, the main concern among Spaniards was the survival of their fragile democracy. In 2000, the 25th anniversary of the dictator's death was barely noticed by most Spaniards, with just a few documentaries on television to mark the occasion. The Spain of the 21st century is a country Franco would barely recognise: full membership of the European Union, with an established democracy, a flourishing modern culture and a solid economy, a country where the regional differences Franco strove so hard to suppress are respected and encouraged. And it all happened so quickly.

A new broom

Prince Juan Carlos was crowned King of Spain on 22 November 1975, just two days after Franco died. The young king had been personally educated and trained by Franco. Few Spaniards had much hope that the dictator's chosen heir would be either able or willing to lead the country out of the system that had nurtured him. But they were proved wrong.

The last years of Francoism had given rise to illegal opposition parties whose leaders realised that Franco's end was near . There was the Communist Party (PCE), the most important of all; the Socialist Party (PSOE), which had lain dormant for years and was revived in the early 1970s by the future Prime Minister Felipe González and his young comrades from Seville; the Christian-Democrats, Social-Democrats, Liberals, Maoists and Marxist-Leninists.

There were also parties on the Right that resisted the move away from fascism; other conservatives, notably the Popular Alliance (AP), led by the former Francoist Cabinet member Manuel Fraga, saw that they would have to adapt themselves to the new system. The king's task was to guarantee political stability at a time when inflation was nearly 30

percent, the prisons still held political prisoners, and the armed forces had lost their leader.

Three weeks after assuming the throne, Juan Carlos charged the last Francoist president, Carlos Arias Navarro, with forming a new government. Arias lasted until July 1976, when the king surprised everyone by appointing Adolfo

Suárez, the former head of the Falange, the only political party allowed under Franco, as the country's new Prime Minister. The king, Suárez and Santiago Carrillo, the Secretary-General of the Communist Party, are the three men generally credited with bringing about Spain's political transition.

Democracy returns

In December 1976 Spaniards participated in the first democratic poll since the Civil War ended in 1939. The "Political Reform Referendum", which was overwhelmingly approved, set the wheels in motion for the first post-Franco general elections in June 1977.

LEFT: the world came to Seville for the Expo in 1992.
RIGHT: Catalan nationalists protesting for independence in Girona, 1988.

One of the first tests of Suárez's experiment came in April, when the PCE was made legal. The Minister of the Navy resigned in protest and the first sabre-rattling could be heard. It would not be the last time that the military threatened to take things into their own hands. Suárez was Prime Minister, but did not belong to any political party that could return him to power. So he created the Union of the Democratic Centre (UCD), a hotchpotch of centrist parties that won 27 percent of the vote.

AGAINST EXPECTATIONS

The former Communist Party Secretary-General Santiago Carrillo mistakenly predicted that the new king would be called "Juan Carlos the Brief".

Attempted coup

In January 1981, Suárez resigned as party chief and Prime Minister. On 23 February 1981, before Leopoldo Calvo-Sotelo could be invested as the country's new head of government, a group of over 300 Civil Guards and military men, led by Lieutenant-Colonel Antonio Tejero Molina, burst into Parliament and tried to stage a military coup d'état. At the same time, an army general declared a state of emergency in Valencia and tanks began rolling down the city

streets. Around six hours after the coup began, King Juan Carlos appeared on television and ordered the insurgents to desist. Twelve hours later they surrendered.

On 12 December 1978, Spanish voters approved the new Constitution, which had previously been passed by Parliament. The abstention rate was 33 percent, and in the Basque Country, the negative votes plus the abstentions were higher than the affirmative votes, indicative of home-rule sentiments in northern Spain. Once the Constitution had been passed, new elections were held, in which the results were similar to those of 1977.

But by this time UCD was beginning to show signs of stress as the different "families" within it began straining at the leash, jealous of each other and desirous of more power. Meanwhile the Prime Minister felt the pressure mounting.

Calvo-Sotelo was invested on 25 February, and two days later an estimated one million Spaniards participated in a demonstration in Madrid in support of democracy. The inherently unstable UCD was back in power but its days were numbered. In October 1982 PSOE swept into power with an overall majority – the first time since 1936 that socialists were in the government and the first time ever that an all-socialist government ruled Spain. In those same elections UCD virtually disappeared; in contrast, the conservative Popular Coalition shot up to 106 seats from the nine it had before. Today's bipartisan system was taking shape.

This short, cluttered electoral chronology illustrates the resolution of the most pressing question following the death of Franco: rupture or reform? Was there to be a clean break with the former regime and the monarchy Franco imposed, or was there to be a gradual adaptation to modern democracy?

Spain joins Europe

King Juan Carlos was initially rejected by many in the anti-Franco opposition who saw him as a continuation of the dictatorship. They wanted to return to the Republican system that had been violently abolished with the Civil War. These same sectors demanded that full-scale purges take place in the police, the armed forces and the judiciary once Franco had died. None of this happened, and they ended up accepting a slower reform as they saw the king was serious when he said he was the "King of all Spaniards" and not just of the victors of the Civil War. The Left and the Right both moderated their position, thus guaranteeing the stability of the new democracy.

One of the most important tasks facing the Spanish government was the re-establishment of Spain as a member of the international community of nations after many years of political isolation. After the Civil War, nearly all the world's countries ceased diplomatic relations with Spain. As a result of President Eisenhower's 1953 visit, however, US military and economic aid was given to the Franco regime, enabling the beginning of an economic recovery after the very difficult post-war years.

In 1975, Spain remained isolated. That year, only one head of state visited the country. By 1986, however, 29 heads of state had come, an indication of the degree to which Spain had gained equal standing with the rest of the world's industrialised countries. Immediately after Franco's death, mutual diplomatic relations were reinstated with most of the world's countries.

LEFT: Lieutenant-Colonel Antonio Tejero Molina attempts a military coup in parliament in 1981.
RIGHT: King Juan Carlos.

> **TOWARDS DEVOLUTION**
>
> Under the terms of the 1978 Constitution, Spain was divided up into 17 "autonomous communities" or regions.

By far the most important sign of Spain's desire to become "part of Europe" was its stepped-up campaign to join the European Community (now the European Union), a process which was completed in 1992, and its entry into NATO, the North Atlantic defence alliance. Spain had tried on and off over a 20-year period to join the EU, but its violations of democratic principles were an obstacle to its entry. After the restoration of constitutional government, Spain finally took its place as a member on 1 January 1986.

Spain's accession to NATO is complicated. The country was originally taken into the alliance in 1981 by the Calvo-Sotelo government despite socialist opposition. When the latter party came to power in 1982 it promised to hold a referendum on NATO membership. Yet over the next four years, Prime Minister Felipe González and his government gradually became convinced of the virtues of NATO and began to campaign in favour of remaining a member. In March 1986 the referendum was finally held after a four-year delay and a massive anti-NATO campaign by the country's peace movement. Membership was accepted by 52 percent of the electorate.

Economic crisis

While Spain was trying to regain its footing politically, it also had an economic crisis to face. When the international recession began to be felt in the early 1970s, other European countries were able to resist the blows, but Spain was saddled with an over-bureaucratic and paternalistic economy that had grown up in isolation over 40 years. It lacked flexibility and when protectionist measures were dropped, business suffered.

The restructuring of key industries caused the loss of more than 65,000 jobs in the early 1980s. As one writer has noted, the two occa-

Gradually, as Spain brought its economy into line with those of other European nations in the 1990s, the unemployment rate was reduced by half, though it continues to be higher than elsewhere in Europe.

Seventeen Spains

One of the most salient features of Spain's democracy is the home-rule structure. In contrast to the strongly centralist approach that had prevailed in Spain, barring a few periods, since the 18th century, the new Spain envisioned by the Constitution is composed of 17 autonomous regions with their own government and legis-

sions in the 20th century when Spain began a democratic experiment, in 1931 and 1976, have coincided with world economic crises. By far the most serious economic problem facing Spanish society is unemployment.

By the early 1990s the number of people who were out of work had reached 3 million, or 22 percent, of the total labour force, and the numbers continued to rise. This dramatic figure would signify social chaos in most other countries. However, the strong family structure in Spain combined with the fact that an estimated 20 percent of the GNP is produced "under the table" provided a cushion against soaring unemployment.

REGIONAL AUTONOMY

The Basque Country, Catalonia and Galicia are considered to be "historic nationalities", and have enjoyed a degree of independence from central government since the unification of Spain in the 16th century. In these regions, local languages are spoken in addition to or instead of Castilian, and the fight to get them treated on an equal basis with Castilian was a main aim of the 1970s "autonomy movement". The Basque Euskera language bears no relation to any other known language, but its origin, though unknown, is now believed by some to date to the Stone Age; Catalan derives from the French Langues d'Oc; Galician is of Roman origin.

lature, and jurisdiction over social services, housing, health, agriculture, education, city planning, culture, some taxes and, in the case of the Basque Country and Catalonia, the police.

Regional sentiment was especially strong in the three so-called "historical regions", Galicia, the Basque Country and Catalonia, each of which has its own separate language. Catalan and Euskera (the Basque language) were severely repressed in the Franco era, as was any other manifestation that could be seen to question Spanish "unity". The creation of Spain's quasi-federal system was a bumpy process, not only because of resistence from the entrenched

order to govern. Needless to say, this support came at a price, in the form of more concessions for self-government.

The region best known for its separatist leanings is Euskadi, or the Basque Country, where the leading party is the Basque Nationalist Party (PNV). The most extreme manifestation of Basque separatism is ETA (standing for *Euskadi Ta Askatasuna*, or "Basque Homeland and Liberty"), an armed organisation founded in the 1960s. Owing to the particularly harsh repression dealt out by the Franco regime to the Basque provinces, the anti-Franco struggle there became inextricably linked to Basque

right wing, but also because of the marked differences between the regions that were seeking to gain home rule.

Catalonia has been particularly successful at encouraging its indigenous culture and the Catalan language, and in gaining control over many aspects of government, largely because the last socialist administration and the conservative government elected in 1996 both had a minority in the Spanish parliament and needed the support of the Catalan regional parties in

nationalism. But even with the death of Franco and the later implementation of Basque autonomous rule, ETA's activities continued unabated, with kidnappings, car bombs, extortion of Basque businessmen (the so-called "revolutionary tax") and assassination. Since the 1960s, ETA has killed nearly 800 people.

The solid voting base of ETA's political arm, Euskal Herritarok (formerly Herri Batasuna), with around 20 percent of the vote; the failure of the government in Madrid to find an effective solution to terrorism; and the ambivalent attitude of the Basque Nationalist Party towards ETA have made Basque separatism Spain's most intractable problem.

LEFT: street demonstration, 1981.
ABOVE: an open-air session of the Basque Parliament on the Day of the Community.

Rapid change

Someone who knew Spain under Franco would have a hard time recognising things today, and a first-time visitor would have a hard time imagining that just a few decades ago most aspects of cultural and intellectual life were rigidly controlled by the authorities, that superstition and clichés were a good substitute for knowledge and that sexual freedom was an unheard-of concept that would have been viewed with the utmost suspicion.

> **NEW WOMEN**
>
> Spain now has one of the lowest birthrates anywhere in the world: an average of 1.2 children per woman aged between 15 and 49.

The crash course in political affairs has been

mirrored, in an even more visible way, by the changes in social questions that affect Spaniards' daily lives. Education, the church, family life, culture and social services – none of these emerged from the post-Franco transition unscathed.

As the conservative laws regarding divorce, birth control, abortion, homosexuality and adultery were gradually relaxed during the centrist and socialist administrations, social behaviour began to resemble that of other European countries. The women's movement was launched in December 1975 and its first campaigns were largely concerned with the demand for birth control, a divorce law and an abortion law.

As women nowadays tend to have fewer children, they have begun entering the workforce, although to a lesser degree than in other OECD (Organisation for Economic Co-operation and Development) countries. This is partly due to the high unemployment rate in general and partly due to sexism. Nevertheless, although the famed Spanish *machismo* is alive and well, fathers often take their children for walks, young couples battle over the division of household tasks just as in other countries and no eyebrows are raised when women enter such professions as law and medicine.

The Church retreats

Despite reform, the education system was largely incapable of responding to the needs of a new society. One indication of this is the enormous popularity of language schools; foreign languages were badly taught – if at all – during the Franco years, but given the country's isolation there was not much need to speak anything other than Castilian Spanish (the country's other languages were prohibited). With Spain's entry into the EU, the increased prosperity that permits travel, and the dramatic inflow of foreign firms, there has been a rush to learn languages, especially English, and regular schools and universities are steadily improving to meet the demand.

The Church as an institution supported the Franco regime, and was generally regarded as a bastion of conservatism. The exceptions were mainly found in Madrid, where there was a certain "worker-priest" tradition, and in the Basque Country, where the separatists found a great deal of support from priests. As the Church has lost battles over birth control, education and divorce, as the number of vocations has declined and as the Sunday Mass-goers have dwindled, so too has the institution lost many privileges afforded it by Franco, most importantly its financial subsidies and tax breaks. During the drafting of the 1978 Constitution, Spain's bishops fought tooth and nail even to get the Constitution to mention the Church, and it did so in a less than adulatory way: "The authorities shall take into account the religious beliefs of Spanish society and maintain appropriate relations...with the Catholic Church and the other denominations."

Media and arts

If the country's youth were to be prepared in schools for the challenges posed by this new society then the adults too needed a daily "school" to adapt and learn to think in new ways. That school for most people was the media.

Spain wasn't lacking in talented journalists, but there were no newspapers that could do justice to their craft. The birth of modern Spanish journalism can be traced to a specific date: 4 May 1976, when the first issue of a national daily, *El País*, appeared. *El País* laid the ground rules for modern Spanish news reporting, including double-checking sources and the use of a clear, readable style to replace the rather turgid, verbose prose favoured by the traditional Spanish press. It continues to be the country's best-selling title, but its prestige suffered greatly in the 1990s due to its close sympathy with the governing Socialist Party. Revealing the Socialists' peccadilloes was left to the emerging competition, notably *Diario 16* and *El Mundo*. *El Mundo's* editor, Pedro J. Ramirez, was credited with playing a key part in the downfall of Felipe González in 1996.

But press readership in Spain continues to be lower than in most European countries, since Spaniards tend to rely more on radio and television news. Regional television stations and private broadcasters were introduced in the 1980s, giving a better balance of news, as well as providing a voice for Basques, Catalans, Galicians and Andalusians.

Books were another medium where Spain had a lot of catching up to do. The claim by a Spanish politician in the 1930s that "if you want to keep a secret in Spain, all you have to do is publish it in a book" is a good indication of Spaniards' reading habits until recently. Bright lights such as Nobel Prize-winner Camilo José Cela, were few and far between, but that began to change as a fresh batch of authors started to produce books entertaining enough to captivate a new generation of readers, such as Arturo Perez Reverte, a former journalist who became a best-selling novelist both in Spain and abroad. By 2000, some 60,000 books were being published annually in Spain, of which around 9,000 were fiction.

LEFT: former Socialist Prime Minister Felipe González before his second electoral victory in 1986.
RIGHT: Expo '92 brought the future to Seville.

Spanish cinema has fared much better, perhaps because it is a relatively new art form. From the late 1970s, after the Ministry of Culture was set up, home-grown films have won international prizes, and directors such as Fernando Trueba and Pedro Almodóvar have become world-famous.

That was the year that was

In 1992, three of the country's greatest cities played host to the world: the first Universal Exposition in over 20 years took place in Seville; the Olympic Games came to Barcelona and Madrid was the EU's Capital of Culture.

Madrid's Palacio de Linares was superbly refurbished and became a centre for Latin American culture, and there were major improvements to the city's museums. It was the year in which the magnificent Thyssen-Bornemisza art collection was put on public display in the restored Palacio de Villahermosa, making Madrid one of the most art-rich cities in the world.

It was also the 500th anniversary of Columbus's exploratory voyage to the New World. Expo '92 was timed to begin and end on the same days as that historic journey, and had as its theme "the Age of Discovery". Millions visited the Exposition site, and Expo also had an ambitious arts programme.

The Alta Velocidad Española (the acronym, AVE, translates as "bird" in Castilian), a high-speed train linking Madrid with Seville, was built in time for Expo '92. The line has a money-back guarantee if the train is late by 5 minutes or more. It has been extended from its central hub, Madrid, northeastwards through Zaragoza and on to Lleida, its eventual destination being Barcelona. In 2003, Spain and Morocco agreed, provisionally, to build a rail tunnel linking Europe and Africa; a joint committee of officials set out a preliminary three-year plan with work beginning as early as 2005.

Expo '92 brought a new energy and stimulus to southern Spain, and helped to put Seville back on its feet. The city acquired a new railway terminus, a much enlarged airport and several new bridges on the Río Guadalquivir. The region as a whole has been transformed from one of the most isolated into one of the most accessible areas of the country. A similar process is gradually taking place in Galicia.

The 1992 Olympics in Barcelona were a genuinely global games, with more countries participating than ever before. Barcelona used the Olympics to transform itself. An ambitious urban renewal project became a reality, opening up the city to the sea, getting rid of slums and creating beaches where previously there had been industrial wasteland. It gained a remodelled airport, a new ring road freeing the centre from traffic congestion and new telecommunications and sewage systems. Culture also received a boost.

The city's latest brainchild lies ahead. This is Diagonal Mar, a newly created residential district of high-rise apartment blocks, parks, a landscaped waterfront and a shopping mall. It has a new metro station, El Maresme/Forum, and is the terminus of the brand-new tram, which speeds up and down Avinguda Diagonal. It is also the venue for Forum 2004, a universal forum of cultures. Sponsored by UNESCO, the forum has three main themes: multi-culturalism, fostering world peace, and sustainable urban development. A huge festival of arts, as well as meetings based on these themes, will take place in summer 2004. The River Besòs has been cleaned up and a new marina and leisure centre is to be built.

The honeymoon is over

The celebrations of 1992 were followed by facing up to the reality of a slowdown in the world economy. This coincided with a loss of credibility of PSOE, which had governed the country since 1982 amid a series of corruption scandals. Party sympathisers convicted for their financial shenanigans included the governor of the Bank of Spain and the civilian head of the Civil Guard. Members of the government were also linked to GAL, a shady hit squad set up to fight a dirty war against ETA terrorists but which ended up kidnapping or murdering people who had nothing to do with the Basque separatist movement.

All this led to the Socialist Party's defeat in

STIRRING STUFF

The 1992 Olympics was not an event that could be said to belong to any one competitor. Rather, the Games left a series of stirring snapshots of the triumph of the human spirit over adversity.

"Magic" Johnson, star of the US basketball "Dream Team", showed how courage could win out in the face of the HIV virus. And Mirsal Buric, a 22-year-old sprinter from Bosnia-Herzegovina, had fought his own personal battle in order to compete. He had been forced to train on the battle-torn streets of Sarajevo when the firing was at its worst, because "that was when the streets were empty".

the 1996 general election. The Partido Popular (PP), headed by José María Aznar, won a relative majority, and were able to govern with the support of the Catalan regionalist parties. Almost immediately after Aznar took over, Spain's economy was once again on an upturn, although this had more to do with the favourable global economic climate than with any clever manoeuvres undertaken by Aznar's ministers. In order to be among the first countries to adopt the euro, sustained economic growth along with reduced inflation, unemployment and interest rates were required. Spain passed the test, and the euro was adopted at a trade level in 1999, and then integrated as currency in 2002.

In 2000, Aznar won a second term in office, this time with an absolute majority. The PP became increasingly transparent in its conservatism, passing tough immigration laws and planning to return to a more traditional approach to education. The government was widely criticized for its handling of environmental disasters such as industrial pollution in the Doñana Wildlife Reserve in 1999 and the *Prestige* oil tanker spilling its cargo of crude oil off the coast of Galicia in 2002. The National Water Plan to divert the natural course of the River Ebro to supply arid areas also met with fierce public disapproval, while Prime Minister Aznar's staunch allegiance to the US in the Iraq war provoked a nationwide outcry.

Terror in Madrid

On 11 March 2004, ten bombs ripped through three commuter trains in central Madrid, killing almost 200 people and injuring a further 1,500. Prime Minister Aznar immediately and insistently laid the blame squarely with ETA. Mass protests were held throughout the country, and more than a quarter of the population held vigils. About 90 percent of Spaniards had been against their country's involvement in the war on Iraq, and the government was judged to be trying to manipulate the outcome of the impending election by blaming ETA and ruling out an Islamist backlash: if ETA had been responsible for the attacks it is probable that PP would have remained in power. Spain's

---

LEFT: the 1992 Barcelona Olympics.
RIGHT: a triumph in titanium: Frank Gehry's Guggenheim Museum, Bilbao.

Socialist Party, PSOE, won the election, though not by an absolute majority. Jose Luis Rodriguez Zapatero, Spain's new prime minister, said his first priority was to fight terrorism. He had been totally opposed to Spain's support for the Iraq conflict and his first decision after winning was a promise to withdraw Spanish troops from Iraq.

No looking back

Spaniards see themselves as citizens of a modern Europe. Some tourists may lament the passing of picturesque old Spain, but Spaniards themselves feel no nostalgia whatsoever for starvation wages, double-digit inflation and life

with no car, television or washing machine. And today's younger generation has little memory of that earlier Spain.

Spain's transition to democracy proved a remarkable and inspiring success, and the past decade has seen an ever-increasing acceleration in modernisation, in an era of IT and globalisation. Along with economic success, Spain has seen a new cultural flowering and has taken fresh pride in its great historical sites and the natural treasures of its wilderness areas. Its rich patchwork of regional cultures have a renewed sense of self-awareness. Today's Spaniards are self-confident and proud of their country. ❑

THE SPANISH PEOPLE

*Proud, fiery and extrovert, a Spaniard is most at home in a crowd,
for where there is no noise, there is no life*

Fun in Spain goes hand in hand with being in a large, noisy crowd. For many reasons, one of them being the sunny weather that keeps everyone outdoors for most of the year, gregariousness is the norm. The larger the gathering, the larger the potential audience. Naturally, there is a fair amount of playing to the crowd, but the pillar of Spanish *joie de vivre* is an internal self-sufficiency that needs no material support. It is expressed through wit, grandiloquence, appearance, courtesy, generosity and pride.

On the town

The best place to appreciate the Spanish art of conversation as performance is in a bar. The "*ambiente*", or the amount of noise and people, is of utmost importance. Where there is no noise, there is no life, and a Spaniard flees from tranquillity. It is hard to determine what makes more racket in a bar, the patrons shouting at each other – for it would be a euphemism to say that they talk – or the waiters thrashing glasses about. What is certain is that the din is so deafening one can hardly hear the television perched on a shelf in the corner with its volume turned on full.

Anything goes as a subject of conversation. Most Spaniards are extremely articulate, and a chat can become a performance punctuated with recitations. While the ratio of book readers is low – in 1999 only 38 percent of Spaniards read a book – those who read do so seriously.

Generosity

A full third of Spaniards' income is spent on food, drink and tobacco. Snobbishness dictates that American cigarette brands are preferable to the perfectly adequate national ones. But with food, it is a different matter. Fast-food hamburger joints and pizza parlours are appreciated by moped-driving teenagers, and

PRECEDING PAGES: dancing in a Menorcan meadow; the Alhambra, Granada, last bastion of the Muslims.
LEFT: reading the news, Barcelona.
RIGHT: at Capileira, high in the Sierra Nevada.

busy office workers. But Spanish food is generally preferred. A feast at a bar might include cured ham, spicy prawns or potato omelette, washed down with wine, beer or dry sherry. One self-satisfied-looking man often conspicuously foots the bill – which may easily add up to half his monthly salary.

The friendly generosity of the Spaniard is one of the characteristics that most astounds first-time visitors to the country. If a local and a stranger embark upon a conversation, it is quite likely to end up with an invitation to a coffee or a beer. In the south, bartenders offer so many drinks on the house it is a wonder they make a profit. Young people rarely seem to buy a cigarette. They approach each other on the street to ask for one, and it is graciously given. A Spaniard will respond wholeheartedly to anything that appeals directly to his emotions. Most beggars make a living, and some have been hauled into jail for amassing a near-fortune.

A Spaniard is also politely helpful and

generous with his time. Strangers asking for an address will often be accompanied to their destination. But the Spaniard is also loath to disappoint, and may indicate the wrong road rather than admit he does not know the way.

Another large chunk of Spaniards' incomes goes on clothes. The traditional style of dressing in dark colours has given way to colourful sporty attire. In rural areas, the habit of dressing in mourning for several years after the death of a relative lingers only among the older generations, who are bound to spend the rest of their lives in black because when one term of grief ends another is likely to begin due to the size of

REGIONAL RULE

Scores of rulers have attempted, by marriage or by iron fist, to unify spiritually and politically this country of 39 million individualists who speak four languages and seven different dialects. Franco went as far as to forbid the use in public of any language except Castilian and banned the christening of babies with local names.

The outburst of regionalism after Franco's death was such that today Spanish-speaking people must arm themselves with a dictionary when they visit Catalonia, Galicia, the Basque country, and parts of Levante and the Balearics, where regional governments encourage the local language through education and the media.

their families. In the cities, however, this custom has largely disappeared.

Everything under the sun

There are marked differences between people from the north, the south, the east and the centre. It has often been said that the Spanish nation is a myth, a dream of politicians and ideologues. Tourism officials coined a phrase that sums up the varied climates, landscapes and types: "Spain, everything under the sun".

Hot and perennially sunny Andalusia personifies the image foreigners tend to identify with Spain. In this vast area, still strongly marked by Arab influence, is joy of life coupled with a piercing tragic fatalism. The Andalusian looks and sees the parched faces of peasants mirroring parched and arid land and knows life is cruel but also exquisitely beautiful. Flamenco is an expression of this particular view of existence.

By contrast the Galicians, who inhabit the green, rainy land of mist-filled valleys in the northwest, are a conservative people, many of them fishermen and subsistence farmers with a sprinkling of smugglers because of the numerous hidden coves. Once they smuggled tobacco – now they run an estimated 60 percent of Europe's cocaine. They have a reputation for melancholy and political cunning. Like other peoples with Celtic roots, they play the bagpipes and have emigrated in droves during centuries of penury.

Further along the north coast is the land of the hardworking Basques, gifted with appetites to match their superb cooking. They have traditionally sought independence from Spain and in recent decades, local nationalism has spilled over into terrorism. The Basque language, Euskera, bears no relation to any other known language. Their rugged sports, such as wood-chopping and boulder-lifting, go hand-in-hand with their skill as bankers, industrialists and engineers.

Very different are the sophisticated Catalans, whose history is linked with the Languedoc area of France beyond the Pyrenees. They share one thing with the Basques, however: a desire to sever their ties with the rest of the country.

Fierce regionalism has been tempered by migrations from the centre and south to the rich northern and coastal lands, and from rural regions to cities. Today, some of the least populated parts of Europe lie just an hour's drive from Madrid.

Sex and the family

The Spanish family is an affectionate clan in which mutual tolerance and staunch support is the norm. Take a stroll through a park on any afternoon and it is immediately evident that the Spaniard is a happy and adjusted being who will never be an outcast in his own circle. The toughest-looking ruffians are out for a walk with a grandfather leaning on one arm and a baby cousin clinging to a hand.

The honour, rights or jobs of sisters, brothers, aunts, second cousins and even in-laws are defended ferociously in Spain. The worst abuse one can hurl at a man is to insult his mother –

However, while men must still be seen to wear the trousers outside the family, women keep a tight grip on the domestic life of their family. Nowadays, most men do not keep a second woman – mainly because they can't afford to – but they still have extramarital affairs. Increasingly, women now have them, too.

The new moral code

The word *noviazgo*, or engagement, referring to a state which among working-class couples used to last up to 10 years while they saved to buy a house, is rarely heard these days. Don Juanism has become characteristic of both

and at a woman, to insult her child. Children accompany their doting parents everywhere and stay up all hours of the night.

Spanish men are viewed as lustful, dominating macho types. Often, they are. Rarely faithful to one woman, until recently it was acknowledged and even accepted that married men kept a mistress. The wife, who ran the household and brought up the offspring, was regarded by him as something close to a saint.

LEFT: coffee and conversation in the warm Pamplona sun.
ABOVE: young women dress up in traditional Aragonese costume.

sexes, who before settling into wedlock change partners with almost equal frequency and ease. The number of people living together without a wedding ring is indicated by the drop in the numbers of marriages, which nearly halved in the two decades after Franco's death.

The changes have been largely due to the liberation of women. For many reasons, including Franco's ability to ward off progress, the pressure of the church and poverty, female liberation happened later in Spain than in the rest of the developed world. As recently as 1970, wives had to present written authorisation from their husbands to travel within the country or to open a bank account in their own name.

Perhaps most astounding was the speed of change in sexual mores. But then, the largest section of society has always regarded morality as something to be broken now and then to add spice to life. Where else could the married vice-president of the government have had a publicly known lover and not caused righteous indignation, even after having an illegitimate child? Who could disapprove, when the voices of restraint are equated with the reviled dictatorship? At the same time, open homosexuality only became acceptable in public life in the late 1990s, through the courage of key figures in the arts, politics and the army.

Religious matters

Strange as it may seem, worldly passion does not clash with religious sentiment. Religious events in Spain are celebrated with wine and dance and every excess that goes hand in hand with merriment. In the early hours of Good Friday in Seville, when Christ was on the way to his crucifixion, a huge float of the Virgin of the Macarena transported on the backs of men sets off down the tightly packed moonlit streets. Thousands of voices shatter the night with cries of "*Guapa! Guapa!*" (Beauty! Beauty!) as the band strikes up and the Virgin, despite the diamond tear in her eye, does a sensuous little dance. Lack of respect? No – just familiarity.

To the believer, God is a patient being who understands the weakness of the human flesh and easily forgives. Spaniards sometimes rely so much on his understanding that the relationship becomes one of complicity. At Mass, people act with less formality than they would in the house of a close friend. They arrive late, greet acquaintances out loud, and drag chairs; at seaside resorts they attend the service in bathing suits. The ceremony lasts only 20 minutes, but before the priest has given his blessing to the congregation there is a stampede for the door.

A distinction must be drawn between the Spaniard's comfortable relationship with God and his relationship with the institution of the Church. To many, the Church represents the repression of the former dictatorship. After winning the Civil War, Franco sat bishops in parliament and in the council of the realm and put the clergy in control of primary and secondary education. People who are now only 35 years old remember endless candle-bearing processions to religious shrines at dawn and being encouraged by priests at school to place small stones in their shoes for penitence. What became frustrating for educated adults was how every form of cultural expression was subject to Church censorship. The unfortunate result was that upon Franco's death, pornography glutted magazine stands and cinemas.

Partly because of resentment of the control that the clergy had over their lives and partly because of new winds from abroad, the number of practising Catholics in Spain has fallen to 50 percent of the population; only 18 percent of these attend Mass on a regular basis.

The new Spaniards

There is a tendency to classify Spaniards either according to their unique history or according to a modern and homogeneous Europe. They are at the crossroads of two cultures and two continents, Africa and Europe, and of two political and economic systems. Awakening from the lethargy imposed by so many years of isolationism, they are stretching and considering the situation. The jostling within Spain's new political framework has produced a revived regional awareness that lends an infinity of different meanings to national identity. At the same time, the men and women on the street are happy to have joined the European Union. They feel as if they are finally members of an advanced society. ❑

The Spanish Gypsies

George Borrow wrote of the Gypsies or *gitanos*: "I felt myself very much more at home with them than with the silent, reserved men of Spain...". When he travelled with them in the 1830s they had been in Spain for over 400 years yet he found them to be foreigners in their own land, clinging to their language and culture long after they had begun to settle in the 18th century.

Today, nearly two centuries later, the Gypsies still hover on the edges of society. A few may catch the limelight as singing or dance stars like Joaquín Cortes or Lola Flores, but more often they remain largely invisible in Spanish art, history and literature – Carmen, for example, the heroine of Bizet's opera, was the creation of Frenchman Prosper Merimée. As one Gypsy patriarch puts it, they are "one of the most unknown people in the world."

Who, then, are the Spanish Gypsies or *gitanos*? Of Hindu descent, from Rajasthan in northwestern India, they left their homeland for unknown reasons – possibly an invasion – and migrated slowly westwards via Persia to arrive in Spain in the 15th century, bringing with them their language *(caló)*, costume, social laws and large flocks of sheep and goats. Travelling in groups to avoid attack, they worked as blacksmiths, professional musicians, fortune-tellers, horse-dealers and sheep-shearers.

Six hundred years later there are an estimated 800,000 Gypsies in Spain and, as the population with the highest birth rate in Europe, their numbers are expected to double in the next 30 years. More than a quarter live in Andalusia. They may be antique- or scrap-dealers, fruit-pickers, market-stall holders, horse-handlers, jewellers, flamenco musicians, or flower-sellers. In less independent jobs they often disguise their origins for fear of racism. Few have accumulated material wealth: a survey in 1998 found that the average Andalusian Gypsy family lived on 35,000 Ptas (£150/€222) a month. Often they are intensely religious. The Gypsy Holy Week processions are among the most moving in southern Spain, and in recent years there have been sweeping conversions to Evangelism in Madrid and in other Gypsy communities. Only a few words of *caló* are sprinkled through their speech, but they remain closely bound by private social

rules, family loyalties, patriarchal authority and cultural pride.

The Gypsies' marginalised position is explained by their history in Spain. Relentless persecution from 1499 was aimed at forced assimilation through restricted movement and eradication of their culture. To quote just one of a dozen laws, Philip IV's Pragmatic of 1633 banned *gitano* language, costume, music, horse-dealing, possession of weapons, marriage and association in public as well as the use of the word Gypsy, on pain of life slavery. Even Charles III's 1783 law granting equal rights of work and residence made Gypsy "behaviour" punishable by red-hot irons or the

death sentence. It is little wonder that half a century later Prosper Merimée found the Gypsies to be "astute, daring but naturally fearful of blows".

Settlement and integration finally began in the 18th century in southern towns where the Gypsies had taken on jobs such as blacksmithing. But it was to be a slow process.

Today the Constitution protects the Gypsies' rights, but the exclusion of *gitano* children from schools and housing schemes are everyday events. In response, the Gypsies have learned to defend their culture and ways not only through Civil Rights movements, but also, more subtly, with humour, art – and, as in Borrow's time, by keeping a safe distance from Spanish society. ❏

LEFT: three generations gather for a traditional big lunch in Madrid.
RIGHT: Gypsy children during playtime at school.

A FOREIGNER'S VIEW

A seasoned visitor commends the Spanish way of life, and Spain's discovery of a genuine national pride

When I first went to Spain, in the early 1950s, travelling was far from easy: roads were very bad, accommodation sparse, comforts minimal. The sun shone however, and it was not long before sun-starved Northerners – Scandinavians, Celts, Germans – began to flock to Spain, spearheading what

provide work. The country surrendered itself to alien hordes for a period of about 20 years, something of an indignity to Spaniards, who referred to tourism as *putería*, or prostitution. The mass intrusion had a fruitful side; it put Spaniards in touch with the rest of the world and showed them other ways of being, so that,

was to become an invasion of mass tourism that reached a peak in 1974, when more than 30 million tourists, one for every native Spaniard, crossed the Spanish frontier during the year.

Broadening the mind?

The author Robert Graves, who rooted himself in the Spanish landscape for 50-odd years, gleefully told of an English secretary, newly returned from Spain, who announced to her friends that she had just been on holiday in Mallorca. "Where's that?" they asked her. "I have no idea," she replied. "I flew."

Franco, however, badly needed tourism to strengthen his foreign currency reserves and to

when the time came to make a new Spain, after Franco, Spaniards impressed everyone with their political sophistication, their native vitality and their determined optimism.

Tourism forced Spain into a whirlwind of change, grafting the trappings of modernity on to rustic foundations and often bringing the old ways and the new into sharp conflict. Tourists, however, kept to the beaten track, to the concrete meccas created for them, and much of Spain remained in rural isolation. The remote villages were sought out by sturdy souls, who found a mix of landscape, mode of being and human rhythms that existed nowhere else.

From the 1950s on, I lived for a part of every

year in a series of Spanish villages, eventually settling in one to which I would return once a year, like a pilgrim. It is in village life that Spanish qualities most reveal themselves. The elements there are so stark, so boned down, the inhabitants so separate and durable, the rituals so essential and so graceful that living in them feels like a simplification, a purification. In the remoter parts of the country, the quality that Spaniards have of being able to do with less, to wear lack with a kind of pride, often seems like a positive resistance to the trappings of civilisation. My village friends always gave off the air of being self-sufficient in their own skin, of having come to terms with their fate, with the help of the stoic proverb and the cosmic shrug. Conversations took as long as they had to, work was done in the course of time, and sometimes, sitting down to a long Spanish lunch, I could feel the world outside withdraw, giving way to the small, rich world of the table and the conversation.

From my first visit on, simply being in Spain has always brought me a sudden joy, a physical tingle, from the light, from the landscape, from the language. It springs from intense Spanish particularities: bare village cafés loud with argument and dominoes, or else sleepy and empty except for flies; sudden memorable conversations, about life and death, with total strangers; the way Spaniards have of imposing human time, so that meals and meetings decide their own duration. There is a durability about people here, an acceptance of fate that, paradoxically, sharpens their sense of the present, their spontaneity. The villages have a sparse, uncluttered look, with bare landscapes and stark interiors. The days seem wondrously long, gifts of time, and existence simplifies itself to a vocabulary of elemental acts, like drawing water and making fire.

Changing roles

Over some 25 years, I watched my own village die, in a sense, losing its agricultural self-sufficiency, when bottled gas replaced the charcoal it had prepared from time immemorial. The population dwindled, as the men left to find work elsewhere, and the school closed when their families eventually followed them.

LEFT AND RIGHT: international brands and consumer values are making an increasing impact in Spain.

Foreigners, in search of silence, occupied the empty houses, and the village evolved a continuing life, the remaining inhabitants playing the part of custodians, the foreigners their honoured guests.

The best of hosts

The tourist occupation of the Franco years was not a destiny that Spain wished on itself, but one which the country has survived well, and has turned to its own advantage. For me, the great satisfaction of recent years has been in seeing the Spaniards themselves assume control of their own destiny, with flair and imagina-

tion, and with a genuine national pride. They have also taken a keen pleasure in maintaining and preserving their country, and in making it comfortably available to its own inhabitants.

Their enthusiasm makes them the best of hosts. Foreigners, consequently, who had grown used to trudging across Spain at will for so long, have now been moved towards the periphery of Spanish life, and behave more as guests to a host, a change of status desirable for Spain's sake, and one that has enhanced the pleasures of being in that inexhaustible human landscape. ❏

Poet and essayist Alistair Reid has written about Spain for the New Yorker magazine for 40 years.

THE BULLS

Despite predictions about the demise of bullfighting, passionate aficionados affirm that it will exist as long as Spain does

First-time visitors to Spain are likely to approach the whole idea of bullfighting with varying mixtures of excitement, fascination and apprehension and possibly revulsion. Sitting in the stands and waiting for the initial pageantry to begin, one knows instinctively that what is about to happen is not

to attack anything that moves or challenges its predominance. A bull has been known to charge an express train that crossed its path.

It is, in fact, the bull's selected bloodlines, responsible for its innate bravery, nobility and proud bearing, which have kept it from the slaughterhouse and granted it an almost envi-

a sport. Spanish newspapers categorise the *corrida de toros* as a spectacle; ardent *corrida* advocates fiercely defend its artistic nature, and bullfighting has left its mark on painting, sculpture, music, dance and literature.

The toro bravo

Spain's brave fighting bull is a fierce, untamed animal, whose bloodlines and pedigrees have been protected over the centuries in order to maintain its purity and the characteristics that make it both fundamental and particularly apt for the *corrida de toros*.

The fighting bull is not trained to charge; this herbivorous creature is born with the tendency

able, if traumatic, life. Pampered as a valuable thoroughbred, the *toro bravo* enjoys four to five years of splendour in the grass before it is faced with the ultimate test, its appearance in the arena.

During Spain's most glorious historic period, bullfighting was an important part of public life. For some 600 years, the aristocracy was responsible for breeding bulls and then fighting them before king and court.

The first man to turn bullfighting into a profession was the Ronda carpenter Francisco Romero, but it was his grandson, the great Pedro Romero, who is considered the father of modern bullfighting. With the *muleta* (the red cloth draped over a metre-long stick) in his left hand and the sword in his right, Pedro Romero manoeuvred the animal until it was in position for placing the sword. He killed more than 5,600 bulls between 1771 and 1799, without suffering so much as a scratch. No matador since has matched his feat in terms of physical immunity.

This then was *toreo* in its most rudimentary form; the object of the "show" was to kill the bull. Today, many are the intricate and artistic manoeuvres that have been created with the cape and *muleta*, and the bullfighter is no longer merely a *matador* (killer); he is a *torero*, who expresses his sentiments and artistic ability through the art of challenging and dominating a wild beast.

The spectacle itself is filled with colour, tradition, pageantry, danger, beauty, daring, blood, excitement and sublime art, and is certainly worth a closer look. Though some view it as an unnecessarily cruel slaughter, others see in the bullfight a dramatic dance between man in all his elegant cognisance and the bull in all its natural, earthy fierceness and brutality.

Death in the afternoon

The *corrida* commences with the pageantry of the *paseíllo* or entrance parade in which the *alguacilillos*, the mounted constables in 16th-century attire, lead the march of the bullfighters into the ring to the tune of the *pasodoble*.

The *alguacilillos* are followed into the arena or *ruedo* by the three matadors who precede in turn the three rows of their respective *cuadrillas* or teams. Each matador has in his service three *banderilleros*; their role is to assist him in the handling of the bull by using the cape and also in the placing of the *banderillas*, the 60-cm (2-ft) crêpe paper-decorated darts.

These *banderilleros* were, in their day, aspiring matadors, though probably few progressed beyond the novice stage to the *alternativa*. This is the ceremony in which a veteran matador symbolically cedes the tools of the trade – the *muleta* and sword – to the neophyte, endowing him with the right to kill fully grown bulls and to hold the coveted title of *Matador de Toros*.

The three rows of *banderilleros* are followed

LEFT: a five-year-old fighting bull sporting the ribbons of his ranch.
RIGHT: close encounter.

> ### RED RAGS AND BULLS
> It is a fallacy that bulls charge only red. Bulls are colour blind, but they have an innate tendency to attack anything that moves.

by the mounted *picadors*. Each matador will have two in his employ, one to stab each of his bulls. The *paseíllo* is completed with the no less pompous entrance of the more mundane bullring employees who will have to put in an appearance in the arena: the *monosabios*, who guide the picadors' horses, the *mulilleros*, who handle the mule team that drags out the dead bull, and the *areneros*, who tidy up the sand afterwards.

Once everyone has taken his respective post, the president of the *corrida* will pull out his

white handkerchief to signal the entrance of the first bull into the ring. This marks the initiation of the first *tercio* (third) of this live drama.

The bull will come charging into the arena through the *toril* gate, which communicates directly with the *chiqueros* – the individual pens where each bull had been enclosed since the morning's *sorteo* (draw). He will be greeted by a *banderillero*, magenta and gold *capote* (cape) in hand, or by an extremely eager matador.

The fight begins

The *torero* will effect some initial cape passes or lances directed to either of the bull's horns in order to determine the animal's natural tendencies: whether it favours one horn over the other, has a long smooth charge or swerves about rapidly, whether it sees well, and if it is strong.

As soon as the matador feels confident about the bull's condition, he will proceed to perform the most classic and fundamental of the passes, the *verónica*. A tandem of *verónicas* are linked together as the matador leads the bull gradually towards the centre of the ring. The series is concluded with a *media verónica* (half turn) in which the bull is abruptly brought about, giving the matador sufficient time and space in which to withdraw from the animal's path.

At this point, the picadors make their en-trance, the least understood and appreciated aspect of the *corrida*. The picadors have a mul-tifold purpose. First, they have the thankless task of preparing the animal for the culmina-tion of the matador's work, the *faena*. In order for the bull to be able to follow the cape smoothly it must be slowed down, but not excessively, and its head must be lowered. To achieve this they goad the bull with lances to weaken its shoulder muscles.

The picador must also try to correct any defects in the bull's charge, such as a tendency to hook to the right or swing up its horns at the end of each pass, which could prove fatal to the

A DRAMA IN THREE ACTS

Three is a magic number for understanding modern bullfighting. The *corrida* itself is a drama in three acts, each marked by trumpet calls.

There are three matadors, who alternate in the fighting of six bulls, which have previously been divided into three pairs of *lotes* in the *sorteo*, or drawing of lots.

The first and most senior matador is responsible for dispatching the first and fourth bulls, the second matador, the second and fifth, and the third and least experienced of the trio, the third and sixth.

Each matador has three *banderilleros*, who plant pairs of *banderillas*, or darts, in the bull's withers.

matador who is unprepared for it. The picador's other important function is to determine the *toro's* bravery, for the bull is just as significant a figure in the bullfight as the matador and the public calls upon both to perform at their best. A sign of bovine bravery is the animal's repetition of buoyant and determined charges against the padding of the picador's horse.

Generally three jabs or *puyazos* are administered, depending upon the animal's strength. The first third of the jabs is bright-ened by the alternating participation of the three matadors in a competitive display. With the cape, known as *quites*, each matador is sup-posed to *quitar* or draw the bull away from the horse and perform, whenever possible, any of the many varied cape adornments, such as *verónicas, chicuelinas, gaoneras, navarras* and *delantales.*

The President will use his white handkerchief once again to mark the beginning of the second *tercio*, the *banderillas*. Some matadors are skilled in the placing of their own *banderillas*, but 80 percent of the time the public will see the assistants place the darts in the most expedient manner. This *tercio* gives the bull the opportunity to recuperate after its cumbersome struggle with the heavily padded picador's horse.

The moment of truth

The trumpet now sounds for the third and final act of the drama. Armed with his sword and the red serge *muleta*, the matador will simultaneously salute and request permission from the President to kill the bull.

The right-handed pass or *derechazo*, in which the sword is used to expand the cloth, and the left-handed *natural* are the two fundamental *muleta* passes. More importance is attributed to the *natural*, in which the *muleta* is held in its natural and more diminutive size, with the sword in the right hand. A series of smooth or tempered *naturales* is usually completed with a *remate* pass, the *pase de pecho*, taking the bull from behind the matador and leading it past and off to the right.

The matador has 15 minutes in which to bring about the death of the bull, creating his artistic masterpiece, the *faena*. In order to kill in the *volapié* fashion, the matador positions the bull, raises the sword to shoulder level and moves in to kill, using the *muleta* to guide the dangerous horns past his right hip. He must move with determination and a steady hand to ensure that the sword hits its mark, a 7.5-cm (3-inch) wide opening just between the shoulder blades. If he misses his target, he will hit bone and the *pinchazo* will not be appreciated by the public.

If the steel *estoque* is not well placed or proves to be insufficient to produce the animal's death, the matador will be obliged to make use of the *descabello*. This is a shorter

---

LEFT: parading at the fiesta of San Fermín held in Pamplona.
RIGHT: a bull charging from the gate meets a *banderillero.*

sword fitted with a crossbar close to the tip. The matador directs the *descabello* to the rachidian bulb at the base of the bull's skull, which produces its instant death, if performed correctly. As soon as the bull drops to the ground, the *puntillero* rushes out with the *puntilla* or dagger to administer the *coup de grâce* to prevent any further suffering.

At this point the public displays its approval – or otherwise – of the bullfighter's performance. Under satisfactory circumstances the crowd waves handkerchiefs to request the granting of an ear to the matador. Nowadays, the *orejas* (ears) and the *rabo* (tail) are

symbolic trophies for a good-to-excellent performance. A matador who performs well but experiences difficulty with the sword, for example, might be applauded by the crowd and invited to take a *vuelta* or lap of the ring.

As the bulls share star billing with the matadors, a brave animal that performs well is applauded as it is drawn out of the arena by the mules. It may even be granted its own turn of the ring and, in exceptional cases, a pardon. A cowardly animal will be the object of irate protests as it is dragged from the ring. The trumpet will sound again and it is time for the second bull to emerge from its dark pen into the bright sunlight of the arena.

The bull has evolved from the fierce, erratic bovine faced by Pedro Romero and his contemporaries in Ronda. Years of selective breeding have produced a more tempered, noble stock, but have also led to a weakening of the caste. Additionally, the pasture areas of many ranches have been sharply reduced, and the limited area for exercise and grazing has debilitated the physical stamina of the bulls.

A cause for celebration

Every town in the country, no matter the size, celebrates its local *fiestas* on behalf of its respective patron saint, and the festivities would be incomplete without bullfighting. Madrid honours San Isidro the Farmer on 15 May with the longest bullfight fair of all: an incredible 27 consecutive days of *corridas*.

Other important *ferias* are the delightful *fallas* of Valencia in March; the incomparably colourful and gay Seville Fair in April; the Corpus Christi celebrations of Granada in June; the *Sanfermines* of Pamplona in July, immortalised by Ernest Hemingway; followed by the Valencia Summer Fair; the *Semana Grande* of Bilbao in August; and the busy month of September with the Salamanca and Valladolid fairs and the Grape harvests of Jerez and Logroño.

WHEN TO SEE BULLFIGHTS

The bullfighting season officially opens on 19 March (St Joseph's Day) and ends on 12 October (Columbus' Day in America; Hispanic Day in Spain), though fights are frequently held before and after these dates.

The bullring audience sits in the *tendidos* (stalls) or the *palcos* (balcony), where the president's box is situated. Seating is normally divided into three sections: the more comfortable and expensive shady side, or *sombra*; the cheaper sunny section, or *sol*, where, depending upon the season, spectators suffer the summer heat; and the intermediate *sol y sombra*.

The *corrida* generally starts at 5pm.

The El Pilar festivities in Zaragoza in mid-October conclude the season. *Festivales* are informal bullfights in which the *toreros* perform merely for their expenses, because the general proceeds of the *corrida* are intended for charity. In order to render these fights less dangerous, the bulls' horns are trimmed or shaved for these festivals. The bullfighters also exchange their silk and sequined *traje de luces* (suit of lights) for the *traje corto* or country costume.

Bullfighting today

Bullfighting, also referred to as the *Fiesta Nacional*, is no longer the unchallenged prime national pastime. It is obliged to share the spotlight with increasingly popular football matches as well as with all other forms of Spanish Sunday afternoon entertainment. Ticket prices have also soared. Added to the costs involved in raising a herd of fighting bulls for four to five years (the age at which they are allowed to fight) is the fact that the *festejo* is heavily taxed.

One thing which surely will never change because it represents the very essence of the *fiesta* is the mortal danger to the bullfighters

SUMMONED BY BULLS

Bulls have inspired countless writers and artists, including Hemingway and Picasso. The poet Federico García Lorca called the bulls "Spain's greatest vital and poetic treasure".

"Burlero" of the Marcos Núñez ranch. The fatal gorings of these star matadors were mourned by an entire Spanish nation.

El Cordobés once thrilled his audience but was sometimes thought guilty of holding the bulls in too much disdain. Today's crowd-pleasers include Enrique Ponce, a stylish performer; Joselito, who has superb technical skills; El Julí, a young *madrileño* star, and Fran Rivera, Paquirri's son. For a brief period during the 1990s, the emergence of star *torera,* Cristina

and of course the injury to, and ultimate death of, the bulls. During the 1980s two top matadors died in the arena. The popular Francisco Rivera, "Paquirri", married to the famous folksinger, Isabel Pantoja, was killed by the bull "Avispado" of the Sayalero y Bandrés ranch in Pozoblanco (Córdoba) on 26 September 1984. The promising 21-year-old José Cubero, "Yiyo", died instantly in the Colmenar Viejo arena of a horn wound inflicted directly to his heart on 30 August 1985. He was a victim of

LEFT: bullfighter Espartaco executing a cape pass called *derechazo.*
ABOVE: he successfully completes a natural pass.

Sánchez, who achieved massive popular acclaim, seemed to herald the end of the age-old male monopoly of the ring. But she retired in 1999, defeated, she said, by machismo.

A touch of madness

The *torero* continues to be a unique human being. The profession calls for an individual with considerable courage, grace, skill, physical prowess and agility, artistic sensitivity, romanticism – and perhaps madness.

The *torero* develops his own personalised philosophy that will enable him to risk his life and regularly face death with periodic precision and serenity. ❑

SPANISH PAINTING

From early cave paintings to Picasso's Guernica, *there is a heightened realism that characterises Spanish art*

The English writer Rose Macaulay, visiting Spain during the 1940s, concluded that the country "grows Roman walls and basilicas and 10th-century churches like wild figs, leaving them about in the most careless and arrogant profusion, uncharted and untended, for travellers to stumble on as they will". Today, in more enlightened and prosperous times, it is not true that Spain's artistic patrimony is, as she put it, "mouldering away". Throughout Spain there are well-catalogued museums and churches, and few important works of art have been neglected.

The majority of Spanish masterpieces were commissioned by the Church, court and higher aristocracy for Spanish eyes only and meant to induce lingering contemplation on subjects such as Christ's Passion, the lives of the saints, the nobility of earthly portrait sitters and the omnipotence of the Church. An invitation to contemplation, careful observation of life as it is, directness of expression and psychological penetration are qualities that come to mind when considering what is particularly "Spanish" about Spanish art.

Primitive wall paintings

The earliest Spanish masterpieces, rediscovered as recently as 100 years ago, are the prehistoric paintings in caves (particularly at Altamira) and early medieval wall paintings previously hidden under whitewash in Spanish churches. The cave drawings consist of marks that appear to have been primitive notational systems, and elegantly rendered bison, reindeer and other animals. The vigorous style and spiritual feeling of both cave drawings and early-Christian murals influenced 20th-century artists, notably Joan Miró and Pablo Picasso.

In the Middle Ages, pilgrims' trails and trade routes brought the stylistic influences of French and Italian, Netherlandish and German, Near

Eastern and North African art into Spain's ecclesiastical network. All artists patronised by the Church were affected by these. Thus, the decorative figures and rich colours of medieval wall paintings are also found in illuminated manuscripts in the libraries of León Cathedral, El Escorial and other cathedrals and museums.

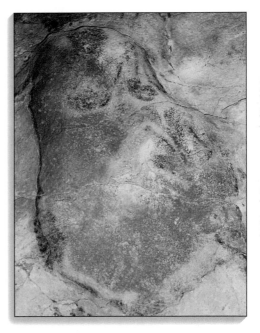

One of the most surprising ensembles of rediscovered early medieval mural paintings is in the little pre-Romanesque church known as "Santullano" (or San Julian de los Prados) in Oviedo, built in the early 9th century. Mosaics from Roman villas have been excavated near Oviedo, and Roman wall paintings similar to those preserved at Pompeii in Italy inspired the *trompe-l'oeil* decoration of this Asturian church.

In León, south of Oviedo, the mid-11th-century Panteón de los Reyes, a royal crypt adjoining the Colegiata de San Isidro, has unusually well-preserved wall paintings dating from 1175. León is on a pilgrimage trail to Santiago de Compostela, so it is possible that

---

PRECEEDING PAGES: Goya's *Marquess of Santa Cruz.*
LEFT: El Greco's *Gentleman with a Hand on his Chest.*
RIGHT: prehistoric cave painting at Altamira.

French artists painted the relatively naturalistic Christ in Majesty and scenes from the New Testament. But one of them, in which the angel appears to the shepherds, is often cited as an example of Spanish realism. Ordinary details such as a shepherd feeding his dog are found in the sacred art of other European schools, too; but in the frequency with which they occur in Spanish art, many people read a special Spanish sense of the dignity of everyday life.

Catalan Romanesque

Catalonia was the most important centre for Romanesque painting in Spain, and there are many superb examples in the Museo de Arte de Cataluña in Barcelona, where the frescoes are displayed in rooms emulating the shapes of the churches from which they have been taken. The Moors, who entered Spain from North Africa in the 8th century, had reinforced the Spanish artists' flair for flat, linear, brightly coloured stylisation. However, the Oriental gift for pattern also wafted across the Mediterranean via Italy from Byzantium. The Catalan Romanesque style, in particular, shows the Byzantine influence. Its ritualistic figures are almost expressionless, even when they undergo horrifying martyrdoms. Some of the finest

AMNESTY REVEALS LOST TREASURES

Many Spanish works of art are still undiscovered in private hands. When the Spanish government offered a tax amnesty in 1986 forgiving back taxes on undeclared works of art and reducing future taxes, 30,000 paintings turned up, including at least 80 previously unknown works by Goya. A number of Goyas are still owned by the families who commissioned them. Under the terms of the amnesty, owners must allow their freshly rediscovered possessions to be shown in public for one month a year, and they may not sell them outside Spain. This will inevitably lead to a more complete picture of the work of many artists.

paintings in this style come from the Pyrenean church of Sant Climent in Taüll, Lérida, dedicated in 1123. Spanish anecdotal detail can be seen in the fresco in which Lazarus, propped on his crutch, is licked by an ecstatic dog.

Regional schools

As the *Reconquista* – the Christian conquest of Spain over the Muslims – progressed, regional Spanish schools developed. The product of their workshops was naive and at times positively homely. However, during the 14th and 15th centuries, the technical breakthroughs of the increasingly realistic northern European and northern Italian schools profoundly affected Spanish painting. It is unclear how many Spanish artists visited Italy or the Netherlands, but in a fresco cycle by the Catalan Ferrer Bassa, thought to have studied in Italy, there are squared, three-dimensional figures and striking narrative scenes strongly reminiscent of Giotto.

In the late 14th century, an International Gothic style spread from the Burgundian and French courts. Integrating the Flemish artists' careful drawing in meticulous detail and the Italo-Byzantine love of pattern and colour, the style was characterised by courtly elegance and a new interest in individual psychology. A

retablo, which was stretched out to become a wall of panels that climbed up to fill and tower over the east end of the church.

Hispano-Flemish

From around 1440 Flemish influence came to dominate Spanish painting. Lluis Dalmau, a Catalan, went to study in Bruges and, returning to Barcelona, passed on his training to the younger Jaime Huguet. The *Virgen des Concellers*, Dalmau's impressive altarpiece in Barcelona, has a Spanish Virgin and Child on a Gothic throne in a Flemish landscape. A panel by Huguet in the same museum contains

superb example is the Flemish painter Rogier van der Weyden's *Deposition* in the Prado, an altarpiece of around 1435 that came into the Spanish royal collection in the 16th century. Lluis Borrassa's altarpiece of Santa Clara in Barcelona (*circa* 1412) is a Catalan version of this International Gothic style.

The altarpiece was the most important commission for the artist of the *Reconquista*. In this lively period, Spanish fresco painting died out, and the altar frontal was replaced by the

LEFT: early 12th-century painted apse, Santa María d'Aneu in the Catalan Pyrenees.
RIGHT: *The Last Supper* by Jaime Huguet (*circa* 1470).

charming Spanish anecdotal details: votive offerings hanging over the corpse of the miracle-working St Vincent, and a tiny devil escaping from the mouth of one of the cured.

The Hispano-Flemish style peaked at the centralising, art-collecting court of the Catholic monarchs Fernando and Isabel from the mid-15th and into the 16th century. Flemish or Flemish-trained artists painted his portrait (now at Windsor Castle) and hers (now in the Royal Palace, Madrid). Fernando Gallego (*Piedad* in the Prado), the outstanding Castilian master of this style, combined the decorativeness of International Gothic with the monumentality that had been developing since Giotto.

Renaissance influence

From the early 16th century a new wave of Italian influence brought the High Renaissance style to Spain. The collecting fever of the monarchy begun by Charles V, who befriended Titian, meant that Spanish painting was exposed to wider influences and lost much of its provincial character. Felipe II moved Spain's capital from Toledo to Madrid, giving the country's artistic life a focus. A great patron of art, he also imported several Italian artists to decorate his

> ### IBERIAN GENIUS
>
> The influences of Spanish cave drawings, early Christian church murals, Goya and Velázquez and the subject of the bullfight, all find their way into Picasso's work.

from Italy to Spain hoping to find employment. But his weird, hovering, Byzantine figures wiped with eerie bluish light did not appeal to Felipe, who had expected something very different from a pupil of Titian. Fortunately, El Greco's portraits and religious subjects commanded an audience elsewhere in Spain. His portraits reveal an unexpected realism: in *The Gentleman with a Hand on his Chest* the dark background emphasises the man's facial features and aristocratic fingers. In his altarpieces for

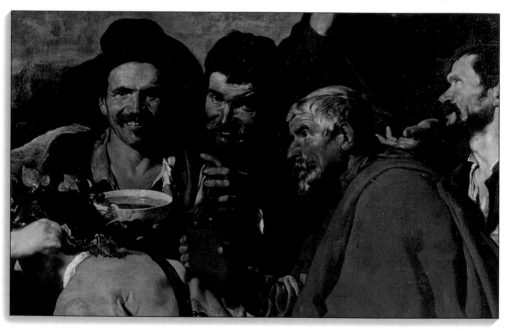

palace at the Escorial, which consequently became a training school for Spanish painters.

But the pagan classical ideals of Italian Renaissance were not initially in tune with the prevailing ethos of priest-ridden Spain, and religious subjects continued to predominate. The Church and the Inquisition militated against the portrayal of idealised nudes and mythological subjects. Similarly, High Renaissance perspective like that in Andrea Mantegna's Italian masterpiece, *The Death of the Virgin*, in the Prado, brought to Spain by Felipe IV, was attempted by only a few Spanish artists.

Felipe II's Escorial project attracted the great Mannerist painter, El Greco, who travelled

Toledo's churches, El Greco displayed his own brand of piety and a streak of mysticism. The Inquisition was ambivalent about religious ecstasy, but the number of contemporaneous copies of his work attest to his popularity.

The Golden Age

The 17th century was a Golden Age for Spanish painting. The era was dominated by three painters from Seville: Francisco Zurbarán, Bartolomé Esteban Murillo and Diego Velázquez; and José de Ribera, a Spaniard who worked in the Spanish kingdom of Naples. Although the range of acceptable subject matter broadened to include history and mythology, religious subjects remained the most important. Paintings had to conform to Counter-Reformation ideals, which decreed that the visual arts should give clear, straightforward expositions of religious subjects to act as an aid to devotion.

This aim is most clearly realised in the work of Zurbarán, whose series of paintings featuring a single figure – usually a saint or monk – in meditation are stark, uncompromising images with violent contrasts of dark and light. Ribera also delighted in painting scenes of bloody martyrdom with the energy and verve of Caravaggio. Murillo's soft-edged treatment of religious themes was more in tune with popular taste, and his compositions were distributed in print form among the middle classes. Favoured subjects were the Immaculate Conception, the Holy Family and the Madonna and Child. Modern taste favours Murillo's pictures of children and beggars in which the vivacity of the subject is tempered by an unsentimental rendering of the reality of their circumstances.

Still life and Velázquez

The 17th century was also a time when the Spanish love of naturalism culminated in a flowering of still-life painting. Unlike Flemish examples, Spanish still lives are often spare compositions: a few fruits, vegetables or pots arranged with austere simplicity. Lovingly delineated still-life details are often inserted into narrative paintings. This is true of the type of painting known as *bodegones* – genre scenes set in a kitchen or tavern. No-one painted these with more assurance than Velázquez, whose *Old Woman Frying Eggs* (National Gallery of Scotland, Edinburgh) is a prime example.

Velázquez enjoyed a successful career, becoming Felipe IV's favourite painter at the age of 24. His sitters ranged from the king to the court dwarves. Pope Innocent said of his portrait by the artist that it was *"troppo vero"* – too truthful. *Las Meninas*, in the Prado, records one of the royal family's visits to Velázquez's studio in the Alcázar. The bold technique, the sense of depth created by the figures in the mirror and, above all, the spontaneous snapshot quality of the royal portrait, have made this picture a masterpiece of world art.

LEFT: *The Drunkards* by Velázquez (detail) shows the artist's realism, sympathy and insight.
RIGHT: self-portrait by Goya.

Apart from *bodegones* and portraits, Velázquez made a few excursions into other fields. His monumental *Surrender of Breda* in the Prado is inspired by Rubens. Painted for Felipe IV's court theatre, Buen Retiro, it recreates a gesture of magnanimity on the part of the victor and vanquished after the Spanish siege against the Dutch stronghold a few miles north of Rubens' studio in Antwerp. Velázquez's *Rokeby Venus,* one of the few paintings of the nude in Spanish art, shows his awareness of the work of Titian, who popularised the subject of Venus gazing at herself in a mirror attended by Cupid.

Goya probably took his cue from this canvas, which belonged to his patron the Duchess of Alba, when he came to paint his *Naked Maja* 150 years later. Like Velázquez, Goya was a court painter, and his portraits of the royal family are suffused with an astonishing realism: Ernest Hemingway claimed that he "painted his spittle into every face" in his portrait of the degenerate *Family of Charles IV* in the Prado.

Goya's realism could also descend to the horrific: following a severe illness that left him profoundly deaf, a darker and highly original side emerged in his work. He produced a series of etchings, *Los Caprichos* (caprices), which took a satirical look at the follies and inadequacies of humanity; a second series of engravings, *The Disasters of War*, depicted atrocities committed by the French troops when they occupied Spain in the Peninsular War. This darker tendency culminated in the late "black" paintings now in the Prado, originally painted directly on the walls of his home, in which the myth of Saturn, the symbol of death and destruction, constantly recurs.

IMAGE MAKER

The strong graphic quality of Miró's work, together with its inherent wit, led the Spanish National Tourist office to ask him to design their publicity.

Goya was an isolated figure of genius in the 18th century, and there was no Spanish painter of comparable stature in the following century.

Yet it was then that Spanish art began to be appreciated in Europe: the French Impressionists were stunned by the realism and expressive paint-handling of Velázquez and Goya.

The 20th century

The 20th century gave rise to several giants of Spanish painting, including Pablo Picasso, who like many modern Spanish artists, spent most of his career outside Spain. Along with fellow Cubist painter Juan Gris, he spent his formative years in Paris, and most of the rest of his life in France. But his work retained its Spanish roots. As Gertrude Stein put it, he "had in him not only Spanish painting but Spanish Cubism, which is

the daily life of Spain". His famous painting *Guernica* was inspired by his distress at the bombing of a town during the Spanish Civil War. Barcelona's Picasso Museum has an unrivalled collection of his early works.

Salvador Dalí, too, lived most of his life in exile, in Paris and the US, and there is a Dalí museum at his birthplace, Figueres. A Catalan like Miró, he took up the thread of realism, but turned it to Surrealist ends, to produce what he called "hand-painted dream photographs".

Joan Miró, on the other hand, after an initial period in Paris, lived in and around his native Barcelona before moving to Mallorca. His Surrealism was of an entirely different complexion to Dalí's, based on imagination rather than external reality, blending primitivism, personal mythology and abstraction. The graphic quality of his work is inspired by the rhythmic forms of traditional Catalan art. The Miró Foundation in Barcelona houses many of his works.

Antoní Tàpies, Spain's most important postwar painter, was a member of the Dau al Set collective; he developed a distinct abstract style in the 1950s, using mixed media to produce works of startling originality *(see page 260)*.

From the 1950s to the mid-1970s much of Spanish art was directed against fascism, the oligarchy and, later, consumer culture. Antonio Saura's violent monochromatic pieces were attacks on the Church and the repression of the individual. Art collectives Equipo Realidad and Equipo Crónica, and painters Eduardo Arroyo, Juan Genovés and Antonio Lopez, used realism or pop art to make ironic social comment.

With Franco's death in 1975 there was a change of direction. Abstract artists Soledad Sevilla and Pablo Palazuelos were inspired by Velázquez, Spanish history and nature. In the 1980s art boom two Mallorcans, both expressionists, received international recognition: Miguel Barceló and Ferrán García Sevilla.

The mid-1980s saw the emergence of new media: installations, video, film and computer technology. An exception is the contemporary painter Dis Berlin, whose nostalgic work harks back to the art of the early 20th century. ❑

LEFT: drawing of Picasso aged 20 by Ramón Casas.
RIGHT: Miró's *The Wine Bottle*.

WILDLIFE

From the high Pyrenees to low-lying marshlands: travel slowly in Spain's
unspoiled countryside and you will find a plethora of wild creatures

Few of the millions of international tourists who crowd the *costas* every year realise that Spain, with its vast areas of unspoiled scenery, is host to a wide range of fascinating wild animals and birds. So extensive is the country's list of rare and exotic creatures that, for some naturalists, Spain is Europe's last Eden. Enthusiasm and concern starts at the top. King Juan Carlos has declared: "Nature conservation is one of the great public endeavours of our age."

The country has more than 200 nature reserves, including 11 national parks. The principal highland parks are Covadonga National Park in the western Picos de Europa, home to the European brown bear as well as to wolves, wild boar and chamois; the Ordesa and Monte Perdido National Park in the Aragonese Pyrenees; the Aigües Tortes and San Mauricio Lake National Park in the Catalan Pyrenees, and Garajonay, the cloud forest-capped peaks of La Gomera in the Canary Islands.

In southwest Spain, flanking the estuary of the Guadalquivir river, is the huge wetland area of Doñana National Park, habitat of six world-protected species including the imperial eagle, and the winter retreat of thousands of migratory aquatic birds. For years Doñana was under assault from developers and commercial pressure groups and in 1998, toxic waste poured through the park from a neighbouring plant. Now its future seems assured. The smaller marshland area of Tablas de Daimiel in La Mancha also supports a wealth of birdlife. The contrasts between Spain's protected wild spaces are also impressive, including marine landscapes such as the islands of Cabrera (Mallorca) and Tabarca (Alicante) and the coastline of the Cabo de Gata (Almería), which teems with underwater life. At the other end of the scale are the moon-like, parched volcanic peaks of Timanfaya (Lanzarote) and Teide (Tenerife).

LEFT: a short-toed eagle feeds a snake to its young.
RIGHT: a well concealed genet in the Coto Doñana; an agile tree climber, it also swims well.

Imperial eagle

Yet with varying attitudes and policies across Spain's autonomous regions, from dedicated and protectionist to indifferent or antagonistic, conservationist ideas may have come at too late a stage. Itself a regal symbol, the Spanish imperial eagle's population has been reduced by

habitat destruction and heedless development. But with patience and luck you may see, high above the coastal heathland in southwest Spain, pairs of these magnificent eagles in flight, displaying their remarkable mating behaviour .

It starts with a series of elegant circlings, with wings and pinions fully extended. After soaring together for a few minutes, one bird takes the initiative and dives at its mate. Male and female then perform a display of aerial swoops and chases. One bird eventually rolls on its back in mid-air and presents its unsheathed talons to the other. Finally, they plunge earthward, interlocked, then level out and fly apart a few hundred feet above ground.

The couple build a large ramshackle nest on top of a cork-oak tree. Two or three eggs produce plump balls of white fluff. At two months, the young eagles, now with cinnamon-brown feathers, learn to soar and to dive at prey. Within a year, the adults are ready to mate again and juveniles are on their own.

Glimpse of a lynx

It could be even harder to see, in the southwestern region, one of the shyest of exclusively Iberian creatures; the Iberian lynx has the look of a leopard cub. There are about 150 wild lynx remaining in Spain, in the national parks of

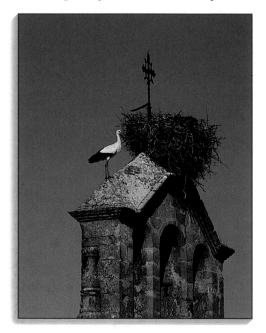

ON THE NATURE TRAIL

Spain's mountain parks are snow-filled from mid-November to mid-April. The best time to visit the Ordesa or Covadonga National Parks is mid-summer. Aigües Tortes can be visited in May, though the highest peaks will still be avalanche-prone. To see migratory birds on the move, visit the wetlands of Doñana and the Tablas de Daimiel in spring or autumn. Spain also has many nature reserves *(parques naturales)*. Cazorla, in southwest Spain, is home to many protected bird species including the golden eagle. Monfragüe, in Extremadura, is a favoured breeding place for the black stork, the black vulture and the black-winged kite.

Andújar in Jaen and Doñana in Huelva, and the species could become extinct within 20 years. The biggest cause for their dwindling numbers was a myxomatosis plague which all but wiped out their main diet, rabbits. The 80 percent reduction in its habitat since 1960 has also contributed to this frightening prospect. In 2002, the World Conservation Union listed the Iberian lynx as a Category One Critical Endangered Species, which means that money was made available for a rescue project. Doñana National Park has begun an active breeding programme.

Weighing around 12 kg (30 lb), it has markings even more pronounced than its first cousin, the European lynx. The lynx is king of Spain's wildcats, a family that includes the slender genet with its characteristic long banded tail. Fur pattern apart, the lynx is distinguished by large and tapering ears, topped with tufts of black hair. These act as antennae, sensitive to air currents during up-wind stalking and to the slightest rustle in the undergrowth. Monitoring sounds inaudible to a human ear, they also compensate for a weak sense of smell. A mottled-ochre coat provides the perfect camouflage in sun-dappled vegetation.

So lithe as to appear boneless, the lynx is a nocturnal hunter. An agile tree-climber, it is also an expert swimmer. With eyes that can be green or amber, it has ultrasensitive sight – enabling it to spot its supper at a considerable distance on a moonless night.

Black storks

Relax under an oak in rural Spain and you may hear the unexpected sound above you of a saw cutting wood. Look carefully for the carpenter. It could be a black stork *(Cigüeña negra)*, in Spain from its winter sojourn in Africa. A big bird with jet-dark plumage, it returns to the same large, untidy nest every year. Unlike the large white stork visible on bell towers and tall chimneys throughout Spain, the black species prefer elm or oak woods, river cliffs or rocky platforms in the *sierras*. The *Cigüeña negra* is a solitary bird, flying alone or in small groups during migration.

Averse to using their heavy wings, the storks do plenty of gliding, and need thermal up-currents to maintain altitude. As there are few thermals over large expanses of water, they seek short crossings, like the Straits of Gibraltar, for their north and southbound journeys.

The black stork shares a curious habit with its white counterpart. On emerging from the egg, the nestling lays its head on its back and makes rapid snapping movements with its bill to signal it is hungry. Though silent at first (the infant stork's bill is soft), in this way begins the bird's lifelong characteristic clacking. And if, in an adult, the habit looks like a warning of attack, it can also signal excitement and love.

When they are courting, the storks throw their heads back and engage in a riot of mutual bill-clapping. When eggs appear, male and female share responsibility for the hatching and, once chicks emerge – three to five of them,

and fiercely protective of their engagingly striped piglets, and have been known to attack.

To see anything of the brown bear families of the Cantabrian mountains of northwest Spain you could do with wings or a stargazer's telescope. Even scientists trying to study them may find only one or two of the shaggy giants (at about 2 metres/7 ft tall, they are among the largest land animals). But a shrunken colony of bears *is* there, forced from the foothills to take refuge in forests near the peaks after centuries of persecution by hunting parties.

Once these brown bears numbered several hundreds. Today some 80 or fewer survive in

with snowy white feathers – the storks are faithful parents. So much so that if the female dies or is killed, the male will remain alone at the nest to guard the eggs and rear the chicks.

Boar and bear

If you're planning a walk through thick forest, watch out for wild boar. The animal that featured prominently in medieval banquets is still the curse of farmers, whose crops it raids, and target of not always legal hunters. The boar are shy

LEFT: white stork and bell-tower nest.
RIGHT: the Cantabrian mountains are the last refuge of Spain's brown bears; only about 100 remain.

the mountain range. In winter the bears disappear entirely, holed up in caves for their long hibernation, a prolonged light sleep on a bed of leaves, during which respiration sinks to some five breaths every couple of minutes. Heartbeats slow down accordingly, though body temperatures drop by only about 10 percent. Females that have given birth lie in the den, making a warm circle for their hairless cubs.

Since 1973 Spanish bears have been legally protected. Hunting or killing carries extremely stiff fines, and possible imprisonment. You still might hear farmers boasting of a trophy, though the kill will be claimed as self-defence or the protection of lambs.

Flamingos

In contrast to the secretive bears, greater flamingos are eminently visible – particularly in the large Fuente de Piedra lagoon north of urban Málaga, or on the mud-flats of the Guadalquivir River estuary in Doñana and the shallow coastal lakes, floodwaters and salt marshes of the south – a sub-tropical climate where there is normally a good food supply of algae, molluscs and crustaceans. The rose-pink and white flamingos, wading or in serried flight, are an

> **BIZARRE BIRD**
>
> Spain is the last European stronghold of the great bustard. This "goose with eagle's wings" is almost grotesque on the ground yet spectacular in flight.

are visited by a mass of migratory birds during the year. Occassionally, trigger-happy hunters can also pose a threat to the wildlife in this area.

Great bustard

Turning from one leggy bird to another, on the plains of Spain you may see the fascinating great bustard. Weighing about 12 kg (30 lb), it has a moustache of white bristles, an ostrich-type head and legs, and barks like a dog when excited. One of the world's largest flying birds, it is legally protected. The courtship of great

ornithological treasure. Their stilt-like legs and long necks allow them to "graze" the shallow water for nutritious algae, feeding with their heads upside-down.

Totally gregarious, greater flamingos "talk" to their companions with much trumpeting and, when flying in formation, goose-like gabbles. They breed in company, building circular, mud-heap nests a few inches above brackish water. In the warm places they favour lies a danger to the flamingo populations: a searing summer will shrink or dry up water habitats. Lakes become salt-pans and the birds can breed there only irregularly. Nevertheless, the salt-pans at Torrevieja and Santa Pola on the Alicante coast

bustards, in spring often performed by dozens of birds in open spaces, is quite a spectacle. Uttering gruff barks, the males (or *barbons*) attract the assembled females with displays of their gorgeously striped plumage and fan-tail, and showy and prolonged dancing rituals. After the ball is over, the female seeks long grass or a field of cereals for her nest. The principal enemy to her hatchlings is the raven.

Other birds

The friendly little hoopoe is found searching the grass for insects all over Spain. If you walk extensively in Spain, you are likely to see its unmistakable fanned crest of black and pale gold, pinkish-brown plumage and barred black-and-white wings. The hoopoe's singularity and its seemingly playful ways give it a considerable charm.

Spain is rich in woodpeckers. A rare prize would be a glimpse of the swamp-dwelling purple gallinule. The lovely, egg-thieving azure-winged magpie of the Coto Doñana is also a notable character which, apart from Spain, inhabits only China and east Asia.

Another striking bird, the Spanish imperial heron, is the most exalted of its species, a dramatic figure with a black crest and long, graceful, boldly striped neck. It nests and breeds in colonies, hidden in beds of dense reeds. The question arises why this bird, *Ardea purpurea*, with its dark plumage, is "imperial" in Spain when elsewhere it is simply a purple heron. The answer may lie in subtleties of sheen or colouring, but the Spanish name seems appropriate – one that is very different, moreover, from the truly purple, red-legged, red-billed gallinule. Virtually all that the two have in common is that they are secretive dwellers of the wetlands.

Two other vastly different creatures inhabit the high Pyrenees: the bearded vulture with its 3-metre (9-ft) wingspan and the odd, mole-sized Pyrenean desman, one of the rarest animals on earth. Related to the mole, the desman is a sightless nocturnal rodent with a long, flattened, red-tipped snout, clawed front feet, large webbed hind feet and a rat-like tail.

Visually unappealing, rarely photographed – and unknown to science before the 19th century – there's nothing like it in the animal kingdom. The local saying is that "God's hand shook when He created the desman". An aquatic mammal, it feeds on caddis – the larva of mayfly and stone flies – probing icy river beds with its sensitive proboscis. Water pollution has driven it ever higher into the mountains; for all its unwholesome appearance, the desman can only survive in the purest water.

Vulture and toad

The bearded vulture (or lammergeyer) is in decline due in part to shooting by hunters and its unfortunate habit of eating poisoned meat put down by shepherds for wolves. Its diet consists primarily of wild or domestic animal remains. As the garbage collectors of the mountains, these birds play a vital role in the scheme of nature.

Splendid gliders, bearded vultures will stay aloft for many hours, scanning the landscape in search of food. Carrion creatures though they are, the birds' flight silhouette is not unlike the falcon's. Lacking the long, bare neck that gives other vultures a repulsive image, the birds in flight are impressive and beautiful.

The bearded vulture supplements its food by a neat trick. Its wings extended – primary feathers outstretched like slim fingers – it will soar

over rocky ground strewn with bones left by predators. Swooping down, it picks up a bone, flies up, then drops it from a height so that the bone cracks, exposing a tasty morsel of marrow. Thus their Spanish name *quebranta-huesos*, or bone-breakers.

Travel slowly and you will see wild creatures virtually everywhere, including near ponds, the strange little Spanish midwife toad, its eggs on its back. You are unlikely to see any of the few remaining Iberian wolves living mainly in the west, but you could be luckier with the striking Iberian ibex in the Gredos mountains near Madrid and, in Galicia, the heathlands' wild horse, the Garrano. ❑

LEFT: Iberian ibex by a mountain stream.
RIGHT: the friendly hoopoe with its distinctive fanned crest can be seen almost anywhere in Spain.

FLAMENCO

A powerful artistic expression of the sorrows and joys of life, flamenco offers

a window on the soul of Andalusia – and touches our deepest emotions

Jazz genius Miles Davis once said: "Sometimes, when I hear flamenco, I fall on my knees." Today, more than ever, flamenco has proved its power to move audiences the world over, yet its musical complexities, lyrics and emotional depth are rarely understood. What is it in flamenco that communicates so directly with musicians and audiences from so many varied cultures?

A music and a way of life

Although deeply rooted in southern Spanish folklore, flamenco is now a complex intertwined art form. Its song, music and dance have each developed separately and responded together to changes in the world at large. In the past 50 years waves of emigration from southern to northern cities and the mushrooming of dance schools all over Spain have left their mark. Yet for all its sophistication flamenco remains eminently popular. The majority of its artists and enthusiasts come from the poorer fringes of society, where life's experiences have taught them to be fiercely independent, proud and sceptical. Above all, they share a profound sense of suffering.

These are the emotions that audiences feel across the divides of culture and language in flamenco. Sparing with words and rich in metaphor, the lyrics strike directly at the emotions. As anthropologist William Washabaugh put it, they share "a rustic poetic style that operates like a psychic key to open up floodgates of passion".

Ancient art, religious roots

Flamenco's roots lie in the distant past. The hedonistic Tartessans (4th–6th century BC), thought to have come from Africa, were famed for their music and primitive dance, and later, in Roman times, dancing girls from Cádiz were shipped off to the imperial capital where they earned a reputation for rhythmic virtuosity and sensuality verging on the lascivious. The Greeks contributed the Oriental patterns of Byzantine liturgical chant forms.

Other elements entered during the Muslim centuries. Fragments of Jewish religious song survive in the *saetas* sung during Holy Week

processions, and 11th-century *andalusí* music shaped southern folk dances such as the *fandango, jarcha* and *zambra,* which provided flamenco's formal framework. *Ziriab*, a music that originated from the Damascan caliphate, may be the source of flamenco's use of repetition to build to a cathartic emotional climax. One Arabic account tells of a fish-seller driven to such a state of ecstatic frenzy by *ziriab* that he ripped open his shirt, just as Gypsy audiences once did in moments of uncontrollable emotion.

After the Christian Reconquest was completed with the fall of Granada in 1492, the plaintive Oriental sounds of Gregorian plain-

LEFT: flamenco dance is essentially an individual art.
RIGHT: Doré etching of the Gypsy camps at Sacromonte, Granada.

song – derived from Visigothic Byzantine chants – filtered right through the Spanish folk tradition. The singer Enrique el Mellizo created one flamenco song-style after sitting outside Málaga cathedral and listening to the monks singing Mass.

Gypsy song

Professional musicians long before their arrival in Spain in the 15th century, the Gypsies *(see page 75)* were also vital catalysts in the creation of flamenco. It was born – alongside bullfighting and banditry – in the rich hybrid culture of the semi-nomadic frontier world they shared

Casanova, noted it in their diaries, leaving some of the first written evidence of flamenco's existence.

In search of black sounds

Song remains flamenco's essential form of expression. The voices are dark and wailing, hoarse and deep, capturing the pain at the heart of flamenco. When flamenco is good, it is said to pinch the listener. The singers, called *cantaores,* shift from a gravelly whisper to an intense musical shout and slide from top to bottom notes within a few seconds in search of what the singer Manuel Torres once called

with converted Muslims and those who had been left landless by the Reconquest. The word flamenco may have its roots in the Arabic *felag-mengu,* meaning wandering peasant.

As the Gypsies learned southern folksong, they added complex rhythms, expressive vocals and, above all, emotional depth. At *ferias,* cattle fairs and horse markets, they sang for money, using the lyrics of Castilian Renaissance romances.

In the 18th century, as Gypsies' persecution became less acute, flamenco also took root in southern towns. From the 1760s travellers began to chance upon flamenco in Cádiz, Jerez and Seville. A few, like Giacomo

MAJOR FLAMENCO FESTIVALS

Festival de Madrid (Feb): themed performances, theatre spaces. **Certamen Nacional de Córdoba** (May): prestigious biennial national contest. **Festival de Jerez** (May): leading dance event. **Festival de la Guitarra de Granada** (summer). **Festival Nacional del Cante de las Minas**, La Union, Murcia (Aug): contest showcasing young singing talent plus performances by leading artists. **Bienal de Sevilla** (Sept–Oct): month-long biannual flamenco festival. **Fiesta de la Bulería de Jerez** (Sep): weekend event held in the bullring; large crowds. There are smaller, open-air festivals throughout the summer in Andalusia.

"black sounds". But for aficionados, technique is secondary to the singers' courage in pushing their voices and emotions to the limits.

Behind this apparently uninhibited improvisation is a strict underlying musical discipline: a canon of more than 50 song-styles *(palos)*, each defined by a different rhythmic pattern *(compás)* and mood. Each style is further subdivided into as many as 30 different variants. Mastery of these is the foundation from which all flamenco artists work, and a basic understanding is important for the audience, whose "*Olés*" give a live show its two-way electricity. In live performances, a *cantaor* often introduces each piece by its song-style.

Two early styles with Gypsy roots remain fundamental today. One is the *seguiriya*, the most tragic style of *cante jondo*, or deep song, which expresses anguish in the face of despair. Its structure illustrates flamenco's rhythmic complexity: each line of its four-line stanzas has seven syllables, except for the third, which has 11, and on to this is grafted a 12-bar rhythm, with the emphasis on the off-beat.

The second early song-style still widely performed today, the *soleá*, has generated more variants than any other. It explores themes from the everyday to the dramatic, filtering them through the wisdom and irony of experience.

A third group of song-styles, *tonás* from the forge and prison, are a surviving example of old flamenco song stripped back to its starting point, the naked voice.

Dancing out emotions

Flamenco dance, always marked out by its sensuality, also emerged as a fusion of earlier forms, among them folk dances and courtly boleros. "The fandango is an excitation to lust when danced by Gypsies," noted the minutes of Cádiz council in 1761. By 1800 it had found its way from the Gypsy quarters of Cádiz, Seville and Granada via taverns and variety theatres to dance academies.

The physical tension between discipline and freedom of movement, evoking a sense of

---

LEFT: *cante*, or song, is the heart of flamenco. Singers push their voices and emotions to the limits.
RIGHT: Paco de Lucia, top flamenco guitarist.

> ### LOST AND FOUND
>
> During the 1950s, romance lyrics that had been lost for centuries were rediscovered in a few Gypsy families who had handed them down by word of mouth.

caged desire, still gives flamenco dance its sexual energy. In pure flamenco the dancers, or *bailaores*, do not follow any choreography. Instead, anchored by the rhythmic pattern of each song-style, they dance out their emotions, which can produce lightning switches from moments of contained inner absorption to unleashed energy in furious rhythmic stamping called *zapateo*.

Flamenco dance has always flirted with other forms, thereby producing hybrid theatrical

versions: operas staged in bullrings around the beginning of the 20th century; Antonio Gadés' film trilogy made in the 1980s; and Joaquín Cortés' spectacular stage musicals today all fall within that tradition.

The *cafés cantantes*

From 1850 onwards flamenco found its way into wider paying audiences via *cafés cantantes*, singing cafés with small stages.

It was in the *cafés cantantes* that performances took their present-day form, with each artist coming forward at various points for solos. Here, too, the guitar finally emerged as an element in its own right. A hybrid of two earlier stringed instruments – one Arab and the other Christian, the first plucked and the second strummed – it was initially used as basic accompaniment to dance and song. But simple early technique quickly gave way to more intricate *tremolos* and *arpeggios* as well as varied personal interpretations.

However, virtuosity is second in importance to depth of feeling. The strong rhythmic baseline, warmth of tone and vast array of chords used give flamenco guitar its particular human quality. Listening to recordings by some of the great concert guitarists of different generations – Paco el de Lucena, Javier Molina,

Into the modern age

Today, after a surge of creativity since Franco's death, flamenco is more popular than ever, and is enjoyed all round Spain, although Andalusia remains its heartland.

In the 1920s, when intellectuals such as poet Federico García Lorca believed flamenco was a dying art form, the myth grew up that only unpaid flamenco was authentic. But in fact, ever since the early cattle fairs, flamenco's paid artists have also been its creative innovators.

In the same century, new dance forms like the *seguiriya, martinete* or *rondeña* were

Ramón Montoya, Niño Montoya, Sabicas and Paco de Lucía, to name but a few – it is extraordinary to think that none of them could read sheet music.

Songs of life

As Gypsy and Andalusian folk singers performed alongside one another in the *cafés cantantes*, the crossover of styles gave rise to new song-forms which to this day remain the base of flamenco's repertoire. In this way the range widened to include the *fandango* dance plus its variants, *malagueñas, granaínas,* and the mining songs that sprung up towards the end of the 19th century.

SO MANY SONG STYLES

The *cantiñas* of Cádiz province – including *alegrías, romeras and caracoles* – grew around the Aragonese *jota* brought south by troops during the Napoleonic war of independence. *De ida y vuelta* (round-trip) are folk songs taken to Latin America, or brought back from there, then flamenco-ised. Some song-styles focus on working life: *livianas* and *serranas* reflect the preoccupations of peasant life in the Andalusian sierras; *cantes mineros* – including *tarantos, tarantas* and *mineras* – stem from eastern Andalusia's mining communities in the late 1800s. Two other song forms, *tangos* and *bulerías,* are closely linked to fiestas.

invented by individual dancers such as Antonio (1921–1996). Another important influence was Carmen Amaya (1913–63), whose footwork revolutionised both men's and women's dance. She was captured on film in *Los Tarantos* (1962), a Gypsy version of *Romeo and Juliet*. Today's key *bailaores* divide into two groups: those who have moved back to flamenco from classical training – like Joaquín Cortés or Antonio Canales – and others, such as Farruquito or Eva Yierbabuena, who stretch the boundaries of flamenco from within the genre.

THRILLING FINALE

Skilled performers can graft *bulerías,* flamenco's liveliest and most vibrant form, on to any other song-style: you will often see them in the *fin de fiesta.*

Each generation has produced great voices. Antonio Mairena and Fosforito marked the revival of unadorned Gypsy and *payo* (non-Gypsy) styles in the 1950s, and in the following generation Camarón de la Isla took *cante jondo* to a far wider Spanish and international audience than ever before. His early death in 1992, at the age of 42, casts a huge shadow over flamenco today. Although there are widely admired singers of great technical breadth and creativity – among them Enrique Morente, José Mercé, Arcangel, Carmen Linares and Mayte Martín – none has acquired his iconic status.

This is also considered a golden age for guitar. Paco de Lucía, who accompanied Camarón de la Isla, remains a towering influence, through his search for harmonic range and jazz influences. He also introduced the *cajón* – or sand box – after a trip to Peru, and it has now been generally absorbed into flamenco.

A flamenco evening

Live flamenco today has been shaped not only by the artists but also by new performance spaces. The golden age of open-air festivals in Andalusian town plazas, in bullrings and stadiums is now waning, as the increasing interest in flamenco has won it a niche in year-round theatre and concert-hall programming.

But however artistically brilliant flamenco may be when performed in a theatre or concert hall, it often loses its essentially improvisational spirit.

In this sense flamenco is at its best in intimate spaces in late-night sessions. In Andalusia there are still several hundred *peñas,* or membership clubs, where you may be allowed in as a guest. Here members sing among friends; and there is a complete rapport between the artist and audience. Then there are the *tablaos,* which range from tourist traps to reliable, if expensive, venues.

In Madrid, Seville and other Andalusian towns and cities, you can find flamenco being performed all year round. Barcelona has produced some exceptionally gifted pure flamenco artists, but everywhere, even in Jerez, the bastion of pure flamenco, young artists are interested in experimenting with other forms of music, too. Now, as much as ever, flamenco is constantly evolving in search of new forms of expression.

Yet the essence of flamenco as a vehicle for deep emotions has not changed. One thing is certain: as long as there is love and despair, innocence and loss, injustice and the search for freedom, there will be flamenco. ❑

LEFT: choreography is often used in modern flamenco performances.
RIGHT: flamenco clubs, or *tablaos*, give the chance to see artists in an intimate atmosphere.

FOOD

Enriched by Roman and Moorish influences and discoveries from the New World, the regional diversity of Spain's food tantalises the tastebuds

"**S**pain is the last large European country in which cuisine *really* varies from province to province," wrote the French historian Jean-François Revel in 1982. Travellers in Spain today will quickly see what he means. The choice in municipal markets, cake-shops, pork-butchers and even lorry-drivers' cafés

varies not only between regions but also between neighbouring towns and villages. And even within the same town each restaurant or *tapas* bar has its own specialities.

A jigsaw of cuisines

Spaniards talk proudly of their regional cuisine, but in reality the map is a far more complicated jigsaw. Along the coast the cooking of each region or province splits between *montaña y mar*, or mountain and sea. Inland there are similar divides between the mountains, river valleys and plains – and all of these are criss-crossed by traditional shepherds', muleteers' and harvesters' routes, which share dishes

like *gazpacho* (cold soup) and *ajo-arriero* (braised salt-cod). Finally there are a few pockets, such as the Empordá in Catalonia, El Bierzo in Castile León or the Maestrazgo in the Levante, and cities such as Segovia, Cuenca or San Sebastián (Donostia), that have nurtured a much more local gastronomy.

Today these local flavours are found not only in *casas de comida* (eating houses), *tascas* (taverns) and *ventas* or *posadas* (roadside inns), but also in Spain's top restaurants. Basque chefs led the way in the 1970s with *nueva cocina*, and today a technically brilliant third generation of avant-garde cooks, trained by star chefs such as Ferran Adrià of El Bulli (Girona) – considered by many chefs and food critics the best cook in the world – and Martín Berasategui (Guipuzkoa), keep a firm sense of their roots alongside dazzling creativity.

Modern transport networks also shape the map. Spaniards are prepared to pay for the freshest fish, and lorries rush from the sea ports to supply markets across the country within hours of the catches being landed. Madrid has the world's second-largest wholesale fish market and its wholesalers and restaurants claim the very best from the Atlantic and Mediterranean ports.

Moorish and New World flavours

For all the wondrous variety of Iberian cuisine, it has a certain character that sets it apart. For example, the influence of French cooking is hardly felt, as the author Alexander Dumas noted to his surprise in the 1840s. Instead, Moorish and New World flavours are close to the surface, and underlying Roman influences are still present.

The impact of the Islamic centuries is most apparent in a crescent swinging south through Valencia, Murcia and Andalusia. Here you will find honey and almond pastries, cumin- and aniseed-spiced breads, and a vast family of rice dishes and iced drinks *(granizadas)*.

LEFT: traditional *churros*, delicious strips of fried dough, often served with a thick chocolate drink.
RIGHT: Basque specialities at a Madrid restaurant.

On the other hand, the food plants brought back from the New World by Columbus and others are staples everywhere. Kidney beans *(alubias)* and potatoes *(patatas)* appear in regional *cocidos* (one-pot stews), while tomatoes and sweet peppers, as well as *pimentón* (paprika), have splashed their fiery red right across Spanish cooking. In the Canary Islands, a stop-off point between Europe and the New World, try *papas arrugadas* – "wrinkled potatoes" boiled in their skins – served with *mojo rojo,* a spicy red sauce.

Bread and olive oil have accompanied meals since Roman times. Today Spain is the world's

the Basque way of life and there are clusters of Michelin-starred restaurants in San Sebastián (Donostia) and Bilbao (Viscaya). Such is the reputation of Basque chefs that you will find them cooking in top restaurants throughout the whole of Spain.

Further west, Asturia favours sturdy country dishes like bean stew *(fabada)*, caramelised rice pudding *(arroz con leche)*, more than 20 farmhouse cheeses and dry cider. Galician cooking has cleaner flavours with excellent beef and a wealth of fish and shellfish, sturdy *empanadas* (meat pies), *lacón con grelos* (boiled ham with turnip greens) and paprika-laced dishes.

largest olive-oil producer (up to 30 percent is exported to Italy and bottled there), and the range of oils is enormous. Try them in a Mediterranean breakfast, drizzled over toast that has been rubbed with fresh tomato and garlic.

Around the regions

It is often said that in the north of Spain you live to eat rather than eat to live. For the Basques food and cooking are a fundamental part of their culture and identity; the table is a gathering place, whether at home, in male gastronomic societies, at restaurants, cooking competitions or open-air communal meals during fiestas. Going out to restaurants is part of

The inland cuisines of the Rioja, Navarre and Aragón share the produce of the fertile Ebro valley: peaches and pears preserved in red wine, braised spring vegetables *(menestras)*, and sweet and spicy red peppers, which, along with tomatoes, are key ingredients of *chilindrón* – lamb, poultry or game stew. Red peppers also go into *patatas a la Riojana*, a potato stew, which the French chef Paul Bocuse pronounced a work of art.

Meseta and the Mediterranean

There is a decidedly medieval air to the dishes of the central plateau *(meseta)* – wood-roast meat such as milk-fed lamb *(cordero lechal)*, messy dishes of tripe *(callos)*, Manchego cheese made with sheep's milk and wonderful garlic soups *(sopas de ajo)*, while those of the Mediterranean seem distinctly contemporary: sun-drenched salads, roasted vegetables *(escalivada)*, fish baked in salt or turned into soups. They all make for deliciously healthy eating.

Catalan cooking has a literary tradition dating from the 14th century. Classics include *romesco* (almond and pepper sauce) served with fish or grilled

> ### TRADITIONAL CURES
>
> Native black-hooved pigs produce Spain's superb but expensive *jamón iberico*, known as the king of hams. Other cured hams, made from white pigs, are called *jamón serrano*.

spring onions, *zarzuela* (seafood stew) and *escudella* (pot-au-feu). Each of the Balearic Islands has its own specialities: Menorca is known for its lobster and Mallorca for its spiral *ensaimada* pastries.

Valencians are justifiably famous as consummate rice cooks. What we think of as *paella* is a kind of synthesised technicolour version of the hundreds of rice dishes on menus in this area – some cooked until dry in the wide flat paella dishes, and others left wet and soupy in earthenware casseroles. Valencians are also great makers of ice-cream and

ABOVE: *tapas* bars allow you to sample many dishes.

iced drinks *(granizada)*: the most original of these is *horchata*, a sublime tiger-nut milk.

The Deep South

Andalusia, often much maligned for its food, also has its classics. Its chilled *gazpacho* soups are a vast extended family. The original Roman white almond soup *(ajo blanco)* is very different from today's better known tomato *gazpacho*. This is the home of *pescadito frito* (mixed dry-fried fish), hams and *potajes* or bean stews. In the sierras you may be lucky enough to find one of the old country dishes that tell of a poorer past: *migas*, made from fried breadcrumbs or flour spiced up with bits of meat, fish or fruit, garlic and herbs. Andalusia and neighbouring Extremadura are also the principal producers of *jamón ibérico,* cured ham made from black-hooved pigs, which have been reared grazing free-range on a mixture of acorns and chestnuts and thus produce meat that has an intensely nutty flavour.

Terrific *tapas*

Tapas, small snacks that are served with drinks in bars, have progressed a long way from their simple Andalusian origins as a mere mouthful of cured ham or cheese on a saucer which was used as a lid to keep the dust off a glass of wine. These days every region, town and bar has its own local *tapas*, and the selection of dishes can stretch the entire length of the bar. Seville is the capital of traditional southern *tapas*, while San Sebastián is the home of sophisticated modern ones.

To *tapear* in the Spanish style you have to keep moving from one bar to the next, picking up just a couple of mouthfuls in each place. There are three different portion sizes – *pincho* (bitesize), *tapa* (snack) and *ración* (plateful) – and a fork will come for each person to graze from the same dish. You can order one *tapa* at a time or in some places, such as San Sebastián, help yourself from the bar, but you never need to pay until the very end of your session, and in the south *tapas* are very often free. Finally, if you really want to blend in with the crowd, remember to chuck away your olive stones, napkins and even your toothpicks onto the floor once you have finished eating. ❑

Spanish Wine

Spain has been exporting wine since Roman times, but travellers to Spain still have many pleasurable discoveries to make on-the-spot. For the past 30 years Spain's *bodegas* (wine shops) and vineyards have gone through a major revolution: investment in state-of-the-art pressing machinery, widespread experimental planting of new grape varieties, larger vineyards and, above all, a shift of mindset from quantity to quality mean that right now a lot of very good-quality and relatively cheap wine is flowing in Spain's bars and *bodegas*.

What you choose to drink will depend on where you are. People tend to think of Spain as a land of red wines, thanks to the fame of its Riojas, but its very first cultivated vines, perhaps grown as early as Phoenician times, were those used to make Jerez- or Montilla-style wines in the sunbaked south. These unique fortified wines, aged using a complex system of stacked casks, range from deliciously dry, nutty, chilled *fino*, swigged all around Andalusia, to dark, syrupy-sweet PX (Pedro Ximénez) wines generally served with desserts. The *bodegas* of Jerez are often nicknamed the "cathedrals of wine", and some are open for visiting.

By contrast, eastern Spain – Catalonia, the Valencian region and Murcia – is rapidly gaining fame for its big, balsamic red wines. Vines were first planted in Priorato, a spectacular area of slate black hills behind Tarragona, by Carthusian monks, and today its steep vineyards produce one of Europe's most powerful and expensive reds. Other little-known Spanish growing areas that are now producing some great modern reds are Priorato's Jumilla (in Murcia) and, further inland, Somontano in Aragon and Toro in Castile Leon. These *denominación de origen* (DO) areas – equivalent to the French *appellation contrôlée* – will appear on good restaurant wine lists along with the better-known names such as Rioja, Valdepeñas, Penedés and Ribera del Duero.

The modern, crisp, fruity whites tailor-made for drinking with Spain's wonderful fish and seafood are another discovery to make on-the-spot. These are generally made from just one variety of grape – Albariño in Galicia and Verdejo in Rueda (Castile León) – and are drunk young. Less well known, but highly rated, are the white wines made with Godello grapes in Valdeorras, also in Galicia, and the

Basque country's Txacoli wines. Demand exceeds supply for nearly all these white wines, and few are shipped abroad, so they are worth exploring.

Finally, there is Cava, once called Spanish champagne, which picked up its name from the underground *bodegas* in Catalonia where it was first made in the late 19th century. Made by exactly the same traditional method as French champagne, it is exceptionally good value for two main reasons: the expensive hand-turning of bottles is entirely mechanised here, and the milder climate offers a low risk of lost harvests. However, the best *brut* Cavas, which are generally from the small makers, are now very sought-after and more expensive.

Spaniards also enjoy semi-sweet Cavas since they very often drink bubbly wine with desserts.

Where, then, is the best place to try these wines? Generally speaking there are few specialist wine bars, so apart from regional specialities – Barcelona has Cava bars, and Galician taverns serve new country wines from small china cups *(tazas)* – restaurants offer the best choice. Even quite modest ones will have a good wine list. And, if you prefer quantity to quality, the fiestas celebrating the grape harvest in each area are fun. You may even find the wine flowing in a fountain – as in Jumilla – but it is worth remembering that while Spaniards appreciate good-humoured tipsyness, they don't generally admire or indulge in drunkenness. ❑

RIGHT: A bottle of young rosé *(rosado joven)* from Mallorca.

A YEAR-LONG ROUND OF FIESTAS

Spain celebrates the great feast days of the
Catholic Church and other special days of the
year with an unbridled intensity and passion

Even the tiniest village in Spain downs tools for
at least one fiesta a year in honour of its patron
saint. Whether it is a day of communal pilgrimage
(romería) to a shrine or a week of parades, a fiesta
offers a chance to dress up in costume, dance
through the night, let off firecrackers or run with
bulls. Ranging from exuberant fun to solemn acts
of worship or pagan fertility rites, Spanish fiestas
have one thing in common: everybody participates;
there are no spectators.

BAROQUE EXCESS

The most bizarre rituals have a distinctly
medieval flavour but many Spanish fiestas are
pure baroque in their excess and ostentation. The
greatest number of celebrations take place at
Epiphany (the arrival of the Three Kings on 6
January); at Carnival (in February or March);
during Easter Week (March or April); on the first
few days of May; at Whitsun
and Corpus Christi (in May or
June); on Midsummer Eve, also
called St John's Night (23–24
June) and around the feast of the
Assumption (15 August).

The picture at the top of this
column shows a scene from
mainland Spain's biggest
carnival, held in Cádiz. It is
characterised by flamboyantly
dressed groups of
revellers who wander
the streets singing
satirical songs.

◁ **CARNIVAL CAPERS**
The days before Lent are
a time for licentious
behaviour, above all
for cross-dressing
and wearing masks.

△ **SAN JOSE'S** *FALLAS*
Hundreds of papier-mâché
monuments *(fallas)* are
filled with fireworks and set
alight at midnight in
Valencia on 19 March.

◁ **HOLY WEEK**
Processions of hooded penitents can be seen in towns and cities all over Spain during the week leading up to Easter Sunday.

△ **EASTER RITES**
Barefoot *picaos* beat themselves on the back on Holy Thursday and Good Friday in San Vicente de la Sonsierra (La Rioja).

SEVILLE'S FAMOUS FERIA

Seville's springtime fair may have started off in the 19th century as a gathering of farmers and businessmen, but it has since evolved into a gigantic party with no other purpose than pleasure. For six days and nights the purpose-built fairground, made up of over 1,000 *casetas* (booths, both corporate and private), reverberates to the sound of Seville's flamenco-related music, the *sevillana*. Both men and women dress for the occasion – the latter in stunning flamenco-style dresses – and parade up and down on horseback or seated in carriages. Bullfights in Seville's Plaza de la Maestranza are also an essential ingredient of the week's celebrations. Many other towns in Andalusia hold smaller but similar fairs.

△ **DRUM CHORUS**
On Good Friday, the incessant beat of masses of drums reverberates throughout towns in Teruel, La Mancha and Andalusia.

▽ **MAY IN MADRID**
Events during the capital's main fiesta, around 15 May, in honour of St Isidore (San Isidro), range from folk dancing to rock concerts.

△ **HUMAN TOWERS**
Tarragona province is the home of *castellers*, who compete to build their daring human structures as high as possible.

▷ **SOUTHERN FINERY**
The *ferias*, originally meaning horse fairs in the south, are an opportunity for women to wear Andalusian dress.

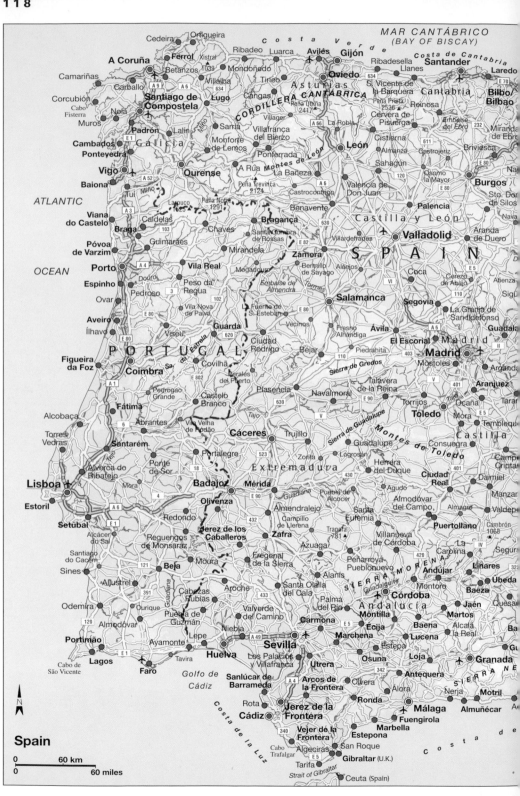

Spain

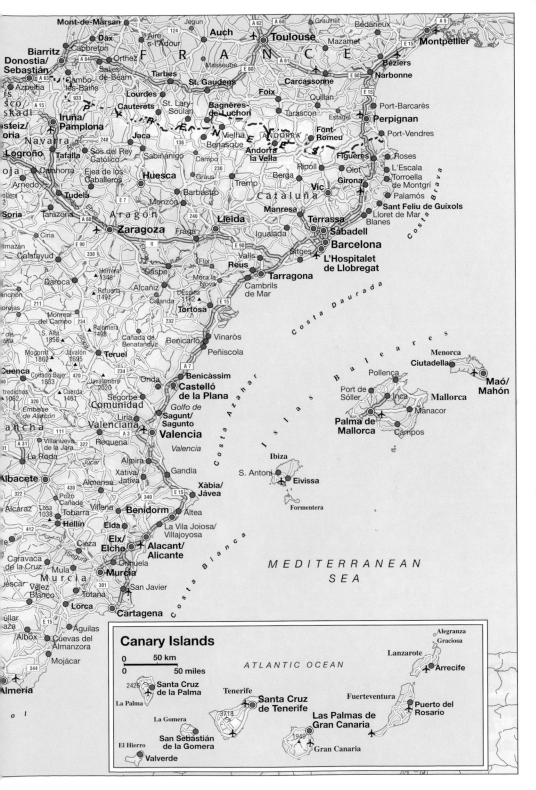

PLACES

From the gorse-covered hills of Galicia to the furnace heat of Seville, Spain is a diverse and beautiful country

The territory covered by Spain's 50 provinces is vast and breathtakingly varied. It is a land of illusions: in the clear, bright air the windmills on the horizon seem close enough to touch, and nearly every journey is longer than it appears on a map.

This following section of the book divides Spain into its four main climatic zones, beginning with the central plateau, or *meseta* of Castile. At its heart is Madrid, home to the Prado Museum. Castile's great medieval cities offer insights into Iberia's mixed cultural past and the stern Catholicism that fuelled its empire. Extremadura, the *meseta* region running southwest to Portugal, is an arid country that has traditionally bred conquistadors and brave fighting bulls.

The second zone is Andalusia, the Spanish South. This is the sunny Spain of legend and travel brochures, with its Muslim architecture and passion for flamenco. In addition to the three great cities of Seville, Córdoba and Granada, Andalusia is sprinkled with lovely white villages. Another Andalusian highlight is the Coto Doñana, a wildlife refuge for migrating birds.

In the Levant, the zone along the Mediterranean coast, you'll find the soil is among the most fertile in Spain. For more than 1,000 years, the cities of Valencia and Murcia have been prospering from agriculture made possible by Muslim irrigation. Tourism, centred on high-rise resorts like Benidorm, brings millions of visitors to the Costa Blanca, Costa Brava and Costa Dorada. These last two flank Barcelona, the capital of Catalonia, a region which rises from coastal plains to meet the Pyrenees.

Finally, the Spanish North is the most mountainous and culturally varied part of the country. Navarre and Aragón offer rugged alpine vistas, Romanesque churches and the splendid festivals of San Fermín and El Pilar. The Basque Country, with its lush hills and attractive beaches, is Spain's gastronomic paradise, adjoining the famous vineyards of La Rioja to the south. The two upland regions of the mid-north coast, Cantabria and Asturias, share between them the magnificent wilderness of the Picos de Europa. Beyond, in the northwest corner of the peninsula, bounded by the Atlantic on two sides, are the green misted landscapes of Galicia, trodden over the centuries by innumerable pilgrims making their way to Santiago de Compostela.   ❏

PRECEDING PAGES: Castilian plain; Arcos de la Frontera; an Andalusian village, dominated by its church. **LEFT:** Festival of San Fermín, Pamplona.

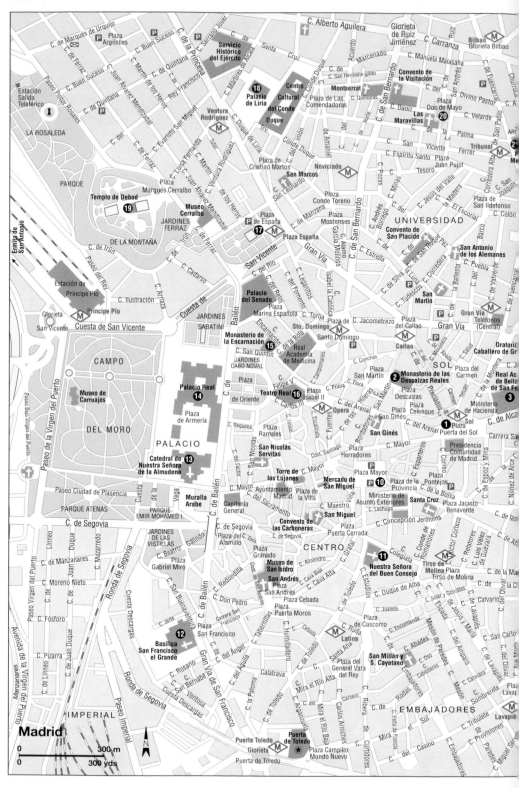

Madrid

0   300 m

0   300 yds

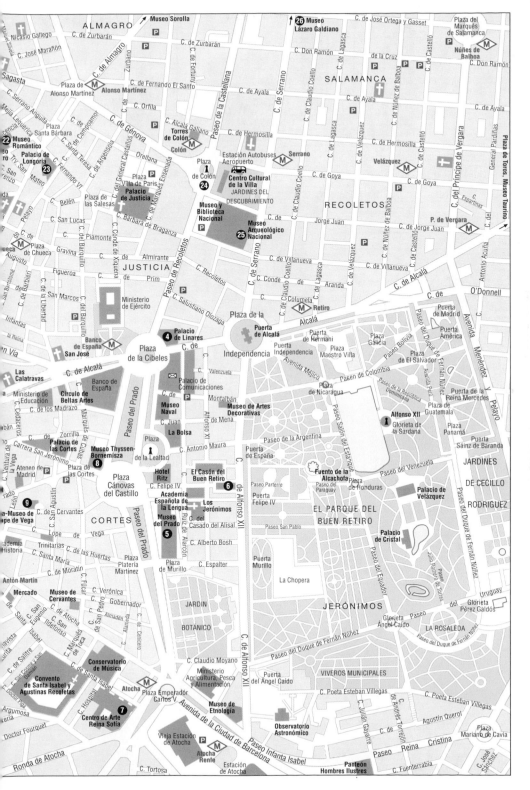

MADRID

The charm of the old quarters, the blue skies and exquisite sierra light, the superb art collections and the vibrancy of the long, long night: these are a few of the attractions of Spain's capital

Map on pages 124–5

Think of Paris or Rome, and familiar images spring to mind. But Madrid is more elusive, with an old heart hidden behind its smart new shopping streets. Over the past 30 years or so, democracy has brought a new dynamism and splendid cultural attractions to the capital, which was created on the caprice of a king in 1561.

The city's evolution

Sixteenth-century Madrid was a placid farming community within sight of the **Sierra de Guadarrama**. The high terrain with its clear, dry air and the dense surrounding forests had attracted the Muslims, who built a fort called *Magerit* on a rise over the **Río Manzanares**, just to the south of today's royal palace. It was captured by the Christians in 1083, but the two religions coexisted here in relative tranquillity, remote from the politics of the larger Castilian cities.

When Felipe II proclaimed Madrid the capital against the advice of his father, Carlos V (known as King Carlos I within Spain), reluctant courtiers speculated that it was simply because the town was convenient to the building works for his royal palace at El Escorial. Noble houses, convents and monasteries were hastily assembled in order to be near royal influence. As the city grew, deforestation led to erosion and drought in the sun-baked city.

When the Bourbons took over the crown in the 18th century, they were horrified by the state of the capital. The streets were filthy and crime-ridden; the housing, tightly packed within the city walls, was squalid; the facades of the churches were, in their eyes, lacking in splendour.

Civic improvements weren't always received gratefully by *madrileños*. Carlos III believed that the long capes and broad-brimmed hats worn by Spaniards were conducive to Madrid's many cloak-and-dagger incidents, but his decree that citizens wear European short capes and tricorner hats caused a mutiny ending in bloodshed. In the early 1800s, Joseph Bonaparte initiated a programme of tree-planting and open spaces, but he had been brought to power by a revolutionary invasion, and his beautification efforts earned him the nickname of *"Rey Plazuelas"* – "King of Little Plazas".

By the turn of the 20th century, imposing bank buildings along **Calle de Alcalá** marked the capital's growing financial power. Sweeping boulevards and monumental fountains had given Madrid a truly majestic appearance, yet she couldn't quite shake off her cow-town reputation. Basque novelist Pío Baroja called Madrid "an overgrown village of La Mancha".

Officially, this city of almost 3 million inhabitants is still called by its Habsburg title of "Town and

PRECEDING PAGES: view of Madrid from atop the Hotel Plaza. **LEFT:** Don Quijote and Sancho Panza in the Plaza de España. **BELOW:** the Retiro Park as studio.

The midday sun can
be intense, so it's a
good idea to retreat
indoors at 2pm for
lunch and a nap, as
the Spanish do. The
lovely long *tarde* –
strolling, café-sitting
and people-watching
– starts in the late
afternoon and lasts
until around 10pm.

Court", and in spite of Madrid's hectic arts scene and sophisticated nightlife, many regard it still as a mass of old-fashioned quarters or *barrios. Madrileños* are known for being open, unaffected and outspoken, and those very traits have eased the city's rapid political and cultural transformation.

On top of the world

At an altitude of 600 metres (2,000 ft), Madrid is the highest capital in Europe. Pollution from the city's 1.2 million vehicles and the continuing use of coal- and oil-fired heating have made the air rather less champagne-like than it was said to have been in the 19th century, when European princesses often came to Madrid to give birth, but on a clear day the Sierra de Guadarrama still seems within walking distance.

The heart of it all is the **Puerta del Sol ❶**, an oval plaza surrounded on all sides by cream-coloured 18th-century buildings. It's Spain's Kilometre Zero, marked by a pavement plaque in front of the clock tower, from which all distances are measured; the bronze statue of a bear and a strawberry tree in the middle of the plaza is the most popular rendezvous point. At midnight on New Year's Eve *madrileños* gather here to eat the traditional 12 grapes, one after each chime of the clock.

Less festive gatherings in the Puerta del Sol included a bloody battle with Napoleon's Egyptian forces, depicted in Goya's *Charge of the Mamelukes*, and an 1830 uprising against Madrid's friars, rumoured to have poisoned the city water supply. The Second Republic was declared here in 1931, and in the 1980s the plaza was the centre of demonstrations against NATO; in 1997 more than 1 million *madrileños* gathered here to protest against ETA terrorism; and large crowds

BELOW: the
neoclassical
Puerta de Alcalá.

protested against their government's support for the invasion of Iraq in early 2003.

Feeding into the Puerta del Sol from the north is **Calle de Preciados**, where you'll find lots of shops, including Madrid's largest department store, **El Corte Inglés**, which stays open all day. Nearby in Plaza de San Martín, a curious island of peace among the shopping crowds, is the **Monasterio de las Descalzas Reales ❷** (open Tues–Sat 10.30am–12.45pm and 4–5.45pm, Fri am only, Sun 11am–1.30pm; entrance fee), founded by Juana, youngest daughter of Carlos I, and still a working convent today, with its own kitchen-garden within the walled precinct. It contains a number of art treasures donated by blue-blooded nuns' families. Many of the works have children as their theme. For the Golden Age painters, they represented the triumph of life over death.

Following Calle de Alcalá to the northeast, you will pass the **Real Academia de Bellas Artes de San Fernando ❸** (open Tues–Fri 9am–7pm, Sat–Mon 9am–2pm; entrance fee). It houses paintings by artists of the Spanish School, including Goya's *Burial of the Sardine*, a portrayal of a mock-tragic funeral that takes place on Ash Wednesday.

Elegant boulevard

Alcalá intersects the **Paseo de la Castellana**, the city's main boulevard, at the spacious **Plaza de la Cibeles**, graced by a fountain dedicated to Madrid's patron goddess Cybeline. The white building opposite resembling a wedding cake is the **Palacio de Comunicaciones**,the central post office. On the northeast corner is the aristocratic **Palacio de Linares ❹** (open Tues–Fri 11am–8pm, Sat and Sun 11am–2pm; free), the palace of a wealthy 19th-century industrialist, which houses a centre for Latin American culture. Guided

Map on pages 124–5

The Infanta Margarita in Velázquez's "Las Meninas".

BELOW: looking up at Velázquez' statue outside the Museo del Prado.

TIP

Entry to the Prado and
the Reina Sofía Art
Centre is free on
Saturday afternoons
and Sundays.

tours, some in English, reveal its fantastic 1870s interiors, the walls groaning with gold leaf, silk and marble, murals and splendid mirrors.

The Paseo de la Castellana runs north and south of here, bisecting the city from Atocha train station (to the south) to the leaning Torres Kio (to the north). Over the next 15 years a 4-km (2½-mile) high-rise extension will be built northwards. Once a shepherd's track running alongside a small river, it was colonised by wealthy families in the 19th century. Most of the palaces along the 19th-century section, the **Paseo de Recoletos**, are now banks, or have made way for new edifices of glass and chrome, but it's still a delightful promenade. Traffic islands shielded by potted palms and privet make oddly intimate outdoor cafés, since the swoop of cars is loud enough to keep conversations private. In summer the open-air *terrazas* are popular nightspots. Starting in 2004, the Paseo de Recoletos and the Castellana's southern stretch, the Paseo del Prado, are to be remodelled by Portuguese architect Álvaro Siza. The new look will recreate the original pedestrian-friendly Paseo, with the addition of two spectacular new museums.

Madrid's art treasures

The Paseo del Prado is also known as the Paseo del Arte because of its three outstanding art museums. Among them, the **Museo del Prado** ❺ (open daily 9am–7pm; entrance fee) remains in a class of its own. Ironically, it was Joseph Bonaparte who first proposed a plan to make the royal art collection available to the Spanish public. Fernando VII completed the project. In 1819 the collection was opened in a building originally designed to hold a natural science museum. As notions of public morals became more enlightened, pictures such as Titian's *Venus* and Rubens' *Three Graces* were unveiled. Today the museum owns a vast

BELOW: emulating a
master's strokes in
the Prado.

collection, of which 5,000 pieces are on permanent display, here or elsewhere.

On arrival, head for the first floor to see the 17th- and 18th-century Spanish masters. Diego Velázquez (1599–1660), the greatest of Spain's Golden Age artists, produced outstanding royal portraits, notably *Las Meninas* (1656), depicting the Infanta Margarita among her courtiers but also including the painter's self-portrait. Also on the first floor are paintings by Francisco de Goya (1746–1828), noted for his brilliantly unflattering portraits of Carlos IV and family, his early tapestry designs and late "black" paintings. Other paintings and drawings by him are on the second floor within the 18th-century European section. The extensive collection of Italian paintings, including works by most of the early Italian masters, is on the ground floor, along with early Flemish, Dutch and German masterpieces and earlier Spanish works, like those of El Greco (1541–1614). Don't miss the roomful of paintings by Hieronymus Bosch. The museum's annexe, **El Casón del Buen Retiro ❻**, is closed. When it reopens, it will be linked to the main building via a Modernist cube designed by Rafael Moneo, and to a new annexe in the old army museum.

The Casón was for years the home of *Guernica*, Picasso's vast painted allegory of the bombing of the Basque town of that name, which, at his request, came to Spain only after democracy was restored. In 1992, amid fierce controversy, the painting was moved to Madrid's new showcase for modern art, the **Centro de Arte Reina Sofía ❼** (open Mon and Wed–Sat 10am–9pm, Sun 10am–2.30pm; entrance fee), on Calle de Santa Isabel just off the Paseo del Prado at its southern tip. The gallery is housed in an 18th-century building which was formerly used as the General Hospital of Madrid and has had its formidable exterior jazzed up by the addition of hi-tech lifts. The Reina Sofía

Map on pages 124–5

*For a refreshing antidote to Madrid's highbrow art treasures, the **Museo de Artes Decorativas**, just a short stroll from the Prado, offers a taste of popular decorative arts (open Tues–Sun; entrance fee).*

BELOW: boating in El Parque del Buen Retiro.

has undergone seemingly endless renovations and rehangings, and a new wing is currently being built on a neighbouring site. Today a room is devoted to the great 20th-century Spanish innovators, Dalí, Picasso, Miró and Juan Gris, while *Guernica*'s enormous canvas, surrounded by Picasso's many preparatory sketches, has a wall to itself. Just down the road is **La Casa Encendida** (open daily 10am–8pm), a lively contemporary arts centre.

The Thyssen trove

The art collection at the **Museo Thyssen-Bornemisza** ❽ (open Tues–Sun 10am–7pm; entrance fee) arrived in 1993 amid hot competition from other countries, for an initial period only, but now it will stay for good in the Palacio de Villahermosa, almost across the road from the Prado. The lion's share of Baron Hans Heinrich Thyssen-Bornemisza's collection, reckoned the greatest in private hands after that of Britain's Queen Elizabeth II, was bought by the Spanish state for 44,100 million pesetas (£230 million/$375 million). Spanning the centuries from 1290 to the 1980s, it is notable for its medieval Northern European paintings, 17th-century Dutch Old Masters, 19th-century North American paintings, and 20th-century Russian Constructivists and German Expressionists.

In the park

Originally, **El Parque del Buen Retiro** (open winter 6am–10pm; summer 6am–midnight) was conceived as an ornamental garden surrounding the royal palace-retreat built to a 17th-century design by Velázquez. Garden parties and water masquerades reached lascivious heights during the reign of Felipe IV. Fountains, statues, the delicate 19th-century **Palacio de Cristal** (open Tues–Sun;

Just up the street from the parliament building on Carrera San Jerónimo is the Museo del Jamón (open daily until midnight), a delicatessen with artful displays of Spanish ham and sausage. Be sure to try serrano, a tender, cured ham.

BELOW: the pedestrianised Plaza Mayor.

entrance fee), the original boating lake and the ruined royal porcelain factory still give the Retiro an air of a royal garden. Joggers, roller skaters, buskers and fortune-tellers are now a part of the landscape, and there are temporary art exhibitions in the park's various buildings.

Map on pages 124–5

The nearby **Real Jardín Botánico** (open daily 10am–8pm, until 7pm in winter; entrance fee) was created in 1774 by Carlos III. Even if you can't tell a Japanese maple from a dahlia, these gardens are an aromatic retreat with desert and tropical greenhouses. Outside the southern wall is the **Cuesta de Moyano**, a year-round outdoor book fair. Sunday morning is the peak browsing time.

On other mornings of the week, literary pilgrims can follow the **Calle Cervantes** from the Paseo del Prado to the **Casa-Museo de Lope de Vega** ❾ at No. 11 (open Tues–Fri 9.30am–2pm, Sat 10am–2pm, closed Aug; entrance fee). Here the great playwright created his most important works. The furnishings and personal effects are not his, but they show how a 17th-century Spanish household might have looked.

Returning to the Puerta del Sol along the Carrera San Jerónimo, you'll pass the parliament building, the **Palacio de las Cortes** (closed to the public). The bronze lions in front are made of melted-down cannons captured in the war with the Moroccans in 1860.

TIP

Old Madrid's best-known bars are in and around Plaza Santa Ana. Try Cervecería Alemana, Viva Madrid or Los Gabrieles.

Old Madrid

Madrid's **Plaza Mayor** ❿ or Main Square, west of the Puerta del Sol, is a 17th-century beauty, even if it is no longer the centre of town as it was in ages past, when *autos-da-fé*, bullfights and coronations took place there. The wide, cobbled pedestrian square is a pleasant if pricey spot to have coffee and watch the world go by.

BELOW: combing the Rastro for the best bargains.

Dancers celebrate the Fiesta de La Paloma in old Madrid.

BELOW LEFT: the new Catedral de Nuestra Señora de la Almudena.
BELOW RIGHT: the 18th-century Palacio Real.

Just west of the Plaza Mayor is the **Mercado de San Miguel** enclosed in a lacy early 20th-century ironwork building. Redolent with *chorizo* and voluptuous heaps of fruit, a Madrid market will also give you an idea of why this city is sometimes called the best seaport in Spain. Fish and shellfish are flown into Castile daily.

Further along Calle Mayor is the **Plaza de la Villa**, a pretty pedestrian square that is a showcase of Madrid architecture from the 15th to the 17th century. The main attraction is the baroque Casa de la Villa, or town hall. Also worth noting is the Torre de los Lujanes, with *Mudéjar* arches and a Gothic portal, one of the few examples of 15th-century secular architecture in the capital. A short walk from here, cutting through the three plazas at the heart of Habsburg Madrid – Cordon, Cruz Verde and Paja – will take you to the **Museo de San Isidro** (open Tues–Fri 9.30am–8pm, Sat & Sun 10am–2pm) in Plaza de San Andrés. Madrid's patron saint, San Isidro – beatified jointly with his wife – supposedly lived and worked for the noble Vargas family here. Recently restored, the museum houses local archaeological finds.

On a Sunday morning, head south to **Nuestra Señora del Buen Consejo ⑪** (open daily) on Calle de Toledo, the church that for centuries has held the popular status of a cathedral. Its gloomy interior houses the remains of Madrid's peasant patron saint, and a Virgin awarded a field-marshal's sash by Franco. Just beyond the church, the **Rastro**, an enormous open-air bazaar, fills the streets for several blocks in all directions on Sunday mornings. Clothes, furniture and animals can all be haggled for, as well as specialist items such as rings of skeleton keys, old liquor stills and fascist memorabilia. (Beware of pickpockets.)

In this area of the city, known as Lavapiés, once the Jewish quarter, Madrid's throaty urban accent is at its thickest. This is the pulse point of the mid-August

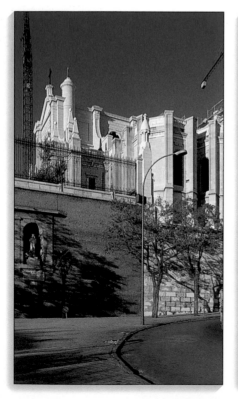

Fiesta de Virgen de La Paloma, when women in colourful kerchiefs and flounced skirts dance through the streets with their waistcoated partners to blasts of traditional *chotis* and rock music.

At the bottom of the Rastro, the neoclassical **Basílica de San Francisco el Grande** ⓬ (open Tues–Sat 11am–12.30pm and 4–6.30pm) was built on the site of a 13th-century monastery purportedly founded by St Francis during a pilgrimage to Spain. The interior is mostly decorated in florid 19th-century style; one mural shows an apparition of St James in the act of killing Muslims. There is also an early fresco by Goya, which contains a bright-eyed self-portrait.

To the north, alongside the Palacio Real is the **Catedral de Nuestra Señora de la Almudena** ⓭, finally consecrated on 15 June 1993 (open daily). The church, something of a monolithic eyesore, houses the image of Our Lady of the Almudena, patroness of Madrid. Work on the building had started in 1883: indeed, King Alfonso XII hoped it would be the burial place of his beloved first wife, María de las Mercedes, a devotee of Our Lady of the Almudena. A century later Madrid's cathedral was complete, but María de las Mercedes had been buried at El Escorial. Just before the cathedral the Cuesta de la Vega winds down to the only surviving stretch of Madrid's Arab wall.

The Palacio Real

The **Palacio Real** ⓮ (open Oct–Mar Mon–Sat 9am–5pm, Sun 9am–2pm; Apr–Sept till 6pm and 3pm; entrance fee) is an opulent 18th-century affair reflecting the French tastes then in vogue. On Christmas Eve, 1734, the Habsburg Alcázar burned to the ground, enabling Felipe V to build a palace more suited to the requirements of a Bourbon monarch. Designed by Italian masters

Map on pages 124–5

BELOW: the popular King Juan Carlos in the 1980s.

SPAIN'S ROYAL FAMILY

When Juan Carlos came to the throne after General Franco's death, he did so in the uncomfortable knowledge that Spaniards had a well-established tradition of unseating Bourbon monarchs they did not like. His reign has been aimed at establishing a monarchy commited to democratic politics. No one can doubt that, against all the odds, he has succeeded.

He has also helped set the tone of a new Spain free of the formality that constricted his country in the past. His easy-going manner has won over many a lifelong Republican. A keen sportsman – he sailed for Spain in the 1972 Olympics – Juan Carlos's hearty image is complemented by the gentler ways of his Greek wife. Queen Sofía's principal enthusiasm is classical music, particularly Bach. Increasingly now, Spaniards' attention is turning towards the next generation: Elena, an accomplished horsewoman, and Cristina, a talented yachtswoman, who lives in Barcelona, both worked before they had their children. Crown Prince Felipe has so far managed to keep his personal life relatively private. He got engaged to Letizia Ortiz Rocasolano, a TV presenter, divorceé, and popular public figure, in late 2003, and they married in Madrid's Almudena Cathedral in May 2004.

TIP

La Bola restaurant, just beside the Monasterio de la Encarnación, is an ideal place for those in search of an authentic taste of Madrid.

Sacchetti and Sabatini, it was so lavish that Napoleon claimed his brother Joseph had better lodgings than his own at the Tuileries in Paris. Inside are the Farmacia Real, with glass cases full of exotic medications, the **Museo de la Real Armería** containing the swords of Cortés and Fernando the Catholic, and the grand royal apartments. Certain areas of the earlier Habsburg Alcázar and Arab wall east of the palace are being excavated.

Alfonso XIII was the last resident of the palace. The present royal family prefers less elaborate quarters outside town and the palace is now used only for official functions. The stately 19th-century **Campo del Moro** gardens, entered from the Paseo de la Virgen del Puerto, are also on view to the public (open daily 10am–6pm; Sun from 9am; closes 8pm summer; entrance fee).

The **Real Monasterio de la Encarnación** ⓯ (open Wed & Sat 10.30am–12.30pm and 4–5.30pm, Sun 11am–1.30pm; entrance fee) was once connected to the royal palace by a passageway. Apparently the convent was meant to be a refuge for the women of the royal family, "in case of some novelty", as its founder, Queen Margaret of Austria, hinted darkly in a letter. The cloister houses royal portraits, including one of an illegitimate daughter of Felipe IV being received into heaven. The church is a splendid example of 18th-century Madrid architecture by Ventura Rodríguez. In the reliquary is a vial of San Pantaleón's blood, which is said to liquefy every year on 27 July.

A grand reopening

The **Teatro Real** ⓰, opposite the royal palace, opened as an opera house in 1850, after 38 years of building work. Legend has it that the cast of one production included live elephants. In October 1997, after lengthy renovations, the

BELOW: Goya frescoes in the Ermita de San Antonio.

Map on pages 124–5

building reopened as one of the largest opera houses in Europe, capable of seating 1,800 spectators (guided tours Tues–Fri 1pm, Sat & Sun 10.30am–1.30pm). The surrounding streets and **Plaza de Oriente**, laid out as formal gardens around a bronze statue of Felipe IV on horseback, designed by Velázquez and engineered by Galileo, have been pedestrianised, making this a pleasant area to take a stroll.

The centre of the western end of Madrid, at the end of Gran Vía, is the **Plaza de España** ⑰, where larger-than-life bronze statues of Don Quijote and Sancho Panza ride towards the sunset. Just north of the Plaza de España is the **Palacio de Liria** ⑱, the magnificent 18th-century home of the Duchess of Alba, which is open for visits by special arrangement only. Designed by Ventura Rodríguez, who worked on the royal palaces of Madrid and Aranjuez, the house contains an outstanding collection of furniture. Close by is the **Centro Cultural del Conde Duque** (open Tues–Sat 10am–2pm, 5.30–9pm; Sun 10.30am–3pm), an 18th-century military barracks now housing exhibition rooms around two giant courtyards.

Goya's extraordinary painting is a good reason for making a pilgrimage to the Paseo de la Florida to visit the neoclassical **Ermita de San Antonio** (open Tues–Fri 9.30am–2.30pm and 4–8pm, Sat & Sun 10am–2pm; entrance fee). In 1798, after completing the frescoed ceiling showing St Anthony raising a murdered man from the dead, Goya was appointed first painter to the court, despite the fact that the fresco's portrayal of street people was a startling departure in church art. Goya died in 1828 and chose to be buried here. The popularity of the shrine's annual fiesta – St Anthony is the patron of disappointed lovers and lost objects – has necessitated the construction of a replica chapel next door.

Views over Madrid from the cable car.

BELOW: the Parque del Oeste.

The archway in the Plaza Dos de Mayo, commemorating those killed in the 1808 uprising against the French.

BELOW: serving drinks in a Malasaña bar.

Other sights in this part of town include the **Templo de Debod** ⓲ (open Tues–Fri, 9.45am–1.45pm and 4.15–6.15pm, Sat & Sun 10am–2pm; entrance fee), which was given to Spain by Egypt in gratitude for helping with the construction of the Aswan Dam. It was originally sited on land flooded by the dam, and was built by the Pharaoh Zakheramon in the 2nd century BC.

Nearby, you can board a cable car *(teleférico)* and sail over the **Parque del Oeste** and the Río Manzanares to the **Casa de Campo**, an enormous open space, with an amusement park (open late on summer nights), zoo and aquarium (open daily 10.30am–sunset). A new sports pavilion here is one of the facilities built as part of the city's bid to host the 2012 Olympics.

Madrid's rebel roots

Madrid's counterculture centre in the heady late 1970s after the fall of Franco, was **Malasaña**, between calles San Bernardo and Fuencarral south of Calle Carranza. By day this area is redolent of old Madrid, with local people going about their lives. A former pharmacy on the corner of calles **San Andrés** and **San Vicente Ferrer** has memorable tiles advertising early 20th-century miracle cures. But when night falls the neighbourhood changes character. Bars resound with rock 'n' roll, grunge, garage, hip-hop and jazz and the streets fill with lively people – young and old ones – looking for a good time until the early hours of the morning. The centre of the neighbourhood, the **Plaza Dos de Mayo** ⓴, was the scene of a fierce battle with Napoleon's forces in 1808; citizens rushed into the streets wielding whatever weapons they could lay their hands on. The casualties on both sides were heavy; the archway in the middle of the plaza commemorates those who fell. Some years ago, when plans were made to tear

down the old houses and put up new apartment blocks, the neighbours once again mobilised in defence of the *barrio*. This time Malasaña was saved without bloodshed and it still thrives as a fashionable bohemian district. Nearby, on the corner of the Corredera Bajo de San Pablo, is the richly frescoed 17th-century church of **San Antonio de los Alemanes** (open daily).

The **Museo Municipal ㉑** (open Tues–Fri 9.30am–8pm, Sat & Sun 10am–2pm; entrance fee) on nearby Calle Fuencarral, is installed in a former poorhouse with an ornate late-baroque facade. The museum contains exhibits on the history of Madrid from the Palaeolithic period to the present day. Among its attractions are Goya's *Allegory of the City of Madrid*, an exquisite 1830 model of the capital, and early photographs.

The **Museo Romántico ㉒** (open Tues–Sat 9am–2.45pm, Sun and public hols 10am–1.45pm; entrance fee) is nearby at Calle San Mateo 13, in a mansion that once belonged to the Condes de la Puebla del Maestre. The 19th-century interior has been preserved by the Marqués de Vega Inclán. Objects associated with the peculiarities of the 19th century include a pair of duelling pistols instrumental in the death of satirist José de Larra, scatological moving pictures and a water closet with a velvet seat, which once belonged to Fernando VII.

While in the area, enthusiasts of Catalan Modernism should see the **Palacio de Longoria ㉓** (closed to the public) on Calle Fernando VI (at the corner with Calle Pelayo). Designed in 1902 by the architect José Grases Riera, of the Gaudí School, the building is the headquarters of the Society of Authors, who have restored it to its original splendour. Between here and Gran Vía runs the neighbourhood of Chueca, another thriving nightlife area with art galleries, restaurants, bars, design shops and meeting places.

Map on pages 124–5

TIP

If you're looking for stylish new clothes, head south of Plaza de Colón for Calle de Almirante, a showcase for Spain's newest fashions.

BELOW: the *barrio* de Salamanca.

Map on pages 124–5

Letter box at the main post office on Cibeles.

BELOW: strolling along Paseo de la Castellana.

Upmarket Salamanca

A few blocks east, the **Plaza de Colón ㉔**, "Columbus Square", is graced by a statue of the adventurer on a carved neo-Gothic column erected in 1885. On the other side of the square are four enormous concrete sculptures that resemble large decayed teeth. They, too, commemorate Columbus, with inscriptions describing the "discovery" of America. At the western end of the square, a waterfall like a giant wave guards the entrance to the Centro Cultural de la Villa, an arts complex with a theatre, concert hall and exhibition space.

Alongside this plaza is a monolithic structure enclosing the **Biblioteca Nacional** (open Tues–Sat 10am–9pm, Sun 10am–2pm) facing west and the **Museo Arqueológico Nacional ㉕** (open Tues–Sat 9.30am–8.30pm, Sun 9.30am–2.30pm; entrance fee) facing east. The library, inaugurated in 1892 to mark the 400th anniversary of Columbus's voyage, contains a small museum open to the general public. The museum is a small gem with treasures controversially gathered here from all over Spain. They include Iberian rarities, such as the mysterious, impassive Lady of Elche, Roman mosaics, a Visigothic crown studded with jewels and two fine *Mudéjar* ceilings. In the garden are reproductions of the Altamira cave paintings in a reconstructed cave.

The *barrio* of **Salamanca** was constructed in the late 19th century for the Spanish aristocracy who wanted to move away from the noise and congestion of the city centre. The project was bankrolled by the Marqués de Salamanca, a soldier, politician and entrepreneur who made and lost three fortunes and whose picaresque business dealings once forced him to flee to France in disguise. Today, however, the neighbourhood is the soul of respectability.

Many of the mansions are now foreign embassies, but the area is still the comfortable enclave of the well-to-do. The main shopping streets are grouped around **Calle Serrano**, where French and Italian boutiques now make room for Spanish names such as Loewe and Adolfo Domínguez.

A trio of museums

Further north, just before Serrano crosses Calle María de Molina, is one of Madrid's loveliest museums, the **Lázaro Galdiano ㉖** (open Tues–Sun 10am–2pm, July–Sept Thur only 7–11pm; entrance fee). The early 20th-century Italianate palace and lush garden was the private residence of a publisher who bequeathed his art collection to the Spanish government in 1948. Medieval enamels, chalices, armour and ceramics are on show alongside paintings from Spanish and Flemish primitives to Constable and Turner.

Close by on the western side of Castellana is another museum full of personality, the **Museo Sorolla** (open Tues–Sat 10am–3pm, Sun 10am–2pm; entrance fee), where the Valencian impressionist's paintings are on show in his own home. A final museum full of *madrileño* character is the **Museo Taurino** (open Mon–Sat 9.30am–2.30pm, closed Mon in summer), next to the splendid 1930s neo-*Mudéjar* **Plaza de Toros** or bullring (Calle de Alcalá 231), well worth a visit for its architecture and an insight into the history of that most Spanish of rituals and spectacles. ❑

Café Life

Most of us think of a café as a place to have a cup of a coffee and a sinful pastry. But not so to the Spaniards. To them a café is variously a place to watch the world go by, an academic arena, a setting for cultural input or a therapeutic refuge from the world beyond its velvet curtains. The 19th century was the heyday of the Madrid café. The repression inflicted by Franco stifled much of the political and philosophical rhetoric that were the mainstay of the capital's cafés before the Spanish Civil War; but the cafés at least provided a welcome refuge from the winter cold. As indoor plumbing and central heating became more common in the 1960s and '70s, the old-world café became almost extinct. But it has made a comeback since the rebirth of democracy.

To experience the Spanish café at its traditional best, visit the **Café Gijón** on the Paseo de Recoletos. More than a century old, this is the *grande dame* of the café as cultural institution. The group at the next table may be immersed in a *tertulia* – a lengthy discussion, usually on some artistic or political issue – or simply downing the powerful gin and tonics. Probably no café in Madrid goes back as far as the Gijón.

The delightful Art Nouveau-style decor of **El Espejo**, also on Recoletos, is deceptive. Its tiled pictures and huge mirrors date from 1978, while the pavilion extension, a seemingly early 20th-century confection of glass and tiles, appeared only in 1990.

Another new entry in the old style is the **Café de Oriente**, opposite the royal palace. Draped with plush velvet trimmed with lace, and incorporating archaeological remains in one room, the café specialises in exotic coffees and homemade patisserie.

In Spain, patronising one café over another is not just a matter of convenience and taste: it is a question of personal conviction. There are cafés for the literati, for yuppies, for the film crowd, for the *outré* and progressive. They come together at the **Círculo de Bellas Artes**, near the Puerta del Sol at Alcalá 42.

The café's fabulous interior – columns, chandeliers, beautifully painted ceilings and a magnificent sprawling nude as you walk in the door – dates from 1926.

Another institution for whiling away a few hours is the mirrored 1920s **Café Comercial** (Glorieta de Bilbao).

Late in the evening at the **Café Central** (Plaza del Angel 10) you can listen to great jazz played live in an Art Deco setting. Stylish modern cafés include **La Fídula** (Calle Huertas 57) and **Star's** (Calle Marqués de Valdeiglesias 5), while trendy **La Sastrería**, at Calle Hortaleza 74, is especially popular with gay couples.

In the summer *madrileños* move outside to the *terrazas* (terraces), positioned in breezy spots, where they can enjoy a cooling drink in the open air until the early hours. The location of many terrace-cafés changes from year to year, but you will always find some along the Paseo de Recoletos and Paseo de la Castellana (these are the most upmarket) and more relaxed ones along the Parque del Oeste and at Vistillas, next to the aqueduct. ❑

RIGHT: bidding a fond farewell on the pavement outside the Gafé Gijon.

MADRID PROVINCE

Map on page 144

Royal palaces, as well as historic towns and villages, lie close to Madrid. El Escorial, Felipe II's monastery-retreat in the foothills of the Sierra de Guadarrama, is the highlight

The "eighth wonder of the world", a "monotonous symphony of stone", and an "architectural nightmare" are just three of the ways that **San Lorenzo de El Escorial** ❶ (tel: 91-890 5902; open Tues–Sun 10am–5pm, Apr–Sept until 6pm, closed public hols; entrance fee), Felipe II's most enduring legacy to Spain and the world, has been described since it was completed in 1584. This combination monastery-palace-mausoleum is just an hour away from Madrid in the foothills of the **Sierra de Guadarrama**. There are frequent trains from Madrid's Chamartín station, via Atocha, or you can drive along the N-VI and turn left on the C-600.

The origin of El Escorial was most likely Felipe II's armies' hard-won victory over the French at the Battle of St Quentin, in Flanders. In honour of St Lawrence (San Lorenzo), on whose feast day the battle took place, Felipe decided to build a tribute to the saint. The king sent two architects, two doctors and two stone masons to seek out a site for the new monastery that was to be neither too hot nor too cold nor too far from the new capital. Philosophers and astrologers were also consulted to find a suitable meeting place for land and sky.

The stony monarch

Felipe II was an introverted, melancholy, deeply religious and ailing man who wanted a place to retreat from his duties as king of the world's mightiest empire. He wanted to be surrounded by monks, not courtiers, and he conceived El Escorial as a monastery for the Order of Jeronimo monks, as well as a royal residence.

Felipe did not permit anyone to write his biography while he was alive, and instead left it himself, written in stone. The battles he won and lost, the glories and defeats of the empire, the succession of deaths and tragedies around him, and his obsession for learning, art, prayer and order are all reflected in El Escorial. The location of the enormous church in the centre of the complex reflected his belief that all political action should be governed by religious considerations.

Construction began in 1563 and took 21 years to complete. The chief architect was originally Juan Bautista de Toledo, a disciple of Michelangelo, but after he died the task was picked up in 1569 by Juan de Herrera, who is credited with having provided the inspiration for the final design.

Statistics give some idea of El Escorial's monumental scale. Built of grey granite, it measures 208 x 162 metres (683 x 531 ft). It has 15 cloisters, 16 patios, 13 oratorios, 300 cells, 86 stairways, nine towers, nine organs, 2,673 windows, 1,200 doors and a collection of more than 1,600 paintings. Some historians

LEFT: San Lorenzo de El Escorial. **BELOW:** portrait of Felipe II as a young man.

believe that the shape of the building is like an upside-down grill, a reminder of the martyrdom of St Lawrence, who was grilled alive.

The northern and western sides of the monastery are bordered by huge patios while the southern and eastern sides are the site of gardens with excellent views of the monastery's fields and the Madrid countryside beyond. In fact, there is a statue of Felipe II there doing just that, looking out beyond the **Jardín de los Frailes**, where the monks rested from their labours. Below the garden on the right is the **Gallery of Convalescents**.

Architecture and painting at El Escorial

Visits are unaccompanied, although guides are available. The route starts in two small new museums (**Nuevos Museos**), the first of which explains the building's architectural history through drawings, plans, tools and scale models. Exhibits include machinery dreamed up by Herrera to cope with technical problems.

Flights of stairs then lead up to nine rooms of magnificent 15th–17th century paintings. As in the Prado, the range and quality – from Bosch to Veronese, Tintoretto and Van Dyck, as well as the Spanish School – illustrate why the Spanish Habsburgs were the greatest patrons of art of their time. The Flemish School, collected by Felipe's grandmother Isabel, and Titian, court painter to his father Carlos I, are especially well represented. The recently restored **Sala de Batallas** includes scenes from the Battle of St Quentin.

The first room of the Habsburg living quarters belonged to Felipe II's favourite daughter, Isabel Clara Eugenia, who took care of him when he was dying. The austerity is broken only by the important collection of paintings and the Talavera ceramic skirting on all the walls in this section of the palace. The simplicity

The word "palace" seems inappropriate for the living quarters at El Escorial. Felipe II himself said that he wanted to build "a palace for God and a shack for the King".

BELOW: inside El Escorial.

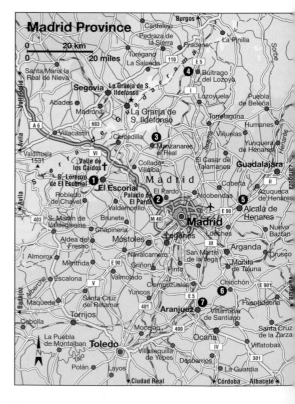

continues in the Sedan Room, where you will find the unadorned wooden chair in which the king was carried from Madrid after his gout had worsened. In the adjacent Portrait Room, so-called for its portraits of the Spanish Habsburg dynasty, you can also see the chair on which Philip rested his painful leg.

A hallway leads on to the Walking Gallery, whose old leaded windows give the best views out over the gardens. The doors, made from 17 different types of wood – surprisingly splendid – were a present from Maximilian of Austria in 1567. These lead through to the Ambassadors' Salon, or waiting room, and, finally, the King's Bedroom, adjacent to the main altar of the church, so that Felipe II could hear Mass from his bed. When his gout permitted, he would walk through a small door that leads directly from his room to the church.

Stairs and corridors lead round to the four Chapter Rooms, where the monks once held their meetings. Now the walls are hung with paintings, among them Velázquez's masterpiece, *Joseph's Tunic*, in the first room and Bosch's *Garden of Pleasures* in the last.

Map on page 144

Portrait of Felipe II's favourite daughter, Isabel Clara Eugenia.

Royal remains

One of Felipe II's motivations for building El Escorial was to construct a mausoleum for his father, Emperor Carlos V (Carlos I of Spain), whose remains were brought here in 1586. But it was not until the reign of Felipe III, in 1617, that this splendid bronze, marble and jasper pantheon began to be built directly below the main altar of the church. The remains of all the kings of Spain since Carlos I lie here, with the exception of Felipe V, who could not bear the gloom of the place and asked to be buried at Segovia, and Fernando VI, whose tomb is in Madrid. The queens who produced male heirs are also buried here, while

BELOW: elegant Bourbon apartments in the otherwise austere El Escorial.

across the way in the 19th-century **Princes' Pantheon** lie the remains of princes, princesses and queens whose children did not succeed to the throne.

Church and library

While some illustrious visitors have praised the church's perfect grandeur – the French writer Alexandre Dumas referred to the Kings' Courtyard as "the entrance to eternity" – others have complained about its oppressive size. French writer and intellectual Théophile Gautier wrote: "in the El Escorial church one feels so overwhelmed, so crushed, so subordinate to a melancholy and inflexible power that prayer appears to be entirely useless". The frescoes on the ceilings and along the 43 altars were painted by Spanish and Italian masters. The retable was designed by architect Juan de Herrera himself. On either side of the retable are the royal stalls and the sculpted figures of Carlos I and Felipe II.

The El Escorial library, second only in size to that of the Vatican, holds the writings of St Augustine, Alfonso the Wise and Santa Teresa. It has the largest collection of Arabic manuscripts in the world, illuminated hymnals and works of natural history and cartography from the Middle Ages. It is the only library in the world to store its books facing backwards, a measure taken to preserve the ancient parchment.

Pope Gregory XIII ordered the excommunication of anyone who stole a manuscript from here. The ceiling, painted by Tibaldi and his daughter, represents the seven liberal arts: grammar, rhetoric, dialectics, arithmetic, geometry, astronomy and music.

During the reign of the Bourbons, part of the living quarters were converted and two small palaces were built near the monastery to be used as hunting

Don Juan, father of the present King Juan Carlos, will be the first non-monarch to be honoured by burial in El Escorial's mausoleum, but not until 25 years after his death – the same as all monarchs. Spaniards believe that his defence of democracy under Franco deserved this final mark of respect.

BELOW: the Royal Pantheon at El Escorial.

lodges and guest houses. **The Prince's Pavilion** (Lower Pavilion; closed for restoration), around a half-hour's walk down towards the train station, is a showpiece of Pompeian ceilings, Italian painting, bronze, marble and porcelain. **The Upper Pavilion**, located 3 km (2 miles) along the road leading to Ávila, is open during summer. Continuing along the Ávila road a bit, and then taking a fork to the left, leads to **La Silla de Felipe II** (Philip II's seat), a group of large boulders up on a hill from where the king supposedly gazed out over his monstrous monastery as it was being built.

In the summer months El Escorial's small, sedate town fills up with *madrileños* escaping the city heat. If you stay overnight, you may be lucky enough to catch a performance in the **Teatro Real Coliseo**.

North from Madrid

The joy of escaping north from the capital is that the Sierra de Guadarrama is almost always in view. The peaks, which reach almost 2,500 metres (8,000 ft), can be snow-covered until early summer. There are three routes: the N-VI, which cuts through the mountains by means of a tunnel; the C-607/601, which goes via the Navacerrada Pass and is the most picturesque; and the main N-I, which goes over the Somosierra Pass.

Just outside the city limits, approximately 15 km (9 miles) northwest of central Madrid off the N-V1, is the **Palacio de El Pardo ❷** (open Tues–Sat 10.30am–5pm, Sun 9.55am–1.40pm; entrance fee), a former royal hunting lodge surrounded by forests of holm oak. Inside, several hundred tapestries are on display, including some designed by Goya. General Franco lived here for a time, as did Juan Carlos I, but the palace is now used mainly for entertaining royal guests.

Map on page 144

The cross above the basilica at Valle de los Caídos.

BELOW: the crypt of Santa Cruz del Valle de los Caídos.

THE VALLEY OF THE FALLEN

Just 13 km (8 miles) from El Escorial, on the road back to Madrid, is Santa Cruz del Valle de los Caídos, Franco's memorial to those who died in the Civil War and subsequently his own burial place (open Tues–Sun 10am–6pm; Apr–Sept 9.30am–7pm; entrance fee). For those without their own vehicle there is a bus to the site that leaves daily from El Escorial.

A total of 40,000 Republican and Nationalist soldiers lie buried here. Built by the sweat of Republican prisoners of war between 1940 and 1958, the concrete basilica is a chilling sight, carved several thousand metres into the rock. Opposite Franco's tomb is that of Falange leader José Antonio Primo de Rivera, son of the 1920s dictator Miguel Primo de Rivera who was killed by the Republicans in 1936. The mosaics in the dome include militaristic details, like a tank, alongside the apostles. Admirers of Franco still gather here every year on 20 November, the day he died.

The tombs lie directly below a massive, 150-metre (490-ft) high cross, which can be seen for miles around. If you wish, you can drive up to the base of the cross, from where there is a splendid view of the surrounding countryside.

A little further north and a good place for a picnic stop is the pretty town of **Manzanares el Real** . The 15th-century **Castillo** (open summer Tues–Sun 10am–1.15pm and 4–7pm, winter Tues–Sun 10am–5.15pm; entrance fee) dominates the town. Just beyond it is **La Pedriza**, a park with walking trails and climbing routes among its spectacularly formed granite rocks.

The walled town of **Buitrago del Lozoya** ❹ lies just off the N-I highway about 14 km (9 miles) shy of the Somosierra Pass. In the basement of the town hall in the Plaza de Picasso is the **Museo Picasso** (open Tues–Fri 11am–1.45pm and 4–6pm, Sat 10am–2pm and 4–7pm, Sun 10am–2pm). The collection belonged to his barber, who accumulated a private hoard of ceramics, sketches and other small works. Close by is the **Monasterio de El Paular**, a Carthusian monastery dating back to the 14th century (tel: 91-869 1425). Part of the monastery is a hotel.

Alcalá de Henares

The old university town of **Alcalá de Henares** ❺, 35 km (20 miles) east of Madrid on the N-II highway, is well worth visiting for the afternoon. The entrance from Madrid is unpromising, but once you're inside, the charm of its university buildings, convents and churches obliterates that impression.

Founded in 1508 by Cardinal Francisco de Cisneros, the **Universidad** (open daily) soon rivalled Salamanca as one of the great seats of learning. It was built at the peak of Plateresque, and many of its courtyards and edifices are fine examples of this Renaissance style, so called because it resembles beaten and worked silver. The most exciting is the facade designed by Rodrigo Gil de Hontañón. Allow at least an hour to see the rest of the old town.

Miguel de Cervantes Saavedra (1547–1661), the genius of Spain's Golden Age of literature, is thought to have been born in Alcalá de Henares. He published his masterpiece, Don Quijote, *in 1605.*

BELOW: Chinchón's rustic Plaza Mayor.

Alcalá de Henares was also the birthplace of the great writer Miguel de Cervantes; on the corner of Calle Imagen and Calle Mayor is the **Museo Casa Natal de Miguel de Cervantes** (open Tues–Sun 10am–6pm), which is dedicated to his life.

South from Madrid

Within very easy reach of Madrid, 52 km (32 miles) to the southeast – is the picturesque town of **Chinchón 6**. It is famous for two things. The first is its splendid and historic **Plaza Mayor**, which has been used for bullfights since at least 1502. Surrounded on three sides with three storeys of wooden galleries, it is both rustic and elegant. Chinchón's other claim to fame is a strong aniseed drink that takes its name from the town and is drunk all over the country as a bump-start before work. One place to taste it, to have lunch or to stay the night is the **Parador Nacional**, set in a former 17th-century convent.

Aranjuez 7 lies just off the N-IV highway 45 km (27 miles) south of the capital. The baroque 18th-century **Palacio Real** (open Tues–Sun 10am–5.15pm, Apr–Sept until 6.15pm; guided tour compulsory; entrance fee) was inspired by Versailles and is stuffed with royal portraits, porcelain, stucco and wooden carving. The lush, green setting at the meeting point of the ríos Tajo and Jarama, is probably the reason why most visitors choose to linger here. There are 300 hectares (740 acres) of royal gardens, including the Jardín de la Isla, close to the palace, and the extensive Jardín del Principe, consisting of many species of trees. The latter contains two museums: the **Casa de Marinos**, housing former royal riverboats; and the **Casa del Labrador**, a royal pavilion built by Carlos I in response to the Petit Trianon at Versailles. ❑

Map on page 144

ABOVE: porcelain detail in the Palacio Real.
BELOW: view of Aranjuez.

CASTILLA Y LEÓN

The architectural splendours of Salamanca, Segovia, León, Ávila and Burgos give way to timeless mountain scenery and the villages of the vast Castilian plain

Map on page 152

"**W**ide is Castile", says the plain-spoken Castilian proverb. For centuries Old Castile has been the geographical heart of Spain. Many of the great notions of Spanish history germinated here, including the unification of the medieval Spanish kingdoms and the *Reconquista*. Felipe II chose the dead centre of Castile as the vantage point from which to rule his empire. The empire in turn grew and then gradually disintegrated as a result of the mismanagement and short-sightedness of Castilian governments. This process caused philosopher Ortega y Gasset to lament, in 1921, that "Castile made Spain and Castile has been her undoing". General Franco increased the force of the Castilian centrifuge by decreeing that *castellano* was to be the nation's only legal language.

Deadpan and dignified, Castilians themselves often express mixed emotions about their landscape. "Nine months of winter and three of hell", runs a wry proverb. But spring and autumn are long and richly coloured, with long hours of dramatically beautiful light. The sierras are stark but beautiful, the wide plains are windswept and intense.

After the democratic government granted autonomous status to Spain's various regions in 1983, Old Castile became the Autonomous Community of Castile-León (Castilla y León), a territory covering one-fifth of the nation, or 94,150 sq km (36,350 sq miles), and made up of the provinces of Ávila, Burgos, León, Palencia, Salamanca, Segovia, Soria, Valladolid and Zamora, each with a capital of the same name. The fragrant native scrubland nurturing holm-oak, thyme and *jara* (rock rose) of past centuries has in large part been replaced by wheat fields, vineyards and olive groves. Provincial capitals, once medieval cathedral cities, now maintain impressive historic quarters surrounded by modern growth.

Many Castilian villages were built as outposts against the Muslims, and they still have a frontier atmosphere. Some, too, are virtually ghost towns with a steadily declining population, as young people leave to look for work.

LEFT: the monumental walls of Ávila.
BELOW: Castilian costume.

Ávila

Sealed within its perfectly preserved medieval walls, **Ávila ❶** has been compared by poets to both a coffin and a crown. It lies 113 km (70 miles) northwest of Madrid. At 1,130 metres (3,710 ft), it is the highest city on the peninsula. Hercules was the city's legendary founder, although it is probably older than the Greek invasion of Spain: stone carvings of pigs and bulls found in the area point to a Celto-Iberian origin. Ávila was passed back and forth between Muslims and Christians until Alfonso VI claimed it

*Shrines to Sta Teresa abound in Ávila.
Egg yolk confections called "yemas de Santa Teresa" are sold as souvenirs.*

definitively in 1090. He promptly transferred his best knights from the northern kingdoms to the city, and they began constructing fortifications. The walls, which average 10 metres (33 ft) in height and 3 metres (10 ft) in width, have 88 round towers and nine fortified entrances. They stretch round the old city for over a mile. You can climb them at the city's gates and look out across the surrounding plains (open Tues–Sun 11am–6pm; entrance fee).

Knights and nuns

The city has been a magnet for pilgrims since the late 16th century, as the birthplace of Santa Teresa, an outspoken nun who founded a reformed religious order and wrote about the presence of God in her life in distinctly physical terms. Teresa de Cepeda y Ahumada was born in 1515 to a noble family with Jewish roots who, possibly to keep their daughter out of the way of the Inquisition, sent her to a convent school. When she left her father's house to enter the Carmelite Order, at her own choice but with misgivings, Teresa wrote: "I did not think the

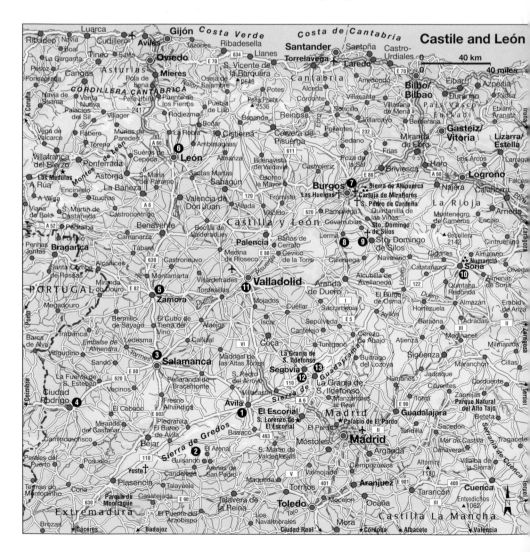

Map on page 152

day of my death would be more upsetting", but as a nun she thrived. She began to have face-to-face conversations with Christ, beginning with an encounter with the child Jesus on the convent stairs.

Her objections to the opulent lifestyle of the Carmelites spurred her to begin her own order, the Barefoot Carmelites. Her insistence on austerity made her unpopular with the nuns of her own city, and her unorthodox writings brought the eye of the Inquisition upon her, but she was canonised in 1622, 40 years after her death, and her personality and austere ideals can be felt throughout the city.

Ávila's **Catedral** (open Mon–Fri 10am–5pm, Sat 10am–6pm, Sun noon–6pm; entrance fee) is set into the city walls, and has a matching military air. This is the oldest Gothic church in Spain. Inside is the mottled red-and-white stonework characteristic of churches throughout the city. Of particular artistic merit are the choir stalls, by the Dutch artist Cornelius, and the retable, painted with scenes from the life of Christ. Of interest to literary pilgrims is the chapel of San Segundo, where playwright Lope de Vega was chaplain.

Follow **Calle Santo Tomás** southeast to the **Monasterio de Santo Tomás**, (open daily 10am–1pm and 4–8pm; entrance fee), which was founded by Fernando and Isabel in 1482. Its adornment includes carvings of pomegranates, or *granadas,* to commemorate the recapture of Granada in 1492. The church has a retable considered to be the masterpiece of Pedro Berruguete, depicting the life of St Thomas Aquinas.

In the late 1970s, Ávila refused to be nominated a National Historical Artistic Monument, but capitulated five years later when the commercial advantages of such a title became impossible to ignore.

Santa Teresa's relics

Enter the town again through **Plaza de Santa Teresa**. The white statue of Santa Teresa was built in honour of the Pope's visit in 1982, at which time she was named Doctor of the Church, the first woman to hold the title. Nearby, the **Convento de Santa Teresa** (open Tues–Sun; entrance fee for museum) is built over the site of her childhood home. Her finger is among the objects on display in the **Convento de San José** (also known as the Convento de las Madres; open daily 10am–2pm and 4–7pm; entrance fee) east of the city walls, the first convent she founded. The more appealing relics in this museum include her saddle and her toy drum.

North of the city walls is the **Monasterio de La Encarnación** (open Mon–Fri 9.30am–1.30pm and 3–8pm; Sat & Sun 10am–1pm and 4–6pm), where Teresa spent nearly 30 years. Guided tours take visitors to her cell, and the **locutorio** where she carried on animated conversations with her confessor and fellow mystic, San Juan de la Cruz. In her memoirs Teresa describes a scene in which she and "my brother Juan" became so ecstatic during a theological exchange that they levitated, each on opposite sides of the wooden screen. Today the cloistered nuns at Encarnación still follow Teresa's dictates, and only leave the convent in cases of personal illness, or to vote.

The southern part of Ávila province is traversed by the **Sierra de Gredos ❷**, beloved by *madrileños* for its fresh air and spectacular mountain scenery. A large area is protected as a national park, set up in royal hunting grounds. The Gredos is full of picturesque

BELOW: landscape of the Sierra de Gredos national reserve.

stone villages, such as **Arenas de San Pedro**, with its 15th-century castle and Gothic bridge, **Mombeltrán** and **El Barco de Ávila**. Driving north of Ávila, an interesting historical detour is **Madrigal de las Altas Torres**, featuring the ruins of the palace where Queen Isabel the Catholic was born.

Salamanca – seat of learning

The honey-coloured sandstone university town of **Salamanca** ❸ "is the pinnacle; the greatest triumph and honour Spain has ever had", wrote a historian in the 15th-century court of Fernando and Isabel. Salamanca was an important Iberian city 2,000 years before the university was founded in 1218. It was Hannibal's westernmost conquest, and an Islamic town until it was captured by the Christians in 1085. The victors filled the city with churches: San Julián, San Martín, San Benito, San Juan, Santiago, San Cristobal and the Catedral Vieja all date from a century of feverish Romanesque construction.

Historians suspect that Alfonso IX of León established the university in response to the foundation of one in Palencia by his cousin and rival, Alfonso VIII of Castile. Salamanca quickly absorbed the latter school, and less than 30 years later the Pope, Alexander IV, proclaimed it one of the four best universities in the world, ranking alongside Oxford, Paris and Bologna.

The Inquisition put an end to the university's reputation as a haven for new ideas and thinkers, and during Felipe II's reign Spanish students were forbidden to study abroad. By the end of the 19th century the colleges were decimated by war and neglect, although the 20th century brought a brief moment of triumph when the philosopher and novelist Miguel de Unamuno became University Rector. Unamuno's *Tragic Sense of Life* is a lucid, poetic exploration of the

LEFT: Salamanca's Old Cathedral. **RIGHT:** the Casa de las Conchas.

Map on page 152

Spanish soul. Unamuno died driven mad by the atrocities of the Civil War, and the Franco period saw Salamanca, like other Spanish universities, fall into a long sleep. Now, however, it is regaining a vibrant cultural life.

A tour of the university

Salamanca has three universities, but the entrance to the original **Universidad** (open Mon–Sat 9.30am–1.30pm and 4–7.30pm, Sat until 7pm, Sun am only; entrance fee) can be found in the **Patio de las Escuelas**. The Plateresque facade contains likenesses of the Catholic Monarchs surrounded by a jungle of symbols.

Downstairs are several historic lecture halls, including the one where Hebrew scholar Fray Luis de León, after five years in the prisons of the Inquisition, began his first lecture with: "As we were saying yesterday…" Upstairs, the **Library** has over 40,000 rare volumes plus valuable ancient manuscripts. Across the Patio are Plateresque doors leading to the **Escuelas Menores** (primary school). One of the old classrooms has a ceiling painted with the signs of the zodiac, a reminder that Salamanca once had a Department of Astrology.

The **Plaza de Anaya** is a graceful quadrangle surrounded on three sides by university buildings from several epochs and dominated by the **Catedral Nueva** (New Cathedral; open Mon–Sat 9am–6pm, Sun 9am–4pm). This imposing Gothic church was begun in 1513, when Salamanca's fame was such that the smaller Catedral Vieja would no longer do. It contains a magnificent gate and choir stalls. The **Catedral Vieja** (Old Cathedral; open Mon–Sat 10am–5.30pm, Sun until 3.30pm), which leans against the new one like a chick under the wing of a hen, is a museum. It is the more attractive church of the two, with its Byzantine dome and Romanesque frescoes.

In the adjacent **cloister** is the **Capilla de Santa Barbara**, where students were quizzed while touching the tomb of a bishop for luck. Exam results were made public, and a crowd of townspeople waited outside to pelt with rubbish those who failed. Those who passed were carried triumphantly around, and painted the word "Victor" on the university walls in bull's blood. Franco, who never attended a class here, also painted his "Victor" on the wall in 1939. Behind the cathedral stands a Modernist mansion, **Casa Lis**, now an Art Nouveau museum.

Many consider Salamanca's **Plaza Mayor** to be the most magnificent in Spain. The square, designed in 1729 by Alberto Churriguera, is bordered by an arcaded walkway lined with fashionable boutiques and delectable pastry shops. A *paseo* (stroll) in the plaza is a tradition beloved by students and locals.

Close to the Plaza Mayor is the odd-looking **Casa de las Conchas**, a noble mansion decorated all over with carved scallop shells, now the main tourist office. Following Calle San Pablo from the Plaza Mayor you will come to two gorgeous examples of the Plateresque style: the 16th-century **Convento de las Dueñas** (open daily; entrance fee), and the **Monasterio de San Esteban** (open daily; entrance fee), as delicate as spun sugar. Continue downhill as far as the river and cross over on the **Puente Romano** for a splendid look at the city rising above the bank.

TIP

For a cheap snack in Salamanca, try the student bars in Plaza del Mercado, which serve delicious sausages called *farinato*.

BELOW: Salamanca's Plaza Mayor.

Historical detours

Southwest of Salamanca, 90 km (55 miles) along the N-620, stands the handsome town of **Ciudad Rodrigo ❹**. Scene of a famous battle during the War of Independence, when the Duke of Wellington captured the town from French forces, marks of shellfire are still visible on the cathedral belfry. Inside the **Catedral** (open daily 10am–1pm and 3.30–6pm; entrance fee for museum) are cloisters sporting Romanesque capitals and racy choir-stalls by Rodrigo Alemán.

The 14th-century castle overlooking the Río Agueda now houses a pleasant Parador, and the old town is crammed with Renaissance palaces – a **Museo de Escultura** is being installed in the Palacio del Principe – and interesting churches. Spend time walking the ramparts, and wandering the narrow streets around the Plaza Mayor. On the square itself is a wonderful old pharmacy. To the southwest of the city lies the lovely Sierra de Francia and its villages; elsewhere bulls destined for the *corrida* graze peacefully beneath ilex trees.

Zamora ❺ lies on the banks of the **Río Duero** 60 km (37 miles) north of Salamanca by the N-630. The town has a 12th-century **Catedral** (open Tues–Sun 11am–2pm and 4–6pm; entrance fee), which makes it well worth a stop. Its Byzantine dome is a striking addition to the Romanesque-Gothic structure. The cathedral contains a painting of *Christ in Glory* by Fernando Gallego, and 15th-century choir stalls whose carvings are spiced up by lewd satires of monastic life.

Outside the cathedral are the remains of Zamora's walls. Sancho II was treacherously murdered here, and the spot is commemorated by the Postigo de la Traicíon (Traitor's Gate) in the ruined **castillo**. The town also has the region's new **Museo Etnografico** (open Tues–Sat 10am–2pm, 5–8pm; entrance fee),

BELOW: Gaudí's Casa de Botines in León is now a bank.

which houses an interesting collection of costumes and artefacts. From Zamora it is worth making the short drive east to **Toro**, a medieval wine town with fine *Mudéjar* churches, delicious tapas, and *bodegas* selling the excellent local wines.

León

Cool, regal **León** is in many respects a gateway city, with ancient ties both to Castile and to the green regions of Asturias and Galicia to the north. It sits at the base of the Cantabrian Mountains, 314 km (195 miles) from Madrid. The city's proudest century was the 10th, when Ordoño II moved his court here. León became a model of reasonable, civilised medieval government, and the assault and burning of the city by the muslim Almansor in 996 is an event still spoken of with regret. The city was recaptured in the 11th century, and was for a time capital of Spain as well as the seat of the Reconquest.

A visit to León should begin with the **Catedral** (open Mon–Sat 8.30am–1.30pm and 4–7pm, Sun 8.30am–2.30pm and 5–7pm; entrance fee for museum), which has nearly 1,800 sq metres (20,000 sq ft) of magnificent stained-glass windows. Construction was begun in 1258, in the Romanesque style, but the soaring upper portions are Gothic at its best. In the morning and afternoon the splendid rose windows should be seen from the inside, while at night the illumination turns the exterior into a glittering jewel box. Inside are several thousand-year-old sepulchres, including the delicate and ornate tomb of Ordoño II. The late-Gothic **cloister** and the **cathedral museum**, containing many Romanesque treasures, may be visited with a guide.

The **Colegiata de San Isidoro** (open daily) is a shrine dedicated to San Isidoro of Seville, whose remains were brought here to escape desecration by

Map on page 152

TIP

Try to visit León's cathedral at least twice, at different times of the day, to see the effect of the changing light on the coloured glass.

BELOW: stained glass in León cathedral.

Carving in the Monasterio de Huelgas, Burgos.

BELOW: strolling on the Paseo del Espolón, Burgos.

the Muslims. Adjacent to the Romanesque and Gothic church is the **Panteón de los Reyes** (open Mon–Sat 10am–1.30pm and 4–6.30pm, Sun am only; entrance fee), which holds the tombs of early royalty of León and Castile. The frescoes in the pantheon are generally described as "The Sistine Chapel of Romanesque art". The old city around León's Plaza Mayor, an attractive quarter of winding cobbled streets, has become the domain of the younger crowd, and nearly every block has a bar or pub offering jazz and quirky decor.

A palatial prison

The **Hostal San Marcos**, on the **Río Bernesga**, is worth a visit even if you aren't a guest at the five-star Parador inside. It was built in 1168 as a hospital for pilgrims on the road to Santiago. The ornate Plateresque facade, by Juan de Badajoz, was added in 1513. The hostel subsequently became a political prison (the poet Quevedo was the most illustrious guest). The cloister and sacristy house the **Museo de León** (open Tues–Sat 10am–1.30pm and 4–6.30pm, Sun am only; entrance fee). Of particular note are the 11th-century ivory Christ and a 10th-century Mozarabic cross.

West of León, the Roman town of **Astorga** has a huge **Catedral** (open Mon–Sat 9.30am–noon and 4.30–6pm; entrance fee for museum and Palacio Episcopal) with some remarkable features, including an altarpiece from the School of Michelangelo and an interesting museum. Even more striking, however, is the **Palacio Episcopal** (Bishop's Palace) designed by Antoní Gaudí. The bizarre edifice caused a great stir when it was built, and the horrified bishop refused to live there. Today it houses the **Museo de los Caminos** (open Tues–Sat 11am–2pm and 4–6pm, Sun am only), which covers the pilgrimage to Santiago.

Further west from Astorga is **El Bierzo**, a mountainous pocket close to Galicia, with its own hybrid gastronomy and excellent wines. South of the town of **Villafranca del Bierzo** lie the Roman gold mines of **Las Medulas**, now a world heritage site, where a museum is set against the dramatic bare-rock formations (tel: 987-422 848).

Burgos

Situated in the middle of the high plains of Old Castile, **Burgos ❼** has been a crossroads for a thousand years. Founded in 884 as a fortification against Muslim invaders, it is a relatively young city. Most of the landmarks have to do with its beloved native son, Rodrigo Díaz de Vivar, better known as El Cid. El Cid (from *Sidi,* Arabic for leader) pursued his own zealous campaign against the Muslims, eventually capturing the city of Valencia in 1094.

Burgos's **Catedral** (open daily 9.30am–1pm and 4–7pm), begun in 1221, was described as "the work of angels" by Felipe II. Perhaps no other cathedral has so many curios, as well as artistic treasures. Visitors are usually as anxious to see the marionette clock **Papamoscas** and the life-size Christ made of animal skin and human hair as they are to admire the **Golden Staircase** by Diego de Siloe, the opulent Isabeline **Capilla del Condestable** and the **Capilla de Santa Ana**, with its magnificent retable showing the Vir-

Map on page 152

gin's family tree. In the **cloister** (entrance fee) you can see the coffer that El Cid filled with sand to trick Jewish moneylenders (the legend adds that he repaid them with interest). El Cid and his wife are buried in the middle of the cathedral transept.

As an antidote to the still, dark air of the church, cross the Plaza Santa María to the esplanade along the Río Arlanzón. The turreted **Arcos de Santa María** were formed of part of the 11th-century city walls and decorated in the 16th century as a tribute to a visit from Carlos I.

Just west of the city centre, the **Monasterio de Las Huelgas** (open Tues–Sat 10am–1.15pm and 3.45–5.45pm; entrance fee) is a 12th-century nunnery combining, uniquely, Cistercian, *Mudéjar* and Almohad architecture. Only women from the highest rank of society were admitted. The abbess was second in rank to the Queen of Spain, and it was said that if the Pope were allowed to marry, only the abbess of Las Huelgas would be worthy of the honour.

Around Burgos: Atapuerca

The **Cartuja de Miraflores** (open daily 10.15am–3pm and 4–6pm), less than 3 km (2 miles) east of Burgos, was built by Queen Isabel as a memorial to her parents, who are buried here in elaborate tombs. Just 10 km (6 miles) southeast of the city is the **Monasterio de San Pedro de Cardeña** (open Mon–Sat 10am–1pm and 4–6pm; Sun noon–1.30pm and 4–6pm), from which El Cid went into exile after being banished from Castile by Alfonso VI.

Also just outside Burgos, 15 km (9 miles) to the east in the **Sierra de Atapuerca**, is one of Europe's most important archaeological sites, where evidence of the continent's oldest human settlement was found in 1994 within an existing

TIP

If you're touring the area, Burgos is a good place to stop for lunch. Try the local suckling pig, *morcilla* (blood sausage), or pork and bean stew.

BELOW: Burgos Cathedral, a mausoleum to the town's hero, El Cid.

*The Visigothic chapel
at Quintanilla de
las Viñas.*

archaeological site. The bones and teeth of "Homo Antecessor", 80,000 years old, will be housed in a new museum, the **Museo de la Evolución Humana**, now being built close to the river in Burgos. Meanwhile, the site itself can be visited on interesting guided tours (take walking boots) that must be pre-booked at the visitor centres in Ibeas de Juarros or Atapuerca (tel: 947-421 462).

Towns and villages of Burgos

The province of Burgos is full of villages that strongly evoke the days of chivalry. A detour from the N-I highway takes in two particularly haunting spots. Some 4 km (2½ miles) east of **Quintanilla de las Viñas** is the ruin of a 7th-century Visigothic chapel, one of the earliest Christian edifices in Spain. Only a square apse and transepts remain of the original church, which can be visited in the company of a guide from the village.

Passing the ruins of the **Monasterio de San Pedro de Arlanza** leads you to the lovely village of **Covarrubias**, with its 10th-century tower where Doña Urraca, one of Spain's most tragic princesses, was imprisoned. The monastery contains the tombs of Doña Urraca's parents. Catching up with the N-I at **Lerma** ❽ allows a stop at this town rising like a mirage over the Río Arlanza. The grandiose baroque buildings here were built by the Duke of Lerma in 1605. Lerma's fortress-like appearance is peculiar considering the time it was built, and is testimony to 17th-century Spain's longing for the glory of the Middle Ages.

About 20 km (12 miles) southeast of Covarrubias, the **Monasterio de Santo Domingo de Silos** ❾ (open Tues–Sat 10am–1pm and 4.30–6pm; entrance fee) is famed for two things: its magnificent 12th-century Romanesque cloister, and its community of Benedictine monks who hit the classical charts in 1994

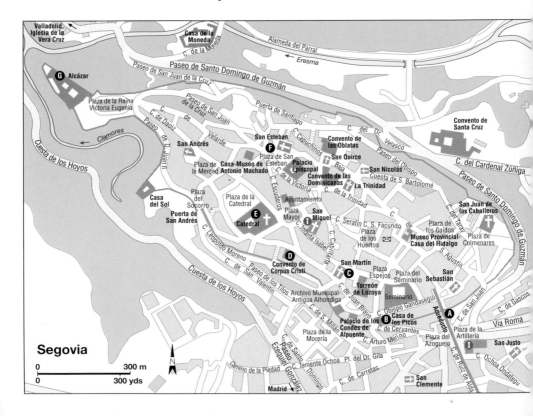

Map on page 152

with their recorded version of Gregorian chant. Visitors can hear live plainsong at the church services (evensong is at 7pm) – a dignified and moving experience. The monks spend the rest of their time gardening, studying and beekeeping. There are guided tours of the splendidly carved and tranquil cloisters; don't miss the fascinating old pharmacy, containing gorgeous Talavera jars and antique distilling equipment.

Following the N-234 southeast brings you to the small, friendly provincial capital of **Soria ⑩**, which attracts comparatively few visitors. The **Museo Numantino** (open Tues–Sat 10am–2pm and 4–7pm; Sun am only; entrance fee) on Calle El Espolón displays archaeological finds from the Celtiberian settlement of Numancia, located just north of the town. The ruined Templar **Monasterio de San Juan de Duero**, beside the Río Duero east of the town centre, can be seen only from the outside while it is being restored and a museum added.

The scenery of flat-topped red hills around Soria is striking. Northwest of the town, tarns glisten against the green wooded hills of the Sierra de Urbíon, a popular spot for excursions.

Valladolid and Palencia

The N-122 runs southwest of Soria to **Burgo de Osma**, a small town with a splendid cathedral, and then along the Duero valley. At **Aranda** you can visit the underground *bodegas*, and then drive through the vineyards to the west where Spain's most legendary wine, Vega de Sicilia, is produced. There is a Museo del Vino (open Tues–Sun 11.30am–2.30pm and 4.30–8.30pm) in the castle at Peñafiel.

Valladolid **⑪**, home to the regional parliament, was once a medieval court city, but is now a sprawling industrial centre with only an austere cathedral and two fine churches – San Pablo to the north of the centre and its neighbour the Colegio de San Gregorio – as oustanding monuments. The latter houses the excellent **Museo Nacional de Escultura** (open Tues–Sat 10am–2pm and 4–6pm; Sun am only), which is a crash course on the Spanish Renaissance. In its bid to improve its cultural standing, the city has also opened museums of contemporary art and science.

Just 45 km (28 miles) north is **Palencia**, nicknamed "the unknown beauty" for its rarely visited but exquisite **Catedral** (open daily 8.45am–1.30pm and 4–6.30pm), which is stuffed with medieval art and sculpture; and **Santa Eulalia de Paredes**, a church which keeps the major collection of locally born artist Pedro Berruguete and other contemporary artists. Southwards 12 km (7 miles) stands **San Juan Bautista** at Baños de Cerrato, one of the earliest Spanish Visigothic churches, dating from 661 (open Tues–Sun 10.30am–1.30pm and 4–6pm).

It is also worth driving 60 km (37 miles) north to visit **La Olmeda** (open Tues–Sun 10am–1.30pm and 4.30–8pm), one of the province's four exceptionally well-preserved Roman villas. This one includes baths and perfect mosaics in situ. A museum is also being built around a newly excavated villa in southern Valladolid, at **Almenara-Puros**, close to the Roman road south to Ávila.

City of poets

Of all the cities of Castile, **Segovia ⑫** may be the one whose charms are most evident at first sight. Only 92 km (57 miles) from Madrid on the N-VI and

BELOW: a painting in the ancient Monasterio Santo Domingo de Silos.

Model of Segovia's famous Roman aqueduct.

N-603 highways, Segovia fills up with *madrileños* every weekend, who come to admire the remarkable Roman aqueduct and the fairytale castle, and feast on the wood-roast pork and lamb for which the province is famous.

Segovia became important under the Romans, who built the aqueduct in the 1st century AD. The city was long favoured by Castilian royalty, and Isabel the Catholic was proclaimed Queen here in 1474. In 1480 it became the headquarters of the dreaded Inquisitor Torquemada. Economic recession, war and a 1599 plague nearly brought Segovia to ruins, but it rose again under the Bourbons, who built their summer palace at La Granja nearby. It became known for its writers and artists, the most famous being the early 20th-century poet Antonio Machado.

Roman marvel

All roads to Segovia lead to the **acueducto** Ⓐ. One of the largest Roman constructions still standing in Spain, it carried water until the 20th century. Its 165 arches rise as high as 29 metres (96 ft) over the **Plaza del Azoguejo**. The huge granite blocks stay in place without mortar, which may have fed the medieval legend that the Devil built the aqueduct in one night. Its future was assured by extensive restoration to the crumbling granite in the 1990s.

From the Plaza del Azoguejo, follow the Calle de Cervantes uphill to the old city, past the **Casa del los Picos** Ⓑ (closed to the public), a noble house decorated in the 15th century with diamond-shaped blocks of stone. A few steps beyond is the **Plaza de San Martín**, with the beautiful Romanesque **Iglesia de San Martín** Ⓒ (open daily in summer) and a circle of Renaissance mansions. In the middle of the plaza is a statue of Segovian hero Juan Bravo, who led the citizens in their disastrous resistance against the army of Carlos I in 1520.

BELOW: Segovia's Alcázar.

The **Convento de Corpus Cristi** , consecrated in 1410, was once the largest synagogue in Segovia. It is currently being restored. The old Jewish Quarter, or *judería*, along Calle San Frutos, still has houses with tiny windows, which allowed the inhabitants ventilation, but not a view of the street.

On **Plaza Mayor** stands the late-Gothic **Catedral** (open daily 9am–5.30pm; entrance fee), designed by Juan Gil de Hontañón and his son Rodrigo. The Isabeline cloister was transplanted here from the old cathedral, which was burned during the insurrection against Carlos I. It contains the tombs of the architects and that of María del Salto, a Jewish woman wrongly accused of adultery. Allegedly, she was flung from a cliff and saved by the Virgin, whom she prayed to as she fell. Beyond Plaza Mayor is the church of **San Esteban** (closed to the public), set on a plaza of the same name. It is one of the most beautiful of the 18 Romanesque churches in Segovia.

Fairytale castle

The **Alcázar** (open daily 10am–6pm; entrance fee) stands at the western end of the city, the prow of the Segovian ship. Destroyed by fire in the 19th century, its 1882 restoration combines reconstruction of some *Mudéjar* elements with contemporary taste in castles, and the result looks like a child's fantasy. Two of the Alcázar's most interesting rooms are the **Sala de Reyes**, containing wooden carvings of the early Castilian, Leonese and Asturian kings, and the **Sala del Cordón**, decorated with a frieze of the Franciscan cord. According to legend, Alfonso the Wise once ventured the heretical opinion that the earth moved round the sun. A bolt of lightning followed his remark and, terrified, he wore the penitential cord for the rest of his life. The arduous climb up the **Torre de Juan II** is rewarded by sweeping views of the Segovian countryside and the Sierra de Guadarrama. Look down from here to the **Iglesia de la Vera Cruz** (open Tues–Sun 10.30am–1.30pm and 3.30–6pm; closed Nov), just outside the walls, a round Templar church.

Little Versailles

The French-style palace of **La Granja de San Ildefonso** (open Tues–Sat 10am–1.30pm and 5–7pm; Sun am only; entrance fee) lies 11 km (7 miles) southeast of Segovia. It symbolises the vast differences between the Bourbon monarchs who built it and their dour Habsburg predecessors. Felipe V of Bourbon commissioned a palace here suitable for the retirement of an enlightened 18th-century despot.

A team of French and Italian architects built something along the lines of a modest Versailles, the royal residence outside Paris. The palace has an interesting collection of Flemish tapestries, with the inevitable Spanish touch of a chapel full of saints' bones and teeth. The most splendid part of San Ildefonso, however, are the gardens, with pools and snow-fed fountains, occasionally turned on at the weekend in spring.

The old road north of Segovia (N-603) will take you to the old hill-town of **Sepúlveda** and the spectacular **Duratón** gorges, where a hermitage stands above, gazing down on the rivers below. ❏

During the Segovian festival of Santa Agüeda in February, women dress in traditional costume and take over the running of the provincial villages. Some say it's time this ritual was no longer treated as a joke.

BELOW: detail from La Granja de San Ildefonso.

CASTILLA-LA MANCHA

Map on page 166

This region is the quintessential Spain – immense rolling plains studded with windmills and castles fill the landscape, interrupted by olive groves, vineyards and dusty medieval villages

O riginally part of New Castile, so-named when the northern Castilian kings wrested the area from Islamic control in 1085, La Mancha is centred around Toledo, capital of Visigothic Spain and national treasury of art and architecture. Cuenca, with its Gothic and Renaissance quarter, unique *Casas Colgadas* (Hanging Houses) and Museo de Arte Abstracto Español is another major historic city. Picturesque towns and villages are everywhere – Tembleque, Sigüenza, Brihuega, Almagro, Oropesa, Ayllón, Chinchilla, Pastrana and many more.

Spectacular landscapes – from the wetlands of the Tablas de Daimiel and the peaks of the Sierra de Alcaraz to the forests and meadows of the Parque Nacional de Cabañeros and the rushing gorges of the Upper Tagus – are abundant and varied. Elsewhere there are spa-hotels, cycling routes and impressive Roman archaeological sites. The medieval castles at Belmonte, Calatrava la Nueva, Alarcón and Sigüenza provide another theme for exploring La Mancha, as does the Don Quijote trail, from the windmills at Campo de Criptana to the Lagunas de Ruidera, all identifiable in Cervantes' great opus, generally considered literature's first modern psychological novel.

"En un lugar de la Mancha de cuyo nombre no quiero acordarme" (In a place in La Mancha, the name of which I do not wish to recall), the opening line of *Don Quijote de la Mancha*, is the most famous sentence in Spanish letters.

Toledo – the essence of Spain

Toledo ❶ is La Mancha's and Spain's historical and cultural heart, former Spanish capital and still today the religious seat of the nation. A natural fortress occupying high ground with the Río Tajo protecting all but its northern flank, the Roman city of Toletum was founded in AD 192. Little is left of the Roman occupation: a **Circo Romano** off the Avenida de la Reconquista, and a few mosaics and reconstructed buildings.

By the 6th century the Visigoths had set up court in Toledo. In AD 711, the city was taken over by the Muslims, and became capital of Christian Spain in 1085 under Alfonso VI. By the 12th century, Toledo was also Spain's most important Jewish centre with over 12,000 Jewish citizens. During the 13th century under Alfonso X el Sabio (the Wise), Toledo became a cultural forum within which Muslims, Jews and Christians lived in mutual tolerance and collaborated in a school of translators responsible for introducing much Arabic and Greek science and philosophy into the early Spanish Romance and, from there, into the budding European Renaissance.

This eclecticism shaped the city's architecture and art. The Mozarabic style of architecture was developed by Christians living under Muslim domination,

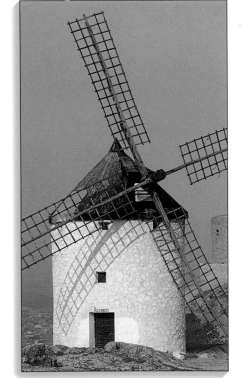

LEFT: Castilian shepherd.
BELOW: windmill country.

while the *Mudéjar* style, well displayed in the **Taller del Moro** *Mudéjar* palace (open Tues–Sat 10am–2pm and 4–6.30pm; Sun am only; entrance fee) behind the cathedral, was the work of Muslims who remained in the areas reconquered by Christians. Less apparent are the remains of Jewish influence in the city. Of the ten synagogues, only two managed to survive the Jewish pogroms. The 1492 expulsion of Muslims and Jews was a blow to Toledo's fortunes, and in 1561 Felipe II moved the Spanish court to Madrid to limit Toledo's power. In the next 100 years the city's population halved.

Today, Toledo is a small regional capital (pop. 62,000), but such is her beauty and history, unusually well preserved by her sudden economic decline, which continued until the early 20th century, that the entire old city is a national monument and one of the UN's World Heritage Sites. The city lies 72 km (45 miles) south of Madrid. The unusual neo-*Mudéjar* train station is a good starting point for a visit. Just outside the station, the city's majestic patrician profile rises above the Río Tajo gorge. Cross the river on the **Puente de Alcántara Ⓐ**, the

Rich, sweet marzipan, a Toledo speciality found in shops and cafés around the city, is a reviving snack or portable souvenir.

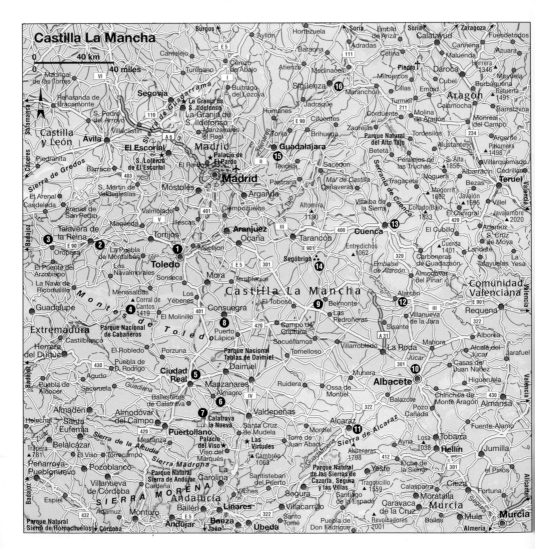

oldest bridge leading into town. It was built by the Romans, then refurbished successfully by the Muslims and the Christians. On the hill opposite the city is the **Castillo de San Servando**, built by the Romans to protect the bridge.

The main entrance to the city is by the **Puerta de Bisagra**, the most impressive of the nine toll-collecting gates along the old city walls. On the **Puerta de Cambrón**, at the west end of the city, you can still read the medieval plaque advising gatekeepers that Toledo residents need not pay.

Churches, synagogues and mosques

Visible from quite a distance on the *meseta* (tableland), the **Catedral Primada** **B** (open daily 10.30am–noon and 4–6pm; entrance fee) itself is testament to Toledo's history as Spain's spiritual capital long after the Royal court moved to Madrid. The Goths worshipped on the site before the Muslim invasion, when the church was converted to a mosque. The present Spanish Gothic structure, with five broad naves around a central choir, was begun in 1226 and finished 300 years later, during which time *Mudéjar*, baroque and neoclassical elements were added. The large polychrome retable depicting the life of Christ; the famously excessive baroque and neoclassical Transparente altarpiece, built to allow in natural light; the sacristy with its collection of paintings by El Greco, Titian, Goya and Van Dyck; the sumptuous walnut and alabaster choir stalls and *Mudéjar* ceiling in the chapterhouse are just a few of the wealth of details here. Allow a good hour to enjoy a complete and leisurely visit.

Ten minutes walk from the cathedral, the **Mezquita Cristo de la Luz** **C**, a church originally built as a mosque, is one of the oldest and loveliest buildings in the city; Alfonso VI held Mass here when he conquered Toledo in 1085. The church is viewed through railings. Nearby is the **Puerta del Sol**, the old Islamic gate. To get a sense of the unique Visigothic presence in Toledo, visit the **Iglesia de San Román** **D** (open Tues–Sun 10am–2pm and 4–6pm; entrance fee), where the Visigothic Culture and Councils Museum has been installed. In the museum are copies of the stunning Visigothic crown jewels.

The major synagogue that survived the 14th-century pogroms is known today as the **Sinagoga de Santa María la Blanca** **E** (open daily 10am–1.45pm, 3.30–5.45pm; until 6.45pm in summer; entrance fee), located on Calle Reyes Católicos. The most striking feature of the synagogue are the capitals, which reflect a Byzantine or Persian influence. The iris, symbol of honesty, and the Star of David play prominent roles in the synagogue's interior ornamentation. Except for the three chapels at the head of the building, added in the 16th century, the synagogue is much as it was before it was converted into a church in the latter half of the 15th century. The other surviving synagogue is **Sinagoga del Tránsito** **F** close by, a simpler, 14th-century structure, with superb Almohad-style plasterwork on the walls. It now houses the **Museo Sefardi** but is closed for refurbishment until at least 2004.

The other major Catholic structure in Toledo, after the cathedral, is **San Juan de los Reyes** **G** (open

Maps:
Area 166
City 168

TIP

Ideally, try to spend the night in Toledo to catch the city's magic when empty of tourist crowds. Also bear in mind that most monuments close for lunch. Only the Museo de Santa Cruz stays open.

BELOW: festival time in Toledo.

Detail from El Greco's "Agony in the Garden". Trained and influenced by Italian masters, El Greco imbued his work with a realism and vigour that makes his paintings seem alive and contemporary even today.

daily 10am–2pm and 3.30–6pm), located in what is left of the *judería*, the old Jewish quarter. The Gothic monastery, with a lovely cloister and church, was built by the Catholic Monarchs, Fernando and Isabel.

El Greco

Toledo is permanently and inextricably associated with the painter Domenikos Theotocopoulos, known as El Greco, born in Crete in 1541. El Greco lived and worked in Toledo from 1577 until his death in 1614. His paintings are spread throughout the city. One of his masterpieces, *The Burial of the Count of Orgaz*, is in the **Iglesia de Santo Tomé** Ⓗ (open daily 10am–5.45pm; entrance fee) on Calle Santo Tomé. The complexity, the blend of the temporal and spiritual and the inclusion of many supposed portraits, including El Greco's own, are just some of the ingredients that make this painting so memorable.

El Greco lived in the Jewish section of the city just behind El Tránsito. His house is no longer standing but a nearby 16th-century dwelling known today as the **Casa-Museo de El Greco** Ⓘ (entrance fee) contains several paintings including the famous *View of Toledo* – painted from the north of the city, where the Parador hotel stands today. The **Museo de Santa Cruz** Ⓙ (open Mon–Sat 10am–6.30pm, Sun 10am–2pm; entrance fee), just off the central plaza, holds fine El Greco paintings as well as several rooms of typically Toledan crafts. The building itself is beautiful, particularly its Plateresque entrance and staircase and the splendid *Mudéjar* wooden ceilings. It hosts spectacular special exhibitions and concerts.

Outside the city walls, the **Hospital de Tavera** (open daily 10.30am–1.30pm and 3.30–6pm; entrance fee), built in the 16th century, houses El Greco's *The*

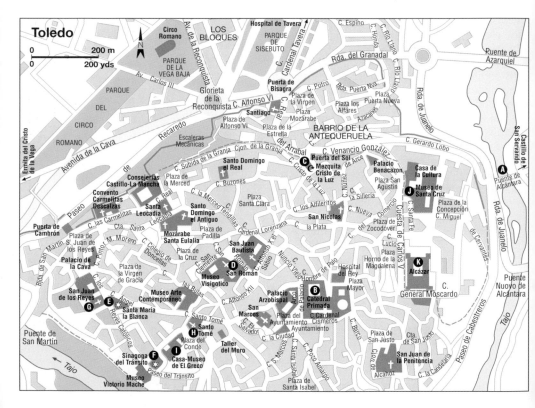

Holy Family, The Baptism of Christ and several important portraits of saints. One of the few Renaissance interiors that has kept intact much of an original art collection, it also has fine paintings by Caravaggio, Titian and Tintoretto. For El Greco fans it is also worth making the effort to see five other magnificent paintings by him in the **Hospital de la Caridad** (open daily; entrance fee) in Illescas, a small town just off the N-401 between Madrid and Toledo.

Maps:
Area 166
City 168

The **Alcázar** Ⓚ (open Tues–Sun; entrance fee) dates back to the era of El Cid, and its occupants, architects and purposes have been numerous. Today's building is the result of the work of Spain's finest 16th-century architects, though now heavily restored; it is now in the process of conversion into a major military museum due to open in 2008.

The best-known crafts in the city are the bequest of the Muslim and Jewish legacies: damascene (a type of black enamel inlaid with gold, silver and copper wire), steel knives, swords and the fine ceramic work from nearby **Talavera de la Reina** ❷, one of Toledo's medieval satellite towns. Here, the **Museo Ruiz de Luna** (open Tues–Sun; entrance fee) near Plaza de San Pedro is the place to view ceramics of all kinds, while the **Ermita de La Virgen del Prado** (open daily) houses traditional ceramic murals depicting religious themes. Talavera has a diverse old quarter, featuring a 15th-century bridge and Roman ramparts.

The charming small town of **Oropesa** ❸, 32 km (20 miles) west of Talavera de la Reina on the N-V, is dominated by the 16th-century **Palacio Nuevo** (open daily; entrance fee), part of which is now a Parador. It has other fine medieval and Renaissance buildings and a long tradition of embroidery.

Covering an area of approximately 1,000 sq km (400 sq miles) to the south of Talavera and Toledo are the **Montes de Toledo** ❹, a low mountain range

BELOW: view of Toledo and the River Tagus.

stretching west towards Extremadura where some of Spain's largest hunting estates may be found. Travelling along the northern edge of the range you will find the **Parque Nacional de Cabañeros** (tel: 926-783 297), consisting mainly of evergreen woodland and sheep pasture. You can take a guided tour of the park in a four-wheel drive vehicle. The wildlife here includes wild boar, red deer and imperial eagles.

Southern La Mancha

Approximately 100 km (60 miles) south of Toledo on the C-401 is the provincial capital of **Ciudad Real ❺**. Today it is a largely modern city, but the central streets within the medieval ramparts (accessed via the 14th-century Puerta de Toledo) are alive with bustling, boisterous bars, cafés and restaurants. The 13th-century **Iglesia de Santiago** and the **Catedral** are the most interesting architectural features. In the surrounding countryside, some of La Mancha's greatest treasures can be found. The **Parque Nacional Tablas de Daimiel** (tel: 926-693 118), just northeast, is one of Spain's most important wetlands, a national park on the Río Guadiana and rallying point for migratory waterfowl from all over Europe. The town of **Almagro ❻**, southeast of Ciudad Real, is the site of an unusual stone Plaza Mayor with wooden porticoes and green-painted balconies. At No. 17 is a 16th-century **Corral de Comedias** (outdoor theatre) where an annual summer theatre festival is held.

Calatrava la Nueva ❼ (open Tues–Sun; entrance fee), on the CR-504 approximately 35 km (20 miles) south of Almagro, is a spectacular sight visible for miles around. Founded in 1217 by the military Order of Calatrava, it was later used as a monastery until it was irreparably cracked by an earthquake in 1802.

BELOW: beloved Don Quijote and Sancho Panza.

THE QUIJOTE TRAIL

A tour of central La Mancha is an ideal opportunity for fans of Don Quijote to trace key points from various chapters of Cervantes' novel – the world's first bestseller. El Toboso, on the N-301 between Albacete and Ocaña, was the village of Dulcinea, Don Quijote's fantasised true love and damsel for whom he was to risk all. A local house (Casa de Dulcinea, open Mon–Sat 10am–2pm and 4–6pm, Sun am only; entrance fee), thought to be that of the woman Cervantes had in mind, has been restored to its 16th-century appearance. The town hall has copies of Don Quijote in three dozen languages. Puerto Lápice, 20 km (12 miles) southeast of Consuegra, matches Cervantes' description of the inn where Don Quijote officially swore in as a knight errant.

Nearby Campo de Criptana has a fleet of hillcrest windmills in on-line formation, which look ominously like the ones that made Quijote's day back in 1605, while Cueva de Montesinos, near the San Pedro lake in the Lagunas de Ruidera valley, is the very cave in which our hero was treated by Montesinos himself to elegiac visions of other bewitched knights errant and of his beloved Dulcinea.

The nearby village of Argamasilla de Alba is a firm candidate, among several, to be the place where it all began: "*En un lugar de la Mancha ...*".

The triple-naved church has since been restored. Nearby **Viso del Marqués** is the site of the 16th-century Renaissance colossus, **Palacio del Viso** (open Tues–Sun 9am–1pm and 4–6pm; entrance fee), built by the Marqués de Santa Cruz don Álvaro de Bazán, the admiral who defeated the Turks at the battle of Lepanto in 1571. The sumptuous interior is decorated with lovely Italian frescoes. A final curious rural sight just off the N-IV motorway is **Las Virtudes**, the site of Spain's oldest identified bullring – a picturesque 17th-century square galleried corral. These sights and the squat villages of the southern plains are set against the vineyards of the Valdepeñas growing region, the largest in Spain. They have existed since medieval times, when they supplied Madrid with its wine, and today, after extensive modernisation, they remain important to the local economy.

Map on page 166

Windmills and castles

Consuegra ❽ is known for its windmills, its 13th-century castle and the late October saffron harvest and fiesta, during which one or more of the windmills are set in motion. **Tembleque**, a little further north and so-named for "trembling" victims of medieval banditry, is built around one of Spain's most beautiful central squares, a triple-tiered, porticoed gem occasionally used as a bullring. About 80 km (50 miles) east, **Belmonte** ❾ has a splendidly preserved 15th-century **castillo** (open Tues–Sun 10am–2pm and 4–6pm; entrance fee), originally built by the Marquis of Villena, Juan Pacheco, to defend the domains he is alleged to have accumulated through a series of adroit court intrigues.

Albacete ❿, at Castilla-La Mancha's southeastern corner, is a plain town largely rebuilt after the Civil War. In the Parque Abelardo Sanchez, the **Museo de Albacete** (open Tues–Sun 10am–2pm and 4.30–7pm; entrance fee) has

BELOW: the windmills at Consuegra.

some good Iberian and Roman objects. More attractive are the smaller castle-crowned towns of **Chinchilla de Monte Aragón** and **Almansa** to the east off the main N-430. Chinchilla is built around a pretty Plaza Mayor, which has some lively bars and restaurants. The 15th-century castle above the town offers sweeping views south over the plains to the picturesque **Sierra de Alcaraz**, where the mountain peaks and fertile green valleys give way to spectacular gorges and little-explored villages. The town of **Alcaraz ⓫**, with its twin Renaissance towers in the attractive Plaza Mayor, is a good base for exploring this area.

The rather singular village of **Alcalá del Júcar**, 50 km (30 miles) northeast of Albacete, literally juts out over the Júcar gorges, with houses excavated into the limestone. Some of the houses even have balconies over the far side, reached via long corridors.

Alarcón ⓬ is one of Spain's best examples of medieval military architecture. Almost completely encircled by the Río Júcar, the triangular castle, now converted to a Parador Nacional, is defended by three defensive ramparts. A Muslim stronghold, the town was subjected to a nine-month siege in 1184 before finally succumbing to the Christian conquerers.

Northeast Castilla-La Mancha

Approximately 55 km (34 miles) to the north is the city of **Cuenca ⓭**. The old part of town, with mainly Gothic and Renaissance buildings, lies north of the modern city at the top of a steep hill. The **Casas Colgadas** (Hanging Houses) teetering on the edge of the cliff over the Río Huécar are the old town's most emblematic feature. Inside one of these houses is the **Museo de Arte Abstracto Español**

BELOW: strange rock formations at Ciudad Encantada, northeast of Cuenca.

Map on page 166

(open Tues–Sun 11am–2pm and 4–6pm, Sun am only; entrance fee), with one of the best collections of abstract art in Spain, including works by Chillida, Tàpies, Saura, Zobel, Cuixart, Sempere, Rivera and others. The 18th-century **Plaza Mayor** and the mainly Gothic **Catedral** (open daily), built on the site of a mosque between the 12th and 16th century, are other key sights. The **Serranía de Cuenca**, to the northeast of the city provides a cooling summer antidote to the sun-baked plains. One of the most unusual sights in this region is the **Ciudad Encantada** (Enchanted City; open daily 10am–dusk), east of Villalba de la Sierra, named for its strange, twisted limestone formations.

West of Cuenca, just off the N-III motorway to Madrid, are the remains of the Roman settlement of **Segóbriga** ⑭ (open Tues–Sun 10am–2pm and 4–6pm; entrance fee). The ruined city includes a 2,000-spectator capacity theatre dating to the 3rd century, which is still sometimes used to stage plays. Close by is **Uclés**, an austere medieval fortress occupied by the Order of Santiago during the Reconquest, and today a school (open daily 10am–6pm).

In the region's far northeastern corner, **Guadalajara's** ⑮ flamboyant Gothic-*Mudéjar* **Palacio de los Duques del Infantado** (open Mon–Fri 9am–9pm, Sat 10am–2pm and 4.30–7pm, Sun am only; entrance fee), with its exquisitely carved facade, is the most notable of the city's half-dozen monuments. The **catedral** at nearby **Sigüenza** ⑯ is the site of the strikingly lifelike El Doncel, tomb of Martín Vázquez de Arce, Isabel of Castile's page who was killed in the taking of Granada in 1486. **La Alcarria**, the area east of Guadalajara, has lovely medieval villages such as **Pastrana**. **Brihuega**, 30 km (18 miles) north-east of Guadalajara, has a picturesque medieval centre notable for its Plaza Mayor, narrow streets and 18th-century cloth factory. ❏

BELOW: the Casas Colgadas in Cuenca.

EXTREMADURA

Walk through the honey-coloured old quarter of an Extremaduran town and step back in time to a land of conquistador gold and baroque palaces

Map on page 176

B ordered to the west by Portugal and to the north and south by granite mountain ranges, the expansive plains and hills of Extremadura are sweet with the scent of wild thyme and eucalyptus. Cattle- and sheep-raising are traditional occupations here, while forests of cork and holm-oaks provide rooting grounds for the native black pigs that are turned into superb cured hams. A complex network of dams built since the 1960s irrigates newer market gardens and vineyards, and provides water and power to large areas of Spain.

"Land of the conquistadors, land of the gods", is a refrain travellers to this region may hear. You might also come across the apocryphal remark attributed to a French soldier, who declared that Extremaduran cooking made Spain worth invading. *Extremeños* are hospitable, straightforward and independent, the legacy of centuries of poverty and isolation.

Archaeological evidence points to an extensive prehistoric settlement of the area. Mild winters and generally fertile soil made this the site of several Roman towns, most notably Mérida, which became a kind of luxury retirement colony for distinguished soldiers. Subsequent invasions of Visigoths and Moors disturbed the *Pax Romana*, however, and during the Reconquest the region became a no-man's frontier land between Muslims and Christians. From the 13th century, as the Muslims were driven south, the Christian military religious orders were granted huge tracts of land to resettle. Rural life in this lonely territory is said to have helped shape the hardy and intrepid character of the conquistador.

An estimated third of the Spaniards who set out to explore and conquer Latin America came from Extremadura; those who survived and triumphed named settlements there and returned to build magnificent palaces in their home towns. Some of the houses are still inhabited by their descendants; others have become hotels or public buildings, or been abandoned to nesting storks. Money and glory passed quickly through this land, leaving it as remote as ever when economic decline began in the 16th century.

Shrine and spiritual heart

Perched amid wooded sierras, 214 km (133 miles) southwest of Madrid, the town of **Guadalupe ❶** is a striking point of entry to the region. Since the late-13th century, when a shepherd chanced upon a buried image of the Virgin Mary purportedly carved by St Luke, Guadalupe has been an important place of pilgrimage. Alfonso XI dedicated a battle to this Virgin in 1340; when she brought him victory he ordered the construction of a splendid monastery in which to house her. Christopher Columbus brought the first Amerindians to be baptised to Guadalupe, where the

LEFT: San Martín church in the Plaza Major, Trujillo
BELOW: a local farmer.

In 1531, the Guadalupe Virgin appeared to Mexican peasant Juan Diego. More than 100 cities in the New World bear her name and, today, she is a symbol of "hispanidad", drawing thousands of pilgrims every year from the Spanish-speaking world.

rite was performed at the town fountain in 1496. Over the next few centuries wealthy pilgrims enriched the monastery's order of Hieronymite monks and donated funds for additions to the original building, which served as a combination palace, church, fortress and royal lodgings (the latter is now converted into a hotel).

By the 15th century the shrine was known as the "Spanish Vatican" and possessed hospitals, schools of fine arts, grammar and medicine, 30,000 head of cattle and what was possibly the world's best library. Guadalupe was also a renowned centre for the treatment of syphilis, and had a hospital specialising in the "sweat cure". The old Hospital San Juan Bautista, with a graceful 16th-century patio, is now the Parador Zurbarán, across the street from the monastery.

Such became the wealth and power of the monastery that a popular refrain went: "Better than count or duke, to be a monk in Guadalupe." The place was sacked by the French in 1809, and in 1835, when the Spanish government ordered the sale of monastic property, the Hieronymites fled. Today, however, it is once again the region's spiritual heart.

The Virgin's treasures

Presently the **Monasterio de Guadalupe** (open daily 9.30am–1pm and 3.30–6.30pm; entrance fee; tel: 927-367 000) is inhabited by Franciscan monks, who provide both lodging for visitors and a tour of Guadalupe's treasures. A visit begins in the 14th-century Gothic *Mudéjar* **cloister**, with its two-tiered horse-shoe archways and lovely fountain surrounded by a miniature temple. The old **refectory** houses a dazzling collection of priests' robes, embroidered with gold threads and encrusted with pearls. Of further interest is the collection of illumi-

BELOW: the Guadalupe Virgin.

nated choir books, and a room containing the Virgin's own rich wardrobe, necklaces and crowns, given to her by kings, presidents and popes.

The artistic highlight of the tour is the **sacristy**, which is locally given the rather grand nickname of the Spanish Sistine Chapel, where portraits of monks by 17th-century master Zurbarán are set against lavishly decorated walls. Finally, up a red marble staircase is the **camarín**, where the Virgin resides. The famous iron grille in the **church**, entered separately off the plaza, is said to be made from the chains of freed slaves.

The cobbled streets of the town wind among traditional Extremaduran slate houses, their wooden balconies full of potted geraniums. In addition to devotional souvenirs and pottery, you can also take home a bottle of *gloria*, a local drink made from a blend of *aguardiente*, grape juice and herbs.

Crossing the **Sierra de Guadalupe** south takes you through the mountain villages of **Logrosán** and **Zorita**, the former boasting the remains of a pre-Roman town on a nearby hillside. Catch up with the main highway, the N-V, at **Miajadas**. From there you can take a 28-km (17-mile) detour to **Medellín**, birthplace of the conqueror of Mexico, Hernán Cortés. Climb up to the ruined **castle** and survey the **Río Guadiana** shimmering below. Medellín is a pleasant, quiet village, noted for its outsize bronze statue of Cortés in the town square – a rare representation, since there are no statues of him in Mexico.

Roman city, modern capital

Formerly known as Emeritus Augustus, **Mérida** ❷ lies 127 km (79 miles) south of Guadalupe, on a sluggish bend of the Guadiana. Founded in 25 BC, the city became a prosperous capital of the Roman colony of Lusitania, and Roman

Map on page 176

The hands and face of the Guadalupe Virgin are dark brown after her 700 years underground and, according to the Franciscan guide, because the Muslims tried to set her on fire.

BELOW: classical drama at Mérida's Roman theatre during its summer festival.

Roman mosaic depicting grape harvest celebrations.

It's worth buying a combined ticket for entry to all the Roman sites in Mérida. Ask at the tourist office by the gates of the Teatro Romano.

BELOW: the Milagros Aqueduct.

ruins are Mérida's pride today. Yet this lovely city, whose buildings and hedges of myrtle and hibiscus give a flavour of the Spanish south, also aspires to modernity. Since becoming capital of the autonomous region in 1981 its skyline has been reshaped by largely brash new development. But there are modern architectural highlights: Calatrava's sleek Lusitania bridge and Rafael Moneo's stunning museum are both strokes of genius.

In July, Mérida hosts a classical theatre festival, which attracts Spanish and international companies and directors. Performances are held in the **Teatro Romano** and **Anfiteatro**, which seat 6,000 and 14,000 spectators respectively. Nearby are the hippodrome, formerly used for chariot races, and the **Casa Romana del Mithraeo**, which was actually a small palace. Of particular interest are the mosaic floors depicting the four seasons, and the remains of a sauna. The **Casa del Anfiteatro** also has exceptionally good mosaics and the remains of some paintings (all sites open daily 9.30am–1.45pm and 5–7.15pm, closes at 6.15pm in winter; entrance fee).

Modern museum

Across the street from the theatres is the brick **Museo Nacional de Arte Romano** (1989), designed by Rafael Moneo, a superb location for the largest collection of Roman artefacts outside Italy (open Tues–Sun 10am–2pm, 4–6pm; 5–7pm Apr–Sept, Sun am only; entrance fee). The main hall of the museum, with its high archways and dramatic use of natural light, has the feeling of a cathedral nave, and is an impressive backdrop for the colossal statues. Two storeys of galleries built around the main hall are dedicated to theme exhibits, such as rare painted friezes, jewellery and glass, replicas of which are on sale.

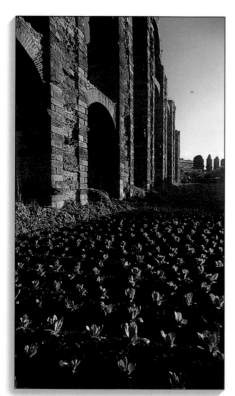

Many other Roman monuments are dotted around town. The **Arco de Trajano**, just off the Plaza de España, dwarfs the narrow street and nearby houses. A short walk away in Calle Romero Leal is the **Templo de Diana** (1st century AD but with Renaissance additions) and the 9th century riverside **Alcazaba**, with ruins inside it. On the edge of town are the **Puente de Guadiana**, with its 60 granite arches (now open only for pedestrian traffic), and the **Milagros Aqueduct**, which until recently brought water to Mérida. Around 8 km (5 miles) to the northeast of the city, within the lovely wooded **Parque de Cornalvo**, are Europe's oldest working dam and reservoir. They once supplied Roman Mérida with water and still supply local villages.

Badajoz

The capital of Extremadura's southern province, **Badajoz ❸** is just 6 km (3½ miles) from the Portuguese border. Originally a Roman town named Pax Augustus, it rose to prominence as Batalajoz, capital of a *taifa* (principality), and once dominated half of Portugal, including Lisbon. It was captured from the Muslims in 1229, but its strategic location made it the site of many bloody sieges over the centuries.

In August 1936 it was captured by Nationalist forces, and, in one of the darkest moments of the Civil War, many Republican defenders (possibly several thousand but the exact figure is unknown) were herded into the bullring and shot.

Badajoz's solid post-war appearance today is given limited spark by its monuments. The ramparts of the **Alcazaba**, or Muslim castle, are best approached from the river, not through the old town's poor quarter. It keeps an octagonal tower, the **Espantaperros** (dog-frightener), so-called because its ancient bell vibrated at a high pitch that terrified dogs. Inside is a provincial **Museo Arqueólogico** (open Tues–Sun 10am–3pm), with interesting displays on local sites that include Cancho Ruano, Spain's only known Tartessan temple, burned down in the 6th century BC. Also worth a look is the Gothic **Catedral** (open daily 11am–1pm and 6–8pm; entrance fee for cloister) which has impressive Renaissance choirstalls, paintings by Morales and Zurbarán, and a stunning tiled cloister.

South of Badajoz is unspoiled countryside dotted with whitewashed towns marked by dramatic military and religious history. **Zafra** is a good base for exploring; it has a magnificent Parador inside the 15th-century palace around which the walled quarter grew. **Olivenza**, to the west, keeps a remarkable cluster of monuments built in the Portuguese Manueline style thanks to its long frontier history; it finally became Spanish in 1803. **Jerez de los Caballeros** was the seat of the Knights Templar and birthplace of Nuñez de Balboa, who "discovered" the Pacific Ocean. Fountains, churches and heraldic shields are found at every turn in the streets sloping down from the ruined castle. The Knights maintained satellite villages in the hilly **Sierra de Fregenal** to the south, where today black pigs snuffle among thick woods. The Order of Santiago was based at **Llerena**, now known as the gateway to Andalusia but once feared as a centre of the Inquisition, and also controlled the tiny 15th-century hilltop **Monasterio de Tentudia** (tel: 924-149 092; open daily), which commands magnificent panoramic views.

Map on page 176

Discovered in 1978 near Zalamea de la Serena in southeastern Extremadura are the remains of a 6th-century BC temple-palace, Cancho Ruano, the world's only known Tartessan monument. Enquire at Zalamea's town hall (tel: 924-780 032) to visit the site.

BELOW: the Museo Nacional de Arte Romano, Mérida.

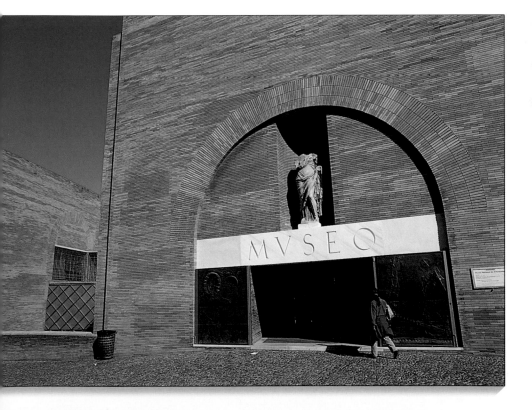

TIP

The best time to wander around Cáceres is at dusk, as the street lights come on. Tip the porter and you may be allowed a peek into the patios of some of the inhabited palaces.

Noble hotheads

Cáceres , capital of the northern Extremaduran province, is a city lifted out of the pages of an illuminated book of chivalry. Over the centuries, it has been spared the sieges and bombardments that destroyed parts of other Extremaduran cities, a longevity that saw it declared a national monument in 1949. The old city is separated from the new by well-preserved walls and towers originally built in Muslim times. It is best approached from the **Plaza Mayor**. For the most dramatic ascent, climb the steps leading through the **Arco de la Estrella**.

During the Middle Ages the atmosphere was rather more hectic. When Alfonso IX took the city from the Muslims in 1229, it became the seat of a brotherhood of knights called the *Fratres de Cáceres,* who eventually became Spain's most noble order, the Order of Santiago, and a wealthy centre of free trade. At one time there were 300 knights in the city, their palaces just a few steps from one another. Each *solar*, or noble house, had its own defensive tower, and the continual factions and rivalries meant that there was always a small war in progress somewhere around town. In the interests of peace Fernando and Isabel ordered the destruction of most of the towers in 1476, save those belonging to their favourites. Of the few that are left, the most striking is perhaps the **Torre de las Cigüeñas**, or Stork Tower, in the **Plaza San Mateo**.

Directly opposite is the **Casa de las Veletas**, a baroque palace built on the site of the Muslim castle (open Tues–Sun 9.30am–2.30pm and 4–8.15pm (closes 7.15pm in winter), Sun 10.15am–2.30pm; entrance fee). In the basement is an enormous arcaded *aljibe*, or cistern, which looks like a flooded mosque. Upstairs is the **Museo de Cáceres** containing artefacts from prehistoric times, Roman coins and local handicrafts and costumes. There are also reproductions of the cave

BELOW: buttercups in an olive grove, Extremadura.

paintings in the nearby caves of **Maltravieso** and contemporary Spanish art on display. Close by is the Jewish quarter, recently restored. To the left of the museum is the church of **San Mateo**, with a beautiful bell tower, and the **Convento de San Pablo** (open daily), inhabited by cloistered nuns who sell their famous *yemas* (candied egg yolks) through a screened dumbwaiter to avoid showing their faces to the world.

While the old town's palaces range in architectural style from Gothic to Plateresque, they blend harmoniously together through their sober grey-gold sandstone and granite facades. Palaces of particular note include the **Casa de los Solís**, with its coat of arms in the shape of a sun, and the **Casa del Mono** (monkey), now a library. Near the 16th-century cathedral church of **Santa María la Mayor** (open Mon–Sat 10am–1pm and 5–6.15pm, Sun 10.45–11.45am) are the **Bishop's Palace**, the **Palace of Ovando**, with its lush green patio, and the **Casa Toledo-Moctezuma**, once inhabited by the descendants of the conquistador Juan Cano and Aztec Emperor Moctezuma's daughter.

Behind Santa María is the **Casa de los Golfines de Abajo**, a house belonging to a family of French knights invited here in the 12th century to help fight the Muslims. According to a contemporary chronicler, "even the king cannot subject them, though he has tried". It is believed that the Spanish word *golfo*, meaning "scoundrel", is derived from this family's surname.

Map on page 176

Cradle of conquerors

Crowning a dusty hill surrounded by pastureland, **Trujillo** ❺ is 47 km (30 miles) east of Cáceres on the N-521. Its number of extraordinarily beautiful monuments make it well worth a two-day visit. The town's long and dramatic history

BELOW: statue of Pizarro in Trujillo's Plaza Mayor.

CONQUERORS OF THE NEW WORLD

The conquistadors of the Americas were not, as they are sometimes depicted, village louts, but often the second or illegitimate sons of aristocrats, with grand surnames and the military training to go with it, but limited expectations in Spain. Francisco Pizarro, for example, was the bastard son of a minor nobleman from Trujillo who, together with his two half-brothers, set out to capture the fabled wealth of Peru. Even in that delirious time the expedition was widely known as *de los locos* – of the mad men – and did not fail to live up to expectations.

During one desperate moment in the jungle, Pizarro drew a line in the sand with the point of his sword and dared his comrades to cross it and head home. All but 13 did. However, the inroads made by those 13 men convinced Carlos I to give Pizarro the ships and armies he so desperately wanted, and with which he was able to conquer the Inca. A few years later, however, Pizarro was assassinated; his body is buried in Lima cathedral.

Other notable conquistadors from Extremadura include Hernán Cortés, who captured Mexico City, capital of the Aztec empire, in 1521; Hernando de Soto, who discovered the Mississippi in 1540; and Francisco de Orellana, who charted the waters of the Amazon.

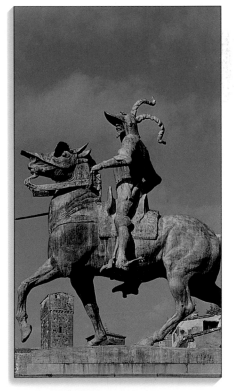

is said to have begun with its founding by Julius Caesar, but Trujillo's proudest moment was clearly the conquest of Peru by native son Francisco Pizarro. His bronze equestrian statue dominates the beautiful **Plaza Mayor** and palaces built with wealth from Inca treasures are sprinkled throughout the city.

The **Palacio del Marqués de la Conquista**, built by Pizarros's brother, Hernando, stands across the plaza from the statue, though disappointingly, it is not open to the public. On the ornate facade are busts of Francisco Pizarro and his wife Inés Yupanqui, sister of the Inca emperor Atahualpa. Above them is the coat of arms ceded to them by Carlos I. Behind the equestrian statue is the 15th-century church of **San Martín** (open daily 10am–1pm and 4–7pm), whose bell and clock towers provide ample nesting ground for several storks.

Pizarro's family played an important role in regaining possession of Trujillo during the Reconquest. Their reward was to be allowed to build their home, now the Casa-Museo de Pizarro, within the old city walls.

Military miracles

Across the street from the church is the **Palacio de los Duques de San Carlos** (open Mon–Sat 10.30am–1.30pm and 4.30–6.30; entrance fee), a 16th-century palace with a striking baroque facade and chimneys inspired by Inca temples. The house is now inhabited by nuns, who are more than willing to give a tour of the patio and splendid staircase.

A few steps outside the plaza's southwest corner is the **Palacio Orellana-Pizarro** (open daily 10.30am–1.30pm and 4.30–6.30pm), also run by nuns, which has an exquisite Plateresque patio. Francisco de Orellana was a Pizarro cousin, and the first European to navigate the Amazon. He claimed the river for Spain, and eventually perished along its banks.

Each step uphill in Trujillo is a step further back into the past. Follow **Cuesta de Santiago** past the **Torre del Alfiler** (Needle Tower) up to the Muslim **castillo** (open daily). Pause for breath at **Santa María la Mayor**, a 15th-century church containing the tomb of Diego Paredes, the "Samson of Spain". As a young child he was said to have carried the stone baptismal font from the church to his mother's bedside, and Cervantes wrote that as an adult soldier, Diego "defeated the entire French army and held them at the end of a bridge". Further up is the **Casa Museo de Pizarro** (open daily 9.30am–2pm and 4–7pm winter, 10am–2pm and 5–8.30pm summer; entrance fee), with exhibits documenting the exploits of the Pizarro family.

BELOW: carving in Plasencia's cathedral.

From the castle walls there is a panoramic view of the surrounding countryside, while inside are the Muslim cisterns. A craft fair is held in the Patio de San Pablo. Upstairs is a chapel dedicated to the Virgin who enabled the Christian armies to take the castle from the Muslims by illuminating a dark fog that had enveloped them. A coin-operated machine allows the visitor to illuminate the granite statue of the Virgin; her bright light can be seen from the Plaza Mayor below.

The two-ton virgin

An attractive town on the banks of the Río Jerte, **Plasencia ❻** is 43 km (27 miles) north of Trujillo by the C-524. Settled by the Berbers, it was conquered by Alfonso VIII, who in 1189 granted it a coat of arms with the title *Placeat Deo et hominibus*

Map on page 176

(Pleasing to God and Man). Up until 1492 the city continued to have large Jewish and Arab populations, reflected by the narrow, winding streets in which they lived, as well as by street names, such as **Calle de las Morenas** (Street of the Dark Women). On Tuesdays, a market takes place in the **Plaza Mayor**, as it has for 800 years.

Plasencia has an impressive **Catedral** (open Mon–Sat 9am–1pm and 4–6pm winter; 5–7pm summer; closed Sun pm), which is actually parts of two cathedrals joined together. The first is 13th–14th-century Romanesque, with some touches of Gothic, while the second is 15th–16th-century Gothic with a Plateresque facade. The older cathedral, reached via a cloister with stone-carving, houses an exceptional collection of religious art including the 2,000-kg (2-ton) stone Virgin of Perdón.

The choir stalls are some of the most beautiful in Spain; the carving represents both sacred and, on the backs of the seats, profane subjects. The sculptor, Rodrigo Alemán, declared that even God couldn't have made such a masterpiece, a blasphemy that got him locked into a nearby castle tower. According to legend, he ended his days by falling from the tower, flapping home-made wings.

Aristrocratic homes

There are several palaces in Plasencia. The **Convento de los Dominicos** has been converted into Spain's newest Parador, and the 14th-century Provincial Hospital on Plazuela Marqués de la Puebla now houses the excellent **Museo Etnográfico-Textil** (open Wed–Sun 11am–2pm and 5–8pm, Sun am only; July–Aug Mon–Sat am only), with some vivid exhibits including regional costumes and traditional crafts.

BELOW: clouds over Trujillo.

To the south of Plasencia is the **Parque de Monfragüe ❼**, a 500 sq km (200 sq mile) national park. The name comes from the Roman "Mons Fragorum" and its Mediterranean woodland and scrub protects a wealth of wildlife, including over three-quarters of Spain's protected bird species. The information centre at **Villareal de San Carlos** (tel: 927-199 134; open daily) on the C-524 between Plasencia and Trujillo makes a good starting point, and has information on walking trails and lookout points.

Coria, 33 km (20 miles) west of Plasencia, was one of Spain's earliest bishoprics (AD 589). The splendid cathedral quarter – surrounded by the best preserved medieval walls in Europe – dwarfs today's town. A good time to visit is during the June fiestas when the gates in the wall are kept shut to allow the after-dark bull-running.

South-east of Coria is **Alcántara**, where the **Puente Romano** (Roman bridge) soars high above the River Tagus to avoid flood water. By contrast, the once magnificent **Convento de San Benito**, sacked by Napoleon in 1807, is an atmospheric ruin. Legend has it that the monks' recipe book was stolen by General Junot, and became the source of some elements of French *haute cuisine*. Further south are the attractive frontier towns are Valencia de Alcántara and Albuquerque.

Cherry blossom

Extremadura's northern sierras and valleys offer an unexpected mosaic of contrasting landscapes. To the north of Coria, the **Sierra de Gata**'s hamlets and green fields border on **Las Hurdes' ❽** slate-black slopes and beehives, caught by Luis Buñuel in his classic documentary *Tierra Sin Pan* (*Land Without Bread,* 1932). The cramped stone dwellings built into the hillsides give a sense of the terrible poverty endured in the villages of this region. Approaching on the C-512 from the west, you'll cross the Río Hurdano at Vegas de Coria where a road turns off, following the river valley to some of the most atmospheric "black villages" of the region. The road continues all the way back to the C-512 at Riomalo de Abajo.

To the east rise the peaks of the **Sierra de Francia** and **Sierra de Gredos'**, sliced through by the lush green Ambroz, Vera and Jerte river valleys. Tobacco, asparagus, paprika peppers and cherries all flourish in the region's gentle climate. In spring the sight of the snowy cherry blossom in the Jerte valley is unforgettable.

Hervás ❾, a mountain village in the Ambroz valley, has one of the best-preserved Jewish quarters in Spain. It is thought that Hervás became a predominantly Jewish settlement in the early Middle Ages, as the Jews fled Christian and Muslim persecution of the larger cities. Perhaps because of the remoteness of the area, Hervás escaped the massive pogroms and fires of 1391. When the Jews were expelled from Spain in 1492, their neighbourhood was left intact, and their possessions ceded to the local Duke of Béjar. Its textile industry flourished until the 18th century. Intricate, maze-like streets make this village an intimate one full of atmosphere. A plaque marks the house thought to be the old synagogue in Calle Sinagoga.

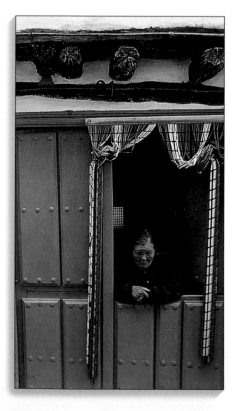

BELOW: in the Jewish quarter, Hervás.

An interesting and worthwhile side trip from Hervás, approximately 22 km (14 miles) west on the other side of the N-630, is the restored village of **Granadilla**. It has been uninhabited since the 1960s when the Embalse de Gabriel y Galán reservoir was created on its doorstep.

Map on page 176

Over the pass

Leading out of Hervás, there is a narrow but spectacular road, which should not be attempted in poor weather, that crosses the treeless Honduras Pass, and then plunges into the **Jerte Valley**. The villages here, including Cabezuela del Valle and Jerte itself, are becoming increasingly popular among travellers, and a number of rural guest houses and country inns have opened. The area is especially popular during the March cherry blossom season. The Holy Roman Emperor Charles V (Spain's Carlos I), passed through here in 1556, on his way to the Valley of La Vera, on the southern side of the Tormantos mountain range. There is now a 28-km (17-mile) walking trail from the pass of Tornavacas, at the tip of the Jerte valley, crossing through the nature reserve of Garganta de los Infiernos to the village of **Jarandilla de la Vera**. The palace where the king rested on his journey, the Castillo de los Condes Oropesa, has been converted into a modern Parador.

Carlos I soon had his own lodgings built at the **Monasterio de Yuste** ❿ (open daily 9.30am–2.30pm and 3–6pm winter; 3.30–6.30pm summer; entrance fee), 10 km (6 miles) to the southwest of Jarandilla. Here he tended to his clock-mending and observed Mass from his bed until he died in 1558. It is the unforgettable setting – above a small lake and the picturesque village of **Cuacos de Yuste** – and the monastery's simplicity that make it so beautiful today. ❑

Las Hurdes is known for the production of high-quality honey, and beehives are in evidence in many villages in the area.

BELOW: collecting honey in Las Hurdes.

AMONG THE CASTLES OF IMPOSSIBLE DREAMS

Imperious, impervious, fantastic, steeped in history and dripping with romance – the castles of Spain are the stuff of fairytales

Castile is the high, arid heart of Spain, Castilian is the country's spoken language. Both derive their names from *castillo* (castle), the building that for years was the most dominant feature of this part of Spain. Castile was where the first significant advances were made against the Muslims, a Wild West of adventurers and pioneers. Frontiers were marked along the Duero, Arlanzón and Ebro rivers where there were no walled cities, monasteries or manorial estates to run to in times of trouble. Strongholds were established about 100 years after the Muslim conquest, notably under Fernán Gonzáles (910–970), first Count of Castile, and over the next 400 years of fighting, castles appeared all over the countryside.

MUSLIM CASTLES

The Muslims were great castle builders, too; at Berlanga de Duero they constructed a fortress with a massive curtain wall and drum towers with a commanding view *(pictured above)*.

As the lands grew safer, castles were adopted as glorified homes. The Fonseca family's Castillo de Coca in Segovia, for example, displays some fine *Mudéjar* military architecture, but it was never intended to be put to the test.

As the Muslims were driven out in 1492, castle building was forbidden, but 2,000 had already altered the landscape forever.

△ **CASTILLO DE GUADALEST**
Alicante's eyries have commanding views. The coast needed protection from pirates.

◁ **PONFERRADA**
On the pilgrim route to Santiago de Compostella, Ponferrada was run by the Knights Templar.

◁ SEGOVIA ALCAZAR

The castle where Fernando and Isabel were proclaimed is the ultimate fairytale fortress. It stands on an 80-metre rocky outcrop.

△ TORRE DE HOMENAJE

Segovia's keep has unusual candlestick-and-snuffer towers. This was the residential and social hub of the castle.

ARISTOCRATIC LODGINGS

The picture above is of the interior of the Parador at Zamora, a 15th-century castle and former home of the counts of Alba y Aliste on the banks of the Duero. The word *parador* (from the Arabic *waradah*, meaning "halting place") had been in use for many centuries before 1928 when the government instigated this chain of state-run hotels in restored historic buildings. Designed to be no more than a day's journey apart, there are around 90 altogether. They are all relatively inexpensive and have a reputation for good service and good food. As a matter of policy, they have always served the best local dishes, and even if you don't stay in one, they are worth a visit for a meal, or a coffee, just to have a look around.

△ PEÑAFIEL

One of a number of early Castilian castles built on the banks of the Duero, Peñafiel dates from the 10th century, but is mostly 15th-century.

◁ VALENCIA DE DON JUAN

The most arrogant castle in León, Valencia de Don Juan has high walls and lofty towers looming above the River Esla, near Coyança.

▽ CASTILLO DE SANTA CATALINA

This 13th-century castle in Jaén was built by Ibn-al-Ahmar, who ceded it to Ferdinand III in 1245 in return for control of Granada. The castle is now a Parador.

SEVILLE

Aside from Seville's immense cultural heritage, its convivial, fun-loving atmosphere makes the city an ideal place to experience Andalusia's sultry nightlife

Map on page 192

Seville. Córdoba. Granada. A resounding triumvirate of southern (Andalusian) Spanish cities whose very names roll off the tongue with a hint of arrogance. Flashy, flamboyant, proud. Warm of weather, attractive of scenery and easily accessible by sea, Andalusia proved vulnerable to the successive settlements of the Phoenicians, Greeks, Romans, Visigoths and Muslims. But it was the Arab and Berber presence that bequeathed Andalusia the richly sensuous medieval culture of silver filigree and ornate mosques that bewitches visitors to the region today.

Under Islamic dominion, Andalusia was the centre of the most highly developed civilisation of the Middle Ages. But its reputation for riches and flair for hospitality hark back to an even earlier incarnation as the Roman province of Baetica, when Andalusia purveyed all make and manner of luxuries to the connoisseurs and cognoscenti of imperial Rome.

Such 19th-century visitors as Washington Irving, George Borrow and Richard Ford were inspired to record its charms in their various travel chronicles and thus helped to convert the salient features of Andalusia into the universal Spanish stereotype. Sherry wines, well-disciplined horses, brave bulls and flamboyant flamenco were the stuff of Andalusia. And who from a colder and soggier climate could resist the promise of 3,000 hours of sunshine annually and a mere 30 cm (12 inches) of rain? Generally, Andalusia's winters are mild and its summers scorching. Throughout, the climatic catchword is "dry", as evidenced by the number of bridges spanning parched riverbeds, some of which are being cultivated.

PRECEDING PAGES: festival gear. **LEFT:** in the Parque de María Luisa. **BELOW:** Torre del Oro, which houses Seville's Maritime Museum.

Fellow *Andaluces*

Until the Reconquest of Granada by the Catholic Monarchs Fernando and Isabel in 1492, Andalusia had rarely been united under one ruler. Internecine strife among the *emirs* and *taifas* (principalities) of Córdoba, Jaén, Granada and Seville undermined Islamic domination until the increasing pressure of Spain's northern Christian kingdoms vanquished it.

Today Andalusia is Spain's most populous region, tallying 87,270 sq km (33,695 sq miles), 7 million inhabitants and comprising Spain's 8 southernmost provinces. Comparable in size to Portugal, it stretches from that country in the west to Murcia in the east. Its northern reaches are marked by the Sierra Morena and its southern boundaries by the Atlantic Ocean and Mediterranean Sea.

The people of the provinces of Almería, Granada, Jaén, Córdoba, Málaga, Cádiz, Seville and Huelva, each with a provincial capital of the same name, are at once fellow *andaluces* and individual *almerienses*,

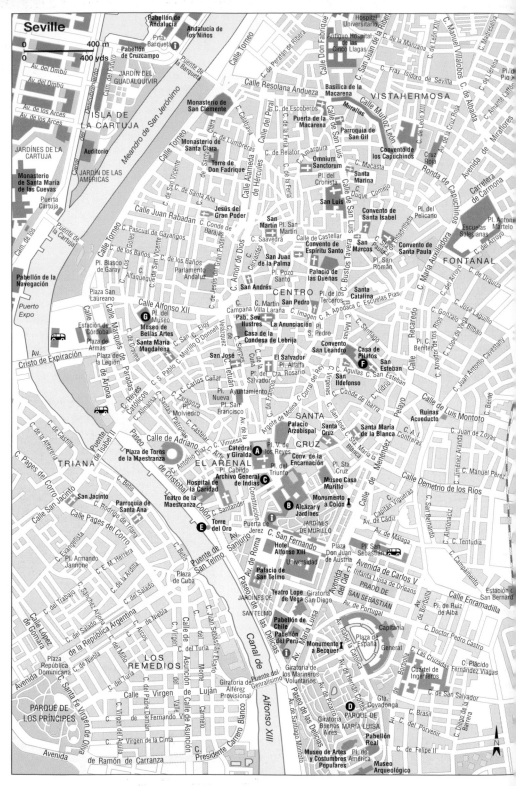

Seville

0   400 m
0   400 yds

granadinos, cordobeses and *sevillanos*. Says one Seville taxi driver: "Seville is different from the rest. Here we are more *simpático* (genial) and more polite in everything. We all call ourselves *andaluces* because we share the same flag. Of course, Cádiz is somewhat similar to Seville, but the *granadinos* are coarse fellows, as if they weren't even *andaluces*." These provincial rivalries have their roots in a not-so-playful past of seesawing fortunes among the former Muslim kingdoms of Granada, Seville and Córdoba.

Map on page 192

Southern outlook

For a long time outsiders have characterised the *andaluces* as lethargic and fond of their afternoon siesta. But at the same time all consider them to be spontaneous and witty, balancing an exaggerated sense of tragedy with a robust sense of humour. "Here are two classes of people to whom life seems one long holiday, the very rich, and the very poor", writes Washington Irving in *Tales of the Alhambra*, "one, because they need do nothing, the other, because they have nothing to do; but there are none who understand the art of doing nothing and living upon nothing better than the poor classes of Spain. Climate does one half and temperament the rest… Talk of poverty! With (a Spaniard) it has no disgrace. It sits upon him with a grandiose style, like his ragged cloak. He is an *hidalgo* (nobleman) even when in rags."

A 19th-century sketch of Seville.

A southern farmer said this about his native *tierra*: "This is a land boiling over, yes, but here the fiestas and other things are born and die; what is important is the ephemeral, the fleeting, paper lanterns and flashes, but one doesn't build, one doesn't put cement to anything. What delights is the arrival of the heat to signal the siesta."

Ever since the Christians eclipsed the Muslims in Andalusia, the south has been largely poor. Not the overt, searing poverty of the Third World, but rather an undercurrent of rural poverty not readily detected by the casual tourist. Fortunately, Andalusia's reputation as "a rich land inhabited by poor men" is declining. While officially, unemployment remains relatively high, there is a thriving underground economy and rural workers, long neglected, now enjoy an unheard-of range of social services.

BELOW: a good-looking city.

Historic leap

The 1980s brought unprecedented prosperity to Andalusia. Spain's entry into the EU in 1986 spurred development, which was further boosted by the investment in infrastructure for Expo '92, the world fair in Seville celebrating Columbus's voyage to the New World. Having Seville native Felipe González as prime minister was helpful, too. Four-lane highways now connect Andalusia with Madrid and the rest of Europe and the AVE high-speed train has halved travelling time from Madrid to Seville.

Abundant sunshine and fertile farmland are two enduring resources. The sunshine has converted the coast, particularly the Costa del Sol, into a favourite holiday and residential area for Northern Europeans, but efforts are underway to open up less-known areas inland to attract hikers and wildlife aficionados. Mod-

Young woman in flamenco costume, a manifestation of an exuberant culture.

ern methods are being applied to farming, and thousands of acres of what once was desert in Almería province have been transformed into plastic-covered greenhouses, where export crops, from melons to carnations, flourish all year.

Flirtatious Seville

Seville, Spain's fourth-largest city and Andalusia's capital, is the most coquettish of the three grand cities of the south. An old Spanish refrain says: *Quien no ha visto Sevilla, no ha visto maravilla.* (He who has not seen Seville, has not known wonderment.) George Borrow, author of *The Bible in Spain*, considered it "the most interesting town in all Spain (beneath) the most glorious heaven…"

Even through a veil of fine December rain Seville is pretty. In the bright Andalusian sunshine, she is dazzling. A fitting setting for Byron's Don Juan, Bizet's Carmen, and Rossini's barber to play out their fictional lives. Some of the real lives that got their start here are those of the poets Gustavo Adolfo Bécquer (1836–70) and Antonio Machado (1875–1939), and the painters Diego de Velázquez (1599–1660) and Bartolomé Esteban Murillo (1618–82). Romance has apparently always coursed through the city's veins. The Muslim historian Al-Saqundi, captivated by its charm, once proclaimed: "If one asked for the milk of birds in Seville, it would be found." St Teresa was so taken with its beauty and boldness that she confessed she felt that anyone who could somehow avoid committing sin in Seville would be doing very well indeed.

Roman rule

BELOW: decorative tiles in the Alcázar.

"Hercules built me; Caesar surrounded me with walls and towers; the King Saint took me." This terse recapitulation of Seville's multi-tiered history was carved long ago on the Jerez Gate. Later, Seville's port would bustle with New World activity as Spain built a lustrous but short-lived overseas empire.

In the era of discoverers, when the Netherlands, England and Spain were fighting for supremacy at sea and in the New World colonies, Seville was one of the richest cities in the world. But it had already known previous fame and fortune. Founded by the Iberians, it was usurped by Julius Caesar for Rome in 45 BC. Made an assize town and named *Hispalis*, it was given the title of *Colonia Julia Romula* and became one of the leading towns of the flourishing Roman province of Baetica, roughly corresponding to present-day Andalusia. There followed several lacklustre centuries under the Vandals and Visigoths, the latter having Seville report to their capital at Toledo.

Glory days

Then in 712 came the Muslims, who renamed it *Ishbiliya*. Later, as part of the Caliphate of Córdoba, Seville rivalled that capital in material prosperity and as a seat of learning. When the Caliphate broke up in the 11th century, Seville pursued an independent course. Beginning in 1023, it saw the successive rule of the Abbadites, Almoravids (1091) and Almohads (1147). Under this last dynasty a new period of prosperity reigned that left behind many of Seville's fine buildings, including the Giralda. In 1248, Seville was reconquered for Christianity by Fernando III, the King Saint, who died and was buried here.

The wave of New World discoveries that raised Seville to the crest of its fortunes in the 16th century also dashed it in its wake when the empire ebbed a century later. In 1519, Magellan set sail from here to circumnavigate the globe. But Seville's moment of glory was all too fleeting, and decline set in again in the early 17th century, subsequently hastened by maritime competition from Cádiz, the snowballing loss of the Spanish colonies that had brought so much trade, the troubled state of 19th-century Spain and a brief French occupation lasting from 1808 to 1812.

Its historic momentum lost, Seville strolled into the 20th century trailing a tarnished heritage that nevertheless stirred great feelings of pride among *sevillanos*. Seized early in the Civil War by the Nationalists, Seville served as a base for attacks on the rest of Andalusia. Emerging from the war physically starving and spiritually spent, the city gradually regained its legendary *alegría* (happiness) under the entrenched Franco dictatorship. But for a long time its gypsy bravado resounded with a tragic note.

Since 1940, Seville's population has almost doubled to the current 700,000. With the granting of regional autonomy, Seville – as capital – received a boost in importance. But Expo '92 brought an influx of professionals from other regions and countries to shake up the status quo in a community where class barriers and conservative attitudes seemed immovable. They brought new money and fresh ideas to a city frozen in its ritualistic ways. Expo also transformed Seville physically and scores of old buildings were restored and fine walkways were built along the riverside.

Map on page 192

AVE high-speed train at Seville's Estación de Santa Justa.

BELOW: exhibits from Expo '92, held in Seville.

ISLA DE LA CARTUJA

The site of Expo '92, on the west bank of the Río Guadalquivir, was once a boggy wasteland with only one building, the 15th-century **Monasterio de Santa María de las Cuevas**. Part of the monastery houses the **Centro Andaluz de Arte Contemporáneo** with a permanent exhibition of modern Andalusian artists (open Tues–Sat; entrance fee). The western part of the island was developed into a high-tech research area. Visitors are still able to view the Expo '92 pavilions but, since most are now privately owned, they are not open to the public. La Cartuja is also home to the 35-hectare (88-acre) **Isla Mágica** theme park (open Mar–Oct daily; entrance fee), with rides, outdoor entertainment, cafés, bars and restaurants.

Other attractions include the oval-shaped **Puente de la Barqueta** and lyre-shaped **Puente del Alamillo**, the **Auditorio** (a large open-air theatre) and the **Teatro Central**, offering regular performances of drama, dance and music. The northern third of the island is occupied by Seville's largest park, the **Parque del Alamillo** (open daily dawn–dusk). The latest addition to La Cartuja is the **Estadio Olímpico**, built to back Seville's (unsuccessful) bid to host the 2004 Olympic Games. The 60,000-seat stadium opened for the World Athletics Championship in 1999.

Seville's monumental cathedral, with the Giralda tower rising behind.

On a huge scale

Virtually everything in Andalusia is of a human scale – with the exception of Seville's **Catedral** (open Mon–Sat 11am–5pm, Sun 2–6pm; entrance fee). Built between 1402 and 1506, it contains five spacious aisles, a large main chapel with a wrought-iron screen and vaulting that towers 56 metres (184 ft) above the transept. Allegedly it was the chapter's aim in 1401 "to construct a church such and as good that it never should have had its equal. Let Posterity, when it admires it complete, say that those who dared to devise such a work must have been mad."

You enter the cathedral through the **Patio de los Naranjos** (Patio of the Orange Trees) – the courtyard of the city's main mosque – a shaded oasis of trees and sparkling fountains used for the ritual ablutions of Islam. From this bright, courtyard, the **Puerto del Lagarto** (Gate of the Lizard) leads into the cathedral interior.

Hidden in its sombre shadows are many relics and treasures, such as paintings by Murillo, Zurbarán and Goya; a cross said to be made from the first gold brought from America by Columbus; and a funerary monument claimed to hold the explorer's remains. In fact, he almost certainly reposes in Santo Domingo, capital of the Dominican Republic. His leaden tomb was taken from Seville to Santo Domingo Cathedral in 1544, and was supposedly returned over three centuries later. But somewhere there was a mix-up and it is believed that the bones in Seville are those of his son, Diego.

BELOW: the tomb of Columbus in Seville's cathedral.

A doorway at the northeastern corner of the cathedral, between the Puerta del Lagarto and the Capilla Real, leads to the base of Seville's trademark **Giralda**, a 93-metre (305-ft) rectangular tower, erected between 1184 and 1196. It is the remaining minaret of the mosque, which was destroyed a century later. Climb to the top by a series of ramps for splendid views of the city.

Across the **Plaza del Triunfo** from the cathedral stands a Moorish fantasy in filigree: the **Alcázar** (open Apr–Sep Tues–Sat 9.30am–7pm, Sun 9.30am–5pm, Oct–Mar Tues–Sun 9.30am–5pm; entrance fee). Built between 1350 and 1369, it is a *Mudéjar* elaboration of an original Islamic citadel and palace. For nearly seven centuries, it was the palace of Spanish kings. Most notorious among them was Pedro the Cruel, who had his half-brother Fadrique assassinated in 1358 and murdered his guest, Abu Said of Granada, for his jewels. The skulls painted over Pedro's bedroom door supposedly suggest the fate of five unjust judges who crossed him during his reign.

Though less grandiose than Granada's Alhambra, Seville's Alcázar has a special cosiness and charm derived from its sense of intimacy and its attention to polychrome detail. Its fanciful floors, ceilings and walls are intricate works of art, reaching heights of richness in Carlos I's room and the **Salón de Embajadores** (Ambassador's Room). The **Patio de las Doncellas** (Maiden's Patio) is noted for its friezes, *azulejos* (tiles) and stucco work. Well-manicured gardens and orange groves, contribute to the sense of a summer sanctuary.

The Jewish quarter

Stretching beyond the walls of the Alcázar is the **Barrio de Santa Cruz**, the former Jewish quarter turned fashionable neighbourhood. The walls are so white, the flowers so bright and the ironwork everywhere so exquisitely wrought that you quite expect a *señorita* in full flounce to come around the corner any minute, castanets clicking. The atmosphere is further enhanced by guitar-playing gypsies, who regularly flock to the local taverns; they often play until dawn for local aficionados at clubs, bars and private gatherings.

Map on page 192

TIP

If you're driving in Seville, be aware of the web of one-way streets. Also watch out for cars parked on the kerbs of already too-narrow streets.

BELOW: relaxing in the Barrio de Santa Cruz.

Amid the chic shops and rustic restaurants of this *barrio* (neighbourhood), you can see many traditional Andalusian homes. Wrought-iron gates mark the entrance porch and iron gratings the windows. An inner courtyard, cool and inviting with its abundant greenery, Moorish tiles and central fountain, is covered with an awning in the summer and used as the living-room.

Near the cathedral, the shelves of the **Archivo General de Indias**  (closed until late 2004; check with the tourist office for details) sag with the weight of history. Since 1785, it has been accumulating the heavy tomes that contain 36,000 files of documents chronicling the adventure of discovery, the trails of colonisation, colonial administration and minutiae of trade that recall a 16th-century Seville that was the headquarters for New World trade and, as a result, one of the richest cities in the Old World.

Park and plaza

The **Parque de María Luisa**  (open daily dawn–dusk) and the **Plaza de España** to the south of the centre have the feel of a bygone Seville. The Plaza de España is marked by a long semicircular series of arches bearing ceramic crests of all the provinces of Spain. Several ceramic-and-brick bridges span the small, concentric stream that flows through this expansive plaza. The park itself is dotted with buildings left over from the Spanish–American exhibition of 1929. One of these now houses the **Museo Arqueológico** (open Tues 2.30–8.30pm, Wed–Sat 9am–8.30pm, Sun 9am–2.30pm; entrance fee except for EU nationals). Artefacts from the Moorish palace at Medina Azahara *(see page 228)* are on display here. The museum also has a collection of mosaics and statuary from the well-preserved ruins of Itálica, 12 km (7 miles) north of Seville.

TIP

Save your feet by hiring one of the horse-drawn carriages outside the cathedral to tour the Parque de María Luisa.

BELOW: Plaza de España.

The river

Seville straddles the banks of the **Río Guadalquivir**. Known by the Romans as "Baetis" and the Muslims as the "Wadi el Kebir" ("great river"), frequent droughts render this river less than impressive, but to citizens of Seville it is every bit as revered as the Nile.

Once, in Seville you could be born on the "wrong side of the river". Over there, across the river from the cathedral, the bullring and the up-and-coming *barrio* of Santa Cruz was the nefarious **Triana** neighbourhood, haven of violence and vice. Long known as the gypsy quarter, with many flamenco movers and shakers originating from the area, today it is largely a residential suburb of a more diverse racial mix.

Back on the "right" side of the river, you'll see along the Paseo de Cristobal Colón the 13th-century, 12-sided, battlemented **Torre del Oro ❺**. In times of danger the tower held one end of a chain that stretched across the river to a companion tower, now vanished, on the other side. The tower now houses a small **Maritime Museum** (open Tues–Fri 10am–2pm, Sat & Sun 11am–2pm; entrance fee).

The ruined Roman amphitheatre at Itálica (open Tues–Sat 9am–5.30pm, Sun 10am–4pm; entrance fee), just off the N-630 north of Seville.

Pilate's house

The 16th-century **Casa de Pilatos ❻** (open daily 9am–7pm; entrance fee), just north of the Barrio de Santa Cruz, was named after the famous Biblical magistrate whose house in Jerusalem inspired some of its features. Also incorporated in this mansion of the first Marquess of Tarifa are *Mudéjar* and Renaissance elements rendered in remarkable *azulejos* and moulded stucco. Also in the Santa Cruz neighbourhood is the **Museo de Bellas Artes ❼** (open Tues 3–8pm,

BELOW: courtyard of the Casa de Pilatos.

Map on page 192

TIP

Seville is best avoided during July and August, when the heat becomes unbearable.

BELOW: parading at Seville's April Fair.

Wed–Sat 9am–8pm, Sun 9am–2pm), housed in a former convent that includes a baroque chapel with fabulous frescoed vaulting and dome, with works by greats such as Murillo, Zurbarán, Velázquez and El Greco.

It is only in the late morning that Seville begins to stir and gradually transmutes into a vibrant city. Along the **Calle Sierpes**, a stylish pedestrian thoroughfare winding from **La Campana** to the **Plaza de San Francisco**, friends meet to do business and pass the time. At No. 85 once stood a prison that quartered the not-yet-prominent Cervantes, author of *Don Quijote*. After dinner, which is usually served between 9pm and 11pm, the bars of both Santa Cruz and Triana across the river burst explosively into life.

Feria de Abril

Every April brings the Spring Fair, the *Feria*, Andalusia's biggest festival. Seville dresses to the nines and lets down her hair in a confluence of Andalusian stereotypes: wine, bulls, horses and flamenco. The day begins around noon with a parade of horses and riders: men in leather chaps with scarlet cummerbunds, short jackets, and broad-brimmed hats and women riding pillion wearing full-skirted flamenco dresses. Amid all the rejoicing, dancers perform the classic *sevillanas*, a light-hearted form of flamenco.

Temporary pavilions, arranged in rows and decorated with flowers, flags and paper lanterns, fill the fairground south of the **Los Remedios** district. Between them, the street is carpeted with layers of smooth, golden sand. In the late afternoon the bullfights begin, amid an atmosphere of tremendous excitement. Beneath the floodlights and fireworks of night, the flirtatious merriment continues until dawn. ❑

Holy Week

The week preceding Easter is Semana Santa, a time of national ritual in Spain. In every corner of the country processions snake their way, day and night, from the local parishes to the main cathedrals and back again. In the larger cities there may be more than 30 different processions in any 24-hour period. Depending on the size of the municipality and its economic means, each day is marked by regalia of varying colour, elaborate floats showing scenes from the Passion and centuries-old music. Since the 16th century, this has been the Spanish way of commemorating Holy Week.

These celebrations attain a feverish pitch of pageantry and colour in the south. From Palm Sunday to Easter Sunday the communities focus on the trials of Christ and the tears of the Virgin. It has often been alleged that the Andaluces are more demonstrative in their faith because of a need to live down the Islamic (specifically Moorish) legacy.

In Seville, a fervent "thunder" fills the cathedral on Wednesday with the rending of the veil of the temple and resounds again on Saturday just before all join in singing "Gloria in Excelsis" and ringing every bell. In Córdoba, on the afternoon of Good Friday, Mass is celebrated in the church within the mosque with a full symphony orchestra and a massive chorus. In Granada, mantilla'd ladies all in black dripping with jewellery and rosaries walk through the city among the floats.

For everywhere *pasos*, or floats, are a fixed feature of Semana Santa. They bear life-size and extremely lifelike polychrome and gilded figures depicting every Passion scene from the Last Supper and the Garden of Olives to the Descent from the Cross. The figures wear wigs and real costumes that can cost thousands of euros.

As the proud parishioners watch their particular Virgin pass by they may weep, applaud, sing, or even throw her some saucy compliments. Some admirers are so moved by a particular *paso* that they spontaneously sing the traditional, melancholy *saeta*.

RIGHT: polychrome figure of Christ on the cross made for Seville's Holy Week.

The trappings of the processions are solemn. Penitents wear robes gathered with belts of esparto grass and tall, pointed hoods covering their faces except for two slits for the eyes. Called *capuchones*, these are the hoods of the Spanish Inquisition and the equally insidious Ku Klux Klan.

But the strong Andalusian sense of fun cannot be long suppressed. The processional ranks are constantly broken as people cross through the parade to greet friends and share a beer or a *boccadillo* (sandwich).

In the side streets off the parade route tables and chairs are set up to provide rest and sustenance. *Torrijas*, a fried, milk-soaked confection, and *flamenquines*, deep-fried slices of veal wrapped around snow-cured ham and cheese, are traditional snacks.

Almost everywhere in Spain, the end of Semana Santa signals the beginning of the bullfighting season. In Arcos de la Frontera a local version of the "running of the bulls" takes place on Easter Sunday, and in Málaga you can go straight from the last Easter Mass to the season's first *corrida*. ❑

Map
on page
202

CÓRDOBA

*The walls of the Mezquita dominate the town, while
the alleyways of Córdoba's old Jewish and Muslim quarters, with
their overflowing pots of geraniums, are a delight to explore*

Handsome, honourable and forthright, Córdoba is harsher than Seville and without the benefit of a marked gypsy grace note to soften its keen masculine edge. In its no-nonsense streets there is an absence of the benign chaos that chokes rush-hour Seville, nor is there in the town centre a subtle layering of eras as in Granada.

There are just the old and the new, clearly demarcated by an intermittent, well-tended Moorish wall. To one side are the twisted ancient alleys, to the other wide, straight streets with a contemporary purpose. Just look at a map of Córdoba and you'll see the old quarter meandering down to the banks of the wide, shallow Guadalquivir in a maze of tiny alleyways doubling back on themselves or sometimes leading nowhere. These will test the mettle of even the most seasoned navigator.

Visitors are advised to leave their cars outside the old quarter and go on foot with good reason. Most of the roads are barely wide enough to accommodate even the smallest of vehicles, and you might well find yourself suddenly backing a hasty retreat down a one-way street under the reproachful gaze of an impatient horse, tourists in tow, eager to return its carriage to the shaded queue outside the Roman walls.

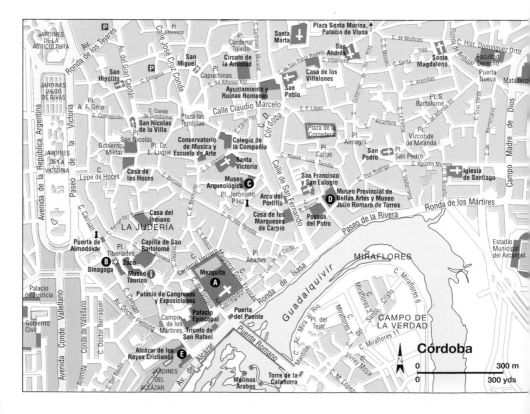

Patrician colony

Looking at Córdoba today, it is hard to imagine the truly heady heights this city achieved in earlier epochs. The history of Córdoba, like that of Granada and Seville, is a dizzying account of soaring success and dismal failure.

Like Seville, Córdoba was an important Iberian town. In 152 BC its fate passed to Roman hands when the consul Marcus Marcellus made it a colony favoured with the title *Colonia Patricia.* As the Roman "Corduba", it became the capital of *Hispania Ulterior;* and under Augustus, it came into its own as the prosperous capital of Baetica Province and Spain's largest city at the time. At this stage in its life it sired Seneca the Elder (55 BC–AD 39) and his son, Lucius Seneca (4 BC–AD 65), noted philosopher and preceptor to Nero. His statue now stands by the **Puerta de Almodóvar**, the principal entrance to the old town.

After the fall of the Roman Empire Córdoba was ruled by the Visigoths until the conquest of Iberia by the Muslims at the beginning of the 8th century. With the help of the city's disaffected Jewish residents, harassed by the Visigoths, the invaders quickly established their supremacy and ultimately raised Córdoba to the pinnacle of prestige and prosperity.

The Caliphate

At the beginning of the 8th century, *emirs* from the Damascus Caliphate had already established themselves in the city; but with the arrival of Abd-al-Rahman I in 756, a discernible dynasty was founded capable of consolidating the power to rule over all of Muslim Spain, which the Moors called *al-Andalus.* Under Abd-al-Rahman III (912–61) and his successor Hakam II (961–76), the blessings of the Caliphate of Córdoba rained down on the city. Its overstuffed coffers, luxurious appointments and richly brocaded cultural achievements defied even the hyperbole that was second nature to the Muslims and is a lingering trait among their present-day Andalusian offspring.

Córdoba was then possibly Europe's most civilised city. In the 10th century it founded a university of great renown. Literature and science were encouraged, schools of philosophy and medicine were strongly promoted and libraries were established. The city's inhabitants, numbering around half a million, were served by 3,000 mosques, 300 public baths and 28 suburbs. At its supreme moment of glory Córdoba was surpassed only by the city of Baghdad.

Disintegration and decline

But bad news was just around the corner. At the beginning of the 11th century internal dissent and revolt laid a foundation for its downfall. In 1031, the powerful Caliphate split up into petty kingdoms called *taifas* (principalities), and some 40 years later Córdoba itself was subsumed by the kingdom of Seville until its recapture by Fernando III in 1236. Many inhabitants fled and the Christians were indifferent to the industry, trade and agriculture that fed the city's affluence. For centuries Córdoba wallowed in the doldrums, but over the past 50 years its spirit has been steadily reviving. Since 1950 its population has grown by over 50 percent to more than 250,000.

TIP

To see Córdoba at its liveliest, visit during the Patio Fiesta, held in the second week of May, or the *Feria*, in the last week of May.

BELOW: view from the Mezquita.

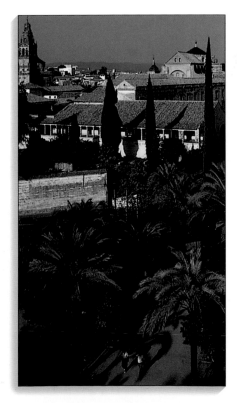

The intricately decorated dome of the Mezquita's mihrab.

Córdoba's mosque

Whether seen as a travesty or a triumph, the **Mezquita** (mosque; open Mon–Sat 10am–6.30pm, Sun 1.30–6.30pm; entrance fee) is a product and a symbol of the grafting of Christianity on to Muslim Spain. As the great mosque of the Umayyad caliphs, it enjoyed such profound artistic and religious stature that it saved the city's inhabitants the arduous pilgrimage to Mecca, whose mosque was the only one of greater size and importance. Begun in 785, the mosque took two centuries to complete, expanding with the city's population before reaching its full size.

Inside, a forest of about 850 columns produces a repetitive motif of criss-crossing alleys not unlike the effect of a hall of mirrors. Uneven in height and varying in material and style, these pillars support an architectural innovation of the time: two tiers of candy-striped arches that lend added height and spaciousness. Most notable and memorable among the Islamic flourishes is the mihrab, or prayer recess, along the wall facing Mecca. The workmanship is a masterpiece of Moorish mosaic art. Interlaced arches sprout from the marble columns surrounding the vestibule; and, more exquisitely decorated still, is the octagonal mihrab itself topped by a shell-shaped dome.

Newly Christian Córdoba soon claimed the mosque as its own church of the Virgin of the Assumption, building chapels against the interior walls and closing up the open northern facade to allow access only through the **Puerta de las Palmas** (Gate of the Palms). Construction of the cruciform church in the centre of the mosque began in 1523, and massive as the church is, you are not immediately aware of its looming presence upon entering the mosque. Only after considerable slaloming beneath the arches do you suddenly stumble

BELOW: columns and arches inside the Mezquita.

upon a 55-metre (180-ft) long Renaissance structure with a choir, a **Capilla Mayor**, a 15-metre (50-ft) wide transept and a lavishly adorned ceiling. Its mixture of styles (Gothic, Renaissance, Italian and baroque) required nearly a century of construction; and when Carlos I, who had given his unthinking permission for the building, first saw the architectural and artistic disfigurement it caused, he reproached those responsible for the transformation. "You have built here what you or anyone might have built anywhere else", he said, "but you have destroyed what was unique in the world."

Outside the mosque but within its surrounding battlemented walls is the **Patio de los Naranjos** entered through the **Puerta del Perdón** (Gate of Forgiveness) at the base of the Christian belfry that replaced the Islamic minaret. From nearby **Calleja de la Flores** (Alley of the Flowers), you can see the belfry framed in postcard splendour between the flower-studded walls of this narrow street.

Map on page 202

Religious persecution

The site and size of Córdoba's **Judería** (Jewish Quarter) indicates that here, as elsewhere, the Jews were long considered a race apart. And like elsewhere, they were a learned, accomplished and wealthy breed that seemed never to be allowed to prosper between periods of persecution. Disgruntled with their lot under the Visigoths, the Jews of Córdoba aided and abetted the Muslim victory; they subsequently enjoyed a welcome period of peace and prosperity under the tolerant Caliphate.

Córdoba was at one time home to the distinguished Muslim physicist, astrologer, mathematician, doctor and philosopher Averroës (who lived here from 1126 to 1198) and to Moses Maimonides (1135–1204), noted Jewish physician and philosopher. In Calle Maimonides today stands his monument, along with the remains of a 14th-century **Sinagoga** ❸ (open Tues–Sat 10am–2pm, 3.30–5.30pm; Sun 10am–1.30pm; entrance fee).

In the plaza named after Maimonides, opening off a beautiful patio is the municipal **Museo Taurino** (Bullfighting Museum; open Tues–Sat 9.30am–1.30pm, 4–7pm; Sun 9.30am–1.30pm; entrance fee except Tues) displaying posters, swords, capes and *trajes de luz*, the "suits of lights" worn by matadors. Córdoba is a famous town for bullfighters and home of two all-time greats, Lagartijo and Manolete.

Córdoba's museums

Heirlooms deposited in the environs of Córdoba by the various tiers of its history are beautifully displayed in the **Museo Arqueológico** ❻ (open Tues–Sat 10am–2pm, 5–7pm; Sun 10am–1.30pm; entrance fee) in the Plaza de Jerónimo Páez. Housed in a Renaissance palace of the same name, the extensive collection contains prehistoric, Roman, Visigothic, Islamic and Gothic remains. Particularly striking among them are a bronze stag from nearby Medina Azahara *(see page 228)*, Iberian sculptures reminiscent of Chinese temple dogs and an original Roman foundation upon which the building rests. The museum also contains the world's largest collections of lead sarcophagi and Arabic capitals.

BELOW: shopping in the Jewish Quarter.

Looking up at the crucifix of El Cristo de los Faroles, north of the town centre.

The 17th-century **Plaza de la Corredera** a little to the north is so named because of its earlier use for bullfights. The four-square, three-tiered structures marking its perimeter have a sagging, B-Western-movie quality, though there is a lively morning food market, as well as a flea market held on most days. In contrast, the **Plaza del Potro** has remained vigorous since the days when Cervantes allegedly stayed at the *posada* in this square and wrote part of *Don Quijote*. The square's fountain-statue of a colt *(potro)* is mentioned in the book.

The **Museo Provincial de Bellas Artes** ⓓ (open Tues–Sun 10am–2pm, 5–7pm; entrance fee), in an old hospital on the plaza, has a large collection of paintings, including several by Murillo, Zurbarán and Goya. Just across the courtyard is the **Museo Julio Romero de Torres** (open Tues pm–Sun am; entrance fee), which is devoted to the Córdoban-born artist (1874–1930). The large collection here includes many sensual studies of Córdoban women.

Everywhere in the town you'll notice shops offering Córdoba's prime crafts in trade: silver filigree and stamped leather. Since the time of the Muslims these crafts have flourished here, but in the 16th and 17th centuries the latter in particular flourished through a prevailing fashion dictating that all walls and seats should be covered with leather, properly embossed, tooled, tinted and gilded.

The Alcázar

Just west of the Mezquita, near the much-restored **Puente Romano** (Roman bridge) spanning the Río Guadalquivir, is the old **Alcázar de los Reyes Cristianos** ⓔ (Tues–Sat 9.30am–1.30pm, 4–7pm; Sun 9.30am–1.30pm; entrance fee except Fri). Built under Alfonso XI in 1328, it was the residence of Fernando and Isabel during their campaign against the Muslims in Andalusia.

BELOW: outlook across the rooftops of Córdoba.

Islamic patios and extensive Arabic gardens, with pools shaded by cypresses, offer a respite from the summer heat. Inside is a museum housing impressive Roman mosaics.

The original Roman bridge has in fact been rebuilt many times but retains its Roman foundations. At its southern end is the 14th-century **Torre de la Calahorra**. Inside the tower is a **museum** (open daily 10am–6pm; entrance fee) with interesting sound and light displays that explain how Christians, Jews and Muslims co-existed in 10th-century Córdoba. Also on display are impressive models of the Alhambra in Granada *(see pages 211–214)* as well as Córdoba's Mezquita.

To the northeast of the city centre, on Plaza de Don Gome, is the **Palacio de Viana** (open Mon–Tues, Thur–Sat 10am–1pm, 4–6pm; Wed, Sun 10am–1pm; entrance fee), an elegant 17th-century aristocratic home that is now a museum. It is packed with artworks and antiques, porcelain and tapestries, but perhaps the most pleasing aspects are the 12 interior courtyards and the delightful garden stocked with a variety of plants, including citrus and roses.

Nearby is the **Plaza Santa Marina** and its monument to Manolete. Born Manuel Rodríguez in 1917, Manolete was a local boy who found fame and fortune in the bullrings. Unfortunately, he encountered an untimely death in 1947, by goring. The equally famous *torero* El Cordobés was actually born Manuel Benítez in 1936 in the town of Palma del Río 58 km (36 miles) west of Córdoba.

If you walk a little further west from Plaza Santa Marina, crossing Calle Alfaros, you will see the well-known crucifix **El Cristo de los Faroles**. It stands starkly in a hidden plaza surrounded by wrought-iron lanterns. A return visit at night is highly recommended, when the lanterns are alight and the crucifix can be seen in all its glory. ❑

The defensive Torre de la Calahorra on the Puente Romano.

BELOW: the Puente Romano at sunset.

GRANADA

*"There is no pain in life so cruel as to be blind in Granada" is
inscribed on the ramparts of the Alhambra. These words
address the unique beauty of Granada*

Nature was generous in Granada, endowing the city with much greenery and placing it at the foot of three mountain spurs, from which it gracefully stretches up towards luminous blue skies against the blue-green backdrop of the Sierra Nevada to the southeast. To the west of the city is a broad, fertile *vega* (plain). To the north, the dainty Darro, a mountain stream, flows through the city between two of its three picturesque hills, those of the **Alhambra** and the **Albaicín**. The third hill, **Sacromonte**, is due north of the Alhambra. After the relative flatness of Seville and Córdoba, Granada's hills are a welcome change of scenic pace. For much of the year you can see snow on the Sierra Nevada, a popular winter retreat for skiers.

While Seville sprawls open-ended under the abundant Andalusian sunshine and Córdoba goes about its business with a minimum of fuss, Granada savours in its municipal valleys the romantic promise of the three hills that are the pillars of its tourism trade and the core of its own unique character.

Early history

Granada, the last stronghold and longest-running kingdom of the Muslims in Spain, began life as the obscure Iberian settlement of Elibyrge in the 50th century BC. From there it went on to become the equally obscure Illiberis of the Romans and Visigoths.

It is to the Muslims, then, that it owes a debt of gratitude for its current national and international stature. Its name derives from the Islamic "Karnattah" and not from the Spanish word for pomegranate (*granada*), which it has nevertheless adopted as the city arms. While Seville and Córdoba both tasted wealth and glory under the Romans, Granada first knew grandeur as a provincial capital during the time of the caliphs of Córdoba. As Córdoba's prominence waned with the fall there of the Umayyads in 1031, Granada's political stock began to rise. For some 60 years the city was the capital of an independent kingdom, but inroads by the Almoravids eventually resulted in its integration into the kingdom of Seville.

When Jaén fell to the Christians in 1246 under the relentless assaults of Ferdinand III, Ibn al-Ahmar moved his capital to Granada and, as Mohammed I, founded the Nasrid Dynasty that ruled for 250 years.

A golden age of prosperity

During this "golden age" under the Muslims, the Jewish presence in Granada was important and strong. In fact, for a time Granada was known as the "City of the Jews". Here, as elsewhere in Muslim Spain, the Jews were doctors and philosophers and even diplomats and generals. Politically, however, Mohammed I

LEFT: the exquisitely decorated Alhambra.
BELOW: the Patio de los Leones (Patio of the Lions), part of the royal living quarters.

TIP

Tickets to the
Alhambra can sell out
quickly, so purchase in
advance: tel: 902 224
460 (from Spain) or 34
913 745 454 (from
abroad). Tickets have
three parts: the Alcaz-
aba, the Generalife and
the Nasrid Palaces; the
latter can only be vis-
ited during the half-
hour slot shown on the
ticket: structure the
rest of your visit
accordingly, saving the
Nasrid Palaces for last,
if possible.

found it expedient to remain on friendly terms with Christian Castile, and even
went so far as to help Fernando III capture Seville, which little helped the
granadinos ingratiate themselves hereinafter with the *sevillanos*.

For the first time in its life, Granada was indisputably on top. In the wake of
successive Christian victories in Córdoba, Seville and elsewhere throughout
al-Andalus, Muslim refugees flocked to Granada, contributing to the trade and
commerce of this up-and-coming kingdom. As surrounding Muslim kingdoms
failed, Granada reaped an unprecedented prosperity. The fertile *vega* to the west
enjoyed elaborate irrigation. Science, arts and the humanities flourished. Out of
this impressive synergy of material, intellectual and spiritual well-being was
born the greatest triumph of Moorish art, the Alhambra. During this period
Granada's population swelled to 200,000, over four times that of the London of
its day and just shy of its current headcount.

A fateful love affair

Then under Muley Hassan (1462–85) it all started to unravel over a family
affair. Hassan fell in love with a Christian and entertained thoughts of repudi-
ating his queen Ayesha, mother of his son Boabdil, for the beautiful Zoraya.
Conjugal jealousy and concern for the regal inheritance of her son caused
Ayesha to flee the city, which was already torn by feuds between the Abencer-
rajes, in support of her, and the Zegris, in support of Zoraya.

Mother and son soon returned, however, to dethrone Hassan and his brother,
weakening the kingdom. Preying upon this weakness, Fernando V of Aragón
captured Boabdil, the Boy King *(El Rey Chico)*, offering him liberty at the price
of remaining passive while the Catholic Monarchs gobbled up more and more

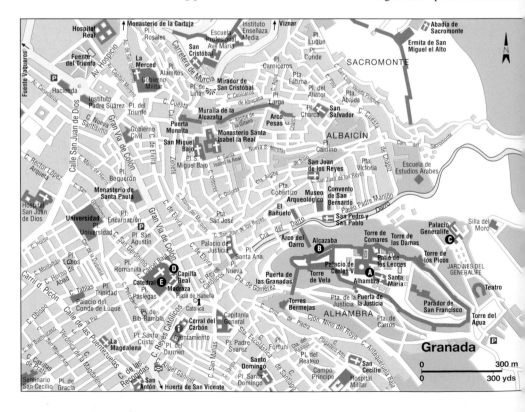

of the Muslim territory. When in late 1491 Fernando and Isabel beat down the door of Granada, the city's spirit had already been broken and Boabdil put up but a token resistance. By 2 January 1492, the capture of the sole remaining stronghold of Muslim Spain was complete.

As the cross and banner of Castile cast their first Christian shadows across the 9th-century Alcazaba, Boabdil and his followers retired to the Alpujarras mountains. As Boabdil turned for a final look at the flickering glory of Granada, his mother allegedly reproved him, saying: "You weep like a woman for what you could not hold as a man." To this day that very spot is known as the *Suspiro del Moro*, the Moor's Sigh.

The resounding God-speed that reverberated throughout Christendom with the fall of Granada never came to fruition. Religious intolerance culminating with the expulsion of the *moriscos* in 1609 drained the city of its most enterprising citizens and the glory they had wrought. By 1800, its population had dropped to just 40,000.

But like the rest of Andalusia, Granada is again enjoying a new prosperity resulting from improved irrigation and intense agricultural activity. Also important are the visitors who enthuse over the artistic legacy that, after almost eight centuries of rule, was the swan-song of the Muslims.

Moorish motifs decorate the pillars

The Alhambra

The **Alhambra** (open daily; combined entrance fee for the Nasrid Palaces, Alcazaba and Palacio Generalife; ticket reservations tel: 902-224 460), the only surviving monument of Islamic Granada's great artistic outpouring, sits on a scarped ridge crowning a wooded hill. No amount of description can prepare

BELOW: the majestic beauty of the Alhambra.

Stunning symmetry of the Patio de los Arrayánes (Patio of the Myrtles).

you for its great playfulness or do justice to its exquisite delicacy and proportions. Proclaimed one of the unofficial wonders of the world, it is the epitome of Islamic imagination and artistry, the consummate expression of a sophisticated culture. For many, it serves as a kind of bridge between Oriental and Western minds, a personal point of contact with the magical world found in the tales of the *Arabian Nights*.

Its pleasing splendour resides not in the architectural structures themselves, but in the masterful ornamentation that makes them seem almost an apparition, in the intricate delicacy of its carved wooden ceilings, the lace-like reliefs of its plaster walls, the repeated motifs of interlaced arabesques and the finely perforated tracery of the arched arcades on slender columns of white marble.

The Nasrid Palaces

Knowing a good thing when they saw it, the Catholic Monarchs had the Alhambra repaired and strengthened after their 1492 conquest and used it whenever they were in town. Subsequently, Carlos I (known as Charles V outside Spain), who had given the uninformed nod to the construction of the church inside Córdoba's mosque, deemed it insufficiently magnificent for him and had a section demolished to make way for his own palace in the 16th century. Beautiful in its own right as an example of the Italian Renaissance style, the **Palacio de Carlos** is nevertheless incongruous in its Aladdin's lamp setting.

BELOW: a tranquil scene in the Alhambra gardens.

The **Nasrid Palaces**, royal residence of the Muslims, lie at the heart of the Alhambra and are highlighted by the **Patio de los Arráyanes** (Patio of the Myrtles), and the **Patio de los Leones** (Patio of the Lions). The former is an open court measuring 37 metres by 23 metres (121 ft by 75 ft) bisected by a narrow

fishpond tucked between hedges of myrtle. At either end, within the arcaded alcoves, you can see fine stalactite vaulting. Off the northern end of this court is the lofty **Salón de los Embajadores**, the audience chamber of the Muslim kings. A dado of *azulejos* underscores the intertwining polychrome patterns and inscriptions stamped upon the stucco. Pairs of horseshoe windows admit enchanting views of Granada. And topping it all off is a domed ceiling of cedarwood.

Leading off the southern end is the Patio of the Lions (measuring 28 metres x 15 metres/90 ft x 50 ft), built around a massive antique fountain resting on the backs of 12 diminutive grey marble lions. Off its northern end is the **Sala de las Dos Hermanas** (Hall of the Two Sisters), containing the most elaborate of the Alhambra's honeycomb cupolas, said to comprise over 5,000 cells.

East of the Nasrid Palaces are the terraced **Partal Gardens** and charming **Torre de las Damas**.

Washington Irving

Some 19th-century writers were fortunate enough to spend some time in the Alhambra. During his three-month stay in 1829, Washington Irving began his *Tales of the Alhambra,* a collection of romantic sketches of the Muslims and Spaniards that continues to sell well in Granada's souvenir shops. Richard Ford, author of the *Hand-Book for Travellers in Spain,* paid the palace a visit in the summers of 1831 and 1833; and George Borrow, author of *The Bible in Spain,* visited in 1836.

The **Alcazaba** ❸ at the western extremity of Alhambra Hill was a 9th-century Islamic citadel. Today, its vista takes in the palace, the Generalife, the Albaicín and Sacromonte sections of Granada, and the Sierra Nevada.

Map on page 210

BELOW: geranium-decked balconies in the Albaicín.

Tombs of the Catholic Monarchs in the Capilla Real.

Gardens of seduction

Adjoining the Alhambra and overlooking both it and the city are the grounds of the former summer palace of the sultans, the **Palacio Generalife** ⓒ (entrance included in Alhambra ticket), dating from 1250. Blessed with gardens that far outclass the sparse beauty of its restored buildings, this palace is cool and green and full of restful pools and murmuring fountains. Known in Arabic as *Jennat al-Arif*, meaning "garden of the architect" (who remains unknown), it is filled with statuesque cypresses, diminutive shrubs, orange trees, hedges and flowers. Rumour has it that Boabdil's sultana kept trysts with her lover Hamet in the enclosed **Patio de los Cipreses**. Who can blame them? This garden is a veritable invitation to indiscretion.

The **Patio de la Acequia** (Court of the Long Pond), within the gardens, has pretty pavilions at either end linked on one side by a gallery and on the other by the palace apartments. At some point be sure to pass along the **Camino de las Cascadas**, where runnels of water cascade down a series of conduits. Every summer from mid-June to the first week in July, the International Music and Dance Festival is staged in the grounds of the Generalife.

City sights

BELOW:
performance at one of the popular flamenco *tablaos* in Granada.

Away from the Alhambra, Granada has plenty more to offer. A decorative royal mausoleum, the **Capilla Real** ⓓ (open daily 10.30am–1pm and 4–7pm; entrance fee) was built when the Catholic Monarchs, proud of their conclusive victory over the Muslims, wished to be buried in the city where Muslim Spain met its final demise. Construction was commissioned by Fernando and Isabel, and took place between 1506 and 1521. Many royal accessories, such as Isabel's crown and Fernando's sword, are on display, and hanging in the sacristy are many works from Queen Isabel's personal art collection, containing Flemish, Spanish and Italian paintings of the 15th century.

The **Catedral** ⓔ (open Mon–Sat 10.30am–1pm and 4–7pm, Sun pm only; entrance fee) adjoins the Royal Chapel. Begun in 1523 in the Gothic style and continued in 1528 in the early-Renaissance style, it has been described as "one of the world's architectural tragedies, one of the saddest of wasted opportunities". Not finished until 1714, it is a rather awkward structure.

Taking a break

Sightseeing in Granada always seems to be more intense, more all-consuming than the other grand cities of the south. Perhaps it's the desire to drink in every last detail of the Alhambra, or to spend an afternoon just smelling the flowers of the Generalife. Whatever it is, there just doesn't seem to be enough time left to give the cafés and bars of Granada their proper due.

In the heart of the city are any number of cafés outfitted with marble columns and counters that evoke images of handlebar moustaches and pomaded hair, but in reality they are frequented by little old ladies in floral-print dresses aggressively fanning themselves in summer alongside leather-clad youths sipping their *café con leche*. In the evening, crowds congregate at the **Plaza Bibrambla**, which was once the site of medieval jousts and bullfights. Just off the square is the maze-like **Alcaicería**, a colourful reproduction of the old Islamic souk that once stood on the same spot (it was destroyed by fire), and is now crammed with souvenir shops.

Map on page 210

Albaicín and Sacromonte

The Albaicín quarter, the oldest part of Granada, covers a slope facing the Alhambra on the north side of the Río Darro. It was home to the first fortress of the Muslims and the haven to which they fled when the Christians reconquered the city. Today it offers the typical tangle of Andalusian alleys and simple whitewashed houses. It is home to popular *tapas* bars and Moroccan-style tea shops. Often the area's long walls signal luxuriant gardens discreetly enclosed. If you climb up the hill, the **Mirador de San Nicolás** offers a postcard view of the Alhambra. Further up, beyond the ruins of the Muslim walls, is the **Mirador de San Cristóbal**.

The Sacromonte hill, packed with picturesque cave dwellings, was at one time a gypsy enclave. Most of the gypsy families moved out decades ago, but the spirit survives in a handful of cave *zambras*, where flamenco shows are staged. It is strictly tourist fare, but among the performers there could be one destined for international fame as more than one flamenco great has started their career here.

Fuente Vaqueros, 16 km (10 miles) west of the city, was the birthplace of Federico García Lorca, one of the 20th century's greatest Spanish poets and dramatists. The house where he lived is now the **Museo Casa Natal** (open Tues–Sun 10am–1pm and 4–6pm; entrance fee). The Huerta de San Vincente, an old farmhouse on Granada's southern outskirts where he wrote several famous works, is also open to the public (Tues–Sun; entrance fee). It contains interesting memorabilia, including Lorca's desk, and is surrounded by a peaceful park. ❏

BELOW: poet and dramatist Federico García Lorca.

FEDERICO GARCÍA LORCA

Born in 1898 in a village not far from Granada and raised in the city, poet and dramatist García Lorca portrayed the gypsy as exemplifying the most profound elements in the Andalusian psyche. *Gypsy Ballads*, published in 1928, brought him national fame. His plays, such as *Blood Wedding* and *Yerma*, were often based on folk themes and tended towards surrealism. But his political views – and his homosexuality – made him many enemies in his home town.

Fatefully, he was in Granada in 1936 at the start of the Spanish Civil War and was arrested with hundreds of others and summarily executed by the Nationalists. A granite block in a memorial park near Víznar, 8 km (5 miles) northeast of the city, marks the spot where he is believed to have been killed. His body was never found, and it was only after the return to democracy that it became possible to speak freely of Lorca's murder and for his work to receive the attention it deserved. His plays are now widely produced and some have been filmed.

Lorca often left Granada, but always yearned to return. He said of these leave-takings: "It will always be like this. Before and now. We must leave, but Granada remains. eternal in time, but fleeting in these poor hands ...".

THEY CAME, THEY SAW, THEY PLANTED

From the intimacy of the patios to the spectacular gardens of the Generalife in Granada, Andalusia is a magnet for gardeners from all over the world

Fertile soil and abundant sunshine make Andalusia a gardener's paradise, and the region is home to some outstanding gardens including Seville's María Luisa Park and the gardens of the Generalife in Granada.

For the Muslims, gardens were intimate places that aimed to appeal to all the senses. Aromatic plants such as mint and basil were key elements, as was the soothing sound of running water. Islamic homes were arranged around interior courtyards that provided a scented refuge from the heat, of which the patios of Córdoba are a living example. After the Muslims departed, the reigning style was the Italian garden of the Renaissance, designed to impress with proportioned layout, manicured aspect, statues and fountains. The Generalife gardens we see now owe more to this style than to the Islamic.

COLOURFUL IMPORTS

Each subsequent lot of settlers brought with them their preferred plants. The Phoenicians, Greeks and Romans introduced olive trees, date palms and grape vines. The Muslims brought orange trees and a great many herbs and flowers native to Asia. Explorations of new continents added to this botanical wealth. Geraniums came from southern Africa, while mimosas are originally from Australia, wisteria from Asia and bougainvillea from South America.

◁ **MODEL LION**
A statue in the Jardín de los Leones (Lions' Garden) in Seville's María Luisa Park recalls the famous Patio of the Lions in the Alhambra, which served as the model.

△ **TILED FEATURES**
Pigeons congregate around a tiled fountain in the María Luisa Park's Plaza de América. This Seville park was donated to the city by Princess María Luisa de Orleans in 1893.

◁ ISLAMIC LEGACY

The gardens of El Partal in the Alhambra. Muslim gardens were designed to appeal to all the senses, and pools and channels of water were key ingredients.

▽ ITALIAN INFLUENCE

The Generalife in Granada is Spain's most famous garden. Originally an Islamic royal summer residence, its present layout owes more to Italian influences.

THE WONDER OF WATER

Thanks to their talent as engineers, the Romans tapped Andalusia's water resources, and their canals and aqueducts turned the region into the breadbasket of the empire. But it was the Muslims who, adapting and improving on the Roman irrigation system, regarded water as an aesthetic element as well. Fountains, pools and elaborate channels, such as the "water stairway" in the Generalife gardens, filled the air with soothing sound and helped keep summer temperatures down. Water had a symbolic significance for the Muslims. Gardens were divided into four sections separated by channels of water representing the four Rivers of Life.

Taking a leaf from the Muslims' gardening book, Christian landscapers capitalised on water's use for dramatic visual effect, especially with exquisite fountains, such as in the Patio de la Madama in the 17th-century Palacio de Viana in Córdoba (above).

▽ COOL OASIS

Potted flowers adorn a patio in Córdoba. These cool, intimate spaces are a legacy of Islamic times. The Muslims, coming as they did from the desert, were specially fond of gardens.

△ NATURALISATION

Geraniums are often considered the quintessential Andalusian flower. Yet, like so many of Andalusia's plants, it is an introduced variety; it was originally from South Africa.

△ EXOTICA

Cupola in La Concepción botanical gardens in Málaga. The garden has a unique collection of palm trees and other exotica.

THE ANDALUSIAN HEARTLAND

There is so much more to discover in the southernmost region of Spain than the Costa del Sol and the three main draws of Seville, Córdoba and Granada

Map on page 220

Madrid

Within the area defined by Seville, Córdoba, Granada and the Mediterranean Sea there lies much to be seen that is little known to the tourist population. This is Andalusia, where life means simplicity, peace and hospitality. Whether you spend your holiday vagabonding from village to village or simply make inland excursions from the coast, you will marvel at the spontaneous beauty and variety of Spain's landscape. Like set changes in the theatre, Andalusia's villages and vistas seem to spring suddenly out of thin, dry air. The only constant in this ever-shifting scene is the ubiquitous olive tree.

Dunes and wetland

The **Parque Nacional de Doñana ❶** (open daily; book guided tours in advance, tel: 959-430 432) is Spain's biggest national park, straddling more than 50,000 hectares (125,000 acres) of the Huelva and Seville provinces. Most of the park is a special reserve but organised tours in four-wheel drive vehicles, starting from the visitors' centre (open daily 8am–7pm) at **El Acebuche**, leave twice a day for a five-hour journey through the inner areas of the reserve. The route follows the beach, where oystercatchers, dunlins and sanderlings scurry among the broken waves, and sandwich terns and black-eyed gulls swoop low across the sand. Once at the Guadalquivir estuary, the convoy swings towards the centre of the park, through pine forest and Mediterranean brush.

LEFT: the Tajo bridge, Ronda.
BELOW: stork nesting in the Parque Nacional de Doñana.

As you travel, guides helpfully point out red stag deer, fallow deer and boars; and even the shy lynx may show itself occasionally. At the edge of the lakes and marshes you may see flocks of pink flamingos, greylags and spoonbills. The rare imperial eagle may also be spotted, surveying his empire from the topmost branches of a pine. The vehicles then turn back towards the ocean, through more pines to the dunes; these moving mountains of sand are slowly burying part of the pine wood.

The outskirts of the park may be explored on foot via a choice of self-guided paths. A pollution scare in spring 1998 threatened a large area of the park.

On the Columbus trail

The small town of **Huelva ❷** lies 80 km (48 miles) west of **Seville** *(see pages 191–201)* along the A-49. It has been somewhat spoilt by industrial development but nevertheless retains a refreshingly innocent small-town atmosphere, especially along its Gran Via. The **Museo Provincial** (Tues–Sat 9am–8pm, Sun 9am–3pm) has exhibits celebrating Columbus's voyage to the New World in 1492; he set sail from Palos de la Frontera, just across the Odiel estuary, on 3 August that year.

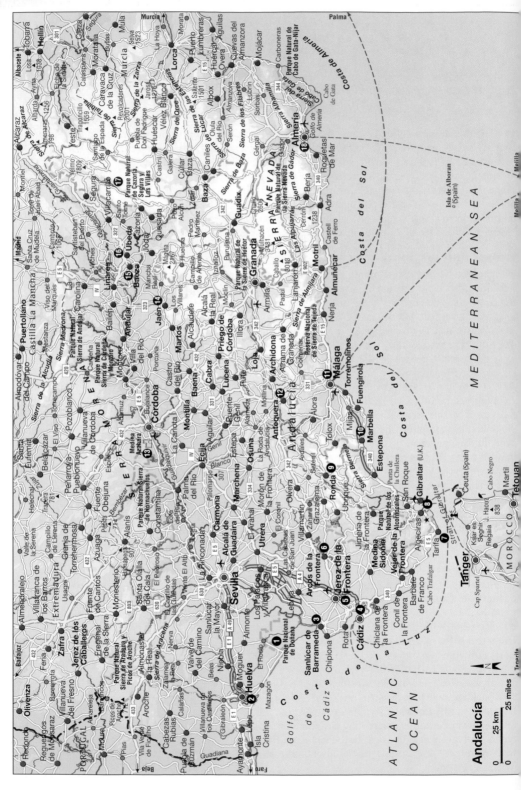

Andalucía

0   25 km
0   25 miles

The 13th-century **Monasterio de la Rábida** (Tues–Sun, closed 1–4 pm; donation encouraged), 4 km (2½ miles) north of Palos, is a complete contrast to the industry around it. This is where Columbus met the friars Antonio de Marchena and Juan Pérez, who took his case to Queen Isabela and persuaded her to back the venture. Inside are the Columbus murals painted by Vázquez Díaz in 1930.

The coast of light

Andalusia's breezy Atlantic coast, the **Costa de la Luz**, stretches south from Huelva all the way to Cádiz and Tarifa, its wide, sandy beaches deserted in comparison with those on the Mediterranean. **Sanlúcar de Barrameda ❸**, best known for its production of manzanilla, a light, dry sherry, is a flourishing resort and fishing port less than an hour's drive from Seville on the A-4 and C-441. The town looks across the mouth of the Guadalquivir to the Doñana Park's marshlands. Sanlúcar is one of the three towns that comprise the "sherry triangle" where the legendary aperitif wine is made. The others are Jerez (*see page 222*) and **Puerto de Santa María**, a crusty port on the Cádiz Bay. Aside from its sherry, Puerto is known for its shellfish, sold at numerous establishments along the seafront promenade, known as Ribera del Marisco ("shellfish row").

Cádiz ❹, whose safe inner harbour first attracted the Phoenicians in 1100 BC, is on the other side of the bay. The Carthaginians arrived in 501 BC, followed by the Romans under whom "Gades", as it was known, prospered. However, its importance declined under the succeeding Visigoths and Muslims. With the "discovery" of America, Cádiz rose again to become the wealthiest port in western Europe and, as a result, the target of attack for the Barbary corsairs and the envious English naval fleet. Sir Francis Drake burned ships at anchor here in 1587, delaying the sending of the Armada and boasting afterwards that he "had singed the King of Spain's beard". The long history of Cádiz can be traced at the **Museo Histórico Municipal** (Tues–Sun; closed 1–4pm and Sat–Sun pm) which contains a remarkable model of Cádiz as it was in 1777, and the **Museo de Cádiz** (Tues pm–Sun am) on Plaza Mina, with its two Phoenician sarcophagi.

The narrow streets of the old city are dotted with churches and monuments, the most notable being the **New Cathedral** (open mornings Tues–Sat; entrance fee), so called because it replaced the "old" cathedral next door, which is now called the church of Santa Cruz ,dating from the 13th century. It is a grandiose 18th-century structure capped by a Byzantine-style dome of golden tiles. In the crypt lies the tomb of composer Manuel de Falla, whose music is evocative of the magic of Andalusia. The **Oratorio de San Felipe Neri** (Mon–Sat 10am–1pm; entrance fee), on Calle Santa Inés, is where parliament gathered in 1812 to proclaim a liberal constitution.

Despite its vacillating fortunes and the somewhat ramshackle appearance of some quarters, the *gaditanos* love their town and have a reputation for being among the liveliest of Andalusians. Many leading flamenco artists hail from the Bay of Cádiz and the city runs wild every year during the crazy days of Carnival.

A little to the south of Huelva at Punta del Sebo is the Monumento a Colón. This 34-metre (112-ft) statue sculpted by Gertrude Vanderbilt Whitney was a gift from the US in honour of the "discoverers" of America.

BELOW: the richly decorated *Mudéjar* doorway of Nuestra Señora de la O, Sanlúcar de Barrameda.

The Tourist Office publishes a useful map of the white towns. If you need a room for the night, just enquire at the local bar.

BELOW: the late Don José Ignacio Domecq, who was popularly known as "the Nose".

Sherry country

The rolling landscape between **Jerez de la Frontera** and the Atlantic, known as The Sherry Triangle, is ideally suited to raising the grapes that the wineries of Jerez convert into extraordinary sherries and brandies. Tours and tastings are informative and readily intoxicating.

The city's annual *Feria del Caballo* (horse show) is held at the start of May. Proud of its pure-bred line of Carthusian horses, Jerez shows them off in racing, dressage and carriage competitions. All year round these handsome Arabian animals can also be seen at the **Real Escuela Andaluza del Arte Ecuestre** (shows Thurs noon; rehearsals other weekdays 11am and 1pm; entrance fee). Also in Jerez are the remains of an 11th-century **Alcazar**, or Moorish fortified palace (daily; entrance fee).

Arcos de la Frontera (pop. 25,000) sits on a sharp ridge above a loop of the Río Guadalete. Steep streets lead up to the panoramic Parador looking out across the mottled browns and greens of Andalusia's farmland and the blue of a large reservoir (Embalse de Arcos). This is considered the archetypal *pueblo blanco* (white village) – the term used to describe the innumerable small villages of the Andalusian hinterland whose sparkling whitewashed houses cap the mountaintops or tumble down their slopes. In common with Arcos, many of the white towns share the tag *de la frontera* ("of the border"), a reminder of their location on the contentious frontier between Christianity and Islam.

North of the Arcos to Grazalema road is **Prado del Rey** (the King's Field). Founded by King Carlos III in 1768 in an attempt to stimulate agricultural reform in Andalucía, this town is something of an early Spanish garden city with wide streets and leafy squares.

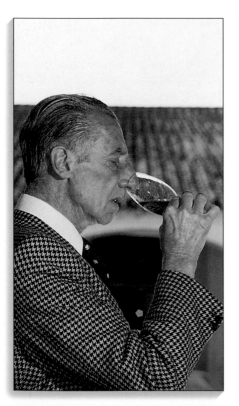

ANDALUSIA'S SHERRY DYNASTIES

About 250 years ago the Gordons, a Catholic family from Scotland, arrived in Cádiz and set themselves up in the wine trade. Not long afterwards, several Frenchmen established wine businesses in the area. Their names are still synonymous with sherry: Domecq, Pemartín, Lustau, Lacave and Delage. In 1765, Juan Vicente Vergara y Dickinson, the son of a Basque father and an English mother, arrived in Puerto de Santa María and entered the wine trade. His great-great-grandson, Javier Vergara, still markets sherry under the label of Juan Vicente Vergara.

Despite the foreign origins of a great many of the sherry families, they developed over the decades into a very Spanish aristocracy. Scions became scholars, priests, poets, painters, politicians, and even bullfighters.

Today's aristocrats are a more subdued breed than their predecessors. With big multinational companies controlling most of the *bodegas*, they have to be very businesslike – the polo grounds at the Chapín Club, where José Ignacio Domecq used to play in Jerez, have not seen a match in years. Nevertheless, when touring the wineries and their cool cellars containing row upon row of venerable oak casks, each holding 500 litres (132 gallons) of sherry or brandy, you'll have the feeling that the good old times are still alive.

Back on the coast road (N-340) south from Cádiz, past the white hilltop town of **Vejer de la Frontera** are the remains of the Roman city of **Baelo Claudia** (follow signs for Bolonia). Founded in 171 BC, today you can see remains of an amphitheatre, paved forum and streets. Visits are by guided tour (Tues–Sun; closed Sun pm and Mon; entrance fee). The road eventually arrives at **Tarifa ❼**. This Moorish-walled town is at the southernmost point of Europe, just 13 km (8 miles) and a 35-minute boat ride from Tangier across the Strait of Gibraltar. It is on the cusp of the Atlantic and Mediterranean and a mecca for windsurfing and kitesurfing. The surrounding unspoilt countryside and vast sandy beaches are becoming increasingly fashionable among those seeking a change from package holidays and rampant development. The ugly industrial chaos around **Algeciras** can be seen from the motorway on the main route to Gibraltar and the Costa del Sol. Algeciras is the main Spanish ferry port for the North African destinations of Ceuta and Tangier.

Map on page 220

The Rock

The unmistakeable profile of the limestone Rock of **Gibraltar ❽** stands at the very tip of the Iberian peninsula, across the bay from Algeciras. Peaking at 425 metres (1,396 ft), the territory measures less than 7 sq. km (3 sq. miles) yet it is home to over 30,000 people. To enter Gibraltar, you need to possess a valid passport or identity card. It is a good idea to leave your car behind in the Spanish border town of La Linea, and take a taxi or bus from the border into Gibraltar town, as the colony's maze of narrow streets is invariably congested, and most sights can be reached easily on foot, or by minibus or cable car.

Since 1704 Gibraltar, one of the ancient Pillars of Hercules, has been a bone of contention between Britain and Spain. But before that it had been passed back and forth between the Spaniards and the Muslims, who first took it in 711 under the Berber leadership of Tariq ibn Zeyad and gave it its name "Gebel Tarik", the mountain of Tariq. The Moorish castle, now in ruins, was his legacy. In 1462, the Spanish regained it one last time before the British seized it in 1704.

Wildlife

This seemingly barren rock enjoys some fame for its wildlife. The origin of its distinctive Barbary apes is not known, but they are not found on the Spanish mainland. Among the variety of birds that stop here on their annual migrations to Europe are honey buzzards, griffons, black storks and short-toed eagles.

A curious military feat are the **Upper Galleries** (daily; entrance fee) tunnelled into the rock at the time of the Great Siege by France and Spain between 1779 and 1783. By the end of this war the tunnel measured 113 metres (370 ft). Curious, too, is the evident cultural mixture on the Rock. Arab women in full-length dress and modified *chador* cross paths with British officers, Spanish-speaking merchants and dark-skinned descendants of the Muslims. Equally mixed are the linguistics. In a local bar the TV plays in Spanish, the radio in English and the bartender speaks with a hybrid accent.

BELOW: Gibraltar's Key Ceremony.

Legend has it that the British will remain in Gibraltar as long as the Barbary apes survive. When extinction threatened them in 1944, Churchill ordered reinforcements.

BELOW: the Plaza de Toros in Ronda, which opened in May 1784.

Bandido country

Heading inland from the coast on the C-369 towards Ronda, the countryside gradually grows wilder. In the 19th century, travelling here meant taking your life in your hands. The hills were full of highwaymen. During and after the Civil War, the more remote of these villages harboured Republican refugees.

To reach **Castellar** (bypassing the "new" Castellar, built in the 1960s), a road signposted "Castillo de Castellar" climbs a rocky hillside. The archetypal castle stands like a lone sentinel on top of a craggy outcrop, enclosing an entire village. The inconvenient location meant it was abandoned and crumbled for years, until new residents moved in. Some houses in the castle grounds were restored as self-catering holiday accomodation. The next castle, too, sits on its own hilltop, crumbling. At its feet, the town of **Jimena de la Frontera** spills like white paint down the hillside where mules graze below on the steep, grassy slopes. Between Jimena and Ronda, a distance of about 56 km (35 miles), stop somewhere by the roadside and indulge your senses. The scent of herbs perfumes a silence smooth as silk.

Whether you approach **Ronda** ❾ from the north or south, you are given no clues that you are about to enter a bustling town of 35,000 perched on a rocky bluff with sheer walls falling away a dramatic 180 metres (600 ft) on three sides. A deep ravine some 90 metres (300 ft) wide divides the old and new sections. Near the **Puente Nuevo** (New Bridge) that links the old and new towns a path leads down to a fine view of this bridge that spans the vertiginous gorge. It is beautifully unobtrusive in design, allowing the magnificent scenery to shine through. Begun in 1755, after a previous effort collapsed, it seems to have been first opened for transit in 1784; its architect José Martín de Aldehuela fell to his

Map on page 220

death inspecting the structure shortly before its completion. Once it was open, tightly corseted Ronda spilled out on to the tableland known as the Mercadillo, which until then had been used mainly for markets and fairs. Thanks to its auspicious position, Ronda was virtually impregnable, remaining the capital of an isolated Islamic kingdom until 1485.

The 18th-century **Plaza de Toros** (daily; entrance fee) is one of the oldest bull-rings in Spain and contains a museum displaying *traje de luces* (bullfighters' suits), documents, photos, posters and Goya prints pertaining to this uniquely Spanish art.

It was in Ronda that bullfighting on foot first began early in the 18th century when a noble and his horse were upended by a bull's charge. A bystander leapt into the ring and, using his hat as a lure, managed to draw the bull away from the hapless rider.

Cut-throat den

Throughout the **Serranía de Ronda**, the mountain range surrounding the city, are more storybook white towns. **Grazalema**, 32 km (20 miles) west of Ronda, boasts that it gets more rain than anywhere else in Spain. Long a haunt of smugglers and brigands, it was described by Ford as a "cut-throat den". These days it is more welcoming with several hotels, and is the gateway to the nature reserve bearing its name. Set up in 1984, the reserve extends from **El Bosque**, where there is a small information centre, to Benaoján in the east and Cortes de la Frontera to the south. Much of the Mediterranean forest of holm oak and Montpelier maple still survives, but some areas have been converted to open ranges or brush. Here mountain goats and a superb range of birds of prey can be seen, including buzzards, griffon vultures and Bonelli's booted and short-toed eagles.

The **Cueva de la Pileta** (guided tours daily 10am–1pm and 4–5pm daily; entrance fee), with some remarkable prehistoric animal paintings, is signposted from the MA-501 about 4 km (2½ miles) south of Benaoján. The paintings were discovered by a local farmer in 1905 while he was out looking for *guano* (bird droppings) to manure his fields. Perhaps the most impressive painting is one depicting a huge fish that seems to have swallowed a seal.

Not far away, through wild, pine-clad sierras, at the foot of a mountain, lies **Ubrique**, specially noted for its leatherwork. Most of these villages have spectacular settings, but that of **Zahara** ("de la Sierra" to distinguish it from Zahara de los Atunes on the Costa de la Luz) is truly breathtaking. A brilliant beacon of white, it stands on a steep crag northwest of Ronda. It offers another ancient castle and superb views. In contrast, much of the village of **Setenil** huddles in a chasm, its houses built right under menacing lips of rock.

Costa del Sol

Most of the Sunshine Coast is in Málaga province, running from east of Gibraltar to the province of Granada. Development has been heavy – often excessive – all along the coast. However, there are still some nooks and crannies where you can avoid the crowds, as in the western section between Gibraltar and San Pedro. **Estepona**, the most westerly of the Costa's swollen fishing villages and now a large town, has so far avoided too many high-rises and remains Spanish, with an old quarter of narrow streets and bars. From here on the pace quickens and the crowds thicken, with lush green golf courses interspersed with luxury villas.

BELOW: landscape around Puerto de la Paloma.

The area between the flashy marina Puerta Banus and **Marbella**  is known as the Golden Mile and is the playground of celebrities, sheikhs, millionaires, royalty and bullfighters. Expensive restaurants, a casino, signs in Arabic and a mosque testify to the presence of Middle East oil money. In the centre of Marbella, the old town remains picturesque, with the Plaza de los Naranjos as its showpiece. On a hot summer night this plaza becomes one vast open-air restaurant and it can delight even hardened Costa-watchers.

The coast goes down-market approaching **Fuengirola**. From there to Málaga tourist traffic is intense. High-rise hotels and apartment blocks crowd the water's edge, summer beaches are packed with bodies and discos and bars compete raucously, reaching a climax at **Torremolinos**, which was a poor fishing village until the early 1960s when it was "discovered"; it has become grotesquely overgrown, with hundreds of bars, lush vegetation and overhead walkways.

Just west of Málaga, at Cerro del Villar, archaeologists have unearthed the largest Phoenician settlement discovered so far on the Iberian peninsula and dating to at least the 8th century BC.

Donkey taxis

Up in the mountains, 8 km (5 miles) above Fuengirola, the white town of **Mijas**, once a quaint mountain village, now uses its donkeys for photo opportunities rather than for farming and seems to have more shops than residences. Despite this, there is fresher air up here and fine views down to the coast.

Málaga ⑪ (pop. 550,000) is the capital of the Costa del Sol. However, it is not a resort but a bustling port founded by the Phoenicians. Its citizens sided briefly with Carthage before becoming a Roman municipium (a town governed by its own laws). In 711 it fell to the Muslims within a year of their invasion of Spain and was the port of the Kingdom of Granada until 1487, when it was taken by the Christians after a four-month siege.

BELOW: regimented beach loungers stretch along the Golden Mile.

Málaga's historical ruins can be found mainly at the eastern end of the city. The 11th-century Islamic **Alcazaba** (Oct–Apr Tues–Fri 9.30am–1.30pm and 4–7pm, Sat 10am–1pm, Sun 10am–2pm; May–Sep Tues–Fri 9.30am–1pm and 5–8pm, Sat and Sun as before; entrance fee) is a maze of pretty gardens and courtyards. It is connected to the ruined 14th-century Islamic **Castillo de Gibralfaro** (open daily) by a formidable double-walled rampart, while a rocky path climbs beside it. A *mirador* gives a view over the harbour and down to Málaga's bullring.

The **Catedral** (Mon–Sat 10am–12.45pm, 4–5.30pm), designed by Pedro de Mena in the 16th century, is further west on Calle Molina Lario, towards the dry riverbed of the Río Guadalmedina. The Cathedral's east tower was never completed, giving it the nickname La Manquita – "the one-armed one". Between the Alcazaba and Cathedral, at Calle San Agustín 8, is the Palacio de Buenavista, housing the **Museo Picasso**, with a collection that spans Picasso's entire career; the majority of works were donated by his daughter-in-law Cristina (Tues, Thur and Sun 10am–8pm, Fri–Sat 10am–9pm; entrance fee). A short walk north from here is the **Casa Natal de Picasso** (Mon–Sat 10am–8pm; Sun am only) at Plaza de la Merced 15, where the artist spent his first years. The Picasso Foundation based here organises lectures on aspects of Picasso's work, and promotes contemporary art.

Map on page 220

By the train station in calle Alemania is the **Centro de Arte Contemporáneo de Málaga** (open summer Tues–Sun 10am–2pm, 5.30–9.30pm; free). Housed in the former wholesale market, CAC Málaga is a cultural initiative whose aim is to promote 20th- and 21st-century art. The project is an innovative one as it combines private management with the aims and ideals of public administration.

For a peaceful and thought-provoking haven from Málaga's careering traffic, visit the **English Cemetery**, which lies beyond the bullring, approached along avenues of orange trees. Founded in 1830, it was Spain's first Protestant cemetery and contains tiny shell-covered graves of a dozen children.

Dolmens and caves

About 50 km (32 miles) north of Málaga on the N-331, **Antequera** ⓬ is an attractive town with innumerable churches and convents. Seek out the Islamic **castillo**, near the 16th-century Iglesia de Santa María la Mayor, for a fine view. To the east, a curiously shaped rock, the Peña de los Enamorados, gets its name from a legend of two thwarted lovers who hurled themselves off the top. Antequera's most unusual attractions are three dolmens which were constructed with huge slabs of rock in around 2000 BC. The **Cuevas de Menga** and **Viera** (Mon–Sat 9am–2pm and 3–6pm, Sun 10am–2.30pm; free) are close together on the edge of town, while the **Cueva de Romeral** is down the road near a defunct sugar factory, where a guardian is on duty. Back on the coast, east of Málaga, **Nerja** is one of the larger resorts on this part of the coast and offers some vast caves nearby. On display inside are some of the Palaeolithic remains discovered on this site along with photos of the excavations. Also, over 500 cave paintings have been uncovered here, but will be accessible only to researchers until study of them has been completed.

Málaga's harbour seen from the Castillo de Gibralfaro.

BELOW: Islamic-influenced modern architecture of Torremolinos.

A 2-km (1¼-mile) path leads through the colourfully lit caverns. As yet, the full extent of this underground wonderland remains unknown. But what there is, is wonder enough. It is like an underground cathedral in an abstract Gaudí style with stalactite pipe organs and stalagmite spires. Every July these bizarre natural sculptures are the backdrop for a festival of music and ballet.

Medina Azahara

Eight km (5 miles) northwest of **Córdoba** *(see pages 202–7)* stand the emerging remains of **Medina Azahara** ⓭ (Tues–Sun; entrance fee), an extensive palace complex begun around 936 by Abd-al-Rahman III to satisfy the caprices of his favourite wife Zahara (meaning "flower").

The new city stretched up the Sierra de Córdoba, the foothills of the Sierra Morena, adapting itself gracefully to the three-level terraced terrain. The highest level contains the **Alcázar**; the middle, the gardens and orchards; and the lowest, the mosque and city proper. The account of its construction, as rendered by Arab historian El-Makkari, gives some impression of its scale. Ten thousand men, 2,600 mules and 400 camels worked for 25 years, he reports, to erect the palace, gardens, fish ponds, mosque, baths and schools. The royal entourage included some 12,000 men, 4,000 servants and 2,000 horses. There were hanging gardens, aviaries, zoos, streams, courts, gold fountains and a quicksilver pool. But the life of the city was as fleeting as its very being was fantastic. In 1010, just 74 years after its conception, the Berbers attacked and burned it.

Two historical towns lie between Córdoba and Seville. **Carmona**, on the main N-IV route, was an important Roman centre. Its well laid-out **Necrópolis Romana** (museum open Tues–Sun; entrance fee) on the western extremity of

BELOW: ruins of the once-glorious Moorish palace of Medina Azahara.

the town shows the walls of the crematorium still discoloured by the heat of the fire. **Ecija**, 56 km (34 miles) east, is built in a valley bowl and consequently has no summer breeze to relieve the heat. The town is littered with (crumbling) baroque church towers, the most notable being that of the **Iglesia de Santa María** (open daily). The covered market is colourful, and Calle Caballeros (north of the main square) has several rambling and ornate merchants' houses, including the **Palacio de Peñaflor** (courtyard open daily), with a very unusual curved balcony.

Map on page 220

Olive trees dominate the landscape in Jaén province.

Jaén province

A massive undulating area of 150 million olive trees, Jaén province has always suffered from being a place to drive through rather than to stay. The north-south artery, the N-323, which brings you into the province, takes you directly to the provincial capital, **Jaén ⓴**. Perched above the western plain with its back to the sierras, the city has surprisingly few monuments. But what it lacks in quantity it makes up for in scale.

The **Catedral** (open daily) is a massive pile built over three centuries, with a wonderful mixture of Gothic to baroque styles. The 11th-century **Baños Arabes** (open Tues–Sun; entrance fee), superbly excavated and restored, are among the largest and best-preserved in Spain. The city streets, in both the commercial zone and the old town stacked against the hillside, have a zip and energy you find only in such self-possessed Spanish provincial cities.

Baeza ⓯, 40 km (25 miles) northeast of the provincial capital, is an architectural gem, its honey-coloured palaces, churches and civic buildings dating chiefly to the 15th–17th century. Star features include the studded **Palacio de**

BELOW: peaks of the Parque Natural de Cazorla.

Ubeda's Parador Condestable Davalos, housed in a 16th-century Renaissance palace.

BELOW: the hillside town of Cazorla.

Jabalquinto and nearby, on Plaza Santa María, the **Santa Iglesia Catedral** (open daily), which was largely rebuilt in the 16th century. The real focus of interest, however, is the **Plaza de los Leones** to the west of the centre, which is clustered with splendid Renaissance architecture. Overlooking the fountain in the middle of the square are the **Puerta de Jaén** and the adjoining **Arco de Villalar**. On the north side of the square you can see the **Antigua Carnicería**, a 16th-century butcher's shop. A few steps away, on Paseo Cardenel Benavides, is the **Ayuntamiento** (town hall; Mon–Fri am only), a magnificent Plateresque building that was once a courthouse and jail.

Only 10 km (6 miles) further north along the N-316 is the larger town of **Ubeda** ⑯, another Renaissance jewel. The **Plaza de Vázquez de Molina** – an architectural set-piece in a class of its own – is unmissable. The rectangular plaza runs down from the stunningly rich domed **Capilla del Salvador**, which was built as a family pantheon and is still privately owned by the Duques de Medinaceli. As it widens out, the plaza reveals a balanced, beautifully proportioned sequence of austere palaces unbroken by modern additions considered by many to be the purest architectural expression of the Renaissance in Spain.

At the far end is the church of Santa María de los Reales Alcázares, built on the site of the old mosque. Also worth seeking out are the **Iglesia de San Pablo** for its impressive Plateresque tower, and the **Hospital de Santiago**, designed by Andrés de Vandelvira and now a cultural centre (open daily), which is sometimes compared to El Escorial for its severity of style.

The town of **Cazorla**, to the east of Ubeda, is a good access point for the **Parque Natural de Cazorla** ⑰ (information and maps at Cazorla's Oficina del Parque Natural, Calle Martínez Falero 11). Buses are scarce, so to get the best

CAZORLA'S FLORA AND FAUNA

One of Spain's most beautiful natural parks, the Parque Natural de Cazorla, Segura y Las Villas (to give it its full name) is a vast protected area in the northeast of Jaén province. Designated a natural park in 1986, it covers more than 200,000 hectares (500,000 acres) of dense forests and mountain peaks. More than 500,000 people visit every year on walking or driving trips to enjoy the diverse natural attractions of the park.

The best times to visit, especially if you plan to walk a lot, are spring and early or late summer, when the Andalusian climate is not so intensely hot. In spring, hikers can see primroses and the dwarf violets unique to Cazorla. At any time of year visitors may spot several species of eagle, bearded vultures, deer, boar and ibex (mountain goats) – the remoteness of the area means that the wildlife is unusually visible. An especially popular spot in the south of the reserve is the small spring where the Río Guadalquivir starts its course, when it is unceremoniously spat out from the depths of a mountain.

The sierras in the reserve are spectacular and rise to more than 2,000 metres (6,500 ft). The main driving route through the park hugs the river bed for much of the way, before reaching the Embalse del Tranco reservoir.

from a visit here you'll need a car or, better still, be prepared to walk – undoubtedly the best way to see the abundant wildlife and spectacular scenery the park has to offer. There is a modern Parador and several campgrounds in the park as well as plenty of accommodation in Cazorla.

Map on page 220

Sierra Nevada and Alpujarras

The **Sierra Nevada** range southeast of **Granada** *(see pages 209–15)*, is also excellent for walking, though many visitors come here to ski at the 2,100-metre (6,890-ft) ski station. More scenic though, is the south-facing slope of the Sierra, the Alpujarras region, which provides prime walking and horse-riding country, and beautiful mountain villages, including Bubion, Capileira and Pampaneira. The autumnal landscape of ravines, streams and terraced farms is spectacular.

Almería

For much of the 20th century, Almería's harsh landscape of sun-scorched sierras and rocky plains was dismissed as a forgotten corner. But now the desert-like climate powers a massive agricultural business spreading over 20,000 hectares (50,000 acres) of the coastal plain.

At the centre of the southern coast sits the provincial capital of **Almería** ⓲, still dominated by the 11th-century **Alcazaba**, its severe Moorish architecture overlaid by the more grandiose Catholic upper courtyard. The coast to the east of Almería runs south to the volcanic headland of **Cabo de Gata**, a protected area since 1980 for its flora, fauna and underwater life. Small resorts and villages line this stretch of coast, culminating at **Mojácar**, which until the 1960s was a quiet white village but is now overrun with chintzy bars and boutiques. ❑

BELOW: Almería's coast is Europe's winter garden.

VALENCIA AND MURCIA

*Together, these two regions are often known as the Levant.
Between them they enjoy more than half of Spain's
eastern coastline, stretching from Catalonia to Almería*

Maps:
City 236
Area 243

Just 3 km (2 miles) from the Mediterranean and straddling the Río Turia, the city of **Valencia ❶** has an enviable location, right in the middle of one of Europe's most fertile regions. The fields surrounding the city can yield three to four crops a year. Orange and lemon trees line the roads. Rice grows alongside sweet corn. Shimmering canals weave their way through the land, giving it life. This is the *huerta*, a cultivated and irrigated plain that was considered by the Muslims to be heaven on earth. Even the Spanish hero El Cid was taken by it. On his entry into Valencia he proclaimed: "From the day when I saw this city I found it to my liking, and I desired it, and I asked God to make me master of it."

The city he so desperately wanted had already seen the glories of past empires. It had been founded as Valentia by the Romans in 138 BC and became known as a retirement town for old soldiers. Chosen for its mild year-round temperatures, the Romans took advantage of the sunshine and the runoff from the surrounding mountains to turn the rich soil into some of the most efficiently irrigated farmland in their domain.

PRECEDING PAGES:
ceramic-covered
house at Manises.
LEFT: Alicante's
seafront.
BELOW: orange
harvest in
Valencia's fertile
huerta.

Earthly paradise

The Visigoths and Muslims knew a good thing when they saw it, and continued to improve the complex system of canals and channels. To the Muslims it was a paradise, and one that could effectively feed their people. They controlled the land for 500 years and built a city impressive enough to draw El Cid's attention. He conquered Valencia in 1094 but after his death it fell back under the jurisdiction of the Muslims. In 1238 the city was finally wrestled from them and incorporated into the kingdom of Aragón by Jaume I, *El Conquistador*.

The 15th century saw Valencia blossom into its Golden Age as it overtook Barcelona as the financial capital of this Mediterranean empire. Aside from its agricultural riches and its burgeoning port, the city held claim to a growing ceramic and silk industry and set up the nation's first printing press in 1474.

The city continued to prosper until 1609, when it was dealt a disastrous blow by Felipe III – the expulsion of the *moriscos* from Spain. No area was as hard hit as Valencia, which lost one-third of its people, most of them farm labourers. Its importance further declined in the early 18th century when the kingdom of Valencia was reduced to a province dependent on Madrid. And during the Spanish Civil War, the city was hard hit as one of the last Republican strongholds.

Valencia recovered much of its prestige when it became the capital of the Comunidad Valenciana, one

of the new autonomous regions of Spain, in 1982. Since then this city of almost 800,000 inhabitants, the third largest in Spain after Madrid and Barcelona, has been feverishly reinventing itself – laying out wide new avenues and investing in daring architectural projects.

The natural place to begin a tour of the city is the main square. Like most main squares, the **Plaza del Ayuntamiento** lies in the city centre and is the location of the city hall, post office, and bus stops. For some years, this triangular plaza was called the "Plaza of the Valencian Nation". While their separatist feelings are not as strong as the Catalans' or the Basques', Valencians do not forget that the city gained its importance long before it was joined to Castile, and are proud of their own traditions and language, *valenciano*.

The history of this nation is told in the **Museo Histórico Municipal** (open Mon–Fri 8.30am–2.30pm) housed on the second floor of the **Ayuntamiento A** (City Hall). Unfortunately, there is nothing here regarding El Cid, since most of the exhibits date from the time of Jaume I of Aragón, who is considered by Valencians as the true saviour of the city from the Muslims. Of special interest is the first map of the city drawn at a time when Valencia, with a population of 80,000, was bigger than Barcelona, Madrid and Genova. This incredibly accurate map, drawn in 1704, took five years to complete as the cartographer, Padre Tosca, measured the city street by street with a tape.

City of ceramics

Valencians are known for their individualism, sensuality, creativity, their desire to show off, and their pride in their city. For evidence of this you need look no further than the railway station, the Estación del Norte, which is decorated on

Valenciano is widely spoken in the region, but is less frequent in the city.

BELOW: view over Valencia.

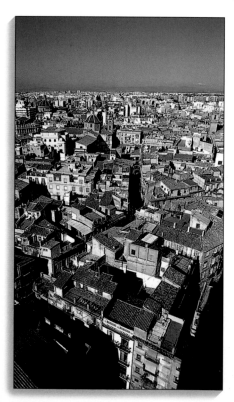

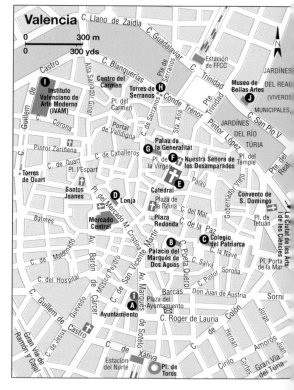

Map on page 236

the outside with bunches of sculpted oranges and inside with stained glass and ceramic mosaics. The craft that Valencia developed into a fine art, ceramics, is represented in the **Palacio del Marqués de Dos Aguas** ❸ on Calle Poeta Querol, which houses the **Museo Nacional de Cerámica** (open Tues–Sat 10am–2pm and 4–8pm; Sun 10am–2pm; free Sat pm and Sun). The industry dates back to the 13th century, when ceramic work came into use as a means of home decoration. Tapestries, which were used in colder climates to help retain heat, were never needed in Valencia and the use of *azulejos* (coloured tiles) became popular.

The oldest pieces in the museum come from two towns in the *huerta*, Paterna and Manises. Their porcelain was once much sought-after by European royalty. Today only Manises keeps up its potteries. The palace itself appears to be made of ceramic. Its grey and rust marble facade is in perfect Churrigueresque style: on either side of the alabaster entryway is a carved muscled Greek pouring water from an urn, illustrating the Marqués' name.

Round the corner from the Ceramic Museum is the Real Colegio de Corpus Cristi, known as the **Colegio del Patriarca** ❸ (open daily 11am–1.30pm; entrance fee), in honour of its founder, the 16th-century archbishop and viceroy of Valencia, St John de Ribera. Grouped around its renowned two-storey Renaissance patio are a church whose walls and ceilings are covered with frescoes and a museum housing an important collection of works of art by both Spanish and foreign masters.

Glorious food

To the north of the Plaza del Ayuntamiento is the Plaza del Mercado, site of the **Central Market** (open Mon–Sat 8.30am–2.30pm). The brick and tile market is a veritable cathedral to food. The domed building with stained-glass windows and ornate doorways is over 8,030 sq metres (9,600 sq yards), which makes it one of the largest markets in Europe.

Opposite is the 15th-century **Lonja** ❸ (open Tues–Sat 9.30am–2pm and 5–7pm; Sun am), built as the commercial exchange for the ever-increasing mercantile industry, and now a World Heritage Monument. The prosperity is reflected in the elegant Transactions Hall. High-ceilinged and supported by eight twisted columns, the hall's delicately traced windows allow the sun to cast shadows across the red and black tiled floor.

Behind the Lonja a maze of narrow streets lead to the Plaza de la Reina, on which stands the cathedral. On the way, you may stumble across the charming **Plaza Redonda**, a circular covered market selling a mixture of haberdashery, clothes and crafts.

The **Catedral** ❸ (open daily, closed lunchtimes), built on the site of a Roman temple to Diana and later a mosque, was begun in 1262 in traditional Gothic style. In the 1700s its interior was covered over with a neoclassical facade, which has been removed. The south side, facing the Plaza de la Reina, is Italian baroque while the east door is Romanesque. The focal point of the structure is the 15th-century octagonal

BELOW: the Miguelete tower.

bell tower known as the **Miguelete** (open daily; entrance fee), or *Micalet* in *valenciano*. From the top is a fine view of the glazed-tile domes of the city and a glimpse of the *huerta* stretching beyond it to the nearby hills. Inside the cathedral is a chapel containing a small purple agate cup purported to be the Holy Grail.

Water power

The cathedral's **Door of the Apostles**, a 14th-century portal adorned with statuary, gives on to the **Plaza de la Virgen**. It is in this antique doorway that once a week, without fail, the ancient Water Tribunal of Valencia meets, in which the proceedings are as they have been for hundreds of years.

On the east side of the plaza and connected to the cathedral by a small bridge is the **Basílica de Nuestra Señora de los Desamparados ᶠ** (Our Lady of the Abandoned, open daily, closed lunchtimes), the patron saint of the city since the 17th century. The image of the Virgin displayed above the altar was carved in 1416 for the chapel of Spain's first mental institution.

Across from the basilica is the **Palau de la Generalitat ᴳ**, housing the regional government (for visits tel: 96-386 6100). This Gothic palace was built in the 15th century but skilfully extended in the 1950s. It is arranged around a handsome inner courtyard, off which is an exquisite reception room, the Salón Dorado, so named for its ornate, gold-coffered ceiling. Upstairs is the assembly hall of the ancient *Cortes*, the Valencian parliament.

Calle de Caballeros, running north from the palace, is the old main street. Its commercial importance has waned but its former glory is seen in the Gothic residences that are interspersed with restaurants, bars and cafés. Most of the houses here retain their beautiful patios, the sure sign of 15th-century Valencian success.

BELOW LEFT: ceramic tiled door jamb of a private house.
BELOW RIGHT: the Palacio de Marqués de Dos Aguas.

Map on page 236

IVAM and the Museum of Fine Arts

The maze of streets that branch off from Caballeros towards the river form the oldest part of the city, the **Barrio del Carmen**. As late as 1762, Valencia was still a network of 428 narrow streets held within fortified city walls. In 1777 the dangers of these dark alleyways gave rise to the establishment of the first corps of *serenos*, or nightwatchmen, who later became a standard feature of most Spanish towns. The Barrio del Carmen, once in ruins, is being rapidly refurbished and its trendy bars are a mainstay of the city's exuberant nightlife.

Calle de Serranos leads from the Palau de la Generalitat to the **Torres de Serranos** ❸ (open Tues–Sun, closed Sun pm; free but a tip appreciated), a city gate built in the 1390s and one of two left standing (the other is the **Torres de Quart** at the end of Caballeros). The tower is a massive fortification, reputedly the finest Gothic gate in Europe and part of the city walls, which were torn down in 1865. The walls, broken by 10 gateways, followed the boundaries set by the streets of Guillem de Castro and Colón, and the bank of the river.

Valencia suffered a disastrous flood in 1957, after which the Río Turia was diverted along an artifical channel lying outside the city.

Calle Guillem de Castro is now the site of the **Instituto Valenciano de Arte Moderno** ❶ (IVAM; open Tues–Sun 10am–8pm; entrance fee), considered to be one of Spain's most dynamic contemporary art galleries. The Valencian artists, sculptor Julio González and painter Ignacio Pinazo, are well represented here. The institute also has a lively programme of temporary exhibitions.

The Torres de Serranos looks out across the dry bed of the Río Turia to the city's largest gardens, the **Jardines del Real** (open 8am–sunset daily). Beside them stands the **Museo de Bellas Artes** ❶ (open Tues–Sun 10am–8pm), one of the most important galleries in Spain. Housed in a former seminary with a stunning blue dome, the museum's most notable works include the 14th- and

BELOW: Water Tribunal judge.

THE WATER TRIBUNAL

Valencia's *Tribunal de las Aguas* (Water Tribunal) has been meeting every Thursday at noon for an estimated 1,000 years, making it not only one of the world's most curious legal institutions but also one of the oldest.

There are eight judges presiding, each of whom is dressed in black and each representing one of the great *acequias* or irrigation canals of the *huerta* – the vast area of cultivated land surrounding the city that is under threat from the encroaching suburbs. These canals were originally built by the Romans over 2,000 years ago, and are still used to distribute water among the farmers of the area. Any questions regarding the intricate system of channels, canals and drains must be brought before the Water Tribunal. Every farmer is told precisely on which days and for exactly how long he can irrigate his fields. If he exceeds his quota – whether through negligence or greed – he is likely to be challenged in public before the tribunal.

The judges, who are farmers themselves, conduct their business in *valenciano*. They rarely need to discuss a case in any detail but usually pass judgement immediately and impose a fine on any farmer who is found guilty of a misdemeanour. The Water Tribunal may be ancient but it represents swift and efficient justice.

15th-century altarpieces by so-called Valencian "primitive" painters. The works of the late 19th- and early 20th-century Valencian artists, inspired by the sea, the colours of the *huerta* and the Mediterranean light, are very evocative.

Following the river to the sea

The redundant course of the Río Turia has been turned into an attractive feature of the city as an elongated ribbon of parks and sports fields crossed by old and new bridges. On the bank downstream stands Valencia's main concert hall, the **Palau de la Musica**, and beyond it a giant figure of **Gulliver**.

Papier-mâché giants celebrating the annual fallas.

Towards the port is the city's exciting new centre of interest, **La Ciutat de les Arts i de les Ciències** (City of Arts and Sciences). Largely designed by Valencian architect Santiago Calatrava, this massive 21st-century complex has five main parts. The **Hemisferic**, an OMNIMAX cinema and planetarium; the **Museu de les Ciences Principe Felipe** (open daily 10am–8pm, Sat 10am–9pm; entrance fee), an interactive science museum; the recently opened **Oceanographic Park**, the largest in Europe; and the **Umbraculo**, a spacious planted walkway. The **Palau des Arts** – an arts centre including state-of-the-art opera house – is due to open in 2004. To purchase tickets, tel: 902-100 031.

A pleasant tram ride from the Pont de Fusta station (near the Museo de Bellas Artes) brings you to the beach, with its wide promenade stretching from the port past the old fishing quarters of El Cabañal and La Malvarrosa. A string of restaurants along Playa de las Arenas (near the penultimate tram stop) serve excellent *paella*. The best-known of Spanish dishes, *paella* has its origins in the rice paddies south of the city around the Albufera *(see page 243)*. The original *paella valenciana* contains vegetables, chicken and rabbit. Favourite Valencian

BELOW: young girls weep at the end of the *fallas* fiesta.

drinks include fresh orange juice, *Agua de Valencia* – a cocktail of orange juice and sparkling wine, and *horchata*, a refreshing drink made from tiger nuts.

The *fallas*

Look on almost any old building in the centre of Valencia for the small plaque guaranteeing that the structure is insured against fire. Fire insurance is essential in the city with the most explosive fiestas in Spain: the *fallas*. The custom dates back to the Middle Ages when Valencia's carpenters burned their accumulated wood shavings in huge bonfires on the eve of 19 March, the feast of St Joseph, patron of woodworkers. Over the years, the traditional woodchips were replaced with papier-mâché figures lampooning politicians, local customs and current events. For a week, hundreds of these are on display throughout the city. The moment of truth, the *cremá*, arrives on 19 March, and the streets, plazas and balconies fill up with citizens, tourists and, most importantly, firemen. The figures are set alight one by one, so that at midnight the entire city, illuminated with an orange glow, appears to be burning down.

The Comunidad Valenciana

The 23,300 sq km (9,000 sq miles) of the Comunidad Valenciana is split into three provinces: Valencia, Castellón and Alicante. This region approximately follows the boundaries of the old Kingdom of Valencia, which was captured from the Muslims in the 13th century by an army of Catalans, who left their language here in the form of the *valenciano* dialect.

Valencia, according to the *paso doble* that has become the region's unofficial anthem, "is the land of flowers, light and love." Thanks to an equable

Confusingly, the name Valencia is used in English to refer to three distinct entities: the capital city, the province that surrounds it, and the autonomous region of the Comunidad Valenciana.

BELOW: Valencia's inferno, culmination of the fiesta.

Wooden rowing boats at the Albufera Lake.

Mediterranean climate, all good things seem in abundance here. Sunshine saturates its many attractive beaches and warm temperatures make for an active outdoor life day and night, almost all year round.

Castellón province

Away from the coast both Valencia and Murcia are mountainous. One of the most picturesque upland areas is **El Maestrazgo** (Maestrat), which straddles the border between Castellón and Teruel. The crags and flat-topped summits form a backdrop to stout medieval towns built in impregnable locations. The most impressive of these is **Morella** ❷, the "capital" of the Maestrazgo, a walled town clinging to a protruding rock. **Ares del Maestre** is also spectacularly sited. Other places that are particularly worth visiting are the two towns **Cinctorres** and **La Iglesuela del Cid**, and the extraordinary shrine of **La Balma**, in a cave half-way up a cliff.

Descending to sea level, the coast of Castellón could not come as more of a contrast. It is aptly named the **Costa Azahar**, the orange blossom coast, after the citrus groves that cover the coastal plain and emit a sweet perfume in spring. The main resorts are **Vinaròs**, **Benicarló**, **Orpesa**, **Benicàssim** and **Borriana** but the most appealing one to visit is **Peñíscola** ❸. The **Castell del Papa Luna** (open daily; entrance fee), at the heart of this fortified town built on a rocky headland, was the refuge of the renegade Pedro de Luna, elected Pope Benedict XIII in the late 14th century during the Great Schism that split the Christian Church, but who was later deposed.

BELOW: the town of Manises, famed for its ceramic productions.

The provincial capital **Castelló de la Plana** ❹ centres on a 16th-century bell tower, El Fadrí. Its most important museum is the **Espai d'Art Contemporani** (Calle Prim s/n; open Tues–Sun 11am–8pm). Other attractions include the **Convento de las Madres Capuchinas**, which houses a collection of Zurbarán paintings (open daily, pm only), the **Planetarium** (open Tues–Sat; Sun am; entrance fee) near the beach, and the **Museo de Bellas Artes** (Avenida Hermanos Bou 28; open Tues–Sat 10am–8pm, Sun 10am–2pm; free Sun) in a new building that has won several awards.

Valencia province

The interior of Valencia is not unmissable but it is worth exploring if you have the time. There are several beauty spots in the valley of the Río Turia (the **Alto Turia**) – a destination for hikers – including the remains of a Roman aqueduct near **Chelva** ❺. **Alpuente**, somewhat out of the way, has a tiny town hall crammed into a tower above a 14th-century gateway. **Requena**, a fine Gothic town to the south of the Turia, is Valencia's principal wine centre. Sensation-seekers make a pilgrimage to **Buñol** in late August for the extraordinary phenomenon of La Tomatina, a free-for-all tomato-throwing fiesta.

Continuing down the coast you come to **Sagunt** (Sagunto) ❻, the Roman town of Saguntum, which was sacked by the Carthaginian general Hannibal in 219 BC, leading to the Second Punic War and the Roman subjugation of Spain. The controversially restored **theatre** that the Romans built into the hillside above the town in the 1st century AD is home to a summer arts festival. The **castle** above it (open Tues–Sat, Sun am; entrance fee) incorporates remains from all the races to have passed this way, from the Iberians to the Moors.

The coast of Valencia province has few resorts or sights, but there are two places south of the capital city worthy of a detour. The first is **L'Albufera ❼**, a freshwater lake separated from the sea by a sandbar. You can learn about the Albufera's birdlife in the visitor's centre at Racó de l'Olla or take a boat trip from the village of El Palmar. El Palmar is also a good place to eat *paella*: it stands on the edge of a maze of paddy fields.

The other place worth a stop is **Gandia ❽**. Its **Palacio Ducal** (Duke's Palace, open Mon–Sat; guided tour obligatory; entrance fee), once home of St Francisco de Borja (1510–72), has sumptuous chambers surrounding a Gothic patio. The palace is now owned by Jesuits.

The most historic town of inland Valencia is **Xàtiva** (Jativa) ❾, said to be the original home of the Borgia family before they went to Italy, with its superb **castle** (open Tues–Sun; entrance fee). This was the first European city to manufacture paper – under the Muslims in the 12th century – but its prosperity came to an abrupt end during the War of the Spanish Succession when it was all but burned to the ground by Felipe V, whose portrait hangs upside down symbolically in the **Museo Municipal** (open Tues–Sun; free Sun).

Alicante province

Getting around inland in this mountainous region can be slow going and the main roads stay close to the coast. A short way beyond Gandia you enter the province of Alicante, whose shoreline has become famous as the **Costa Blanca**. Although some parts of it are now dominated by high-rise hotels and seas of whitewashed villas built for expatriate residents, it is still an attractive stretch of coast with unspoiled

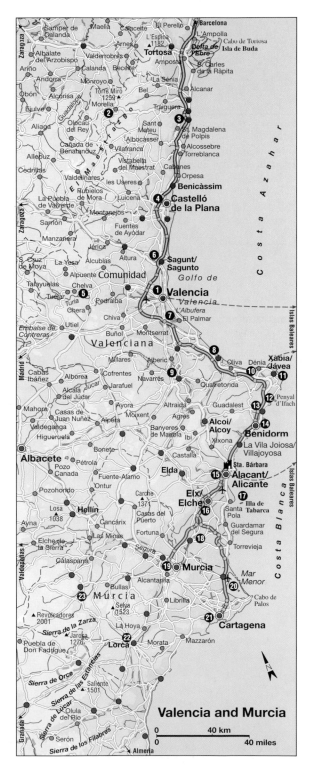

Valencia and Murcia

0 ___ 40 km

0 ___ 40 miles

sandy beaches, hidden coves, cliffs and headlands. The first two resorts you come to, **Dénia** ⑩ and **Xàbia** (Jávea) ⑪, could not be more dissimilar, although both are worth seeing. They are separated by the distinctive hump of Mount Montgó, now a *parque natural*. Dénia was originally a Greek settlement. Its main monument is the largely Arab **castle** (open daily; entrance fee) which looks down on the fishing port that supplies the excellent local restaurants here. Xàbia, built around an unusual, fortified church, gives access to the lovely coastline landscape and beaches on **Cap (Cabo) de la Nau.**

The northern Costa Blanca is dominated by a huge, natural feature, the **Penyal d'Ifach** (Peñón de Ifach) ⑫, a limestone crag that juts into the sea and towers above the resort of **Calp** (Calpe). It can be climbed from the visitors' centre at its base for tremendous views and rare plants and birds.

The rise of Benidorm

A rocky gorge separates Calp from the next resort, **Altea** ⑬, whose upmarket old town is a picturesque jumble of white houses, narrow streets and steps. Around the next headland is **Benidorm** ⑭, a mini-Manhattan set down beside two bays of golden sand. If you can penetrate past the cut-price, high-rise hotels (including the tallest hotel in Europe) and restaurants, and Terra Mítica, a Mediterranean theme park, it has quite a pleasant old town centre. From the Balcón del Mediterráneo you get a good view of the resort.

For a more authentic local flavour, **La Vila Joiosa** (Villajoyosa), a chocolate-making town to the south, is a better choice. From Benidorm it is a short excursion into the nearby hills to **Guadalest**, the Costa Blanca's most spectacular tourist spot. You have to go through a pedestrian tunnel to enter the old vil-

As recently as the 1950s, Benidorm was an obscure fishing village. For much of the year it is now overrun with sun-seeking tourists, and its summer clubbing scene is notorious.

BELOW: taunting bulls at the lively Dénia fiesta *Bous a la mar.*

lage, at the top of which are the remains of a castle. On an adjacent rock sits the church's quaint belfry. Coach loads of tourists regularly leave Benidorm for Guadalest; quieter inland villages to visit include **Xaló** (Jalón) and the picturesque hamlets of the **Vall de Gallïnera**.

Map on page 243

Southern Costa Blanca and the interior

Continuing south along the coast brings you to the resort town of **Alacant** (Alicante) **⑮**, a busy port and the capital of the province, overlooked by the **Castillo de Santa Bárbara** (open daily; entrance fee). Other sights worth seeing are the baroque **city hall**, the **Museo de la Asegurada** (open Tues–Sun) housing an interesting collection of modern art (including Miró, Tàpies and Chillida), and the MARQ "21st century" archaelogical museum (open Tues–Sun; entrance fee).

The lobster catch on the Illa de Tabarca.

Approximately 50 km (32 miles) inland from Alicante on the N-340 the landscape changes dramatically. The industrial city of **Alcoi** (Alcoy) is worth visiting in April for its famous Moors and Christians fiesta, and as a base for exploring a beautiful mountain area, including the nearby nature reserve of Font Roja. Not far away the Sierra de Mariola mountains are best approached through the village of **Agres** and the lovely historic town of **Cocentaina**.

Elx (Elche) **⑯** is renowned for its palm groves at **El Palmeral**, a World Heritage site; the **Huerto del Cura** garden (open Tues–Sun; entrance fee); and the Dama de Elche, an enigmatic Iberian sculpture found on the site of classical Illici (now Alcúdia) housed in the National Museum of Archaeology in Madrid. The Misteri d'Elx, a medieval mystery play performed in August in the **Basílica de Santa María** is one of the few masterpieces of oral heritage in Europe.

BELOW: the Moors and Christians fiesta at Alcoi.

South of Alicante, the Costa Blanca is less spectacular, though the **Illa de Tabarca ⑰**, a marine reserve, makes a pleasant day-trip from the fishing port of **Santa Pola** (ferry information tel: 680-330-422). A sea and fishing museum has opened in the castle of Santa Pola, and the salt pans here attract flamingos. There are more salt pans and flamingos around **Torrevieja**, a town that grew exponentially during the 1980s as estates of cheap villas were sold to Spanish families looking for their own piece of the sun.

Orihuela ⑱, inland on the N-340 and to the south of Elx, is a smaller town that was the second most important city in the Kingdom of Valencia. It has some handsome churches, especially the Gothic **Catedral** (open daily) with an elegant two-storey patio, tower and museum attached to it.

Murcia: the old frontier

Covering just 11,317 sq km (4,369 sq miles), Murcia is one of Spain's smallest *comunidades*. Compared with its larger neighbours, Andalusia and the Comunidad Valenciana, Murcia is little known but it has its superlatives too.

Murcia ⑲, the capital, stands inland in a fertile river valley. At the heart of the city is the **Catedral** (open daily), built on the foundations of a former mosque between the 14th and 18th centuries. Notable features of the cathedral include its great baroque

facade and two exquisite side chapels. The **Cathedral Museum** (open Mon–Sat; entrance fee) is also worth a visit for its Gothic altarpieces and Roman frieze. A short walk away is the lively **Museo de la Ciudad** (open Tues–Sun), which tells the story of the city.

A modern counterpart to the city's baroque flair is the **Casino** (ask doorman for permission to enter; tip appreciated), a late 19th-century caprice full of details such as a *Mudéjar*-style entrance patio and paintings on the ceiling of the ladies' cloakroom.

Murcia's taste for extravagance can also be seen during Easter Week when a series of baroque *pasos* (floats) are taken on procession. Those which are the work of the sculptor Francisco Salzillo can be admired during the rest of the year in the **Museo Salzillo** (open Tues–Sat, weekdays only July–Aug; entrance fee). If you want something more down-to-earth, at **Alcantarilla**, just outside the city, is a giant waterwheel and excellent folk museum on the *huerta* (open Tues–Sun).

The Costa Cálida and Cartagena

Murcia's coastline, the **Costa Cálida** (the "Warm Coast"), possesses one unique natural feature in the **Mar Menor** ❷⓪, a large, calm lagoon popular for swimming and other watersports where the water is usually several degrees warmer than the Mediterranean. On the sheltered landward shore are the old-fashioned resorts of Los Alcázares and Santiago de la Ribera, which still have quaint wooden boathouses on their beaches. These small towns look across the lagoon at La Manga de Mar Menor, a narrow line of high-rise hotels and apartment blocks marching along the sand bar that all but cuts off the Mar Menor (literally "the Smaller Sea") from the Mediterranean.

BELOW: Murcia's cathedral by night.

Map on page 243

Cabo de Palos, the fishing port where La Manga is attached to the mainland, is famous for its restaurants, and just to the west of it lies **Calblanque**, a natural park enclosing fine sandy virgin beaches.

Cartagena ㉑, the region's seaport and the principal Carthaginian city in Spain, has an interesting cultural heritage. A sign of that ancient history is the excavated stretch of the **Muralla Bizantina** (Byzantine Wall; open Tues–Sat 11am–1.30pm and 5.30–8.30pm) built in the 6th century. The **Museo Nacional de Arqueología Marítima** (Maritime Archaeology Museum; open Tues–Sun 10am–2pm; entrance fee) also explores Spain's early history, while the splendid **Roman theatre** (open Mon–Sat 11am–1.30pm and 4–6pm; Sun am only) and the recently opened **Augusteum** should not be missed.

The old frontier between Murcia and Andalusia is guarded by the town of **Lorca ㉒**, which is overlooked by a ruined castle. The **Colegiata de San Patricio** and the town hall, in the handsome Plaza de España, were erected at the height of Lorca's prosperity in the 17th and 18th centuries. Lorca's immensely popular Good Friday procession is typical of Valencia and Murcia fiestas in its love of finery, in this case, the colour and dazzle of the spectacularly embroidered costumes.

Further inland are some splendid tracts of unspoiled countryside. The wine from around **Jumilla**, once cheap and plentiful, is now well regarded internationally. **Caravaca de la Cruz ㉓** is well known in Spain for the double-armed cross said to have appeared miraculously in 1231 in what is now the **Santuario de la Vera Cruz** (Sanctuary of the True Cross). Its pilgrimage, which is held every seven years, has now been blessed by the Vatican. Other places in the vicinity that are worthy of a leisurely detour are the **Segura Valley** villages north of the spa of **Archena** and the **sierras de Espuna** and **Moratalla**. ❏

On the evening of Good Friday, the town of Lorca stages one of the most extraordinary processions in Spain, involving thousands of people dressed as Biblical characters.

BELOW: windmills in the sunset, Murcia.

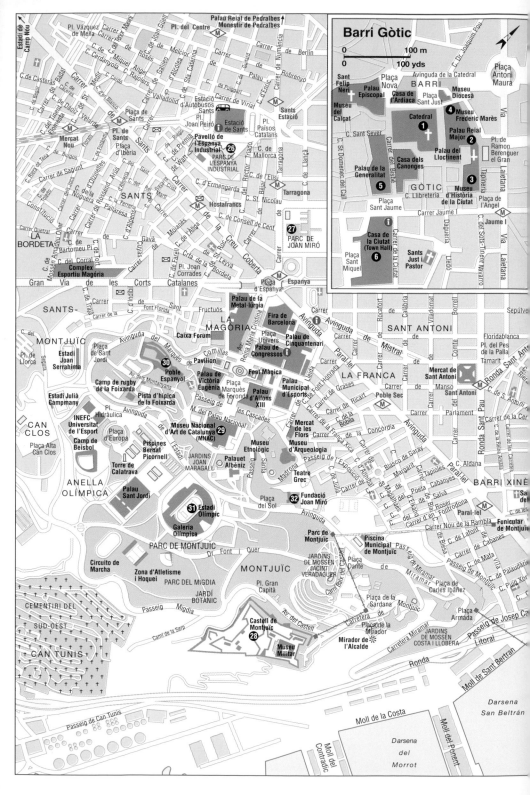

Barri Gòtic

0 — 100 m
0 — 100 yds

Plaça Antoni Maura

Sant Felip Neri

Plaça Nova

BARRI

Palau Episcopal

Casa de l'Ardiaca

Plaça Sant Just

Museu Diocesà

Museu del Calçat

Catedral **1**

4 Museu Frederic Marès

C. Sant Sever

Palau Reial Major **2**

C. St Domenec del Call

Casa dels Canonges

Palau del Lloctinent

Pl. de Ramon Berenguer el Gran

Palau de la Generalitat **5**

GÒTIC

3

Museu d'Història de la Ciutat

Plaça Sant Jaume

C. Llibreteria

Carrer Jaume I

Plaça de l'Àngel

Jaume I

Casa de la Ciutat (Town Hall) **6**

Plaça Sant Miquel

Sants Just i Pastor

BARRI XINÈ

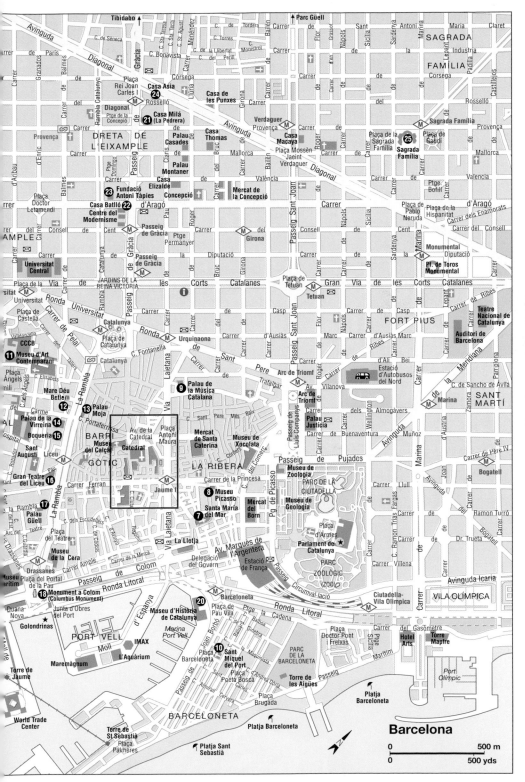

Barcelona

BARCELONA

*As well as being the largest city on the Mediterranean,
Barcelona is one of Europe's most brilliant centres, at the
forefront of modern architecture, fashion and design*

Map
on page
248–9

The capital of Catalonia and a key Mediterranean port, Barcelona is a bilingual city, its citizens speaking both Castilian Spanish and Catalan. With one foot in France and the other in traditional Spain, in many respects the city seems almost as close to Paris as it is to Madrid, and has long been Iberia's link to the rest of Western Europe. The city most characterised by the *modernista* architect Antoni Gaudí has also produced other world-figures in the arts – Miró, Tàpies, Pau Casals, Josep Carreras and Montserrat Caballé, for instance. For the 1992 Olympic Games, it was given an enormous facelift. Many fine medieval buildings were renovated, modern structures erected, a ring road created, and the port and waterfront districts comprehensively overhauled.

Catalonia's relationship with Spain

Understanding Barcelona requires some insight into the Catalan-Spanish duality. Although about half of Greater Barcelona's 3 million inhabitants have emigrated from other parts of Spain, Barcelona is historically and culturally a Catalan city, the capital of Catalonia and the seat of the Generalitat, the Catalan autonomous government. Catalonia was an independent nation with a parliament – the Council of 100 – well before the formation of the Spanish State. Catalo-

LEFT: *castellers*
perform in Plaça
Sant Jaume during
the Fiestas de
la Mercè.
BELOW: a carved
door at Gaudí's
Casa Batlló.

nia became a commercial power in the Mediterranean during the 14th and 15th centuries, developing a merchant class, banking and a social structure significantly different from the feudal model that continued in most of Spain. Later, while the rest of Spain colonised, mining New World wealth, Catalonia industrialised, becoming the world's fourth manufacturing power by 1850.

Catalan, a Romance language derived from the speech of the occupying Romans, is closely related to the Provençal and Langue d'Oc French spoken in southern France. The strength of Catalan culture has fluctuated with the region's political fortunes. After uniting with the kingdom of Aragón in the 12th century, Catalonia found itself part of a new nation – Spain – when Fernando II of Aragón married Isabel I of Castile in 1469. Centuries-old privileges and institutions were suppressed by Castilian centralism over the next 300 years, most notably in 1714 when the newly installed Spanish King Felipe V, grandson of Louis XIV of France, militarily seized Barcelona and abolished all local autonomous privileges.

During the 19th century Catalonia's industrial success fostered new independence movements and a renaissance of Catalan nationalism. But in 1939 its last experiment in autonomy was crushed by Franco's victory in the Spanish Civil War. Since Franco's death in 1975, Catalonia has undergone a spectacular cultural

Picasso fresco on Barcelona's Chamber of Architects.

resurgence. Catalan, forbidden for 36 years, is the language used in state schools and universities, books and newspapers, radio and TV, theatre and cinema, the arts and sciences and official documents. It is the co-official language. The Barcelona Olympics was a high point of this new cultural golden age, with Catalan accepted as an official language, and since then it has continued to flourish.

Bordered by the sea on one side and by the Collserola hills to the west, Barcelona is intersected by great avenues such as the **Diagonal** and the **Passeig de Gràcia**, and punctuated by open spaces that provide welcome relief from the city's human and architectural density. The two promontories of Montjuïc (by the port) and Tibidabo (behind and inland) tower over the city's chaotic sprawl.

After 1850 Barcelona broke out of the old Gothic city to create the **Eixample**, the orderly grid of wide avenues planned by Ildefons Cerdà, which occupies the middle ground between the old city and its backdrop of hills. In 1992 this grid system was extended down to the seafront when the old industrial area of **Poble Nou** was pulled down to build the Olympic Village and the Port Olímpic. Construction continues as the waterfront is being developed to create residential areas.

A tour of the Gothic Quarter

BELOW: on the steps of the Palau Reial Major.

Barcelona's old city, the **Barri Gòtic** or Gothic Quarter, is a wonderful display of solid stone, sprinkled with small shops, cafés, taverns and gourmet restaurants. Although most of the major architecture was completed between the 13th and the 15th centuries, there are traces of Roman civilisation. Barcelona's acropolis – the highest elevation in the Barri Gòtic – was originally the Iberian village of Laia. The Romans conquered the town in 133 BC, erected the Temple of Augustus and fortified their *Mons Taber* with defensive walls in the 4th century.

Map on page 248–9

The itinerary that best clarifies the city's archaeology and history begins at the **Catedral** ❶ (open daily, closed lunchtime; museum open daily 10am–1pm and 4.30–7.30pm; entrance fee) at Plaça Nova. Known as La Seu (the "seat" of the Bishopric), construction began in 1298 and was completed over the next two centuries, with the exception of the main facade which was not finished until the late 19th century. The two octagonal bell towers are, perhaps, the cathedral's most monumental features, while the interior cloister with its magnolias, palms, orange trees and resident geese is one of the city's most beautiful spots. The Canonja, Degà and Ardiaca houses that ring the square outside the cathedral, as well as the Capella de Santa Llúcia at the corner of Carrer del Bisbe, are also important architectural gems. Follow Bisbe towards the Plaça Sant Jaume, with a detour into the timeless Plaça Sant Felip Neri. The sounds of street musicians playing medieval compositions are echoed and amplified by the acoustics of stone.

Return to Plaça Nova and continue round to the right down Carrer Tapineria to the Plaça de Ramón Berenguer el Gran, where you can see the eastern limit of the **Roman walls**. After another section of Carrer Tapineria, cross through Plaça de l'Angel and along the Carrer Sots-tinent Navarro where more sections of the walls are clearly visible. After cutting in behind the wall to Plaça Sant Just and doubling back up to Carrer Llibreteria, the Carrer Veguer leads up to the Plaça del Rei and the royal buildings of Catalonia's sovereign count-kings.

The **Palau Reial Major** ❷ (Tues–Sun 10am–8pm; closed Sun pm and lunchtime during winter; entrance fee) and the Capella de Santa Agata are located at the foot of the tower of St Martí, worth climbing for the view over the old city. Santa Agata is an extraordinarily pure example of Catalan Gothic construction and was the chapel of the Royal Palace, the residence of the counts of Barcelona, who became kings of Aragón in 1137. The **Museu d'Història de la Ciutat** ❸ (Tues–Sat 10am–8pm, Sun am; closed lunchtime during winter; entrance fee) is a part of this complex, built over Roman foundations still visible in its basement. The impressive Saló del Tinell, the early Gothic Great Hall of the Royal Palace, and the adjacent Palau del Lloctinent complete the buildings around this regal square, widely considered the Barri Gòtic's loveliest. Nearby, on Plaça de Sant Iu is the **Museu Frederic Marès** ❹ (Tues–Sat 10am–7pm and Sun am; entrance fee). The collection was donated by the sculptor Marès in 1946, with pieces dating from the Middle Ages.

Catalonia's seat of government

Down Carrer del Bisbe and to the right emerging into Plaça Sant Jaume is the **Palau de la Generalitat de Catalunya** ❺ (2nd and 4th Sunday in the month, 10.30am–1.30pm), the seat of the autonomous Catalan government since the 14th century. Any lingering doubts about Catalonia's view of herself as a nation are quickly laid to rest with a tour of the stunningly ornate Generalitat building. Constructed from the 15th to the 17th century, the main points of interest are the Gothic patio with its exterior staircase, the Sant Jordi chapel, the Patí dels Tarongers (Patio of the Orange Trees) and the Saló Daurat (Gilded Room), with its lovely murals.

BELOW: the tranquil Cathedral cloister.

The Plaça Sant Jaume, originally part of the Roman forum, is regularly a focal point for popular festivities and political demonstrations. The neoclassical facade directly across the square from the Generalitat is the **Casa de la Ciutat ❻** (town hall; open on key public holidays or by appointment; tel: 93-402 7364). Inside the building, a black marble staircase leads to the main floor, the Saló de Cent (Hall of the Hundred), which was the meeting place for one of Europe's first Republican parliaments.

The mariner's church

The **Barri de Santa María**, also known as the Born or La Ribera, is the area around the superb **Santa María del Mar ❼** (open daily, closed lunchtime), a supreme example of Mediterranean Gothic architecture. Begun in 1329, the basilica was the centre of Barcelona's new seafaring and merchant community and the crowning glory of Catalonia's hegemony in the Mediterranean. "Santa María!" was a war cry of the Catalan sailors and soldiers as they stormed into Sicily, Sardinia and Greece. It is one of the simplest and most elegant structures in the city: the three naves are vast and of similar height, reducing interior support to the bare minimum. The basilica's massively tall stone columns, rose window, two bell towers and virtually all of the side chapels and stained-glass windows are striking, with graceful, pure lines. The acoustics here are also worthy of note – they produce a six-second delay that is capable of converting a dulcet medieval melody into a polyphony of powerful echoes and overtones.

Tucked behind the church is Montcada, one of Barcelona's most aristocratic streets in the 14th century and one of the most beautiful today. Many of its 14th-century palaces now house museums. Five have been well restored to

The El Born area on the eastern side of Santa María del Mar was the site of jousts and tournaments from the 13th to the 17th century, and became the central marketplace for maritime Barcelona. The area is now fashionable again, and is the place to head to after 9pm for trendy bars and hip nightclubs.

BELOW: religious icons, a speciality of Barcelona.

become the **Museu Picasso** ❽ (Tues–Sat 10am–8pm, Sun am; entrance fee); the buildings are almost as interesting as their contents. The museum provides an insight into the early evolution of the artist's talent. From caricatures of his teachers in school texts to studies of anatomy as an art student and his first great paintings in the styles of the Masters – Goya, Velázquez, El Greco – Picasso's extraordinary vitality comes through.

Continue over Princesa into Corders, and turn left for the **Plaça de la Llana**, a small medieval square. From there, wind up past the Mercat de Santa Caterina to the **Palau de la Música Catalana** ❾ (guided tours 10am–3.30pm; entrance charge). Erected in 1908 by the *modernista* architect Domènech i Montaner, this magnificent concert hall, flagship of Barcelona's Art Nouveau architecturehas been declared a World Heritage building by UNESCO. The only concert hall in Europe to be naturally lit, it was cramped uncomfortably in all its ornate splendour between dull neighbours. However, in a major renovation plan by Oscar Tusquets, architect of an earlier extension, it has been liberated and a new chamber for concerts, the Petit Palau, and offices have been contructed. Visits are possible since the resident orchestra, the Orquestra Simfònica de Barcelona i Nacional de Catalunya (OBC), moved to the grand new **Auditori**, near Glorès *(see page 261).*

Map on page 248–9

The artist's signature at the Museu Picasso entrance.

Barcelona's beaches and Olympic port

Next, you could head for the beach in **Barceloneta**. The narrow alleys here have the feel of a fishing town, with brightly painted houses, laundry hanging over the pavement, and the delicious aroma of seafood from its restaurants. From the church of **Sant Miquel del Port** ❿ (open daily), which stands in a

LEFT: the Olympic Village seafront. **BELOW:** diners at the Olympic port.

Snowflake, the former star of Barcelona's zoo.

lovely square just off Passeig Joan de Borbó, it's a short meander out to the beach and the start of the 4-km (2-mile) waterfront, encompassing seven beaches – a legacy of the Olympics. The Port Olímpic marina is lined with restaurants, music bars and cafés especially popular in summer. The Olympic Village, originally for athletes, has become a residential district. Beyond it is the Forum 2004 site. The Universal Forum of Cultures, held in Barcelona from 9 May to 24 September 2004, has three main themes – to promote cultural diversity, conditions for world peace and a sustainable urban environment. The forum will involve debates, exhibitions and a world festival of the arts. All the events will simultaneously reach every corner of the world via a virtual forum, in keeping with one of the key aims, which is to transcend the limitations of nationality.

Where Avinguda Diagonal meets the sea a huge showground has been constructed, comprising a new-age zoological park, exhibition areas and a port. It is an impressive and hugely ambitious project. For further information and ticket sales visit www.barcelona2004.org. On the port side of Barceloneta is the tower station for the cable car that crosses to the hill of Montjuïc *(see page 262)*, providing a spectacular panorama.

Ciutadella Park

BELOW LEFT: the restored Gran Teatre del Liceu.
BELOW RIGHT: strolling on the Rambla.

Felipe V built a citadel in this park in reply to Barcelona's long and bitter resistance in the siege of 1714. Over 1,000 houses were torn down in the waterfront district known as the Barri de la Ribera to make way for the fortress, which became a focal point of subsequent anti-centralist resentment. It was razed in 1888 and became an attractive and popular city park, home to the **Zoo**, the museus de Zoologia and Geologia, and the Hivernacle, an elegant tropical greenhouse.

Map on page 248-9

La Rambla and the port

Barcelona's famous **Rambla**, its lively, mile-long pedestrian thoroughfare, has something for everyone. Originally a seasonal riverbed, the Rambla runs from Plaça Catalunya to the Columbus monument at the port, and now extends across a wooden walkway, the Rambla del Mar, to the Maremàgnum shopping and leisure complex (including the Aquarium and IMAX cinema), somewhat ironically called the Port Vell (Old Port).

At the top of the Rambla is Café Zurich, rebuilt in El Triangle shopping centre, a legendary place to have coffee and meet friends. The section of Rambla at **Font de les Canaletes**, around a cast-iron drinking fountain, is a traditional gathering point for soccer enthusiasts passionately debating the fortunes of Barcelona's *fútbol* club. Turning off the Rambla at Carrer Bonsuccés, you'll come to the impressive white slab of the new **Museu d'Art Contemporani** ⓫ (MACBA; Wed–Mon 11am–7.30pm, closed Sun pm; entrance fee), with its large abstract works, sculpture and installations. Next door is the CCCB (Centre for Contemporary Culture) in the beautifully restored Casa de la Caritat, a former orphanage. The next section, the **Rambla dels Estudis**, has the renovated **Mare Déu Betlem** ⓬ church on the right and, on the left, the **Palau Moja** ⓭, an 18th-century palace now used for exhibitions and a Generalitat bookshop.

The **Rambla de las Flors** or **Rambla de Sant Josep** is the next section of the main promenade, lined with flower stalls and overlooked by the **Palau de la Virreina** ⓮ and the **Boqueria** ⓯ market. The 18th-century Virreina Palace houses the city's cultural information centre, booking office and an exhibition space. The Boqueria is Barcelona's largest market, covered by a high-roofed, steel-girdered hangar. The fruits and vegetables, the fresh iodine aroma of the seafood and the busy din of the marketplace, with its marble-countered bars, make it one of the city's most exhilarating places to visit. Ramón Casas, Catalonia's first Impressionist painter, is said to have discovered his best model and, subsequently, his wife among the beautiful flower-sellers of the Rambla.

The **Rambla del Centre** or **Rambla dels Caputxins** begins at the small square – which has a pavement mosaic by Joan Miró – in front of Barcelona's opera house, the **Gran Teatre del Liceu** ⓰ (1862), destroyed by fire in 1994 but reopened in 1999. The Café de l'Opera opposite is a popular meeting spot. Just off the Rambla on Carrer Nou de la Rambla is Gaudí's magnificent **Palau Güell** ⓱ (guided tours Mon–Sat 10.15am–4.30pm; entrance fee). This palace (1890), with its mighty balcony, is one of the finest works that Gaudí constructed for his patron, Count Güell. Gaudí was also responsible for the interior decoration; the wooden and metal decorations are particularly impressive.

Back on the Rambla is the Hotel Oriente, located in one of the few surviving former convents that once lined this side of the Rambla. It was originally the Franciscan Sant Bonaventura convent. The **Rambla de Santa Mònica** is the next and final part of the Rambla, extending from the entrance to Plaça Reial down to the port. The Plaça Reial, with its palm trees and uniformly porticoed 19th-century facades, is one

BELOW: the Boqueria market.

of Barcelona's most appealing spots, sunny by day and buzzing at night. The bars and restaurants tucked in under the columns are picturesque places for refreshments but beware the pickpockets. The bottom of the Rambla is flagged by one of the city's most famous landmarks, the **Monument a Colom** ⑱ (Columbus Monument), designed by Gaietà Buïgas for the Universal Exhibition of 1888. A lift takes visitors up to the top of the 60-metre (200-ft) column. This was the former landing point for the city; today small tour boats – called *golondrinas* (swallows) – explore the port while larger ones go to the Olympic port.

At the end of the Rambla is the excellent **Museu Marítim** ⑲ (open daily 10am–7pm; entrance fee), in the vast Gothic shipyards that once turned out 30 war galleys at a time. The exhibits include models, documents, galleon figures, maps and nautical instruments. The centrepiece is a life-size replica of the *Galera Real*, the flagship of the Christian fleet that under Don John of Austria defeated the Turks at the Battle of Lepanto in October 1571. The cafeteria is a pleasant spot. The *Santa Eulàlia*, a sailing vessel dating from 1918 and part of the museum, is afloat nearby in the Port Vell (daily visits, closed Mon).

The Rambla continues over a walkway, so you can stroll all around the **Port Vell**, or the Maremàgnum leisure complex. Apart from its shops and restaurants, **L'Aquàrium** is great for kids (9.30am–9pm). On the adjacent quay is the Palau de Mar, with restaurants downstairs and the **Museu d'Història de Catalunya** ⑳ (Tues–Sat 10am–7pm, Sun and hols am only; entrance fee) above. Opened in 1996, this state-of-the-art museum takes you from Catalan prehistory to 1980, with hands-on exhibits that will appeal especially to children. Information panels are mostly in Catalan but this shouldn't put you off trying your hand at a medieval joust or experiencing the terror of a civil war air-raid.

BELOW: the Rambla de Mar at the modernised Port Vell.

Gaudí's Barcelona

Few architects have marked a city as Gaudí has Barcelona. Born in nearby Reus in 1852, Antoni Gaudí i Cornet created revolutionary forms that coincided with the Art Nouveau or *modernisme* artistic movements. For more information on the *modernisme* movement, *see pages 264–265*. The young Gaudí's work can be found in Josep Fontseré's Cascada in the Ciutadella Park where, as a student, he designed the rocks of the cascade. The Plaça Reial lampposts are also early Gaudí products. His 1889 house, **Casa Vicens**, in the **Gràcia** neighbourhood (24–26 Carrer de les Carolines), was his first major project and the debut of totally polychromatic architecture. Gaudí's most important works in Barcelona are Güell Park, Casa Batlló, Casa Milà (also known as La Pedrera) and, of course, his extraordinary temple of the Sagrada Família.

Map on page 248–9

Parc Güell (daily 10am–8pm) was commissioned by the Barcelona financier Eusebi Güell as a garden suburb above Gràcia. Between 1900 and 1914 Gaudí designed a covered market, a large central square, a series of paths across the side of the mountain and the plots for houses; only two were finally built, one of which houses a small museum – the **Casa-Museu Gaudí** (open with park; entrance fee); Gaudí lived in it himself for 20 years. The wall surrounding the park, decorated with a ceramic mosaic, is the first notable feature of Güell Park, followed by the two houses near the entrance with their bizarre shapes, multi-coloured roofing and wild, mushroom-like towers.

The market is known as the Sala de les Cent Columnes (Hall of the Hundred Columns). There are actually 86 Doric columns supporting an undulating ceiling decorated with mosaics. The central square is surrounded by an ingeniously decorated serpentine bench which uses a wide range of found objects, tiles and rubble, all spontaneously mixed and built into the ceramic finish. A pathway winds up the mountainside giving panoramic views of the city.

Casa Milà ㉑ (daily 10am–8pm; entrance fee) and **Casa Batlló ㉒** (Mon–Sat 9am– 2pm, Sun till 8pm; entrance fee) are houses on the **Passeig de Gràcia** in the Eixample. Casa Batlló (at No. 43) forms part of the famous "Illa de la Discòrdia" (block of discord), so named for the contrasting architectural styles of the three neighbouring buildings designed by the city's greatest 19th-century architects. Apart from Gaudí's Casa Batlló, there is Domènech i Montaner's 1905 Casa Lleó Morera at No. 35 and Puig i Cadafalch's 1900 Casa Ametller at No. 41 (the centre of the "Ruta del Modernisme", which offers discounts to visit key modernist sites). Casa Milà, an apartment block at No. 92, is a more natural fantasy by Gaudí – repetitions of sandcastle waves, shadows and elaborate wrought-iron balustrades. Even the mouldings, the door knobs and the window casings of the apartments were designed or inspired by Gaudí. A visit here includes the "Espai Gaudí" exhibit, the spectacular rooftop and "El Pis", a flat decorated in the style of the era.

Round the corner at Carrer d'Aragó 255 is another astonishing building, this time designed by Domènech i Montaner between 1881 and 1886. Since 1990 it has housed the **Fundació Antoni Tàpies ㉓** (Tues–Sun

BELOW: chimneys of Gaudí's La Pedrera.

10am–8pm; entrance fee), set up by the artist himself to promote modern art and culture. Some of Tàpies' own abstract works, which are noted for their use of innovative new materials such as sand, rubbed marble and varnish as well as iron and concrete, are displayed here along with works by other modern artists. There is a shop at the entrance, selling books on Tàpies and his work.

At Diagonal No. 373 is Puig i Cadafalch's **Casa Quadras**. Built for Barón de Quadras in 1904, it has been beautifully adapted and modernised to become **Casa Asia** ㉔ (Tues–Sat 10am–8pm, Sun 10am–2pm; free), a cultural centre to link Spain with Oriental countries. It holds exhibitions and conferences and has a restaurant.

El Temple Expiatori de la Sagrada Família ㉕ (daily 9am–6pm, to 8pm in summer; entrance fee), on the north side of the Avinguda Diagonal, was begun in 1882 as a neo-Gothic structure under the direction of Francesc P. Villar. In 1883 Antoni Gaudí took over, completed the crypt and designed an enormous project that would reach a height of over 150 metres (500 ft).

Gaudí worked on the Sagrada Família until his death in 1926. Conceived as a symbolic construction, the cathedral has three gigantic facades still being built: the Nativity facade to the east, the western side representing Christ's Passion and Death and the southern facade portraying Christ's Glory. The four spires of each facade symbolise the 12 apostles; the tower over the apse represents the Virgin Mary; the central spire (as yet unbuilt), dedicated to Christ the Saviour, is surrounded by four lesser towers representing the Evangelists: Matthew, Mark, Luke and John. The decorative sculpture and ornamentation covering the different elements of the structure are of extraordinary quality and density. Work is still in progress here, but much of the site can be visited.

BELOW: west facade of the Sagrada Família, with recent sculptures by Subirachs.

Notable in Gaudí's buildings is the extent to which the architect attempted to integrate the shapes and textures of nature. The influence of the peaks and heights of Montserrat *(see page 275)*, Catalonia's holy mountain near Barcelona, is certainly evident in the Sagrada Família. A deeply religious man and a mystic, Gaudí was struck by a trolley car at the age of 74. His appearance was so unassuming that he was unidentified for some time and died in paupers' accommodation at the Hospital de la Santa Creu, the early medieval hospital behind the Boqueria market. His body is buried in the crypt of the unfinished temple, which continues to grow around his tomb. Just beyond the Sagrada Família is Plaça de les Glòries Catalanes where Els Encants fleamarket takes place every Monday, Wednesday, Friday and Saturday morning. Nearby is the Plaça de les Arts, comprising the Teatre Nacional de Catalunya, designed by Barcelona architect Ricardo Bofill, and Rafael Moneo's concert hall L'Auditori.

Map on page 248–9

Pedralbes

From Glòries the Diagonal traverses the city to the upper part of town not far from the smart residential area of Pedralbes. The **Palau Reial de Pedralbes** was built for Alfonso XIII in 1925 and part of it houses the fine **Museu Ceràmica** and the **Museu de les Arts Decoratives** (Interior Design Museum; Tues–Sat 10am–6pm, Sun am only; combined entrance ticket). Both o ld and contemporary ceramic creations by Miró, Picasso and others are displayed in the stylish palace. A spectacular dragon wrought-iron gate by Gaudí on the road up to the right of the palace is a clue that this was all once part of the Güell farm estate. Continue past it to reach the beautifully preserved **Reial Monestir de Pedralbes** (Tues–Sun 10am–2pm; entrance fee), where early masterpieces from the collection of Baron Thyssen-Bornemisza are the icing on the cake in the lovely triple-tiered cloister. The bell tower, cloister and Sant Miquel Chapel are perfect examples of Catalan Gothic architecture.

Enjoy historic and contemporary ceramics at the Palau Reial de Pedralbes.

BELOW: cloister of the Reial Monestir de Pedralbes.

Along the road from Pedralbes is **Sarrià**, a small town swallowed up by the city, which has managed to maintain its special flavour, some of its peace and a sense of community. Near the station is the Plaçeta de Sant Vicens, a picturesque spot that still has the air of a village square.

On the south side of the Diagonal, below Pedralbes Palace, is the home of FC Barcelona, where visitors can see the trophies and view the pitch from the Presidential box. Designed in 1957 by Francesc Mitjans, **El Camp Nou** (Mon–Sat 10am–6.30pm and Sun am; entrance fee) has a capacity of 120,000 and is one of the most beautiful soccer stadiums in the world. Fútbol Club Barcelona, for 40 years of Francoism the *only* means of expressing Catalan nationalism, is a monolithic organisation with top professional and amateur teams competing for every amateur national championship from ice hockey to baseball.

Between here and the hill of Montjuïc is **Sants**. The area around Sants was one of several that benefited from the 1992 Olympic Games. The station was redesigned with the **Parc de l'Espanya Industrial** ❷⑥ nearby, where boats may be hired on the small

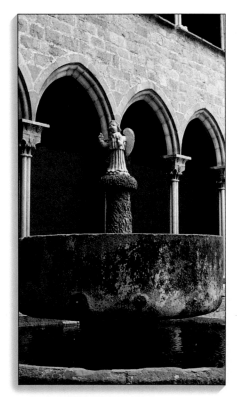

lake. Beyond it on the Carrer Aragó is another urban park, **Parc de Joan Miró** , dominated by the artist's colourful 22-metre (70-ft) statue *Woman and Bird*.

Gràcia, the district above the Diagonal at the top of the Passeig de Gràcia, has a young, radical and traditionally working-class tradition and ambience. Mercé Rodoreda's moving novel, *La Plaça del Diamant* (translated as *The Time of the Doves* by David Rosenthal), gives an excellent account of life in Gràcia during the 1930s and 1940s. La Torre de Rellotge (the clock tower) at Plaça de Rius i Taulet is one of the centres of life in Gràcia.

The 1992 Olympic site

Barcelona's seafront hill overlooking the port, **Montjuïc**, was the main site of the 1992 Olympic Games. Attractions include the **Castell de Montjuïc** ❷, which guards the harbour, its **military museum** (Tues–Sun 9.30am–7.30pm), the **Botanical Garden**, sports facilities, including Olympic swimming pools, the Grec (summer festival) amphitheatre and some of the city's key museums.

Start at **Plaça d'Espanya** and either walk up or take the escalator between the exhibition pavilions past La Font Màgica (Magic Fountain), which comes to life Thurs–Sun 8pm–midnight in summer and Fri–Sat 7–9pm in winter, towards the Palau Nacional. Here, the **Museu Nacional d'Art de Catalunya** ❷ (MNAC; Tues–Sat 10am–7pm, Sun am; entrance fee) houses a fine collection of Romanesque art. Most of the murals are from the Catalan Pyrenees and date from the 10th to the 12th century. The Gothic collection is superb. The **Museu d'Art Modern** (Tues–Sat 10am–7pm, Sun am only; entrance fee), formerly in the Parc de la Ciutadella, and now rehoused in the national museum, includes works by Casas, Miró, Nonell and Sert.

BELOW: the ultra-modern Olympic complex.

To the right of the Magic Fountain is Mies van der Rohe's restored **Pavilion** (daily 10am–8pm; entrance fee), built originally for the International Exhibition of 1929 like the Palau Nacional and most of Montjuïc's grand edifices. Opposite is the **Caixa Forum**, a wonderful cultural centre in a restored *modernista* factory, with a full programme of exhibitions and concerts (Tues–Sun 10am–8pm; free), as well as the Contemporary Art Collection of La Caixa Foundation. Most popular of the 1929 exhibition projects is the **Poble Espanyol** ❸ (open daily, closes 4am weekends; entrance fee), built to show the different architectural styles of all the regions of Spain. Today it is flourishing as a tourist centre with a good selection of bars and restaurants, and a *tablao* with a flamenco show. Fashionable now for its late nightlife, one of the city's most famous clubs, the Torres de Avila, is at the entrance gates, its interior the work of designers Alfredo Arribas and Javier Mariscal.

Behind the Palau Nacional are the principal Olympic sites: the brown sandstone **Estadi Olímpic** ❹, enlarged from Pere Domènech i Roure's 1927 original; and beside it on the Plaça Europa – a wide and elegant terrace overlooking the delta of the Llobregat and the sea – are the modern lines of Arata Isozaki's **Palau Sant Jordi**, one of the largest sports halls in the world.

On the way up to the hill-top castle is the **Fundació Joan Miró** ❷ (Tues–Sat 10am–7pm, until 9.30pm Thurs, Sun am; entrance fee). One of Europe's finest modern galleries, it was built in 1974 by the artist's friend Josep Lluís Sert. More than 150 paintings, sculptures and over 5,000 drawings are on display in the light, airy rooms, covering each of the artist's surrealist creative periods. Works from Miró's contemporaries can also be seen here, and special exhibitions are devoted to leading modern artists.

"The Hunter" by Joan Miró.

Hill-top spectacular

Barcelona's other hill, **Tibidabo**, the highest point of the Collserola hills behind the city, derives its name from the Devil's temptation of Christ as reported by Saint Matthew: *Haec omnia tibi dabo si cadens adoraberis me* (I will give you this if you adore me). Catalans say that the view from the 518-metre (1,700-ft) peak, towering over the city of Barcelona on one side and looking out over the interior of Catalonia to the north and west, was the most diabolical temptation imaginable. Part of the charm of a visit to Tibidabo is the process of getting there. At the foot of Avinguda Tibidabo, take the old Tramvia Blau (blue tram) to an excellent restaurant called La Venta, where the funicular to the summit departs. The nearby Museu de la Ciència is temporarily closed for major refurbishment, but promises to reopen as a stimulating science museum well worth visiting.

The **Temple Expiatori de Sagrat Cor** (Church of the Sacred Heart), the Hotel Florida and the popular amusement park are points of interest at the top of Tibidabo, as well as the magnificent panorama. The tremendous views of the city and the Mediterranean on one side, the fields of Catalonia and the jagged peaks of Montserrat *(see page 275)* on the other and, to the north, the snowcaps of the Pyrenees are a tempting display of the city's and Catalonia's riches. ❑

BELOW: thrills and spills at the Parc d'Atraccions.

THE FANTASTIC VISION OF ANTONI GAUDÍ

Antoni Gaudí's amazing buildings in Barcelona established him as the most original European architect in the early years of the 20th century

Antoni Gaudí (1852–1926) was born in Reus, Catalonia, the son of a coppersmith, and spent almost all his career in Barcelona. He was a patriotic Catalan and is said to have insisted on using the Catalan language even when talking to the King of Spain. The other major forces that shaped his life were a devotion to his work and a devout Christian faith. In 1878 he graduated from the Escuela Superior de Arquitectura, Barcelona, and soon afterwards met Eusebi Güell (1847–1918), a wealthy industrialist and Catalan nationalist who became his main patron, commissioning the Parc Güell *(above)* and other works.

A BIZARRE STYLE

Gaudí's work was influenced by various sources, including Gothic and Islamic architecture, and it has features in common with the Art Nouveau style fashionable at the time. However, his buildings have a sense of bizarre fantasy that sets them apart from anything else in the history of architecture. Walls undulate as if they were alive, towers grow like giant anthills, columns slant out of the vertical, and surfaces are encrusted with unconventional decoration, including broken bottles.
Gaudí died after being hit by a trolley bus. He cared so little for material success that – in spite of his great reputation – he was mistaken for a tramp and taken to a paupers' ward in hospital.

▷ **RAISING THE ROOF**
The undulating roof of the Casa Batlló, with its overlapping scale-like tiles, has been compared to the writhing of a dragon.

◁ **VIBRANT DECORATION**
Richly coloured ceramic decoration in playful, abstract designs typifies Antoni Gaudí's work at Parc Güell.

△ PARC GÜELL

The Parc Güell is part of a garden suburb that Gaudí worked on for his patron Eusebi Güell from about 1900 to 1914 but never completed.

▽ COLOURED FACADE

Gaudí used blue-green ceramic material on the facade of the Casa Batlló; the artist Salvador Dalí compared it to "the tranquil waters of a lake."

RESIDENTIAL BUILDINGS

In 1904–06 Gaudí remodelled a house for José Batlló y Casanovas, a Barcelona textiles manufacturer. The house had been built in the 1870s and was elegant but unremarkable. Gaudí completely transformed the exterior, adding an extra storey, topping it with a spectacular roof, and adorning the windows with flowing frames and balconies. Inside the house, the subtle interplay of forms continues *(above)*. Immediately after the Batlló house, Gaudí designed an apartment block (1906–10) for Don Pedro Milà, Batlló's partner. The Casa Milà has been aptly nicknamed "*la pedrera*" (the quarry) because the curving facade looks like a strange cliff-face. The sense of movement and fantasy continues on the roof, where the chimneys and ventilation stacks are a riot of exuberant shapes – see the example below.

◁ SLOW EVOLUTION

Gaudí began work on his masterpiece, the Sagrada Familia (Holy Family), in 1883. The huge church remains unfinished, though roofing is almost complete.

▽ DRAGON GUARDIAN

The dragon gate linking two entrance lodges (1884–88) for Eusebi Güell's estate in the upper part of Barcelona is one of Gaudí's finest pieces of ironwork.

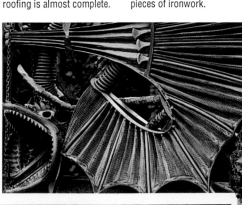

CATALONIA

Covering the area from the Pyrenees in the north to the Mediterranean in the east and the Ebre valley in the southwest, this region offers diverse scenery and attractions

Map on page 268

Madrid

Catalonia appears to have everything: rocky coasts, sandy beaches, lush plains, steppe, foothills and high sierra, all within a couple of hours of the major European metropolis of Barcelona *(see pages 251–263)*. There are historic cities and towns, tiny fishing villages, mountain hamlets, some 1,000 Romanesque chapels, Roman bridges, centuries-old stone farmhouses, vineyards, wheat fields, orchards, trout streams and wild boar – all in this one autonomous community. The presence of so much variety and density within such a small area, which has struggled to keep its own identity and language, is a continual surprise, even to longtime admirers of this corner of the earth.

Catalonia's 31,910 sq km (12,320 sq miles) comprise 6 percent of Spain's share of the Iberian peninsula, and are divided into four provinces, Barcelona, Girona, Lleida and Tarragona, plus 38 *comarques*, or counties. But the most obvious components of Catalonia for the visitor are the Mediterranean, the Pyrenees and the interior.

The Costa Brava

The term *Costa Brava* (sheer, bold, rocky coast) was originally coined by the Catalan journalist Ferran Agulló in 1905 and initially only referred to part of the rough coastline north of Barcelona. It is now taken to include all of the seafront that is in Girona Province, from **Blanes ❶**, which has one of the Costa Brava's longest beaches, all the way up to the French border. Also at Blanes is the **Jardí Botànic Mar i Murtra** (open daily; entrance fee), in a spectacular setting on the cliffs above the town, with a fantastic collection of Mediterranean and tropical plants. All along the coast, a series of *cales* or inlets, with small, intimate beaches, restaurants and hotels punctuate rocky cliffs rising out of the blue-green Mediterranean. Passenger boats ply their way from one inlet to another, picking up and dropping off travellers.

The hermitage of Santa Cristina, and the two beaches just below, lie between Blanes and **Lloret de Mar ❷**. Santa Cristina is the closest Costa Brava inlet to the city of Barcelona – barely an hour by coast road – and, though exquisite, can also be crowded. Above the populous and busy Lloret de Mar are the beaches at Canyelles and the Morisca inlets. Further north are the extraordinarily wild and unspoiled *cales* of Bona, Pola, Giverola, Sanlionç and Vallpregona. Close by, **Tossa de Mar ❸** has a pretty old town as well as a lovely beach. A little further north, **Canyet de Mar ❹** is a delicious inlet typical of this piney, rocky coastline. The coast road from Lloret de Mar to **Sant Feliu de Guixols ❺** or the local ferry boat are the best ways to see the breathtaking coastal scenery.

LEFT: the monastery at Montserrat.
BELOW: fishing boats along the Costa Brava.

Beautiful scenery can be enjoyed along the coast at Begur.

Further north are S'Agaro, the smart 1920s resort, and the more commercial **Platja d'Aro**, which has a big disco scene. **Palamós ❻** is the next main town along the coast. Founded in 1277, it had its heyday in the Middle Ages and is now a resort and an important cork-exporting and fishing harbour. From here on there are a series of beaches and *cales* that rank among the simplest and most attractive stretches on the Costa Brava. S'Alguer is a tiny fishing inlet with boat houses on the sand and natural rock jetties, and Tamariu is a particularly picturesque *cala*. Aiguablava's Parador Nacional is just over the top from Tamariu, although many maps don't show this road. Aiguablava's sheer cliffs high over the water are among the Costa Brava's most spectacular sights.

There is a superb view out across the sea from **Begur ❼**, a village 200 metres (650 ft) above the steep coastline. Distinctive features of Begur are its ruined 15th-century castle and its medieval watchtowers, which served as a defence against pirates. About 8 km (5 miles) south and a little inland, the Sunday markets at **Palafrugell ❽** are always festive and refreshing. **La Bisbal ❾** has held its Friday markets since 1322; earthenware products of all kinds, as well as the School of Ceramics, are traditional specialities. This area, El Baix Empordà, has a wealth of medieval villages to explore that can only be entered on foot.

Cultural centre

The city of **Girona ❿** (Gerona in Castilian), originally a Roman settlement, was completely surrounded by walls up until modern times. It was so regularly besieged that it became known as "the city of a thousand sieges". In its medieval district is one of Europe's biggest and best-preserved Jewish quarters, the *Call*, with a **Museum of Jewish History** (open daily; entrance fee). The former monastery of **Sant Pere de Galligants** lies to the north of the old town beside the Riu Galligants and now houses an **archaeological museum** (open Tues–Sat and Sun am; entrance fee). Across the river, the **Banys Arabs** (open Tues–Sun 10am–2pm, all day in summer) were built in 1295 not by Muslims but by Christians.

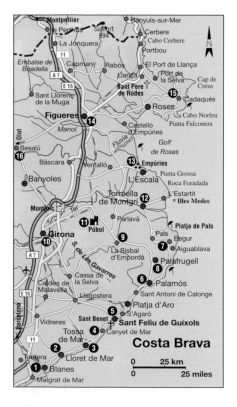

Girona's **Catedral** is famous for its single nave, the widest Gothic nave in the world. Construction of this superb basilica began in 1312 and took over four centuries to complete; several architectural styles, including Renaissance and Romanesque, have left their mark on it. Its **Museu Capitular** (open Tues–Sun; entrance fee), has a fine collection of ecclesiastical treasures, including medieval tapestries and manuscripts.

Dalí's legacy

The northernmost section of the Costa Brava stretches from the town of **L'Escala** across the bay of Roses and north to France. Heading to the coast on the C-66 from Girona, stop at the atmospheric Castell Gala Dalí in **Púbol ⓫** (open Tues–Sun 10.30am–5.15pm, mid-June–mid-Sept until 7.15pm, closed Nov–Mar; www.salvador-dali.org; entrance fee), a Gothic and Renaissance castle bought by Dalí for Gala, his adored wife. Inside, the rooms are furnished in Dalí's outlandish surrealist style. Dalí lived here between 1982 and 1984, but a fire that broke out almost killed him and he subsequently abandoned the castle.

Map on page 268

Heading north to **L'Estartit** you pass through **Torroella de Montgrí** ⑫, known for its summer music festival and dominated by the 300-metre (985-ft) rocky outcrop with the Castillo de Montgrí perched on top. The old part of the town is enclosed by a wall, and two of the former six gates still exist. Just north of L'Escala, the (mostly) Greek ruins at **Empúries** ⑬ (open daily 10am–6pm; entrance fee) are an impressive glimpse into the area's rich history. This important site includes the Greek temples of Jupiter Serapis and Asklepios, a market place and assembly hall, as well as the remains of two Roman villas and an amphitheatre. The nearby beaches are very attractive and ideal for children. **Roses** is an important fishing port across the bay and a popular resort.

Figueres ⑭ is the area's main town, known for its 18th-century **Castell de Sant Ferrán** and its role in the development of the *sardana* – Catalonia's national dance – but mostly for its **Teatre-Museu Dalí** (open Tues–Sun, also Mon Jul–Sept; entrance fee). This houses a startling collection of some of Salvador Dalí's most extraordinary creations. Born in Figueres in 1904, Dalí converted the former theatre building himself in the 1960s and early 1970s. Among the most memorable exhibits are the Sala de Mae West and the Cadillac car awash with water on the inside, both created for the museum, and the recently opened room to exhibit Dalí's extravagant jewellery. The museum is understandably popular, so be prepared to queue.

Back on the coast, **Cadaqués** ⑮ is a sparkling white fishing village heavily populated with artists and literati, especially in summer, while Dalí's house in neighbouring **Portlligat** can be visited (book in advance, tel: 972-677 500). **Cap de Creus**, a *parc natural* 8 km (5 miles) north, makes an invigorating trip, especially if the prevailing wind, known as the *Tramuntana*, is blowing. Nearby,

Dalí's emotional ties to Figueres were strong. He moved into a tower adjoining his theatre-museum in 1984, living there until his death in 1989. He is buried in the museum.

BELOW: white-washed houses along the seafront at Cadaqués.

Fortified bridge in medieval Besalú.

the fishing town of **Port de la Selva** remains unspoiled and attractive. On the hillside above is the magnificent Romanesque monastery of **Sant Pere de Rodes** (open Tues–Sun 10am–5pm, until 8pm in summer), now fully restored and very striking, set against the panorama of the bright coastal towns and the sweep of the Mediterranean.

A worthwhile trip from Figueres is to the medieval village of **Besalú** ⑯, 20 km (12 miles) further inland along the N-260. The village, now a national monument, is set beside the Riu Fluvià, and was once the capital of an enormous county covering present-day Barcelona and Girona provinces. It has many beautiful Romanesque buildings and a striking fortified bridge.

The Golden Coast

With its long sandy beaches, the coast south of Barcelona is known as the **Costa Daurada** (Costa Dorada in Castilian), the "Golden Coast". In contrast to the rugged Costa Brava with its picturesque coves and fishing boats, these beaches

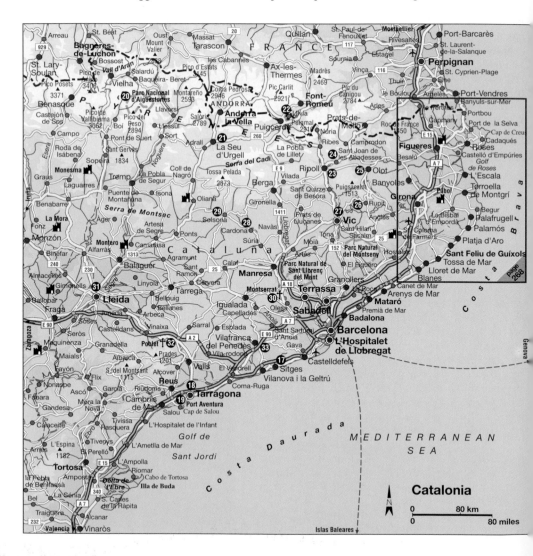

Maps: pages 268 & 270

and resorts have less personality, but there are still rewarding spots to explore. At the southernmost point is the Delta de l'Ebre where even in August you can walk for miles over strands with barely a glimpse of another human – vast and empty spaces of sand, sea, sky and sun.

Castelldefels is the closest beach to Barcelona, but it is worth going the extra 20 minutes to **Sitges** ⓱, a lively town with good beaches and restaurants. Its **Museu Cau Ferrat** (open Tues–Sun; entrance fee) has a fine collection of *modernista* objects donated by artist Santiago Rusiñol on his death in 1931.

Tarragona ⓲ is rich in Roman art and archaeology. It also has an impressive 12th-century **Catedral** and a provincial freshness which, all together, create a unique blend of past and present, town and country. Roman remains of the **Aqüeducte de les Ferreres** and the **Arc de Berà** are located on the city's outskirts. The **Passeig Arqueològic** (closed Sun pm and Mon), a walkway through the city's ancient walls, including massive boulders set in place in the 3rd century BC, is one of Tarragona's most spectacular sights. The ruins of the **Amfiteatre** (closed Sun pm and Mon), built near the beach in order to use the natural incline of the shore, are also well preserved. Tarragona's **Rambla**, an elegant, broad walkway down to the sea, is a key spot.

Salou is famed for package holidays and **Port Aventura** ⓳, part of the Universal Mediterranea theme park (open daily Apr–Oct; entrance fee). The thrills and spills have been extended to include an aquatic park and two hotels. The park has its own train station, with several services daily from Barcelona and Tarragona.

Cambrils is an excellent fishing port and marina known for superb seafood. **L'Ametlla de Mar** and **L'Ampolla** are good beaches to the south, but the most interesting area is the **Delta de l'Ebre**, known for its wildlife and rice paddies; El Trabucador and La Punta de la Banya are two of the wildest stretches of sand anywhere in Spain.

The Catalan Pyrenees

The sharp peaks and lush valleys of the Pyrenees provide opportunities for skiing, snowboarding, climbing, hunting, fishing and endless walking – the outdoors experience enhanced by the region's long history of human settlement. Medieval bridges span trout streams, and gourmet restaurants welcome skiers at the foot of ski lifts.

The **Val d'Aran** is Catalonia's northwest corner. "L'Aranès", the language of the valley, is a linguistic branch of Gascon French. **Baqueira-Beret**, frequented by Spain's royal family, is one of the country's top ski resorts. There are mountain trails and superb views to be found on foot or horseback in the summer, or on skis in winter. The peculiar mountain architecture of the Val d'Aran, like Alpine or Tyrolean high country design – steep, slate roofs – reflects the stone *cordillera* that surround these Pyrenean dwellings. The 12th-century church at **Bossòst** is one of the most extraordinary religious monuments of the valley. The 12th/13th-century church at **Salardú** houses the "Sant Crist de Salardú" crucifix, one of the treasures of Pyrenean art.

The best route east from the Val d'Arán would be to start south, passing through the **Túnel de Vielha** and

BELOW: Romanesque church in the Boí Valley.

Illuminated manuscript at the Museu Diocesà, La Seu D'Urgell.

driving down to the **Vall de Boí**, which connects to the **Parc Nacional d'Aigüestortes** ⑳ and Espot. The Boí Valley's set of churches is the most important collection of Romanesque architecture in the Pyrenees. Aigüestortes National Park, Lake Mauricio and the Vall d'Espot are all spectacular, as is the Vall d'Assua and its Llessui ski area, accessible from the town of **Sort**.

East from Sort is **La Seu d'Urgell** ㉑ and its important medieval **Catedral de Santa María** and **Museu Diocesà** (open Jun–Sept Mon–Sat am only; entrance fee), containing sculptures, altarpieces and illuminated manuscripts. The cathedral is an outstanding example of Lombard Romanesque architecture, notable for its purity of line and proportion. The eastern Pyrenees extend almost to the Mediterranean sea. **La Cerdanya** is an especially luminous east–west running valley, which history has divided between France and Spain.

Sun and snow

Solar energy projects, solar-powered bakeries, and year-round tennis are a few results of the Cerdanya's record number of sun-hours (2,500 annually). About 45 minutes from **Puigcerdà** are a dozen ski resorts in three countries: Spain, France and Andorra. Boar, chamois and wild mushrooms are hunted in the autumn, while in spring and summer the **Riu Segre** is one of Europe's premier trout streams. The hiking and camping on the upper slopes of the Eastern Pyrenees *(Pirineus Orientales)*, which reach heights over 2,900 metres (9,500 ft), are superb. **Llívia** ㉒, a Spanish enclave within French territory – thanks to the wording of the 1659 Treaty of the Pyrenees ceding certain "villages" to France (Llívia was a "town") – has ancient stone streets and buildings, Europe's oldest pharmacy, and one of the area's best restaurants, **Can Ventura**, located in a

BELOW: the rushing waters of the Riu Segre offer excellent trout fishing.

farmhouse in the centre of town. La Cerdanya abounds in things to do: skiing, hiking, horseback riding, hunting, fishing or just browsing through tiny villages. **Guils**, **Aja**, **Vilallovent** and **Bellver de Cerdanya** have retained the rustic Pyrenean flavour of the early mountain towns. La Cerdanya is open and lush, brilliant and broad compared to the Val d'Aran's steep, angular pitch.

Map on page 270

Cradle of Catalonia

Southeast of La Cerdanya, the *"cremallera"* (zipper) cogwheel train from Ribes de Freser up to Núria, one of Spain's earliest winter sports stations, is a spectacular excursion. Ribes is an easy daytrip by train from Barcelona. Just to the south, **Ripoll ㉓** is an important medieval capital. A Christian stronghold and starting point of the *Reconquista,* it is considered the *bressol* (cradle) of Catalonia. The carved portal of Ripoll's **Santa María** monastery church is among the best Romanesque works in Spain. Also in this valley, the Camprodon are a ski area at Vallter and two fine Romanesque churches at **Molló** and **Beget**.

Just east of Ripoll on the C-26 is the little town of **Sant Joan de les Abadesses ㉔**. The main attraction here is the **Iglesia de Sant Joan** (open daily, closed weekdays Nov–mid-Mar; entrance fee), which was originally part of a Benedictine monastery founded in the 9th century. The highlight is the Calvary on the main altar, a masterpiece of Romanesque carving dating to 1250.

La Garrotxa is an attractive volcanic area, good for cycling. Its capital, **Olot ㉕**, known for its 19th-century school of landscape artists, has a **volcanic museum** (open daily, closed Sun pm and Tues). Between Olot and Figueres is **Banyoles** with its large lake. Here the terrain smooths out into the moist and fertile lowlands of the Empordà.

BELOW: the richly decorated portico of Santa María in Ripoll.

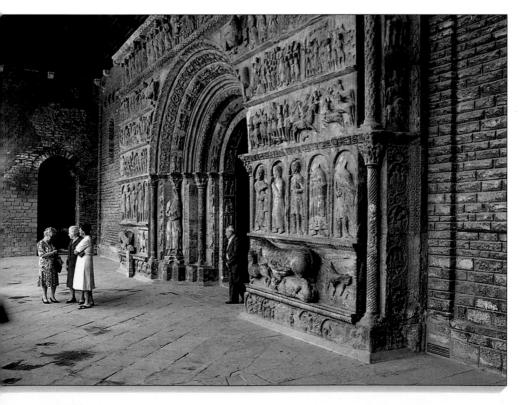

Lleida's Old Cathedral, looking more like a castle than a church, was used for many years as a military barracks.

BELOW: the Monestir de Poblet, which is once again run by monks.

The interior

Most Catalans take it for granted that one lifetime isn't enough to browse through everything the provincial towns of Catalonia have to offer. North from Barcelona is the Montseny mountain range – smooth, placid, massive heights from which there are excellent views out on to the coastal plain of Catalonia. **Rupit** ㉖, 20 km (12 miles) south of Olot in a beautiful landscape, is a picturesque medieval village with restaurants serving *Patata de Rupit*, potato stuffed with herbs, as well as duck, lamb and veal.

The roads around Barcelona

An hour north of Barcelona is the thriving provincial capital of **Vic** ㉗ with a beautiful central square, **La Plaça Major**, and a cathedral famous for the energetic murals of Catalan painter Josep María Sert. Sert's work was defaced by anti-clerical vandals at the beginning of the Civil War in 1936, but was restored by the painter himself before his death in 1945. Many of the faces are said to be satirical representations of fascist leaders, although Franco failed to catch on when he toured the cathedral. The newly built **Museu Episcopal** has a famed collection of medieval art (open Tues–Sat, Sun am only; entrance fee).

Cardona ㉘, 50 km (30 miles) to the west, is notable for its Parador Nacional at the site of the ancient castle and church that overlook the Vall de Cardoner. The **Salt Mountain**, a 150-metre (500-ft) hill of almost pure salt, is one of the most extraordinary geological curiosities in Catalonia; guided tours include a ride into the mountain. **Solsona** ㉙, further northwest, a town steeped in medieval mystery – silence, stone, tiny streets – is known for its **Catedral** and its **Museu Diocesà** (open Tues–Sun; entrance fee), where you can view local

Map on page 270

archaeological finds. The two main squares are typical of early provincial architecture. Solsona's charm, however, is the *feel* of the place – the sense of time, the serenity of its antique granite world. There's even a town crier, *el pregoner*, one of Europe's last, who can be heard chanting the town news daily.

The Black Virgin of Montserrat

Every visitor to Catalonia should see the sacred mountain of **Montserrat** ㉚ (tel: 93-877 7701; open daily), hear the boys' choir and visit its museum. The spectacular site is thrillingly reached by cable-car from the Aeri de Montserrat station (regular trains from Barcelona). A Catalan religious shrine of great power and mystery, during the Franco regime Montserrat performed the only marriage ceremony and celebrated the only Masses in the Catalan language. *La Moreneta*, Catalonia's beloved Black Virgin, presides over the church nestled among the natural stone spires that rise up from the valley floor.

Cava – *the Catalan answer to champagne.*

Lleida (**Lérida** in Castilian) ㉛, 75 km (45 miles) west of Montserrat, is an ancient city, perched on the edge of Spain's central plateau with a magnificent **Old Cathedral** (La Seu Vella), high on a hill above the old part of the city. **La Paeria** (the town hall), on the Carrer Major, and the Gothic **Hospital de Santa María**, with pretty, arcaded inner courtyards, are two of Lleida's best early structures. The church of **Sant Llorenç**, in a square of the same name, represents the transition from Romanesque to Gothic. The delicate, octagonal bell tower, 76 metres (250 ft) high, is particularly striking.

The **Monestir de Poblet** ㉜ (open daily, closed lunchtimes; entrance fee), 40 km (25 miles) north of Tarragona, was founded after the reconquest of Catalonia from the Muslims. Surrounded by a 1.8-km (1-mile) wall, the complex of buildings is more reminiscent of a secular royal residence than a monastic refuge. Ramón Berenguer IV, Count of Barcelona, completed his drive from Lleida, via the Segre and then the Ebro, to the sea and made the initial donation for the founding of the monastery in 1150. Surrounded by rough, austere country, Poblet reflects this severity in its sober, powerful architecture. A self-sufficient unit, the monastery has always controlled vast tracts of land. It was ransacked in 1835 but subsequently rebuilt.

BELOW: vineyard near Vilafranca.

Celebrating with wine

Vilafranca del Penedès ㉝, about 40 km (25 miles) west of Barcelona, is the centre of Catalonia's largest wine-producing region, the Penedès. Its famous *cava* is a champagne-like sparkling white wine – 90 percent of it made from grapes grown in nearby **Sant Sadurní d'Anoia**.

Vilafranca is a town with an aristocratic architectural presence and has plenty to offer visitors: its **Museu del Vi** (open Tues–Sat, closed lunchtimes except June–Aug, Sun am only; entrance fee) on Plaça Jaume I is one of the best wine museums in Europe. Also worth seeing at the right time of year is the *Fira del Gall* (fowl market) just before Christmas, and the *La Calçotada* feast in February – where new onions dipped in delicious *romesco* sauce are served. All of it accompanied by plenty of good *cava*, of course. ❑

ARAGÓN

The towns and cities of this little-known region offer a feast of Mudéjar architecture. In sharp contrast are the dramatic landscapes of the Parque Nacional de Ordesa

A ragón is known throughout Spain for the highest Pyrenees, the snowiest ski stations and as the home of the *jota*, the country's best-known folkloric music and dance. In winter, skiers race up the region's major roads in search of the perfect slopes in the Pyrenees, passing by Romanesque churches, villages that are dying from lack of attention and walled cities that hide wonders of *Mudéjar* architecture.

Home of kings

The Romans founded Caesaraugusta, known today as Zaragoza, in 25 BC. Not much evidence of their presence remains today. Aragón was invaded along with the rest of Spain by the Muslims in AD 711; resistance to the occupation began around 100 years later. In 1035, Ramiro I, the bastard son of Sancho III of the neighbouring kingdom of Navarre, inherited the kingdom of Aragón, which was united with Castile in 1469. At its height it included parts of France, the Balearic Islands, Naples and Sicily, and stretched as far south as the southeasterly region of Murcia.

Zaragoza was recaptured by the Christian armies at the orders of Alfonso I in 1118. But, despite the Reconquest, Christians and Muslims lived alongside one another for centuries; the Muslims who remained were responsible for the *Mudéjar* architecture characteristic of the region. At the beginning of the 16th century it is estimated the *moriscos*, Muslims living under Christian domination, comprised 16 percent of the region's population. But in 1502 all Muslims were ordered to convert or leave the country, and the definitive expulsion order made in 1609 by Felipe III ended the cohabitation.

Although Fernando II was from Aragón (his marriage to Isabel of Castile in 1469 marked the unification of Spain), he was not overly sensitive to the social realities of his home region. Ignoring the protests of his lords, he imposed the Inquisition, with the unpleasant result of having his Inquisitor-General murdered in the Seo Cathedral in Zaragoza in 1485. The swords supposedly used to commit the crime can be seen today next to the altar.

Geographically, Aragón is divided into three areas that roughly correspond to its three provinces: the Pyrenees (Huesca), the Ebro River Valley (Zaragoza) and the Iberian mountains (Teruel). It is the least densely populated of Spain's regions.

Zaragoza province

There are fine examples of *Mudéjar* architecture throughout the province of Zaragoza. **Tarazona ❶**, 72 km (45 miles) northwest of the capital, is known as

LEFT: Pyrenean peaks in the Parque Nacional de Ordesa.
BELOW: slate roof typical of the Aragón region.

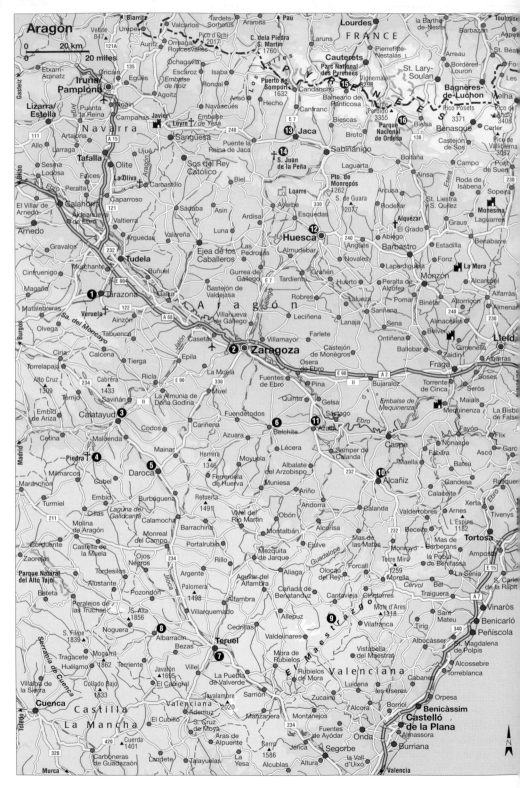

"The *Mudéjar* City" and offers a spectacle of Islamic and Sephardic history. The cloisters of the 12th-century brick-domed **Catedral** (closed for restoration), have some particularly fine Moorish tracery. The twisting, cobbled streets, crossed by *Mudéjar* arches, of the old Jewish district (located behind the Palacio Episcopal) are worth exploring on foot. Not to be missed are the 8th-century **Iglesia de Santa María Magdalena** and the marvellously decorated **town hall**.

The capital of the region, **Zaragoza ❷**, has a population of around 615,000. The visitor will find few monuments indicating the city's past grandeur since time, neglect and two terrible sieges suffered during the Napoleonic Wars (1808–09) destroyed a great deal. The old part of town, on the south bank of the Río Ebro, is the place to head for first – it contains most of the sights and plenty of hotels as well as lively bars and restaurants.

Zaragoza has two important religious structures, the **Catedral de San Salvador**, known as **La Seo** (open daily, entrance fee), which was consecrated in 1119 on the site of the old mosque, and the basilica, known as **El Pilar** (open daily), built in honour of Spain's patron saint, the Virgin of Pilar, who supposedly appeared there on top of a pillar to St James in AD 40. The Parroquieta chapel's *Mudéjar* wall and ceiling, the Gothic altarpiece and the baroque choir stalls are the cathedral's most outstanding features.

Francisco Goya y Lucientes, born in Fuendetodos in 1746, rose to become court painter to Carlos IV.

The Basílica de Nuestra Señora del Pilar, with its 11 domes, is the most distinctive feature of the city. The present building, dating from the 17th and 18th centuries, is the third on the site. Massive pillars split the church into three bays, some of the frescoes on the cupolas being the work of Goya. But the focal point is the Lady Chapel. There you will see the legendary marble pillar that supports the much-venerated Virgin, a tiny wooden image encrusted in silver, whose rich mantle is changed every day. The altarpiece in the basilica is alabaster. The day of El Pilar, 12 October, a national holiday, is attended by lavish celebrations in Zaragoza, with city processions of cardboard giants.

BELOW: rooftops of El Pilar cathedral.

Moorish pleasure palace

The **Aljafería** (open daily,, closed Sun pm) to the west of the old town has been fully restored. It was first built in the 11th century by the ruling Islamic king and could well have been taken from the *Arabian Nights*, according to testimonies of the time. The Catholic Monarchs transformed part of the palace into their headquarters – later used by the Inquisition – and then as an army barracks in the 19th century. Ferdinand and Isabel's throne room, with its remarkable ceiling, and the Moorish chapel are the best-preserved parts of the interior. Outside, Santa Isabel's courtyard has some splendid *Mudéjar* arches.

The **Museo Camón Aznar** (open Tues–Sun; entrance fee), on Calle de Espoz y Mina, has a large collection of Spanish art, but the main draw are the fine etchings by Goya on the top floor of the building. Goya was born in the village of **Fuendetodos**, 50 km (30 miles) directly south of Zaragoza. The house where he was born is now a **museum** (open Tues–Sun; entrance fee), after being abandoned for years. The rooms are furnished in a simple style appropriate to the period.

Calatayud , 60 km (35 miles) southwest of Zaragoza on the N-II, is justly famous for its *Mudéjar* towers, the best example of which rises above the Colegiata de Santa María. Nearby is the **Monasterio de Piedra** ❹ (open daily; entrance fee), founded by Alfonso II in 1195 and now an oasis of gardens, lakes and waterfalls around a 12th-century Cistercian monastery (now a hotel).

Also in the southern part of Zaragoza province is the beautiful but rather neglected town of **Daroca** ❺. Surrounded by nearly 3 km (2 miles) of walls with more than 100 towers, Daroca appeared in the annals of the Greek voyagers. The walls are now in ruins, although some of the towers have been restored. Visitors who want to understand Spain's more recent history would be well advised to visit **Belchite** ❻, 40 km (25 miles) southeast of Zaragoza. This town was the site of one of the most ferocious battles of the Civil War, and its ruins have been preserved as a reminder of the horrors of war. A new town, completed in 1954, was built alongside the original devastated site.

Lovers of Teruel

Of the three Aragonese provinces, Teruel is the least known, and the capital city of **Teruel** ❼ has the smallest population of all Spain's provincial capitals. It is a province in which *Mudéjar* architecture abounds, both in the capital itself and in towns so far off the beaten track that most Spaniards don't know they exist.

The **Catedral** (open daily; entrance fee) is justly famous for its remarkable ceiling, a masterpiece of the 14th century in which daily life in the Middle Ages is depicted in portraits painted on wood. Another outstanding *Mudéjar* monument is the **Iglesia de San Pedro** on the eastern side of the former Jewish quarter. The church has an adjoining funerary chapel (open daily; entrance

BELOW: restored towers in Daroca's medieval walls.

fee) known for housing the tombs of the Lovers of Teruel, a tragic couple immortalised in poems and plays, whose fame in Spain exceeds that of Romeo and Juliet. A relief by Juan de Avalos depicts the lovers and, if you peer into the tomb, you can see the mummified bodies. Diego Marcilla and Isabel Segura were in love, the story goes, but their parents opposed the marriage. Diego left to make his fortune, and thus endear himself to his lover's father. He came home in 1217 a rich man, only to find his beloved walking down the aisle with another. He died of a broken heart the next day and Isabel kissed the cadaver and passed on to a better world with her Diego.

Visitors should also stop to admire the twin *Mudéjar* towers of San Martín and El Salvador, supposedly the result of a contest between two Muslim architects in love with the same woman. The winner won his love and the loser (who built San Martín) jumped off the tower.

Of all the mountain villages in Teruel, **Albarracín** ❽ is the best preserved. Located 30 km (18 miles) west of Teruel, it is a place to stroll through, admiring the town walls, the towers, the harmony between nature and man-made structures and the architectural magic of a fortified town rising high above a river.

Moving southeast of Teruel, to the harsh mountains and spectacular gorges of **El Maestrazgo** ❾, stop at **Mora de Rubielos** to see its immense castle, built between the 13th and 15th centuries, and the nearby **Rubielos de Mora** (they shouldn't be confused). The truth is that nearly any road through the mountains of Teruel will lead to *Mudéjar* towers, castles, city walls or outstanding churches. **Alcañiz** ❿, to the northeast of Teruel, is famed for its castle, with murals depicting the history of the Calatrava Order, and the Colegiata de Santa María, with its great baroque portal. North of Alcañiz, towards Zaragoza on the N-232, is **Azaila** ⓫, which has been declared a national monument due to the discovery of an ancient Celtic-Roman *castro* (hill fort).

Romanesque region

If the dominant architectural or historical motif in Zaragoza is *Mudéjar*, moving north to the province of Huesca the traveller is surrounded by Romanesque buildings. The stream of pilgrims on their way to Santiago during the Middle Ages encouraged the construction of churches from Catalonia to Galicia, of which Jaca's cathedral *(see page 282)* is one of the most important. In addition to offering literally hundreds of well-preserved examples of the Romanesque style, Huesca is a paradise for hikers, skiers, walkers and climbers.

The capital of the province is **Huesca** ⓬, whose age of splendour was the 13th century. Pedro IV founded the University of Huesca in the 14th century, but it was abolished in 1845, by which time the city had been reduced to the status of an insignificant provincial capital. Huesca's **Catedral** (open daily; entrance fee), dates from the 15th and 16th centuries, built on the earlier foundations of the old mosque. Of particular interest is the alabaster Renaissance altarpiece by Damián Forment. Nearby is the **Palacio Municipal** (City Hall; open Mon–Fri; entrance fee), built in 1578, with a mural depicting the story of

Map on page 278

Map on page 278

TIP

To explore El Maestrazgo, which straddles southern Aragón and Valencia, you'll need to hire a car – few buses serve the area.

BELOW: tomb in the Iglesia de San Pedro, with the barely touching hands of the Lovers of Teruel.

Saint's statue adorning Jaca cathedral.

BELOW: cathedral nave, Jaca.

"The Bell of Huesca", one of the bloody legends of Spanish history: Ramiro II, a former monk who ruled Aragón in the 12th century, was disturbed by his nobles' refusal to submit to his rule. After consulting with the abbot of his former monastery, Ramiro summoned the nobles to a banquet to celebrate the casting of a new bell that the king said would be heard throughout Aragón. When they arrived Ramiro had them all decapitated, piling up their heads in the form of a large bell, and order was restored.

The other major city in the province is **Jaca** ⓭, whose **Catedral** is one of Spain's treasures of Romanesque architecture. The beautifully restored **Museo Diocesano** (open Tues–Sun; entrance fee) contains a remarkable collection of Romanesque frescoes. **La Ciudadela**, a fortress built by Felipe II, is currently under the jurisdiction of the army but is open for guided tours.

Soon after the kingdom of Aragón was established, King Sancho Ramirez founded the **Monasterio de San Juan de la Peña** ⓮ (open daily; entrance fee), which became the point of religious inspiration for the Christian Reconquest campaign. Located 27 km (17 miles) southwest of Jaca, the monastery is wedged between enormous boulders and under a sheer rock cliff. It contains an extraordinary Romanesque cloister and a 10th-century church, the monks' sleeping quarters and the Nobles' Pantheon, which houses the tombs of early Aragonese kings.

West of Jaca are **Los Valles**, a series of valleys that eventually lead to Navarre and that maintain the old architectural, linguistic and cultural traditions of Aragón. The villages of **Hecho** and **Ansó** feature houses with odd-shaped chimneys distinguishing one town from another, and the windows are outlined in white. Another showcase town worth a detour in northwest Aragón is **Sos del**

Map on page 278

Rey Católico, birthplace of Fernando II (the "Catholic King") and one of the Five Towns (Cinco Villas) honoured by Felipe V for their support during the War of the Spanish Succession. The entire town is a monument of grand stone mansions and quaint, flower-decked houses. The frescoed **Iglesia de San Esteban** and the Gothic **Lonja** (exchange building) are worth tracking down. The town's Parador makes a comfortable touring base.

Mountaineering

North of Hecho is the Los Valles National Reserve, and directly north of Jaca is the **Puerto de Somport** marking the border with France and the starting point for many trails into the high country. To the northeast of Jaca lies the **Viñamala National Reserve**. To get there you pass through the towns of Sabiñánigo and Biescas, as well as a host of tiny towns along the C-136 road that contain Romanesque churches and usually little else. Branching off the road leads you to **Balneario de Panticosa** ⓕ, with a lake, hotel facilities and stores where you can stock up on provisions, buy a trail map and head off into the wild. The highest peaks in this area are over 3,000 metres (9,800 ft).

Further to the east is one of Spain's most famous national parks, **Ordesa** ⓖ, part of a chain of reserve areas that lead hikers across the border to France or east into the Catalonian Pyrenees. The park is a fabulous wilderness of gorges, forests, waterfalls and dramatic cliffs. Many species of flora and fauna thrive here, including the sarrio (Pyrenean chamois). The weather here can be unpredictable – the best time for hikers is between June and September, but violent thunderstorms are a hazard. In winter the ski resorts of **Candanchú** and **Canfranc**, on the road from Jaca to Somport, and the towns of **Panticosa** and **Formigal** are all popular. ❑

BELOW: the strategically located Monasterio de San Juan de la Peña.

Map on page 288

Madrid

THE BASQUE COUNTRY

Peaceful green river valleys set against dour peaks
form the backdrop to the lively fishing ports, inviting resorts and
sandy beaches of the Basque Country

Mountain chains, like "bones showing through skin" as one historian has described them, extend along the Bay of Biscay west of the Pyrenees, separating much of the rolling farmland of the Basque Country from the rest of Spain. In this clearly defined geographical area, known locally as Euskadi, the Basques and their anthropologically mysterious ancestors have lived since the end of the last Ice Age.

A world apart

Basques live on either side of the Pyrenees; in the French region of Pyrénées-Atlantiques, Spanish Navarre and the three Spanish provinces that have made up the autonomous Basque community since 1980: **Guipúzcoa** and **Vizcaya** on the coast and landlocked **Álava** on the edge of the Iberian *meseta*. In addition to possessing physical characteristics that have led some anthropologists to believe they are directly descended from Cro-Magnon Europeans, the Basque language, Euskera, sets this people apart from their French and Spanish countrymen.

Of Western Europe's living languages, only Euskera does not belong to the Indo-European family. It has fascinated linguists since the Middle Ages, when scholars traced it to Tubal, the grandson of Noah who settled the peninsula after The Flood. More recently, philologists comparing the Basque words for axe, *aitzor*, and stone, *aitz* have raised the possibility that the language dates from a time when tools were made of stone.

Basque was mostly preserved among rural families during the Franco years and possesses a very small written literature. It is now taught along with Castilian in Basque schools and at night courses, although it takes the average adult some 500 hours of study to be able to carry on a conversation. Road signs in Basque can confuse visitors, thus Donostia stands for San Sebastián, Bilbo for Bilbao, and Gasteiz (of Visigothic origin) for Vitoria.

Indomitable

Fiercely proud of their ancient past, Basques like to say they have never submitted to outside conquerors, including Muslims and Romans. Guipúzcoa and Vizcaya possess prehistoric caves and dolmens, but are notably lacking in Roman and early-Christian remains. However, both the Romans and Christianity made inroads into the mountain strongholds, and the Basques' Catholicism has stood firm ever since. They are considered the most religious people in Spain. Appropriately, Ignacio de Loyola, the warrior who founded the influential Society of Jesus or Jesuits,

PRECEDING PAGES:
the Valle de Atxarte
in Vizcaya.
BELOW: inline
skaters, Santander.

was born in this region, near Azpeitia, 52 km (32 miles) from San Sebastián (Donostia). On his saint's day, 31 July, large crowds flock to the monastery with its basilica topped by a lofty cupola.

To a certain extent it was religious feeling that brought the Basques into the 19th-century Carlist Wars. But, ironically, it was mainly to protect their *fueros* (local laws) that they chose what turned out to be the losing side in both the Carlist and the Civil wars, thus losing their independence. The terrorist incidents for which the Basque Country has become known since the 1970s are seen by radical separatists as a continuation of the struggle for the restoration of self-rule.

Relatively few non-Basques make a comprehensive tour of the interior of the region. Visitors typically spend the summer on the mild and misty Basque coast, as Spaniards and an increasing number of French have done since the 19th century, when the point of resort life was to rest in the shade.

Guipúzcoa

The smallest province on the peninsula and one of the most densely populated corners of Europe, **Guipúzcoa** has had close cultural connections with the other side of the Pyrenees since prehistoric times. More recently, the fortified Basque ports a few miles from the frontier have been easy targets for the French in wartime.

Eugenie de Montijo (1826–1920), daughter of a Spanish nobleman who fought on the French side in the Peninsular War and Empress of France after her marriage to Napoleon III, is credited with setting the style for summering on the Basque coast. Once she introduced the Emperor to Biarritz in the French Basque Country, other royals, including Queen Victoria, arrived. By the end of the 19th century, the Spanish and South American aristocracy had made **San Sebastián** (Donostia) ❶ their chosen summer residence.

BELOW: La Concha Beach, San Sebastián.

From this period date the **Casa Consistorial** (town hall), formerly the Gran Casino; the royal family's Tudor-style **Palacio Miramar**, dividing the two long curving beaches; and the high-style **Puente Zurriola** bridge over the canalised Río Urumea.

Although it is now a city of 182,000 with a diverse economy, San Sebastián is still one of the most beautiful resorts in Europe: elegant and cosmopolitan during the jazz and film festivals, favoured by the Spanish aristocracy – including the king – during the warm autumn months, but still humming with street life in the old town. If you happen to arrive in the morning, proceed to the efficient tourist bureau on Reina Regente, near the end of Puente de la Zurriola. The beaches lying beyond a windbreak of tamarisks on the elegant **Paseo de la Concha** will rarely be full. This would be a good time to take the inexpensive funicular or to drive to the top of **Monte Igueldo**, the westernmost of the wooded promontories overlooking the Bay of La Concha.

On 31 August, as the summer ends, a torchlight procession in the **Parte Vieja**, or Old Quarter, at the foot of Monte Urgull commemorates the virtual destruc-

San Sebastián is famed for its gourmet restaurants.

tion of San Sebastián during the Peninsular War. Among the surviving structures belonging to the old walled port are the cavernous 18th-century **Basilica of Santa María del Coro**, with its apsidal portal deeply recessed to protect the sculptures from hard winters and its graceful statue of the city's namesake in a niche; and the 16th-century Dominican monastery of **San Telmo** in the Plaza de Zuloaga. This has been converted into a wonderful museum (open Tues–Sun), devoted mainly to Basque culture and art but also including works by artists such as El Greco.

Part of the ethnographic collection is devoted to the history of the seafaring Basques. The Spanish colonisation of America depended partly on the skills of Basque navigators and shipbuilders with their long experience of deep-sea fishing. Other exhibits introduce *pelota*, the Basque national sport, and typical Basque cuisine, costume and customs. In this traditionally rainy country, the matriarchal kitchen and adjoining stable, reconstructed in the museum, became the most important rooms of the Basque farmhouse, the stone-and-timber

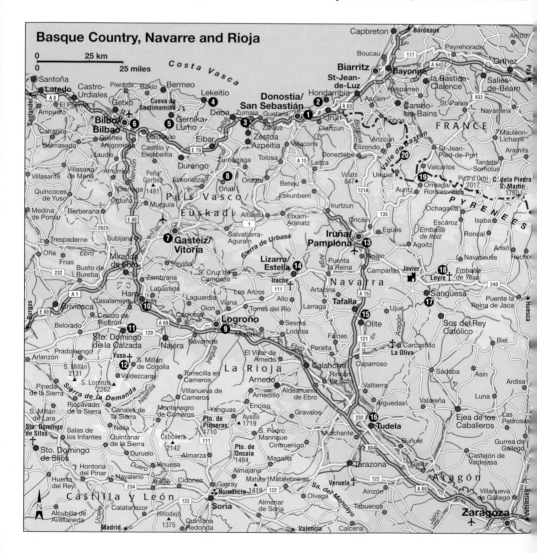

Basque Country, Navarre and Rioja

Map on page 288

caserío. The Fine Arts collection ranges from Hispano-Flemish to contemporary. Occupying a place of honour, the Basque painter Ignacio Zuloaga's best-known work shows three hearty Basque men enjoying a meal.

Eating clubs

Private, men-only gastronomic societies *(txokos)* were founded here in the Parte Vieja in the 1870s. Basque cookery, with its fresh vegetables, dairy products and fish from the Bay of Biscay, seasoned with subtle sauces, is generally acknowledged to be the best on the peninsula.

The neoclassical **Pescadería** (fish market), a short walk south of the Plaza de Zuloaga near the arcaded **Plaza de la Constitución**, has, appropriately, one of the grandest facades in the Parte Vieja. At the nearby market ask for Idiazabal, cheese from the long-haired Laxa sheep that has been cured and smoked, and *txakoli*, the thin white Basque wine drunk with shellfish.

The Basque coast

Northeast of San Sebastián, the fishing port and seaside resort of **Hondarribia** ❷ (Fuenterrabía in Castilian) lies just south of the border with France and, over the centuries, has consequently suffered many attacks by the French. Its charming old town, entered through the **Puerta Santa María**, has somehow survived and still has many old houses with splendidly carved wooden balconies. The town has a fine beach and excellent fish restaurants.

A pleasant way to see this stretch of coast is to drive west from San Sebastián all along the hilly coast of Guipúzcoa and Vizcaya, stopping whenever you feel like visiting one of the family beaches or enjoying a freshly caught fish dinner. Typical port resorts have at least one old church near the water, several good restaurants and sandy beaches. **Zarautz**, with its nice long beach, and **Getaria**, which has a smaller one, are two of the best-known producers of *txakoli*. This part of the coast may be the best place in Spain to order *chipirones en su tinta* (squid in its own ink) or *besugo* (sea bream).

In Getaria, formerly a whaling port, is a monument to Juan Sebastián Elcano, Magellan's Basque navigator, and skipper of the round-the-world voyage after Magellan was killed in the Philippines. Also born in Getaria was Cristobal Balenciaga (1895–1972), the widely respected and highly disciplined couturier.

Past Getaria is the pretty resort of **Zumaia** ❸, where the painter Ignacio Zuloaga's summer villa and studio, in a former convent, was turned into the excellent **Museo Zuloaga** (Carretera de San Sebastián, open Jan–Sept Wed–Sun; entrance fee) after his death. Zuloaga was an important collector, and the museum includes one of El Greco's many versions of Saint Francis receiving the stigmata; a painting by Morales il Divino; and two by Zurbarán, who came from a Basque family. After Zumaia the craggy shoreline of the **Cornisa Cantábrica** begins. Although it does not look far on the map, **Lekeitio** ❹, one of the most interesting ports on the Basque coast, is a good two-hour drive from San Sebastián. The 15th-century church at Lekeitio with its flying buttresses and

BELOW: surfing the waves at Getaria.

Gernika,
photographed
shortly after the air
raid in 1937.

baroque tower is a few yards from a pretty beach where, in the morning, you may see fishermen painting their boats, or groups of children being given swimming lessons. From Lequeitio it is only a short drive south to Gernika.

Gernika (Guernica)

The bustling modern market town of **Gernika-Lumo** ❺ is sacred to the Basques for its associations with their ancient tradition of self-government. At least since the early Middle Ages, their representatives met here to elect a council of leaders and witness the titular monarch's oath to uphold their *fueros*. An event of enormous consequence for today's Basques, the election of José Antonio Aguirre at the **Casa de Juntas** (open daily), the parliament building, in the 1936 election, revived this tradition. Members of his government were sworn in under the **Gernikako Arbola**, the symbolic oak of Gernika. (The original oak that had stood for centuries was evidently destroyed by the French in the Peninsular War. The present one, it is claimed, grew from the original tree's acorn or sapling.)

The declaration of an independent Basque state was met with swift retribution by the Nationalists under General Mola. Miraculously, the Casa de Juntas, the oak and the neighbouring **Iglesia de Santa María** (begun in the 15th century) survived the almost total destruction of Gernika on Monday 26 April 1937, one of the most infamous episodes of the 1936–39 Spanish Civil War.

Mondays, then as now, were market days and the narrow streets were crowded with farming families and refugees. A third of the civilian population was killed in the attack, and many more were wounded, when German aircraft dropped 50 tons of bombs, then flew low to shoot at the Basques fleeing into the fields.

BELOW: the
symbolic oak of
Gernika.

Caseríos in the hills were also bombed. "In the night these burned like candles", one of the dazed correspondents covering the war wrote in *The Times* of London. International outrage probably discouraged the use of such air attacks again in Spain.

The very word "Gernika" became synonymous with the horrors of war, symbolised in Picasso's famous painting *Guernica*, which now hangs in Madrid's Reina Sofía Museum. "General Franco's aeroplanes burned Gernika and the Basques will never forget it", predicted *The Times* correspondent. Repression under the Franco regime only stiffened resistance to domination by the central government and on the night of the dictator's death Basques danced in the streets. The 1979 Statute of Gernika finally gave the 2 million Basques autonomous government, although significant, sometimes violent, pressure continues for a greater degree of self-rule. Oddly enough, some of the most fervent Basque nationalists are young descendants of non-Basques who migrated to the region's industrial cities in Franco's time.

The Casa de Juntas is the only significant sight to see in Gernika and it is mainly visited for its symbolic importance. However, the room next door to the assembly chamber has a magnificent stained glass ceiling showing the Tree of Gernika, the various traditional economic activities of the Basque people and (round the edges) the most important

Map on page 288

monuments of Bizkaia province. There are also some interesting murals under the eaves of the Caja de Ahorros Municipal de Bilbao at the intersection of the Gran Vía and the Calle Adolfo Urioste (between the tourist bureau and the Casa de Juntas).

The castellated country house at Arteaga, 8 km (5 miles) to the north of here, where the Empress Eugenie spent part of her early life, is seen in one of the murals. Eugenie's castle is visible from the highway, but the principal attraction on the outskirts of Gernika-Lumo, to the northeast, is the **Cueva de Santimamiñe** (open Mon–Fri) and its prehistoric wall paintings, first discovered in 1916.

Bilbao and the Guggenheim

The Basque capital, **Bilbao** ❻ has had its ups and downs. In 1300 the then small fishing and ironmongering village received *villa* status from Diego López de Haro. His statue stands on a high plinth sometimes hung with the *Ikurriña*, the red, white and green Basque flag inspired by the Union Jack, at the foot of the pink and black Banco de Vizcaya tower in the **Plaza Circular** near the **Puente de la Victoria**. This is the main bridge joining old Bilbao on the east bank of the Ría Nervión and the newer bourgeois quarter that grew up on the west bank in the 19th century. Once you locate the Gran Vía de López de Haro, the main traffic artery running east to west from the Plaza Circular to the large **Parque de Doña Casilda Iturriza**, or the smart new Metro designed by British architect Norman Foster, it is easy to find your way around.

The spectacular **Museo Guggenheim Bilbao** (Abandoibarra Et 2; open Tues–Sun 10am–8pm; entrance fee) has put Bilbao firmly on the cultural map

BELOW: the new Metro at Bilbao.

Entrance to the city's railway station.

and, in the opinion of many, launched the entire Basque Country into a rebirth of general optimism. (For more information about the museum and its collection, *see pages 296–7.*) As a result of the excitement caused by the Guggenheim, Bilbao has become one of Spain's hottest tourist destinations. Book well ahead – Bilbao is booming.

Despite the air pollution and a wide ring of grim apartment blocks, the city has a good deal to offer visitors. If you are here in August, it is worth staying for the *Semana Grande*, the biggest of the week-long festivals in the three provincial capitals. The events usually range from heavy culture to heavy metal to bull-fights, Basque folk music and traditional contests of stamina and strength.

Early Bilbao

The earliest settlements here are said to have been made near the present 15th-century Iglesia de San Antón in the Atxuri district along the Ribera east of the Siete Calles, the "Seven Streets" of the **Casco Viejo**, or Old Town. The prosperous Casco Viejo was pillaged by the French during the Peninsular War, and much of it was destroyed in the Carlist Wars, but narrow streets and a number of pre 19th-century structures remain.

The **Museo Arqueológico, Etnográfico e Histórico Vasco** (open Tues–Sun; entrance fee) is in a converted Jesuit monastery in Calle de la Cruz, which was once attached to the baroque Iglesia de los Santos Juanes. Along with prehistoric exhibits, it contains a copy of an important piece of Basque folk art, the Kurutzi-aga Cross from Durango, and a scale model map of Vizcaya.

You can look over Greater Bilbao from the terrace of the **Santuario de Nuestra Señora de Begoña** (*circa* 1511 and later). To get there, take the lift in

BELOW: a new route into the city.

Calle Esperanza Ascoa behind the 15th and 18th-century **Iglesia de San Nicolás de Bari**, the original Father Christmas and patron saint of Bilbao's children, sailors, prisoners and prostitutes.

Map on page 288

Industry and art

In the 1870s, at the end of the Second Carlist War, Bilbao began to exploit its natural iron deposits and industrialise in a big way. By the end of the century, half the Spanish merchant fleet came from Basque shipyards, much of its steel industry was located near Bilbao, and Basque bankers and businessmen wielded great financial power. The **Teatro Arriaga** (1890) on the Paseo del Arenal, the **Ayuntamiento** (1892) at the bend in the river north of the Puente de la Victoria, and the **Palacio de la Diputación** (1897) were built, and a ground-swell of popular sentiment for going it alone and declaring a Basque State developed.

The wealthy, cosmopolitan aspect of Bilbao is reflected in the excellent **Museo de Bellas Artes** (open Tues–Sun; entrance fee) in Iturriza Park. It contains the most important collection of paintings in northern Spain. In addition to its Flemish, Catalan and classical Spanish holdings, it has a modern wing with some pieces showing the influence of various international art movements on those artists who grew up under Franco, including Isabel Baquenado, Juan José Arqueretta, Andrés Nagel and Javier Morras.

The Basque interior

The capital of Álava, **Vitoria** (Gasteiz) ❼ is the largest and least Bascophone of the three Basque provinces, and the seat of the autonomous Basque govern-

BELOW: Bilbao's industrial port.

The Basques are proud of their musical traditions.

ment. While Vitoria is best known for the bloody battle of 1813 in which Wellington defeated the French general Jourdan, it received its name as early as 1181 when Sancho the Wise founded a walled city here.

The narrow, concentric alleyways of the old town, some named for the crafts that flourished here – Zapatería, Cuchillería, Pintorería, Herrería – underwent a certain amount of urban renewal in the mid-19th century; medieval arcades were demolished and the alleys were widened out as far as possible. But this quarter, with its three Gothic churches, town houses decorated with escutcheons and carved doorways, and shops and cafés, still imparts an authentic feeling of the prospering commercial town of the Middle Ages and Renaissance.

The White Virgin

The **Feria de la Virgen Blanca** in August pays homage to the "White Virgin", standing in her jasper niche in the porch facade of the 14th-century **Iglesia de San Miguel** (open daily). The Gothic sculpture is of high quality. The city's protector, she overlooks the glassed-in balconies or *miradors* of the busy Plaza de la Virgen Blanca and the monument erected in 1917 to commemorate the Battle of Vitoria. Inside the church is a retable by Gregorio Fernández, an important Golden Age sculptor. Notice the bagpipe player in his *Adoration of the Shepherds*.

BELOW: Vitoria's old town, viewed from the air.

The adjacent **Plaza del Machete**, named for the large knife on which oaths to uphold the town's *fueros* (laws) were sworn, marks the southern end of the old town. Walk north from here, stopping to admire the sculpture in the porch and on the column capitals of the **Catedral de Santa María** to the **Museo de**

Arqueología (open Tues–Sun). This well-designed small museum, accommodated in a 15th-century merchants' house in the **Correría**, distinguished by half-timbering and horizontal brickwork, is a wonderfully sensitive adaptation of an historic structure. The tens of thousands of years of local history to which it is devoted range from the Lower Palaeolithic era through to the Middle Ages.

To the south, in a neighbourhood of large private houses between the Jardines de la Florida and the 19th-century park called El Prado, is the **Museo de Bellas Artes** (Paseo Fray Francisco, 8; open Tues–Sun). Its varied holdings include a Crucifixion by José de Ribera and a Virgin by the irascible Sevillian painter and sculptor Alonso Cano (1601–67), one of the most picaresque personalities in the history of Spanish art. There are paintings and sculptures by various Basque artists and a growing modern collection featuring the work of Miró, Picasso and Antonio Tápies (born 1923), the best-known Spanish abstract painter.

Seat of learning

About 30 km (20 miles) from Vitoria along the GI-627 is the lovely town of **Oñati ❽**, where the **Universidad de Sancti Spiritus** (open daily for guided tours; times vary from summer to winter; entrance fee) is a Renaissance gem, particularly the magnificent facade. Built in the 16th century, the university taught a range of subjects, including law and medicine, until its closure in 1902. A stroll around the town reveals other architectural jewels, especially the Gothic **Iglesia de San Miguel**, with a cloister that spans the river, and the baroque *ayuntamiento* (town hall).   ❑

Map on page 288

A part of the Rioja winegrowing district lies inside the Basque Country. The narrow streets of the fortified town of Laguardia are lined with bodegas (wine cellars) offering tastings and tours.

BELOW: shrimp bar in Vitoria.

THE GUGGENHEIM IN BILBAO

Bilbao's famous museum is the talk of the art world. This spectacular "Metallic Flower" beside the River Nervión has breathed new life into the city

The Guggenheim Museum in Bilbao opened in October 1997 to a blaze of publicity. The city's $100-million investment in the spectacular titanium "Metallic Flower" was the keystone of the plan to redevelop the city and recover Bilbao's early 20th century place on the international cultural map. Matched by Bilbao's other architectural triumphs – Norman Foster's designer Metro, Santiago Calatrava's La Paloma airport and his Zubizuri footbridge over the Nervión at Ubitarte – the Guggenheim reconfirmed the Basques as a people of vision and taste.

HELP FROM AEROSPACE

Set by the River Nervión, the 24,290-sq metre (257,000-sq ft) museum building was designed by Californian architect Frank Gehry. It is made up of inter-connected blocks, clad in limestone and topped with a shimmering titanium roof. Light floods through glass walls and a skylight in the 50-metre (165-ft)-high central atrium *(pictured above)* and from here walkways, lifts and stairs lead through the spacious galleries set on three floors. The Basque administration and the Solomon R. Guggenheim Foundation, based in New York, jointly administer the museum, while the Guggenheim provides curatorial expertise, as well as the core art collection and programming.

While almost everyone who visits the Guggenheim marvels at the daring of the building itself, it means that the exhibitions themselves have a hard act to follow, and some people come away disappointed. What's on offer varies widely from classical and contemporary fine art to more populist subjects such as clothes by Giorgio Armani and "the Art of the Motorcycle". Choose your exhibition carefully.

△ **THE COLLECTION**
The permanent collection has works from international artists from 1960 onwards. Site-specific work has also been specially commissioned.

▷ **VIEW FROM THE STREET**
The titanium "Metallic Flower" looms up in the heart of the town and is designed to have a "sculptural presence" reflecting the waterfront, downtown buildings and surrounding hills. Within easy walking distance are the town hall and the city's existing fine arts museum.

▷ **ARTS CENTRE**
The museum has a book shop, café and restaurant, and a 300-seat auditorium with multi-media technology. Note it closes on Mondays.

◁ **THE ARCHITECT**
Frank Gehry, the California-based architect, was attracted to the city's "tough aesthetic appeal".

MODERN MUSEUMS FOR MODERN ART

The Guggenheim is just one of a number of spectacular museums and galleries to open its doors in the last decade of the 20th century. The events of 1992 – the Seville Expo, the Barcelona Olympic Games and the naming of Madrid as cultural city of Europe – concentrated the minds of planners, architects and visionaries into turning the cities' leisure areas into modern temples for high art. There was no xenophobia: competition brought top architects from all over the world. And there was no lack of imagination: modern was set against medieval; boldness won.

Spain is not short of gallery space: vast halls and monumental buildings are dotted everywhere, and many have been enlisted for imaginative development. A prime example is the four-storey 18th-century General Hospital in Madrid, which reopened in 1992 as the magnificent Centro de Arte Reina Sofía, to house the city's 20th-century art collection. More daring is the 1997 Galician Centre of Contemporary Art, a blazingly modern building by Alvaro Siza Viera in the medieval centre of Santiago de Compostela in Galicia.

The Museu d'Art Contemporani in the Raval District of Barcelona was designed by Richard Meier. This gleaming glass and stone venture, *(pictured above)* opened in 1996 to general acclaim.

◁ **RIVERSIDE SIGHT**
The building occupies a 4.2-hectare (8-acre) site on a bend in the River Nervión, by the busy Puente de la Salve. It used to contain a factory and parking lot in an old dockland area. Another renowned architect, Cesar Pelli, has designed the adjacent waterfront development.

▽ **THE LONG GALLERY**
"Snake", by Richard Serra, is a centrepiece in an exhibition of modern American art in the 130-metre (427-ft), column-free "volume" running under the Puente de la Salve.

NAVARRE AND LA RIOJA

Map on page 288

The medieval kingdom of Navarre has an abundance of monuments, and its capital, Pamplona, hosts the world-renowned San Fermín fiesta. La Rioja's vineyards produce the best red wine in Spain

In the year 778, the mighty Charlemagne, King of the Franks, made an unsuccessful attempt to conquer the lands to the south. As he headed home with his tired army, he was ambushed at Roncesvalles by Basques, who annihilated the rearguard. There died the Frankish hero Roland, later to be immortalised in the epic poem *Chanson de Roland*, with the Basques conveniently replaced by Muslim attackers. Soon after, a group of Basque warlords declared themselves independent, and the state they founded was destined eventually to become the kingdom of Navarre. Navarre was only finally demoted to the status of province in 1841. The greatest of its kings was Sancho III, El Grande, one of a line of Sanchos that ran from the 10th to the 13th century. Sancho III doubled Navarre's territories through astute politics, military campaigns and marriages, and introduced the beginnings of a modern legal system and a process of church reform.

Fueros and Carlism

The period immediately following the death in 1035 of Sancho III marked an enormous advance for Navarre, as the prosperous and secure kingdom initiated the *fueros* system, or the guarantee by the monarchy that towns and cities could enjoy a certain autonomy with their customary laws. Beginning in the 13th century, Navarre was ruled by a succession of French dynasties. But due mainly to a series of weak rulers, the Duke of Alba was able to seize the kingdom in 1512 in the name of King Fernando.

Navarre was no longer independent but it did have its *fueros*, and the monarchs in Madrid were obliged to uphold them. This system made Navarre into a very pro-monarchist region, and it is not surprising that the new ideas of liberalism, republicanism and anti-clericalism penetrating Spain in the late-18th and 19th centuries were not well received in Navarre. The centralist tendencies these movements implied was a threat to Navarre's autonomy.

When Fernando VII died in 1833, there was bitter disagreement as to who should succeed him, his daughter Isabel or his brother Carlos. Navarre supported Carlos, in the hope that a strong ruler like him would restore its traditions. The last of the Carlist wars ended in 1876 but the Carlists resurfaced during the Civil War, when they actively participated with Franco and played a crucial role in the coup that began the war. Franco, in fact, praised Navarre after a visit in 1936 as "the cradle of the nationalist movement".

This set Navarre off from the neighbouring Basque Country, with which it has so many ties. Even though Northern Navarre is Basque-speaking and shares a common past and many customs, the more industrial provinces of Vizcaya, Álava and Guipúzcoa sided

LEFT: a quiet street in Pamplona.
BELOW: hard at work in a Rioja vineyard.

The best Rioja wines come from the limestone soil of the Rioja Alta. The Rioja region takes it name from the Río Oja, one of the rivers draining the Sierra de la Demanda.

with the Republic, and lost. As the Basque nationalist movement began to grow in the early 20th century, there were vain attempts to unite with Navarre, but the centuries-old *Navarrismo* of the more conservative sectors has always impeded attempts at unity.

Vineyards of La Rioja

La Rioja has been ruled by Gascons, Romans, Muslims, Navarrans and Castilians. From 573 to 711 this area, separated by the Río Ebro from the Basque country to the north and Navarre to the east, was part of the Duchy of Cantabria. The Asturian kings reconquered La Rioja in 1023, but by 1076 Alfonso VI had made it part of the crown of Castile. From the 15th to the 17th century, the region was divided between Castile and Navarre. When Spain became 52 provinces in 1822, one of them was Logroño, including all 8,000 sq km (3,000 sq miles) of the natural area of La Rioja. Fernando VII revised the map of Spain the following year, however, reducing Logroño to just over 5,000 sq km (1,900 sq miles) as part of the historic region of Old Castile. La Rioja only regained its name in 1980, and was recognised as an autonomous community in 1982.

The Rioja Alta is the moist and mountainous western part, and the Rioja Baja the flat and arid eastern half. **Logroño ❾**, its busy capital, lies between the two zones. The old quarter, bordered by the Ebro and the medieval walls, has the most charm. Traditionally a centre for pilgrims, many monuments, such as the **Puente de Piedra** and the **Iglesia de Santiago El Real** (open daily), with its equestrian statue of Saint James over the main door, are pilgrimage-connected. The twin baroque towers of Logroño's **Catedral de la Redonda** (open daily) are easily distinguished among the narrow streets.

BELOW: the grape harvest near Haro.

Haro ⓾, 35 km (22 miles) northwest of Logroño, is the undisputed wine capital of La Rioja. The flamboyant Gothic, single-naved **Iglesia de Santo Tomás** (open daily), constructed in 1564, is the town's main monument. The old quarter is filled with taverns and cafés where you can sample local wines. Many of the town's manufacturers offer guided tours and tasting visits, which can be easily arranged at the tourist office (Plaza Monseñor Florentino Rodriguez; tel: 941-303 366; www.haro.org). The Batalla del Vino festival on 29 June is a Bacchanalian free-for-all when participants hurl wine at one another as well as drinking it.

Leaving Logroño on the main N-120 west brings you to **Nájera**, in earlier times court of the Kings of Navarre. Here you will find their royal pantheon at the **Monasterio de Santa María La Real** (open Tues–Sun; entrance fee). Not to be missed are the 11th-century Gothic cloister, the Claustro de los Caballeros and the Plateresque windows over the grassy patio. About 20 km (12 miles) further west is **Santo Domingo de la Calzada ⓫**, a town dedicated to the Santiago pilgrimage route. The Romanesque-Gothic **Catedral** in the medieval quarter houses the 11th-century Santo Domingo's tomb.

San Millán de la Cogolla ⓬ (open daily, guided tours only; entrance fee), about 10 km (6 miles) south of Nájera, is the site of the Monasterio de Yuso, where a 10th-century manuscript on texts by Saint Augustine, the *Glosas Emilianenses*, contains the first words to have been written in Castilian Spanish.

Navarre

The Roman city of Pompaelo, **Pamplona** (Iruña) ⓭ was from the 10th to the 16th century the capital of the Kingdom of Navarre. Since the Civil War, the conservative, religious and hard-working Navarrans have transformed their an-

Map on page 288

TIP

Entertain the children at Spain's "Jurassic Park", near Enciso in the Rioja Baja. Dinosaur footprints from 150 million years ago are embedded in the rocks here.

BELOW: the towers of Pamplona's cathedral, with the snowy Pyrenees as a backdrop.

The running of the bulls in Pamplona appealed to Ernest Hemingway. By making its particulars universal in "The Sun Also Rises", he changed it for good by drawing the thousands of visitors who now come every year to the fiesta.

BELOW: watching the bulls from a safe distance.

cient citadel into a prosperous industrial city. High-rise apartment blocks, manicured boulevards and factories form a protective ring around the lovely old city, which perches on the banks of the **Río Arga**.

The centre of this area is the **Plaza del Castillo**, lined with outdoor cafés. Novelist Pío Baroja once said of the *paseo* in this plaza that the varying degrees of aristocracy were as evident as if they were separate floors of a building. Industry and democracy may have made a difference here, but the city's noble past is close at hand in the **Palacio de Navarra** (visits by appointment only; tel: 948-107 000) at the western end of the plaza. The building contains a magnificent throne room decorated with portraits of the kings of Navarre.

Most of Pamplona's historical buildings are located north of the Plaza del Castillo. Near the old city walls, in the Plaza Santa María La Real, is the 14th-century **Catedral** (open Mon–Sat; entrance fee), with an 18th-century facade by the neoclassical architect Ventura Rodríguez. Inside are the lovely alabaster tombs of Carlos III of Navarre and his wife Leonor. The adjoining Gothic cloister is considered to be the best of its kind in Spain. The **Museo de Navarra** (open Tues–Sun; entrance fee), situated in a 16th-century hospital in Calle Jaranta, has interesting pieces of Navarrans archaeology, frescoes taken from Romanesque churches around the province and Goya's portrait of the Marquis of San Adrián.

Beginning at the south end of the Plaza del Castillo, the tree-lined **Paseo de Sarasate**, named after the native violinist, is Pamplona's main promenade. It runs past the Monument to the Fueros and the 13th-century **Iglesia de San Nicolás**, skirting the grassy Ciudadela, a fortress built by Felipe II and now the site of outdoor concerts in warm weather. The Paseo finishes in the **Parque de la Taconera**, a park resplendent with tame deer, fountains and monuments to Navarrans heroes. The **Iglesia de San Lorenzo**, located in the middle of the park, has a chapel dedicated to the city's saint, San Fermín.

The fiesta

There is a measured, stately air to Pamplona much of the time. Native *pamplonicas*, proud of their industriousness, look down upon southern Spain's legendary indolence, although the University of Navarre's student throng lead a furious bar life. But at noon on 6 July, the Eve of San Fermín, a *chupinazo* (rocket) fired from the balcony of the 16th-century **Ayuntamiento** (town hall) puts an end to the order that has made the city flourish. For the following week, Pamplona becomes delirious. It has been said that this wildest of wild fiestas is an extension, rather than an aberration, of the Navarrans personality. The festival isn't about flowers or gorgeously dressed virgins, but sheer endurance. It might be true that a certain amount of stoical Basque blood is necessary to produce a celebration in which the revellers drink, dance and sing for seven days, then, once worn down by exhaustion, throw themselves in front of a herd of charging bulls.

Since there's no place in the city where a visitor can merely stand and watch; everyone who arrives has no choice but to put together a semblance of the red and white costume and join in the dance. Occa-

Map on page 288

sionally, the *sanfermines* are the scene of human, as well as taurine mayhem, and by the end of the week the heat and confusion may make the merriment seem less romantic.

Lest you become too seduced by the prevailing fiesta mood, it ought to be pointed out that fatal gorings really do occur, although not often, at the morning running of the bulls. It's a much better idea to watch an *encierro* (literally, enclosing) from behind a grille. You will undoubtedly find that vicarious terror, or a confused bull charging the barricade you are peering through, is thrilling enough. If you start at the town hall with all of your fearful peers, it takes about 4-minutes to reach the bullring. The closer you get to the bulls, the greater the danger, adrenaline and catharsis. By the end, you'll be singing the *"pobre de mí"* (poor me) with a lump in your throat and missing *sanfermines* before it's even over.

The southwest countryside

Navarre province is enormously varied, ranging from the western Pyrenees to vineyards near Rioja to the desert-like Bardenas Reales north of Tudela. Pilgrims on their way to Santiago from France were obliged to travel through Navarre, with the result that Romanesque churches abound. It is a province to take one's time in, drive slowly (or better yet, ride a bike) and allow plenty of time to sit down and eat, for among the many things that makes Navarre a Basque province is its fine cuisine.

Southwest of Pamplona is **Lizarra** (Estella) ⑭, one of Navarre's most monumental cities and the closest thing to a holy city for the Carlists. Among the splendid Romanesque churches in Lizarra are **Santa María Jus del Castillo** (which used to be a synagogue), **San Pedro** and **San Miguel**, while the 12th-century **Palacio de los Reyes** is a rare example of secular Romanesque architecture.

Not far southwest of Lizarra, at the foot of **Montejurra**, site of an historic Carlist victory over the Republican troops in 1873, is the **Monasterio de Irache** (open Tues–Sun 10am–2pm), which had its own university in the 16th century. And further down the N-111 highway is **Viana**, founded in 1219 by Sancho the Strong. The Crown Princes of Navarre held the title of Prince of Viana until they assumed the throne. In the **Iglesia de Santa María** you can see the tomb of Cesare Borgia, who died in battle here in 1507.

The C-132 road takes you to **Tafalla**, where the Iglesia de Santa María has a beautiful Renaissance altarpiece. Before reaching Tafalla, veer to the left to visit **Artajona**, a fortified town that rises up in the distance like a ghost from the Middle Ages.

Olite

South from Tafalla is **Olite** ⑮, the former residence of the kings of Navarre from the 15th century. Their castle has been restored – *too* restored, in the opinion of some – and is used for theatre and music festivals, as well as being a government-run Parador. Two side trips from Olite are well worth the time: the village of **Ujué** has barely been touched since the Middle Ages and

BELOW: the medieval village of Ujué.

The Parador in the 15th-century castle at Olite is a comfortable base if you're touring the area.

BELOW: Tudela's Plaza de los Fueros, at the heart of the the old town.

has miraculously survived intact; and the **Monasterio de la Oliva** (open daily), used today by Trappist monks, was founded in 1134 by King García Ramírez.

Tudela

South of Olite on the A-15, **Tudela** is one of those remarkable Spanish cities that illustrate the harmony in which Christians, Muslims and Jews lived for several centuries. It was founded in 802 by the Moors, the remains of whose mosque can be seen today inside the **Catedral**, a brilliant example of the transition from Romanesque to Gothic. The Last Judgement doorway in the main facade is a sculpted vision of the rewards and punishments supposedly awaiting us all. Tudela's old Jewish district *(aljama)* is one of the best known in Spain. It is situated between the cathedral and the junction of the Ríos Queiles and Ebro.

Northeast from Tudela, just before you reach the N-240, is **Sangüesa** , located at the foot of the Navarre Pyrenees. This is another 11th-century town, founded by Alfonso I, the Warrior, with another **Iglesia de Santa María**. This one has one of Spain's most beautiful Romanesque porticos.

Nearby, above the Yesa Reservoir and surrounded by rugged mountains, is the **Monasterio de Leyre** (open daily; guided tours only; entrance fee), Navarre's spiritual centre in the 11th century and pantheon of Navarre kings. Consecrated in 1057, it features beautiful Romanesque architecture, including a magnificent vaulted crypt. Abandoned in the 19th century, the monastery has been restored by Benedictine monks and now includes a hotel for those in search of tranquillity. Between here and Sangüesa is the 16th-century **Castillo de Javier**, dedicated to San Francisco Xavier, the great

Jesuit missionary who was born in a house on this site. Pilgrims still visit the castle to pay homage to Xavier, and they say that one of the crucifixes there bled the day the saint died in 1552.

Map on page 288

A tour of the valleys

To the north of Leyre and the N-240 highway are a series of beautiful green valleys dotted with small villages that extend west to Guipúzcoa and east to Huesca and the High Pyrenees. These valleys have few monuments *per se* to offer, although there are isolated Romanesque churches and hermitages, but rather stand out more for their setting and traditional architecture. **Roncal** and **Isaba** are two of the major villages in the Roncal Valley, which is surrounded by peaks reaching as high as 2,000 metres (6,560 ft).

North of Ochagavía in the Salazar Valley is the **Irati Forest**, one of Europe's densest and largest beech forests, supplier of masts for the "invincible" *Armada* and said to be inhabited by witches. Continuing west you reach **Orreaga ⓭** (Roncesvalles), where pilgrims coming from France would stop for the night at one of the most important hostelries along the road to Santiago. Today it is an Augustine monastery. Also in Orreaga you can see the **Colegiata Real**, an overly restored Gothic construction in whose chapterhouse lies the enormous tomb of Sancho VII, the Strong (1154–1234), and his queen.

Smugglers and witches

Up the road from Orreaga at **Valcarlos** is the steep canyon where the famous ambush of 778 featured in the *Chanson de Roland* took place, and you can understand how Charlemagne's men didn't stand a chance against the Basque warriors perched high on either side. This is smugglers' country, and Valcarlos has more than a few families who have made small fortunes by carrying merchandise back and forth over the French border, as do all the mountain villages in this area.

The last of the valleys before entering Guipúzcoa is the beautiful **Valle de Baztán ⓴**, with its 14 villages of stone houses, many of them with noble coats-of-arms. There are noticeably more heraldic crests in Navarre than in most other provinces, where an estimated 20 percent of the population during the heyday of the kingdom belonged to a noble family.

The capital of the Baztán is **Elizondo**, a resort town and residence of many *indianos* – Basques who went off to the New World, made money and returned to live out their days in their villages. North of Elizondo is **Arizcun**, one of the villages partially inhabited by *cagotes*, who suffered centuries of persecution due to their supposed descent from lepers, Jews, Muslims, Visigoths or even Cathars, depending upon which story one chooses to believe. Further north still is **Zugarramurdi**, where witches once gathered in caves to hold *akelarres* or covens. The caves were already inhabited in the Neolithic period, but their fame as the site of witches' gatherings arose from an Inquisition trial in Logroño in 1610, when 40 unfortunate women were accused of witchcraft and 12 of them were burned at the stake. ❑

BELOW: stone houses by the river in Elizondo.

CANTABRIA AND ASTURIAS

*Few parts of Spain have greater natural beauty than
Cantabria and Asturias, where sandy beaches and rocky headlands
are backed by the soft greens and greys of the rugged landscape*

The autonomous regions of Cantabria and Asturias lie between the Basque Country and Galicia along the Bay of Biscay or *Mar Cantábrico*. Each region consists of one narrow province: Santander and Asturias, respectively. A formidable mountain chain, the **Cordillera Cantábrica**, separates the coast and its narrow strip of lush, green valleys from the arid *meseta* plateau of central Spain.

There are 72 beaches in Cantabria, stretching east to west from Castro-Urdiales to San Vicente de la Barquera, while the 290 km (180 miles) of coastline in Asturias comprises a succession of beaches, estuaries and promontories. From the 91-metre (300-ft) **Cabo de Peñas**, north of Gijón and Avilés, you can see a large part of it. On rainy days you may see the tiny figure of a solitary fisherman on a long stretch of sand at the foot of an immense weatherbeaten cliff. On a sunny day, the same spot will be filled with bathers and beach tents.

Even in summer there is snow on the spectacular **Picos de Europa**, which rise to over 2,640 metres (8,660 ft), the highest mountains in the Cordillera. The region containing the mountains that are the source of the rivers flowing into the Cantabrian Sea has long been called *La Montaña*.

LEFT: in the medieval village of Santillana del Mar. **BELOW:** the Iglesia de Santa María above the harbour in Castro-Urdiales.

From prehistory to modern times

Small nomadic bands of hunters and food-gatherers belonging to the Stone Age cultures decorated the walls and ceilings of the limestone caves in this region with pictures of the migratory animals they followed. The similarity between the decorated prehistoric caves in the limestone area of southern France and those of northern Spain led to the designation of a prehistoric "Franco-Cantabrian" cultural area, which includes a number of sites in the foothills of the Pyrenees in the Basque Country and in Asturias.

Castro-Urdiales ❶, once an important Roman seaport, is the easternmost and one of the oldest ports on the coast of Cantabria. The **Playa de Brazomar** and the **Playa de Oriñón** at the mouth of the Ría Agüera are characteristically long, sandy Cantabrian beaches, a short walk from both summer resort facilities and an old quarter with medieval remains. From the small fortified peninsula, a ruined Templars' hostel, the "Castle" of Santa Ana and the Gothic **Iglesia de Santa María**, with French sculptures, flying buttresses and uncompleted towers reminiscent of Notre Dame in Paris, overlook the photogenic harbour filled with fishing boats.

The most important medieval pilgrimage trails led to Santiago de Compostela and, in the opposite direction, to Rome and on to Jerusalem. The powerful, rich

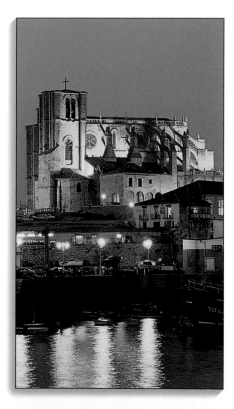

*A splendid coast
for sailing.*

BELOW: beach life in
Santander.

military Order of Knights Templars, ascetic monks in arms distinguished by their white habits embroidered with the red Crusaders' cross, was founded in 1120 to protect pilgrims on their way to Palestine. At Castro-Urdiales the Templars ministered to the pilgrims of St James and recruited suitable members for their main work in the Holy Land.

At **Laredo ❷**, the long, sandy beach attracts so many summer visitors that the off-season population of over 10,000 will have multiplied by a factor of 10 by mid-August. This explains the high-rises and summer houses that follow the curve of the beautiful beach.

In the Castilian Golden Age that followed the Reconquest, this part of the coast was the administrative centre of Cantabria, and Old Castile's only outlet to the sea. The size of the Cantabrian fleet that operated here increased dramatically in the 16th century. The ports on the Bay of Biscay were the jewels in the Spanish emperor's crown and were the basis of Spain's superior maritime capability. Ships carrying Spanish wine and wool sailed from San Sebastián, Laredo, Santander and La Coruña to Flanders and England, or into the Mediterranean through the Strait of Gibraltar. All along this coast churches were enhanced by the massive building campaign instigated by the Catholic Monarchs as well as from their location on the pilgrim trail. In Laredo, for example, a 16th-century doorway was added to the 13th-century Gothic **Iglesia de Nuestra Señora de la Asunción**.

In 1556 Carlos I, having abdicated in favour of his son Felipe II, sailed into Laredo from Flanders on the way to the Monastery of Yuste, in Extremadura. With him arrived his sister, Mary of Hungary, ruler of the Netherlands, and the art treasures accumulated by both these great Habsburg collectors. The Spanish

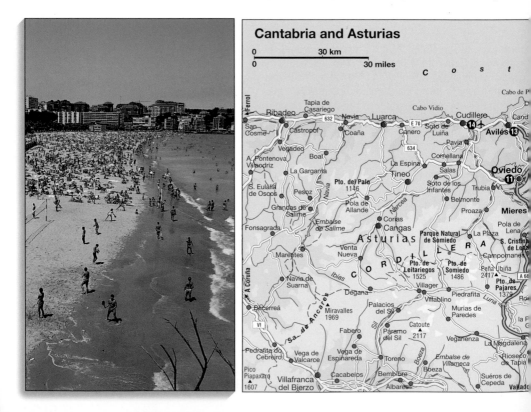

public collections still hold most of the priceless works of Flemish art carried across Spain from Laredo more than 400 years ago.

Across **Santoña Bay** from Laredo is the port and resort of **Santoña ❸**. It has another church begun in the 13th century and several beaches, including the splendid 2-km (1-mile) long **Playa de Nueva Berria**.

Castilian summer retreat

The important modern port of **Santander ❹** has been the provincial capital since the 18th century, when the French plundered the coastal area to the east. The city centre, rebuilt after much of it was destroyed by a fire in 1941, looks south across a beautiful protected bay. On a clear day you can see the snow-capped peaks of the Cordillera Cantábrica from the busy quay.

There are fine beaches (El Camella, La Concha, La Primera and La Segunda, all joined at low tide) facing out to sea in the older residential and resort quarter, **El Sardinero**. Here, too, are the Gran Casino del Sardinero, the International Menéndez Pelayo University, which offers summer courses to foreign students, and the large old-fashioned resort hotel, the Hotel Real. On the **Península de La Magdalena** is the neo-Gothic summer palace of the royal family, an imitation of Balmoral, built by Alfonso XIII in 1912 for his English queen. It is now part of the International University.

On a rainy day, visit the **Museo de Bellas Artes** (open Mon–Sat; entrance fee) on the Calle Rubio west of the Plaza Porticada. It shares a building with the library donated by the Santander literary scholar, Marcelino Menéndez y Pelayo (1856–1912), whose statue is in the garden leading to the house. The museum has an interesting small collection ranging from Zurbarán to contemporary

Map below

TIP

A good time to visit Santander is during July or August, when the town hosts an international festival of music, dance and drama.

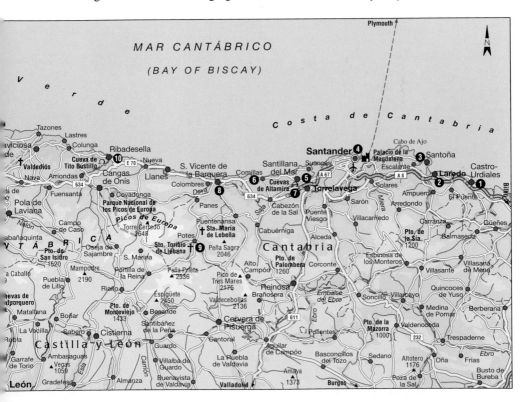

Cantabrian artists and roomy galleries for temporary exhibitions. Here hang portraits of three of Spain's less-beloved rulers: Fernando VII, Isabel II, deposed in 1868 while summering in the Basque Country, and General Franco. The portrait of Fernando, one of several painted by Goya of this weak and cruel king, is believed to have been commissioned by the city of Santander. Nearby Goya's four famous series of etchings are displayed: the *Caprichos*, the *Disasters of War*, the *Tauromaquía* and the *Disparates* or *Proverbios*.

The **Museo de Prehistoria y Arqueología** (open Tues–Sun; entrance fee) in the Diputación Provincial near the Puerto Chico, where fishing boats are moored, provides an insight into the Lower-Palaeolithic cave art found in this region.

Medieval to *modernista*

The resorts of **Santillana del Mar ❺** and **Comillas ❻** on the coast west of Santander are crowded in summer with well-heeled Spaniards from further south. This is an agreeable area of first-rate beaches, pretty farms overlooking the sea, medieval and Renaissance churches and balconied, galleried and escutcheoned granite Golden Age palaces or town houses.

Santillana is an amazingly well-preserved medieval village, with fine stone mansions and cobbled streets. The 12th to 13th-century Romanesque **La Colegiata** contains the bones of one of the virgin saints, the 4th-century Santa Juliana. "Santillana" is derived from the Latin *Sancta Juliana*. The Colegiata itself, like many other churches in the French-influenced Romanesque style, was designed to serve as a roomy reliquary entered through the elegant round-arched west portal. Despite the cosmopolitanism it has acquired over a thousand years or so, Santillana has been able to preserve the character of a market town.

BELOW: Gaudí's handiwork in Comillas.

The Parador Nacional Gil Blas on the main square, one of the most popular parZDFTS LQ 6SDLQ LV QDPHG IRU WKH SLFDUHVTXH KHUR RI *LO %ODV GH 6DQWLOODQH, parTGRUV LQ 6SDLQ, is named for the picaresque hero of *Gil Blas de Santillane*, a novel by the 18th-century French satirist Alain-Rene Le Sage, and later a verse play by Victor Hugo. Both attacked social problems in France while pretending to write about Spain.

In Comillas, follow the signs to **El Capricho**, the summer house built to the designs of the Catalan architect Antoni Gaudí in 1883–85. At El Capricho, Gaudí combined references to the squat Romanesque columns, the minaret, *Mudéjar* brickwork, the traditional Spanish iron balcony, the pink neo-Gothic **Palacio Sobrellano** adjacent to it, and – most imaginatively of all – the shapes and colours of the Cantabrian countryside and seashore.

Map on pages 308–9

Cave art from 12,000 BC

Altamira ➐ is about 1.5 km (less than 1 mile) south of Santillana del Mar. The "Sistine Chapel" of cave art was the first, and arguably is still the finest, Palaeolithic-decorated cave identified. Altamira's authenticity was not generally accepted until the early 20th century, when other caves, to which the entrances had been blocked – ruling out any possibility of a hoax – were discovered. Ironically, the quality and precise detail of figures such as the pregnant bison were the greatest impediment to the recognition of Altamira's antiquity.

The Costa Verde

San Vicente de la Barquera ➑, 10 km (6 miles) west of Comillas, is one of the nicest surprises on the Cantabrian coast. As you travel west, the little harbours on which the old ports were built become wider, the river valleys look

BELOW: polychrome painting of a bison, Altamira.

PREHISTORY AT ALTAMIRA

In 1879 Don Marcelino de Sautuola, who lived in a villa near the site and who had seen some small engraved Palaeolithic art objects that were accepted as genuine at the Universal Exposition in Paris the year before, realised by their similarity that the paintings at Altamira were prehistoric. The bison, hinds, wild boar, horses and other animals on the ceiling at Altamira are the largest known group of "polychromes", that is, figures which were painted using several colours of pigment (ochres, manganese oxides, charcoal, iron carbonate). The three most important polychrome sites in the world are Altamira, Tito Bustillo (in Asturias) and Lascaux in Perigord, France. Some of these sophisticated figures of about 15,000 years ago are large – over 2 metres (6 ft) long – while the ceiling is low, so the best way to view them is by lying on your back.

To preserve the paintings' condition, visitor numbers are controlled – booking at least ten months in advance is essential. Write to: **Museo de Altamira**, 39330 Santillana del Mar, Santander, specifying the number of people and naming a date. The museum itself, with exhibits explaining the significance of the paintings, is open Tues–Sun (am only; entrance fee; www.mcu.es).

The Picos de Europa form the biggest national park in Europe. The limestone mountain range offers excellent climbing and hiking trails. Good roads through the park also make the spectacular scenery accessible by car.

greener and the mountains are higher. The fortified walls and castle, and the 13th to 16th-century **Iglesia de Santa María de los Angeles** (open daily) on the pine-clad headland, are reflected in the inlet spanned by the 17th-century **Puente de la Maza**, a stone bridge with 28 arches. The beach, the **Sable de Merón**, is almost 3 km (2 miles) long and as much as 100 metres (328 ft) wide when the tide is out.

Mozarabic art

Leave the coast at San Vicente and take the road that follows the **Ría Deva** valley to **Panes**, and then up into the eastern end of the **Picos de Europa** in the direction of the village of **Potes** ❾.

The narrow Desfiladero de la Hermida may be slow going as it criss-crosses the Santander-Asturias border, but it widens north of Potes to form the austere mountain setting for one of the jewels of Mozarabic architecture, the **Iglesia de Santa María de Lebeña**. Founded by Alfonso, Count of Liébana (924–63), and his wife Justa, possibly immigrants from Andalusia, it combines the architectural concepts of the mosque with the forms of local pre-Romanesque Asturian churches, with its small agglomerative compartments and tunnel vaults, which had developed independently north of the Cordillera Cantábrica from the 8th century, based to some degree on Visigothic prototypes. Like the Asturian churches, Santa María was completely vaulted over.

Entered by a side door, the church has the feeling of a mosque, due in part to its horseshoe arches. Its 15th-century red, white and blue Virgin is now part of an 18th-century retable. A stone stele re-used by a 9th-century builder is carved with Visigothic designs in roundels. A primitive human figure in the lower left corner of the stele was painted, it is said, with a mixture of blood and ashes. At the time Santa María was built, this remote area had been a centre of monastic culture for several centuries. It was in the monastery of **Santo Toribio de Lebaña**, a few miles south, that the 8th-century monk Beatus wrote his commentaries on the Apocalypse and the Book of Daniel. The *Beatos*, as they were called, were illuminated in the scriptoria of various monasteries in the following centuries. As examples of Mozarabic art, they are as important as Santa María. Santo Toribio also possesses what is claimed to be the entire right arm of Christ's wooden cross.

The Fuente Dé Parador west of Potes is located at the source of the Ría Deva and surrounded by high peaks. It is open all year, and climbers use it as a base. The view from the **Mirador del Cable**, reached by a cable car that runs all year from Fuente Dé, takes in Potes, the Deva Valley, the nearby wildlife reserves and the mountains.

Asturias

Returning to the coast and entering the kingdom of Asturias, you will find yourself on an increasingly irregular shoreline. Sandy beaches and port resorts lie between high promontories. Pretty **Llanes** has a cliff walk, the **Paseo de San Pedro**, and 30 small beaches. Ask when the charming Asturian folk dance called

BELOW: looking out from the Mirador del Cable.

El Pericote is to be performed. A prehistoric menhir carved with an anthropomorphic figure called Peña Tu is at Vidiago close by; at **Colombres** is one of the more important decorated caves, El Pindal.

Ribadesella ⑩ occupies the east bank of the estuary of the Río Sella. One of the most important Franco-Cantabrian caves, **Tito Bustillo** (open April–Sept Wed–Sun; entrance fee; www.3errres.com), is west of the port across the bridge over the estuary. The original entrance has been lost, so that it is uncertain whether the paintings here were exposed to daylight. On a red ochre-painted wall overhanging the habitation site, more than 20 animals were painted in other colours and then engraved with flint tools. The size of these well-observed animals is considerable, averaging over 2 metres (6 ft). They include at least one reindeer, a species rarely encountered in Cantabrian Palaeolithic art. To prevent deterioration of the paintings, the number of visitors per day is strictly limited, so be sure to arrive early, especially in high season.

Asturian cider advert dating from the late 19th century.

Sea and cider

An overwhelming mural painting by the Uria Aza brothers, depicting the horrors of modern war in the church at Ribadesella, is worth a sobering look, as is the view of mountains and port life from the quay.

In any of the fishing villages here, you can eat excellent *caldereta* (fish stew), hake in cider or locally caught shellfish such as sea urchins. Cider, the traditional Asturian drink, is aerated by being poured from a bottle held some distance from the glass to activate carbonation. Visitors tend to spill a lot, but it does not seem to matter. You may be treated to the local folk songs; Asturian voices are said to have both the depth of the mountain valleys and the lilt of the sea.

BELOW: the grandeur of the Picos de Europa.

The region's traditional footwear.

From Ribadesella it is a pleasant excursion to **Covadonga** in the Parque Nacional de los Picos de Europa. In a green, tree-shaded valley lies the important national shrine of Covadonga, where in the 8th century Pelayo, an Asturian warrior, crushed a Muslim force, thus becoming a symbol of Christian resistance to the invaders. A statue of Pelayo stands near a neo-Romanesque church. Continuing into the park, you reach two glacier-formed lakes, Enol and La Ercina. In the background are the snow-capped peaks of the Picos.

Oviedo – the capital of Asturias

Unless you are able to make an extended visit to Asturias, you should go first to **Oviedo ⓫** (pop. 205,000), the provincial capital of the kingdom of Asturias. It is on a plain of meadows, surrounded by fields of maize, apple orchards and small prosperous towns.

Get your bearings by going to the large park in the city centre, the **Parque de San Francisco**. With the tall grey post office tower on your left, walk straight ahead to the old ecclesiastical district much damaged in the anti-fascist uprising of working-class parties led by the miners in 1934 and in the Civil War soon afterwards. The tourist office, with its models of Asturian churches, is on the Plaza Alfonso II El Casto, next to the remains of the pre-Romanesque **Iglesia de San Tirso** built by that king. The flamboyant Gothic cathedral, the **Basilica del Salvador** (open Mon–Sat; entrance fee), its perforated spire damaged in the 1930s and subsequently restored, contains the Pantheon of the Asturian Kings and the Cámara Santa, their reliquary chapel.

BELOW: Santa María de Naranco as night falls.

Behind the cathedral is a burial ground for pilgrims to Santiago de Compostela and a superb **Museo Arqueológico** (open Tues–Sun; entrance fee) in the

Monasterio de San Vicente. The museum's treasures include prehistoric arte-facts, Roman mosaics and pre-Romanesque artwork.

Several of the finest pre-Romanesque Asturian buildings can be found in Oviedo, including the basilican church of San Julián de los Prados (*circa* 830) with illusionistic wall paintings. It was built in the reign of Alfonso II to adjoin one of the king's palaces. On **Mount Naranco**, the barrel-vaulted Santa María de Naranco, originally a royal hall built for Ramiro I in the mid-9th century, and the incomplete San Miguel de Lillo of the same period, are close together on the same hillside.

Mountain views and fishing villages

It is only an hour's drive directly south to Puerto de Pajares (1,380 metres/4,530 ft), a pass in the Picos on the border between Asturias and León. At **Mieres**, a steelworkers' town along the way, the Socialist Republic was proclaimed on 5 October 1934. Past Mieres, and accessible only by doubling back through **Pola de Lena**, the single-naved early 10th-century pre-Romanesque **Iglesia de Santa Cristina** is perched on a hill and visible from the highway.

Heading back towards the coast, the fishing-port resorts around **Gijón** with their folkloric festivals, and all of the pre-Romanesque churches in the area, are within easy driving distance. Gijón itself is an industrial port and the biggest Asturian city, with a population of 260,000. The old part of town is located on a narrow isthmus, centring around the arcaded **Plaza Mayor**.

Avilés ⓭, further west, also has a charming old town concealed within its industrial shell. The area around the Plaza de España is ancient and intimate, and filled with bustling bars and restaurants. Continuing approximately 20 km (12 miles) further west along the N-632 brings you to **Cudillero** ⓮, one of the most extraordinary Asturian fishing villages, with houses hanging from steep rock walls over the ramp leading down to the harbour. Restaurants serving fresh sardines and cider line either side of the dramatic ravine.

Luarca is really not much more than a cluster of slate-roofed houses but is a lively village and a good place to stay the night if you are touring this section of the Costa Verde. Just beyond the nearby village of Navia, a left turn up the AS-12 leads to the Celtic *castro* (hill fort) at **Coaña**, a cluster of circular stone foundations dating from the Iron Age.

Less than 20 km (12 miles) inland from the coast along the N-634 is the memorable old quarter of **Salas**, where the Valdés Salas castle, former residence of the Marquis of Valdés Salas, a leader of the Inquisition, is now a hotel and restaurant. From the Espinass Pass, which has a superlative 360-degree view, descend south to **Tineo** on the AS-216. Tineo is known for its ham industry and for the 14th-century García-Tineo and 16th-century Meras palaces.

The **Parque Natural de Somiedo**, southwest of Oviedo, surrounds the Teverga and Quirós valleys, extending into the peaks of the neighbouring province of León. The park is populated by wolves and a few surviving European brown bears, and more than a dozen glacial lakes dot the landscape. ❏

Map on pages 308–9

TIP

Delicious Asturian specialities include *fabada*, a rich white bean stew. The local pork and sausages are also good, as are cheeses such as the pungent *Cabrales* and spicy *Los Beyos*.

BELOW: lush pastures in the Parque Natural de Somiedo.

GALICIA

Spain's green northwestern corner keeps a spectacular coastline. Inland, historic pilgrimage routes cut across empty sierras to meet at Santiago de Compostela

Map on page 318

Madrid

Criss-crossed by myriad rivers and mountain ranges, Galicia is a green, rugged land of unforgettable vistas and ocean-chiselled coastline. Across this nature-blessed region can be found treasures left by the Celts, the Seubi, the Romans and the Visigoths who conquered and settled it. Isolated from the rest of Spain by a bulwark of mountains on the east and south and bounded to the north and west by the tumultuous North Atlantic, Galicia's natural formations include craggy mountains, long, loping valleys and distinctive *rías* or estuaries.

While mountains ring the interior, separating the region from the Spanish provinces of Asturias, León and Zamora to the east and Portugal to the south, Galicia's stormy, westernmost point is *Finisterre*, or Land's End, as the Romans named it. In winter, the fishing fleet braves storms famed for their fury.

In spring and summer a striking palette of colours – deep green, yellow and orange – blooms on the inland moors, and the milder weather attracts thousands of tourists to its beaches. Lining the 380 km (240 miles) of its bold, indented coastline are quaint fishing villages, busy resorts and the major ports of Vigo and A Coruña. The spectacularly wild *rías* in the north are known as the **Rías Altas**, while the gentler southwestern ones are called the **Rías Baixas**. Parts of the coast are still recovering from the catastrophic effects of the *Prestige* oil tanker spill off the coast near Cabo Finisterre in November 2002. The ageing vessel released its cargo of 77,000 tonnes of crude oil into the sea, much of which was washed towards shore provoking Spain's worst ecological disaster.

LEFT: modern-day pilgrims on the road to Santiago. **BELOW:** fisherman putting out to sea in the Ría de Coruña.

Celtic roots

Galicia and its people retain many traces of the Celts, who swept through from 900–600 BC and established a hold on this windswept, rain-soaked land that they did not relinquish until the arrival of the Romans in 137 BC. The region's name is derived from "Gallaeci", the name by which the Celtic tribes were known to the Romans; they coexisted for three centuries, the golden age of Celtic culture. Hundreds of ruined hilltop *castros*, or fortified Celtic settlements, survive: those at Viladonga (Lugo), Boroña and Monte Tecla (both Pontevedra) are especially worthwhile.

Even before the Celtic centuries, the native people lived in *pallozas*, conical-shaped stone houses with thatched roofs. In isolated inland areas, such as Os Ancares in Ourense Province and parts of Lugo Province, *pallozas* survived as family homes until recently, but Os Ancares (O Piornedo village) survives largely as a tourist sight. However, Galicia's population remains overwhelmingly rural; even today the population of nearly 3 million is scattered among

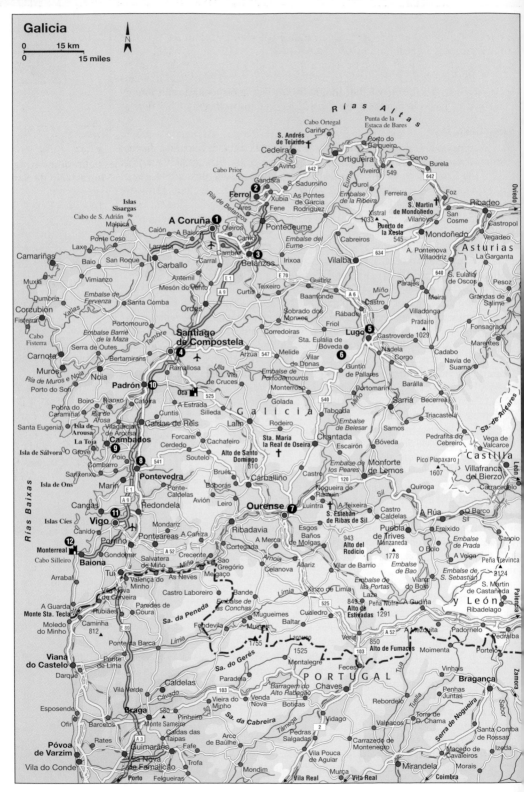

Galicia

0   15 km
0   15 miles
N

the region's 40,000 parishes and three out of ten Galician families still live off the land, the highest proportion of any European region. A regional herd of a million dairy and beef cattle provide superb quality meat and milk. The latter is used to make farmhouse cheeses such as breast-shaped *tetilla*. Galicians are also renowned for their belief in magic, witches and superstition. In many cases this pagan belief in the spirit world has grafted itself on to Christianity.

Pilgrims' land

Galicia remained relatively free from Muslim influence and developed a distinct cultural personality. Linguists place the beginning of the Galician language in the early 11th century, by which time it had been an independent kingdom for 500 years, albeit ruled from Asturias and León between the 8th and 11th centuries. The Galician culture showed greater affinity for Portuguese culture than for that of Spain until the final separation of the two countries in 1668. But by the time Galicia came under the rule of the Catholic Monarchs, who established the *Junta* of the kingdom of Galicia in 1495, the region had firm economic and religious ties to the central kingdom because of the importance of Santiago de Compostela as a pilgrimage destination.

A Coruña

A good point of departure for travellers planning to tour the **Rías Altas** is the port city of **A Coruña ❶**. It has been a key shipping centre for nearly 2,000 years. Julius Caesar sailed in here from Gaul (France) in AD 60 to re-establish Roman rule, and Felipe II's Armada set sail from here. The old part of the city (La Ciudad Vieja) rises from a narrow strip of land pointing out into the Atlantic, while the new section (La Pescadería) rests on the edge of the mainland and an isthmus. Because of its position near a great sea route between northern Europe and South and Central America, A Coruña continues to play an important role as a major Atlantic port and oil refinery.

The city's showpiece is its **Torre de Hércules** (open daily; entrance fee), the world's only Roman-era lighthouse, which is 10 minutes by car or tram from the city centre. It dates from the time of the Celtic chieftain Breogan and was rebuilt during the reign of Trajan, the Roman Emperor born in Spain in AD 98. It looks down on the spot where the *Mar Egeo* oil tanker ran aground on the rocks in 1992.

The characteristic enclosed glass balconies *(miradores)* of the pretty white buildings lining the seafront permit residents to admire the bay while protecting them from stiff ocean winds. To take in the sun, cross the old city and stop at the downtown beach, **Riazor**, or take a short cab ride and swim at **Santa Cristina** beach on the isthmus. In the old section, pass along the gardens lining **Avenida de la Marina** and then walk over to the grandiose **Plaza de María Pita**, named after the heroine who courageously gave the alarm alerting citizens of an attack by the English admiral, Sir Francis Drake, in 1589. A few streets south is the **Castillo de San Antón**, once a prison and now an archaeological museum with a varied collection of

The Celts have a genius for poetry and music, and a deep love of what they call "Terra Nosa" (Our Land). Today, this is expressed in everything from Celtic rock music to the revival of the local "gallego" language.

BELOW: the Torre de Hércules lighthouse near A Coruña.

TIP

From O Ferrol, take a train ride along the wildest stretch of the Rías Altas to the magically atmospheric headland of Cabo de Bares.

Roman, Visigothic and even Egyptian artefacts (open Tues–Sun; entrance fee).

The churches of **Santiago** (12th century), **María del Campo** (13th century) and **Santo Domingo** (17th century) are in the city's old section, as is the stunning **Museo de Arte Sacro de la Colegiata**, with exhibits of religious silver (open Tues–Fri and Sat am). Just south of the old section and overlooking the harbour is the **Jardín de San Carlos**, an enclosed garden containing the granite tomb of Sir John Moore, the Englishman who died in 1809 while helping to defend the city against the French during the Peninsular War.

More modern attractions include **Domus** (open daily; entrance fee), a striking interactive museum of mankind, and the **Casa de Los Peces** (open daily; entrance fee), an aquarium on the Playa de Orzáno.

Franco's birthplace

An hour's drive east along the coast from A Coruña leads to the major upper *ría* on whose edge lies the city of **O Ferrol ❷**, founded during the Middle Ages. The large estuary, 6 km (4 miles) wide, forms a near-perfect, protected deep-water port where one of Spain's principal naval bases has existed since the 18th century. Shipbuilding flourished here until the closure of the yards in the 1980s, since when the town has struck hard times.

General Francisco Franco was born and grew up here, the son of a navy supply clerk, and until 2002 his huge equestrian statue dominated the Plaza de España. During his rule the city was officially known as El Ferrol del Caudillo (of the Leader). Although a native son of Galicia, Franco viewed regional loyalty as anti-Spanish, and prohibited the teaching and official use of the Galician language. He is just one of a host of famous Galician politicians – others include the Cuban president, Fidel Castro; the founding father of Spanish socialism, Pablo Iglesias; and the former Argentine president, Raul Alfonsín. Among Spaniards, Galicians are believed to make astute politicians because of their cunning nature and conservatism. It is sometimes said that if a Galician is seen on a staircase it is hard to determine whether he is going up or down.

The roads to Santiago

Betanzos ❸, a lovely unspoiled port, lies at the mouth of a *ría* easily reached (20 minutes east by car) from A Coruña. The city reached its apogee in the 14th and 15th centuries when the nearby **Las Marinas Valley** provided wheat for the entire A Coruña province. Three impressive but small Gothic churches, **Santa María del Azogue** (founded late 1300s), **San Francisco** (1387) and **Santiago**, have been well preserved and serve as an illustration of the town's best moments. The road runs north from here to the spectacular cliffs and headlands of the **Rías Altas**, Galicia's wildest coast.

Today, **Santiago de Compostela's ❹** horizon is still clearly identified by the distinctive sight of the twin baroque towers of the city's **Catedral** (open daily 7am–9pm; museum Mon–Sat 11am–1.30pm and 4.30–6.30pm; Sun 10am–1.30pm and 4–7pm), which shelters the tomb of St James, the patron saint of Spain. After the discovery of the tomb between AD

BELOW: Cabo Finisterre, Spain's westernmost point.

Map on page 318

812 and 814, support from the Asturian king and his successors and later the offering – *voto de Santiago* – of the Spanish Monarchs created a bustling town within an otherwise turbulent province. Over the saint's tomb, King Alfonso II of Asturias ordered the erection of an earthen temple, later replaced by a stone church under the rule of Alfonso III. In 997, al-Mansur Abu Jafar (military commander of the Caliphate of Córdoba) destroyed the entire town except for the tomb. But in 1075 work began on the present cathedral by order of King Alfonso VI of León and Castile.

The well travelled path of thousands of pilgrims through Navarre and Galicia became known as *El Camino de Santiago* (Road to Santiago). The number of pilgrims increased dramatically after Pope Calixto II conceded the Roman Catholic Church's greatest privileges to the See of Santiago de Compostela and designated as Holy Years those in which the day of St James fell on a Sunday. Pilgrims who reached Santiago in those years obtained a plenary indulgence and absolution for one year. The shrine became the greatest place of Christian pilgrimage after Rome and Jerusalem and the city itself emerged as one of Europe's most brilliant, attracting outstanding artists, scholars and silver- and goldsmiths. Santiago is still a bustling pilgrimage city; an estimated 11 million pilgrims now visit during a Holy Year. It is also a major university town as well as the region's administrative capital.

The cathedral

This Romanesque building (consecrated in 1211) occupies the east end of the **Praza do Obradoiro**. Its baroque facade by Fernando Casas y Novoa has graced the entrance to the cathedral since 1750. The interplay of curved and

BELOW: the harbour at Betanzos.

St James looks out from the cathedral.

BELOW: the shrine of St James in Santiago de Compostela.

straight lines on the carvings appears to culminate in flickers of flame at the height of the two slender towers. Walk around the cathedral's contrasting four plazas, unique in Spain, for views back on to the building. Inside the baroque facade is *El Pórtico da Gloria*, the tripartite porch depicting the Last Judgment by Maestro Mateo, considered one of the greatest masterpieces in the Romanesque style.

Inside the cathedral, the high altar is dominated by a sumptuously attired 13th-century statue of St James. Some pilgrims mount the stairs behind the altar to kiss the saint's mantle. Below the altar, a crypt constructed in the foundations of the 9th-century church holds the remains of the saint (which went missing from 1589–1879) and two of his disciples, St Theodore and St Athanasius. Other obligatory stops include the *Puerta de las Platerías* (Silversmith's Door), a Romanesque doorway so named because it led outside on to a plaza lined by silversmith shops, and the *Puerta Santa* (Holy Door), opened during Holy Years.

Across the spacious Praza do Obradoiro from the cathedral stairs, the **Pazo de Raxoi**, an impressive 18th-century mansion designed by French architect Charles Lemaur, serves as the City Hall. It is capped by a bronze sculpture of - Santiago the Moor Slayer in battle gear, riding a charging stallion *(see panel below)*. At the plaza's south end is the **Colegio de San Jerónimo**, a 17th-century building attractive for its 15th-century-style gateway. The north side of the plaza is occupied by the **Hostal de los Reyes Católicos**, begun in 1501 under orders of Ferdinand and Isabel as an inn and hospital for pilgrims. It is now a flagship Parador. The building's facade features an ornate Plateresque doorway of great beauty, and the wrought-iron work and carved columns in a chapel inside are of exceptional artistic merit.

THE SANTIAGO LEGEND

A ccording to legend, a Spanish peasant led to a field by a shower of stars – *campus stella* – discovered the tomb of the Apostle of Jesus. St James had been martyred in Jerusalem in AD 44 but his remains are said to have returned by boat with his followers to Spain, where he had supposedly travelled and evangelised.

The discovery became a focus of unity for Christians who were then separated politically and spread across a narrow strip of northern Spain. It inspired Christian efforts to carry out the Reconquest that would eventually force Muslims off the Iberian peninsula. Whether St James ever visited Spain in the first place has always been disputed, but there is no doubt that the idea of the possession of the sacred remains of the saint aroused tremendous passion and pride, and emboldened the Christians. As their battle cry, the Christian soldiers shouted "*Santiago y cierre España!*" (St James, and close Spain!") to urge their brethren to defeat the Muslims. Christian fighters also gave their patron the name of *Matamoros* (Slayer of Moors).

Numerous testimonies by Spanish champions have talked of being spurred on by "visions of a white knight on horseback brandishing a fear-inspiring sword and wearing a vengeful grimace".

Map on page 318

Tourists and pilgrims

Heading out of the plaza between the cathedral and the Colegio de San Jerónimo, turn into the **Rua do Franco**, where university students, tourists and pilgrims mingle among bars, shops and colleges. The **Colegio de Fonseca** (finished in 1530) has a remarkable Renaissance doorway. Also worth visiting are the **Colegio de San Clemente** (1601), the **Convento de San Francisco**, said to have been founded by St Francis of Assisi in 1214, and the **Monasterio de San Martiño Pinario**, now a seminary, founded in the 10th century and rebuilt in the 17th century.

Just outside the Porta do Camiño in the northeast of the old city, the **Museo do Pobo Galego** (open Mon–Sun) has a wide-ranging display of Galician trades, arts and crafts, musical instruments and traditional costumes. The adjacent **Centro Galego de Arte Contemporánea** (open Tues–Sun) has temporary exhibitions of modern art. To tour the **University of Santiago de Compostela**, walk from the Praza do Obradoiro along descending cobblestoned streets. The university was established in 1532, although its present building dates from 1750. The **Ciudad de la Cultura**, an ambitious complex of museums, libraries and other cultural facilities, is now being built to complement it.

A formidable fireworks display at midnight on 25 July each year initiates the week-long festivities dedicated to Santiago.

Inland to Lugo and Ourense

Cutting across Galicia from all points of the compass are the roads that pilgrims travelled to Santiago: the original Cantabrian *camino* from the Asturian coast; the French *camino* from the Pyrenees via the Benedictine monastery at Samos and Lugo; the so-called English *camino* from A Coruña and Betanzos; the Portuguese coastal route via Tui and Pontevedra; and, finally, the route up

BELOW: Santiago Cathedral.

It is estimated that in the past 500 years one in three Galician men left his homeland. Most went to Cuba, Argentina, Uruguay or Venezuela – perhaps the most famous immigrant's son is Cuban President Fidel Castro.

BELOW: the Roman walls of Lugo.

from Central Spain via Ourense. **Lugo ⑤**, the main Galician town on the French *camino*, is 95 km (60 miles) east of Santiago on the N-547 highway that twists and turns through jagged mountains. The drive is worth the effort, for circling the town is one of the best-preserved Roman walls to be found anywhere in the world. The massive schist walls, now declared a World Heritage site, are 2 km (1¼ miles) long and 10 metres (33 ft) high and date from the 3rd century; the walk around the top takes just 30 minutes.

Lugo's position on the French *camino* explains the strong French influence in the Romanesque parts of its **Cathedral**, begun in the 12th century (open daily). It was expanded in the Gothic period and enlarged in the 18th century. The **Capilla de Nossa Señora dos Ollos Grandes** (Virgin of the Big Eyes), a chapel at its east end features an exquisite baroque rotunda, which contrasts with the Romanesque carving on the north and south doors. Across from the north door on the lovely Praza de Santa María is the 18th-century **Palacio Episcopal**, a typical *pazo*, or Galician manorhouse. The **Museo Provincial** (open Mon–Sat 10.30am–2pm and 4.30–8pm, Sun until noon) houses a large mixed collection representing provincial history and includes a country cottage kitchen and Roman mosaics discovered while building a city-centre car park.

In summer you can join the largely local crowds who flock to Lugo's coast and its relaxed fishing ports-turned-beach resorts; **Viveiro** and **Ribadeo** both have beautiful old towns that are pleasant to stroll through. Alternatively, you can explore the interior. **Santa Eulalia de Bóveda ⑥**, 25 km (15 miles) from Lugo, is a palaeo-Christian monument that was unearthed in the early years of the 20th century, with a vestibule open to the sky and a rectangular chamber decorated with exquisite frescoes of birds and leaves (open Tues–Sun

Map on page 318

11am–2pm and 3.30–5.30pm, until 7.30pm June–Sept). Slightly further afield, **Mondoñedo** and **Monforte de Lemos** are country towns that are also worthy of a visit if you have the time.

Feudal remnants

The highways and byways of Lugo and Ourense, the two eastern inland provinces, provide an insight into Galician history. Old men with weatherbeaten and wrinkled faces plough small plots with the help of a pair of oxen. Old women in the rigorous black of widowhood trudge along roads, their long-handled scythes on their shoulders as they follow carts piled high with long grass.

Farming methods here vary little from the strip farming done in the Middle Ages. Abundant rainfall gives the appearance of a bucolic paradise, but severe erosion and the uneven terrain make the mechanisation of farming almost impossible in many areas, while the division of the land into small family farms, known as *minifundio*, averaging just 250 sq metres (300 sq yds) thwarts political attempts to bring about agricultural reforms. Everyone has some land and no one wants to give up their small parcels, which are usually spread apart because of the way land has been passed down through inheritance. In fact, a semi-feudal society continues to exist. Dominant *caciques* (bosses) maintain great influence and power over peasants in villages in many areas where communication by road off the major highways remains difficult despite improvements. The provinces of Lugo and Ourense have the lowest income per capita in all Spain and much of the population still emigrates to the cities, the coast or overseas to find work. The other side of the same coin are the region's weatherbeaten castles and *pazos*, or manorhouses, built with the rents or *foros* paid by the local aristocracy. An outstanding example of their distinctive architectural and gardening style is the **Pazo de Oca**, south of Santiago on the N-525.

Ourense ❼ is said to have received its name because of the gold mined by the Romans in the Valdeorras hills of the Sil valley. Although it is now a busy commercial town, it retains the **Puente Romano** (Roman bridge) that was rebuilt on its original foundations in the 13th century. In the **Museo Arqueológico** (open Tues–Sun; entrance fee), just behind Praza Maior, prehistoric, pre-Roman and Roman-era specimens are kept alongside later pilgrimage art. Close by, the **Catedral de San Martiño**'s Romanesque Pórtico del Paraíso (Paradise Door) inside the west front illustrates the 24 Old Men of the Apocalypse and still has its medieval colouring. The province's river valleys to the east are dotted with monasteries and steeply terraced vineyards along the Sol; to the west the Miño Valley road (PO 400) is an impressive drive taking you up to **Ribadavia**, a medieval wine-town, and along the Portuguese border to **Tui**, with its splendid hilltop cathedral.

"Cradle of sailors"

You can visit most of the impressive **Rías Baixas** with relative ease by car from Pontevedra and Vigo. According to legend, **Pontevedra** ❽ was founded by Teucer, half-brother of Ajax. But historians say the town probably dates from the Roman period and its

For hundreds of years, Ourense has attracted visitors who come to sample the mineral waters from three springs in Praza das Burgas. The water emerges at a temperature of 67°C (153°F).

BELOW: Ourense's Puente Romano.

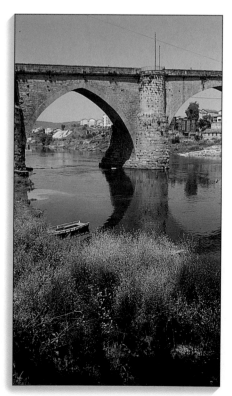

name from the Latin "*Pons Vetus*" (Old Bridge) that described the 11-arch span over the Río Lérez. The trading port had a brilliant life during the Middle Ages and Columbus's *Santa María* was built in its shipyards. But after the harbour silted up, a new port built at Marín surpassed it in importance. Today the islet in the river has been converted into an open-air sculpture museum.

Pontevedra is the birthplace of great sailors, including the explorer Pedro Sarmiento de Gamboa, a skilled 16th-century navigator and cosmographer who wrote "Voyage to the Straits of Magellan".

Pontevedra preserves the charm of an old country town with fine examples of *cruceiros*, the stone crosses marking crossroads, in its streets. The **Santa María La Mayor** Plateresque church (open daily 9am–2pm, 5–8.30pm), nestled among the alleyways in the fishermen's quarter, was built late in the 15th century by the mariners' guild. Its interior features an impressive mix of Gothic notched arches, Isabelline twisted columns and ribbed vaulting in the Renaissance style. Close by in Praza de la Leña is the small but stunning **Museo Provincial** (open daily; entrance fee), with Bronze Age jewellery, paintings by Zurbarán and Goya and the work of Alfonso Castaleo, a 20th-century Galician artist. His images of the Civil War are particularly moving.

Behind Pontevedra is a lovely rolling hill country with hamlets steeped in rural traditions. In the municipality of **As Neves** in southern Pontevedra province, every year on 29 July, people whose lives have been saved in one way or another during the previous year gather to thank St Marta for her saving grace; the "saved" people dress up in funeral clothes and get inside coffins which are then paraded around the church of **Ribarteme** by their families. Carnival here, and in the Lugo and Ourense countryside, is a hedonistic week of revelling with a mass of medieval rituals, fancy-dress, eating and drinking.

BELOW: Galician women preparing octopus.

From Pontevedra, the coastal highway C-550 zigzags north around the Salnés peninsula, which has grown wealthy on tourism, intensive fish farming,

smuggling and vineyards. **Combarro** is one of the picturesque fishing villages in this area. Round a cape on the southern side of the **Ría de Arousa** is the extraordinary **La Lanzada beach**. In summer hundreds camp out on this long, picturesque strand which shines like a white clam shell. At the far end is a nature reserve with protected dunes and marshland. Further north is the island of **La Toja**, where Galicia's beach tourism began. A sick donkey was the first creature to benefit from the mineral waters of a spring here. Now a luxury hotel offers everything from blackjack to beauty treatments. Neighbouring **O Grove** is a seafood lover's paradise, with excellent restaurants, an aquarium and submarine trips in the *rías*.

In the smuggling town of **Cambados ⑨**, savour the strong Albariño varietal wine produced nearby that goes so well with seafood. A 17th-century church and the adjoining **Fefiñanes Pazo** (mansion), along with a row of arcaded houses, form the attractive **Plaza de Fefiñanes** at the town's north entrance. A little further down the highway is a lovely promenade overlooking the bay.

Rosalía de Castro

Padrón ⑩ is believed to be the coastal town where the boat bearing the body of St James arrived in Spain. The boat's mooring stone can be seen under the altar of the local church, beneath the bridge over the **Río Sar**. Galicia's most famous poet, Rosalía de Castro (1837–85) lived for many years in a stone house near the Sar. The house is now a **museum** (open Tues–Sun). She and her husband, the historian Manuel Murguía, formed the nucleus of a group of poets and writers who were influential in stimulating the *Rexurdimento* (renaissance) in Galician letters. The *Rexurdimento* stirred latent nationalist sentiment, and by

Map on page 318

BELOW: the *horreo*, or Galician granary, is built on stilts to keep out vermin.

Rosalía de Castro's penetrating studies of country folk sparked a new interest in Galician culture. Her "Cantares Gallegos" (Galician Songs, 1863) is one of the greatest works of Spanish literature.

BELOW: view of Galicia's Rías Baixas.

the beginning of the 20th century, several nationalist parties had been formed.

Rosalía de Castro felt a fundamental affiliation with the tribulations of the poor of rural Galicia because of the pain she experienced in her own life. The illegitimate daughter of a priest, she was rejected by family and society, lived for many years in an unhappy marriage and in her old age she was wracked by cancer. She is a universally revered figure for Galicians, who know her poetry well. In more recent times, Padrón was the birthplace of the Nobel-prizewinning novelist Camilo José de Cela, whose home is now a literary foundation.

The coastline to the north of Padrón is called the **Costa da Morte**, meaning the Coast of Death, so named because of the number of ships wrecked and lives lost along the rocky shoreline. The land leads out to Cabo Finisterre – literally the end of the earth to the Romans – via a winding road that snakes its way through fishing villages and past a stunning 8-km (5-mile) stretch of virgin beach at **Carnota**.

Riches old and new

Vigo ⓫, just an hour's drive south of Pontevedra along the A9, is Galicia's largest and most industrialised city. It dates back to Roman times, but flourished and grew wealthier in later centuries when Carlos I authorised commercial trade with America in 1529. In 1702, a Spanish treasure convoy was intercepted and destroyed by the British in Vigo Bay. To this day, it is believed that tons of gold lie at the bottom of the bay in the hold of lost galleons.

In more recent decades, Vigo's wealth has been based on manufacturing industries such as fish-canning, car production, shipbuilding and the sleepless port, which is home to half of Spain's deep-sea fishing fleet, one of the largest

Map on page 318

in the world. Although not a traditionally beautiful city, the old quarter and Modernist buildings give it character; and the Galician art collection in the **Pazo de Quiñones**, a 17th-century manor-house set in the peaceful Parque de Castrelos (open Tues–Sun; entrance fee), is unmissable.

Above all, Vigo is a city for sea-lovers. Enjoy the sun at one of several sparkling beaches, including **Samil**, **Alcabre** and **Canido**. Or take a ferry ride from the port to the charming fishing village of **Cangas** on the north side of the *ría* or to the **Islas Cíes**, small, uninhabited isles in the mouth of Vigo Bay, now protected as a natural park. Back on the mainland, an ambitious **Museo del Mar** was inaugurated in 2002 (open Tues–Sun 10am–9pm; entrance fee).

To reach the port where Columbus's flagship *Pinta* docked in 1493 with news of the discovery of the New World, drive south for an hour on coastal highway C-550 to **Baiona**, a chic and wealthy resort with smart yachts bobbing in the bay. **Castelo de Monterreal ⑫**, a massive castle fortress with a long defence wall, was built on this promontory rock in about 1500. It later became the governor's residence and has now been converted to the Parador **Conde de Gondomar**, which has a commanding view of the Atlantic, the **Islas Estelas** in the mouth of the bay and the coast south to **Cabo Silleiro**.

At this point, the crowds appear to drop away for the final stretch of coastline running down to Portugal. The climate in the Miño estuary has a mild, tropical quality, enabling such species as kiwis, vines and subtropical flowers to flourish. **A Guarda**, the border town, is a beautifully unspoiled fishing port offering both fine beaches and wonderfully scenic, panoramic views from the Celtic **Museo de Monte de Santa Tecla** (open daily; entrance fee), located south of the town centre.   ❑

Seafood is abundant and super fresh along this southern stretch of coast. Try fried shrimp with garlic, scallops, hake, raw oysters with lemon, boiled lobster or clams.

BELOW: Vigo's deep-water bay.

THE CANARY ISLANDS

Map on pages 334–5

This isolated archipelago is often forgotten in any survey of Spain. Yet eight million tourists a year come here, lured by the continuous sunshine, endless beaches and volcanic landscapes

The Canary Islands offer some remarkable contrasts. Here you'll find one of the highest mountains in Europe, beaches of black sand and seas of still-hot volcanic lava; and moss-cloaked and mist-shrouded forests that have survived from the tertiary era. Some of the islands in this archipelago are razor-sharp, steep and volcanic, their tops in cloud; a couple of them are slivers of sand, like slices cut from nearby mainland Africa and rolled flat by blistering sunshine.

Parts of this archipelago, marooned out in the Atlantic Ocean, are better known to Europeans escaping the mid-winter blues than to Spaniards. At the height of the season, tourists outnumber locals by five to one. They are attracted by a remarkably consistent climate: the average temperature of 17°C (63°F) in winter increases to 24°C (75°F) in summer, with a cooling offshore breeze.

The Canaries have been transformed by tourism from an isolated outpost of Spain into a diverse, multicultural society. The seas are covered in fluttering sails, and apartment blocks cling to the slopes. The well equipped resorts are little cities in themselves, with a babel of different languages filling the streets and bars. You can buy genuine fish and chips cooked up by a man from Macclesfield, and authentic sauerkraut dished up by a woman from Stuttgart.

PRECEDING PAGES: sunbathing on Gran Canaria. **LEFT:** Las Teresitas beach, Tenerife. **BELOW:** working partnership.

A touch of history

Despite this annual invasion, there are many parts of the islands that are almost untouched by tourism and have retained their individuality. Elegant colonial architecture, introduced by the Spanish conquerors who arrived in the 15th century, has been lovingly restored in several cities on Tenerife and Gran Canaria. The influence of years of trade with and immigration to South America is evident in food, language and a certain indefinable atmosphere. World events have touched the islands at various times: Colombus stopped here for essential ship repairs on his great voyage of discovery; Nelson tried and failed to take the port of Santa Cruz in 1797 and lost his arm while trying to capture a Mexican fleet; and General Franco launched the Civil War from Tenerife in 1936.

There are seven main islands in the Canaries: Gran Canaria, Fuerteventura and Lanzarote in the eastern Las Palmas Province, and Tenerife, La Palma, La Gomera and El Hierro in the western Santa Cruz Province. There are also four uninhabited islets, and countless reefs and rocks in the archipelago.

The eastern Canaries

Tenerife and Gran Canaria share equal status as capital of the autonomous region of the Canary Islands, and the presidency alternates between them every four years. **Gran Canaria** is the third largest island (1,532

The promenade at Playa del Inglés, the largest resort on the south coast of Gran Canaria. It has a long white-sand beach stretching for 10 km (6 miles).

sq km/592 sq miles) and has a population of 760,000. Its capital, **Las Palmas de Gran Canaria ❶** (pop. 360,000), covers its northern tip.

Las Palmas is both elegant and seedy. It has one of the largest ports in Europe and an excellent beach, Playa de las Canteras, which is very popular with tourists from mainland Spain. Not far from the port is the new, state-of-the-art science museum, **Museu Elder** (open Tues–Sun 10am–8pm; entrance fee). Vegueta, the old Spanish colonial quarter to the south, is centred on the Gothic **Catedral de Santa Ana** with the adjacent **Museu de Arte Sacro** (open daily; entrance fee to museum). Nearby, the **Museu Canario** (open Mon–Fri 10am–8pm, Sat–Sun 10am–2pm; entrance fee) exhibits mummies and other artefacts from the pre-Hispanic period when the aboriginal *Guanches* inhabited the islands. Also in Vegueta's narrow streets, the **Casa de Colón** (open Mon–Fri 9am–7pm, Sat–Sun 9am–3pm; entrance fee), a lovely Renaissance building, is a museum dedicated to Columbus and the maritime past.

En route to the main tourist destinations in the south, make time for some attractive old towns such as Telde, with San Juan Bautista, the oldest church on the island; and **Agüimes ❷**, whose attractive Casco Historico and a couple of hotels dedicated to rural tourism make it worth a visit. Then follow the steep, winding road through the wild, scenic interior to the **Pico de las Nieves ❸** (1,950 metres/6,398 ft). There is an excellent view of the central summits from the Cruz de Tejeda. Some inland areas, notably the lovely village of Artenara, have inhabited caves and the island's most famous ravine, the **Barranco de Guayadeque**, wonderful for serious walking, has cave bars and restaurants.

Wind back down to the coast (or return to the coast-hugging motorway, GC1) to reach the huge, strident resorts of **Playa del Inglés** and **Maspalomas ❹**, where

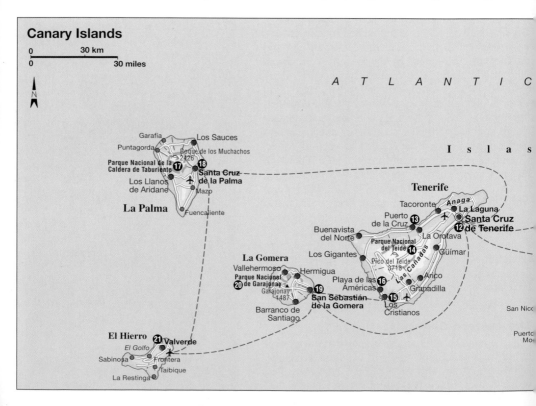

Canary Islands

0   30 km
0   30 miles

N

ATLANTIC

Islas

Garafia
Los Sauces
Puntagorda
Roque de los Muchachos
▲ 2426
Parque Nacional de la
Caldera de Taburiente ❶⓻
Santa Cruz
Los Llanos ❶⓼
de Aridane
de la Palma
La Palma
Mazo
Fuencaliente

Tenerife
Tacoronte Anaga
Puerto La Laguna
de la Cruz ❶⓷
Santa Cruz
Buenavista
La Orotava ❶⓶ de Tenerife
del Norte
Parque Nacional
del Teide ❶⓸
Los Gigantes
Güimar
La Gomera
Pico del Teide
▲ 3718
Vallehermoso Las Cañadas
Hermigua
Parque Nacional
Playa de las ❶⓺ Arico
❷⓪ de Garajonay
Américas
Granadilla
Garajonay
1487
San Sebastián ❶⓹
Barranco de
de la Gomera
Santiago
Los
San Nico
Cristianos

El Hierro ❷⓵ Valverde
El Golfo
Puerto
Sabinosa
Frontera
Mo
Taibique
La Restinga

Map below

there are endless hours of guaranteed sunshine and wonderful stretches of sand dunes. Until the early 1960s the south was a remote, arid spot; now the southern shoreline is virtually one continous urbanisation, with high-rise hotels and apartment blocks, water theme parks and streets full of bars, clubs and restaurants.

Beyond the attractive and more up-market resort of **Puerto de Mogán ❺**, where bougainvillaea-covered houses surround a harbour bobbing with yachts, the coast returns to its semi-wild state, with locals still making their living by fishing or agriculture. In the northwest are the attractive towns of **Agaete**, and its fishing port, the **Puerto de las Nieves**, built around a picturesque rocky bay; and **Gáldar**, ancient capital of the Guanches, although the remains of their splendour are currently under wraps, as they undergo lengthy renovation.

A land without rain

The second largest of the Canary Islands at 1,670 sq km (645 sq miles), **Fuerteventura** also has one of the smallest populations (30,000). Like neighbouring Lanzarote and not-so-distant Africa only 96 km (60 miles) away, Fuerteventura doesn't have the height to prod the passing clouds into releasing their water. The island is consequently very barren and sandy, and its fragile economy is based on goat-rearing and tourism, although recent initiatives in *turismo rural* have led to the renovation of many of the island's landmark windmills and the establishment of ecological museums, such as the **Eco-Museu La Alcogida** (open Tues–Fri and Sun; entrance fee) at Tefia. The main town of **Puerto del Rosario** is straggling and unattractive, although an extensive renovation of the harbour front should brighten it up when completed. The old capital city of **Betancuria ❻**, a pretty spot in the centre of the island, is far more

Before the arrival of the Europeans, several indigenous tribes, known collectively as Guanches, *lived on the Canary Islands. Examples of stone and bone implements, and other* Guanche *artefacts, can be seen in museums all over the islands.*

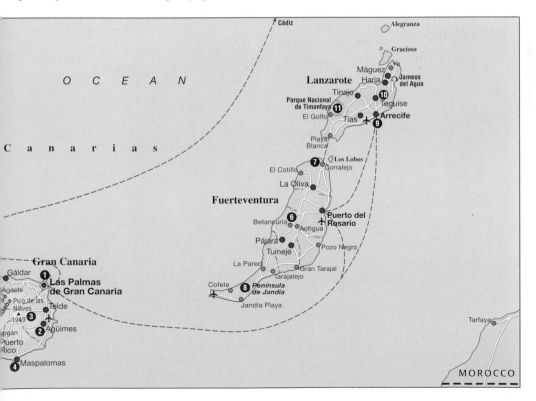

Demonstration of volcanic heat at the Parque Nacional de Timanfaya.

interesting, with a cathedral, the Iglesia Santa María, and a fascinating **Museu Arqueológico y Etnográfico** (open Tues–Sun; entrance fee).

Fuerteventura has the Canaries' best beaches. At the northern tip lie the idyllic sands of **Corralejo** ❼, where the old part of town retains its character, although surrounded by apartment blocks and shopping malls. In the south the **Peninsula de Jandía** ❽, once separated from the rest of the island by a wall, La Pared, is a region of glorious golden beaches, glittering seas and water-sports facilities and the inevitable over-development of the coast.

Volcanic island

The fourth largest of the seven islands, **Lanzarote** (810 sq km/315 sq miles) has a population of 86,000. At times, when the light is sluggish, the island looks like the scab on a volcanic wound, still bubbling hot, red and raw underneath, but there are moments of rare beauty in this barren landscape, where the prickly pear cactus is the most commonplace plant, and the islanders paint their windows and doors green to compensate for the lack of vegetation.

Arrecife ❾, the island capital, is a modern town, although waterfront promenades and a pleasant beach add interest. As on Fuerteventura, the former capital has all the historic interest: **Teguise** ❿ has a 15th-century church, a lofty convent, an old palace, a castle and an excellent Sunday market (open 9am–4pm).

Lanzarote's **Parque Nacional de Timanfaya** ⓫ (open daily 10am–6pm; entrance fee) is a massive volcanic wasteland of mangled rock and twisted lava created by early 18th-century eruptions. During tours of the park (by bus and camel) park rangers give dramatic demonstrations of the earth's continuing power, and the El Diablo restaurant cooks with volcanic heat.

BELOW: lighthouse on Tenerife.

Lanzarote's star resort is **Puerto del Carmen** but there are numerous other attractive spots around the southern tip. Most of the tourist developments are tastefully done, reflecting the influence of local artist, César Manrique, who died in 1992 and whose sculptures can be seen all over the island. The **César Manrique Foundation** (open daily 10am–6pm; entrance fee) in Tahiche, just north of the capital, is one of Lanzarote's greatest attractions.

The western Canaries

The western islands – Tenerife, La Palma, La Gomera and El Hierro – are more beautiful than the eastern group with craggy mountains, lush valleys, deep and ancient forests and a mixture of sunshine, cloud and mist.

The largest of the islands (2,354 sq km/910 sq miles), **Tenerife** has a population of 700,000 and the highest mountain in Spain, the volcanic El Teide, rising to 3,720 metres (12,200 ft), with forests, green valleys and finally beaches on its lower skirts. Tenerife's capital, **Santa Cruz de Tenerife ⓬**, is a pleasant colonial town, rather smaller than Las Palmas. Among sites worth visiting are the Iglesia de Nuestra Señora de la Concepción (open daylight hours, like most Tenerife churches); the Museu de la Naturaleza (open Tues–Sun 10am–8pm; entrance fee), with excellent collections of artefacts from the Guanche era; and the **Museu Militar** (open Tues–Sun 10am–2pm; entrance fee), which exhibits the cannon reputed to have removed Admiral Nelson's arm in 1797.

About 8 km (5 miles) north lie the gleaming white sands of **Las Teresitas**, one of the largest man-made beaches in the world. Santa Cruz lies in the shadow of the Anaga mountains, which form the northern part of the island, and conceal remarkable, rugged scenery and tiny hidden villages in their green folds.

Map on pages 334–5

Local architect César Manrique designed many memorable cave conversions in Lanzarote, notably the Jameos del Agua complex on the northeast coast, which includes a nightclub, restaurant and formal gardens.

BELOW: La Orotava during the flower festival.

The history of tourism in Tenerife began in 1850, with the first steamship service from Cádiz. Only gentry could afford to travel, of course, and they came to **Puerto de la Cruz** ⓭ and **La Orotava** in the fertile Orotava Valley on the northwestern coast, an area still known for its banana plantations. Both these attractive towns, with their elegant colonial-style mansions and narrow cobbled streets, retain some of their earlier gentility. However, because the northern coast is rough and wild, Puerto lacks one major feature that the modern tourist expects – a sandy beach. This problem has been circumvented by the elegant **Lago de Martiánez**, a series of swimming pools sculpted out of the rock at sea level by Lanzarote architect César Manrique.

In the 1880s, Mrs Olivia Stone, a formidable Victorian traveller, toured the Canary Islands on donkey-back. Visitors began pouring into the islands after her book, "Tenerife and its Six Satellites", was published.

The **Parque Nacional del Teide** ⓮ encompasses Las Cañadas, the area left by the collapse of the ancient crater around El Teide. There are good roads into the park, but because of erosion you are not allowed to climb right to the peak; instead, you can take a cable-car (teleférico), which stops 160 metres (525 ft) short of the summit. There are stunning views and some very unusual rock formations. A helpful Visitors' Centre (open daily 9am–4pm) at the El Portillo entrance offers advice and there's a Parador if you want to stay overnight.

The largest resorts, **Los Cristianos** ⓯ and **Playa de las Américas** ⓰, are in the south of the island, where the sunshine is guaranteed. Big, brash and ever busy, with 24-hour entertainment, they are close to the main airport, Reina Sofía, and are easily reached from Santa Cruz via the TF1 motorway.

The best of the rest

BELOW: balconies in La Palma.

La Palma, the greenest and fifth largest of the islands (730 sq km/282 sq miles), has retained much of its 80,000-strong population, thanks to its suitability for

agriculture. The island is very steep, rising to 2,426 metres (7,960 ft) at the **Roque de los Muchachos**, and falling away sharply to the sea around the rocky coast, thus denying mass tourism much of a foothold. The **Parque Nacional de la Caldera de Taburiente** ⑰ (Visitors' Centre open Mon–Sat), with its massive volcanic crater 9 km (5½ miles) in diameter, occupies much of the northern part of La Palma. On the rim of the volcano is the Observatorio Astrofísica, with one of the largest telescopes in Europe. Colonial **Santa Cruz de la Palma** ⑱ is acknowledged to be the most beautiful of the Canary Islands' capitals.

The second smallest of the islands (378 sq km/146 sq miles), **La Gomera** has a population of around 20,000, with tourism on the increase. The main town of **San Sebastián** ⑲, which may not have changed much since Columbus stopped here for supplies in 1492, is linked to southern Tenerife by a regular ferry service. The Parador here is one of the finest in Spain. La Gomera's limited tourist areas are the **Valle Gran Rey**, a deep, luxuriant valley in the southeast corner of the island, which attracts longer-staying backpackers, and **Playa de Santiago**, the site of the upmarket **Jardín Tecina** hotel complex. Beach areas are limited: the island rises steeply to its highest point (Mount Garajonay at 1,487 metres/4,880 ft) in the centre of **Parque Nacional de Garajonay** ⑳, notable for its ancient tertiary-era forest made up of moss-cloaked laurel and cedar trees.

The smallest of the islands at 278 sq km (107 sq miles), **El Hierro** is also the least developed and least populated, with around 6,000 inhabitants. Cattle and livestock are the mainstay, and wines and cheeses are produced. The principal town, **Valverde** ㉑ is the only island capital situated inland. El Hierro also has its own massive volcanic crater, although one side has collapsed into the sea; the result is **El Golfo**, a calm, wide gulf, this friendly island's most peaceful spot. ❏

Map on pages 334–5

La Palma was the scene of the most recent volcanic activity in the Canaries, when an eruption in the side of the old volcano of San Antonio in 1971 formed a new cone.

BELOW:
El Teide's summit.

THE BALEARIC ISLANDS

Map
on page
344

Writers and artists have long flocked to Mallorca, Menorca, Ibiza and Formentera, finding inspiration in the idyllic climate, the magnificent landscapes and, above all, the peace and quiet

The Balearic islands are well known for their sunshine and beaches, but just a short distance away from the resorts lies a wealth of beautiful scenery and handsome old towns. On Mallorca, the largest island, the spectacular Serra de Tramuntana forms one of Europe's most dramatic coastlines, while Menorca is more gentle, with a timeless landscape and a surprising number of undeveloped little coves and beaches. Ibiza is famous for its nightlife, while tiny Formentera just about manages to retain its uncluttered simplicity.

These islands make up the autonomous region of the Balearics (Balears). Their name comes from the Greek word for sling, *ballo.* So famous were the ancient natives of the Balearics for their skill in hurling deadly lead pellets with slings that the Romans called the two larger islands *Balear Maior* and *Balear Minor.*

Skeletal remains indicate that the islands were inhabited as early as 4000 BC but the oldest architectural ruins date from the 3rd millennium BC. The Talayotic Age, which extended from 1000 BC to the Roman conquest, left the most archaeological testimonies; stone structures called *talayots,* believed to have been built by a people who came from the Eastern Mediterranean. The Carthaginians, whose occupation dated from the middle of the 7th century BC, recruited Balearic mercenaries whose slings were the terror of the Romans. It was not until 20 years after the destruction of Carthage (146 BC) that Rome was able to subjugate the islands.

PRECEDING PAGES: Sant Joan Festival, Menorca. **LEFT:** the rocky coast of the Formentor peninsula, Mallorca. **BELOW:** tower at Banyalbufar, Mallorca.

Conquest and reconquest

As the Roman Empire was falling apart, the Vandals swept into the islands in AD 426 and remained until they were driven out by the Byzantines 100 years later. Three centuries of Muslim domination of the Balearics, made tributary to the Emirate of Córdoba in 848, left a heritage of Moorish place-names (beginning with "Bin" or "Al") and whitewashed architecture.

The Christian Reconquest took place in Mallorca in 1229 under King Jaume of Aragón. The event proved decisive in the final evolution of the islands' culture. They fell under the influence of Catalonia, and to this day each island speaks its own variant of Catalan. In the 13th century the Balearic Islands became important stops on the trade route between northern Italy and northern Europe. Mallorca produced great artists and craftsmen whose work may be seen in Palma's cathedral and the Castel de Belver.

With the rise of the Turkish Empire in the 16th century, the Balearic Islands became a bastion of the expanding Spanish Empire. Watchtowers or *talaies* throughout the islands testify to the constant need to keep watch against sudden raids of Muslim corsairs in search of booty and slaves. Ibiza city's magnificent walls date from this period.

With the resurgence of Mediterranean commerce in the middle of the 17th century, Mallorcan merchants once again began to benefit from the islands' strategic location. Many of the country mansions or *possessiós* that grace the countryside date from this period, and their Italian-inspired architecture illustrates the strong links between Mallorca and Italy. In 1708 the British seized Menorca during the War of the Spanish Succession. Except for a brief occupation by the French, they remained in control until 1781.

Artists' colony

In Palma the sky is turquoise, the sea is blue, and the mountains are emerald. The air is just as blue as the sky. In a word, life here is delicious.

—FRÉDÉRIC CHOPIN

In the mid-19th century, foreign tourists began to discover the delights of the Balearics. A five-month stay by Aurore Dupin, Baroness Dudevant, better known by her pen name of George Sand, and the pianist and composer, Frédéric Chopin, inaugurated a whole era of tourism.

George Sand's book, *A Winter in Mallorca*, was the first of what is now an extensive travel literature on the islands. Writers such as Charles Wood, Gaston Vouillier and the eccentric Archduke Louis Salvador of Habsburg Bourbon followed. This descendant of one of Europe's oldest royal families discovered Mallorca in 1867. He returned five years later to settle down and acquired the estate of Miramar. He maintained a large household presided over by a Mallorcan peasant girl, Catalina Homar, the great love of his life. Archduke Louis Salvador was not an idle aristocrat; he wrote a total of 60 books headed by his seven-volume work, *Die Balearen – The Baleares Described in Words and Images*.

A steady stream of writers and artists looking for secluded picturesque places continued to visit Mallorca and Ibiza. Some, like Robert Graves, settled down and stayed for life.

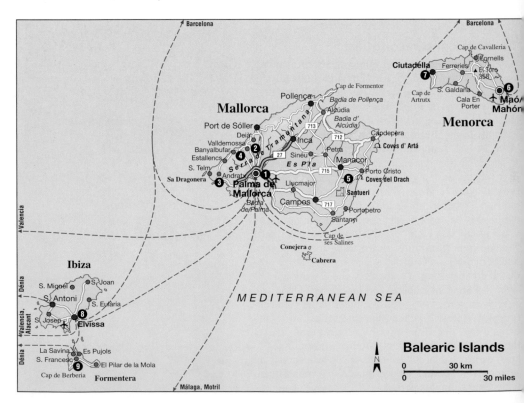

Mallorca

Although most people arrive by air, the most impressive way to reach Mallorca is by boat from Barcelona or Valencia to **Palma** ❶. From a distance the city's medieval Gothic masterpiece, the **Catedral** (open Mon–Fri 10am–6.15pm, Sat 10am–2.15pm; entrance fee for museum), stands out like a huge, rose-coloured, craggy rock. Work on the cathedral began in the 13th century and was not completed until the 16th century. Its beautiful rose windows makes it the most luminous of Mediterranean cathedrals. You enter through a small **museum** which has splendid silver monstrances and some medieval paintings.

As the boat draws closer, the city's profile is crowned by other ancient monuments. The **Castel de Bellver** (open Mon–Sat 8am–8.30pm, Oct–Mar closes 7pm, Sun 10am–6.30pm, Oct–Mar closes 4.30pm; entrance fee), perched on a hill to the west of the city, was a prison until the early 20th century, although it was originally built as a summer palace. The 13th-century **Palau de l'Almudaina** (open Mon–Fri 10am–6.30pm, Sat 10am–2pm; entrance fee but free to EU citizens on Wed), beside the cathedral on the foundations of an Arab *alcàsser* or fortress, is used for official functions by the royal family and has some interesting royal portraits. In the courtyard is the Gothic Capilla de Santa Ana.

The area around the cathedral was the site of the Arab city known as *Medina Mayurka*. The only architectural remnants are an arch on Carrer Alumudaina and the two small chambers of the **Banys Àrabs** (open daily 9.30am–8pm, Oct–Mar 9.30am–6pm; entrance fee) in Carrer Serra. This neighbourhood is especially interesting for wandering around, poking into ancient churches and admiring the houses of wealthy noblemen and merchants. The nearby streets of **Almudaina**, **Zanglada** and **Morey** have noble houses dating from the 16th through to the

Map on page 344

TIP

For a lively (and loud) night out in Palma, the narrow streets immediately west of Passeig d'es Born and Avenida Antonio Maura have the best selection of bars. The other major nightlife area is further west, around Passeig Marítimo and Avda Gabriel Roca.

BELOW: Palma's Gothic *Catedral*.

Ramón Llull (1235–1315), a Christian monk, wrote 500 books including poetry, allegorical novels and works of medicine and mathematics. At the age of 80 he was stoned to death while trying to convert Muslims.

BELOW: nets drying in the sun at Port de Sóller.

18th century. On the **Plaça San Francesc** is a church of the same name built during the 13th century, although its baroque façade dates from the 17th century. One of its eight-sided chapels, all of which are decorated with Renaissance and baroque art, contains the 15th-century sarcophagus of Ramón Llull. Outside is a statue of missionary Father Junípero Serra *(see page 349)*.

A symbol of Palma's prosperous past is the magnificent 15th-century building known as **Sa Llotja** (open Mon–Fri 11am–2pm), which used to house the merchants' stock exchange; today the wonderfully airy interior is used for art exhibitions. Its four crenellated, octagonal-cornered towers and galleried windows serve as a counterweight to the majestic cathedral. The 17th-century **Consolat de Mar** next door has an impressive Renaissance-style gallery.

About 5 km (3 miles) southwest of the old town (regular bus services) at Carrer Joan de Saridakis 29, the **Fundacío Pilar i Joan Miró** (open Tues–Sat 10am–7pm, Oct–Mar 11am–6pm, Sun 10am–3pm; entrance fee) is worth a visit to admire the architecture of the modern building, designed by Rafael Moneo, as well as to see the changing display of work from the Miró collection.

Scenic drives

Inland, Mallorca divides into two: the Serra de Tramuntana, which runs along the northern coast, and the fertile plain that makes up the bulk of the rest. The bays of **Alcúdia** and **Pollença**, on the northeastern side of the island, are particularly attractive. Most heavy tourist urbanisation is within the Bay of Palma and along some of the coves of the eastern coast.

If time is short, head straight towards **Valldemossa ❷**, about 25 km (15 miles) north of the capital, to see **La Real Cartuja de Valldemossa** (open

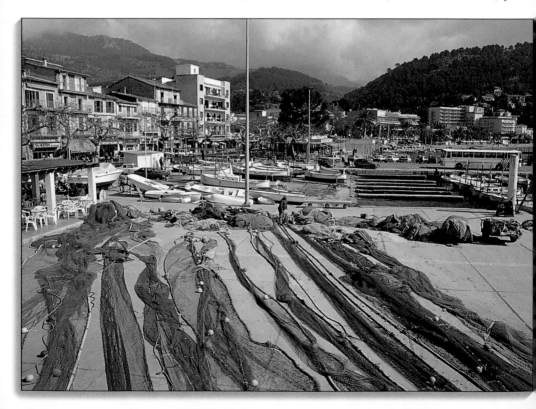

Mon–Sat 9.30am–6pm, Sun 10am–1pm, Nov–Feb 9.30am–4.30pm; entrance fee), where George Sand and Chopin spent the winter of 1838–9. In spite of having a rather primitive borrowed piano to work with, Chopin composed some of his most beautiful pieces here, including the *Raindrop Prelude*. The monastery was originally built as a palace by King Jaume II in 1309, but was later given to the Carthusian order to establish a monastery. The neoclassical chapel has frescoes on the ceiling painted by Goya's brother-in-law, Manuel Bayeu. The owners of the well-kept houses of this village make a point of keeping their front doors open for passers-by to admire the decor of their entrance halls.

If taking the coastal route to the west of Palma you will come to **Andratx ❸**, which has an attractive port nearby. Despite tourist-oriented development, **Port d'Andratx** has kept its colour as a fishing village. Like many towns in the Balearics, the main town of Andratx was built some miles inland for protection from pirates and was surrounded by *talaies* or watchtowers. The fortified **church**, like many on the islands, was once surrounded by a moat. The somewhat isolated village of **Sant Telm** has also retained its identity and affords a striking view of the island of **Sa Dragonera**. Nearby is the abandoned monastery of **Sa Trapa**, which makes for an excellent walk from Sant Telm. During the summer there are boat trips around Sa Dragonera, believed to be the beachhead of the Christian expedition that conquered Mallorca in 1229.

The northwest coast route

The C-710 coastal road from Andratx follows one of Europe's most breathtaking routes, hugging the mountainside high above the sea. The village of **Estellencs**, which straddles the steep slopes of **Mount Galatzó**, has a defensive

Map on page 344

BELOW: terraced fields overlooking the sea at Banyalbufar.

For additional rugged countryside next to the sea, visit the northern peninsula of Formentor. On the way, you'll pass the lovely town of Pollença, which has a Roman bridge on its outskirts.

tower used in the days when pirates were a menace. A little further along this road is the village of **Banyalbufar** ❹, set amid agricultural terraces carved out of the mountain, shored up with meticulous stone walls and irrigated by a network of canals. The town still has half of the dozen fortified towers built as a defence against the marauding Turks in the 16th and 17th centuries.

About 5 km (3 miles) past Valldemossa is the estate of **Miramar**, the nucleus of various properties owned by Archduke Louis Salvador. The most notable of these is **Son Marroig** (open Mon–Sat 9.30am–2pm, 3pm–sunset), on the way to Deià. This splendid mansion, built around an ancient defensive tower, has a museum of Mallorcan folklore, but is best known for its marble belvedere, with views of the rocky promontory of Na Foradada and the coast to the west.

Deià has kept much of its original architecture. It has resisted the ravages of hotel complexes and tourist shops thanks largely to the efforts of its artists' colony led by Robert Graves, who first settled here in 1929 at Gertrude Stein's suggestion. "It's paradise, if you can stand it," she is reported to have told him. From here the road wriggles its way through the hills before descending to **Sóller**, a lovely town set amid orange and lemon groves, and linked to its port (3 km/2 miles to the north) by a delightful old-fashioned tram service. Sóller is also the terminus for the early 20th-century wooden train from Palma, which runs five times daily (six on Sunday).

The east coast

The extensive **Coves del Drach** ❺ and **Coves d'Artà** (both open daily, entrance fee) in the eastern part of the island are worth seeing. A chamber-music ensemble performs next to the largest of the subterranean lakes of the more commer-

BELOW: Georgian town house in Maó.

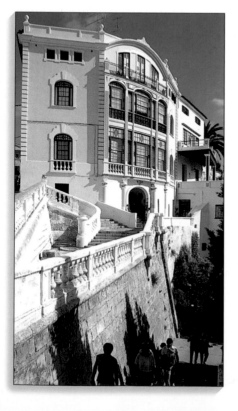

PREHISTORY IN MENORCA

Three different types of prehistoric constructions exist in Menorca. *Talayots* are usually round, conical stone towers, two or three storeys high. Satisfactory explanations for the purpose of *talayots* have yet to be given, although it is clear that they were useful for defence and as dwellings. A *naveta* has the shape of an upside-down hull of a ship and was used as a mausoleum. The most fascinating and puzzling of the prehistoric monuments to be found in Menorca are called *tales,* from the Catalan word for table. A *taula* is one multi-ton megalith balanced on top of another in the form of a "T". About 30 have been identified, but only seven are still standing. They were most likely religious in purpose.

Another prehistoric wonder can be seen in **Cales Coves**, a network of some 140 man-made caves, most dating from the 9th century BC. In one of them there are Latin inscriptions from the 2nd century BC. In the two main Menorcan cities of Maó and Ciutadella, bars and discotheques have been installed in caves. The most spectacular discotheque on the islands is located in **Cala'n Porter**, set in a series of natural caves overlooking the sea.

cialised Coves del Drach, near Porto Cristo. There are guided tours along the 2-km (1¼-mile) route. The town of **Artà** has a great fortress, the **Santuari de Sant Salvador**. Just to the north of it lies **Capdepera**, which also has an impressive walled citadel (open daily April–Oct 10am–8pm, Nov–Mar 10am–5pm).

Petra, in the agricultural heartland of the island, is just a few kilometres from the C-715 running between the capital and the east coast. Father Junípero Serra, the founder of California's first missions, was born here in 1713. In Carrer Barracar Alt, the **Casa Museu Fray Junípero Serra** (visits by arrangement, tel: 971-561 149; entrance fee), the house in which the missionary was brought up, has been preserved and furnished much as it was, and displays scale models of Serra's missions in California and Mexico as well as maps and letters.

Menorca

The island of **Menorca** has an abundance of prehistoric structures. The people who built them are thought to be responsible for similar structures in Sardinia and at Stonehenge, England. Menorcan culture was also heavily influenced by British occupation in the 18th century, most clearly seen in and around **Maó ❻**. Nowhere else in Spain are sash windows a regular feature of the architecture. Menorcan gin, introduced by Englishmen, has a distinctive taste and is popular throughout Spain. The Menorcan dialect has even assimilated a number of English words from that period of occupation.

The city, which the English made the island's capital, is situated at the end of a 5-km (3-mile) fjord, the only geological formation of its kind in the Balearics. **Es Port**, the large and beautiful harbour, lined by a tree-shaded promenade, is one of the liveliest areas, but there is much to see and do in the old city centre.

TIP

The best time to visit Ciutadella is during the Festa de Sant Joan, 23–24 June. Horsemen in medieval costume parade their horses while crowds gather round.

BELOW: soaking up the sun on Ibiza.

Map on page 344

Menorca's other large town, the golden city of **Ciutadella ❼**, lies at the western extreme of the island. It was the capital under Muslim rule and from the time of the Christian conquest until 1722. Its Gothic **Catedral** has a tower built on the foundations of a mosque. The broad squares and stately houses of the nobility, dating from the 16th to the 19th century, give Ciutadella a dignified air.

Ibiza

Ibiza is a very popular destination among British ravers. This is one of the places where acid-jazz began and a haven for anyone wanting to experience club culture at its best.

Founded as *Ibosim* by the Carthaginians in the middle of the 7th century BC, **Eivissa (Ibiza Town) ❽** developed a flourishing economy, based on the export of salt, ceramics, glassware and agricultural products. Testimony of this prosperity are the Ibizan coins found throughout the Mediterranean.

But if Ibiza had a flourishing ancient past, its present is no less prosperous. For some 20 years it has been a mecca, first for jet-setters in search of a highly sophisticated nightlife as well as sun, sand and surf; later as a package holiday destination for young travellers, whose nightlife is no longer so sophisticated, but begins in bars and discos near the port and doesn't end until well after dawn.

In contrast to the hustle and bustle around the port is the dignified serenity of the oldest part of Eivissa, **Dalt Vila**, enclosed within a complete ring of walls. Crowning the hill of Dalt Vila, the sombre-looking **Catedral** (open daily) is built on truly holy ground since its predecessors on the spot were a mosque, a palaeo-Christian church, a Roman temple dedicated to Mercury and a Carthaginian temple. The basic street plan of this part of Eivissa has changed little since it was first laid out by the Carthaginians. There are archaeological relics of this period at the **Museu Arqueologic** (open Tues–Sun; tel: 971-301 701; entrance fee) in Plaça de la Catedral. The museum has one of the world's best collections of Punic articles. **Puig des Molins** (open Sun; entrance fee), on Via Romana at the foot of the hill, is a huge necropolis with more than 400 Carthaginian tombs.

BELOW: boating in the Balearics.
RIGHT: sunny islander.

Formentera

The small island of **Formentera** is separated from Ibiza by 7 km (4 miles) of straits and islets. A regular boat service links Ibiza's port to Formentera's port of **La Savina**. This limited access is an advantage for those who want to get away from the hordes of tourists on Ibiza – nightlife is limited to a few clubs, and the island has a low-key feel. Yet besides peace and quiet, Formentera offers the visitor the superb, long beaches of **Illetes**, **Levant** and **Migjorn**. There are also the package-tour-oriented beach of **Es Pujols** and a number of small *cales* or coves. **Sant Francesc ❾**, the island's capital, is 3 km (2 miles) south of La Savina. The agricultural character of the island is reflected in its name, which is derived from the Latin word for grain.

The best way to get around the island is by motor-scooter, which may be rented at La Savina. The drive up to the plateau on the far eastern side of the island known as **La Mola** is recommended. The winding road to the top affords incomparable views of the island and of Ibiza. At the end of the road a lighthouse presides over sheer cliffs and a plaque commemorates the fact that Jules Verne chose this spot for the blast-off for his novel, *From the Earth to the Moon.* ❏

TRAVEL TIPS

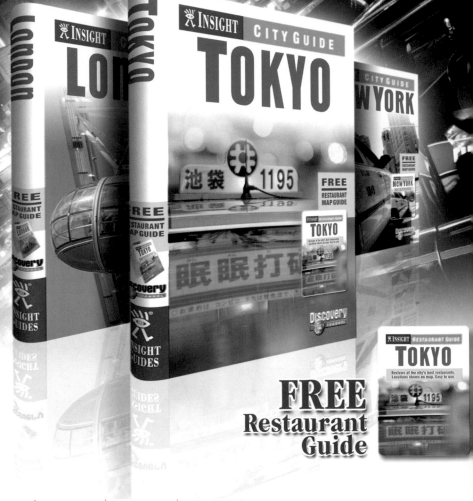

The Guides That Are Streets Ahead

London

Tokyo

INSIGHT CITY GUIDE

TOKYO

池袋 1195

FREE
RESTAURANT
MAP GUIDE

TOKYO

眠眠打破

Discovery

CITY GUIDE
NEW YORK

FREE
RESTAURANT
MAP GUIDE

NEW YORK

Discovery

INSIGHT RESTAURANT GUIDE

TOKYO
Reviews of the city's best restaurants.
Locations shown on map. Easy to use.

池袋 1195

眠眠打破

FREE
Restaurant
Guide

Barcelona Beijing Los Angeles St Petersburg

*Insight Guides to every major country
are also available*

INSIGHT CITY GUIDES

www.insightguides.com

CONTENTS

Getting Acquainted

The Place

Area 504,880 sq km (194,885 sq miles).
Capital Madrid.
Population 41 million.
Language Spanish (Castilian), plus Catalan, Basque and Galician.
Religion Roman Catholic.
Time zone GMT +1 hour (November–March), +2 hours (April–October), except for Canary Islands which are on GMT in winter and GMT +1 hour in summer.
Currency the euro (€).
Weights and measures Metric.
Electricity 220 volts.
International dialling code 34.

Climate

Spain's climate ranges from the cool and rainy northwest to the hot and arid plains of Andalusia. All of the country away from the north coast is hot and sunny in summer. The weather during the rest of the year is more changeable, but there is plenty of sunshine in all months.

See indvidual regions for more details on climate.

Government

The Kingdom of Spain is a constitutional monarchy under King Juan Carlos I of the House of Bourbon, who has been on the throne since the death of Franco in 1975. Parliament (the *Cortes*) consists of a Senate and a Chamber of Deputies. Elections are held every four years unless there is an early dissolution of parliament.

Some aspects of government are highly decentralised. The country is divided into 17 autonomous regions, each with its own legislature, and each of the mainland regions elects four senators. The Deputies in the lower house are elected by proportional representation.

Spain is a member of the European Union, the North Atlantic Treaty Organisation and the Organisation for Economic Cooperation and Development.

Public Holidays

There are so many holidays, what with national and local fiestas, that it's said there is no one week in the whole year when all of Spain is working.
National holidays:
● 1 January (New Year's Day)
● 6 January (Epiphany)
● Good Friday (date varies)
● 1 May (Labour Day)
● 15 August (Assumption)
● 12 October (Columbus Day or *Día de la Hispanidad*)
● 1 November (All Saint's Day)
● 6 December (Constitution)
● 8 December (Immaculate Conception)
● 25 December (Christmas Day).
Each town is also entitled to two local holidays in honour of its patron saints. Madrid celebrates 2 May, *Fiesta de la Comunidad de Madrid*; 15 May, *Día de San Isidro*; and 9 November, *Día de la Almudena*.

Economy

Spain's economy has largely followed the pattern of western Europe, shedding traditional industries in favour of the service sector, which now provides just over 66 percent of the country's GDP. Since the birth of the package holiday industry in the 1960s, tourism has been a particularly lucrative source of income and for decades Spain has maintained its place as one of the world's most popular holiday destinations.

Agriculture and fishing have declined dramatically over the past 20 years, although Spain is still a largely rural country operating one of the largest fishing fleets in Europe. Manufacturing (mainly vehicles for export) has also declined but remains important. A property boom, partly fuelled by tourism, has given the construction industry a more significant share of the economy than elsewhere in Europe. Despite its generally healthy economy, Spain has one of Europe's highest levels of unemployment.

Planning the Trip

Getting To Spain

For information on getting to Spain, please see the *Getting There* information relating to individual regions.

Entry Regulations

Visas & Passports: visitors from EU countries require only a valid National Identity Card (or passport) from their home state to enter Spain. Citizens of Andorra, Austria, Liechtenstein, Monaco and Switzerland enjoy a similar privilege.

Citizens of the USA, Canada, Australia, New Zealand and South Africa require a valid passport and are automatically authorised for a three-month stay, which can be renewed for another three months by applying for a *permanencia* in Madrid at the Comisaría de Policía, Sección de Extranjería, Calle Los Madrazo, 9, Madrid, tel: 91-521 9350. For all except EU citizens, a *Visado de Residencia* must be obtained for any extended stay in Spain.

A *Tarjeta de Estudiante* or Student Card can be applied for at district police stations or at Calle Los Madrazo, 9, Madrid, by presenting a valid passport, an ordinary visa (from the Spanish Consulate in the country of origin), proof of financial means to cover one's stay, medical insurance and proof of enrolment in an officially recognised school.

All official documents must be accompanied by a corresponding photocopy (two are necessary if a work permit is also requested). Three passport-size photographs are needed for each application.

EU citizens wishing to stay in Spain longer than 90 days should apply for a resident's card. This is a lengthy bureaucratic process. Consult a Spanish consulate before you go or check at the local police station in Spain, where you will be required to show your passport, provide photos, and give evidence that you have the necessary funds to live without working in Spain.

US citizens can stay for three months in a calendar year which can be extended to six months providing the request is made before the first three months expire. After six months they can apply for a *residencia*. This requires a visa which should have been requested prior to leaving the US.

If you know before travelling that you will be staying longer than the permitted time, it can save trouble to apply for the necessary visa at a Spanish consulate in your home country.

Customs

Visitors to Spain can bring the following items into the country duty-free: any personal effects, such as jewellery, a laptop computer, cameras etc. If you are visiting from within the EU there are no restrictions on what you bring in for your personal consumption. If you are visiting from outside the EU, you can also bring the following items duty-free:
● 200 cigarettes or 100 small cigars or 50 cigars or 250g of tobacco
● 1 litre of alcohol of 22°
● Limited amounts of perfumes, coffee and tea.

If your camera, laptop computer, camcorder or other equipment is new and you do not have the purchase receipt, it would be wise to ask a customs official to certify that you brought it with you.

Pets may be taken into Spain as long as you have a suitable Health Certificate for the animal signed by an officially recognised vet from the country of origin. This form should indicate the dates of the last vaccines, in particular the anti-rabies shot.

Health

No special inoculations are required for entering Spain, unless you are visiting from an area where there has been a recent outbreak of cholera or yellow fever.

Tap water can be drunk without reservations but bottled water tastes better and is widely available. Food hygiene is generally good but you should

nevertheless exercise a little caution. In modest establishments avoid seafood on Sunday and Monday (it may not be as fresh as it should be) and be wary too of dishes containing raw egg, such as mayonnaise.

In summer, come prepared with a sun hat and protective suncreams.

Bring with you any prescription medicine you require. Although Spanish pharmacies are amply stocked and many drugs can be purchased without prescription, your particular medication may not be available. Chemists in Spain do not honour foreign prescriptions. Over-the counter remedies are available at *farmacias*, recognisable by a green cross, usually flashing neon.

Money Matters

The euro is Spain's official currency. It comes in coins of 1 cent of a euro, 2 cents, 5 cents, 10 cents, 20 cents, 50 cents, 1 euro and 2 euro. Bills are worth 5, 10, 20, 50, 100, 200 and 500 euro.

Best rates for travellers' cheques (available in euro) and foreign currency are obtained at banks, but you can also change money in cities at currency exchange shops, *Casas de Cambio*. In Madrid there is one at Calle Alcalá, 20 and many in the Gran Vía, especially in the Callao area, the American Express Office (Plaza de las Cortes, 2), hotels (where the rates are lower), major department stores and shops frequented by tourists – shop around.

Banks

Practically all Spanish banks will change foreign currency and travellers' cheques, for a fee. It is also possible to obtain cash at any bank against your credit card. However, personal cheques are not readily accepted in shops, even though they may be drawn on local banks. Always carry ID with you when you go to the bank.

Banking hours vary slightly from one bank to another. Most are open 8.30am–2.30pm weekdays, and some are open Saturday until 1pm, though not usually between June and

September or on Thursday afternoons. All are closed on Sunday and holidays (this includes Madrid fiestas in May – *see Public Holidays below*). Several banks open their major branches in the business districts until 6pm or later.

Unless you are importing very large sums of cash, it is best to avoid transferring money via banks. Many tourists have been left stranded for weeks waiting for cash that inexplicably gets delayed in the pipeline. Even telexed cash can take days or weeks to arrive.

Value Added Tax (VAT)

In order to be eligible, as a tourist, for a refund of the Spanish IVA (Value Added Tax), you must spend €100 or more on one item. This tax can range from 6 to 12 percent on the item, although on certain luxury goods it may be as high as 33 percent. The refund procedure is awkward and there are usually long waits at the department store offices that process the requests (www.globalrefund).

In any event, this is how it is done: first, obtain a triplicate form from the shop, indicating your purchase, its cost and the incorporated tax. If you are a citizen of the EU, show all copies of the form to your local customs, with the goods, and you should receive a cheque from the shop for the tax.

If you are not an EU citizen, turn the form over to Customs officials before you leave Spain. If you go from Madrid Barajas or any of the other major international airports, you can present the validated blue copy of the form at the Banco Exterior de España and they will refund the sum of the tax to you in the currency you wish.

If you leave the country from another Customs post, get them to validate your form and then send the blue copy back to the shop.

Tipping

Service is not usually included in restaurants, so it is customary to leave the spare change (€0.30– 0.60 per person) in the dish when eating at a modest restaurant and a few cents at a bar. At an averagely smart restaurant, 10 percent of the bill is appropriate, unless you're charged for service.

A €0.20 tip is fine for an average taxi ride, and bathroom attendants expect around €0.10–0.20 per person.

What to Wear

If you go sightseeing in shorts or a miniskirt you may not be admitted to churches and other religious sites. Shoulders be also covered; some churches provide shawls (you may have to leave your passport as a deposit).

Spanish Tourist Offices Abroad

● **New York**: 666 Fifth Avenue, New York, 10103,
tel: 212-265 8822
● **Chicago**: 845 N. Michigan Avenue, Suite 915-E, Chicago, Illinois, IL 60611, tel: 312-642 1992.
● **Los Angeles**: 8383 Wilshire Blvd, Suite 960, 90211 Beverly Hills, California, CA 90211
tel: 323-658 7188.

● **Miami**: 1221 Brickell Avenue, Suite 1850, FL 33131,
tel: 305-358 1992.
● **Toronto**: 2 Bloor Street West, 34th floor, Toronto M4W 3E2,
tel: 416-961 3131.
● **London**: 22/23 Manchester Square, London W1M 5AP,
tel: 020-7486 8077.

Practical Tips

Driving in Spain

Foreign motorists in Spain must have either an international driving licence or a valid licence from their country of origin, the car's registration papers and valid insurance. Those who are not EU nationals will also require a *Carta Verde* or Green Card, which can be purchased at the border.

Spain has greatly expanded its motorway network since the mid-1990s. **Tolls** are payable on some motorways *(autopistas)*, which have rest areas, bars and service stations. Other motorways *(autovías)* are toll-free. Roadside telephones are placed at convenient intervals for assistance in case of emergency or breakdown.

The **speed limit** is 120 kph (75 mph) on motorways, 100 kph (60 mph) on all other roads and 60 kph (35 mph) going through cities and towns. **Seatbelts** must be worn by the driver and all passengers, and the car should be equipped with a spare set of headlight and rear-light bulbs or you could face a penalty fine.

Business Hours

Although some **offices** have adopted a standard 8 or 9am–5pm work day, smaller shops usually have a midday break for the long lunch and siesta, which are still very much a part of Spanish life, especially in summer, but then stay open until 8 or 9pm. Large stores tend to open 10am–9pm. Many Spaniards return home for lunch, the main meal of the day, while supper is light.

Shops are open 9.30 or 10am–1.30 or 2pm and then reopen again in the afternoon from 4.30 or 5 until 8pm, or a little later in summer. Many close on Saturday afternoons in summer and all day Sunday. However, the major department stores like El Corte Inglés, the FNAC centre, and shops in the city centres are open without interruption six days a week, 10am–9pm, and frequently on Sunday, despite the protests of small shopkeepers. *Panaderías* (bakeries) are open every morning, including Sunday.

Religious Services

The following are in Madrid:
● **British Embassy Church of St George**, Anglican/Episcopalian, Nuñez de Balboa, 43, tel: 91-576 5109.
● **Catholic Masses** held in English (Sun 11am) in the **Capilla de Nuestra Señora de la Merced**, Avenida Alfonso XIII, 165, tel: 91-259 3010.
● **Synagogue**, Balmes, 3, tel: 91-445 9838.
● The **Centro Cultural Islámico** (Mosque), tel: 91-326 2610, above the M-30 highway on Calle Salvador de Madariaga, 4, is a splendid example of Islamic architecture, featuring a large auditorium, library and several exhibition halls.

Media

TELEVISION & RADIO

There are two nationwide television channels in Spain, TVE 1 and TVE 2, and each region has its own local stations. The better hotels have access to satellite programming, which includes a variety of channels, several of which broadcast in English.

MAGAZINES & NEWSPAPERS

The Spanish daily papers are *El País*, *ABC*, *Ya*, *Diario 16* and *El Mundo*. They provide full local information on cinema, theatre and TV programming, and which pharmacies are open late at night. *El País*, *El Mundo* and *Diario 16* publish handy supplements with their Friday editions, which give complete listings on all the activities, exhibitions, art shows and film schedules that week, along with lists of restaurants, entertainment, television, etc.

You will also be able to find the *International Herald Tribune* and *Time* and *Newsweek* magazines at newsstands in most major cities, and other papers such as the *Times*, *Financial Times*, *Guardian* and *Wall Street Journal* can be easily purchased.

There are a few magazines about Spain, printed in English, which you can buy. You can also pick up free English magazines with articles, events, reviews, listings and classified ads in most Irish pubs, bookshops, universities, language schools and tourist offices. *In Madrid* and *The Broadsheet* are the most popular and useful for Madrid and Barcelona. There is also a free music mag that you can find in pubs and record shops called *Mondo Sonoro*, which is good for gig listings. The major newspapers have regional editions, and regions have their own dailies.

Postal Services

The district post offices are only open 9am–2.30pm on weekdays, and some close on Saturday mornings. All post offices close on Sunday. Principal post offices are open 9am–2pm and 4–7pm for general services, including preparation and postage of packages. Stamps can also be purchased at tobacconists *(estancos)* 9am–10pm every day. Fax services are also available within these hours.

Estancos are distinguishable by their brown and gold sign with the word "Tobacos". They are useful establishments, for in addition to selling tobacco, they can provide you with all you need for writing home – and will even weigh your letter to tell you what postage it requires.

Telephones

All telephone numbers in Spain begin with their respective regional code for both local and international calls. Coin and card operated telephone booths are plentiful. Wait for the tone, deposit a coin and dial the number. It is possible to place a **long-distance call** by depositing several coins at once. Most bars have coin-operated or meter telephones available for public use. You can also purchase phonecards of various values at any tobacconist.

For **overseas calls**, it's probably better to go to privately run telephone shops where one can talk first and pay later and not have to worry about having enough coins. (Although it is convenient to ring from your hotel room, and all top hotels have direct-dialling facilities, you will be charged much more than you would on a public phone – at least 16 percent VAT will be added to the cost of your calls.)

Telephone Contacts

The following numbers may be helpful – though for some, you'll need to speak good Spanish.
1003	Telephone info (Spain)
025	International information
1008	Operator Assistance for Europe
1005	Operator Assistance for the rest of the world
093	The time
095	News in Spanish
096	Wake-up service (automated)
097	Sports Information
010	Citizen's Information in Madrid, Barcelona, Valencia, Seville, Bilbao and major cities. Information about the city from extremely helpful staff. Generally open 8am–9pm Mon–Fri.

Emergency Numbers

- **General Emergency Number,** tel: 112
- **National Police,** tel: 091
- **Municipal Police,** tel: 092
- **Fire Department,** tel: 080
- **Emergency Medical Care,** tel: 061
- **Red Cross Emergency,** tel: 91-522 2222 in Madrid

For **lost or stolen credit cards:**
- **American Express,** tel: 900 994 426
- **Diner's Club,** tel: 902 401 112
- **Eurocard, MasterCard,** tel: 900 991 124
- **Visa,** tel: 900 971-231

To make a direct overseas call, first dial 00 and then the country and city code without the initial '0'. It is cheaper to call before 8am and after 10pm. There are no additional discounts at weekends. Retevision, an alternative company to Telefónica, has started functioning in Spain. If the hotel or private number is registered with them, you need to dial 050 00 plus the country and city codes to call abroad.

US access codes: **AT&T:** 900 990 011; **MCI:** 800 099 357; **Sprint:** 900 990 013.

Embassies and Consulates in Madrid

Australia: Plaza Descubridor Diego de Ordás, 3, tel: 91-441 6025 www.embaustralia.es
Canada: Núñez de Balboa, 35, tel: 91-431 4300; www.canada-es.org
Ireland: Claudio Coello, 73, tel: 91-576 3509;
South Africa: Claudio Coello, 91, tel: 91-436 3780; www.sudafrica.com
United Kingdom: Fernando el Santo, 16, tel: 91-319 0200
United States: Serrano, 75, tel: 91-587 2200; www.embusa.es

Emergencies

Spain these days is no more dangerous than any other cosmopolitan community, but, as in any country, it makes sense to take a few elementary precautions.

Bag-snatching and pick-pocketing are probably the worst problems, so don't allow yourself to be distracted and take care in crowds and busy tourist areas. Avoid flashing money around. Keep valuables in the hotel safe and don't carry large sums of money or your passport (take a photocopy instead), unless you are going to exchange money. Never leave valuables in a parked car.

If you are robbed, contact the local police station or phone the **Emergency Police** on 091. Most insurance companies require an official statement (*denuncia*) before they will accept a claim.

Medical Services

Citizens from EU countries are entitled to free medical treatment in other EU countries under a reciprocal arrangement. However, you must obtain a European Insurance Card (EHIC) in your home country prior to your departure. These are valid for five years and can be applied for on-line by logging onto www.dh.gov.uk/travellers. As Seguridad Social facilities are often over-stretched, visitors are also advised to take out private health insurance. Private health insurance is essential for non-EU visitors.

There is also a reciprocal arrangement with many foreign medical insurance companies. Also available is a Spanish insurance policy, ASTES, which will cover any medical or hospital care if you fall ill or have an accident during your stay in Spain. This Spanish Tourist Insurance, created and promoted by the Spanish state and backed by a group of 80 private insurance companies, covers full medical and hospital care, hotel lodging if an extension of your stay is recommended by a physician, repatriation and even lost luggage.

PHARMACIES

Spain has countless pharmacies (*farmacias*), each identifiable by a large, white sign with a flashing green cross. They are usually open from 9.30am–1.30pm and 5–8pm Mon–Fri; 9am–1.30pm Sat. In most towns an effective system of rotation operates whereby there is always one chemist open round-the-clock in each area. A sign in front of each should indicate which chemists are on duty from 10pm–10am that night, and which is closest to where you are.

A list of duty chemists is printed in daily newspapers or available by dialling 010. Most chemists have a list of the nearest clinics and hospitals posted in their windows.

Central Spain

Getting Acquainted

GEOGRAPHY

The high *meseta* plateau of central Spain ranges from 600–1,000 metres (2,000–3,000 ft) above sea level. The northern *meseta*, the Castilla y León region, is dominated by cereal crops; the southern *meseta* – Castilla-La Mancha and Extremadura – is a land of olive groves, vineyards, sheep-grazing and pig-rearing. Forested sierras break up the tableland right across central Spain.

Madrid is the one of the highest capital cities in Europe, situated at an altitude of 650 metres/2,130 ft, flanked to the north and east by the sierras of Somosierra and Guadarrama, to the west by the Gredos, and to the southwest by those of Toledo.

Climate

Central Spain has a continental climate, with hot summers and cold winters. The rainfall is generally low, though the winter snow can be heavy on the sierras. The southern *meseta* is also exceedingly dry.

Autumn and spring are both pleasant seasons, with afternoon temperatures around 15°C (60°F) in March, 22°C (72°F) in May, 25°C (77°F) in September, and 20°C (68°F) in October. Although spring can be quite wet at times, most days are dry and sunny, and the countryside is green and lush.

In the dry summer, the land bakes under the fierce sun and temperatures can rise to 38°C (100°F), although 32°C (90°F) is more typical. The air is dry, and mountain breezes make the evenings pleasantly cool. The average winter daytime temperature is 8°C (46°F), although it can drop below freezing (0°C/32°F) in January and February, the most unsettled months of the year. You'll need to bring your winter coat and although it does not rain often (rainfall averages 438 mm/17 inches per year), the wettest time is January to April with some rain on an average of 8 to 10 days per month.

Getting There

BY AIR

Airlines offering direct links between the UK and Madrid include **British Airways**, tel: 0870 850 9850, www.britishairways.com; BMI **British Midlands**, tel: 0870 6070 555, www.bmi.com; **Iberia**, tel: 902-400 500, www.iberia.es; **Air Europa**, tel: 0870 2401501, www.aireuropa.com; and **Easyjet**, tel: 0870 600 0000, www.easyjet.com. **Aer Lingus**, tel: 01-886 8844 (Ireland)/0845 084 4444 (UK), www.aerlingus.ie flies to Madrid from Dublin. Airlines connecting the US and Latin America to Madrid include **Iberia** *(for contact details, see above)*; **Delta**, tel: 800-241-4141, www.delta.com; **Continental**, tel: 1-800-231-0856, www.continental.com; and **American Airlines**, tel: 1-800-433-7300, www.americanairlines.com.

BY RAIL

There is only one direct service, which links **Paris Austerlitz** and **Madrid Chamartín** and takes 13 hours overnight. Other trains involve changing at the west Pyrenean border town of Irún. The super-fast AVE line running from Madrid to Barcelona is in its final stages of construction, and will speed up connections with southeastern France; the high-speed TGV from Paris to Avignon takes just over 2½ hours, from where a connection takes 6 hours to Barcelona.

BY ROAD

Fast routes connect Madrid to the Basque coast and France.

Getting Around

BY AIR

Iberia is Spain's national airline, servicing national routes *(for contact details, see above)*. Iberia has ticket offices at Calle Velázquez, 130, Madrid, tel: 91-587 8787. However, Iberia is relatively expensive, so shop around – try logging on to www.priceline.com or www.expedia.com. **Spanair**, tel: 902-131 415, and **Air Europa**, tel: 902-401 501, are carriers competing with Iberia. **Aviaco**, Iberia's subsidiary airline, also offers domestic flights.

Halcón Viajes, a chain of travel agents, is very popular and offers competitive prices. Tel: 91-300 600 for information about your nearest office. **Viajes Marsans**, tel: 91-115 947, is also good, and there are always offers in the national press.

Trainspotting

Spanish trains come in a variety of categories, with progressively higher fares payable on the premium services.

The AVE is Spain's finest rail experience, whisking you from Madrid to Seville in 2½ hours and Madrid to Lleida in 2 hours 40 minutes. **Talgo, T200, Alaris** and **Euromed** trains are fast, comfortable expresses operating on certain routes; slightly less luxurious are **Arco** and **InterCity**

From Madrid Airport

Madrid's **Barajas** airport (tel: 902-353 570; www.aena.es) is 16 km (10 miles) out of the city. A bus service runs regularly to the underground bus terminal at Plaza Colón from 4.45am until 1.30am. From 4.45–5.45am the buses are hourly; after that they are every 15 minutes until 7am; from 7am–10pm, they are every 10/11 minutes, and then every 15 until 1.30am. For bus information, tel: 91-431 6192. Easy connections can be made at Colón to the Madrid Metro (Underground), bus and taxis.

The **Metro** from Barajas (Terminal 2) runs via Line 8 to Nuevas Ministerios in 12 minutes. From here a change to Line 10 takes you to Plaza España at the end of the Gran Vía in 15 minutes. Official Madrid **taxis** are white with red stripes across the doors. Several surcharges may be added to the metered fare: an airport surcharge, a small charge for each large piece of luggage, and a further surcharge for journeys on Sunday, holidays and after 11pm. All surcharges are displayed prominently inside the cab.

BY RAIL

Madrid has two main train stations: **Atocha**, near the city centre, handles trains to Andalusia and the Mediterranean coast from Valencia southwards, as well as the "suburban" Cercanías lines extending out to Ávila, Sigüenza, El Escorial, Soria, Toledo, Segovia, Cercedilla and Navacerrada.

Chamartín station, in the north of Madrid, is the terminus for routes to the north and Barcelona. Trains to Extremadura and Lisbon operate from either station.

You can obtain **train information** from RENFE (tel: 902-240 202; www.renfe.es), the state-owned Spanish railway system. Tickets can be delivered to you for a small fee. They can also be bought at the RENFE offices (Alcalá, 44, and Paseo de Recoletos and Nuevos Ministerios RENFE stations, among others), the stations themselves

(IC). Standard long-distance daytime (non-sleeper) trains are called **Diurnos (D)**. **Estrellas (Estr)** are night trains on which a *cama* (small, private compartment) or inexpensive *litera* (a couchette in a shared compartment) is usually available. Luxury night trains are called **Trenhotel**.

Cercanías are local stopping trains, while **Regionales** and **Rapidos** run longer distances but make frequent stops along their route.

or from most travel agencies.

There are many ways to save money on rail travel in Spain. Ask at a travel agent about Eurailpass, Blue Days *(Días Azules)* and the *Tarjeta Turística* offers.

BY BUS

Buses covering the inter-city routes are air-conditioned, with video entertainment to pass the time, and sometimes toilets. Buses are cheaper than trains. They make frequent stops at rest areas, giving passengers a chance to eat something and to stretch their legs.

There are various bus companies in Madrid that service specific areas of the country. Most leave from the **Estación Sur de Autobuses**, Méndez Alvaro. For information, tel: 91-468 4511/4200; www.estaciondeautobuses.com.

Auto Res, Calle Fernández Shaw, 1, near Plaza Conde de Casal, has a large network of bus lines that operates across the country. For information, tel: 902-422 242; www.auto-res.net.

The Continental bus line at Avenida de América, 34, tel: 91-745 6300; www.continental-auto.es, covers local routes and also points in northern Spain.

Enatcar buses leave from the Estación Sur de Autobuses, Méndez Alvaro, tel: 91-468 4511/4200, for points all over Spain. For information, tel: 91-467 3577.

CAR RENTAL

To rent a car in Spain you have to be at least 19 years of age with either an international licence or a valid licence from your own country.

It is usually necessary to pay for the car rental with a credit card, otherwise you might have to leave a large deposit. You also need insurance.

Cars can be rented on a daily basis, with an additional fee according to mileage used. Alternatively a package deal, which is available for a set number of days at unlimited mileage, is an option; consider which will be most

advantageous for your journey's purpose. It is sometimes possible to pick the car up in one city and leaving it in another.
There are many car hire agencies in Madrid (most have a branch at the airport), including the following:

● **Atesa**, several branches in and around Madrid. Central booking number 902-100 101; airport branch, tel: 91-542 5015; www.atesa.es
● **Avis**, several branches in and around Madrid. Gran Vía, 60, tel: 91-548 4205/547 2048; www.avis.es
● **Econocar**, Felix Boix, 2, tel: 91-359 1403.
● **Europcar**, several branches in and around Madrid, tel: 902-105 030; airport branch, tel: 91-393 7235. www.europcar.es
● **Hertz**, several branches in and around Madrid. Atocha railway station tel: 91-468 1838; airport branch, tel: 91-393 7228. www.hertz.es

MADRID TRANSPORT
Metro Systems

The Madrid underground or Metro system is the fastest, cheapest and most efficient way of getting around the city. (If you are claustrophobic, avoid rush hours: 8–9.30am, 1.30–2.30pm and 8–9pm.) Most trains have air conditioning.
The Metro was opened by King Alfonso XIII in 1919, and today has over 200 stations, which will take you to just about every corner of the city. It operates from 6am–1.30am and is used by over 1 million people daily. Fortunately, most trains are air-conditioned. The ticket that was originally known as the Bonobús is now

called Metrobús; it costs €5.20 and is valid for 10 journeys. A single ticket costs €1.10 regardless of your destination.
For more detailed information on the Madrid Metro, tel: 902-444 403 or log on to www.metromadrid.es

City Buses

Single tickets cost €0.95 regardless of length of journey, and are valid for three hours. You enter from the front and pay the driver preferably with change or small notes. Press the buzzer to tell him to let you out at the stop you want. Leave by the rear door.
Tickets can be purchased from the bus information booths at Puerta del Sol, Plaza Callao, Plaza Cibeles, Plaza de Castilla, etc., all newspaper stands and tobacconists. Stamp your ticket in the slotted box behind the driver.
Buses operate 6am–midnight. There are also Night Buses called Búhos (owls) that operate from midnight–6am departing from Plaza Cibeles. For municipal bus information (EMT), tel: 91-406 8810.
If you are planning an extended period of time in Madrid and doing a lot of bus and Metro travelling, it is a good idea to purchase an Abono. This card can be applied for at any tobacconist by completing a form and providing a passport-size photograph and a photocopy of your passport or national identity document.

Taxis

Taxis in Madrid are plentiful and relatively inexpensive. They are white, bear a diagonal red stripe on the sides and the Madrid coat of arms. They are available if they are displaying a green

libre (free) sign on the windscreen or at night have a little green light on. If a red sign with the name of a Madrid neighbourhood is displayed, it means they are on their way home and are not obliged to pick you up unless you are on their route. All taxis are metered.
Taxis can be hailed with relative ease in main thoroughfares, found at a Parada de Taxi (taxi stand, indicated by a large white "T" against a dark blue background) or requested by phone from the following companies: Radio-Teléfono Taxi, tel: 91-547 8200; Radio-Taxi Independiente, tel: 91-340 5121 or 91-405 5500; Teletaxi, tel: 91-371 2131; or Radio Taxi Asociación Gremial, tel: 91-447 5180.

Media

Many of the main Spanish daily newspapers, e.g. El País, ABC, El Mundo and Diario 16, are published in Madrid, and they contain listings pages with details of forthcoming cultural events. The weekly magazine Guía del Ocio is useful for what's on listings. The TV station Telemadrid reports on events in and around Madrid. The state-owned Radio 3 (FM 93.2) is popular with young people for its varied range of music – from free jazz to flamenco.

Medical Services

The following Madrid hospitals have 24-hour emergency rooms: **La Paz**, Paseo de la Castellano, 261, tel: 91-358 2600 and **Ramón y Cajal**, Ctra de Colmenar Viejo, tel: 91-336 8000 in the north; **Doce de Octubre**, Avda de Córdoba s/n, tel: 91-390 8000 in the south; and, in the centre of the city, the **Gregorio Marañón**, Calle Doctor Esquerdo, 46. Accident and Emergency, tel: 91-586 8500; Maternity, tel: 91-586 8833; Babies and Children, tel: 91-586 8765; Information, tel: 91-586 8556/7.
Dental treatment can be accessed at **Cisne Clínica**, calle Magallanes, 18, tel: 91-446 3221.

Security & Crime

As in all major cities, it is essential to be on your guard against theft. Never leave valuables on view in a car and do not wear valuable jewellery or carry expensive camera equipment. Be especially vigilant in the Rastro flea market, in the metro, at night in the Malasaña quarter or on Gran Vía. Among the ruses often employed by pickpockets are street theatre artists who distract unsuspecting holidaymakers, and staged accidents or fights.

Local Tourist Offices

Madrid
Plaza Mayor, 3, tel: 91-588 1636; www.spaintour.com/madrid
Duque de Medinaceli, 2, tel: 91-429 4951/902-100 007; email: turismo@madrid.org
Castilla-La Mancha
Albacete: Tinte, 2, tel: 967-580 522.
Ciudad Real: Avda Alarcos, 21, tel: 926-200 037.
Cuenca: Glorieta Gonzalez Palencia 2–3, tel: 969-178 800.
Guadalajara: Plaza de las Caidos, 6, tel: 949-211 626.
Toledo: Puerta de Bisagra, s/n, tel: 925-220 843.
Castile-León
Avila: Mercado Chico 1, tel: 920-354 013; www.avilaturismo.com
Burgos: Teatro Principal, 7, tel: 947-288 851; www.aytoburgos.es
León: Plaza de la Regla, 3,

tel: 987-292 189;
email: dituris@argired.com
Palencia: Mayor, 1, tel: 979-718 134; www.palencia-turismo.com
Salamanca: Plaza Mayor, 19, tel: 923-218 342; www.aytosalamanca.es
Segovia: Plaza Azaguejo, 1, tel: 921-462 914; www.infosegovia.com
Soria: Plaza Mayor s/n, tel: 975-234 100; email: soriainfo@ayto-soria.org
Valladolid: Augustics, 48, tel: 983-427 259; www.asumatevalladolid.org
Zamora: Plaza Viriato s/n, tel: 980-534 047; www.zamoradipu.es
Extremadura
Badajoz: Plaza de la Libertad, 3, tel: 924-222 763; email: otbadajoz@brne.es
Cáceres: Plaza Mayor, 3, tel: 927-010 834; email: otcaceres@brne.es

Where to Stay

Choosing a Hotel

With over 60,000 beds, Madrid has accommodation to meet every need and budget. Hotels are classified in five categories, reflected in the number of stars they have been awarded. *Hoteles-residencias* are also classified according to quality and services; these do not have a restaurant, but often have bar and cafeteria facilities. *Hostales* are more modest, and classified according to only 1, 2 or 3 stars. *Pensiones* or guesthouses are useful for those on limited budgets, and most are family-run. Rooms can be rented with home cooking included, and there is usually a family room that is shared with the other guests for watching television or reading.

An official notice should be posted behind the door, indicating the daily price of the room, although the rate can vary according to season. Breakfast is not normally included in the room rate. Remember that 7 percent IVA (VAT) will be added to your bill, except for those of the Grand Luxury category, which charge 15 percent VAT.

An increasingly popular idea for longer stays is to rent a furnished apartment.

If planning excursions out of Madrid, your best bet may be to make a reservation at any of the Parador (state-run inns) on your route. The Parador system, first planned in 1926, was started in the 1970s by the Ministry of Information and Tourism. Run-down castles and palaces were taken over and converted into charming and luxurious hotels at affordable prices. Reservations can be made at the central office: Calle Requena, 3, Madrid, tel: 91-516 6666, www.parador.es

Our listings

The price guide given here refers to a standard double room, but most city hotels offer up to 50 percent discount at weekends. Reserve well in advance, specifying a room not facing the road for quiet, or a double bed if required. Note that s/n in an address signifies *sin número* (no number); ctra means *carretera* (highway). Hotels are listed in order of price category.

MADRID

Ritz
Plaza de la Lealtad, 7
tel: 91-701 6767
www.ritzmadrid.com
email: commercial@ritz.es
One block away from the Prado Museum. Luxury in the old style. €€€€€
Santo Mauro
Zurbano, 36
tel: 91-319 6900
email: santo-mauro@ac-hoteles.com
www.achotelsantomauro.com
An old palace converted into a plush hotel with a quiet atmosphere. €€€€€
Colón
Dr Esquerdo, 119
tel: 91-400 9900
email: colon@fiestahotelgroup.com
Smart hotel located in a quiet residential area. €€€€

Price Guide

For a standard double room
€€€€€ = Over €350
€€€€ = €120–350
€€€ = €90–120
€€ = €50–90
€ = Under €50

Orfila
Orfila, 6
tel: 91-702 7770
email: comercial@HotelOrfila.com
www.hotelorfila.com/
Beautifully converted belle époque mansion with 35 rooms. €€€€
Hotel Suecia
Marqués de Casa Riera, 4
tel: 91-531 6900
email: bookings@hotelsuecia.com
www.hotelsuecia.com
Centrally located beside the Fine Arts Circle. Its restaurant is noted for the typical Swedish smorgasbord served on Thurs and Fri evenings. €€€€
Gran Hotel Reina Victoria
Plaza de Santa Ana, 14
tel: 91-531 4500
email: reinavictoria@trypnet.com
Remodelled and upgraded hotel with cultural and bullfighting links. €€€€
Villamagna
Paseo de la Castellana, 22
tel: 91-587 1234
email: villamagna@hyattintl.com
www.madrid.hyatt.com
A grand, luxury hotel maintained in a modern style. Good atmosphere. €€€€
Wellington
Velázquez, 8
tel: 91-575 4400
email: wellington@hotel-wellington.com
www.hotel-wellington.com
An old-fashioned, stylish hotel close to good shops. Small outdoor swimming pool and a fine restaurant. €€€€

Palace
Plaza de las Cortes, 7
tel: 91-360 8000
www.palacemadrid.com
Classic hotel, with a cultural/international ambience, across the street from the Parliament. €€€€
Emperador
Gran Vía, 53
tel: 91-547 2800
email: comercial@emperadorhotel.com
www.emperadorhotel.com
With a rooftop pool and good views. Open June–Sept. €€€–€€€€
Gran Hotel Conde Duque
Plaza Conde Valle de Suchil, 5
tel: 91-447 7000
www.hotelcondeduque.es
In the Argüelles area. €€€
La Residencia de El Viso
Nervíon 8
tel: 91-564 0370
email: elviso@estanciases.es
Converted 1930's townhouse with garden. Excellent service. Close to business area. €€€
NH Alcalá
Alcalá, 66
tel: 91-435 1060
email: nhalcala@nh-hotels.com
www.nh-hotels.com
Across the street from Retiro Park and near good shops. €€€
Best Western Madrid
Carretas, 10
tel: 91-521 6520
email: hotelmadrid@hotelatlantico.com
An older hotel, one block away from the Puerta del Sol. €€
Claridge
Plaza Conde de Casal, 6
tel: 91-551 9400
Located in the city outskirts at the start of the Madrid–Valencia highway. €€
Inglés
Echegaray, 8
tel: 91-429 6551
email: comercial@hotelingles.com
Cosy hotel with parking, close to the Puerta del Sol. Good value. €€
Puerta de Toledo
Glorieta Puerta de Toledo, 4
tel: 91-474 7100
email: hpto@hotel-puertadetoledo.es
www.hotel-puertadetoledo.es
Close to the Rastro fleamarket and the Puerta de Toledo Market complex. €€
Regina
Alcalá, 19
tel: 91-521 4725
email: info@hotelreginamadrid.com
Centrally located. €€
Alameda
Avda Logroño, 100
tel: 91-747 4800
email: tryp.alameda.aeropuerto@solmelia.com
www.solmelia.com
Near the airport, 14 km (9 miles) from the city. Courtesy service for clients to the airport. With pool. €€

Continental
Gran Vía, 44
tel: 91-521 4640.
www.hostalcontinental.com
Comfortable, good-value hotel close to main shops, bars and cinemas. €

Hostels

Astoria
Carrera de San Jerónimo, 32
tel: 91-429 1188
email: info@hostal-astoria.com
www.hostal-astoria.com
Located across the street from the Palace Hotel and Parliament building. €

Hospedaje Madrid
Esparteros, 6, Second Floor
tel: 91-522 0060
email: reservas@hospedajemadrid.com
www.hospedajemadrid.com
Near Puerta del Sol. Private bathrooms and air conditioning. €€

Las Brisas
Cruz, 8, first floor
tel: 91-531 4403
www.hostalbrisas.com
Near Puerta del Sol. Private bathrooms and TVs. €

Persal
Plaza del Angel, 12
tel: 91-369 4643
www.hostalpersal.com
Former 19th-century townhouse, close to Santa Ana Square noted for its ultra friendly staff and comfortable rooms. €

Hostal La Plata
Gran Vía, 15, 4th floor
tel: 915-211 725
www.hostal-laplata.com
Clean, modern rooms; central area; private bathrooms; air conditioning. €

Apartments

Four to six people can sleep in *apartamentos* for around €180 per night. Look at the website www.apartinmadrid.com for a wider selection of apartments.

Centro Colón
Marqués de la Ensenada, 16
tel: 91-308 6507
All mod cons. Close to Colón Square and within easy walking distance of all central amenities. €€€

Goya 75
General Pardiñas , 13
tel: 91-435 6346/91-781 8930
email: info@ apartmentosgoya75.com
www.apartamentosgoya75.com
Apart-hotel in the Salamanca zone. Near some of the best shopping. €€€

CASTILLA-LA MANCHA

Alarcón

Parador de Alarcón
Amigos de los Castillos, 3
tel: 969-330 315
email: alarcon@parador.es
www.parador.es

Built into a cliff overlooking the Júcar river, restored in 2003. Their roast lamb is especially good. €€€€

Albacete

Parador de Albacete
Route N 301, km 251
tel: 967-245 321
email: albacete@parador.es
www.parador.es
Just outside of Albacete, this rangy ranch-like parador is elegant and comfortable. €€€

Almagro

Parador de Almagro
Ronda de San Francisco, 31
tel: 926-860 100
email: almagro@parador.es
www.parador.es
This 16th-century convent is thought by many to be Spain's most beautiful Parador, with circular stone and brick floor designs copied from the nearby castle of Calatrava and more than 12 interior patios. €€€

Ayna – Sierra de Alcaraz

Felipe II
Avda Manuel Carreras, 9
Carretera Albacete-Elcha
tel/fax: 967-295 083
www.hotelfelipeiiayna.com
This otherwise undistinguished modern building has spectacular views and swimming pools. €€

Beteta

Hotel Los Tilos
Extrarradio, s/n
tel: 969-318 097
email: lostilos@faec.org
This northern Cuenca base camp for exploring the Beteta and Tragavivos gorges has comfortable rooms and serves game in season, and *morteruelo*, a country pâté. €€

Cuenca

Posada de San Jose
Julián Romero, 4
tel: 969-211 300
email: info@posadasanjose.com
www.posadasanjose.com
Converted 16th-century convent with most rooms overlooking the Huécar canyon. Situated in the heart of the old historic quarter of Cuenca. Multi-levelled house with lots of fascinating nooks and crannies. €€€

Daimiel

Las Brujas
Carretera Córdoba-Tarragona, km 231,5
tel: 926-852 289
This hotel and restaurant is an ideal stop-off place for an excursion through the wetlands of Tablas de Daimiel. Simple accomodation and regional cuisine. €€

Oropesa

Parador de Oropesa
Plaza del Palacio, 1
tel: 925-430 000
email: oropesa@parador.es
www.parador.es
This feudal stronghold, with the Sierra de Gredos in the distance, merits a trip just to stay within its medieval walls in modern comfort. Good restaurant. €€€

Puerto Lápice

Aprisco de Puerto Lápice
Ctra Madrid-Cádiz, km 134
tel/fax: 926-576 025
This rustic building was once a shelter for livestock. The circular dining room has an open wrought-iron fireplace in the centre under a conical roof. Unique. €

Riópar – Sierra de Alcaraz

Hotel Riópar
Choperas, 2
tel: 967-435 191
email: hriopar@paralelo40.org
www.hotelriopar.com
This hotel near the source of the Mundo river is tastefully constructed in local wood and stone; a good place to stay for fishing. €€

Sigüenza

Parador de Sigüenza
Plaza del Castillo
tel: 949-390 100
email: siguenza@parador.es
www.parador.es
This elegant and comfortable medieval castle overlooking the town is a top lodging spot; a cosy refuge. €€€€

Toledo

Parador Nacional de Toledo
Cerro del Emperador, s/n
tel: 925-221 850
email: toledo@parador.es
www.parador.es
A splendid hotel outside of town and restored in 2003, with El Greco's famous view of Toledo. €€€€

Pintor El Greco
Alamillos del Tránsito, 13
tel: 925-285 191
email: info@hotelpintorelgreco.com
www.hotel-pintorelgreco.com
Located next to the painter's house-museum, on the premises of a 17th-century bakery. €€€

La Almazara
Ctra Toledo-Arges y Polan, km 3.4
tel: 925-223 866
email: reservas@hotelmazara.com
www.hotelalmazara.com
An old summer palace on the river. €€

Tragacete

Hospedería Real del Jucar
Muñoz Grandes, 7
tel: 969-289 204
email: hospjucar@hosteriasreales.com

www.hosteriasreales.com
Simple but good accommodation in the Cuenca highlands, and a perfect base camp for excursions to the waterfalls and the source of the Cuervo river. €€

CASTILE-LEÓN

Ávila

Palacio Valderrábanos
Plaza de la Catedral, 9
tel: 920-211 023
www.palaciovalderrabanoshotel.com
Smartly furnished traditional hotel in historic mansion next to the cathedral. Good restaurant. €€€€

Parador de Ávila
Marqués de Canales y Chozas, 2
tel: 920-211 340
email: avila@parador.es
www.parador.es
Charming hotel set in the 15th-century Piedras Albas, overlooking the cathedral. €€€€

La Hostería de Bracamonte
Bracamonte, 6
tel: 920-251 280
A 16th-century palace-turned-hotel/restaurant, with stone-walled interior, tapestries and beams. €€

Burgos

Fernán González
Calera, 17
tel: 947-209 441
www.hotelfernangonzalez.com
Traditional hotel on the river's south bank, with an elegant restaurant. €€€

Mesón Del Cid
Plaza de Santa María, 8
tel: 947-208 715
www.mesondelcid.es
Superbly placed opposite the cathedral, a conventional hotel with an excellent restaurant and garage parking. €€€

Norte y Londres
Plaza de Alonso Martinez, 10
tel: 947-264 125
www.hotelnorteylondres.com
Quiet, inexpensive hotel, handily placed for the tourist office and main sights. €€

León

Conde Luna
Avda Independencia, 7
tel: 987-206 600
lesein.es/condeluna
With a garden and pool. €€€€

Parador Hostal de San Marcos
Plaza de San Marcos, 7
tel: 987-237 300
email: leon@parador.es
www.parador.es
Top-class Parador in one of Spain's most palatial Renaissance buildings. Acclaimed restaurant and luxurious bedrooms.€€€€

Quindós
Gran Vía San Maros 38
tel: 987-236 200
www.hotelquindos.com

Clean, modern hotel on a fairly busy central corner. Quiet, stylish interior. €€

Palencia

Castilla Vieja
Avda Casado del Alisal, 26
tel: 979-749 044
email: sedecentral@hotelesuco.com
Centrally located with good services; pets allowed. €€

Rey Sancho
Avda Ponce de León, s/n
tel: 979-725 300
www.reysancho.com
A comfortable hotel with a large garden, swimming pool and tennis court. €€

Price Guide

For a standard double room
€€€€€ = Over €350
€€€€ = €120–350
€€€ = €90–120
€€ = €50–90
€ = Under €50

Salamanca

Gran Hotel
Plaza del Poeta Iglesias, 5
tel: 923-215 401
www.hotelgranvia.net
A classic hotel, popular with the bullfighting crowd and complete with a "feudal restaurant". €€€€

Parador de Salamanca
Teso de la Feria, 2
tel: 923-192 082
email: salamanca@parador.es
www.parador.es
Modern building on the Tormes River with spectacular views of the cathedral. €€€

Rector
Paseo del Rector Esperabé, 10
tel: 923-218 482
email: hotelrector@teleline.es
Beautifully furnished converted mansion. Family-run, small and personal. €€–€€€

Emperatriz II
Rua Mayor, 18
tel: 923-219 156
www.emperatrizhotel.com
Quaint medieval building near university quarter, with clean, simple rooms. Very good value. No credit cards. €€

Segovia

Parador de Segovia
Ctra de Valladolid s/n
tel: 921-443 737
email: segovia@parador.es
www.parador.es
A modern Parador, some way out of town, but with a magnificent view. Comfortable and well equipped. €€€€

Infanta Isabel
Isabel le Católica, 1
tel: 921-461 300
www.hotelinfantaisabel.com

Elegant B&B hotel just off the main square, with spacious, comfortable rooms. Good value. €€€

Acueducto
Padre Claret, 10
tel: 902-250 550
www.hotelacueducto.com
Outside the walls in the lower town, but quite convenient for sightseeing. Modern facilities. Rather noisy location. €€

Los Linajes
Dr Velasco, 9
tel: 921-460 475
www.loslinajes.com
Traditional hotel in a quiet spot by the city walls. Excellent views from some rooms. Parking is tricky. €€

Soria

Parador de Soria
Parque del Castillo, s/n
tel: 975-240 800
email: soria@parador.es
www.parador.es
Spacious, stylish, modern interior. Hilltop location, with excellent views over the park and the Duero valley. Dedicated to the poet Antonio Machado, who made Soria his home and immortalised it in his work. €€€

Valladolid

Felipe IV
Gamazo, 16
tel: 983-307 000
www.hfelipeiv.com
Comfortable and centrally located hotel with good food. €€

Parque
García Morato, 17
tel: 983-220 000
fax: 983-475 029
www.hotelparque.com
Conveniently located with the bus station round the corner. Has a fine restaurant. €€

Lasa
Acera de Recoletos, 21
tel: 983-390 255
email: hotel-lasa@terra.com
Renovated 19th-century apartment block located on the Campo Grande towards the southern end of town. €

Zamora

Parador de Zamora
Plaza de Viriato, 5
tel: 980-514 497
email: zamora@parador.es
www.parador.es
Installed in a 15th-century palace with a splendid Renaissance cloister. €€€

Hostería Real de Zamora
Cuesta de Pizarro, 7
tel: 980-534 545
www.hosteriasreales.com
This beautiful 16th-century mansion is located near the river and city walls. Features include cloister and fountain courtyards in traditional Islamic style. €€

Hostal Rey Don Sancho
Ctra N-630, Villacastín-Vigo, km 276
tel: 980-513 822
email: hrds@mixmal.com
Great hotel with superb restaurant and
a 24-hour cafe-bar. €

EXTREMADURA
Badajoz
Monasterio de Rocamador
Ctra Badajoz-Huelva, km 41
tel: 924-489 000
www.rocamador.com
Luxurious hotel in 16th-century Franciscan
monastery. Wonderful restaurant. €€€€

Cáceres
Meliá Cáceres
Plaza de San Juan 11,
tel: 927-215 800
www.solmelia.com
Luxurious lodgings in a restored 16th-
century palace. €€€€
Parador de Cáceres
Ancha, 6
tel: 927-211 759
email: caceres@parador.es
www.parador.es
Situated in the heart of the restored
monumental quarter in the 14th-century
Palacio del Comendador. €€€€

Plasencia
Parador de Plasencia
Plazoleta San Vincente Ferrer
tel: 927-425 870
email: plasencia@parador.es
www.parador.es
Installed in a restored 15th-century
convent with Gothic features. €€€

Guadalupe
Parador de Guadalupe
Marqués de la Romana, 12
tel: 927-367 075
email: guadalupe@parador.es
www.parador.es
In a 16th-century hospital,with rooms
overlooking a magical Mudéjar patio. €€€€

Mérida
Parador de Mérida
Plaza de la Constitución, 3
tel: 924-313 800
email: merida@parador.es
www.parador.es
This gracious 18th-century Franciscan
convent is now a supremely elegant
and comfortable Parador. €€€€

Trujillo
Parador de Trujillo
Santa Beatriz de Silva, 1
tel: 927-321 350
email: trujillo@parador.es
www.parador.es
Good regional cooking marks out this
Parador built within a converted
convent. €€€€

Where to Eat

What to Eat

In Spain, restaurants, like hotels, are
classified into five categories, this time
symbolised with forks. In addition to
restaurantes, there are bares, or all-
purpose drinking establishments, where
one can order anything from a coffee or
a cola to a bocadillo (a sandwich made
with crusty bread) or a sandwich (on
sliced white bread). Mesones are
typical taverns with appropriate fare.
Casas de comidas, or eating houses,
are informal and good-value
restaurants. Modern cafeterías or
coffee shops are places where you can
get toasted sandwiches or meals
throughout the day. And of course,
there are the fast-food hamburger and
pizza restaurants.
The main meal of the day is usually
a hearty, three-course affair, served
between 2 and 4pm, while the evening
meal is light and generally eaten after
9.30pm.
Tapas are also an important part of
daily life. Whether pinchos, montaditos,
or raciones, tapas are delicacies
designed to please the palate and are
the ideal accompaniment to wine, beer
or fino (dry sherry).
Spaniards tend to have a light
breakfast before going to work and then
a coffee break at mid-morning when
they indulge in pastries, churros (fried
dough rings) or a pincho de tortilla (a
wedge of potato omelette served with
crusty bread). One o'clock is aperitivo
time, when a vast array of tapas are
laid out along the bar counters. Early to
late evening is tapas time again at 8pm
and the idea is to go from one bar to
the next, sampling the specialities each
offers.
Spaniards usually wash down their
tapas with draught beer (una caña de
cerveza), a botellín (a small bottle of
beer), or a small glass of wine (un
chato de vino), tinto being red and
blanco, white. In the south one should
sample the dry sherry, fino or jerez,
which comes from Jerez de la Frontera
and Montilla.
In recent years, Spanish wine has
improved dramatically in quality. The
country is particularly proud of its
Riojas from the north, the different
varieties of sherry from Jerez, and the
champagnes or cavas (sparkling wines)
from Catalonia. Inexpensive ordinary
table wines from around the regions
can be palatable.
Although you can find just about
every alcoholic beverage in Madrid, the
country also has an interesting
selection of after-dinner drinks: the
famous anisette of Chinchón, pacharán
(sloe liqueur) of the Basque country,
Galicia's herbal aguardientes, and
assorted eaux de vie and ponches from
diverse regions of the country.
Despite the wide range and
availability of alcohol and its relatively
low price, drunkeness is rare.
Should you have any serious
problems with the food, service or the
bill in a restaurant, request the hojas
de reclamación, the complaint forms.
When they are filled out, the proprietor
is obliged to send one copy to the local
police station. Always phone to check
when restaurants are closed, as this
varies considerably.
Restaurants are listed in order of
price category.

Price Guide

Approximate cost per person,
including house wine:
€€€€€ = over €35
€€€€ = €30–35
€€€ = €20–30
€€ = €15–20
€ = under €15

Eating Out

MADRID
Top Class
La Broche Sergi Arola
Miguel Angel 29–31
tel: 91-399 3437
www.labroche.com
Cool white restaurant where Catalan
rock guitarist-turned-chef Sergi Arola
serves up stunning cuisine, high on
flavours and textures like foams and
gelatines, but built on traditional
Mediterranean produce. Two Michelin
stars. Book well ahead. Closed at
weekends. €€€€€
Pedro Larumbe
Serrano, 61
tel: 91-575 5111
www.larumbe.com
Pedro Larumbe specializes in fish, with
a Cantabrian style evolving all the time
towards other ethnic cuisines.
Spectacular terrace view. €€€€€
Viridiana
Juan de Mena, 14
tel: 91-523 4478
tel: 91-346 9040
email: www.restauranteviridiana.com

A quirky, avant-garde, top-class restaurant where Abraham García serves whackily experimental cuisine and, arguably, offers the city's best Spanish wine list. Dress as you like. €€€€€

El Amparo
Callejón de Puigcerdá, 8
tel: 91-431 6456
email: rte.elamparo@terra.es
The fashionable clientele, wonderful split-level dining room, unfussy haute cuisine like prawn risotto and scallop salad, the exemplary service and wine list combine for a good but pricy dinner. €€€€€

El Olivo
General Gallegos, 1
tel: 91-359 1535
www.jrnet.com/olivo
Jean Pierre Vandelle's modern European creative cooking showcases Spanish olive oils and Jerez sherries, served to match his contemporary fish, game and vegetable cooking. Unmissable for olive-oil lovers. €€€€€

Príncipe de Viana
Manuel de Falla, 5
tel: 91-457 1549
email: p.viana@teleline.es
A classic, contemporary venue for upmarket modern, light Navarrese-Basque cuisine emphasising artichokes, asparagus and other regional vegetables. Smart but casual dining room; ace service. Closed Sat afternoon and Sun. €€€€€

La Terraza del Casino
Alcalá, 15
tel: 91-532 1275
www.casinodemadrid.com
Lavish 19th-century casino setting with great modern Spanish food. €€€€€

Traditional Madrileño

Botín
Cuchilleros, 17
tel: 91-366 4217
www.botin.es
Founded in 1725 and claims to be the oldest restaurant in the world. Famous for its wood-roast pig and lamb. €€€€

Posada de la Villa
Cava Baja, 9
tel: 91-366 1880
Once a coaching inn and still a Castilian restaurant. Try the curly endive with garlic salad. Good value for money. Book upstairs for a rooftop view. Specialises in roasts and *callos* (tripe). €€€€

Casa Paco
Plaza de Puerta Cerrada, 11
tel: 91-366 3166
Don't be fooled by the laidback air: the cooking here remains a byword with gourmets, drawing a stylish crowd, young and old. Try the *carne de buey* (beef ragoût). €€€€–€

La Bola
Bola, 5
tel: 91-547 6930
A 19th-century dining room where all-comers make the trip for one of Madrid's most authentic versions of *cocido*, or stew, cooked in individual earthenware pots. €€€

Malacatín
Ruda, 5 (metro: La Latina)
tel: 91-365 5241
This modest eating house is a legend for its *cocido* (stew), which comes with its own set-menu. Summer terrace. Order at least the day before; two weeks before for weekends. In the Rastro flea market. €€€

Price Guide

Approximate cost per person, including house wine:
€€€€€ = over €35
€€€€ = €30–35
€€€ = €20–30
€€ = €15–20
€ = under €15

Andalusian

La Dorada
Orense, 64
tel: 91-570 2004
trabajadoresdorada@empresarial.com
Notable fish restaurant serving expert dry-fried rockfish (*fritura malagueña*), salt-baked bream and good fishermen's rices and soups, using fresh fish of the day. Large noisy dining room. €€€€

Alborán
Ponzano, 39–41
tel: 91-399 2150
email: alboran@alboran-rest.com
www.alboran-rest.com
Salt-baked fish, shellfish and paella. €€€

Asturian

Casa Portal
Doctór Castelo, 26
tel: 91-574 2026
www.casa-portal.com
The menu rarely shifts – and why change it when the bean stew (*fabada*), chorizo or hake cooked in cider remain deliciously home-made? Located in the smart Salamanca district. €€€€€

Casa Mingo
Paseo de la Flórida, 34
tel: 91-547 7918
Cavernous cider-house serving roast chicken and Cabrales cheese. Large roof terrace. Good value and a great atmosphere at weekends. €€€

Basque

Casa Julián de Tolosa
Cava Baja, 18
tel: 91-365 8210
Impeccable Basque and Navarrese

cooking; try grilled beef on the bone served with roasted red peppers in a stripped-back rustic dining room. Everything here is good. €€€€–€

Hurly Burly
Marqués de Cubas, 2
tel: 91-523 2367.
Light-filled central restaurant and tapas bar with creative modern Basque cooking in a hip young atmosphere. The set lunches are a bargain. €€€

Castilian

Nuevo Horno de Santa Teresa
Santa Teresa, 8
tel: 91-308 0590
A family-owned restaurant that cooks stews and casseroles the old way, giving them the quality missing elsewhere. €€€€

Casa Ciriaco
Mayor, 84
tel: 91-548 0620
Pick up a tapa and an apéritif at the bar while you soak up the memorabilia on the wall, then settle down to Castilian dishes-of-the-day and stews in character local company. €€€

Catalan

Paradís Madrid
Marqués de Cubas, 14
tel: 91-429 7303
www.paradis.es
A Catalan designer dining room serving excellent modern Mediterrananean cooking with luxury touches: *gazpacho* with shellfish garnish, wild mushrooms and rice, plus modern Mediterranean wines. Near the Prado. €€€€

Can Punyetes
Señores de Luzón, 5
tel: 91-542 0921
canpunyetes.com
Small eatery where a young crowd tuck into grilled *butifarra* sausages, vegetables, toast with tomato and olive oil and wine at bargain prices. €€

Galician

Combarro
José Ortega y Gasset, 40
tel: 91-577 8272
www.combarro.com
Do not look for creative cooking, just enjoy the quality of the supreme quality fish, very simply prepared to show it off at its best. Conservatively smart, but welcoming. €€€€€

CASTILLA-LA MANCHA
Almagro

El Corregidor de Almagro
Jeronimo Cevallos, 2
tel: 926-860 648
This one-time medieval inn is famous for its rustic elegance and offers excellent modern cooking. €€

Almansa
Mesón del Pincelín
Las Norias, 10
tel: 967-340 007
Famed for its excellent shellfish and *gazpacho manchego*, a hot game stew served with flat bread. €€

Brihuega
Asador El Tolmo
Avda de la Constitución, 26
tel: 949-281 130
www.asadoreltolmo.com
Perfect setting for fine Manchego dining in the heart of partridge country. The roasts are peerless. €€

Cuenca
Mesón Casas Colgadas
Canónigos, s/n
tel: 969-223 509
www.mesoncasascolgadas.com
This minimalist white dining room is dramatically located in one of Cuenca's emblematic *casas colgadas* (hanging houses) perched on the cliff over the Huécar gorge. Updated regional cuisine. €€€
Plaza Mayor
Plaza Mayor, 5
tel: 969-211 496
Traditional Castilian spot in the heart of Cuenca's old town. A local favourite for quality, value and *gazpacho pastor* (a hearty stew) or *morteruelo* (pâté). €

Guadalajara
Amparito Roca
Toledo, 19
tel: 949-214 639
www.amparitoroca.com
This restaurant, named after a famous *pasadoble* written for the eponymous singer by Maestro Teixidor, specialises in *cabrito* (roast kid) in *breve* (sauce with aromatic herbs). Excellent wine list. €€€

Illescas
El Bohío
Arda de Castilla La Maneta 81
tel: 925-511 126
Pepe Rodvejrez Rey's excellent roadhouse restaurant turned into a local mecca for avant-garde cuisine. €€€

Las Pedroñeras
Las Rejas
Borreros, 49
tel: 967-161 089
lasrejas.restaurantesok.com
If you go to one restaurant in Castilla-La Mancha, choose this one. Inspiring regional cooking by Mantel de La Osa. €€€€

Puerto Lápice
Venta del Quijote
El Molino, 4
tel: 926-576 110
This is a stop that should not be missed, the legendary *venta* (inn) where Don Quijote is thought to have pledged allegiance to Dulcinea and justice, love and truth. The Manchegan cuisine is excellent. €€

Sigüenza
El Doncel
Paseo de la Alameda, 3
tel: 949-390 001
www.eldoncel.com
This inn and restaurant named after the slain pageboy of Isabela la Católica prepares traditional and modern dishes based on regional produce. €€

Talavera de la Reina
Anticuario
Avda de Madrid, 5
tel: 925-807 600
www.restauranteanticuario.com
The restaurant for the Hotel Beatriz, with light modern versions of local dishes; specialises in partridge. €€€

Toledo
Hostal del Cardenal
Paseo Recaredo, 24
tel: 925-220 862
An 18th-century urban palace with wood ovens where suckling pig and lamb are roasted to perfection. €€€
Restaurante Adolfo
La Granada, 6
tel: 925-227 321
The 14th- and 15th-century decor in this traditional gem deep in the Jewish quarter is no less impressive than the fresh local produce served here. €€€
Hierbabuena
Callejon de San José, 17
tel: 925-229 186
The dining room here is on an interior Moorish patio. The imaginative cuisine changes with the market. €€

Tragacete
El Gamo
Plaza de Fuente del Pinu, 2
tel: 969-289 008
For both dining and lodging, this little hotel and restaurant in the mountains of Cuenca is a perfect hideout. €

Villalba de la Sierra
Mesón Nelia
Ctra De La Ciudad Encantada, s/n
tel: 969-281 021
www.mesonnelia.com
This rustic spot on the banks of the Júcar river is ideal for trying the game on your way to the *Ciudad Encantada* (Enchanted City). Updated versions of local dishes. €€

Los Yébenes
Los Montes de Toledo
Carretera Nacional, s/n, km 401
tel/fax: 925-320 175
This hotel and restaurant overlooking olive groves and the Alberquillas mountains is the best place around for both dining and lodging. €€€

CASTILE-LEÓN

Avila
El Molino de la Losa
Bajada de la Losa, 12
tel: 920-211 101
www.elmolinodelalosa.com
Housed in a 15th-century mill, the restaurant offers classic Castilian cuisine, including local beans (*judías*) and lamb. Closed 15 Oct–15 March. €€€

León
Vivaldi
Platerías, 4
tel: 987-260 760
www.elvivaldi.com
Highly original modern cooking with local produce – the province's top restaurant. Good tapas bar, too. €€€
Casa Pozo
Plaza de San Marcelo, 15.
tel: 987-223 039
Specialities include crayfish with clams, *morcilla* (blood sausage) and San Marcos pie. €€–€€€

Palencia
Casa Damián
Ignacio Martínez de Azcoitia, 9
tel: 979-744 628
Specialities include vegetable stew, fried hake and partridge. €€€

Salamanca
Chez Victor
Espoz y Mina, 26
tel: 923-213 123
Nouvelle Franco-Spanish cuisine. Specialities include duck and, for dessert, crêpes. €€€
Río de la Plata
Plaza del Peso, 1
tel: 923-219 005
Castilian cuisine. Specialities include the meats and fish of the region, and clams. Closed Mon and July. €€–€€€

Segovia
La Cocina de Segovia
Po Ezequiel Gonzalez, 26
tel: 921-437 462
Overlooking the aqueduct, this excellent spot offers old dishes with a new twist. €€€
Casa Amado
Fernandez Ladreda, 9
tel: 921-432 077
Reasonably priced northern Spanish cooking, with excellent Atlantic fish and varied wine list. €€–€€€
Mesón de Cándido
Plaza Azoguejo, 5
tel: 921-425 911
www.mesondecandido.es
Always crowded, and full of atmosphere. There is a collection of photos of famous people tasting the suckling pig. Some tables overlook the 2,000-year-old aqueduct. €€–€€€

Price Guide

Approximate cost per person, including house wine:

€€€€€ = over €35
€€€€ = €30–35
€€€ = €20–30
€€ = €15–20
€ = under €15

Valladolid

La Perla de Castilla
Avda Ramón Pradara 15–19
tel: 983-371 828
Creative versions of Castilian and other Spanish dishes. Large wine cellar. €€
Mesón Cervantes
Rastro, 6
tel: 983-306 138
Family-run establishment specialising in hare, fresh vegetable stew, stuffed partridge, venison with sweet and sour sauce and roast pig and lamb. €€

Zamora

Pizarro
Cuesta de Pizarro, 7
tel: 980-534 545
A 16th-century mansion occupied by Hostería Real de Zamora, with good Castilian and Basque cooking. €€€
La Casita
Ctra de Carrascal, km 4
tel: 980-539 046
In an old house on the edge of town offering good home cooking. €€

EXTREMADURA
Badajoz

Monasterio de Rocamador
Ctra Badajoz-Huelva, km 41
Tel: 924-489 000
www.rocamador.com
Inspired reworking of local dishes by Basque chefs, in a graceful setting. €€€
Los Monjes de Zurbarán
Paseo de Castelar, s/n
tel: 924-222 142
Traditional cuisine, including partridge salad, pork sirloin, lamb stew and excellent cheeses. €€–€€€

Cáceres

Atrio
Avda de España, 30
tel: 927-242 928
www.restauranteatrio.com
Extremadura's leading restaurant. Creative modern cooking based on regional specialities accompanied by fabulous desserts. €€€
El Figón de Eustaquio
Plaza de San Juan, 12–14
tel: 927-244 362
Traditional regional classics include venison and wild mushroom dishes. €€

Nightlife

Entertainment Listings

The most complete listings magazine is the *Guía del Ocio*, published every Friday. On the internet try www.descubremadrid.com

Concerts, Ballet & Opera

Concerts and recitals can be enjoyed throughout the year in Madrid. Main venues are the **Teatro Real**, Madrid's opera house (Plaza de Oriente s/n; information, tel: 91-516 0660; international, tel: 34-91-558 8787,

Calendar of Events

January
Madrid: *Día de los Reyes* (Three Kings Cavalcade). Procession through the streets commemorating the kings' pilgrimage to meet baby Jesus. Takes place on 5/6 January.
February
Madrid: *Carnaval*. Week before Lent celebrated with the curious Entierro de la Sardina (Burial of the Sardine) on Paseo de la Flórida.
Zamarramala, Segovia Province: Santa Agueda festivals, medieval costumes, and even older customs.
Madrid: ARCO (Contemporary Art Fair). Spain's largest international art fair, usually the second week in February.
March/April
Semana Santa (Holy Week). Every town and city has striking processions of the penitent and other religious manifestations. In cities with famous cathedrals, such as Toledo and Segovia, the spectacle is unforgettable. The colourful town of Cuenca, 165 km (100 miles) southeast of Madrid, is noted for its splendid processions.
May
Madrid: Fiestas de San Isidro (St. Isidore the Husbandman), the capital's patron saint. Half a month of noisy neighbourhood parties, contests, plays, concerts and daily bullfights.

www.teatro-real.com; box office, tel: 91-516 0606); the **Auditorio Nacional de Música** (Príncipe de Vergara, 146, tel: 91-337 0140, www.auditorionacional.mcu.es), the home of the National Orchestra; the **Teatro Monumental** (Atocha, 65, tel: 91-429 1281), the official concert hall for the National Radio and Television Orchestra; the **Teatro de la Zarzuela** (Jovellanos, 4, tel: 91-524 5400, teatrodelazarzuela.mcu.es) and the **Centro Cultural de la Villa** (Plaza Colón, tel: 91-480 0300).

The Teatro Real reopened recently after many years of renovations and is now on a par with all the major opera houses in Europe. It has a 1,800 capacity, a high-tech stage and brand new rehearsal facilities. Here you can see opera and ballet companies from around the world. You can also see concerts, opera and ballet at the other venues mentioned above.

Zarzuela (light opera) is a Spanish genre which you can see in the Auditorio Nacional and the Teatro de la Zarzuela, and other Madrid theatres (check press for details). In the summer (late July–end Aug) you can

June
Toledo: Corpus Christi. The Spanish primate leads a solemn religious procession through the streets.
Toledo Province: Camuñas. An ancient religious play is presented in mime, with spectacular costumes.
Fiestas de San Juan and San Pedro. Dances, bullfights, fireworks. June 17–24.
July
Ávila: Summer festival with poetry, art, theatre, sports, bullfights, all outdoors.
August
Madrid: *Castizo* fiestas of San Caeyetano, San Lorenzo and La Virgen de la Paloma.
August 15th is a major national holiday and many towns have local celebrations on this day.
September
Ávila Province: Candeleda. Pilgrimage of Our Lady of Chilla, medieval religious ceremonies plus dancing and bullfights.
October
Toledo Province: Consuegra. Saffron Rose Festival in the heart of the windmill country of La Mancha.
December
Madrid: *Nochevieja* (New Year's Eve). Traditional celebration in the Puerta del Sol, swallowing grapes at each chime of the clock.

watch *Zarzuela* in the traditional open-air setting of **La Corrala** (Calle Tribulete, 12, and Calle Sombrerete, 13 – no phone, check press for details).

There are several festivals that feature visiting theatre and dance companies and orchestras – the main ones are **Veranos de la Villa** (music festival, July–mid-Sept), **Festival de Otoño** (theatre and dance festival, October) and **Festival Mozart** (classical music, June–July). See press for details or tel: 010 (Mon–Fri 8am–9pm, except holidays).

You can purchase tickets at the venues themselves (check local press for opening hours of individual box offices, as they may vary), or in the FNAC building, Calle Preciados, 28, tel: 91-595 6100, open all day; or by phone from Tel-Entradas, tel: 91-538 3333.

Clubs with Live Music

Café Central
Plaza del Angel, 10
tel: 91-369 4143
www.cafecentralmadrid.com
Open 1pm–2.30am; Fri–Sun closes 3.30am. Live jazz.

Café del Foro
San Andrés, 38
tel: 91-445 3752
Open daily 7pm–3am. Live acts, magicians, salsa.

Chesterfield Café
Serrano Jover, 5
tel: 91-542 2817
www.chesterlounge.com
Open daily 1.30pm–4.30am. Live show Wed–Sun at 11.30pm. Blues, soul, new country, rock and pop. American restaurant and bar.

Clamores
Alburquerque, 14
tel: 91-445 7938
www.salaclamores.com
Open 6pm–3am approx. Shows at 10pm. Mainly a jazz venue, also live pop, blues, soul, reggae, Latin and flamenco.

El Sol
Jardines, 3
tel: 91-532 6490
www.elsolmad.com
Open Tue–Sat 1–5am. Concerts 10.30pm. Pop, funk, rock, live bands.

Honky Tonk
Covarrubias, 24
tel: 91-445 6886
Open 9.30pm–5.30am daily. Wednesday night is Magic Night. Wide selection of country, blues and rock.

Moby Dick
Avda de Brasíl, 5
tel: 91-555 7671
www.mobydickclub.com
Open 9pm–4am daily. Live pop, blues and rock.

Suristán
Calle de la Cruz, 7
tel: 91-532 3909
Open 10.30pm–5.30am, Fri–Sat. Closed Sun and Mon. Every night a different style – African, Latin, reggae, flamenco. Live bands most nights.

Clubs and Discos

Cool
Isabel la Catolica, 6
Santo Domingo
tel: 91-548 2022
Film set-style disco with laidback crowd. View the beautiful scene from one of two balconies.

Fun Factory
Orense, 24
Open till late.

Kapital
Atocha, 135
tel: 91-420 2906
Macro-disco with seven floors.

Kathmandú
Señores de Luzón, 3
Ultra-lively basement disco with deafening music.

Magik Room
Colón, 12

Flamenco

There are a number of venues offering live flamenco performances. You can watch flamenco dancers at *tablaos flamencos* or listen to the expert *cante flamenco* singers at other venues. Be warned that the prices in *tablaos* will probably be high.

Tablaos Flamencos shows:
Café de Chinitas
Torija, 7
tel: 91-547 1502, www.chinitas.com
Open 9pm–2am Mon–Sat.

Casa Patas
Calle Cañizares, 10
tel: 91-369 0496, www.casapatas.com
Open midday–3am. Performances Mon–Thurs 10.30pm, Fri–Sat 9pm and midnight. Bar-restaurant.

Corral de la Morería
Morería, 17
tel: 91-365 8446,
www.corraldelamoreria.com
Open 9.30pm–3am daily.

Las Carboneras
Pl Conde de Miranda, 1
tel: 91-542 8677,
www.tablaolascarboneras.com
Upmarket atmosphere and good artists.

Suristán
de la Cruz, 7
tel: 91-532 3909
Holds flamenco nights once a week, usually Wednesday. A good place to see the new, young flamenco artists.

Casinos

The **Casino Gran Madrid** is at Ctra de la Coruña, km 28.3 near the town of Torrelodones, tel: 918-561 100. Open 4.30–11.30pm daily, but phone first to check. You have to be over 18, carry proper identification and be correctly dressed (for men this means a tie, except during August). A free bus service is provided from Plaza de España and Plaza de Colón.

tel: 91-531 3491
Small but friendly psychedelic-style disco co-owned by Oscar nominee Javier Bardem. Thursday to Saturday.

Pachá
Barceló, 11
tel: 91-447 0128
Stylish crowd.

Palacio de Gaviria
Arenal, 9
tel: 91-526 6069
www.palaciogaviria.com
Spiral staircase, gilt bars, Hellenic statues and ornate ceiling frescoes, plus music ranging from salsa to techno.

Pasapoga
Gran Vía 37, Callao
tel: 91-521 50 27
Frescoes, chandeliers, stairways and balconies in this elegant multi-level disco.

Room at Stella
Arlabán 7, Sevilla
Lively after-hours spot featuring house/techno music and a tiny packed dance floor. Fri–Sun 1–7am.

Dinner and Dance with Shows

Florida Park
Paseo de Coches del Retiro, s/n (in Retiro Park)
tel: 91-573 7805
www.floridapark.net
Open 9pm–3am (shows at 10.30pm).

Scala Meliá Castilla
Rosario Pino, 7
tel: 91-571 4411
A fine Las Vegas-style show, with dinner or drink; daily 9/10pm–3am, but changes frequently, so phone first.

Shopping

Corner Shops

Many small **corner shops** sprung up around Madrid in the late 1990s. Apart from a large selection of alcohol and crisps, you can also find some basic items available there, such as bread and milk – the shops are open until very late. Two chains, **VIPS** and **7–11** are also open late, and on Sunday. €0.10–0.20 per person.

Where to Shop

Madrid, as the capital, offers the visitor the whole range of shopping possibilities found in the different regions of Spain.

Spain has always been noted for the variety and quality of its craftwork from colourful hand-sewn, embroidered shawls, leather and suede goods, to its widely exported footwear and furniture.

The major department stores and tourist shops are to be found in the centre of Madrid between the Puerta del Sol and Plaza Callao, and along Gran Vía. The more select shops and international boutiques line Calle Serrano and its adjoining streets in the Salamanca area, while the most avant-garde designers have their shops in Calle Almirante, just off the Paseo de Recoletos.

There are also possibilities for antique shopping in Madrid: the Calle del Prado is a good hunting ground. Madrid Rastro, the open-air flea market, operates on Saturday, Sunday and holiday mornings, and you can find everything and anything there from valuable antiques, second-hand clothing and old books, to souvenirs and live canaries. Watch out for pickpockets.

The main department-store chain is El Corte Inglés (branches at Serrano, Preciados, 3; Princesa, 41; Goya, 76; and Raimundo Fernández Villaverde, 1).

Shopping Centres

ABC Serrano, Serrano, 61. A mall in the chic Salamanca area. More than 100 shops in a beautiful building, which has a rooftop summer terrace bar.

Galería del Prado, Plaza de las Cortes, 7 is probably the most elegant of the Madrid shopping complexes. On the ground floor of the Palace Hotel, with its main entrance on the Carrera de San Jerónimo, this lavishly decorated centre contains 38 exclusive shops and boutiques, together with a pleasant restaurant.

Madrid 2, La Vaguada, Avda Monforte de Lemos, 36, in the north of Madrid. An ultra-modern shopping centre with shops, supermarkets, bars, restaurants and cinemas.

Mercado de Fuencarral, Fuencarral 35. The city's only hip fashion centre, in a street lined with independent shoe and clothes shops.

Mercado Puerta de Toledo, Ronda de Toledo, 1. A former fish market transformed into a bright, spacious shopping centre where shops are to be found alongside exhibition and cultural areas, restaurants and bars.

Moda Shopping, in the Azca complex off the Paseo de La Castellana, is one of the newest centres with 100 shops and an atmosphere designed to induce a feeling of relaxation.

Multicentros, Serrano, 88 (the smallest of the *Multicentros* with 30 top boutiques); Princesa, 47 and Orense, 6.

Food Markets

El Mercado de Chamartín
Potosí, 11
Quality market on two levels; first-rate produce.

Centro Comercial la Paz
Ayala, 28
De luxe market in prime area of Salamanca. Cheeses at La Boulette counter exceptional.

La Cebada
Plaza de la Cebada s/n
tel: 91-365 9176
Large traditional market in La Latina serving range of produce.

Mercado de Maravillas
Bravo Murillo, 122
Largest and most colourful market in Madrid. Superb fish.

San Miguel
Plaza de San Miguel, Austrias
tel: 91-548 1214
Showpiece 19th-century market with iron grill façade. Good range of meat, fish and produce.

Sport

Participant Sports

GOLF

Madrid's golf courses include:
Club de Campo, Carretera Castilla, km 2, tel: 91-550 2010, www.clubvillademadrid.com. Sports complex with 71-par course. Tennis, horse-riding, swimming, hockey and clay pidgeon shooting are also available here.
Club de Golf de Puerta de Hierro, km 4, Madrid-La Coruña highway, tel: 91-316 1745, www.golfinspain.com. 36 holes.
Las Matas, Carretera de La Coruña, 26, tel: 91-630 0820.
Somosaguas Club, Somosaguas, tel: 91-352 1647. Classic club.
Nuevo Club de Golf de Madrid, Las Matas, Ctra de la Coruña, 26, tel: 91-630 2001. Open Tues–Sun; summer 9am–8pm; winter 9am–7pm.

TENNIS

Club de Campo, Ctra de Castilla, km 3, tel: 91-464 9167, www.clubvillademadrid.com.
Club de Tenis Chamartín, Federico Salmón, 2, tel: 91-345 2500, www.ctchamartin.es.
Club Internacional de Tenis, Carretera de El Plantío a Majadahonda, 3, tel: 91-639 25 51.
Parque Deportivo la Ermita, Sepulveda 3/5, tel: 91-470 0111.
Real Club Puerta de Hierro, Avda de Miraflores, s/n, tel: 91-316 1745.

SKIING

The nearest ski slopes are:
Navacerrada, 50 km (30 miles) from Madrid along the N-601. Five chair-lifts and six ski-lifts.
The **Valcotos** ski resort is 65 km (40 miles) along the N-601. Two chair-lifts and four ski-lifts.
Nearby **Valdesquí** has six ski-lifts and a ski-tow.
The **La Pinilla** resort, 113 km (70 miles) from Madrid, at Cerezo de Arriba in the province of Segovia. One ski-chair, six ski-lifts, one ski-tow and two cable cars. Information: 921-550 641. For recorded information (in Spanish) on snow conditions, tel: 91-350 2020.

HORSE RIDING

Central stables are located at: the **Club de Campo** complex, Carretera de Castilla, km 3, tel: 91-307 0395.

CLIMBING

For information on mountaineering, trekking and climbing in the region of Madrid, contact Espacio y Accion, Salustiano Olozaga, 14, first floor, tel: 91-578 0033. For maps, contact La Tienda Verde, Maudes 38 (Cuatro Caminos), tel: 91-535 3810.

Spectator Sports

FOOTBALL

Real Madrid's stadium, **Estadio Santiago Bernabéu**, is at Avenida de Concha Espina, 1, tel: 91-398 4300, (metro: Santiago Bernabéu) in the north of the city; they will soon move out to a purpose-built stadium by the airport.

The **Estadio Vicente Calderón**, Paseo de las Melencólico, tel: 91-366 4707, (metro: Pirámides) is home to Atlético Madrid and is in the south beside the Manzanares river; match tickets can be obtained daily 10am–1.30pm and 5–7.30pm, as well as on match days from 11am till kick-off.

At both stadiums you should expect to pay around €40 for a seat with a reasonable view.

JAI-ALAI

This fast, exciting Basque sport can be seen at **Frontón Reyzabal**, Avda Moratalaz, 40, tel: 91-328 3189.

BASKETBALL

Games are held in the Real Madrid Baloncesto installations, north of the Plaza de Castilla, or in the Palacio de Deportes on Avenida Felipe II. Two teams at the top of the Spanish league are Adecco Estudiantes and Real Madrid.

BULLFIGHTS

These are held in the **Plaza de Toros de Las Ventas** bullring, Calle Alcalá, 237, tel: 91-356 2200, www.las-ventas.com (Metro: Las Ventas). Box office: Thur–Sun 10am–2pm and 5–8pm. Tickets can be purchased a day in advance at Las Ventas. The season runs from mid-March to mid-October, with bullfights scheduled for Sundays and public holidays, and Thurs evenings during the summer.

The big **San Isidro Festival**, over three weeks of daily bullfights featuring top matadors and bulls from the best ranches, starts mid-May into June (check locally for exact dates). The autumn fair is held at the end of September.

During the San Isidro Festival, the corrals at **El Batán** in the Casa de Campo park exhibit the bulls due to be fought and for a modest fee you can take a closer look at these impressive animals. There is also an outdoor bar and restaurant.

Children's Activities

● **The Casa de Campo Park** is in the west of the city. The main entrance is at the El Lago metro stop. The park can also be reached by way of a soaring cross-town ride on the **Teleférico** cable car, which can be taken from the Paseo Pintor Rosales (tel: 91-541 7440). There are three swimming pools and a nearby lake, where rowing boats and canoes can be rented.

The park is also the setting for the modern **Madrid Zoo Aquárium**, tel: 91-512 3770, where it is possible to feed and pet the goats, sheep and deer. The zoo, home to over 3,000 animals, is located near the Batán Metro stop. Open 10.30am–8.30pm weekdays, and Sun 9.30pm. The Dolphin Show in the **Delfinario** is worth seeing. Open 10am–sunset. Dolphin Show: Mon–Fri 10.30am– 8.30pm; Sat–Sun and holidays 10.30am–9pm.

Also in the Casa de Campo is the **Parque de Atracciones** or Amusement Park, tel: 91-463 2900, www.parquedeatracciones.es, with a wide variety of rides and, in summer, performances by top Spanish and international singers. Situated near the Batán Metro stop; buses 33 and 65. Open daily from noon.

● In **Retiro Park** there are marionette shows at noon on Sat, Sun and public holidays, May–Oct, and in August the puppet festival **Titirilandia** brings puppets from around the world – shows on Fri and Sat at 7.30pm and 10.30pm. You can also take the children rowing on the lake (boats can

be rented 9.30am– 7.30pm; motorboats 10.40am– 2.30pm and 4–7.30pm) or enjoy the playgrounds.

Trips can be taken through the park in a *calesa* (horse-drawn carriage). The carriages wait near the *estanque* (lake), 10am–6pm.

● **Acciona** – Museo Interactivo de la Ciencia (Interactive Science Museum), Pintor Murillo, s/n, Parque de Andalucía, Alcobendas, tel: 91-661 3909. Chemistry, optics, palaeontology, energy. Exhibitions in which children can participate are staged in this museum. Open 10am–8pm daily. Bus: Interbus 151, 152, 153, 154 from Plaza Castilla.

● **The Planetarium** in the Tierno Galván Park, tel: 91-467 3898. Shows start at 5.30pm and 6.45pm during the week and at 11.30am, 12.45pm, 5.30pm and 6.45pm on weekends and holidays. Metro: Méndez Alvaro; bus: 148. There is a nice playground outside.

● **Safari**, tel: 91-862 2314, is a wild animal reserve located in the town of Aldea del Fresno, on National Highway V near Navalcarnero about 40 km (25 miles) from Madrid. Open daily Mar–Nov 10.30am–sunset. It also has a museum, trained animal shows, a boating lake, miniature golf, swimming pools and restaurants.

● **Baby West "La Ermita"**, Paseo del Santo, 48, tel: 91-526 0178 is a children's amusement park with a Far West "town", Santa Fe train, rides, trampolines. Open Tues–Fri 5–11pm; Sat noon–midnight, Sun noon–10pm.

● **Parquesur**, Avenida Gran Bretaña, s/n, Leganés, tel: 91-686 3798. This amusement and aquapark is next to a large shopping centre, which also offers entertainment on summer evenings Mon–Fri 5–9pm, Sat–Sun 11am–10pm.

● **Faunia**, Avenida de las Comunidades, s/n, tel: 91-301 6210; www.faunia.es (metro: Valdebernardo). This additon to Madrid's outlying open-air attractions is a blend of zoo and theme park with around 200 animals and a thousand plants from all over the world. Open Mon–Fri 10.30am–8pm, till 9pm Sat Sun.

● IMAX **Madrid**, Parque Tierno Galván, tel: 91-467 4800, www.imaxmadrid.com. (metro: Méndez Alvaro). Three-dimensional cinema showing documentaries.

● **Teatro San Pol**, Plaza San Pol de Mar, s/n, tel: 91-541 9089, www.teatrosanpol.com. Entertaining plays for children.

● **Minigolf**, Calle Montesa, 11. Open 3–8pm.

● **Tren de la Fresa**, tel: 91-328 9020/90-222 8822. Steam train with early 20th-century carriages and actors in costume entertaining passengers. Leaves for Aranjuez from Paseo de Las Delicias, Apr–Oct holidays and weekends. Reservations recommended.

● Another possibility is one of the travelling **circuses**, which come to Madrid in the months of December, January and May (see the newspapers for details).

Southern Spain

GEOGRAPHY & POPULATION

Andalusia covers 87,000 sq km (34,000 sq miles), 17 percent of Spain's total area. Most of the approximately 7 million inhabitants live on the coast or along the Guadalquivir river valley. The 660-km (410-mile) long Guadalquivir is the backbone of the region, draining a vast basin and providing water for power and irrigation as well as drinking. The alluvial sediments bordering the river provide fertile soil for crops.

North of the Guadalquivir, the hills of the Sierra Morena are a barrier to easy communication between Andalusia and the rest of Spain. To the south, the Cordillera Baetica runs from Gibraltar to Murcia, forming another higher barrier between the Guadalquivir basin and the Mediterranean coast.

Mulhacén in the Sierra Nevada is the peninsula's highest mountain at 3,478 metres (11,402 ft) and the ranges bristle with dramatic crags. These sierras shield the coasts of Almería, Granada and Málaga from frost and snow.

Economy

Andalusia is Spain's most important agricultural region. Traditional products such as olive oil, cereals and grapes have lost ground to new crops and methods, and irrigation has been extended. Cotton, sunflowers, citrus fruits, sugar beet and rice are the major crops of the region. Strawberries are a money-spinning export from Huelva and along the sheltered Mediterranean coast avocados, sweet potatoes, kiwi fruit and custard apples flourish. Fish-farming is a fast expanding industry.

The mining of copper, lead, silver and gold, which dates from ancient times, is declining but service industries are growing and the regional authorities are striving to attract high-tech industry.

Climate

Andalusia's position at the southern edge of Europe gives it a privileged climate. Summers are hot and winters generally mild. However, there are considerable variations due to the size of the region, its mountainous character and the fact that it is bordered by both the Atlantic and Mediterranean.

Summers can be extremely hot in the interior with temperatures rising to 40°C (104°F) and even higher in the provinces of Seville and Córdoba. Almería has an extremely arid, desert-like climate. Snow covers the Sierra Nevada from November to June and frost is common in upland areas.

The Levante wind has considerable influence, often blowing hard for days on the Cádiz coast and creating a persistent cloud over the Rock of Gibraltar. June to October is usually dry, except for sporadic torrential downpours. Heavy rain in the winter months is usually interspersed with brilliant sunshine. The best months to tour the region are in spring and autumn.

Since the 1960s there has been phenomenal growth in tourism, which has brought prosperity to what was previously one of Spain's poorest areas. Apart from the annual influx of package-tour visitors, several hundred thousand northern Europeans have permanent or semi-permanent residences on or near the Mediterranean coast.

Getting There

BY AIR

Flights between the UK and Málaga are served by **Air Europa**, tel: 0870-240 1501, www.aireuropa; **British Airways**, tel: 0870-850 9850, www.britishairways.com; **BMI British Midland**, tel: 0870-607 0555, www.britishmidland.com; **BMI Baby**, tel: 0870-262229, www.bmibaby.com; **Easyjet**, tel: 01582-443355, www.easyjet.com; **Flybe**, tel: 0871-700 0123, www.flybe.com; **Globespan**, tel: 0870-556 1522, www.flyglobespan.com; **Iberia**, tel: 0845-601 2854, www.iberia.com; **Jet 2**, tel: 0870-737 8282, www.jet2.com; **Monarch Crown**, tel: 0870-040 5040, www.monarch-airlines.com; **Mytravellite**, www.mytravellite.com; and **Palmair**, tel: 01202-200700, www.bathtravel.com. **Aer Lingus**, tel: 0845-084 4444 (UK), 01-886 8844 (Ireland), www.aerlingus.ie and **Cityjet**, tel: 01 870 0300 fly from Dublin to Málaga. International flights also serve Seville, Jeréz, Granada, Almería and Gibraltar.

BY SEA

Trasmediterránea vessels, carrying passengers and vehicles, travel between Almería, Málaga, Algeciras, Cádiz and ports on the African coast and on the Canary Islands.

There are frequent ferry services across the Straits of Gibraltar from Algeciras to Ceuta and Tangier, and from Tarifa to Tangier.

Getting Around

BY RAIL

A high-speed rail service, the AVE, links Seville to Madrid, reducing travelling time to just over two hours. The fast service between Madrid and Málaga takes just over four hours.

The special AVE track is also used on other services, such as the Madrid–Málaga Talgo, which is also fast and very comfortable. AVE and Talgo services are best booked in advance.

Timetables and reservations are available through the RENFE website; www.renfe.es/ingles.

Regional trains between cities tend to be slower than the national services. The Costa del Sol between Málaga and Fuengirola is served by an efficient commuter service, every 20 minutes. A train ride in the grand style of the Orient Express is offered by the Al-Andalus Expreso. Operating May–October, this deluxe train visits Seville, Córdoba, Granada and Málaga, with the option of a visit to Jerez .

BY ROAD

The road network in Southern Spain has improved dramatically in the past few years as part of a massive expansion of the motorway system throughout Spain. The Autopista del Mediterráneo (toll) runs all the way from the French border at La Junquera along the coast to Alicante; from there, four-lane motorways run directly to Almería or to Granada and Seville. Madrid is also connected by a four-lane motorway to Seville (via Bailén and Córdoba) and Málaga (via Jaén and Granada).

The bridge across the Guadiana River at Ayamonte allows easy access to Andalusia from Portugal's Algarve coast.

Car Rental

International chains have airport offices, and offer collect and deliver services. Local companies are cheaper and will arrange to meet you on arrival if you book.

Avis airport offices (www.avis.com):
Almería, tel: 950-298 221.
Granada, tel: 958-446 455.
Jerez de la Frontera, Cádiz,
tel: 956-150 005.
Málaga,
tel: 952-048 483/222 4949
Seville,
tel: 954-449 121/453 7861.
Europcar airport offices (www.europcar.es):
Almería, tel: 950-292 934.
Granada, tel: 958-245 275.
Jerez de la Frontera, tel: 956-150 098.

Hertz airport offices (www.hertz.com):
Almería, tel: 950-292 500.
Córdoba (railway station),
tel: 957-402 061.
Granada, tel: 958-242 577.
Jerez de la Frontera,
tel: 956-150 038.
Málaga, tel: 952-233 086.
Seville, tel: 954-449 125.

Media

Several English-language publications
serve the large number of expatriates
living along the Mediterranean coast.
Absolute Marbella and Essential
Magazine are devoted to the glitzy

Local Tourist Offices

Almería
Regional tourist office: Parque Nicolás
Salmerón, tel: 950-274 355,
email: otalmería@andalucia.org

Cádiz
Regional tourist office: Plaza de San
Juan de Dios 11, tel: 956-241 001.
Jerez de la Frontera: Plaza del Arenal,
tel: 956-359 654.

Córdoba
Regional tourist office: Torrijos 10
(Palacio de Congresos), tel: 957-471
235, email: otcordoba@andalucia.org

Granada
Regional tourist office: Corral del
Carbón, tel: 958-221 022,
email: otgranada@andalucia.org

Huelva
Regional tourist office: Avda de
Alemania 12, tel: 959-257 403,
email: othuelva@andalucia.org.

Jaén
Regional tourist office: Maestra 13,
tel: 953-190 455,
email: otjaen@andalucia.org.
Baeza: Plaza del Pópulo s/n,
tel: 953-740 444.
Ubeda: Palacio Marqués del
Contadero, Baja del Marqués,
tel: 953-750 897.

lifestyle of the famous resort. SunGolf
is a monthly magazine focusing on the
popular golfing scene.
   Various free papers come out
weekly, with details of events and
activities in the expatriate community,
as well as property pages. They include
Sur in English, Costa del Sol News and
The Entertainer. There are also several
radio stations broadcasting in English
such as the long-established OCI, which
broadcasts on FM 101.6.

Medical Services

Cities and large resorts have numerous
private clinics and dental clinics. The
public hospitals run by the Andalusian
health service (Servicio Andaluz de
Salud) are the best equipped to deal
with serious medical emergencies.
Those on the Costa del Sol have teams
of volunteer interpreters.
   For first aid go to the Urgencias
entrance of the Centro de Salud, the
public health centres in most towns.

Security and Crime

Thefts from tourists and their cars have
increased in recent years. Common-

Málaga
Regional tourist office: Pasaje de
Chinitas 4, tel: 952-213 445.
Municipal tourist office: Avda
Cervantes 1, Paseo del Parque,
tel: 952-604 410; also at airport,
tel: 95-224 0000.
Antequera: Plaza de San Sebastián,
tel: 952-702 505.
Benalmádena-Costa: Avda Antonio
Machado 10, tel: 952-242 494.
Estepona: Avenida San Lorenzo 1,
tel: 952-800 913.
Fuengirola: Avda Jesús Santos Rein 6,
tel: 952-467 457.
Marbella: Glorieta de la Fontanilla,
tel: 952-822 818.
Nerja: Puerta del Mar 4,
tel: 952-521 531.
Ronda: Plaza de España 1, tel: 952-
871 272.
Torremolinos: Plaza Blas Infante,
tel: 952-379 511.

Seville
Municipal Tourist office: Avenida de
la Constitución 21, tel: 954-221 404.
Municipal tourism office: Paseo de
las Delicias 9, tel: 954-234 465.

Tarifa
Regional tourist office: Paseo La
Alameda, tel: 956-680 913.
Puerto de Santa María: Luna 22,
tel: 956-542 413.

Emergency Numbers

National police: 091
Local police: 092
Medical emergencies: 061
Fire brigade: 085

sense precautions should prevent your
holiday being spoiled in this way. Cities
are black spots. Never leave anything
of value in your car, including when
parking near a beach. Don't leave cash
or valuables unattended while you are
swimming. When staying overnight,
take all baggage into the hotel and, if
possible, park your car in a garage or a
guarded car-park.
   Particularly when driving into Seville,
do not leave anything of value within
sight. When walking, women should
keep shoulder bags out of view if
possible. Avoid badly lit back streets at
night in such quarters as Santa Cruz in
Seville. Police patrols have been
stepped up, but this area is a magnet
for muggers, often working in groups.
Carry photocopies of your passport and
other important documents and leave
the originals in the hotel safe.
   If confronted, do not resist, as
thieves often carry knives. If you are
robbed, remember that muggers usually
want easily disposable cash and swiftly
dispose of unwanted items, so check
the nearest gutters, rubbish containers
and toilets for your personal
possessions.

Where to Stay

Accommodation

Parators charge between a luxury and moderate hotel double room rate. You'll find that prices are lower for a double room in other types of accommodation. You can book online by visiting: www.parador.es. In a *pensión*, expect to pay in the region of €18; in 1- and 2-star *hostales*, prices will range from €18–55. Hotels are listed in order of price category.

ALMERÍA

Almería

Gran Hotel Almería
Avda Reina Regente, 8
tel: 950-238 011
fax: 950-270 691
www.granhotelalmeria.com
Almería's top-class hotel, with good views over the harbour. €€€
Torreluz II
Plaza Flores, 1
tel/fax: 950-234 399
www.torreluz.com
Mid-range, clean and modern hotel. €€

Mojácar

El Moresco
Avda De Encamp
tel: 950-478 025
fax: 950-478 262
A good choice for those who want to stay in Mojácar itself, rather than on the beach 3 km (2 miles) below the village, with good views of the surrounding countryside. €€
Parador Reyes Católicos
Ctra de Carboneras, Mojácar Playa
tel: 950-478 250
fax: 950-478 183
www.parador.es
Splendid beachside location is the main attraction of this modern Parador. €€€

Price Guide

For a standard double room
€€€€ =   Over €150
€€€ =   €90–150
€€ =   €50–90
€ =   Under €50

El Puntazo
Paseo del Mediterraneo
tel: 950-478 265
fax: 950-478 285
www.hotelelpuntazo.com
Bright, modern and next to beach. €

Pechina

Sierra Alhamilla
Pechina, s/n
tel: 950-317 413
fax: 950-160 257
A pleasant, small hotel, 10 km (6 miles) north of Almería, built next to a thermal spring. €€

San José

Hotel San José
Correos, San José
tel: 950-380 116
fax: 950-380 002
Rooms overlook a secluded cove in the relatively unspoilt Cabo de Gata. €€€

CÁDIZ

Algeciras

Reina Cristina
Paseo de la Conferencia, s/n
tel: 956-602 622
fax: 956-603 323
www.reinacristina.es
Surrounded by luxuriant gardens, this British-style early 20th-century hotel is a classic. €€€

Arcos de la Frontera

Parador de Arcos de la Frontera
Plaza del Cabildo, s/n
tel: 956-700 500
fax: 956-701 116
www.parador.es
Perched on a cliff and offering spectacular views. Large rooms are furnished in typical parador style. €€€
Los Olivos
Paseo Boliches, 30
tel: 956-700 811
fax: 956-702 018
www.terra.es
An old Andalusian townhouse arranged around a courtyard. Good value. €€
El Convento
Maldonado, 2
tel: 956-702 333
fax: 957-704 128
www.webdearcos.com/elconvento
Eleven rooms, occupying part of a former convent. €€

Cádiz

Atlántico
Duque de Nájera, 9
tel: 956-226 905
fax: 956-214 582
www.parador.es
State-run hotel in a modern, stylish building, the best for staying in the picturesque old part of the city. €€€

Grazalema

Villa Turística de Grazalema
El Olivar, s/n
tel: 956-132 136
fax: 956-132 213
www.tucasa.com
Part of the Andalusian "Villa Turística" network, with self-catering units in addition to a small hotel. €€

Jeréz de la Frontera

Jeréz
Avda Alvaro Domecq, 35
tel: 956-300 600
fax: 956-305 001
www.jerezhotel.com
In a pleasant, leafy residential part of town, this classic hotel has a swimming pool and tennis courts. €€€
Montecastillo
Ctra de Arcos, km 9
tel: 956-151 200
fax: 956-151 209
www.montecastillo.com
Just outside Jeréz, near the motor-racing track, a luxurious neo-Moorish palace adjoining a golf course. €€€€

Puerto de Santa María

Monasterio de San Miguel
Larga, 27
tel: 956-540 440
fax: 956-542 604
www.jale.com/monasterio
Tasteful and comfortable, installed in a former 18th-century monastery, which retains the original cloisters, chapel and enclosed garden. €€€

Tarifa

Hotel Dos Mares
Ctra N340, km 78
Tel: 956-680 090/684 035
Fax: 956-681 078
www.dosmareshotel.com
Ideal beachside location 2 km from town. Riding, tennis, gym. Windsurfing and kitesurfing tuition. €€€

CÓRDOBA

Córdoba

Amistad Córdoba
Plaza de Maimónides, 3
tel: 957-420 335
fax: 957-420 365
Comfortable rooms in two former mansions overlooking the Plaza Maimónides. €€€
Parador de Córdoba
Avda de la Arruzafa, s/n
tel: 957-275 900
fax: 957-280 409
www.parador.es
Modern hotel offers fine views from a hill on the outskirts of the city. €€€
Albucasis
Buen Pastor, 11
tel/fax: 957-478 625
www.hotelalbucasis.com

Family-run with clean, comfortable rooms around a patio in the heart of the old town. €€

Palma del Río

Hospedería San Francisco
Avda Pío X11, 35
tel: 957-710 183
fax: 957-710 236
Renowned for its fine food, the hotel is in a former 15th-century Franciscan monastery. €€€

GRANADA

Almuñecar

Sol los Fenicios
Paseo de Andrés Segovia, La Herradura
tel: 958-827 900
fax: 958-827 910
www.solmelia.com
Bright, modern and situated on the beach of a quiet fishing village, near Almuñecar; good coastal views. €€€

Bubión (Alpujarras)

Villa Turística de Bubión
Barrio Alto
tel: 958-763 111
fax: 958-766 255
www.ctv.es/alpujarr
The first of the Andalusian *Villas Turísticas* network, with modern self-catering apartments, built in the traditional Alpujarras style. €€

Granada

Parador de Granada
Alhambra, s/n
tel: 958-221 440
fax: 958-222 264
www.parador.es
In a converted 15th-century Francisco monastery within the Alhambra gardens. €€€€
Alhambra Palace
Peña Partida, 2
tel: 958-221 468
fax: 958-226 404
www.h-alhambrapalace.es
At the foot of the Alhambra walls, an ochre-coloured neo-Moorish fantasy. Good views over the city. The bar is a popular meeting place. €€€€
Reina Cristina
Tablas, 4
tel: 958-253 211
fax: 958-255 728
www.hotelreinacristina.com
Friendly and comfortable hotel in an old Granada home between the cathedral and Plaza de Bib-Rambla. €€

Loja

La Bobadilla
Finca La Bobadilla
tel: 958-321 861
fax: 958-321 810
www.la-bobadilla.com
Deluxe hotel in the Andalusian country-

palace style. Top-rated restaurant, champagne for breakfast, and prices to match. €€€€

Quéntar

Quentarhotel
Calle San Sebastián
tel: 958-485 426/7
fax: 958-485 242
www.quentarhotel.net
Situated 12 km (8 miles) from Granada and near the Sierra Nevada ski station, in a small unspoilt white village. Fabulous views from the 15 fully equipped rooms. €–€€

Sierra Nevada

Melia Rumaykiyya
Dehesa de San Jerónimo
tel: 958-481 400
fax: 958-480 032
Comfortable modern hotel offering good services to skiers. €€€
Ziryab
Plaza Andalucía
tel: 958-480 512
fax: 958-481 415
www.hotelziryab.com
Conveniently close to the ski lifts and reasonably priced; the newest hotel in Granada's ski resort. €€

HUELVA

Ayamonte

Parador de Ayamonte
El Castillito, s/n
tel: 959-320 700
fax: 959-022 019
www.parador.es
Modern Parador overlooking the Guadiana river, and Portugal on the farther shore. €€€

El Rocío

Toruno
Plaza Acebuchal, 32
tel: 959-442 323
fax: 959-442 338
www.toruno.es
Small hotel, with 30 comfortable rooms, in hamlet of El Rocío, a favourite with bird watchers, with some rooms overlooking Doñana marshes. €€

Huelva

Tartessos
Avda Martín Alonso Pinzón, 13
tel: 959-282 711
fax: 959-250 617
www.hoteltartessos.com
Good location in a quiet residential area of the city. €€

La Rábida

Hostería de la Rábida
La Rábida, s/n
tel/fax: 959-350 035
www.hosterialarabida.com
This five-room hostelry is comfortable

and next door to the beautiful 15th-century Monastery of La Rábida. €

Matalascañas

Tierra Mar
Matalascañas Parc, 120 Sector M
tel: 959-440 300
fax: 959-440 720
www.vimehoteles.com
Matalascañas is a vastly overbuilt beach resort but this beachside hotel is handy for the national park. €€

Mazagón

Parador de Mazagon
Ctra Huelva-Matalascañas, km 24
tel: 959-536 300
fax: 959-536 228
www.parador.es
Pine-shaded, modern hotel with beach view; rooms open onto a garden. €€€

JAÉN

Baeza

Casa Juanito
Avda Arca del Agua, s/n
tel: 953-740 040
fax: 953-742 324
www.juanitobaeza.com
Simple and inexpensive, with an excellent restaurant. €
Fuenteventura Hospedería
Paseo Arca del Agua
tel: 953-743 100
fax: 953-743 200
www.fuentenueva.com
A friendly and tastefully decorated small hotel installed in what used to be the town's women's prison. €

Jaén

Parador Castillo de Santa Catalina
Castillo de Santa Catalina, s/n
tel: 953-230 000
fax: 953-230 930
www.parador.es
On a hill overlooking the city, right next to Jaén's Muslim castle and built in the same style, with magnificent views of the sierra. €€€

Parque Natural de Cazorla

Parador El Adelantado
Sierra de Cazorla
tel: 953-727 075
fax: 953-727 077
www.parador.es
This modern parador is an excellent base from which to explore the wilderness of the Parque Natural de Cazorla. €€€
Sierra de Cazorla
Ctra Sierra de Cazorla, km 2, La Iruela
tel: 953-720 015
fax: 953-720 017
www.hotelsierradecazorla.com
Functional but comfortable small hotel located just beyond the village of La Iruela, at the park's entrance. €€

Price Guide

For a standard double room

€€€€ = Over €150
€€€ = €90–150
€€ = €50–90
€ = Under €50

Ubeda

Parador Condestable Dávalos
Plaza Vázquez Molina, 1
tel: 953-750 345
fax: 953-751 259
www.parador.es
Situated in a 16th-century palace at the centre of Ubeda's old Renaissance region, with spacious rooms. €€€

MÁLAGA

Antequera

Parador de Antequera
García del Olmo, s/n
tel: 95-284 0261
fax: 95-284 1312
www.parador.es
Airy, modern Parador with good views of the sweeping plain of Antequera. €€

Benalmádena-Costa

Alay
Puerto Deportivo, Benalmádena-Costa
tel: 952-441 440
fax: 952-445 702
www.hotelalay.com
Modern hotel, next to the lively yacht harbour of Benalmádena – one of the nightlife hubs of the Costa del Sol. €€€

Estepona

El Paraíso
Urb. El Paraíso, N-340, km 134
tel: 952-883 000
fax: 952-882 019
www.hotelparaisocostadelsol.com
Modern hotel on a hill east of Estepona, next to a golf course with views of the Straits of Gibraltar. €€€€
Las Dunas
La Boladilla Baja, N-340, km 163
tel: 952-809 400
fax: 952-794 825
www.las-dunas.com
Luxurious 5-star spa hotel, housed in several Andalusian-style buildings next to the beach, east of Estepona, with large, sumptuously decorated rooms. €€€€

Málaga

Don Curro
Sancha de Lara, 7.
Tel: 952-227 200
Fax: 952-215 946
www.hoteldoncurro.com
A classic Málaga hostelry, with an old-fashioned atmosphere, on a quiet side street off central Málaga's main shopping district. €€€

Larios
Marqués de Larios, 2
tel: 95-222 2200
fax: 95-222 2407
www.hotel-larios.com
Modern hotel in a restored old building, in a convenient central location. €€€
Las Vegas
Paseo de Sancha, 22
tel: 952-217 712
fax: 952-224 889
Near the Málaga bullring and next to the city's seafront promenade, with a pool and a large garden. €€€
Parador de Turismo Gibralfaro
Monte de Gibralfaro
tel: 952-221 902
fax: 952-221 904
www.parador.es
This charming small parador is on the hill overlooking the city, next to an old Muslim fortress. Reservations and a car essential. €€€

Mijas

Byblos Andaluz
Urb. Mijas-Golf, Mijas Costa
tel: 95-247 3050
fax: 95-247 6783
www.byblos-andaluz.com
A super-deluxe spa hotel adjoining a golf course. Top-class restaurant and stylish atmosphere. €€€€
Hotel Mijas
Urb. Tamisa
tel: 95-248 5800
fax: 95-248 5825
Modern, airy hotel with ample gardens at the entrance to Mijas, offering fine views of the coast. €€€

Marbella

Los Monteros
N-340, km 187
tel: 952-771 700
fax: 952-825 846
www.monteros.com
Luxurious resort hotel adjoining a golf course near the beach 5 km (3 miles) east of Marbella. €€€€
Marbella Club Hotel
N-340, km 178,2
tel: 952-822 211
fax: 952-829 884
www.marbellaclub.com
This 1950s classy hotel was the birthplace of the Marbella legend. Bungalow-style accommodation among gardens reaching the beach. €€€€
Puente Romano
N340, km 177,7
tel: 952-820 900
fax: 952-866 164
www.puenteromano.com
A landmark palatial hotel designed like a Moorish-Andalusian *pueblo*, with gardens and fountains and, within, marble sumptuousness. €€€€
Hotel El Fuerte
Avda El Fuerte

tel: 952-920 000
fax: 952-824 411
www.fuertehoteles.com
Well-run hotel on the Costa del Sol; the best option in the centre of Marbella, at the end of the town's seafront promenade, with sea-view rooms. €€€

Nerja

Parador de Nerja
Almuñécar, 8
tel: 952-520 050
fax: 952-521 997
www.parador.es
Modern parador on a cliff overlooking the beach, with rooms arranged around a pleasant garden. €€€

Ronda

Parador de Ronda
Plaza de España, s/n
tel: 952-877 500
fax: 952-878 188
www.parador.es
One of Spain's newer paradors, perched on a cliff next to the famous gorge; the restored facade of an old building conceals a striking modern interior design. €€€
Polo
Mariano Souvirón, 8
tel: 952-872 447
fax: 952-872 449
www.hotopolo.net
Comfortable and friendly, with a nice atmosphere, in the town centre. €€

Torremolinos

Cervantes
Las Mercedes, s/n
tel: 952-384 033
fax: 952 384 857
www.hotasacervantes.com
Large, modern hotel, the best option for those who want to stay close to the centre of Torremolinos. €€€
Miami
Calle Aladino, 14.
Tel: 952-385 255
www.hoteltropicana.es
This small family-run hotel in a traditional Spanish villa next to the Carihuela beach is inexpensive, friendly and informal. No credit cards. €€
Tropicana
Trópico, 6
tel: 952-386 600
fax: 952-380 568
Right on the beach at the western end of the popular fish-restaurant quarter, La Carihuela. Fun atmosphere. €€€

SEVILLE

Carmona

Casa de Carmona
Plaza Lasso, Carmona (33 km/ 20 miles east of Seville)
tel/fax: 95-419 0189
www.casadecarmona.com

One of Andalusia's most stylish hotels, installed in a 16th-century aristocratic mansion. Exquisitely decorated. €€€€

Parador Alcázar del Rey Don Pedro
Carmona
Alcázar
tel: 95-414 1010
fax: 95-414 1712
www.parador.es
A Mudéjar-style building on a hill viewing the town, with spacious rooms. €€€

Seville

Alfonso XIII
San Fernando, 2
tel: 954-917 000
fax: 954-917 099
www.hotel-alfonsoxiii.com
Old-style elegance in this classic hotel, built in Neo-Mudéjar style. €€€€

Casa Imperial
Imperial, 29
tel: 954-500300
fax: 954-500 330
www.casaimperial.com
Restored 16th-century palace with four inner patios. There are 24 suites, each decorated differently, with enormous bathrooms. €€€€

Inglaterra
Plaza Nueva, 7
tel: 95-422 4970
fax: 95-456 1336
www.hotelinglaterra.es
Comfortable and friendly. A good location for touring the city. €€€€

Las Casas de la Judería
Callejón de Dos Hermanas
tel: 95-441 5150
fax: 95-444 2170
www.intergrupohoteles.com
Three old palaces in Santa Cruz quarter converted into this maze-like hotel, with several inner courtyards. €€€

Villa de le Palmera
Avda de la Palmera, 57
tel: 95-423 8560
www.villadelapalmera.com
Twelve air-conditioned rooms located near the cathedral. €€€

Puerta de Triana
Reyes Catolicos, 5
tel: 95-421 5404
fax: 95-421 5401
www.hotelpuertadetriana.com
Conveniently located, friendly, efficient and good value, with attractive reception area and pleasant rooms. €€

Simón
García de Vinuesa, 19
tel: 95-422 6660
fax: 95-456 2241
www.hotelsimonseville.com
One of the best-value choices in the centre of the city, not far from the cathedral, offering pleasant no-frill lodgings in an 18th-century house around an Andalusian patio. €€

Where to Eat

Eating Out

It is not necessary to step into a restaurant to eat well in Andalusia. Fast food was a part of Spanish culture when the hot dog was hardly more than a puppy. *Tapas*, tasty snacks varying from grilled birds to stewed tripe and chick peas, are served in many bars. Sometimes they come free with the drinks; sometimes you have to order them and pay extra. If you want more, you can ask for a *ración* (plateful), or *media ración* (half plateful).

In bars calling themselves cafeterias, you can order a *plato combinado*. This is usually a variation on pork chop, fried eggs, ham, salad and chips. Even the smallest village usually has a bar serving *tapas* or a *fonda* (inn) serving set meals at budget prices.

Restaurants usually offer a *menú del día*, a three-course meal, including wine, at an economical price. Note also that on the Atlantic and Mediterranean coasts you can eat well on the beaches in restaurants known as *chiringuitos* and *merenderos*. Some of these have become quite sophisticated, with prices to match. Others remain simple, with the best bet probably being "fish of the day", guaranteed to be fresh.

Restaurants in inland cities keep Spanish hours (lunch at 2.30 or 3pm, dinner at 9pm onwards), but those on the Costa del Sol make more allowances for foreign tourists, serving lunch from 1pm and dinner from 7pm.

Moderate to Expensive restaurants usually accept at least one of the credit cards; MasterCard and Visa are more widely accepted than AmEx or Diners. Cheaper establishments prefer cash. Restaurants are listed in order of price category.

ALMERÍA

Almería

Club de Mar
Muelle de las Almadrabillas
tel: 950-235 048
Within Almería's yacht club and near the beach, this classic Almería restaurant has built a solid reputation on its fresh seafood dishes. €€€

La Gruta
Ctra N-340, km 436
tel: 950-239 335
Inside a cave overlooking the sea between Almería and Aguadulce. Grilled meat is the speciality. Closed Sun and all of Nov. €€€

Mojácar area

Terraza Carmona
Manuel Giménez, 1 Vera
tel: 950-390 760
fax: 950-391 314
www.terrazacarmona.com
Set in the beachside community of Vera, north of Mojácar, a long-established restaurant offering a good combination of local (mainly fish) and international fare. Closed Mon. €€

CÁDIZ

Arcos de la Frontera

El Convento
Marqués de Torresoto, 7
tel: 956-703 222
www.webdearcos.com/elconvento
Dining area decorated in painted tiles with plants arranged around interior courtyard in a 17th-century palace. Menu features some unusual regional dishes for the more daring. €€€

Cádiz

El Faro
San Felix, 15
tel: 956-211 068
www.elfarodecadiz.com
The best-known of Cádiz's restaurants, in the old quarter of town, and renowned for its seafood served in its wood-beamed dining room. There's also a large *tapas* bar. CC: AmEx, MasterCard, Visa. €€€€

Ventorillo del Chato
Ctra de San Fernando, km 647
tel: 956-250 025
In an 18th–century inn on the sandy isthmus that joins Cádiz to the mainland, specialising in seafood, although good meat too. Closed Sun. €€€

Jerez de la Frontera

La Mesa Redonda
Manuel de la Quintana, 3
tel: 956-340 069
A small (eight-table) restaurant, serving impeccable Jerez dishes, most based on recipes from aristocratic sherry families. One of the best restaurants in Andalusia. Reservations essential. Closed Sun, holidays, and Aug. €€€€

Price Guide

Approximate cost per person, including house wine:

€€€€ =	above €25
€€€ =	€12–25
€€ =	under €12

Venta Antonio
Ctra Jerez-Sanlúcar, km 5
tel: 956-140 535
Just 5 km (3 miles) outside Jerez on a country road, former roadside inn, Venta Antonio has earned an enviable reputation for its fresh seafood. €€€

Puerto de Santa María
El Faro del Puerto
Ctra El Puerto-Rota
tel: 956-858 003
www.elfarodecadiz.com
Sister restaurant to the famous El Faro of Cádiz, run by young chef-proprietor Fernando Córdoba, with equally fresh seafood, but a more imaginative approach, set in a pleasant villa outside the town centre. You may need to reserve. Closed Sun dinner. €€€€

San Roque
Los Remos
Finca Villa Victoria, Ctra La Linea-Gibraltar, km 2, Campamento San Roque
tel: 956-698 412
Delicious seafood served in style in a magnificent colonial house surrounded by gardens. Best to reserve. €€€€

Tarifa
Mandragora
Independencia
tel: 956-681 291
Located in the old town, this friendly, family-run restaurant is famous for its stuffed anchovies and Moroccan dishes. Real home cooking. Dinner only. Closed Sun. No reservations or credit cards. €€€

CÓRDOBA
Córdoba
Bodegas Campos
Los Lineros, 32
tel: 957-497 500
www.bodegascampos.com
Colourful restaurant in a former wine cellar near the Plaza del Potro, decorated like an upmarket tavern, serving classical Córdoba and Spanish dishes. Closed Sun dinner. €€€€

El Caballo Rojo
Cardenal Herrero, 28
tel: 957-475 375
www.elcaballorojo.com
The longest-established and best-known of Córdoba's restaurants is still a good bet. Aside from traditional Spanish dishes, the menu incorporates some unusual Moorish preparations, such as Cordero a la Miel (lamb in honey). Reservations essential. €€€€

La Almudaina
Campo Santo de los Mártires, 1
tel: 957-474 342
www.restaurantealmudaina.com
Installed in a 15th-century house near the Alcázar gardens, serving local recipes based on fresh produce. Seven different dining areas, around a central courtyard. Closed Sun dinner, all day Sun in summer. €€€€

Casa Pepe de la Judería
Romero, 1,
tel: 957-200 744
www.casapepejuderia.com
At the entrance to the Jewish quarter, a typical Andalusian townhouse, decorated with bullfighting themes. Traditional Andalusian fare. €€€

El Churrasco
Romero, 16
tel: 957-290 819
www.elchurrasco.com
The name suggests grilled meats (a speciality here), but this is also a good place to try salmorejo, a thick Córdoba version of gazpacho. Also worth checking is the wine museum and wine cellar housed in an annexe. Best to reserve. Closed Aug. €€€

Price Guide

Approximate cost per person, including house wine:
€€€€ = above €25
€€€ = €12–25
€€ = under €12

Montilla
Las Camachas
Ctra Córdoba-Málaga, km 48
tel: 957-650 004
A rambling old roadside restaurant where the landed gentry of the wine district dine out. Sturdy, good food, and local Montilla wines on sale. €€€

GRANADA
Almuñécar
Jacqui-Cotobro
Edificio Río, Playa Cotobro
tel: 958-631 802
The simple bare brick walls give little indication that this restaurant by the beach is famous all over Spain for its French cuisine. The best plan is to order the Menú Degustación, including three different courses and dessert. Best to reserve. Closed Mon. €€€

Granada
Ruta del Veleta
Ctra Sierra Nevada, km. 5.4, Cenes de la Vega
tel: 958-486 134
www.rutadelveleta.com
On the old road to the Sierra Nevada, 5 km (3 miles) from the city, it has served consistently good food for decades. Spacious, well-decorated dining rooms, and an outdoor terrace. Classic Spanish food is the speciality. Best to reserve. Closed Sun dinner. €€€€

Sevilla
Oficios, 12
tel: 958-221 223
granadainto.com/sevilla
This Granada classic close to the cathedral is a good place to sample traditional Granada dishes such as Jamon con Habas (cured ham with broad beans) or Tortilla Sacromonte (omelette with lambs brains, ham and vegetables). Closed Sun dinner. €€€

Los Manueles
Zaragoza, 2
tel: 958-223 413
Very atmospheric, traditional tiled tavern serving classic Granada dishes such as Tortilla Sacromonte. €€

HUELVA
Aracena
Jose Vicente
Avda Andalucía, 53
tel: 959-128 455
In an unassuming location on the outskirts of the village, this small restaurant is a true gem in the heart of Huelva's northern Sierra and the best place to try fresh pork. €€€

Huelva
Las Candelas
Avda Huelva, Aljaraque
tel: 959-318 301.
Six km (4 miles) from the centre, Huelva's best-known restaurant offers good value and quality fresh seafood and fish stews. Closed Sun. €€€

JAÉN
Baeza
Juanito
Paseo Arca del Agua, s/n
tel: 953-740 040
www.juanitobaeza.com
Spacious and friendly, one of the best-known restaurants in Andalusia due to its owner's zeal in recovering traditional recipes, in which the virgin olive oil of Jaén plays a key role. Closed Sun dinner, Mon dinner. €€€

Cazorla
Cueva de Juan Pedro
Plaza de Santa María
tel: 953-721 225
www.cuevajuanpedro.com
Literally a hole in the wall, this tiny, informal cave-restaurant specialises in grilled meat. €€

Jaén
Mesón Vicente
Francisco Martín Mora, 1
tel: 953-232 816/222
Popular restaurant near the cathedral, serving traditional Jaén dishes and game. Also a good mesón (tavern) serving tapas. Closed Sun dinner. €€€

MÁLAGA

Antequera

El Angelote
Plaza Coso Viejo
tel: 95-270 3465
Popular restaurant serving traditional Andalusian dishes, in central Antequera near the museum. Closed Mon. €€

Málaga

Café de Paris
Velez Málaga, 8
tel: 95-022 5043
On a back street near the lighthouse, this is Málaga's most sophisticated restaurant, serving imaginative dishes in an elegant atmosphere. Reservations are essential. Closed Sun. €€€€

Escuela de Hostelería
Finca La Consula, Churriana
tel: 95-262 2562
Málaga's official hotel and catering school, 8 km (5 miles) west of the city, serves some of the best food on the Costa del Sol. Reservations essential. Lunch only. Closed Sat–Sun. €€€€

Casa Pedro
Quitapenas, 121, El Palo
tel: 95-229 0013
In the fishing district of El Palo, this beachside restaurant is a favourite with families for its fried fish. Very crowded on Sundays. Closed Mon. €€€

Chinitas
Moreno Monroy, 4
tel: 95-221 0972
www.chinitas.arrakis.es
Typical Andalusian decor, just off Calle Marqués de Larios in the centre of Málaga. Classic regional dishes. €€€

Ronda

Tragabuches
José Aparicio, 1
tel: 95-219 0291
www.tragabuches.com
Strikingly innovative treatment of classic Andalusian dishes. Stylish modern decor and a picture window overlooking the valley. Closed Sun and Mon dinner. €€€€

Pedro Romero
Virgen de la Paz, 18
tel: 95-287 1110
www.ronda.net/pedroromero
Unashamedly touristy, but serving good traditional Andalusian fare. Located just across from the Ronda bullring, and the taurine theme prevails in the decor (bull's heads, posters) and the *menú (Rabo de Toro)* is the speciality. €€€

COSTA DEL SOL

Estepona

Alcaría de Ramos
Ctra N-340, km 167
tel: 95-288 6178
Located in an Andalusian-style house

with good views, serving very well-prepared classic Spanish dishes. Dinner only. Closed Sun dinner. €€€

La Rada
Avda España, s/n
tel: 95-279 1036
Fresh fish served in an informal atmosphere, at the eastern end of Estepona. Closed Wed. €€

Fuengirola

El Bote
Paseo Marítimo, Torreblanca del Sol
tel/fax: 95-266 0084
Spacious and popular, next to the beach at the eastern end of Fuengirola's seafront promenade, serving fresh fish dishes. Closed Tues. €€€

Portofino
Paseo Marítimo, 29
tel: 95-247 0643
Friendly and lively Italian-owned restaurant on the seafront in central Fuengirola, enormously popular, and serving consistently good international dishes, with a few Italian specialities as well. Best to reserve. Closed Mon, and no lunch in summer. €€€

Marbella

La Hacienda
Urb. Las Chapas
tel: 95-283 1267
www.restaurantehacienda.com
Pleasantly set in a villa in the hills east of Marbella, this restaurant, started in the 1960s, was among the first truly top-class international dining spots on the Costa del Sol. Its French-Belgian cuisine adapted to local recipes set a model for others. Reservations essential. Closed Mon, Tue and mid-Nov–mid-Dec. €€€€

La Meridiana
Camino de la Cruz
tel: 95-277 6190
www.meridiana-notte.com
Near the gleaming modern Marbella mosque, this elegant dining spot is a favourite among the famous resort's glitterati. Fresh ingredients are given imaginative treatment. Reservations essential. Dinner only. Closed Jan 5–Feb 12. €€€€

Torremolinos

El Roqueo
Carmen, 35, La Carihuela
tel: 95-238 4946
In Torremolinos's fishing quarter, La Carihuela, it's hard to go wrong: every other house is a seafood restaurant, and they're all good. This one, facing out onto the seafront promenade, is among the longest established. Closed Tue and all of Nov. €€€

Frutos
Ctra de Cádiz, km 235 (next to Los Alamos petrol station)
tel: 95-238 1450

Midway between Torremolinos and the airport, a spacious restaurant that for decades has been known for its hearty helpings of traditional Spanish fare, with excellent meat and fish. Closed Sun dinner. €€€

SEVILLE

Seville

Corral del Agua
Callejón del Agua, 6
tel: 95-422 0714/560 014
In the Barrio Santa, this elegant restaurant occupies a restored 18th-century house, centred on a pleasant patio with plenty of potted plants and a fountain. Try the Dorada al Tio Pepe (sea bass in sherry). Closed Sun. €€€€

Egaña-Oriza
San Fernando, 41
tel: 95-422 7254
www.restauranteoriza.com
The Basque-inspired cuisine of this attractive restaurant, near the Murillo gardens facing the old tobacco factory, is acclaimed as among the best in Andalusia. Imaginative presentations in an elegant, modern setting. Best to reserve. Closed Sun, Sat lunch and Aug. €€€€

La Albahaca
Plaza Santa Cruz, 12
tel: 95-422 0714
A pretty restaurant in the heart of Seville's Barrio Santa Cruz, in an early 20th-century townhouse. The accent is on the decor – three stylish dining rooms, each with a different colour scheme – as well as on the food, an imaginative mixture of Andalusian, French and Basque influences. Best to reserve. Closed Sun. €€€€

Mesón Don Raimundo
Argote de Molina, 26
tel: 95-422 3355
Near the Seville cathedral, this large, popular restaurant, decorated with assorted bric a brac, offers a classic Sevillano dining experience. The speciality is meat and game, and the portions are large. Closed Sun dinner. €€€

Hostería del Laurel
Plaza de los Venerables, 5
tel: 95-422 0295
www.hosteriadellaurel.com
On a small square in the Barrio de Santa Cruz. Popular, both as a good-value dining spot and a *tapas* venue. Traditional Andalusian cuisine, informal atmosphere. €€

Casa Robles
Alvarez Quintero, 58
tel: 95-456 3272
A Seville classic, serving regional specialities in a cosy dining room, while the bar is justifiably famous for its *tapas*. €€

Nightlife

After Dark

Seville has a lively nightlife. The **Santa Cruz** area has countless bars, mainly of the traditional Andalusian tavern type, but also others with modern decor and the latest music. Other areas that come to life in the evening are the bustling **Calle Betis**, running along the Guadalquivir River in the Triana quarter; the **Torneo**, running along the river north from the Plaza de Armas bus station and especially popular in summer; and the streets around the **Plaza Alfalfa**, where you'll find the loudest music. But Seville's most frantic night-time scene is centred on the elongated **Alameda de Hércules** square, with lots of late-night clubs and disco bars, including many gay venues. Seville also has some good live music bars, the best of which is **La Carbonería** on Calle Levies in the Santa Cruz area, featuring everything from genuine flamenco to blues, folk and jazz. **La Naima** is a good jazz venue on Calle Trajeno, while **Weekend** on Calle Torneo combines flamenco with dance music.

Granada's large student population tends to gravitate towards the **Plaza de Principe**. Other favourite hangouts are the **Albaicín** district, the **Plaza Nueva**, and the **bullring**, underneath whose grandstands are a number of restaurants and bars. In summer, the **Paseo de los Tristes** (the misnamed "Sad Peoples' Promenade") below the Alhambra buzzes with bar life.

Torremolinos, on the Costa del Sol, is one of Spain's most popular gay venues.

Marbella, down the coast, has a thriving nightlife scene, especially in summer. The action revolves around the bustling **Puerto Banus** marina – the **Sinatra Bar** is the traditional meeting place. **La Comedia**, **News Café**, **Old Joy's Pub** and **The Living Room** are other popular watering holes. There are also great discos nearby, the most exclusive being the palatial **Olivia Valere** club on Carretera de Istan, past the Mosque. Nearby is the art deco piano club, **La Notte**. In summer the liveliest scene is in Marbella's beach clubs: **Babaloo Beach** and the **Café del Mar** in the Hotel Puente Romano.

Flamenco

There are a number of venues offering live flamenco performances. The best places to see flamenco are Seville and the Santiago district in Jerez. Most venues open 10pm until very late.
A few recommended venues:

El Arenal, Rodo, 7, Seville, tel: 95-421 6492, www.tablaoelarenal.com
Tablao Los Gallos, Plaza Santa Cruz, 11, Seville, tel: 95-422 8522, www.tablaolosgallos.com
Peña Antonio Chacón, Salas, 2, Jerez de la Frontera (Cádiz), tel: 956-347 472
Peña La Buena Gente, Plaza de San Lucas, 9, Jerez de la Frontera (Cádiz), tel: 956-338 404
Mesón La Bulería, Pedro Lopez, 3, Córdoba, tel: 957-483 839
Tablao Cardenal, Torrijos, 10, Córdoba,

Calendar of Events

The following is a list of some of the more important or interesting festivals and events that take place in the region. Exact dates tend to change from year to year, so it is always a good idea to consult the local tourist office for details.

THROUGHOUT ANDALUSIA
January: Three Kings Parades, on the eve of the Epiphany (Jan 5).
March/April: *Semana Santa* processions, from Palm Sunday to Easter Sunday.
June: *Noche de San Juan*, midsummer bonfires lit at midnight 23 June in many Andalusian towns.
July: *Virgen del Carmen*, the patron of fishermen, is honoured with seaborne processions in fishing communities along the coast in mid July.

CÁDIZ
February: Cádiz city hosts one of Spain's best carnival celebrations.
March/April: coinciding with Holy Week, bull-running in Vejer de la Frontera and Arcos de la Frontera.
May: World Motorcycling Championship at Jerez race track. Jerez Horse Fair: display of horses and horsemanship.
August: Sanlucar de Barrameda: horse races along the beach. Sotogrande: international polo matches throughout the month.
September/October: Jerez: *Fiesta de Otoño* (Autumn Festival), including sherry harvest festival.

CÓRDOBA
May: Córdoba: Festival of the Patios (first week of month) and annual fair (last week of month).
June: Cabra *Romería de los Gitanos* – pilgrimage of the gypsies.
July: Córdoba: International Guitar Festival at the Gran Teatro.

GRANADA
May: Granada: *Cruces de Mayo* festival.

June/July: Granada: International Festival of Music and Dance. One of Spain's leading festivals offers a varied programme of music and dance by national and international companies. Concerts in the Auditorio Manuel de Falla and the Palacio Carlos V in the Alhambra, dance in the Generalife gardens.
November: Granada International Jazz Festival.

HUELVA
May: Romería del Rocío, Spain's biggest pilgrimage, to the shrine of the Virgin in El Rocio (Doñana).

JAÉN
February: Linares: International chess tournament.
April: Andújar: *Romería de la Virgen de la Cabeza*, a major pilgrimage.

MÁLAGA
July: International Music and Dance Festival in the caves of Nerja.
August: Málaga fair, the second biggest in Andalusia.
September: Ronda: Goyesca Fair, with colourful carriage displays and bullfight.
October: Fuengirola: *Fiesta del Rosario*, the Costa del Sol's biggest annual fair.
December: Festival of Verdiales, a primitive mountain music, in Málaga (28 Dec).

SEVILLE
April: Seville: Spring Fair or *Feria*. The biggest Andalusian festival. Seville: Antiques fair.
July: Italica, International Festival of Theatre and Dance. Contemporary dance and classical ballet performed by prestigious international companies. Held in the Roman amphitheatre.
September: Bi-annual Flamenco Festival. Held every two years (2006, 2008, 2010 etc). Represents the best in flamenco.

tel: 957-483 112, www.tablaocardenal.com
The best flamenco to be found at the festivals and contests are held between the end of June and the middle of September in small towns – there's at least one every Saturday in Andalusia. The best known are the **Potaje in Utrera** (Seville) at the end of June; **La Caracolá** in Lebrija (Seville) in mid-July; the festival in **Mairena del Alcor** (Seville) in early September; and **Fiesta de la Bulería** in the Jerez bullring in mid-September.

Events Guide

Granada's events guide, *Guía Cultural y de Ocio*, published fortnightly in Spanish and English, gives useful information about cultural events. Seville has a useful entertainment guide, *El Giraldillo*. On the Costa del Sol, numerous publications offer information about what's on including the weekly *Sur in English*. For the Costa de la Luz both the monthly *Visitante* and *What's On* are free and www.andalucia.com has a comprehensive regional calendar of events.

Shopping

ALMERÍA

Principal buys are in handicrafts: **ceramics and pottery** from Albox, Níjar, Sorbas and Vera; **basketwork** from Almería, Alhabía and Níjar; *Jarapas* (rugs made with rags and strips of cotton) from Nijar, Huercal Overa and Berja; **bedspreads and blankets** from Albox, Berja and Macael; **marble items** from Macael.

CÁDIZ

Sherry from Jerez and Puerto de Santa María (such as Harveys, Williams and Humbert, Pedro Domecq and Osborne); finc **leather** from Ubrique; **carpets** from Arcos de la Frontera; **capes and ponchos** from Grazalema; **guitars** from Algodonales; **wickerwork** from Jerez; **saddlery** from Olvera.

CÓRDOBA

Silver filigree jewellery, for which Córdoba is particularly noted; **Montilla wines** (*bodegas* in Montilla, 46 km/28 miles from Córdoba); **anís liquor** from Rute; **ceramics**, **Lucena pottery** with geometric green and yellow design, and *botijos* (spouted drinking pitchers) from La Rambla; **leatherwork**; **decorative metalwork** in copper, bronze and brass from Espejo and Castro del Río.

GRANADA

Cured mountain hams from the Alpujarras villages; **pottery**, most typical is Fajalauza with a distinctive blue and green design; **leather**, (especially embossed); **marquetry** (technique of inlaying wood with bone, ivory, mother of pearl or with other woods) **chests**, **chess boards**, **small tables**; **metal craftwork**, **lanterns** made to traditional Islamic designs; **rugs**, **cushions** and **bedspreads** from the Alpujarras villages; **hand-made guitars** from workshops on the Cuesta de Gomerez in the city; **silver filigree jewellery**.

HUELVA

Cured hams from Jabugo; **white wine** from the Condado de Huelva; **pottery** from Aracena and Cortejana; **rugs** from Ecinasola; **embroidery** from Aracena, Alonso and Puebla de Guzmán; **handmade leather boots** from Valverde de Camino.

JAÉN

Glass and ceramics from Andújar, Bailén and Ubeda; **carpets** and **wickerwork** from Ubeda, Jaén and Los Villares; **iron objects** and **lanterns** from Ubeda; **guitars** from Marmolejo.

MÁLAGA

The colourful **street markets** are sometimes the best place to find bargains. Markets are open: Monday **Marbella**; Tuesday **Fuengirola** and **Nerja**; Wednesday **Estepona**; Thursday **Torremolinos** and **San Pedro de Alcántara**; Friday **Arroyo de la Miel** and **Benalmádena Pueblo**; Sunday **Estepona port** and **Málaga**.

SEVILLE

Antiques around the streets Mateos Gago, Placentines and Rodrigo Caro; **ceramics** and **tiles** from Santa Ana (factory in Triana) and La Cartuja de Sevilla (factory at Ctra de Mérida); **saddlery** and **leather items**, **boots** and **chaps**; **fashion** – Seville's own designers Victorio and Lucchino have showroom at Sierpes, 87; **fans** and **castanets**.

Sport

Participant Sports

GOLF

Southern Spain, particularly the Costa del Sol, is a golfer's paradise, with Europe's biggest concentration of golf courses. For more information, contact the **Andalusian Golf Federation**, Sierra de Grazalema, 33, Málaga, tel: 952-225 590, www.golf-andalucia.net

SCUBA DIVING

The rocky shoreline around much of the coast offers plenty of scope for **underwater exploring**. There are a number of scuba clubs offering courses for beginners and guidance for licensed divers. For details, contact the **Federación Andaluza de Actividades Subacuáticas**, Playa de las Almadrabillas, 10, Almería, tel: 950-270 612.

Bullfighting

Andalusia is the cradle of bullfighting, the controversial struggle between man and beast, and the town of Ronda is regarded as the birthplace of modern bullfighting. Many of Spain's top *matadors* come from the region, as do many of the most respected fighting bulls.

There are occasional charity fights in winter, but the season really gets under way at Easter and with the series of *corridas* (bullfights) during the Seville Fair in April.

Seville's Maestranza bullring is the most important arena; daily fights are held during the fairs in other towns, throughout the summer. Six bulls are killed during a *corrida*, which usually starts at 6pm.

Tickets are expensive, particularly if you want to be in the shade *(sombra)* and near the *barrera*, the ringside. Cheaper tickets are sold for *sol*, the sunny side of the arena. In some communities, bull-runs are held in the streets during local festivities.

SKIING

There is skiing in the **Sierra Nevada** 32 km (20 miles) from Granada, the southernmost ski slope in Europe. Facilities include equipment to rent, instruction, with a special school for children, first aid and rescue service and emergency clinic.

The exceptional conditions of the Pyrenean geography has led to the establishment of several winter resorts. **Panticosa**, is a good place for beginners. Zaragoza, 170 km (105 miles) is the nearest airport.

Baqueira Beret, in the Val d'Aran, is Spain's largest skiing resort. It is located 200 km (124 miles) from Barcelona. There is skiing for all abilities here. It has a modern lift infrastructure and a lively apres-ski scene, with reasonable Spanish prices.

TENNIS

There are too many tennis clubs in the region to list. A number have outstanding facilities, including tuition in some cases by ex-international champions. Some top clubs include:
Don Carlos Tennis Club, Hotel Don Carlos, Urb. Elviria, s/n, Marbella, tel: 952-768 800/833 429, www.hoteldoncarlos.com
El Casco Tennis Club, Urb. El Rosario, s/n, Marbella, tel: 952-837 651, www.elcasco.com
Hotel Puente Romano Tennis Club, Ctra N340, Marbella, tel: 952- 820 900, www.puenteromana.com
Lew Hoad's Tennis Ranch, Ctra Mijas–Fuengirola, s/n, Málaga, tel: 952-474 858.
Los Monteros Tennis Club, Hotel Los Monteros, Ctra N340, s/n, Marbella, tel: 952-771 700, www.monteros.com
Manolo Santana Raquets Club, Ctra de Istan, km 2, Marbella, tel: 952-778 580, www.manolosantana.com

WATERSPORTS

Facilities for sailing, windsurfing, scuba diving, snorkelling and waterskiing are available on the Atlantic and Mediterranean coasts.

Windsurfing: many beaches have schools and rent equipment. The best area is near **Tarifa**, Cádiz. The good winds attract surfers from all over Europe and various competitions are held throughout the year.

Spectator Sports

Football (soccer) and **basketball** are Spain's most popular spectator sports. Andalucía's leading soccer teams are Real Betis and Sevilla (both of Seville) and Cádiz. Games usually start at 5pm on Sunday. Basketball attracts a fanatical following.

There is a **motor-racing** circuit in Jerez (Cádiz), with occasional car races, but the biggest event is the **Motorcycling Grand Prix**, on the first weekend in May (Circuito de Jerez, tel: 956-151 000, www.circuitodejerez.com).

Horse races are staged at Seville La Pineda hipódromo weekly Jan–Mar; there are horse races on the beach in Sanlúcar de Barrameda (Cádiz), during Aug, a tradition dating back more than 150 years. Horse races are held throughout the year, with night races in summer at the Hipódromo Costa del Sol in Mijas-Costa (Urb. El Chaparral, s/n, tel: 952-592 700. The biggest events are held during the winter.

Spas

Andalusia has a number of *balnearios* (spas) where the waters have medicinal properties. These are tranquil spots with doctors on hand to offer advice. Further information can be obtained from the **Asociación de Balnearios de Andalucía**, Calle Nueva de la Virgen 25, Granada, tel: 958-964 022, www.balneariosdeandalucia.com

Eastern Spain

GEOGRAPHY

Eastern Spain comprises the three autonomous regions of Catalonia, Valencia (officially the Comunidad Valenciana) and Murcia.

Valencia and Murcia are often known as the Levant. Between them they enjoy more than half of Spain's eastern coastline from Catalonia to Almería. Catalonia covers an area of approximately 32,000 sq km (12,355 sq miles). The Catalan Pyrenees, some peaks up to 2,950 metres (9,700 ft) high, are snow-covered for many months of the year.

The Val d'Aran in Lleida and the Cerdanya in Girona are typified by green, rolling foothills and broad, fertile valleys; the *comarca* of La Garrotxa is a volcanic region and a swathe of wooded hills follows the coast down to Barcelona.

The Catalan coast is over 580 km (350 miles) long and is divided into four main parts: the Costa Brava, from the border to Blanes, mainly an area of rocky coves; the Costa del Maresme, to the north of Barcelona, with long sandy beaches; the shorter Costa Garraf, reaching as far south as Cubelles; and the Costa Daurada, which stretches the length of Tarragona province.

In the Empordà, in the province of Girona, and the Ebro delta, in Tarragona, the extensive marshlands are important for migratory birds and areas of rice cultivation. The Penedès, in Barcelona, is a big wine-producing region, and the plain of Alcanar at the southern end of the Costa Daurada has citrus groves. Valencia and Murcia share similar geographical characteristics: a fertile coastal plain rising to mountain areas inland. Valencia's coast is split into the Costa Azahar, the Costa de Valencia and the Costa Blanca. Murcia's coast is called the Costa Calida.

Economy

About 25 percent of Spain's industry is in Catalonia, mainly in textiles, chemicals and mechanical equipment. Some 35 percent of the population is engaged in industry, 60 percent in services and 5 percent in agriculture. Valencia and Murcia have strong agricultural and manufacturing sectors.

Population

Catalonia has a population of about 6.5 million, of whom 1.7 million live in Barcelona and 1 million more in the suburbs. The population of the Comunidad Valenciana is just over 4 million and the population of Murcia, 1.2 million. Valencia is Spain's third largest city with roughly 775,000 inhabitants.

Getting There

CATALONIA

By Air

Numerous charter and economy flights connect many European cities with Barcelona, Girona and Reus airports.

By Road

The French border is 149 km (92 miles) north of Barcelona at La Jonquera on the A7 motorway. This motorway also provides speedy access to Valencia and the Costa Blanca. Motorways also run to Madrid and the Basque country.

By Rail

Fast Talgo trains connect Barcelona directly with Paris, Milan and Zurich. The AVE (high-speed) line to Madrid is under construction, but may not be ready in 2004 as scheduled (www.renfe.es).

VALENCIA & MURCIA

By Air

There are international airports at Valencia (Manises Airport), Alicante (El Altet Airport) and Murcia (San Javier airport, by the Mar Menor).

By Sea

Ferries connect the port of Valencia with the Balearic islands.

Climate

In Andorra and the Pyrenees the temperature can drop to below freezing in winter. In the Costa Brava winds seem to whip up from nowhere and last for days. The climate is more reliable further south, with little rain in summer. The average temperature in coastal resorts is 25°C (77°F) in summer and 11°C (52°F) in winter. Inland it's hotter, and spring and autumn are more pleasant.

By Road

Good roads link Madrid to the three main cities: the N-111 (mainly dual carriageway or *autovía*) and A3 motorway to Valencia; the N-330 *autovía* to Alicante and the N-301 to Murcia. The A7 motorway links the region to Barcelona and Andalusia.

By Rail

Main rail lines run from Valencia to both Madrid and Barcelona. Alicante and Murcia also have services to Madrid and Barcelona. The fast Euromed service connects Alicante to Barcelona, stopping at Valencia, Castellón and Tarragona.

Getting Around

CATALONIA

From Barcelona Airport

Barcelona airport, El Prat (tel: 93-298 3838), 12 km (7 miles) south of the city, is easily accessible by train or bus. A smooth, efficient bus service, the Aerobús, runs every 15 minutes between the airport and Plaça de Catalunya, and vice versa, stopping at Sants and other strategic places en route. It takes about 35 minutes. There are also trains to Sants and Plaça de Catalunya every 30 minutes, and the journey takes about 20 minutes.

By Rail

The main RENFE stations in Barcelona are **Estació de França** terminal by the port and **Sants**, west of the city centre. If you are on a train that is not terminating in Barcelona, it may be more convenient to get off at Passeig de Gràcia or Plaça de Catalunya. For all rail enquiries, tel: 93 490 0202 (international) or 93 490 1122 (national). Further up-to-date information on general rail networks and connections can be obtained by visiting: www.eurorail.com, www.routesinternational.com or www.europonrail.com

Barcelona also has a suburban line, run by the Ferrocarils de la Generalitat de Catalunya (FGC). Trains go from Estació Plaça d'Espanya to Montserrat, Igualada and Manresa. Get off at Santa Coloma de Cervelló to see Gaudí's Colònia Güell. From Plaça Catalunya FGC trains go to Sabadell, Terrassa and Sant Cugat, useful for getting to the Parc Collserola just behind the city.

By Road

Catalonia is well served by motorways: the A7 runs from the French border towards Valencia. The A19 motorway, which runs north from Barcelona almost to Blanes, and a ring-road, known as the "Ronda", have greatly

Taking Taxis

There are prominently marked ranks in central areas and fares are very reasonable (a 10 percent tip is usual, though in no way required or expected). Although public transport is adequate and you won't need a car for visiting any of the major towns, to make the most of the country you really do need private transport.

improved the city's traffic problems.

Catalonia is also criss-crossed by a network of regional and local roads, mainly going north-south, following the rivers coming down from the Pyrenees and making hard work of east-west journeys. The roads themselves are of varying quality; some more than compensate – by scenery and absence of traffic – for what they may lack in width or smoothness.

By Bus

The bus company SARFA has excellent services up to the Costa Brava and Girona from Estación de Autobuses Barcelona-Nord, tel: 932-651 158; www.sarfa.es

VALENCIA & MURCIA
By Public Transport

Coaches (long-distance buses) are often more direct and more frequent than trains. There are coach stations in the cities and coach services linking the towns of the region. Narrow-gauge rail lines run along the Costa Blanca (more scenic than practical), between the Mar Menor and Cartagena, and around the outskirts of Valencia.

By Road

New motorways in Valencia, Alicante and Murcia have made road travel much faster; the A7 motorway runs along or near the coast from Catalonia to Andalusia. North of Alicante, except for a stretch circumnavigating Valencia, it is a toll road *(autopista)*; south of Alicante it is toll free *(autovía)*. The old main roads, N-340 and N-332, provide alternatives to it but they can be slower and congested. Other main (N) roads are good. Inland, however, many smaller roads wind tortuously around the contours.

Local Tourist Offices

CATALONIA

For information on individual towns:
Barcelona: Main City tourist office, Plaça Catalunya, 17 (underground); information from abroad: 932-853 834,

from within Spain, tel: 932 384 000. Office open daily 9am–9pm; Sants station: daily 8am–8pm. El Prat airport: 9am–9pm. Information on the city is available by dialling 010 or logging on to www.barcelonaturisme.com or www.bcn.es
Figueres: Oficina de Turisme, Plaça del Sol, tel: 972-503 155.
Girona: Oficina de Turisme, Rambla Llibertat, 1, tel: 972-226 575.
Lleida: Oficina de Turisme, Major 31, tel: 902-250 050.
Reus: Oficina de Turisme, Plaça Libertat, tel: 977-773 715.
Tarragona: Patronat de Turisme, Carrer Major, 39, tel: 977-245 203.
Andorra: Oficina de Turisme del Principat d'Andorra, World Trade Centre, Moll de Barcelona Ed. Nord Planta Baixa, 27, tel: 91-431 7453, www.andorra.es

Regional Offices

For information on the regions:
Barcelona: Centre d'Informació Turística de Catalunya, (for all Catalonia and Spain), Palau Robert, Passeig de Gràcia, 107; open 10am–7pm Mon–Sat, 10am–2pm Sun, tel: 93-402 7000; www.gencat.es/probert.
Girona: Rambla Llibertat, 1, tel: 972-226 575; www.costabrava.org
Lleida: Avinguda Madrid, 36, tel: 973-270 997.
Puigcerdà: Oficina de Turisme de la Cerdanya, Cruïlla (crossroads) N152–N260.
Tarragona: Oficina de Turisme, Carrer Fortuny, 4, tel: 977-233-415.

VALENCIA

Alicante: Rambla Méndez Núñez, 23, tel: 96-520 0000.
Benidorm: Avda Martinez Alejos, 16, tel: 902-100 581.
Castellón: Plaza María Augustina, 5, tel: 96-435 8688.
Dénia: Plaza Oculista Buigues, 9, tel: 96-642 2367.
Santa Pola: Plaza de le Diputacion, 6, tel: 96-669 2276.
Valencia: Calle de la Paz, 48, Valencia, tel: 96-398 6422; www.comunidad-valenciana.com

MURCIA

Murcia: Plaza Cardenal Belluga, tel: 968-358 749; www.murciaturistica.es
La Manga: Km 0 Los Amoladeras, tel: 968-146 136.
Cartagena: Plaza Almirante Bastarreche, tel: 968-521 427.

Media

Television: There are nine television channels. TVE 1 and La 2 are national,

the first broadcasting almost exclusively in Castilian, the second mostly in Catalan. The two Catalan channels supported by the Generalitat are TV3, a popular channel, and Canal 33/K3 which is slightly more high-brow, covering the arts, sports and minority interests. There are three private channels: Antena 3 and Tele 5, both Madrid-based, and Canal Plus, a subscription-only channel linked to its French counterpart. French television can be seen in some northern areas and people in Tarragona can pick up Valencian television, which is on the same wavelength as Canal 33. There is also a useful device available that allows viewers the choice of watching some films either in their dubbed version or in their original language. Canal 9 broadcasts in Valencian and Canal Sur broadcasts from Andalusia; these can both be received in Murcia. Punt 2 is a cultural channel in Valencian.
Radio: Between 9.30am and 4.30pm on weekdays during July and August Râdio Associació de Catalunya broadcasts an hour each of Catalan, English, German, Italian and French (105 mHZ on FM). There are local radio stations in every town and in summer foreign languages burst through the airwaves to advertise shops, discos and events. The most popular radio station is Cadena SER, a national radio with high local input (828 kHZ MW). Radio 3 (98.7 FM) is a very good national music station and FM101.5 is Catalonia's classical channel.

Print: Catalonia's two main daily newspapers are *El Periódico*, in Catalan and Castilian editions, and *La Vanguardia*, in Castilian. The popular Madrid daily, *El País*, has a large Barcelona staff producing a Catalonia edition, which alters about six news and features pages plus the sport. *Avui* (Today) is the Catalan region-wide daily, but there are a number of local daily papers such as *El Nou* in Vic, and the *Diari de Girona*. *Metropolitan* is an English monthly magazine, very useful for listings.

Medical Services

The main towns have hospitals with 24-hour emergency departments. In Barcelona, the number to call in an emergency is 93-218 1800. Town halls post surgery hours of clinics.

Chemists are helpful with minor complaints. Called *famàcies* or *farmàcias*, they are identified by a green or red cross. They should display notices giving details of a local emergency service; otherwise ask the police who will be able to help.

In Barcelona, pharmacies are

generally open 9.30am–1.30pm and 5–8pm. Centrally located 24-hour pharmacies includ Farmàcia Clapés Antoja, La Rambla 98, tel: 93 301 2843.

Security & Crime

There's a relatively high risk of theft at the tourist centres along the costas and in Barcelona, so the following rules apply: never leave anything in your car, never carry more money on your person than you need, and leave your passport or identity card at your hotel. Be especially careful when withdrawing money from cashpoint machines.

Criminals frequent tourist areas and major attractions such as museums, restaurants as well as hotel lobbies and trains. Theft from vehicles is also common. Items such as luggage, cameras and laptop computers, are often stolen from cars. Travellers are advised not to leave valuables in parked cars and to keep their windows locked. Drivers should be cautious about accepting help from anyone other than a uniformed Spanish police officer or Civil Guard.

Where to Stay

Hotels

CATALONIA

Barcelona City

After a notorious shortage of accommodation, new hotels are now mushrooming – although it is still advisable to book in advance, especially during peak periods and trade fairs.

Increasingly popular is the idea of B&B or apartment renting. A well-respected agency is BCN Rooms, tel: 93-226 5467, fax: 93-226 2269; www.bcnrooms.com

Hotels are listed in order of price category.

Colón
Avinguda Catedral, 7
tel: 93-301 1404
fax: 93-317 2915
www.hotelcolon.es
In the Gothic quarter, a comfortable classic, though the cathedral bells may keep you awake. Front rooms have a view. €€€€

Condes de Barcelona
Passeig de Gràcia, 73–75
tel: 93-445 0000
fax: 93-445 3232
www.hotelcondesdebarcelona.com
Top-of-the-range hotel in a converted Modernist mansion in the elegant Eixample quarter. €€€€

Hotel AC Front Marítim
Passeig Garcia i Fària, 69
tel: 93-303 4440
fax: 93-303 4441
www.hotelfrontmaritim.com
One of the new wave of hotels near Diagonal Mar, HQ of forum 2004. Ask for a room with a sea view. €€€.

Hotel Banys Orientals
Argenteria, 37
tel: 93-268 8460
fax: 93-268 8461
www.hotelbanysorientals.com
Very good value for such a stylish new hotel near Santa María del Mar. €€

Hotel España
Sant Pau, 9 i 11,
tel: 93-318 1758
fax: 93-317 1134
www.hotelespanya.com
Though the bedrooms are plain, its public rooms have outstanding

Modernista work by Domènech i Montaner. Just off La Rambla. €€

Hotel Gran Via
Gran Via de les Corts
Catalanes, 642
tel: 93-318 1900
fax: 93-318 9997
www.nnhotels.es
Well placed near Passeig de Gràcia, with a brocaded, Regency feel and a charming, individual personality. €€

There are lots of inexpensive *pensiones* and hotels on the roads and lanes leading off both sides of the Rambla, and they are generally progressively more seedy towards the port. Near Plaça Catalunya at the top there are 1- and 3-star hotels on Carrer de Santa Anna: the **Cortes**, tel: 93-317 9112, fax: 93-412 6608; and the **Nouvel**, tel: 93-301 8274, fax: 93-301 8370, www.hotelnouvel.com. Further down off to the right on Carrer del Carme, there are several: the **Carmen**, tel: 93-317 1076; **Aneto**, tel: 93-301 9989, fax: 93-301 9862, www.hotelaneto.com; **Selecta**, tel: 93-301 4484. The **Peninsula** on Sant Pau is good value, with a delightful inner courtyard, tel: 93-302 3138, www.hotelpeninsular.net. The **Sant Agustí**, Plaça Sant Agustí, 3, tel: 93-318 1658, fax: 93-317 2928, www.hotelsa.com, is pleasantly situated in a quiet square behind the market; on the opposite side of La Rambla overlooking two attractive squares is the very popular (book early) **Hotel Jardí**, Plaça St Josep Oriol, 1, tel: 93-301 5900.

Barcelona Province

Balneari Termas Victòria
Carrer Barcelona, 12,
Caldes de Montbui
tel: 93-865 0150
fax: 93-865 0816
www.termasvictoria.com
A trendy spa hotel. €€€

El Bruc
Ctra Nacional II, Km 570, El Bruc
tel: 93-771 0036
fax: 93-771 0086
www.hotel-bruc.com
This is a well-appointed hotel set in this legendary valley beneath the sacred mountain of Montserrat. It also has an excellent restaurant: listen out for the mythical drummer boy while you eat traditional Catalan cuisine. €€€

Price Guide

For a standard double room
€€€€ =   Over €180
€€€ =   €120–180
€€ =   €60–120
€ =   Under €60

Parador Nacional Duques de Cardona
Cardona
tel: 93-869 1275
fax: 93-869 1636
www.parador.es
A hilltop castle overlooking the town and salt mines, authentically complete with squeaking floorboards. The restaurant in the baronial hall is pricey but the food is fine and the portions large. €€€

Sant Bernat
Finca el Cot, Montseny
tel: 93-847 3011
fax: 93-847 3220
A pleasant small hotel situated near the forest and mountains of the Montseny natural park. €€€

Parador Nacional
Vic, 15 km (10 miles) northeast of Vic off the N-153
tel: 93-812 2323
fax: 93-812 2368
Very popular, this relatively new building lacks the charm of the historic Paradors but is set in a pine forest by the Sau reservoir. The restaurant serves good traditional Vic dishes. €€

Lleida/Lérida Province

Caldes de Boi
Alfores, 5/n (Val de Boi side)
tel: 973-696 210/20
fax: 973-696 058
www.caldesdeboi.com
This spa hotel is worth the extra for a luxury stay and it has a good restaurant. Open from June–Sept. €€€€

Hotel Andria
Passeig Joan Brudieu, 24
tel: 973-350 300
fax: 973-351 425
www.hotelandria.com
Comfortable, inexpensive hotel. €€

Hotel Terradets
Ctra C13, km 75 s/n (the main Balaguer–Tremp road), Cellers
tel: 973-651 120
fax: 973-651 304
www.hotelterradets.com
Beautifully set by a lake. Good value for families and with an inexpensive restaurant serving local dishes. €€

Parador Nacional
Carrer Sant Domènec, 6,
La Seu d'Urgell
tel: 973-352 000
fax: 973-352 309
www.parador.es
The menu is excellent. €€

Gran Sol
Ctra Manresa s/n, Solsona
tel: 973-480 975
fax: 973-481 000
www.gransolhotel.net
Just a kilometre from Solsona, this hotel and restaurant is better known for its cuisine than for lodging. €

Hotel Principal
Plaça de la Paeria, 8, Lleida

tel: 973-230 800
fax: 973-230 803
A comfortable, medium-priced hotel in the heart of the old town. €

Val D'Aran

Hotel Casa Irene
Carrer Major, 3, Arties
tel: 973-644 364
fax: 973-642 174
www.hotelcasairene.com
Attached to the renowned restaurant run by Irene España Plagnes. €€€

Parador Nacional Gaspar de Pórtola
Ctra Baqueira, s/n, Arties
tel: 973-640 801
fax: 973-641 001
A 16th-century house, once home to the explorer who supposedly discovered California, now converted into an intimate inn, catering for skiers. €€€

Girona Province

La Torre del Remei
Camí Reial s/n
Bolvir de Cerdanya
tel: 972-140 182
fax: 972-140 449
www.torredelremei.com
The most luxurious spot in the Pyrenees, José and Lola Boix have created a masterpiece of fine cuisine and elegant hospitality. Exceptional. €€€€

Hotel Empordà
Antiga Carretera a França, Figueres
tel: 972-500 562
fax: 972-509 358
www.hotelemporda.com
This was one of Josep Pla's favourites, and is often credited as the birthplace of the "new" Catalan cuisine. The perfect base for Dalí tourism. €€€

Hotel del Lago
Avda Dr. Piguillem, 7, Puigcerdà
tel: 972-881 000
fax: 972-141 511
www.hotellago.com
This cosy spot next to Puigcerdà's fabled lake is elegant, quiet and a couple of minutes' walk from the town centre. €€€

Peninsular
Carrer Nou, 3, Girona
tel: 972-203 800
fax: 972-210 492
www.novarahotels.com
Established hotel, new side of town. €€€

Cal Sastre
Cases Noves 1, Santa Pau
tel: 972-498 479
fax: 972-680 481
www.calsastre.com
Delightful small hotel in old stone building. Ideal for visiting La Garrotxa. €€

Durán
Lasauca, 5, Figueres
tel: 972-501 250
fax: 972-502 609
www.hotelduran.com
Has a traditional interior of tiles and

Price Guide

For a standard double room
€€€€ =   Over €180
€€€ =   €120–180
€€ =   €60–120
€ =   Under €60

high-backed chairs and a *porrón* of Muscatel does the rounds at the end of the meal of Empordà dishes. €€

El Reixac
Sant Joan de les Abadesses
tel: 972-720 373
www.elreixac.com
Farmhouse tastefully converted into comfortable apartments in beautiful scenery near this historic town. €€

Güell
Plaça Espanya, 8, Camprodón
tel: 972-740 011
fax: 972-741 112
Elegant, inexpensive and central. €€

Hotel Llívia
Avda de Catalunya, 111, Llívia
tel: 972-896 000
fax: 972-146 000
Excellent and friendly spot for exploring the Cerdanya. €€

Mulleres
Can Mulleres, s/n
17176 Sant Privat d'En Bas
tel: 972-693 257
Pretty country *pensión* only a couple of miles outside Olot in the Val d'En Bas. Its walls are covered with paintings by local artists. Bread and tomatoes with ham for breakfast and an inexpensive evening set menu. €€

Ultònia
Gran Via de Jaume I, 22, Girona
tel: 972-203 850
fax: 972-203 334
www.husa.es
In the centre of town with modern, renovated rooms. €€

Costa Brava

El Far
Platja de Llafranc, Palafrugell
tel: 972-301 639
fax: 972-304 328
www.elfar.net
Spectacular location above a lighthouse at the top of cliffs. Built around a courtyard, it has been magnificently renovated and is very attractive. €€€€

La Gavina
Plaça de la Rosaleda, s/n, S'Agaró
tel: 972-321 100
fax: 972-321 573
www.lagavina.com
A grand 5-star hotel with a warm atmosphere and a long history. €€€€

Aiguablava Hotel
17255 Platja de Fornells
tel: 972-622 058
fax: 972-622 112
www.hotelalguablava.com

The classic Costa Brava hotel, beautifully situated in Fornells Bay. Book well in advance. €€€

Hostalet 1701
Plaça Jaume I, 1, Monells
tel: 972-630 012
fax: 972-630 815
www.hostalet1701.com
In one of the pretty medieval villages away from coastal bustle, tastefully decorated with antiques and modern touches in a 17th-century village house, this is a real find, complete with swimming pool and jacuzzi. €€€

Hotel Portlligat
Portlligat
tel: 972-258 162
fax: 972-258 643
The only commercial establishment in Dalí's bay, with a salt-water swimming pool alongside it. Go for a treat, either staying overnight or just for a meal in the dining room overlooking the bay. €€€

Parador Nacional Costa Brava
Platja d'Aiguablava
tel: 972-622 162
fax: 972-622 166
Modern Parador with good local dishes in a very pretty Costa Brava cove. €€€

Trias
Passeig del Mar, s/n, Palamós
tel: 972-601 800
fax: 972-601 819
www.hoteltrias.com
Rather pricey, but another of the coast's well-known hotels that has been going for years. €€€

Hostal Empúries
L'Escala, Empúries
tel/fax: 972-770 207
www.hostalempuries.com
Out of town, right by the ruins and right on the beach. Basic but fun. €€

Costa Daurada

Calípolis
Passeig Marítim, s/n, Sitges
tel: 93-894 1500
fax: 93-894 0764
www.hotelcalipolis.com
A large hotel well situated near the church on the seafront. €€€

Ciudad de Castelldefels
Passeig de la Marina, 212
Castelldefels
tel: 93-665 1900
fax: 93-636 0832
Quieter than the beach-front hotels and has good-quality cuisine. €€€

Hotel Subur Marítim
Pg. Marítim s/n, Sitges
tel: 93-894 1550
fax: 93-894 0427
www.hotelsuburmaritim.com
Away from the crowd, overlooking the sea, this is one of Sitges' most charming hotels, with a pool and garden. €€€

Rey Don Jaime
Avinguda de l'Hotel, 22, Castelldefels
tel: 93-665 1300

fax: 93-664 5151
This is expensive, but worth it for the beautiful hilltop view of the costa as far as Barcelona. Fine restaurant. €€€

Terramar
Passeig Marítim, s/n, Sitges
tel: 93-894 0050
fax: 93-894 5604
www.hotelterramar.com
Older-style hotel at the end of the seafront with gardens and good sports facilities. A 1950s period piece. €€€

Tarragona Province

España
Rambla Nova, 49, Tarragona
tel: 977-232 712
fax: 977-232 079
A small, old-fashioned reasonably priced hotel right in the middle of town. €€

Residència-Casa de Pagèsia Carrerada
Carrer Carrerada, 8, Porrera
tel/fax: 977-828 021
mobile: 630 32 45 78
One of the first of several *casas de pagès* to supply rural accommodation on a small scale. This old house, beautifully converted into two modern apartments, is a great family option. In the fascinating wine region, the Priorat. €€

Torreblanca
Carrer Josep M Fàbregas, 1, Valls
tel: 977-601 022
fax: 977-606 323
Attractive *pensión*. €

VALENCIA

Valencia (city)

Astoria Palace
Plaza Rodrigo Botet, 5
tel: 96-398 1000
fax: 96-398 1010
www.hotelastoriapalace.com
Centrally located luxury hotel in the style of an old grand establishment. €€€€

Ad Hoc
Boix, 4
tel: 96-391 9140
fax: 96-391 3667
www.adhochoteles.com
A small hotel, centrally located, with more character than the city's large chain hotels. €€€

Melia Inglés Boutique Hotel
Marqués de Dos Aguas, 6
tel: 96-351 6426
fax: 96-394 0251
www.solmelia.com
Attractive hotel in a historic building, next door to the Ceramics Museum. €€€

Reina Victoria
Barcas, 4
tel: 96-352 0487
fax: 96-352 2721
A stylish old-fashioned hotel built in 1913, close to the main square. €€€

Hostal Antigua Morellana
En Bou, 2
tel: 96-391 5773

fax: 96-391 5979
www.hostalam.com
An 18th-century building recently converted into a modern hotel, in the historic centre between the cathedral and market. Very good value. €

Valencia Province

Hostería de Mont Sant
Subida al Castillo, Xátiva
tel: 96-227 5081
fax: 96-228 1905
www.mont-sant.com
A small, welcoming hotel occupying a restored Cistercian monastery with a beautiful garden. €€€€

Monte Picayo
Urb. Monte Picayo, s/n, Puçol
tel: 96-142 0100
fax: 96-142 2168
This is a luxurious 5-star complex complete with casino and within reach of Valencia. Some bedrooms have their own swimming pool and garden. €€€€

L'Estació
Parc de L'Estació, s/n, Bocairent
tel: 96-235 0000
fax: 96-235 0030
www.hotelestacio.com
This is the town's former railway station, which has been transformed into a small, modern hotel. €€

Alicante (city)

Hotel Sidi San Juan
Partida Cabo La Huerta
tel: 965-16 13 00
fax: 965-16 33 46
www.sidisanjuan.com
A fine hotel with excellent amenities; restaurants, swimming pools, etc., situated on the beach. €€€€

Mediterranea Plaza
Plaza del Ayuntamiento, 6
tel: 965-210 188
fax: 965-206 750
www.hotelmediterraneaplaza.com
A refurbished historical building in the main square. €€€€

Meliá Alicante
Plaza Puerta del Mar
tel: 965-205 000
fax: 965-204 756
www.solmelia.com
A very comfortable hotel with a pool. €€€

Alicante (Province)

El Montiboli
Partida Montiboli, s/n,
La Villajoyosa
tel: 965-890 250
fax: 965-893 857
www.elmontiboli.com
A seaside hotel perched on a low cliff outside a small resort south of Benidorm. €€€€

Huerto del Cura
Porta de la Morera, 14, Elx
tel: 966-610 011
fax: 965-421 910

www.hotelhuertodelcura.com
Located across the road from the
beautiful gardens of the same name,
the hotel enjoys a similarly lovely
situation in the midst of Elx's extensive
palm groves. €€€

Parador de Xàbia Jávea
Avda Mediterrâneo, 7, Xàbia
tel: 965-790 200
fax: 965-790 308
www.parador.es
A purpose-built Parador with beautifully
maintained gardens, situated beside
the beach. €€€

Castellón

Cardenal Ram
Cuesta Suñer, 1, Morella,
tel: 964-173 085
fax: 964-173 218
www.cardenalram.com
This handsome 16th-century mansion
dominates the porticoed main street of
Morella. €€

Fábrica de Giner
Ctra Morella-Zorita del Maestrazgo,
Morella
tel: 964-173 142
fax: 964-173 197
www.ghihoteles.com/fabrica
A modern hotel in an old textile
factory 4.5 km (3 miles) from Morella,
with a duck pond in the grounds. €€

Hostería del Mar
Avda Papa Luna, 18, Peñíscola
tel: 964-480 600
fax: 964-481 363
www.hosteriadelmar.net
A modern hotel with an interior in a
mock-medieval style, just across the
road from the beach. €€

Palau del Ossets
Plaza Mayor, 16, Forcall
tel: 964-177 524
fax: 964-177 556
www.phihoteles.es
An attractively restored 16th-century
palace on the main square of the
village. €€

For a good selection of rural
accommodation, tel: 964-173 117, or
visit www.morella.net

MURCIA

Murcia (city)

Arco de San Juan
Place de Ceballos, 10
tel: 968-210 455
fax: 968-220 809

Price Guide

For a standard double room
€€€€ =	Over €180
€€€ =	€120–180
€€ =	€60–120
€ =	Under €60

www.arcosanjuan.com
Regarded as one of Murcia's best
hotels, the Arco de San Juan is a
modern building behind an old facade
and stands on one of the main
squares. €€€

Conde de Floridablanca
Princesa, 18
tel: 968-214 626
fax: 968-213 215
www.hoteles-catalonia.com
This hotel, which is decorated with
stained glass, antiques and crafts, is
across the river from the city centre but
within walking distance of the main
sights. €€

Murcia Province

Hotel Hyatt Regency La Manga
Los Belones, La Manga del Mar Menor,
s/n
tel: 968-331 234
fax: 968-331 235
lamanga.regency.hyatt.com
Also known as the Príncipe Felipe, this
hotel forms part of the luxurious La
Manga Club complex, built in the style
of a Spanish village. Among its many
sports facilities are golf courses,
swimming pools, tennis courts and a
health centre. €€€€

Amaltea
Ctra de Granada, s/n, Polígono de los
Peñones, Lorca
tel: 968-406 565
fax: 968-406 989
A modern hotel with attractive gardens
planted with palm trees. This
comfortable enclave offers a swimming
pool and good food. €€

Termas de Archena
Balneario de Archena
tel: 902-333 222
fax: 968-671 002
www.balneariodearchena.com
A spa hotel decorated in a superb
Mozarabic style with domes, patios and
ornate plasterwork. €€

Los Habaneros
San Diego, 60 Cartagena
tel: 968-505 250
fax: 968-509 104
www.hotelhabaneros.com
A modest and functional hotel with
rooms at reasonable prices situated
very close to the harbour. €

Where to Eat

Eating Out

CATALONIA

Barcelona

Barcelona's restaurants are nearly too
numerous and mouth-watering to
begin to describe or recommend.
Gourmet options might begin with
Jean Luc Figueres, Santa Teresa, 10,
tel: 93-415 2877 in Gràcia or **Tram-
Tram**, Major de Sarrià, 121, tel:
93-204 8518, up in the pleasant
village-like Sarrià, easily reached by
train (FGC from Plaça Catalunya). Back
down near the port the classic **Set
Portes**, Passeig Isabel II, 14, tel: 93-
319 3033, www.7portes.com, serves fine
fare in old-world elegance from
1pm–1am, while **Los Caracoles**,
Escudellers, 14, tel: 93-302 3185, is
high on atmosphere, though crammed
with tourists. **Cal Pep**, Plaça de les
Olles, 8, tel: 93-310 7961, serves
the best, hottest, freshest *tapas* in
Barcelona. If there are people waiting,
don't hesitate to join them – it's
worth it. **Botafumeiro**, Carrer Gran de
Gràcia, 81, tel: 93-218 4230,
www.galinor.es is an excellent Galician
seafood restaurant and oyster bar,
offering continual service, at a price,
from 1pm–1am.

Passadís D'en Pep, Plaça de
Palau, 2, tel: 93-310 1021, is a small
but "in" restaurant that's expensive
but excellent, where most diners are
happy to eat what they are given.
Santa Maria, Comerc 17, tel: 93-315
1227, www.santamania.biz, is an example
of new Catalan cooking: unusual
combinations, delicious flavours in
tapa-sized amounts, served with
excellent wines. To get an artistic
flavour more than a gourmet
experience, visit **Els Quatre Gats**,
Carrer Montsió, 3, tel: 93-302 4140,
fax: 93-317 40 33, www.4gats.com, more
a cafe than a restaurant. The
paintings are copies, but the building
is spectacular and evocative of the
days when Rusiñol, Casas and
Picasso sat here.

Other spots with great character
include **El Gran Café**, Carrer de Avinyó,
9, tel: 93-301 32 55, fax: 93 301 35
74, www.grupcacheiro.com. A late 19th-

Price Guide

Prices are per person for a three-course meal, excluding wine
€€€€ = more than €30
€€€ = €12–30
€€ = under €12

century sewing machine factory, which nostalgically retains its decor and serves good Catalan dishes bistro-style. The **Egipte** at La Rambla 79 spreads over several floors full of antiques and is fun and cheap. Or try the bars in the nearby Boqueria market, where you usually have to queue for food fresh from a neighbouring stall-holder. Excellent value and great atmosphere.

Lleida/Lérida Province

Casa Irene
Major, 3, Arties Val d'Aran
tel: 973-644 364
www.hotelcasairene.com
Exceptional cooking – dishes include home-smoked salmon with crab sauce and duck with truffles. Green walnut liqueur is the house speciality. €€€€
La Huerta restaurant
Avda de Tortosa, 13, Lleida
tel: 973-245 0400
Typical Lleidan food and wines. €€€
Cal Pacho
de la Font, La Seu d'Urgell
tel: 973-352 719
Typical dishes of the Alt Urgell region. €€
Solterra
Plaça de Sant Roc, 4, Solsona
tel: 973-480 627
Local cheese, wine and food. €€

Girona

You will eat heartily, especially meat dishes such as beef with prunes, at any of the restaurants in the rural village of Setcases, 13 km (8 miles) to the north of Camprodón.
Can Borrell
tel: 972-880 033
fax: 972-880 144
www.canborrell.com
High in the hills at Meranges, Cerdanya. For years a leader of Catalan nouvelle cuisine, Can Borrell is excellent. The drive up is spectacular, the cuisine superb, and the restaurant is chic rustic. There are eight rooms to rent. €€€€
La Tieta
de las Ferrers, 20,
Puigcerdà, Cerdanya
tel: 972-880 156
Built into a restored 16th-century townhouse, once part of Puigcerdà's ramparts. Excellent fare. €€€

Costa Brava

El Bulli
Cala Montjoi Roses
tel: 972-150 457
fax: 972-150 717
www.elbulli.com
Probably the most famous Spanish restaurant in the world thanks to genius chef Ferran Adrià and his laboratory-like kitchen. €€€€
La Xicra
Estret, 17, Palafrugell
tel: 972-305 630
www.restaurantlaxicra.com
Fine local specialities. Closed Tues pm and Wed (except Aug) and all of Nov. €€€
La Pizzeta
Ventura i Sabater 2
Begur
tel: 972-623 884
www.lapizzeta.com
Wonderful value for all the family, unusual pizzas and pasta in lovely surroundings. €€
Plaça Murada
Plaça Murada, 5, Palamós
tel: 972-315 376
Excellent seafood. €€

There are a number of excellent fish restaurants around the port.

Costa del Maresme

Emma
Baixada de l'Estació, 5,
Caldes d'Estrac

tel: 93-791 1305
Cosy little restaurant for fresh fish and local cuisine. €€

There are several good fish restaurants in the port of **Arenys de Mar**, such as: **Posit de Pescadors**, Zona Puerto s/n, tel: 93-792 1245/4468. €€€€
And nearby is the famous **Hispania** in Reial, 54, tel: 93-791 0306, www.restauranthispania.com, celebrated for its Catalan cuisine. €€€€

Costa Daurada

Joan Gatell
Passeig Miramar, 26
tel: 977-360 057
www.joangatell.com
Owned by the Gatell family of famous restaurateurs. Classic Tarragona fish dishes. €€€€
Vivero
Passeig Balmins, Sitges
tel: 93-894 2149
fax: 93-881 3000
www.elviverositges.com
A basic place with tables outside which overlook the small beach and serving mainly seafood. Closed Tues from Feb–Apr. €€–€€€
Els 4 Gats
Sant Pau, 13, Sitges
tel: 93-894 1915
A reasonably priced, quality restaurant located on a narrow street descending to the sea. €€

Catalonian Wine Routes

Wine producers, co-operatives and *bodegas* (*bodegues* in Catalan) are hospitable places, and at most of them you will be able to taste the wine before buying.
Empordà-Costa Brava: In the most northeasterly corner of the region, stretching between Figueres and the French border to the sea. There are co-operatives at Roses, Pau, Vilajuïga, Garriguella, Mollet de Peralada, Capmany, Sant Climent Sescebes, Rabós and Espolla, a village whose wines Catalan writer Josep Pla thought the best. The centre for the local *cava* industry is Peralada, a delightful medieval town that's worth a visit.
Penedès: Catalonia's largest and best-known wine region, just west of Barcelona, centres on the towns of Vilafranca del Penedès and Sant Sadurní d'Anoia. The famous high-tech Torres winery is just outside Vilafranca (closed Aug). There is a good selection of the local producers' wines in the shops, plus the excellent Museu del Vi (closed Sun). Sant Sadurní is the *cava* town, home of

Catalonia's two top producers of this *méthode champenoise* sparkling wine, Codorníu and Freixenet. Caves Codorníu on the edge of the town is a fine Modernist building designed by Puig i Cadafalch and well worth a visit.
Priorat: Perhaps the most delightful of the regions, overlooked until recently, but now producing some of Spain's most expensive and highly regarded wines. The precipitous slopes are attractive to look at but hard to work, and few young people remain at home to help out on the land. There are co-operatives at Bellmunt del Priorat, Lloà, Gratallops, Porrera, Torroja del Priorat, La Viella Alta, La Viella Baixa, Pobleda, La Morera de Montsanand Scala Dei.
Tarragona: De Müller, supplier of altar wine to the Vatican, is the surviving grand old viniculturist in Tarragona, in the Carrer Reial, open during weekday office hours. There are several cavernous *bodegas* in the town. Outside Tarragona, on the N-240 towards Valls, is the modern Lopez Bertrán wine producer.

Tarragona

Les Voltes
Trinquet Vell, 12
tel: 977-230 651
Built into the Roman amphitheatre, this
is a local favourite for everything from
fresh fish to *calçots* (spring onions).
€€€

Restaurant Masía Bou
Ctra de Lleida, km 21,5, Valls
tel: 972-600 427
www.masiabou.com
This is the place to eat *calçots*. There
are countless photos of celebrities,
from Dalí to Suarez, wearing bibs and
wolfing down their onions. It is smart
and on the pricey side, but the *calçots*
are the real thing, grown at the back
of the restaurant, cooked in the
backyard and followed by the
traditional meal of spicy sausage and
lamb. **€€€**

Restaurant Pi
Rambla, 2, El Vendrell
tel: 977-660 002
A cafe-restaurant done in a
rather overblown Modernist style.
It serves local dishes, such as *xató*
salad and its own version of *calçots*.
€€€

Les Coques
Baixada Nova del Patriarca, 2
Tarragona
tel: 977-228 300
Serves good regional dishes; both
Mediterranean-style and mountain
specialities. **€€**

Restaurant Piro
Carrer Piro, 21, Gratallops, Priorat
tel: 977-839 004
Serves really good *platos típicos* with a
menu that changes daily according to
local ingredients (they collect their own
rovellon mushrooms). Closed Mon.
€€

VALENCIA

Valencia (city)

Eladio
Chiva, 40
tel: 96-384 2244
A classic restaurant in Valencia,
particularly noted for its fish dishes and
desserts. Closed Sun, and all of Aug.
€€€

La Riua
de Mar, 27
tel: 963-17172/924000
A good choice in the centre, notably for
its *paella*. **€€€**

Price Guide

Prices are per person for a three-
course meal, excluding wine
€€€€ =   more than €30
€€€ =   €12–30
€€ =   under €12

Marisquería Civera
Lleida, 11
tel: 96-347 5917
www.marisqueriacivera.com
Fresh seafood, *paella* and vegetables.
Closed Sun evening; Mon and all of
Aug. **€€€**

A line of restaurants at Las Arenas
Beach, near the port, specialise in
paellas, rice and great seafood:

L'Estimat
Avda Neptuno, 16
tel: 96-371 1018
www.lestimat.com
Closed Sun and Mon evening and Tues,
and 15 Aug–15 Sept. **€€€**

La Marcelina
Avda Neptuno, 8
tel: 96-371 2025
Closed Mon and from 7–31 Jan. **€€€**

La Pepica
Avda Neptuno, 6
tel: 96-371 0366
www.lapepica.com
Closed from 15–30 Nov. **€€€**

Valencia Province

Venta L'Home
Autovía Madrid-Valencia, km 294,
Bunyol
tel: 96-250 3515
www.lahoya.net
On the main road between Madrid and
Valencia. Specialities include
Mediterranean salad. **€€€**

Racó de L'Olla
Carretera del Palmar, s/n,
El Palmar
tel: 96-162 0172
www.racodelolla.com
In a village beside the Albufera and its
paddy fields, near Valencia.
Specialising in rice dishes and *all i
pebre de anguilas* (eels in a garlic and
pepper sauce). Closed Mon from
Sept–June, Sun in July and Aug; and for
ten days in Jan. **€€**

Alicante (city)

Dársena
Muelle de Levante, 6
tel: 965-207 589
www.darsena.com
Unbeatable for rice dishes and fish.
More relaxed at dinner than lunch.
Closed Sun evening, and Mon in
summer. **€€€**

Alicante Province

El Girasol, Ctra Moraria-Calpe, km 1.5,
Moraira
tel: 965-744 373
Star-chef cooking aiming at Parisian
standards. Reservations essential.
Gastronomic menu. Closed Mon,
except in summer, and all of Nov.
€€€€

Ca L'Angeles
Gabriel Miró, 36, Polop de la Marina

tel: 965-870 226
A simply furnished village house, with a
menu varying according to season.
Closed Tues and from 15 June–15 July.
€€€

La Lubina
Avda de Bilbao, 3, Benidorm
tel: 965-853 085
Specialities include sea bass, baked
and encrusted with salt. Closed 1
Dec–28 Feb. **€€**

L'Escaleta
Subida Estación del Norte 205,
Cocentaina
tel: 965-592 100
www.lescaleta.com
Exquisite food, elegantly presented.
Closed Sun evening, Mon, Easter Week
and last fortnight in Jan. **€€**

L'Obrer
Ctra de Alcoy, 27, Benimantell
tel: 965-885 088
Local delicacies including *olleta de blat*
(mountain stew), roast lamb and
almond and chocolate pie. Closed Fri
and 26 June–5 Aug. **€€**

Castellón

Hostería del Mar
Avda Papa Luna, 10, Peñíscola
tel: 964-480 600
www.hosteriadelmar.net
Belonging to the hotel of the same
name, specialises in rice dishes.
Medieval banquets staged at
weekends. **€€€**

Mesón del Pastor
Cuesta Jovani, 5, Morella
tel: 964-160 249
www.mesondelpastor.com
In the centre of a historic town,
specialising in local dishes including
Sopa de Pastor (shepherd's soup).
Closed Wed, except in summer. **€€**

Murcia (city)

El Rincón de Pepe
Plaza Apóstoles, 34
tel: 968-212 239
Highly recommended, with a varied
menu. Closed Sun evening.
€€€

Hispano
Radio Murcia, 3
tel: 968-216 152
A classic restaurant serving local
cuisine. Closed Sat in July and Aug.
€€€

Nightlife

Clubs & Discos

CATALONIA

The brightest night spots tend to be in the crowded resorts: the spectacular razzmatazz of the **Grand Palace** in Lloret de Mar or the **Galas** in Salou; or the **laser shows** of La Platja d'Aro, which has the greatest concentration of discos on the coast.

In the summer months open-air discos spring up in all major resorts, charging around €25 to get in and adding several euros to the price of a drink. With meals eaten late, nightlife doesn't begin to get going until after midnight, continuing until around 5am when the tradition is to have fresh *churros* (sugared strips of batter) dunked in thick hot chocolate.

Many of the late drinking places in Barcelona have no entrance fee: they just demand a lot of money for their drinks. Others, such as *Otto Zutz*, like you to queue up so they can then refuse you entrance if they disapprove of you. It is hard to recommend any of these, not least because they come in and out of fashion so fast. **Otto Zutz**, Lincoln 15, appears to be here to stay; **Luz de Gas**, Muntaner 246, has good live music, and **Jamboree**, Plaça Reial, 17 and **La Boite**, Diagonal 477 are jazz clubs. **Bikini**, Deu i Mata 105 and **Razzmatazz**, Almogàvers 122, are popular venues for concerts and DJs. **Nick Havanna**, Rosselló 208, the original 1980s designer bar now has a hip DJ scene on Thursday. **La Paloma**, Tigre 27, is having a new lease of life, with its traditional dance orchestra from Thur–Sat and DJs after 2am. Its old charms remain as enticing as ever.

VALENCIA & MURCIA

Nightlife in the largest cities of the region revolves around *pubs*, which are not to be confused with British and Irish public houses. These late-night bars strive to create an atmosphere by providing few places to sit, attractive bar staff, loud music, and often but not always a dance floor. Few people go out before midnight and many pubs do not come alive until around 2am. It is common to go around several pubs

Casinos

Catalonia
The three casinos in Catalonia open from around 7pm–4am. There is a small entry fee of around €4 and you must take your passport.
Peralada The casino is part of the castle. The gaming rooms are hung with tapestries and the hostesses in glittering top hats and tails look a little out of place. Tel: 972-538 125.
Lloret de Mar Part of the Hotel Casino de Lloret, this casino has all the usual games, plus a slot-machine room, restaurant, disco and pool. Carrer de Tossa, s/n, tel: 972-366 116.
Barcelona Formerly near Sitges, this casino has moved, amid some controversy, to the Olympic port. Gran Casino de Barcelona, Marina, 19–21, tel: 93-225 7878.
Valencia & Murcia There are casinos at Monte Picayo (near Valencia), between Benidorm and La Vila Joiosa on the Costa Blanca and at La Manga on the Mar Menor.

before going on to a disco. The old *barrio* El Carmen in **Valencia** is famed for its throbbing nightlife and designer bars. The place to be in **Alicante** is either El Barrio (the old city) or the new port, full of restaurants and bars. Ask around if you want to find the latest places. In the summer, there is also plenty of nightlife in the larger resorts.

Shopping

What to Buy

CATALONIA

Leather goods and **fashion items** are still good value, as are kitchen, garden and decorative **ceramics** available in small shops, at markets and in huge roadside emporiums. La Bisbal is the largest Catalan ceramic centre. Miravet in Tarragona is also an important pottery town, as is Verdú in the Urgell (Lleida) where most of the ceramic ware is black. You can find **hand-made lace** in L'Arboç in Baix Penedès, Tarragona. **Olive oil** and **wine vinegar** are good value (especially in the Lleida region and the Alt Empordà) and wine and spirits are still cheap. A good Rioja or Valdepeñas can be had for less than €6 and good Spanish brandies for under €12 per litre.

VALENCIA & MURCIA

Valencia and Murcia are rich in crafts, particularly **ceramics**. Manises, near Valencia, is known for its colourful tiles. Lladró porcelain figures are made in Tabernes Blanques near Valencia; where you can visit the factory.

Traditional **blankets** are made in Morella, in the Maestrazgo, and **recycled glassware**, with an attractive green tinge, is manufactured in L'Ollería. Fine **lacework** is on sale in Guadalest, Beniardá, Callosa d'Ensarriá and Jalón Valley. Valencia has a **fan**-making tradition and in Murcia you can buy Christmas **nativity figures**.

An interesting place to shop for presents is Gata de Gorgos, near Xàbia; the main street is lined with shops selling **basketry**, **olive wood bowls** and other local crafts.

Sport

Sailing

CATALONIA

There are 41 marinas along the 580 km (360 miles) of Catalonia's coast, but berths can still be hard to obtain in summer and quite expensive. There are some anchorage points along the rockier northern coast; and temporary berths on public jetties or in harbours are either very cheap or free – see the port authorities on arrival. A helmsman's certificate is required for any boating activity. Many of the new marinas run sailing courses and charter yachts are available. The municipal school in Barcelona is excellent, tel: 93-225 7940; www.vela-barcelona.com

VALENCIA & MURCIA

There are a great many sailing clubs and marinas all along the coast. Some of them offer sailing courses and have yachts for hire. They can usually provide **windsurf** boards too. A good option in Murcia is the Estación Náutica Mar Menor, tel: 902-17 17 18, www.enmarmenor.com

Golf

CATALONIA

There are over 40 golf courses active throughout the year in Catalonia, including pitch and putts.
Club de Golf Costa Brava, La Masía, Santa Cristina d'Aro, province of Girona, tel: 972-837 055, www.golfcostabrava.com Just inland between Sant Feliu de Guíxols and La Platja d'Aro, this course has some narrow doglegs. Open all year round. Closed Wed Oct–May.
Club de Golf Pals, Platja de Pals, Pals, on the Costa Brava, tel: 972-636 006. Set among pine woods beside the long sandy beach at Pals, the main hazard is the Tramuntana wind. Open all year round. Closed on Tues Sept–June.
Golf Fontanals de Cerdanya, Queixans, Girona. This spectacular course, across and down river from the Reial Club de Golf de Cerdanya, takes full advantage of the broad Cerdanya valley. There are

18 holes and many water hazards.
Reial Club de Golf de Cerdanya, Apartat de Correus, 63, Puigcerdà, Girona, tel: 972-141 408/ 141 040. Open all year.
Club de Golf Sant Cugat, Sant Cugat del Vallès, Barcelona, tel: 93-674 3908, www.golfsantcugat.com Just inland from Barcelona city. Where Severiano Ballesteros made his professional debut. Closed Mon.
Club de Golf Vallromanes, Afores, s/n Vallromanes, province of Barcelona, tel: 93-572 9064, www.golfvallromanes.com Behind Mataró on the Maresme coast. Open all year round, closed Tues.
Reial Club de Golf El Prat, Apartat de Correus, 10, 08820 El Prat de Llobregat, tel: 93-728 10 00, www.rcgep.com A very grand course near Barcelona airport. Open all year.

VALENCIA & MURCIA

With over 20 courses in Valencia and 5 in Murcía there's plenty of choice. Well-known are:
El Saler, outside Valencia, Ctra Saler, km 18, tel: 96-161 11 86, fax: 96-162 70 16, www.parador.es
La Manga Club, Los Belones, La Manga, tel: 968-17 5000, fax: 968-33 1235, www.lamangaclub.com
Others include Xàbia, Calpe, Altea and Torrevieja.
Panoramica San Jorge, tel: 964-49 30 25, fax: 964-49 30 62, www.inmopanoramica.com Inland from Vinarós in Castellón, this is a new, well-equipped course, designed by Bernhard Langer

Calendar of Events

CATALONIA
There are numerous colourful national and local festivals, especially in spring and early summer. Important ones are:
Epiphany: The Three Kings arrive by boat, by camel or even helicopter throughout the region on the eve of January 6 to distribute presents.
Carnival: celebrated everywhere for a week before Ash Wednesday.
Semana Santa: Holy Week, religious processions in most towns.
St George's Day, Sant Jordi: 23 April. Also Shakespeare's and Cervantes' birthdays, hence day of books and roses – lovers' day (Catalonia only).
Corpus Christi: flower carpets and other religious celebrations, usually in early June.
St John's Eve: 23 June. Bonfires, fireworks and all-night partying to welcome summer.
Fiesta del Carmen: The fishermen's feast day on 15–16 July is

celebrated at ports.
Vendimia: the wine harvest festivals are in mid-September.
La Mercè festival: 24 September. Barcelona's largest festival – a wild week of music, dragons, giants. *Castells* (human towers) and more for the city's patron saint.

VALENCIA and MURCIA
Valencia and Murcia, like many other regions in Spain, have their fair share of fiestas throughout the year:
Las Fallas Valencia and surrounding towns, culminating 19 March, San José. Involving ceremonial burning of satirical papier-mâché models.
Moors and Christians Alcoi (Alicante) 22–24 April. Parades and mock battles with costumed armies.
La Tomatina Free-for-all tomato fight in Buñol (Valencia) takes place on the third Wednesday of August.
Semana Santa Murcia and Lorca hold their famous Easter processions.

Walking

CATALONIA

You can walk your boots off here. 3,000 km (1,875 miles) of footpaths have been mapped out by trail-blazing Catalans.
Most long-distance "GR" *(gran recorrido)* footpaths are marked with red-and-white stripes painted on rocks and trees. If they are accompanied by an arrow it shows a change of direction. If the two lines are crossed it shows you where not to go. There are some ambitious routes, which have small signposts with the numbers of the routes and the names of the next village. The GR 92 stretches the length of the coast from Portbou to Ulldecona; the GR 11 covers the entire Catalan Pyrenees, from Cap de Creus to Aragón.

VALENCIA & MURCIA

An increasing number of maps and guides have opened up the inland areas of the region for **hiking** and **hill walking**. Suitable areas include the Maestrazgo, the Upper Turia region of Valencia province, the hills behind the Costa Blanca, and the area around Alcoy.

Skiing

CATALONIA

There are 17 resorts in the region, including Alpine and Nordic skiing, all in the Pyrenees. Their season extends from the beginning of December to the end of April.

Main Alpine Ski Resorts:

Baqueira-Beret, 43 pistes from 1,500–2,500 metres (4,820–8,200 ft). Where Spain's royal family go.

Tuca-Mall Blanc, 20 pistes from 1,000–2,250 metres (3,280–7,380 ft). Also in the Vall d'Aran, this is 2 km (1 mile) from Vielha. With some tricky trails and a slalom stadium.

Boï-Taüll, 14 pistes from 2,040–2,455 metres (6,685–8,060 ft). Its lack of sophistication is compensated for by the fine Romanesque villages.

Super Espot, 24 pistes from 1,490–2,320 metres (4,890–7,610 ft). At the entrance to the Aigüestortes Park.

Llesui, 22 pistes from 1,445–2,430 metres (4,740–7,970 ft). Just north of Sort. The bare slopes of the mountains make it obstacle-free.

Rasos de Peguera, 9 pistes from 1,895–2,050 metres (6,215–6,725 ft). South of the great Cadí range and 13 km (8 miles) north of Berga, this is Barcelona's closest resort.

La Molina, 29 pistes from 1,590–2,465 metres (5,215–8,085 ft). Always popular, sometimes full. Can be easily reached by train from Barcelona.

Masella, 88 pistes from 1,600–2,530 metres (5,248–8,300 ft). Next to La Molina, on the north face of Tossa d'Alp.

Vall de Núria, 9 pistes from 1,965–2,270 metres (6,440–7,440 ft). Inaccessible by road, skiers must take the "zip" train up the Freser Valley from Ribes. Uncomplicated slopes, plus ice skating on the lake.

Vallter 2000, 16 pistes from 2,010–2,500 metres (6,595–8,201 ft). The most easterly resort.

Sporting Climate

In Catalonia adventure sports have become more and more popular, especially in the Pyrenees, as well as cycle routes – from sightseeing tours in the cities to demanding mountain trails. For details check www.gencat.es/turistex Valencia and Murcia are ideal for a range of sports, particularly watersports. Most beaches are safe and suitable for **swimming**; many have a blue flag. Normally it is warm enough to swim from June to September. The rockier parts of the Costa Blanca are good for **snorkelling** or **scuba diving** and equipment can be hired from all major resorts.

Most cities have **tennis** courts, like Club Tenis Valencia, Botánico Cavanilles, 7, tel: 96-369 0658. There are also excellent courts, with instructors available, in La Manga Club, tel: 96-833 1234.

Northern Spain

Getting Acquainted

GEOGRAPHY

From Aragón in the east to Galicia in the west, the region spans the Iberian peninsula across a width of about 1,000 km (620 miles), and a depth from north to south that varies between about 175 km (110 miles) and 75 km (45 miles). Apart from Aragón, situated directly below the Pyrenees, the region is bounded on the north by the Bay of Biscay; the Cordillera Cantabrica runs parallel to the coast for its entire length, the highest stretch being in the Picos de Europa which reach 2,648 metres (8,866 feet). The west of Galicia is bounded by the Atlantic Ocean.

Language: Spanish (Castilian – Castellano) throughout, in addition to Basque (Euskera) being spoken in the Basque Country, and Galician (Gallego) in Galicia.

Economy

Northern Spain has Europe's largest fishing fleet in Vigo. It's known for being the industrial area of Spain, with industries based around Bilbao. The Basque Country is also a financial centre – the Banco de Bilbao is one of the nation's leading banks.

There is poverty in the remoter hills and valleys, and Galicia is the poorest region of Spain.

Climate

In Northern Spain, there is a great deal of variation in climate, both regionally and seasonally, so you need to pack for all eventualities. Green Spain, which stretches from the Basque Country along the Atlantic coast through Cantabria and Asturias to Galicia, is obviously so-named because it rains a great deal, so take waterproofs, umbrellas and suitable footwear – even in summer. Bilbao and Santiago are renowned for being very rainy and the pasture-clad hills are often swathed in mist.

Winters in the north and northwest can be very wet, and it may snow. Summers, on the other hand, can be blessed with lavish amounts of sunshine and warmth everywhere, increasing in intensity as you travel inland and cross the mountains of the Cordillera Cantábrica.

The north is, therefore, a good destination for a summer beach holiday. There are hundreds of beautiful coves and beaches (many sheltered and backed by green fields), as well as seaside resorts that have long been popular among Spaniards in the hot season.

Getting There

BY AIR

From the UK

Iberia, Spain's national airline, operates direct flights from London Heathrow to Bilbao and Santiago de Compostela, as well as flights to Santander (via Barcelona), Vitoria (via Madrid or Barcelona), San Sebastián (via Barcelona), Vigo (via Madrid) and A Coruña (via Madrid). Visitors can also fly direct, non-stop to Oviedo from London Gatwick or continue on the same plane to A Coruña.

Iberia also flies from Manchester and Dublin to Barcelona and Madrid, where you can pick up connections to the destinations in the north detailed above. For further information, contact Iberia's London enquiry/reservations service on 0845-601 2854; www.iberia.com

British Airways operates one direct service to Northern Spain – from Heathrow to Bilbao. A Coruña, Santander, Vitoria, San Sebastián, Bilbao, Vigo, Santiago de Compostela, Gijón and Avilés can be reached by flying BA to Barcelona or Madrid and then transferring to a domestic carrier, or catching a train. For information and reservations on all its flights, telephone British Airways in the UK on 0845-7733377; www.british-airways.com.

EasyJet flies to Bilbao and Barcelona from Gatwick and Stansted airports near London. Tel: 0870-600 0000, www.easyjet.com

From the USA and Canada

If you are visiting from North America, **Iberia**, tel: 800-772-4642, flies from Los Angeles, New York, Montreal and Miami to Barcelona; and from Los Angeles, New York, Montreal, Toronto and Chicago to Madrid. From these two destinations, you can then make a connection to any of the cities in Northern Spain mentioned above.

Delta airlines, tel: 800-241-4141; www.delta.com, has direct flights to Barcelona.

BY SEA

Brittany Ferries operates a year-round service from Plymouth to Santander, Cantabria (24 hours' sailing time). Call Brittany Ferries in the UK on 0870-366 5333 for details, or log on at www.brittany-ferries.com

P&O Ferries run a year-round service from Portsmouth to Bilbao. Telephone them in the UK on 0870-242 4999 for more information, or log onto www.poportsmouth.com.

BY RAIL

There are numerous trains from Paris to the border at Irún, from where the line continues to San Sebastian and Bilbao, with serpentine branches to Pamplona, Vitoria-Gasteiz and Logroño.

BY CAR

The motorway route from Calais, France to the Spanish border at Irún takes about 15 hours, from where fast routes run to San Sebastián, Bilbao and Santander.

Getting Around

The region is adequately served by both **bus** and **train** services, though the fastest main road and rail links are with the capital, Madrid, and cross-country travel is slower. The centralised telephone number for all rail enquiries is 902-240 202.

Narrow-gauge rail lines run from Bilbao all the way along the coast to A

Local Tourist Offices

These tourist offices (oficinas de turismo) are open all year:
Aragón Plaza de Catedral, 1, Huesca.
Tomás Nogues, 1, Teruel.
Torreón de la Zuda, Glorieta Pío XII, s/n, Zaragoza.
Navarre Eslava, 1, Pamplona.
La Rioja Calle Portales 46.
Basque Country Paseo del Arenal 1, Bilbao.
Reina Regente, San Sebastián.
Asturias Plaza de Alfonso II El Casto, 6, Oviedo.
Cantabria Plaza Porticada Santander, Municipal information: Jardines de Pereda.
Picos de Europa Avda de Covadonga, Cangas de Onís, Asturias.
Galicia Avda de la Marina, A Coruña.
Rúa do Vilar, 43, Santiago de Compostela.
Estación Marítima de Transatlánticos, Vigo.

Emergencies

- **Emergencies** (health and security) 112
- **Police** 091
- **Telephone Information** 1003

Coruña. This scenic route is also covered by the luxury El Transcantábrico train.

Media

There are two nationwide television channels in Spain, TVE 1 and TVE 2, and three private networks: Antena 3, Tele 5 and Canal Plus. There are also local-language stations. Satellite and cable TV are also available.

This is not a cosmopolitan part of Spain, so you won't find the world's press outside major towns.

Health

Generally all tap water across the north of Spain is safe and sanitary. In the high Pyrenees, however, the "hard" local water can sometimes cause gastric problems. Drinking from streams, no matter how clear they appear to be, is a risky business even in the upper reaches of the Picos de Europa and the Pyrenees.

Security & Crime

Northern Spain is, on the whole, pretty safe, but the usual rules apply. Keep money secure in a hidden belt to deter pickpockets. Never leave anything of value in your car, including when parking near a beach. Don't leave cash or valuables unattended while you are swimming. When staying overnight, take all baggage into the hotel and, if possible, park your car in a garage or a guarded car-park.

Where to Stay

Hotels

Following is our selection of hotels in the Northern Spanish regions of Aragón, Asturias, Cantabria, the Basque Country, Galicia and Navarre. Hotels are listed in order of price category.

ARAGÓN

Huesca

Pedro I de Aragón
Del Parque, 34
tel: 974-220 300
fax: 974-220 094
www.gargallo-hotels.com
Elegant, modern hotel in a pleasant area west of the old town. Good facilities. €€€
Sancho Abarca
Plaza de Lizana, 13
tel: 974-220 650
fax: 974-225 169
www.hotelsanchoabarca.com
Situated in the centre of town, with an excellent restaurant. €€

Jaca

Gran Hotel
Paseo de la Constitución, 1
tel: 974-360 900
fax: 974-364 061
www.inturmark.es
Modern, central hotel located near a park; Jaca is convenient for skiiing in the Pyrenees. €€€
Conde Aznar
Paseo de la Constitución, 3
tel: 974-361 050
fax: 974-360 797
www.condeaznar.com
Simple hotel in a fine house on the same smart street as the Gran Hotel. €€

Teruel

Parador de Teruel
Ctra N-234 (Sagunto-Burgos)
tel: 978-601 800
fax: 978-608 612
www.parador.es
Purpose-built, secluded Parador on the city outskirts; good restaurant. €€€

Zaragoza

Hotel Palafox
Casa Jiménez, s/n

tel: 976-237 700
fax: 976-234 705
www.palafoxhoteles.com
Modern hotel with rooftop pool. One of
Zaragoza's top two choices. €€€€

Meliá Zaragoza Corona
Avda César Augusto, 13
tel: 976-430 100
fax: 976-440 734
www.solmelia.com
Luxurious hotel near city centre with a
good restaurant. €€€€

Don Yo
Bruil, 4–6
tel: 976-226 741
fax: 976-219 956
hotelzenitdonyo.zenithoteles.com
Lively hotel two minutes from city's
main sites; pleasant tavern. €€€

Orus
Escoriaza y Fabro, 45
tel: 976-536 600
fax: 976-536 163
A one-time chocolate factory, now an
elegant hotel with an intimate touch. €€€

Tibur
Plaza de la Seo, 2
tel: 976-202 000
fax: 976-202 002
Conveniently located, comfortable and
well-equipped, with the excavated Roman
forum outside the front door. €€€

Conde Blanco
Predicadores, 84
tel: 976-441 411
fax: 976-280 339
www.hotelcondeblanco.com
Modern, good-value hotel in a quiet,
attractive street. Excellent service. €€

Price Guide

For a standard double room
€€€€ =	Over €120
€€€ =	€90–120
€€ =	€50–90
€ =	Under €50

Monasterio de Piedra
Nuevalos
tel: 902-196 052 or 976-849 011
fax: 976-849 054
www.monasteriopiedra.com
A 12th-century monastery transformed into
a hotel. Next to a famous beauty spot. €€

ASTURIAS

Gijón/Xijon
Parador Molino Viejo
Parque de Isabel la Católica, s/n
tel: 985-370 511
fax: 985-370 233
www.parador.es
The only Asturias Parador, Molino Viejo is
near the end of Playa de San Lorenzo.
€€€

Castillo Valdés-Salas
Plaza Campa, Salas

Rural Asturias

For information about country
houses and other accommodation in
Asturias, tel: 901-300 600.

tel: 985-830 173/4
fax: 985-83 01 83
www.castillovaldesalas.com
A 16th-century converted castle in the
middle of a small town. €€

Principe de Asturias
Manso, 2
tel: 985-367 111
fax: 985-334 741
www.hotelprincipeasturias.com
This excellent hotel overlooks the
beach and Bay of Gijón, with most
rooms enjoying great sea views. €€

Oviedo
Hotel de la Reconquista
Gil de Jaz, 16
tel: 985-241 100
fax: 985-241 166
www.hoteldelareconquista.com
This spectacular 17th-century building
houses what is universally considered
to be Oviedo's finest hotel. €€€€

Principado
San Francisco, 6
tel: 985-217 792
fax: 985-213 946
www.nh-hotels.com
A good-value hotel with friendly service.
€€

Ribadesella
Hotel Rural l'Alceu
Camango, s/n
tel: 985-858 343
fax: 985-860 661
www.ribadesella.com/alceu
The Rural l'Alceu lies 4 km (2½ miles)
outside Ribadesella, in Camango at the
mouth of the River Sella. A 16th-
century house with a perfect *hórreo*
(raised granary) next to it. €

Taramundi
La Rectoral
La Villa, s/n
tel: 985-646 760
fax: 985-646 777
www.larectoral.com
A 17th-century country house – rustic,
romantic and surrounded by one of the
most character-filled towns in Asturias;
don't miss a stopover here. €€€

Villaviciosa
La Casona de Amandi
Villaviciosa, s/n
tel: 985-890 130
fax: 985-890 129
www.lacasonadeamandi.com
This graceful mansion is surrounded by
fields just outside Villaviciosa. Much to
explore in the area. Good value. €€

BASQUE COUNTRY

Bilbao
Carlton
Plaza Federico Moyúa, 2
tel: 944-162 200
fax: 944-164 628
www.aranzazu-hoteles.com
Orson Welles, Ernest Hemingway, Ava
Gardner, and many great bullfighters
have stayed here. The Republican
Basque government headquarters was
here, and later, Franco's general staff.
The place breathes history. €€€€

Ercilla
Ercilla, 37–39
tel: 944-705 700
fax: 944-439 335
www.hotelercilla.es
Highly popular and the centre of the city's
bullfighting and theatrical activity. With a
fine restaurant, the Bermeo. €€€€

Villa de Bilbao
Gran Vía, 87
tel: 944-416 000
fax: 944-416 529
www.nh-hotels.com
Centrally located with excellent service,
this business hotel offers a fine
breakfast and La Pergola, a gourmet
dining choice. €€€€

Nervión
Paseo Campo Volantín, 11
tel: 944-454 700
fax: 944-455 608
www.bchoteles.com
This monolithic operation beside the
estuary offers up-to-date comforts. €€

San Sebastián
Londres y de Inglaterra
Zubieta, 2
tel: 943-440 770
fax: 943- 440 491
www.hlondres.com
Lovely hotel by the beach. €€€€

María Cristina
Calle Oquendo 1
tel: 943-437 600
fax: 943-437 676
www.starwoodhotels.com
Originally opened in 1912, the María
Cristina has been entirely remodelled and
is once again the city's top hotel. €€€€

Monte Igueldo
Monte Igueldo, s/n
tel: 943-210 211
fax: 943-215 028
www.monteigueldo.com
This is a romantic retreat with seascapes
in almost every direction. €€€

Rural Basque Country

Staying on farms is a popular way to
visit the Basque Country. For
information, contact: Office for
Agrotourism, 48200 Garai (Biskaia);
tel/fax: 946-211 188.

Avenida
Paseo de Igueldo, 55
tel: 943-212 022
fax: 943-212 887
www.hotelavenida.net
On the road up to one of San Sebastián's mountains overlooking the sea. €€
Parma
General Javregui II
tel: 943-428 893
fax: 943-424 082
www.hotelparma.com
This tiny hotel offers good value and great views. €€

CANTABRIA
Santander
Real
Pérez Galdós, 28
tel: 942-272 550
fax: 942-274 573
www.hotelreal-santander.com
This elegant hotel close to Santander's beaches was built in the early 20th century for the Spanish royal family's summer holidays. Rooms on the sea side have spectacular Atlantic views. €€€€
Ciudad de Santander
Menéndez Pelayo, 13–15
tel: 942-319 900
fax: 942-217 303
www.nh-hotels.com
This small and well-run hotel is one of Santander's best. €€€
Santemar
Joaquín Costa, 28
tel: 942-272 900
fax: 942- 278 604
www.hotelsantemar.com
Centrally located and endowed with a fine restaurant, this is a sure bet for comfort and service. €€€
Sardinero
Plaza de Italia, 1
tel: 942-271 100
fax: 942-271 698
www.gruposardinero.com
On Sardinero beach, this simple but sound establishment has fine views. €€

GALICIA
A Coruña
Finisterre
Paseo del Parrote, 2
tel: 981-205 400
fax: 981-208 462

Rural Galicia

Turgalicia operates a well-organised network of tourist accommodation in country houses ranging from vineyard homes to *pazo* manor houses,
tel: 981-542 527.

www.hesperia.com
Panoramic views, comfort and service make this A Coruña's top hotel. €€€
Riazor
Avda Barrié de la Maza, 29
tel: 981-253 400
fax: 981-253 404
www.riazorhotel.com
A city-centre hotel with sea views, this is a bright, cheery and spacious place. €€

A Garda
Convento de San Benito
Plaza de San Benito, s/n
tel: 986-611 166
fax: 986-611 517
www.hotelsanbenito.es
This converted convent is an ideal base for exploring the Miño estuary. €€

Lugo
Hostal Piornedo
Piornedo de Ancares, Cervantes
tel: 982-161 587
This rustic hotel is an ideal base from which to explore the Os Ancares sierra. €€
Méndez Núñez
Raíña, 1
tel: 982-230 711
fax: 982-229 738
www.hotelmendeznunez.com
A classic 19th-century hotel in the centre of the old town, this is one of the best-value lodgings in the area. €

Ourense
Parador de Verín
Monterrei, Verín, s/n
tel: 988-410 075
fax: 988-412 017
www.parador.es
This handy stop off the Madrid road overlooks Monterrei castle, a good example of upland *gallego* architecture. €€

Pontevedra
Parador de Ponteredra
Barón, 19
tel: 986-855 800
fax: 986-852 195
www.parador.es
A traditional *pazo* or manor house converted into a Parador with fine, regionally inspired cooking, this is a comfortable and cosy refuge. €€

Santiago de Compostela
Parador Los Reyes Católicos
Plaza de Obradoiro, 1
tel: 981-582 200
fax: 981-563 094
www.parador.es
Luxury hotel near Santiago Cathedral, with lots of creature comforts. One of Europe's great historic hotels. €€€€
Hogar San Francisco
Campiño de San Francisco, 3

Price Guide

For a standard double room
€€€€ =   Over €120
€€€ =   €90–120
€€ =   €50–90
€ =   Under €50

tel: 981-572 463
fax: 981-571 916
Tucked behind the Parador los Reyes Católicos, this former convent is an historic site and a comfortable lodging.€€

Sanxenxo
Rotilio
Avda del Porto, s/n
tel: 986-720 200
fax: 986-724 188
www.hotelrotilio.com
A family hotel in a fishing village with views of the port and an excellent restaurant. €

Vigo
Bahia de Vigo
Canovas del Castillo, 24
tel: 986-226 700
fax: 986-437 487
www.hotelbahiadevigo.com
Located in the centre of the city. The hotel faces the estuary, yachting harbour, and the old town. Suites available. €€€
Ciudad de Vigo
Concepción Arenal, 5
tel: 986-227 820
fax: 986-439 871
www.ciudaddevigo.com
Well located for shops and the beach. €€€

NAVARRE
Pamplona
Iruña Palace-Los Tres Reyes
Jardines de la Taconera, s/n
tel: 948-226 600
fax: 948-222 930
A beautiful hotel. During the bull-running (6–15 July), this is an oasis of peace, but near the action. €€€€
HUSA Iruña Park
Arcadio María Larraona, 1
tel: 948-173 200
fax: 948-172 387
One of Pamplona's newest and most complete luxury hotels, the Iruña Park is lacking in tradition, but flawless. €€€
Ciudad de Pamplona
Iturrama, 21
tel: 948-266 011
fax: 948-173 626
A modern and sleek hotel near Plaza del Castillo, this is one of Pamplona's top-value places. €€
La Perla
Plaza del Castillo, 1

tel: 948-227 706
fax: 948-211 566
The oldest hotel in town and best in value for romantics. From these balconies, Hemingway witnessed his first corralling. Prices increase during San Fermín. €€

Leyre
Leyre, 7
tel: 948-228 500
fax: 948-228 318
www.hotel-leyre.com
A San Fermín favourite, with easy access to the bullring and Plaza del Castillo. €€

Maisonnave
Nueva, 20
tel: 948-222 600
fax: 948-220 166
www.hotelmaisonnave.es
Another peaceful refuge during San Fermín, quiet and comfortable. €€

Yoldi
Avda de San Ignacio, 11
tel: 948-224 800
fax: 948-212 045
www.hotelyoldi.com
A favourite of the international taurine set, this place buzzes after *corridas*. €€

Where to Eat

Eating Out

Northern Spain, and especially the Basque country, is justly proud of its culinary tradition, combining upland and coastal ingredients in roasts, sauces, vegetables, stews and soups of exquisite quality. Ask your waiter for recommendations on local food and wine and he will invariably steer you in the right direction.

The following recommended restaurants are listed in order of price category.

ARAGÓN

Huesca
Navas
Vicente Campo 3
tel: 974-212 825
Traditional dishes include brains with thyme, tuna with mountain herbs, cod with red peppers and a variety of home-made desserts. €€€€

Las Torres
María Auxiliadora, 3
tel: 974-228 213
www.lastorres-restaurante.com
Imaginative cooking, including cod with black noodles, hake *al chilindrón* (tomato-based sauce), pig's feet, and liquorice ice cream. Closed Sun and the second half of Aug. €€€

Jaca
La Cocina Aragonesa
Paseo de la Constitución 3
tel: 974-361 050
Excellent Aragonese fare in a rustic setting with a roaring fire in winter. Roasts, stews and game specialities. €€€

Zaragoza
Los Borrachos
Paseo de Sagasta, 64
tel: 976-275 036
Specialities include pâtés, fresh fish, wild boar, venison and homemade ice-cream and sorbet. Closed Sun and all of Aug. €€€

La Matilde
Predicadores, 7
tel: 976-433 443
Aragonese cuisine. Specialities include chicken in *chilindrón*, lamb and, for dessert, peaches with wine. €€

NAVARRE

Pamplona
Josetxo
Principe de Viana, 1
tel: 948-222 097
fax: 948-224 157
www.restaurantejosetxo.com
Navarrese cuisine. The restaurant's specialities are regional: Tudela artichokes and asparagus, cod, lamb *al chilindrón*, and flounder in champagne. Closed Sun, and throughout Aug. €€€

Rodero
Arrieta, 3
tel: 948-228 035
www.restauranterodero.com
Navarrese cuisine. Specialities include croquettes, mixed vegetables in the spring, and hake *a la navarra*. €€€

THE BASQUE COUNTRY
Bilbao

Gorrotxa
Alameda Urquijo, 30 (Gallery)
tel: 944-443 4937
Exquisite cuisine featuring *vieiras* (local shellfish) with mushrooms, foie gras pastry with peregourdine sauce, lobster, and excellent desserts. Closed Sun and 2 weeks between July and Sept. €€€€

Price Guide

Prices are per person for a three-course meal, excluding wine
€€€€ = more than €25
€€€ = €10–25
€€ = under €10

Guria
Gran Vía, 66
tel: 944-441 5780
www.restauranteguria.com
The home of the Codfish Wizard, although it offers many other dishes. Closed Sun. €€€€

San Sebastián
Akelarre
Paseo Padre Orcolaga, 56
Barrio Igueldo
tel: 943-311 209
www.akelarre.net
Basque cuisine, including asparagus spears in hollandaise sauce, endive salad with apples and walnuts, and sea bass with green pepper. Closed Sun evening, Mon afternoon, and first two weeks of Oct and Feb. €€€

Arzak
Alto del Miracruz, 21
tel: 943-278 465
www.arzak.info
Basque cuisine. Specialities include baby squid cooked in their ink, flounder in champagne, and exceptional vegetable dishes. Closed

Price Guide

Prices are per person for a three-course meal, excluding wine

€€€€ =   more than €25
€€€ =   €10–25
€€ =   under €10

Sun, and Mon afternoons, and during the first two weeks of June. €€€

CANTABRIA
Santander
El Molino
En Puente Arce, Ctra N-611, km 12
tel: 942-575 055
Cantabrian cuisine. Specialities include *pastel de setas* (a pastry with wild mushrooms), sea bass salad, and celery sorbet between courses. Closed Mon. €€€

Chiqui
Avda de García Lago, s/n
tel: 942-282 700
www.hotelchiqui.com
Cantabrian cuisine. Specialities include roasted brill and *tocino del cielo* (a sweet flan). €€

Gran Casino del Sardinero
Plaza de Italia, s/n
tel: 942-276 054
www.grancasinosardinero.es
International cuisine. Specialities include hake, filet mignon and apple tart. €€

ASTURIAS
Gijón
Bella Vista
Avda Garcia Bernardo, 8
tel: 985-362 936
www.bellavista-gijon.com
Known for its fish and seafood, this local favourite has its own live tank where you are welcome to select your own crustacean. €€

Casa Victor
Carmen, 11
tel: 985-350 093
www.casavictor.com
Victor Bango's original approach to traditional seafood dishes fills this place with excited diners. €€

Oviedo
Casa Fermín
San Francisco, 8
tel: 985-216 452
One of Oviedo's most famous gourmet spots, and a favourite among local food lovers. Reserve in advance. €€€

El Raitán
Plaza de Trascorrales, 6
tel: 985-214 218
Waiters in regional costume serve a lunchtime taster menu of nine traditional local dishes – a crash course in Asturian cuisine. €€

Taramundi
El Mazo
Cuesta de la Rectoral
tel: 985-646 760
Set in a restored rectory, serving good mountain cuisine and specialising in seasonal meats and game. Try the local *caldo de Taramundi* soup. €€

GALICIA
A Coruña
Casa Pardo
Novoa Santos, 15
tel: 982-207 614
www.casapardo.com
Seafood croquettes, monkfish, Galician cuisine. Closed Sun, and 15–30 June. €€€

Mesón Coral
Callejón de la Estacada, 4
tel: 981-200 569
www.galinor.es
Specialities include hake, seafood soup and *bonito* in tomato sauce. €€

Pontevedra
Casa Solla
Avda Sineiro 7
tel: 986-872 884
Galician specialities include flounder with clams. Closed Thurs, and Sun evening. €€€

Doña Antonia
Soportales de la Herrería, 4, 1st Floor
tel: 986-847 274
Galician specialities include *tosta de vieiras* (shellfish on toast). €€€

Santiago de Compostela
Casa Vilas
Rosalía de Castro, 88
tel: 981-591 000/592 170
Galician cuisine. Specialities include octopus with potatoes, lamprey in red wine, and the native *tarta de Santiago*, a moist almond cake. Closed Sun. €€€

Don Gaiferos
Rua Nova, 23
tel: 981-583 894
Galician specialities, including flounder stuffed with seafood, seafood brochette, hake in cider, *caldo gallego* (a light broth). €€€

Vigo
El Mosquito
Plaza de Villavicencio, 4
tel: 986-433 570
Specialities include flounder, roast kid and grilled meats. Closed Sun, and 15 Aug–15 Sept. €€€

Puesto Piloto Alcabre
Avda Atlántida, 98
tel: 986-241 524
www.puestopiloto.es
Galician cuisine, including *arroz de vieiras* (rice with shellfish) and *tarta de yema*, a cake made egg yolks. Closed Sun evening, and two weeks in Nov. €€€

Nightlife

A–Z of Where to Go

A Coruña The main area for *tapas* and *copeo* (drinking) is between Avenida de la Marina and Calle de la Franja from the Plaza de María Pita to Calle de la Estrella. Other streets with significant concentrations of taverns, bars and restaurants are Calle de la Galera, Calle de los Olmos and Calle de la Estrella.

Bilbao The Casco Viejo (also known as Siete Calles) is filled with taverns and *tapas* bars. Other areas known for pub crawling include Calle Licenciado Pozas, Calle Ledesma, certain sections of Alameda Mazarredo and the zone of Indautxo.

Gijón You will find the action throughout the Cimadevilla district, between (and including) the yacht harbour and the end of Playa de San Lorenzo.

Haro *La Herradura* (The Horseshoe) begins and ends at the Palacio de Beldaña at the upper left hand corner of Plaza de la Paz. This loop is thick with fine *tapas* and *bodegas*. Don't miss Bar Los Caños.

Huesca The area around the cathedral, which is in the centre of the *Casco Viejo* (the old quarter), and the section of Huesca known as *El Tubo* are the main tavern and *tapa* spots. *El Tubo* includes Calle San Lorenzo, Calle San Orencio and Calle Padre Huesca.

Jaca Jaca's *copas* (bars) and *tapas* are concentrated in the middle of the old

Shopping

The most rewarding souvenirs are in **traditional art** and **craftwork**. The many woodlands make carved objects and utensils abundant. In Galicia, Camariñas is still a centre for **lace making**, Noya for **black-banded straw hats**. Sargadelos is a centre for **black Asturian pottery**. **Wooden clogs** are still made in Carmona, Cantabria. The ubiquitous **beret** comes from Tolosa. The Basque country's specialities are **tapestries** and **white pottery**. **Woollen blankets** come from Ezcaray in Navarre. Also, every town has a morning market.

part of town, around the Town Hall and the cathedral – don't miss the Bar Fau or the famed garlic potato at La Campanilla behind the Town Hall. Plaza Ramiro I and Calle Gil Verges are filled with pubs, taverns and musical bars, as are Calle Bellido and Calle San Nicolás.

Logroño Calle Laurel, Calle Bretón de los Herreros, Plaza del Mercado and Calle Mayor in the old part of town are all excellent grazing areas in Logroño. The *tapeo* (tapa-eating) and *copeo* (bar-hopping) continue until around midnight. To find where the bright young things hang out late at night, ask for directions to La Zona, south of Gran Vía de Juan Carlos I.

Oviedo The *antiguo* is the old part of Oviedo around the cathedral and is the area of maximum nocturnal *movida* or *marcha* (action). You will find *tapas*, pubs, taverns and music bars all along Calle del Rosal, Calle Pérez de la Sala and Calle Martínez Gil.

Pamplona The busiest parts of Pamplona at night are around the central Plaza del Castillo and along the length of Calle San Nicolás.

San Sebastián The best wandering cocktail party is in the Parte Vieja, around the Plaza de la Constitución, between the fishing port and the mouth of the River Urumea. The port itself has excellent little taverns serving very fresh sardines. Along La Concha, there are music bars and discos, and around the Amara Viejo FEVE (narrow-gauge) railway station are some good *tapas* bars.

Santander Plaza Cañadío, the Paseo de Pereda and the streets just back from the waterfront are all well stocked with taverns, *bodegas*, bars, cafés and restaurants of all kinds. Calle Hernán Cortés, Calle Daoíz y Velarde and the streets just in from Puerto Chico all house a lively succession of bars and bistros.

Santiago de Compostela The prime streets for wine and *tapas* are Calle del Franco and Calle A Raíña, while pubs and music bars are found behind Plaza de la Quintana in the San Paio de Antealtares district.

Vigo The main bar and *tapas* area is right in the centre of town. Calle Real, Calle Churruca and Calle Rosalía de Castro are all filled with lively bars.

Calendar of Events

January
19–20January, groups of uniformed drummers parade through the streets of San Sebastián in honour of the city's patron.

February/March
The Carnival festival marking the start of Lent is celebrated all over the region, most famously at Laza, in the province of Ourense, Galicia; and in the town of Lanz in Navarre.

Easter Week
All over Spain there are processions with floats depicting biblical scenes. In San Vicente de la Sonsierra, in La Rioja, the barefoot, hooded *picaos* whip their own backs as they walk in procession.

May
Santo Domingo de la Calzada, in La Rioja, commemorates the miracles performed by its patron, St Dominic, with a series of processions ending on 12 May.

There are many religious rites around Whitsun and Corpus Christi. On the Sunday between them, the men of Lumbier, in Navarre, dress from head to foot in black and go in pilgrimage to a nearby chapel carrying crosses.

In Pontéareas, near Vigo, Galicia, the townspeople create elaborate carpets with flower petals in the path of the Corpus Christi procession.

June
Haro, the wine capital of La Rioja Alta, declares its Wine Battle on the day of St Peter (San Pedro), 29 June. In this messy free-for-all, thousands of people soak each other with red wine.

Irún, on the French border, mobilises its men on the last day of June to commemorate the Basques' defeat of an invading French army in 1522.

July
Throughout the summer, villagers in several parts of Galicia round up herds of wild horses so that their manes and tails can be cut. The biggest is at San Lourenzo de Sabucedo near A Estrada, in Pontevedra province, at the beginning of July.

The famous running of the bulls spectacular, *Los San Fermínes*, takes place in Pamplona/Iruña in the second week of the month *(see page 302)*.

St James' Day (25 July) is the biggest celebration of the year in Santiago de Compostela.

At the Pilgrimage of the Coffins at Ribarteme (near As Neves in Pontevedra province) on 29 July, those who have narrowly escaped death in the course of the previous year are carried in open coffins in procession.

August
Jaca, in Aragón, stages the Pyrenees Folklore Festival every other year in late July or early August. In the intervening years it takes place on the French side of the mountains.

The first Sunday in August is Asturias Day, the major festival in Gijón, celebrated with a procession of floats and groups in folk costume, and with folk dances.

All three major Basque cities hold their biggest fiestas in August: Vitoria has the fiesta of the White Virgin (the city's patron) from the 4th, while both Bilbao and San Sebastián celebrate their respective "Great Week" around 15 August.

Betanzos (in the province of A Coruña in Galicia) celebrates its two main fiestas in quick succession, beginning on 14 August with San Roque (St Roch), when a giant paper balloon is released in the main square. A few days later, there is a pilgrimage on garlanded boats up the River Mandeo for a picnic in the countryside.

September
The patroness of Asturias, Nuestra Señora de Covadonga, is fêted at her chapel near Cangas de Onis in the Picos de Europa National Park on 8 September. On the same day, Galicians congregate at their principal shrine, San Andrés de Teixido, in the Rías Altas.

The various wine regions of Northern Spain celebrate the grape harvest in August or September. One of the biggest celebrations is in Logroño, capital of La Rioja, on 21 September

November
1 November is All Saints' Day, on which people take flowers to cemeteries to remember their dead. On 11 November, several towns in Galicia, including Santiago de Compostela, celebrate Os Magostos, a fiesta in honour of the sweet chestnut, thousands of which are roasted on bonfires.

Sport

Football

First division football matches are a Sunday afternoon ritual across Northern Spain – matches are usually played in Santiago de Compostela, A Coruña, Santander, Bilbao, San Sebastián, Logroño and Pamplona. Check with the tourist office for dates and ticket information.

Jai-Alai

For jai-alai matches in Bilbao, try the Club Deportivo de Bilbao, Alameda Rekalde 28, tel: 944-231 108. In San Sebastián, *cesta punta* is played at Galarreta (on the Hernani road south of town). In Pamplona, try Euskal Jai Berri in Huarte, 10 km (6 miles) west of Pamplona, tel: 948-331 160.

Local Sports

Ox-pulling, scything, stone-lifting and many other rural sporting events are held during the fiestas in the Basque Country. Bilbao's mid-August *Semana Grande* has Basque sports and *trainera* (whale boat) racing in the Nervión. The whale boat races in San Sebastián draw the province of Guipúzcoa to the beach in mid-September. July in Oviedo is when cider-pouring contests are held, with contestants judged by the amount of cider they spill.

Horse Racing

San Sebastián's racetrack at Zubieta, Paseo del Hipódromo s/n, Zubieta, tel: 943 373 087, has meetings between June and September.

Canary Islands

Getting Acquainted

The Canary Islands form an archipelago made up of seven major islands – Tenerife, Gran Canaria, Fuerteventura, Lanzarote, La Palma, La Gomera and El Hierro – plus several small islets, set in the Atlantic Ocean to the west of Morocco. They are an autonomous region of Spain and the status of capital is shared between Tenerife and Gran Canaria, rotating every four years. The main islands are:

Tenerife, the largest island, with a population of 700,000. Its topography is varied, with an impressive mountain range. The volcanic El Teide, at 3,718 metres (12,197 ft), is the highest mountain in Spain. The capital is Santa Cruz de Tenerife.

Fuerteventura is the second largest island but has a population of only 52,000. The capital is Puerto de Rosario.

Gran Canaria is the third largest in size, but has the greatest population, 760,000. Terrain ranges from mountains, ravines and cliffs to sand dunes and subtropical forests. The highest point is Pico de las Nieves at 1,949 metres (6,395 ft). The capital is Las Palmas.

Lanzarote is a largely arid island with a population of 86,000. The capital is Arrecife.

Climate

The islands enjoy a sunny subtropical climate with mild temperatures all year round. Daytime temperatures range

What's On

For the latest information on what's on where, buy a copy of the weekly *La Guia* or pick up *The Island Sun, Canarian Weekly, Island Connections* or *The Paper*. They are very parochial publications but there are nuggets of genuinely valuable information. They tend to target Tenerife and the southern resorts of Gran Canaria.

from 21°C (70°F) in January to 26°C (79°F) in August. There are some wet days in winter, particularly on north-facing coasts and in the mountains on Tenerife, La Palma and Gran Canaria. Fuerteventura and Lanzarote are drier.

Getting There

The Canary Island archipelago is situated 96 km (60 miles) off the African coast. Cádiz, the nearest point on the Spanish peninsula, is around 1,100 km (680 miles) away.

BY AIR

The archipelago is served by the main airlines; direct flights from Madrid take about two hours. Most flights go to Las Palmas, Gran Canaria or Reina Sofía, Tenerife. Most visitors arrive on one of the many charter flights from Europe. Many deals exist, so shop around.

BY SEA

Trasmediterránea (tel: 902-454 645) runs several services a week between mainland Spain (Cádiz) and Gran Canaria, Lanzarote and Tenerife.

Getting Around

BY AIR

A number of airlines operate flights between the islands. Binter Canarias, tel: 902–400 500, a subsidiary of Iberia, has the most flights; others are Air Europa, tel: 902-401 501; Spanair, tel: 902–131 415; NAYSA, tel: 928-137 408, fax: 928- 579 196; and Atlantic Airways, tel: 928-341 000, reservations tel: 928–786 531.

BY ROAD

Car Hire

All the big international companies have offices at the airports and in the major cities and there are numerous local companies, although generally they are local to each island. CICAR (Canary Islands Car), tel: 928-822 900; www.cicar.com, is the only firm to have offices on each island and a ready availability of automatic cars.

Always carry your driving licence with you. Speed limits are 120 km/h (74 mph) on motorways, 100 km/h (62 mph) on dual carriageways, and 50 km/h (31 mph) in built-up areas.

Roads vary from a six-lane highway (in Santa Cruz de Tenerife) to primitive tracks in some rural areas. In every main city, and even in smaller provincial towns, traffic is often heavy and one-way systems confusing.

Calendar of Events

5 January: Epifanía del Señor, Parade of the Three Kings in Santa Cruz de Tenerife and Las Palmas de Gran Canaria.

February: The popular and colourful carnivals of Santa Cruz de Tenerife and Las Palmas de Gran Canaria.

May: Santa Cruz festivities in Tenerife, including the celebration of the founding of the capital on 3 May.

20 May: The *Romería* or Pilgrimage of San Isidro the Farmer in Los Realejos (Tenerife).

June: Corpus Christi Day. Flower carpets are woven along the streets in La Orotava (Tenerife), Villa de Mazo (La Palma) and other towns. Processions in Las Palmas de Gran Canaria and La Laguna (Tenerife).

June: Octava de Corpus. Held eight days after Corpus Christi Day in La Orotava on Tenerife, including a pilgrimage to the San Isidro Sanctuary.

25 July: Fiesta of Santiago Apóstol (St James' Day) celebrated throughout Tenerife. Santa Cruz de Tenerife commemorates the heroic defence of the city against Lord Nelson's naval attack.

26 July: Nuestra Señora del Carmen celebrated in ports throughout the Canaries.

4 August: *Bajada de la Rama in Agaete*, Gran Canaria.

16 August: San Roque pilgrimage in the town of Garachico (Tenerife).

25 August: San Ginés fiestas celebrated in Arrecife (Lanzarote).

17 September: Fiestas of Special Touristic Interest in honour of Cristo del Calvario in Icod de los Vinos (Tenerife).

October (second Sat): Pilgrimage of Nuestra Señora de la Luz in Las Palmas de Gran Canaria including a procession of boats.

Buses

Bus services within the large towns run often and are fast and cheap, with tickets purchased on board and change given. Bus services around the islands vary in frequency and scope.

Taxis

The letters SP *(servicio público)* on the front and rear bumpers of a car indicate that it is a taxi. It might also have a green light in the front windscreen or a green sign indicating "libre" when it is available. Taxis are unmetered in tourist areas. There are fixed prices displayed on a board at the main taxi ranks, giving the fares to the most popular destinations. These are usually

reasonable. If in doubt, ask the driver before you set off.

BY SEA

There are numerous ferry services between the islands (and even the Spanish mainland). The main operators are Líneas Fred Olsen, www.fredolsen.es; Trasmediterránea, www.trasmediterranea.es; Naviera Armas, tel: 928-227 282; and Trasarmas, tel: 922-534 050.

Tourist Offices

Gran Canaria: Leon y Castillo, 17, Las Palmas, tel: 928-681 336.

Tenerife: Plaza de España s/n, Santa Cruz, tel: 922-239 592.

Lanzarote: Parque Municipal, Arrecife, tel: 928-811 860.

Fuerteventura: Avda Constitución, 5, Puerto del Rosario, tel: 928-530 844.

La Palma: O'Daly, 23, Santa Cruz de la Palma, tel: 922-413 141.

La Gomera: Real, 1, San Sebastián, tel: 922-141 512/870 281; fax: 922-140 151.

El Hierro: Licenciado Bueno, 1, Valverde, tel: 922-550 302.

Media

Television and Radio

Most hotels have satellite TV with several stations in many languages. The larger islands all include some English-language news and tourist information in their programming. Local radio stations broadcasting in English include Waves FM 96.8.

Newspapers and Magazines

Major British and Continental newspapers are on sale in the Canaries the day after publication. English-language publications with the free *Holiday Gazette & Tourist Guide* (monthly), and the *Island Sun* (every fortnight), carry what's on listings.

Medical Services

Almost all doctors in the tourist centres speak English. Chemists *(farmácias)* open Mon–Fri 9am–1pm and 4–8pm, Sat 9am–1pm, and have a green cross on the sign outside. The smaller villages usually have a first-aid station run by the Red Cross (Cruz Roja). In the larger towns there will always be at least one chemist open at night.

Gran Canaria Hospitals

The Inter Clinic, Calle Sagasta 62, Las Palmas, tel: 928-278 826), specialises in treating foreign nationals with medical travel insurance. Public hospitals in Las Palmas include

Residencia Sanitaria Nuestra Señora del Pino in the Calle Ingel Guimerá, tel: 928-441 192; the Hospital Insular, in Plaza Dr Pasteur, tel: 928-444 000; or the Clínica de Urgencias, León y Castillo 407, tel: 928-263 208.

In the south, the Scandinavian Clinic, Avda Gran Canaria 30, Playa del Inglés, tel: 928-771 538, has a good reputation. There is also the Clínica Rosa, Buganvillas 1, Playa de San Agustín, tel: 928-769 004.

Tenerife Hospitals

Private hospitals accepting medical insurance and running freephone 24-hour emergency service are Hospiten Rambla, Santa Cruz (tel: 922-291 600, fax: 922-291 088), Hospiten Norte, Puerta de la Cruz (tel: 900-200 145) and Hospiten Sur, Playa de las Américas (tel: 922-750 022, fax: 922-793 618).

Security and Crime

Around the tourist centers there are incidents of bag-snatching and theft. Do not court trouble and only carry your passport and other papers around when absolutely necessary, eg. when changing money. In Las Palmas, the area beyond and behind the Sansofé hotel is not particularly safe at night but is perfectly easy to avoid. Be extra careful with bags, wallets and cameras in busy areas, such as markets.

The majority of hotels and apartments have security boxes and it is advisable to use them at all times. Never leave valuables in your car unattended.

Where to Stay

Hotels

Hotels are listed in order of price category.

FUERTEVENTURA

Atlantis Palace
Avda Grandes Playas, Corralejo,
tel: 928-536 050
fax: 928-535 367
www.atlantishotel.com
Luxurious and centrally located for the beach. Palatial reception, large sound-proofed rooms, fitness centre and swimming pools. €€€

Riu Fuerteventura Playa
Urb. Cánada del Río, Polígono C 1
Costa Calma
tel: 928-547 344
fax: 928-541 097
www.sunandbeachhotels.com
Tennis courts, swimming pools, events programme, live music and shows – you name it. €€

Pension Tamasite
Calle León y Castillo, 9
Puerto del Rosario
tel: 928-850 280/850 300
Small hotel near the harbour. €

EL HIERRO

Parador del Hierro
Las Playas 26, Valverde
tel: 922-558 036
fax: 922-558 086
www.parador.es
Low-rise hotel with pool and gardens on seafront by lonely cliffs. Rustic decor and a comfortable, friendly atmosphere. €€

Boomerang
Dr Gost 1. Valverde
Tel/fax: 922-550 200
This simple but sprucely kept place on a quiet side-street in the town centre makes a convenient touring base. Bedrooms are clean and spacious. €

Price Guide

For a standard double room
€€€ = Over €120
€€ = €60–120
€ = Under €60

Hotel Ida Ines
Camino del Hoya, Belgara Alta,
Frontera.
Tel: 922-559 445
Fax: 922-556 088
www.hotelitoidaines.com
Attractive little hotel with modern facilities and small rooftop swimming pool. Magnificent views, interesting walks, very peaceful. €

GRAN CANARIA
Las Palmas

Meliá Las Palmas
Gomera, 6
tel: 928-267 600
fax: 928-268 411
www.solmelia.com
Facing Las Canteras, this 316-room hotel has a pool, cocktail bar, restaurants, discotheque El Coto, convention halls and a secure parking facility. €€€

Sansofé Palace
Portugal, 68
tel: 928-224 062
fax: 928-270 784
Located on the beach front, with bar, restaurant and 110 rooms. €€

Madrid
Plazoleta de Cairasco, 4
tel: 928-360 664
fax: 928-382 176
A Las Palmas institution. The wood-panelling and atmosphere make up for the antiquated plumbing. €

Maspalomas/Playa del Inglés

Ifa-Faro Maspalomas
Plaza del Faro, 1
tel: 928-142 214/142 342
fax: 928-141 940
Open-plan hotel with convention hall, restaurant, bar, nightclub and pool; 188 rooms. €€€

Maspalomas Oasis
Plaza de Maspalomas,
tel: 928-760 170/141 448
fax: 928-141 192
Elegant hotel set in secluded subtropical gardens with pools and tennis courts, a short distance from the magnificent dunes. Famed for its cuisine and nightly live music. €€€

Parque Tropical
Avda de Italia, 1, Playa del Inglés,
tel: 928-760 712
fax: 928-768 137
www.hotelparquetropical.com
Attractive hotel in traditional Canarian style with pagoda entrance and water gardens. Direct access to the beach. €€€

Puerto de Mogán

Club de Mar
Urb. Puerto de Mogán
tel: 928-565 066
fax: 928-565 438
Right on the quayside, with apartments as well as rooms. €€€€

LA GOMERA

Hotel Jardín Tecina
Playa de Santiago
tel: 922-145 850
fax: 922-145 851
www.jardin-tecina.com
Overlooking a little fishing port, this luxury hotel has three pools, live entertainment, and welcomes children. €€€

Parador de la Gomera
San Sebastián
tel: 922-871 100
fax: 922-871 116
www.parador.es
Cliff-top country house hotel with gorgeous views and gardens. €€€

Hotel Gran Rey
Valle Gran Rey
tel: 922-805 859
fax: 922-805 651
www.hotel-granrey.com
Right by the sea; rooms with balconies. Good restaurant. €€

LA PALMA

Parador de la Palma
El Zumacal, Brena Baja
tel: 922-435 828
fax: 922-435 999
www.parador.es
In a good coastal location, this Parador is in traditional Canarian style with a pool surrounded by gardens. €€€

La Palma Romántica
Topo de las Llanadas, Barlovento
tel: 922-186 221
fax: 922-185 400
www.hotellapalmaromantica.com
On the northern tip of the island, this peaceful hotel has a gym, small astronomical observatory, and an indoor pool (it's chillier here than further south). €€

LANZAROTE
Arrecife

Lancelot
Avda Mancomunidad, 9
tel/fax: 928-805 099
Attractive seafront hotel opposite a sandy beach and coral reefs. All rooms have sea views. €€

Puerto del Carmen

Los Fariones
Roque del Este, 1, Playa Blanca,
tel: 928-510 175
fax: 928-510 202
On the beach with subtropical gardens, facilities and a traditional feel. €€€

La Penita
Chalana, 2
tel: 928-514 262
fax: 928-514 263
www.apartamentoslapenita.com
First resort complex in Puerto del Carmen. Central location. €

TENERIFE

Santa Cruz

Mencey
Dr José Naveiras, 38
tel: 922-609 900
fax: 922-280 017
www.sheraton.com
Deluxe hotel on central but tranquil
tree-lined boulevard. First-class food
and helpful staff. Pool, tennis, and
gardens. €€€

Contemporaneo
Rambla General Franco, 116
tel: 902-120 329
fax: 922-271 223
www.hotelcontemporaneo.com
Modern hotel geared to business
travellers, with a bright bar-cafe and
restaurant. €€

Puerto de la Cruz

Meliá Botánico
Richard J. Yeoward, s/n
tel: 922-381 500
fax: 922-381 504
www.hotelbotanico.com
Luxury rooms near the Botanical
Gardens with magnificent views of El
Teide. Quiet, exclusive atmosphere and
Olympic-sized swimming pool. €€€

Marquesa
Quintana, 11
tel: 922-383 151
fax: 922-386 950
www.hotelmarquesa.com
Carefully refurbished 18th-century building;
courteous service and an outside terrace
where you can eat by candlelight. €€

Monopol
Quintana, 15
tel: 922-384 611
fax: 922-370 310
www.monpoltf.com
Beautiful Canarian mansion in the
heart of the old quarter, with a plant-
filled atrium and wooden balconies. €€

El Teide National Park

Parador Cañadas del Teide
Las Cañadas del Teide
tel: 922-386 415
fax: 922-382 352
www.parador.es
Spectacularly located in the National Park
overlooking strange rock formations.
Good Canarian restaurant with log fire;
self-service café and visitor centre. €€€

Playa de las Américas

Hotel La Siesta
Avda del Litoral, s/n
tel: 922-792 252
fax: 922-792 220
www.lasiesta-hotel.com
Rooms are air-conditioned and have
spacious terraces. Friendly staff, three
pools and an easy walk to beach. €€

Where to Eat

Eating Out

Local cooking features a lot of fish and
seafood, although Canarian specialities
are *papas arrugadas* (salty potatoes
boiled in their skins), spicy *mojo* sauce,
conejo salmorejo (rabbit marinaded in
oil and herbs), *sancocho* (fish and
vegetable stew), and *puchero canario*
(hotpot).

The influx of tourists has provided
business for the many international
restaurants that have opened in all the
major cities.

Restaurants are listed in order of
price category.

GRAN CANARIA

Las Palmas

El Cerdo que Rie (The Laughing Pig)
Paseo de Las Canteras 31 (no
telephone number – it's too popular for
phone reservations). Large but cosy
basement restaurant. Flambée and
fondue specialities. Open daily
1.30pm–midnight, closed all July. €€

El Herreño
Mendizábel 5
tel: 928-310 513
Pure Canarian cooking, specialising in
gofio (roasted maize meal). Closed
Sun. €€

El Pescador
Marina 8
tel: 928-223 068/432 924
fax: 986-441 484
www.o-pescador.com
Fresh fish and seafood in attractive
surroundings; good mix of business
people, locals and tourists.
Open daily. €

Outside Las Palmas

Tenderete II
Edificio Aloe, Avda de Tirajana, 3
Playa del Inglés
tel: 928-761 460
Attractive place – the walls are
decorated with farm implements.
Try fish baked in salt, *sancocho*,
papas with *mojo* sauce, and island
wines. Open daily, booking essential.
€€€

El Barranco
Riera del Carmen 2,
Puerto de Mogán

Price Guide

Prices are per person for a three-
course meal, not including wine
€€€ =   more than €25
€€ =   €10–25
€ =   under €10

An international menu, well cooked and
good value. Open for lunch and dinner.
Closed Mon. €€

Mesón La Silla
Artenara
Set on a mountain ledge, this is one of
the most spectacularly sited
restaurants in the Canaries. There's a
sun-trap terrace and kitchens in the
caves. Open daily until sunset. €

TENERIFE

Café del Príncipe
Plaza del Príncipe, Santa Cruz
Typical Canary Island cuisine. Closed
Mon and Easter week. €€

Casa de Miranda
Plaza de Europa, Puerto de la Cruz
tel: 922-373 871
Housed in one of Puerto's finest old
mansions is an elegant restaurant and
a rustic *tapas* bar both serving
excellent food. €€

La Posada
Mendéz Nuñez 61, Santa Cruz
tel: 922-246 772
www.laposada.net
Tuna and *solomillo al cabrales* (fillet
steak with cheese sauce) are among
the specialities. €€

Mama Rosa
Apartamentos Colón II
Playa de las Américas
tel: 922-794 819
A smart place with an international
menu, good vegetarian options, and a
large wine list. Reservations
recommended. €€

Nightlife

Bars stay open until early morning; the shorts are triple the British size and it's best to take a siesta in the afternoon and to eat before an outing. Prices are lowest in small Spanish bars.

The throbbing hearts of Tenerife nightlife are in Puerto de la Cruz in the north and Playa de las Américas in the south, although Santa Cruz can attract party animals too, especially in summer when the Carpas de Verano – open-air discos – are worth a visit.

Shopping

The most rewarding souvenirs are in **traditional art** and **craftwork**. The many woodlands make carved objects and utensils abundant. In Galicia, Camariñas is still a centre for **lace making**, Noya for **black-banded straw hats**. Sargadelos is a centre for **black Asturian pottery**. **Wooden clogs** are still made in Carmona, Cantabria. The ubiquitous **beret** comes from Tolosa. The Basque country's specialities are **tapestries** and **white pottery**. **Woollen blankets** come from Ezcaray in Navarre. Also, every town has a morning market. €0.10–0.20 per person.

Finding a favourite bar in Las Palmas demands a great dedication to drinking. Parque Santa Catalina is really one giant bar from one end to the other. Playa de Las Canteras is a 3-km (2-mile) promenade of bars. It's really a matter of choosing the ambience and company you enjoy. Clubs and discos are many and varied in all resort areas, especially in Playa del Inglés, Gran Canaria. The entry fee usually includes the first drink; women are often admitted free.

In Lanzarote there is plenty of nightlife in Puerto del Carmen and to a lesser extent in Playa Blanca and Costa Teguise.

Sport

The Canaries have plenty to offer in the way of sports and outdoor activities. **Golf** is very much on the increase, and is popular with both Canarians and visitors. Tenerife and Gran Canaria each have three courses of championship standard.

Windsurfing is popular on all the islands. Equipment can be hired by the hour or day. All along the south coast of Gran Canaria there are training schools, monitors and equipment for hire: at Bahía Feliz, Playa del Inglés, Melaneras, Patalavaca and Puerto Rico. Tenerife's main spot is Playa de la Médano. The best months for **surfing** are normally January and February. **Jet-skiing** and **water-skiing** are possible in the resorts.

Deep-sea fishing excursions are made from Puerto Colón and Puerto los Cristianos in Tenerife, Muelle Santa Catalina (Las Palmas) and in Puerto Rico, Gran Canaria; enquire at any travel agency.

The waters around the islands are pleasantly warm for **scuba diving** and the archipelago has interesting volcanic rock formations with coral reefs, wrecks and much marine life.

The islands of La Gomera, La Palma and El Hierro have some excellent **walking** regions, with a limited amount of diving and fishing.

Other popular activities include **horse-riding**, **parachuting**, **hang-gliding** and **mountain biking**. There are **whale-watching trips** from most of the islands.

Balearic Islands

Getting Acquainted

The Balearic archipelago, located between the mainland of Spain and the North African coast, consists of the principal islands of Mallorca, Menorca, Eivissa (Ibiza) and Formentera, with surrounding and outlying smaller islands.

The islands, which have autonomous status, have a population of some 800,000, in a combined area of 5,000 sq km (1,930 sq miles).

Formentera: With a pop. of 5,900, covers 82 sq km (31 sq miles), receives 15,000 visitors annually.

Eivissa: With a total of over 70,000 residents (about 5,000 are foreigners) and an area of 572 sq. km (220 sq miles), receives over 1 million visitors every year.

Menorca: With 65,000 residents and 699 sq km (270 sq miles), gets visited annually by some 600,000 people.

Mallorca: With some 628,000 residents and a surface 3,640 sq. km (of 1,405 sq. miles), receives over 6,000,000 visitors every year.

In total, the Balearics receive around 8 million visitors annually.

Climate

The three main islands enjoy similar weather conditions, with local variations caused by phenomena such as Mallorca's mountain ranges. The average afternoon temperature varies between 14°C (57°F) in January and 29°C (84°F) in July. Summer is almost invariably dry and sunny. From September to May there are occasional wet days, but it is mostly sunny.

Getting There

BY AIR

There is a wide range of cheap flights from various airports in the UK and around Europe direct to Mallorca and, to a lesser extent, Eivissa and Menorca. Scheduled services also operate from several Spanish mainland cities.

BY SEA

The Balearic Islands are connected to mainland Spain by regular ferry and hydrofoil services from Barcelona and Valencia. Visitors to Formentera, must make their connections from Eivissa. Ferries also operate from Alicante and Denia to Eivissa and Formentera. The main service operator is Trasmediterránea, tel: 902-454 645.

Getting Around

BY SEA

There are inter-island ferries, and a fast hydrofoil (2 hours) runs between Palma and Eivissa.

BY RAIL

Mallorca has two railway lines, both starting at the adjoining Plaça Espanya stations in Palma. The privately owned Sóller railway (tel: 902-364 711, www.sollernet.com) makes five trips a day along the scenic narrow-gauge route between Palma and Sóller, from where an old tram trundles 2 km to the port. The state-run Tren de Isca connects Palma with Inca 20 times a day.

BY ROAD

The islands have a good road network. Always have your driving licence and passport with you when driving. Highway police levy fines on the spot for non-use of seat belts.

Car Hire

All the major international car rental companies have offices at the airports; it's well worth comparing prices; the best rates may be obtained by pre-booking on the internet.

Tourist Offices

MALLORCA

Palma Municipal Tourist Offices are located at Santo Domingo, 11, tel: 902-102 365/902-102 365, fax: 971 225 966, www.majorca-mallorca.co.uk and just off the Plaça Espanya (next to the railway station), tel: 971-754 329.
Consell de Mallorca (for the whole island): airport arrivals building, tel: 971-789 556; Plaça de la Reina 2, tel: 971-712 216, www.conselldemallorca.net . Most towns and resorts have tourist offices, although many of them are closed in winter.

MENORCA

Consell de Menorca, airport arrivals building, tel: 971-157 115; Plaza

Esplanada, 40, Maó, tel: 971-356 050. The Municipal Tourist Office is at Carrer Sa Rovellada de Dalt 24, Maó, tel: 971-363 790.
Ciutadella Tourist Information, Plaça de la Catedral, 3, tel: 971-382 693

EIVISSA (IBIZA)

Eivissa Tourist Information, Vara de Rey 3, tel: 971-301 900, Eivissa.
Municipality of San Antoni, Passeig de ses Fonts, San Antoni, tel: 971-340 111.
Santa Eulàlia Tourist Information, Marià Riquer Wallis, Santa Eulàlia, tel: 971-301 900.

FORMENTERA

Formentera Tourist Information at the ferry terminal, Port de la Savina, tel: 971-322 057. If you have difficulty, try calling the Govern Balear in Palma for information.

Business Hours

The islands traditionally observe the noon-time siesta, with businesses and shops generally open from 9am–1pm, and 4 or 5pm–8pm. Some close on Sat afternoon. Banks and post offices are usually open Mon–Fri 9am–2pm. The main post office in Palma also opens in the afternoon and on Sat from 9am–1pm. In certain sectors these traditional hours are changing. For example the big department stores such as El Corte Inglés, and the out-of-town hypermarkets generally open all day, from 10am–9pm, but close on Sun. In main tourist resorts many stores stay open all day in summer, until about 9pm.

Media

Newspapers

There are several Spanish-language newspapers published in the islands. Some of these are the *Diario de Ibiza*, *Diario de Mallorca*, *Última Hora*, and *Diario Insular de Menorca*. The listings magazine *del Ocio*, available at newsstands, is a useful source of information on What's On as well as information on restaurants.

English-speakers in Mallorca have the *Majorca Daily Bulletin*, otherwise known as the *Daily Bee*. World news sometimes appears a day late as it

Useful Numbers

Trasmediterránea (ferries)
tel: 902-454 645
Palma de Mallorca airport,
tel: 971-789 000.

Emergencies

The **general emergency number** is 112.

The emergency number for local **police** (Policia Municipal) is 092. For the National Police dial 091.

For the **Fire Service** *(bomberos)* in Palma dial 080, elsewhere 085.

Ambulances are operated by the Spanish Red Cross as well as by private operators.
General number: 061
Palma, tel: 971-202 222.
Eivissa, tel: 971-390 303.
Maó, tel: 971-361 200.
Ciutadella, tel: 971-381 993.

All the emergency numbers are found in the first few (green) pages of the telephone directory.

often needs to be translated from the Spanish parent-paper *Última Hora*. There is also a weekly newspaper called *The Reader*.

Radio

Radio stations are varied in both quality and content, and more than one of the Spanish stations broadcasts continuous music. In Eivissa, two local stations carry about one hour a day of English broadcasting, one being on Radio Popular on FM 89.1.

BBC World Service reception is good in most places on the islands.

Medical Services

All major tourist centres on the islands have *centros medicos*, where minor problems can be dealt with promptly; they usually require immediate payment (roughly €50/£30 a consultation). Hotel receptionists will help organise medical care in case of illness, too. The local Red Cross *(Creu Roja)* will take care of minor knock injuries free of charge.

The Clínica Femenía, tel: 971-452 323, is the hospital used by most foreigners in Mallorca.

Chemists *(farmácias)* are open during normal shopping hours, but in Palma and larger resorts there will be a 24-hour rota chemist. In Palma, the Farmácia March on Carrer Joan Miró, to the west of the city (opposite McDonald's) is open 24 hours a day.

Security and Crime

Petty theft is a bit of a problem in the Balearics. The usual rules apply – never leave valuables in your car, don't carry more money than you need, don't wear expensive jewellery and leave your passport or identity card at your hotel.

Where to Stay

Hotels

Hotels are listed in order of price category.

MALLORCA

Palma

Hotel Palacio Ca Sa Galesa
Miramar, 8
tel: 971-715 400
fax: 971-721 579
www.palaciocasagalesa.com
In a grand 17th-century palace, this tiny hotel – the only one in Palma's old quarter – has an indoor pool, Jacuzzi and sauna. Wheelchair access. €€€€

Hotel Palau Sa Font
Carrer Apuntadores 38
tel: 971-712 277
fax: 971-712 618
www.palausafont.com
Designer chic in a 16th-century building. Business meeting facilities. €€€€

Saratoga
Passeig de Mallorca, 6
tel: 971-727 240
Great location close to the heart of the city, with spacious rooms and comprehensive facilities. €€€€

Costa Azul
Passeig Marítim, 7
tel: 971-731 940
Listed as an old favourite with families and business travellers over the years. Right on the harbour front. €€€

Hotel Born
Carrer Sant Jaume, 3
tel: 971-712 942
fax: 971-718 618
www.hotelborn.com
In a restored 16th-century palace, in the heart of the city, with a beautiful courtyard under Romanesque arches. Very good value for money. Reserve well in advance. €€€

Price Guide

For a standard double room
€€€€€ =   Over €180
€€€€ =   Over €120
€€€ =   €90–120
€€ =   €60–90
€ =   Under €60

San Lorenzo
San Lorenzo, 14
tel: 971-728 200
fax: 971-711 901
www.hotelsanlorenzo.com
In a 17th-century house in a lively section of town. Just six rooms, all individually decorated. Small swimming pool. Book well in advance. €€

Apuntadores
Carrer Apuntadors 8
tel: 971-713 491
Cheerful, English-owned hostal with downstairs café in the busy restaurant quarter. Some shared bathrooms. €

Outside Palma

Hotel Formentor
Playa de Formentor
tel: 971-899 101
fax: 971-865 155
www.hotelformentor.net
Overlooking the beach, this peaceful, traditional hotel is family-run and exclusive. Surrounded by pine trees and gardens. €€€€€

L'Hermitage
Carretera de Alaró a Bunyola
tel: 971-180 303
In a converted 17th-century mansion a few kilometers east of the village of Orient, this fine hotel is set at the foot of the mountains in a beautiful valley. Excellent restaurant and marvellous exotic gardens. Closed Dec–Jan. €€€€€

Bon Sol
Passeig de Illetes, 30, Illetes
tel: 971-402 111
fax: 971-402 559
www.ila-chateau.com
Beautiful location surrounded by a subtropical garden, this well-run hotel is handy for Palma yet supremely relaxing. €€€€

Es Molí
Carretera Valldemossa, Deià
tel: 971-639 000
fax: 971-639 333
www.esmoli.com
Traditional luxury hotel, in a manor house surrounded by lush vegetation and with a spring-fed pool. €€€€

Mar i Vent
Carrer Major, 49, Banyalbufar
tel: 971-618 000
fax: 971-618 201
www.hotelmarivent.com
Attractive hotel with sea views and a rooftop pool. Closed Dec–Jan. €€€

MENORCA

Maó

Port Mahon Hotel
Avda Fort de l'Eau, 13
tel: 971-362 600
fax: 971-351 050
The Port Mahon overlooks the fjord-like port, once the Mediterranean base for

Nelson's Royal Navy. It makes a quiet base for a business or holiday visit. €€€–€€€€

Hotel del Almirante
Carretera de Villa Carlos, near Maó
tel: 971-362 700
fax: 971-362 704
www.hoteldelalmirante.com
Attractive conversion of British Admiral Collingwood's home, with views of Maó harbour. A hacienda-style hotel set around a pool. Closed Nov–Apr. €€–€€€

Ciutadella

Sant Ignasi
Carretera Cala Morell
tel: 971-385 575
fax: 971-480 529
www.santignasi.com
Eighteenth-century *finca* on the outskirts of Ciutadella, surrounded by palm trees. Quiet luxury. Ground floor rooms have gardens. €€€€

Fornells

Hostal Fornells
Carrer Major 17
tel: 971-376 676
fax: 971-376 688
www.hostalfornells.com
A modern and friendly small hotel in this attractive port, advertised as a "health eco resort" offering sports activities from diving, windsurfing, water skiing and golf to exercise and nutrition programmes. Small pool. Closed mid-Oct–Apr. €€

EIVISSA (IBIZA)

Although there are city-centre hotels in Eivissa the noise level is high. As distances around the island are relatively short, it is best to stay outside and make trips into town for shopping or nightlife.

Pikes Hotel
Camino Sa Vorera, km 12
San Antonio
tel: 971-342 222
fax: 971-342 312
www.pikeshotel.com
Owned and run by Australian yachtsman Tony Pikes, this idiosyncratic hotel provides a relaxing retreat popular with the jet set. Set in a restored farmhouse, there is a pool and garden, and a good restaurant. €€€€

Palmyra
Dr Fleming
tel: 971-332 551
fax: 971-312 964
Handsome, modern hotel with attractive palm-shaded terrace, about 1 km (½ mile) from the town centre. €€€

Ca's Català
Calle del Sol, Santa Eulàlia
tel: 971-331 006
www.cascatala.com

Nicely furnished single and double rooms, a pool and garden. English-style afternoon tea and cakes. €€

Rey
San José 17, Santa Eulàlia
tel: 971-330 210
Clean, well-run family boarding house, within easy reach of beach and town centre. €

FORMENTERA
Platja de Mitjorn

Hotel Formentera Playa
tel: 971-328 000
fax: 971-328 035
Located in a scenic area, with a pool, playground and cafeteria. Closed Nov–Mar. €€€€

Riu Club La Mola
tel/fax: 971-327 000
www.riu.com
In a picturesque setting, with a pool, tennis, mini-golf, children's playground and cafeteria. Closed Nov–Apr. €€€

Agua Clara
Ca Mari, Platja de Mitjorn
tel: 971-328 180.
Well-kept hotel on the beach. €€

Costa Azul
Ca Mari, Platja de Mitjorn
tel: 971-328 024
A good-quality, low-budget boarding house at the water's edge. Fine seafood restaurant. €

Platja Es Pujols

Hotel Rocabella
tel: 971-328 130
fax: 971-328 002
Situated near the beach, with a swimming pool. Closed Nov–Apr. €€–€€€

Where to Eat

Where to Eat

There is sometimes no menu visible at local bars, but you can generally ask what they have on offer and you could be pleasantly surprised with a thick home-made stew or a fresh salad with grilled fish.

There are all sorts of typical dishes on the islands, from suckling pig and tender lamb to *caldereta de langosta* (a lobster stew), *tumbet* (a kind of ratatouille) or *calamares en su tinta* (squid in a sauce of their own ink). *Paella* is ubiquitous, although it is not really an island dish.

Restaurants are listed in order of price category.

MALLORCA
Palma

Casa Gallega
Passeig Marítim 25
tel: 971-721 141
www.galinor.es
Top-quality Galician seafood restaurant. €€€

Koldo Royo
Passeig Marítim 3
tel: 971-732 435
www.koldoroyo.com
Koldo is one of the most admired chefs among gourmets. Exquisite Basque cuisine, with views of Palma Bay. Closed Sat lunch and all day Sun. €€€

Porto Pí
Carretera Joan Miró 174
tel: 971-400 087
Well-known, expensive and excellent. Serves gourmet Basque and nouvelle cuisine. Closed Sat lunch and all day Sun. €€€

Bon Lloc
Carrer Sant Feliu 7
tel: 971-718 617
Inventive vegetarian cuisine in the heart of Palma. €€–€€€

Caballito del Mar
Passeig de Sagrera 5
tel: 971-721 074
Fish cooked in sea-salt, expensive and takes time to cook, but must be tried once, with alioli. €€–€€€

Es Parlament
Conquistado 11
tel: 971-726 026

Price Guide

Approximate cost per person, not including house wine:
€€€€ = above €25
€€€ = €12–25
€€ = under €12

www.restaurantparlament.com
A favourite with politicians, and well-known for its *paella*. Beautiful interior. Closed Mon. €€–€€€

La Bóveda
Botería 3
tel: 971-714 863
www.laboveda.com
Lively *tapas* bar and restaurant. Good food; always busy. €

Outside Palma

Bens d'Avall
Urb. Costa, Deià
tel: 971-632 381
www.bensdavall.com
Spectacular location, reached by a precipitous road off the main Deià–Sóller route. French cooking with fresh produce from the Sóller valley, and excellent fish. €€€

Ca N'Olesa
Plaça Major 12, Pollença
tel: 971-532 908
Attractive old building, on the popular main square. Has a good-value lunchtime *menu del día*. €€

Ca'n Trompé
Avda Bélgica, Cala d'Or
tel: 971-657 341
Excellent authentic Mallorcan cookery – the only place you'll find it in this sprawling, sophisticated coast resort. €€

Celler C'an Ripoll
Carrer Jaune Armengol 4, Inca
tel: 971-500 024
Cosy and inviting *celler* serving good Mallorcan cuisine. The nearby Celler C'an Amer is also recommended. €€

Ses Porxeres
Carretera Palma–Sóller, km 17 (just before tunnel)
tel: 971-613 762
www.sesporxeres.com
Catalan cuisine, specialising in game dishes. Reservations essential. €€

El Barrigon
Archiduc Lluis Salvador 13, Deià
tel: 971-639139
www.xelini.com
Loud and lively, this popular place on the main road specialises in *tapas*. The stuffed squid is extremely good. €

MENORCA
El Pescador
Carrer Rosario 5, Fornells
tel: 971-376 538
Another excellent sea-front fish restaurant with a wide menu. €€–€€€

Es Pla
Passaig Es Pla, Fornells
tel: 971-376 655
One of the most popular of Fornells'
fish restaurants. The authentic
caldereta de langosta is highly
recommended. €€–€€€
Casa Manolo
Marina 117–21, Port de Ciutadella
tel: 971-380 003
One of the most popular, reliable and
longest established of the many
seafood restaurants lining the port. €€
Pilar
Forn 61, Maó
tel: 971-366 817
Menu fuses Menorcan dishes with
Asian influences. The *menú del día* is a
good deal. €€
Es Foquet
Moll de Llevant 256, Maó
tel: 971-350 058
Some of the freshest seafood in the
port, at excellent prices. Good home-
made desserts. €

EIVISSA (IBIZA)

Can Pujol
Port des Torrent, San Antoni
tel: 971-341 407
Renowned seafood restaurant at the
water's edge. The house speciality is
fish in garlic and cream sauce. €€
Celler Ca'n Pere
San Jaime 73, Santa Eulàlia
tel: 971-330 056
Reputedly the oldest restaurant in
town. Classical local specialities. €€
El Brasero
Barcelona, 4, Eivissa
tel: 971-311 469
Duck and salmon specialities. German
owned. €€
La Oliva
Santa Cruz 2, Eivissa
tel: 971-305 752
www.ibiza-restaurants.com
Fine Provençal cuisine with *Ibicenco*
touch. €€
Mesón de Paco
Bartolomé Roselló, 15,. Eivissa
tel: 971-314 224
Country-style décor, tiled walls, carved
wood furnishings. Wonderful *Ibicenco*
cooking. €€
Sausalito
Plaza Sa Riba, Eivissa
tel: 971-310 116
Elegant yet relaxed, with great French-
influenced food. €€

Price Guide

Approximate cost per person, not
including house wine:
€€€€ = above €25
€€€ = €12–25
€€ = under €12

Calendar of Events

5 January The Three Magi
Procession, Palma, Mallorca.
16–17 January St Anthony's fiesta
throughout Mallorca.
17 January Quirky and colourful
Processó d'els Tres Trocs
(Procession of the Three Knocks) in
Ciutadella, Menorca.
19 January St Stephen's fiesta in
Pollença, Mallorca.
February *Vuelta ciclista*, one of
Mallorca's biggest cycle races.
March Clay goods fair at Marratxí
(Mallorca).
April *Mostra de Cuina Mallorquina*,
culinary week, specialising in home-
grown cooking, in Palma.
Good Friday Processions
everywhere, two of the best of which
are the night *devallaments* in Sineu
and Pollença, Mallorca.
1 May Agricultural show in Sineu,
Mallorca.
9 May Brave Women of Sóller
festival in Sóller, Mallorca.
June Palma book fair.
23–4 June St John's (Sant Juan)
Fiesta in Cuitadella, Menorca.
July *Cala Ratjada* summer festival of
classical music (Mallorca).
August Chopin Festival at
Valldemossa, Mallorca.
September Procession of the Beata
in Santa Margalida, Mallorca (first
Sunday).
October Alcúdia cattle and crafts
festival, Mallorca.
November Craft fair, Inca, Mallorca.
16 December Patron saints
procession in Palma, Mallorca.

Local tourist offices have a complete
list of events.

FORMENTERA

Bergantín
Port de la Sabina
tel: 971-341 461
International menu. €€
Capri
Es Pujols
tel: 971-328 352
Seafood. €€
Truy
Es Pujols
tel: 971-325 073
International menu. €€
Casa Rafal
Sant Francesc
tel: 971-322 205
Very reasonable prices for simple rustic
cooking in a modest setting in the
heart of the village. €

Nightlife

Eivissa (Ibiza) is well known as one of
the nightlife centres of Europe, with a
clubbing scene second to none. The
resorts of Mallorca also have their fair
share, as does Palma. Menorca is
much quieter.

Nightclubs

MALLORCA

Arenal & Can Pastilla Areas
Bolero, Laud 32.
Joy Palace, Misión San Gabriel.
Makiavelo, Padre Bartolomé Salvà 3.
Riu Palace. One of the biggest and
best-known of the many discos along
Platja de Palma, between Can Pastilla
and s'Arenal.
Zorba's, Avda Son Rigo 4.

Cala Mayor Area
La Sirena. One of the oldest discos on
the island. Latest music.

Port d'Alcúdia Area
Menta. Beautiful people congregate
around the swimming pool until dawn.
Great music.

Palma
Bésame Mucho, Avda Joan Miró 3.
Perfect for a romantic evening. Slow
dancing to live music. No fee.
Club de Mar. One of the most select
discos in town.
Tito's Palace, Plaça Gomila. One of the
most modern and exclusive discos in
Europe.
Pacha, Passeig Marítimo. Beautiful
people.

Palma Nova, Magalluf & Paguera Areas
BCM. Possibly the largest disco in
Europe.

MENORCA
Jaleo, in San Luis. Beautiful
people.
Cueva d'en Xeroi, Cala d'En Porter.
Scores extra points for its original
location – inside a large cave on the
cliff face above the beach. Open nightly
10pm to dawn.
Adagio's, in Ciutadella.

Shopping

The islands all produce good **leatherware**, with footwear factories in Mallorca (particularly in the town of Inca) and Menorca, and nicely designed leather clothing everywhere.

Mallorca has **artificial pearl** and **glass-blowing** factories (especially in and around Manacor). Menorca has a well-developed **costume jewellery** industry, and produces excellent **cheese** (Queso de Mahón) and **gin**. Eivissa is known for its **fashion**, and has a large cottage-industry making **jewellery**

Locally produced **pottery** and **ceramics**, particularly cooking-vessels, are a good buy and there is a choice of good **embroidery** and **basketwork**. **Paintings** by local artists are also worth looking at, and these can be seen in galleries, or at lower prices in the flea markets.

Jazz Cava, in Maó centre. A casino turned into a disco. Live music.
Flinstones, San Jorge 10, Villacarlos.

EIVISSA (IBIZA)

The island has some of the best and most extravagant nightclubs and discos in the world. The action doesn't really get going until around 2am, when everything is possible as long as you are willing to stay up all night. Following is a list of the largest and most popular in Eivissa (Ibiza town):
Privilege, on Carrer Sant Rafael.
Pacha, on Passeig Marítimo.
El Divino, on Passeig Marítimo.
Space, on the Platja d'En Bossa. Opens when the other discos close, at dawn.

Other discos (smaller in size but more cosy) are:
Amnesia, on Carrer San Rafael.
El Dome, on Alfonso XII. Eccentric and pink.

FORMENTERA

The quietest island when it comes to nightlife, Formentera has no large discos. But there are plenty of small bars and cafés along the narrow stretch of land, and the Hotel La Mola is a good option for dancing or having a drink.

Sport

Participant Sports

All three main islands have golf, tennis, scuba, horseriding, soccer, squash, windsurfing and other popular sports available for visitors to enjoy. Formentera tends to specialise in windsurfing and watersports, including scuba diving.

Hang-gliding, go-karting and other activities, including several fun water parks, are also available. On the islands there are around 40 tennis clubs, 10 golf courses, innumerable soccer and sports grounds, and a large number of other organised sports.

The following list details various sporting bodies in the Balearics, but for more information contact local tourist offices

GOLF

The following are a few of Mallorca's most prestigious golf courses.
Capdepera Golf
Carretera Artà-Capdepera, km 3.5, tel: 971-818 500, fax: 971-818 193; www.golfcapdepera.com . Open 7am–7pm. In the east of Mallorca, with a golf school and restaurant.
Club de Golf Santa Ponça
In Torrenova, the busy headland bordering Palma Nova and Magaluf.
Pula Golf
Carretera Son Servera-Capdepera, km 3, tel: 971 817 034, fax: 971-817 035; www.pulagolf.com .
Attractive course in the east of the island.
Son Vida Club de Golf, tel: 971-791 210; www.sonvidagolf.com . In the exclusive *urbanización* of Son Vida, 5 km (3 miles) northwest of Palma.

TENNIS/SQUASH

Mallorca Tennis Club, Mestre d'Aixa, Palma, tel: 971-454 717, fax: 670 343 414, www.mallorcatenisclub.com
Elite Club, Avda. Joan Miró 334, Palma, tel: 971-402 080, www.eliteclubfitness.com

HORSERIDING

Rancho Colorado, El Arenal, Mallorca, tel: 971 264595, mobile: 607-862 447

www.rancho-colorado.com
Horse Riding School, Bunyola, Mallorca, tel: 971-613 157.

WATER-SKIING

Ski Club Calanova, Son Ferrer, Calvià, Mallorca, tel: 971-100 328.

PARACHUTING

Real Aeroclub de Baleares, Marratxí, tel: 971-600 675.

HANG-GLIDING

Club Parapente Mallorca, tel. 971-891 366.

SCUBA

Tritón. tel: 971-466 125.
Unidad Costa Norte, Calvià, Mallorca, tel: 971-102 676.

Outdoor Activities

HIKING AND CLIMBING

Hiking and climbing holidays on the islands are increasingly popular, and Mallorca in particular is perfect for dedicated hikers and novice walkers. Simple hikes in the flatter parts of the island can be undertaken alone, but guides are essential up in the Serra de Tramuntana, where walkers face differences in height of up to 1,000 metres (3,330 ft). The major dangers are sudden rainstorms and deep ravines.

There are a number of interesting hiking excursions, one of which goes from Valldemossa in Mallorca to the Puig del Teix – a six-hour walk that takes hikers to the top of the mountain with a panoramic view of Deià and the Mediterranean coast. For more information, contact one of the many tourist offices in Palma.

For information on mountain climbing call GEM, tel: 971-711 314.

CYCLING

Cyclists will encounter all levels of difficulty in Mallorca. The flat stretches of coast in the north, the nature reserve of Albufera at Alcúdia, and the island's flat interior present no trouble. The northwest coast, however, has marvellously steep parts for the particularly ambitious cyclist.

Every kind of bicycle, including mountain bikes (and even Harley-Davidson motorcycles), can be hired at the resorts. In Eivissa and Formentera, cycling is highly recommended, and presents no trouble, even for the unfit, because of their flatter topography.

BIRDWATCHING

Mallorca has a huge variety of wildlife, mainly on its neighbouring uninhabited islet of Dragonera, and in the Albufera nature reserve, in Alcúdia. Contact GOB (tel: 971-721 105) for more information.

Spectator Sports

Spaniards are avid football fans. During the winter soccer season there are games all over the islands on Sundays, and even the smaller villages have teams.

Tennis tournaments, horse-racing, car and motorcycle races, sailing regattas, handball, basketball, billiards and other competitions all have either paid or gratis entry for spectators. Bull-fighting does not have a popular following on the islands. although there are bullrings in Palma and Muro, Mallorca.

The high point of the sailing season in Mallorca is the Copa del Rey (King's Cup) in August. ,

Language

In addition to the national language of Spanish (Castilian), which is spoken throughout the country, some regions use another language. Catalan (spoken in Catalonia), Valenciano (Valencia), Mallorquín (the Balearics) and Gallego (Galicia), like French, Italian and Portuguese, are all Romance languages derived from the Latin spoken by the Romans who conquered the Iberian peninsula more than 2,000 years ago. The exception to these linguistic origins is Euskera, the language of the Basques, which is notoriously complex and difficult. Euskera is unrelated to any other Indo-european tongue, and experts are not even sure what its origins are, though some linguists now believe it may date back to the Stone Age.

The Balearic people speak a variant of Catalan, which in Mallorca is known as *mallorquí*, in Menorca as *menorquí*, and in Eivissa as *eivissenc*. These dialects differ slightly from one another in accent, local vocabulary and expressions. Their source language, Catalan, is similar to Provençal.

Interesting left-overs from the time when Britain's Royal Navy had its Mediterranean base in Menorca are words and expressions used by modern-day Menorquíans in daily conversation.

Examples:
A bow-window is called a *boinder*
A screwdriver is a *tornaescru*
A bottle becomes *bòtil*
Marbles are *mervils*
A leg of pork (shank) is *un xenc*
A black eye is *un ull blec (ull* is eye in *menorquí)*

To rap a door with your knuckles is to *toc de necles*

Following the Latin derivations that formed the basis of the Romance language of Spanish, the Muslims who settled in the peninsula centuries later contributed a great number of new words *(see panel, right)*. Following the discovery of America, Spaniards took their language with them across the globe. Today, Spanish is spoken by 250 million people in north, south and central America and parts of Africa.

Unlike English, Spanish is a phonetic language: words are pronounced exactly as they are spelt, which is why it is somewhat harder for Spaniards to learn English than vice versa (although Spanish distinguishes between the two genders, masculine and feminine, and the subjunctive verb form is an endless source of headaches for students). The English language is one of Britain's biggest exports to Spain. Spaniards spend millions on learning aids, language academies and sending their children to study English in the UK or Ireland, and are eager to practise their linguistic skills with foreign visitors. Even so, they will be flattered and delighted if you make the effort to communicate in Spanish.

Basic Rules

English is widely spoken in most tourist areas, but even if you speak no Spanish at all, it is worth trying to master a few simple words and phrases.

As a general rule, the accent falls on the second-to-last syllable, unless it is otherwise marked with an accent (´) or the word ends in D, L, R or Z.

Vowels in Spanish are always pronounced the same way. The double L (LL) is pronounced like the y in "yes", the double R is rolled. The H is silent in Spanish, whereas J (and G when it precedes an E or I) is pronounced like a guttural H (similar to the end sound of Scottish *loch*).

When addressing someone you are not familiar with, use the more formal

Islamic Connections

The Muslims arrived in Spain in AD 711, and occupied parts of the peninsula for the next eight centuries. They left behind hundreds of Arabic words, many related to farming and crops, as well as place names including those of towns (often identified by the prefix Al-, meaning "the" or Ben-, meaning "son of") and rivers (the prefix Guad-means "river"). Some of these Arabic words passed on to other languages,

including French, and from there into English.

Among those present in both Spanish and English are:
sugar *(azúcar)*, coffee *(café)*, apricot *(albaricoque)*, saffron *(azafrán)*, lemon *(limón)*, cotton *(algodón)*, alcohol *(alcohol)*, karat *(kilate)*, cipher *(cifra)*, elixir *(elixir)*, almanac *(almanaque)*, zenith *(cenit)*, and zero *(cero)*.

"usted". The informal "tú" is reserved for relatives and friends.

Words & Phrases

Hello *Hola*
How are you? *¿Cómo está usted?*
How much is it? *¿Cuánto es?*
What is your name? *¿Cómo se llama usted?*
My name is... *Yo me llamo...*
Do you speak English? *¿Habla inglés?*
I am British/American *Yo soy británico/norteamericano*
I don't understand *No comprendo*
Please speak more slowly *Hable más despacio, por favor*
Can you help me? *¿Me puede ayudar?*
I am looking for... *Estoy buscando*
Where is...? *¿Dónde está...?*
I'm sorry *Lo siento/Perdone*
I don't know *No lo se*
No problem *No hay problema*
Have a good day *Que tenga un buen día, or Vaya con Diós*
That's it *Ese es*
Here it is *Aquí está*
There it is *Allí está*
Let's go *Vámonos*
See you tomorrow *Hasta mañana*
See you soon *Hasta pronto*
Show me the word in the book *Muéstreme la palabra en el libro*
At what time? *¿A qué hora?*
When? *¿Cuándo?*
What time is it? *¿Qué hora es?*
yes/no *sí/no*
please *por favor*
thank you (very much) *(muchas) gracias*
you're welcome *de nada*
excuse me *perdóneme*
hello *hola*
OK *bien*
goodbye *adiós*
good evening/night *buenas tardes/noches*
here *aquí*
there *allí*
today *hoy*
yesterday *ayer*
tomorrow *mañana (note: mañana also means "morning")*
now *ahora*
later *después*
right away *ahora mismo*
this morning *esta mañana*
tomorrow morning *mañana por la mañana*
this afternoon *esta tarde*
this evening *esta tarde*
tonight *esta noche*

On Arrival

I want to get off at... *Quiero bajarme en...*
Is there a bus to the museum? *¿Hay un autobús al museo?*
What street is this? *¿Qué calle es ésta?*

Which line do I take for...? *¿Qué línea cojo para...?*
How far is...? *¿A qué distancia está...?*
airport *aeropuerto*
customs *aduana*
train station *estación de tren*
bus station *estación de autobuses*
metro station *estación de metro*
bus *autobús*
bus stop *parada de autobús*
platform *andén*
ticket *billete*
return ticket *billete de ida y vuelta*
hitch-hiking *auto-stop*
toilets *servicios*
This is the hotel address *Ésta es la dirección del hotel*
I'd like a (single/double) room *Quiero una habitación (sencilla/doble)*
... with shower *con ducha*
... with bath *con baño*
... with a view *con vista*
Does that include breakfast? *¿Incluye desayuno?*
May I see the room? *¿Puedo ver la habitación?*
washbasin *lavabo*
bed *cama*
key *llave*
lift/elevator *ascensor*
air conditioning *aire acondicionado*

Emergencies

Help! *¡Socorro!*
Stop! *¡Pare!/¡Alto!*
Call a doctor *Llame a un médico*
Call an ambulance *Llame a una ambulancia*
Call the police *Llame a la policia*
Call the fire brigade *Llame a los bomberos*
Where is the nearest telephone? *¿Dónde está el teléfono mas próximo?*
Where is the nearest hospital? *¿Dónde está el hospital más próximo?*
I am sick *Estoy enfermo*
I have lost my passport/purse *He perdido mi pasaporte/bolso*

On the Road

Where is the spare wheel? *¿Dónde está la rueda de repuesto?*
Where is the nearest garage? *¿Dónde está el taller más próximo?*
Our car has broken down *Nuestro coche se ha averiado*
I want to have my car repaired *Quiero que reparen mi coche*
It's not your right of way *Usted no tiene prioridad*
I think I must have put diesel in my car by mistake *Me parece que he echado gasoil por error*
the road to... *la carretera a...*
left/right *izquierda/derecha*
straight on *derecho/todo recto*
near/far *cerca/lejos*

The Alphabet

Learning the pronunciation of the Spanish alphabet is a good idea. In particular, learn how to spell out your own name. Spanish has three letters in its alphabet that don't exist in English: the "ñ", the "ch" and the "ll".

a = *ah*, **b** = *bay*, **c** = *thay* (strong th as in "thought"), **ch** = *chay*, **d** = *day*, **e** = *ay*, **f** = *effay*, **g** = *hay*, **h** = *ah-chay*, **i** = *ee*, **j** = *hotah*, **k** = *kah*, **l** = *ellay*, **ll** = *ell-yay*, **m** = *emmay*, **n** = *ennay*, **ñ** = *enyay*, **o** = *oh*, **p** = *pay*, **q** = *koo*, **r** = *erray*, **s** = *essay*, **t** = *tay*, **u** = *oo*, **v** = *oovay*, **w** = *oovay doe-blay*, **x** = *ek-kiss*, **y** = *ee gree-ay-gah*, **z** = *thay-tah*.

opposite *frente a*
beside *al lado de*
car park *aparcamiento*
over there *allí*
at the end *al final*
on foot *a pie*
by car *en coche*
town map *plano de la ciudad*
road map *plano de carreteras*
street *calle*
square *plaza*
give way *ceda el paso*
exit *salida*
dead end *calle sin salida*
wrong way *dirección prohibida*
no parking *prohibido aparcar*
motorway *autovía*
toll highway *autopista*
toll *peaje*
speed limit *límite de velocidad*
petrol/petrol station *gasolina/gasolinera*
unleaded *sin plomo*
diesel *gasoil*
water/oil *agua/aceite*
air *aire*
puncture *pinchazo*
bulb *bombilla*

On the Telephone

How do I make an outside call? *¿Cómo hago una llamada exterior?*
What is the area code? *¿Cuál es el prefijo?*
I want to make an international (local) call *Quiero hacer una llamada internacional (local)*
I'd like an alarm call for 8 tomorrow morning *Quiero que me despierten a las ocho de la mañana*
Hello? *¿Dígame?*
Who's calling? *¿Quién llama?*
Hold on, please *Un momento, por favor*
I can't hear you *No le oigo*
Can you hear me? *¿Me oye?*
He/she is not here *No está aquí*
The line is busy *La línea está ocupada*

I must have dialled the wrong number
Debo haber marcado un número equivocado

Shopping

Where is the nearest bank? *¿Dónde está el banco más próximo?*
I'd like to buy *Quiero comprar*
How much is it *¿Cuánto es?*
Do you accept credit cards? *¿Aceptan tarjetas?*
I'm just looking *Sólo estoy mirando*
Have you got...? *¿Tiene...?*
I'll take it *Me lo llevo*
I'll take this one/that one *Me llevo éste/ese*
What size is it? *¿Qué talla es?*
size (clothes) *talla*
small *pequeño*
large *grande*
cheap *barato*
expensive *caro*
enough *suficiente/bastante*
too much *demasiado*
a piece *un trozo*
each *cada una/la pieza/la unidad (eg. melones, dos euros la unidad)*
bill *la factura* (shop), *la cuenta* (restaurant)
bank *banco*
bookshop *librería*
chemist *farmacia*
hairdressers *peluquería*
post office *correos*
department store *grandes almacenes*

MARKET SHOPPING

Supermarkets *(supermercados)* are self service, but often the best and freshest produce is found at the town market *(mercado)* or at street markets *(mercadillo)*, where you place your order with the person in charge of each stand. Prices are usually by the kilo, sometimes by *gramos* (by the gram) or by *unidad* (by the piece).

fresh/frozen *fresco/congelado*
organic *biológico*
flavour *sabor*
basket *cesta*
bag *bolsa*
bakery *panadería*
butcher's *carnicería*
cake shop *pastelería*
fishmonger's *pescadería*
grocery *ultramarinos*
green grocery *verdulería*
tobacconist *estanco*
market *mercado*

Slang

¡Guay! **Great! Swell!**
Bocata **Sandwich**
Litrona **a litre-bottle of beer**
Guiri **foreigner**

supermarket *supermercado*
junk shop *tienda de segunda mano*

Sightseeing

mountain *montaña*
hill *colina*
valley *valle*
river *río*
lake *lago*
lookout *mirador*
city *ciudad*
small town, village *pueblo*
old town/quarter *casco antiguo*
monastery *monasterio*
convent *convento*
cathedral *catedral*
church *iglesia*
palace *palacio*
hospital *hospital*
town hall *ayuntamiento*
nave *nave*
statue *estatua*
fountain *fuente*
staircase *escalera*
tower *torre*
castle *castillo*
Iberian *ibérico*
Phoenician *fenicio*
Roman *romano*
Muslim *árabe*
Romanesque *románico*
Gothic *gótico*
museum *museo*
art gallery *galería de arte*
exhibition *exposición*
tourist information office *oficina de turismo*
free *gratis*
open *abierto*
closed *cerrado*
every day *diario/todos los días*
all year *todo el año*
all day *todo el día*
swimming pool *piscina*
to book *reservar*

Dining Out

In Spanish, *el menú* is not the main menu, but a fixed menu at a lower price. The main menu is *la carta*.

breakfast *desayuno*
lunch *comida*
dinner/supper *cena*
meal *comida*
first course *primer plato*
main course *plato principal*
made to order *hecho por encargo*
drink included *bebida incluida*
wine list *carta de vinos*
the bill *la cuenta*
fork *tenedor*
knife *cuchillo*
spoon *cuchara*
plate *plato*
glass *vaso*
wine glass *copa*
napkin *servilleta*

ashtray *cenicero*
waiter, please! *camarero, por favor*

Liquid Refreshment

coffee *café*
   black *sólo*
   with milk *con leche/cortado*
   decaffeinated *descafeinado*
sugar *azúcar*
tea *té*
herbal tea *infusión*
milk *leche*
mineral water *agua mineral*
   fizzy *con gas*
   still *sin gas*
juice (fresh) *zumo (natural)*
cold *fresco/frío*
hot *caliente*
beer *cerveza*
   bottled *en botella*
   on tap *de barril*
soft drink *refresco*
diet drink *bebida "light"*
with ice *con hielo*
wine *vino*
   red *tinto*
   white *blanco*
   rosé *rosado*
   dry *seco*
   sweet *dulce*
house wine *vino de la casa*
sparkling wine *vino espumoso*
Where is this wine from? *¿De dónde es este vino?*
pitcher *jarra*
half litre *medio litro*
quarter litre *cuarto de litro*
cheers! *¡salud!*
hangover *resaca*

Menu Decoder

BREAKFAST AND SNACKS

pan **bread**
bollo **bun/roll**
mantequilla **butter**
mermelada/confitura **jam**
pimienta **pepper**
sal **salt**
azúcar **sugar**
huevos **eggs**
   cocidos **boiled, cooked**
   con beicon **with bacon**
   con jamón **with ham**
   escalfados **poached**
   fritos **fried**
   revueltos **scrambled**
yogur **yoghurt**
tostada **toast**
sandwich **sandwich in square slices of bread**
bocadillo **sandwich in a bread roll**

MAIN COURSES
Meat/Carne

buey **beef**
carne picada **ground meat**

Numbers, Days and Dates

Numbers

0	cero
1	uno
2	dos
3	tres
4	cuatro
5	cinco
6	seis
7	siete
8	ocho
9	nueve
10	diez
11	once
12	doce
13	trece
14	catorce
15	quince
16	dieciseis
17	diecisiete
18	dieciocho
19	diecinueve
20	veinte
21	veintiuno
30	treinta
40	cuarenta
50	cincuenta
60	sesenta
70	setenta
80	ochenta
90	noventa
100	cien
200	doscientos
500	quinientos
1,000	mil
10,000	diez mil

1,000,000 *un millón*

Saying the Date

20 October 2003, *el veinte de octubre del dos mil tres* (no capital letters are used for days or months)

Days of the week

Monday *lunes*
Tuesday *martes*
Wednesday *miércoles*
Thursday *jueves*
Friday *viernes*
Saturday *sábado*
Sunday *domingo*

Seasons

Spring *primavera*
Summer *verano*
Autumn *otoño*
Winter *invierno*
Months
January *enero*
February *febrero*
March *marzo*
April *abril*
May *mayo*
June *junio*
July *julio*
August *agosto*
September *septiembre*
October *octubre*
November *noviembrè*
December *diciembre*

---

cerdo **pork**
cabrito **kid**
chorizo **paprika sausage**
chuleta **chop**
cochinillo **roast pig**
conejo **rabbit**
cordero **lamb/mutton**
costilla **rib**
entrecot **beef rib steak**
filete **fillet steak**
jabalí **wild boar**
jamón **ham**
jamón cocido **cooked ham**
jamón serrano **cured ham**
lengua **tongue**
morcilla **black pudding**
pierna **leg**
riñones **kidneys**
salchichón **sausage**
solomillo **sirloin steak**
ternera **veal or young beef**
a la brasa **charcoal grilled**
al horno **roast**
a la plancha **griddled**
asado **roast**
bien hecho **well done**
en salsa **in sauce**
en su punto **medium**
estofado **stew**
frito **fried**
pinchito **skewered snack**

poco hecho **rare**
relleno **stuffed**

Fowl/Aves

codorniz **quail**
faisán **pheasant**
pavo **turkey**
pato **duck**
perdiz **partridge**
pintada **guinea fowl**
pollo **chicken**

Fish/Pescado

anchoas **salted anchovies**
anguila **eel**
atún **tuna**
bacalao **salt cod**
besugo **red bream**
boquerones **fresh anchovies**
caballa **mackerel**
calamar **squid**
cangrejo **crab**
caracola **sea snail**
cazón **dogfish**
centollo **spider crab**
chopito **baby cuttlefish**
cigala **Dublin Bay prawn/scampi**
dorada **gilt head bream**
gamba **shrimps/prawns**
jibia/sepia **cuttlefish**
langosta bogavante **lobster**

langosta **crayfish**
langostino **large prawn**
lenguado **sole**
lubina **sea bass**
mariscada **mixed shellfish**
mariscos **shellfish**
mejillón **mussels**
merluza **hake**
ostión **Portuguese oyster**
ostra **oyster**
peregrina **scallop**
pez espada **swordfish**
pulpo **octopus**
rape **monkfish**
rodaballo **turbot**
salmón **salmon**
salmonete **red mullet**
sardina **sardine**
trucha **trout**

VEGETABLES/CEREALS/SALADS

verduras **vegetables**
ajo **garlic**
alcachofa **artichoke**
apio **celery**
arroz **rice**
berenjena **aubergine/eggplant**
brocolí **broccoli**
calabacín **courgette/zuccini**
cebolla **onion**
champiñón **mushroom**
col **cabbage**
coliflor **cauliflower**
ensalada **salad**
espárrago **asparagus**
espinaca **spinach**
guisante **pea**
haba **broad bean**
judía **green bean**
lechuga **lettuce**
lenteja **lentil**
maíz **corn/maize**
menestra **cooked mixed vegetables**
patata **potato**
pepino **cucumber**
pimiento **pepper**
puerro **leek**
rábano **radish**
seta **wild mushroom**
tomate **tomato**
zanahoria **carrot**

FRUIT AND DESSERTS

fruta **fruta**
aguacate **avocado**
albaricoque **apricot**
cereza **cherry**
ciruela **plum**
frambuesa **raspberry**
fresa **strawberry**
granada **pomegranate**
higo **fig**
limón **lemon**
mandarina **tangerine**
manzana **apple**
melocotón **peach**

melón **melon**
naranja **orange**
pera **pear**
piña **pineapple**
plátano **banana**
pomelo **grapefruit**
sandía **watermelon**
uva **grape**
postre **dessert**
tarta **pie**
pastel **cake**
helado **ice cream**
natillas **custard**
queso **cheese**

HERBS & SPICES

albahaca **basil**
azafrán **saffron**
cilantro **coriander/cilantro**
comino **cumin**
cúrcuma **turmeric**
hierbabuena **mint**
orégano **oregano**
perejil **parsley**
pimentón **paprika**
polvo de curry **curry powder**
romero **rosemary**
salvia **sage**
tomillo **thyme**

Catalan

Catalonia, and to a much lesser extent Valencia, is bilingual in Castilian (Spanish) and Catalan or Valenciano. Everybody in the main cities can speak Spanish, but Catalans in particular prefer to speak their own language.

Catalan is a fully fledged Romance language, closer to Provençal French and Occitanian or Langue d'Oc than to the Iberian language group, which includes Spanish, Portuguese and Gallego. Its teaching and publication were banned during the Franco era and it has since undergone a resurgence.

It is used in conversation, in business and in the media. Most books are in Catalan. All street and place names have been changed to Catalan and any remaining notice in Castilian Spanish may well have *En*

Table Talk

I am a vegetarian *Soy vegetariano*
I am on a diet *Estoy a régimen*
What do you recommend? *¿Qué recomienda?*
Do you have local specialities? *¿Hay especialidades locales?*
I'd like to order *Quiero pedir*
That is not what I ordered *Esto no es lo que he pedido*
May I have more wine? *¿Me da más vino?*
Enjoy your meal *Buen provecho*

Català scrawled across it, for language is a vital part of Catalan nationalism.

A few Catalan words and phrases:
Good morning *Bon dia*
Good evening *Bona tarda*
Hello/Goodbye *Hola/Adéu*
Please *Si us plau*
Thank you *Gràcies/Merci*
You're welcome *De res*
How much is? *Quant val?*
Where is? *On està?*
At what time? *A quina hora?*
Open/Closed *Obert/Tancat*
Where can I change money? *On puc canviar moneda?*
What's your name? *Com us diu?*
My name is... *Em dic...*
Pleased to meet you *Molt de gust*
Do you have any rooms? *Per favor tenen habitacions lliures?*

Further Reading

General

Los Andaluces. Madrid: Ediciones Istmo, 1980. Collection of wide-ranging essays on the people, their history, economy and culture to the present day.

The Art of Flamenco, by D.E. Pohren. Musical New Services Ltd, 1984. The aficionado's bible.

A Way of Life. Madrid: Society of Spanish Studies, 1980. Colourful, humorous account of a disappearing Andalusian lifestyle.

As I Walked Out One Midsummer Morning, by Laurie Lee. Penguin, 1983. Romantic young man's vision of pre-Civil War Spain. Also by Lee **A Rose for Winter**. Penguin, 1983. Lee's post-war return to Andalusia.

The Assassination of Federico García Lorca, by Ian Gibson. Penguin, 1983. Banned by Franco because it revealed the truth about Lorca's death.

Federico García Lorca: A Life, by Ian Gibson. Faber & Faber, 1989. Award-winning biography.

The Bible in Spain, by George Borrow. First published 1842. Eccentric, opinionated and entertaining.

La Civilización Hispano-árabe by Titus Burckhardt. (Original title: *Die maurische Kultur in Spanien.* Munich: Verlag Georg D.W. Callwey, 1970.) Madrid: Alianza Editorial, 1977. Examination of Moorish culture.

Cooking in Spain, by Janet Mendel. Fuengirola, Málaga: Santana. Details of many typical Andalusian dishes.

Los Curiosos Impertinentes, by Ian Robertson. Published in Spanish by Serbal, 1988. English travellers' adventures in and comments on Spain between 1760 and 1855.

Death in the Afternoon, by Ernest Hemingway. (1932).

Death's Other Kingdom, by Gamel Woolsey. Virago Press, 1988. Vivid account of outbreak of Civil War by this American poet, the wife of Gerald Brenan.

Handbook for Travellers in Spain, by Richard Ford. Centaur Press, 1966; and *Gatherings from Spain*. Dent Everyman, 1970. Classic 19th-century travels.

Here in Spain, by David Mitchell. Fuengirola, Málaga: Lookout Publications. Views of foreign travellers through the centuries.

Histoire de l'Espagne Musulmane, by

Travellers' Tales

Although Spain did not figure in the Grand Tour of the early tourists, from the 19th century it attracted a succession of foreign travellers in search of the "exotic" such as Henry Swinburne, Joseph Townsend, and Richard Ford. Ford did the most to awaken interest in the region with witty and shrewdly observed accounts of his travels between 1830–1833.

In the 20th century, Gerald Brenan, who lived much of his life in Andalusia, stands out as a writer whose great affection for the region did not diminish his critical faculties.

Evariste Lévi-Provencale. Three volumes. Erudite history of Spain under the Moors.

In Hiding: The Life of Manuel Cortes, by Ronald Fraser. Penguin, 1982. How a village mayor stayed hidden for 30 years for fear of execution.

Inside Andalusia – A Travel Adventure in Southern Spain, by David Baird. Fuengirola, Málaga: Lookout Publications, 1988. Informative account of Andalusia and its people, well illustrated.

Los Moriscos del Reino de Granada, by Julio Caro Baroja. Madrid: Ediciones Istmo, 1985. One of Spain's foremost historians relates the last days of the Moors of Granada.

The Modern State of Spain, by J.F. Bourgoing. (1808).

Or I'll Dress You in Mourning, by Larry Collins and Dominique Lapierre. Simon & Schuster, 1968. Brilliantly documented insights into Spain's post-Civil War hardships which moulded the Andalusian matador El Cordobés.

The People of the Sierra, by Julian A. Pitt-Rivers. Weidenfield & Nicolson, 1954. Social anthropologist's dissection of a remote mountain community.

The Pueblo: A Mountain Village in Spain, by Ronald Fraser. Pantheon. Villagers of Mijas tell their own story.

The Presence of Spain, by James Morris. (1964, reissued as *Spain* by Jan Morris).

The Road from Ronda, by Alastair Boyd. Collins, 1969. Vivid account of a horse-ride through the Serranía de Ronda.

A Romantic in Spain, by Théophile Gautier. (1926, first published 1845 as *Voyage en Espagne*).

South from Granada, by Gerald Brenan. Cambridge University Press, 1988. Classic account of life in a remote Granada village. Also by Brenan **The Face of Spain**. Penguin, 1987.

Brenan's grim view of an impoverished post-war Spain.

The Spaniards: *A Portrait of the New Spain*, by John Hooper. (1986).

A Spanish Raggle-Taggle, by Walter Starkie. (1934).

Tales of the Alhambra, by Washington Irving. Granada: Miguel Sánchez. Legends and colourful view of Granada in the early 19th century.

Tartessos, by Adolph Schulten. Madrid: Espasa-Calpe. Controversial attempt to establish the site of Tartessos near the mouth of the Guadalquivir.

Travels into Spain, Mme d'Aulnoy. (1930, first published 1691).

White Wall of Spain, by Allen Josephs. Iowa State University Press. Fascinating examination of Andalusia's roots and the creation of a unique culture.

Other Insight Guides

Other Insight Guides which highlight destinations in this region include:

Insight Guide: Southern Spain is your key to Andalusia, often regarded as the soul of the country.

Insight Guide: Northern Spain Discover "Green Spain", including the Pyrenees, Galicia, Asturias and the Basque Country.

Insight Guide: Barcelona explores the trendy cosmopolitan city, which is the largest in the Mediterranean.

Insight Guide: Madrid covers Spain's big city and its cultural capital in glorious colour.

Insight Pocket Guides

Insight Pocket Guides will take you straight to the best of the Spanish cities in day-by-day itineraries specially created by local hosts. They include a full-size fold-out map which can be used independently of the book. Titles in this series include: **Madrid, Barcelona, Bilbao & Northwest Spain, Costa Brava, Ibiza, Mallorca, Costa del Sol, Gran Canaria** and **Tenerife**.

Insight Compact Guides

Insight Compact Guides: Barcelona, Costa Brava, Gran Canaria, Ibiza, Madrid, Mallorca, Marbella/Costa del Sol, Menorca and **Tenerife** are just some of titles taken from Apa Publications' third series of guidebooks. These mini-encyclopaedias are packed with facts, photographs and maps, all carefully cross-referenced, and are the ideal easy-reference books for practical use on the spot.

Insight Flexi Maps

These maps combine clear cartography with useful travel information and come in an easy-to-fold, rain-resistant laminated finish. Spanish titles in this series include: **Barcelona, Costa Blanca, Costa Brava, Mallorca, Menorca, Ibiza, Madrid, Seville, Gran Canaria** and **Tenerife**.

ART & PHOTO CREDITS

AGE **Fotostock** 52L&R, 77, 103, 130T, 257, 259, 340/341
AKG 193T
AISA 4/5, 87, 142, 144, 153, 200, 280, 281, 304, 308, 311, 325, 328T, 329
Oriol Alamany 94
M Angeles Sanchez 167, 240, 241
Archivo Océano 215
Gonzalo M Azumendi 6/7, 68/69, 151, 157, 165, 179, 284/285, 286, 289, 290, 291, 292, 293, 294, 295, 299, 300, 305, 306, 307, 312, back cover left, spine top
David Baird 104
G Barone 198, 201, 213, 267
F Lisa Beebe 102, 105, 196, 214, 228, 240T
Dani Codina 250
Cover/Santos Cirilo 75
Cover/X. Gómez 177, 256L
Cover/Sofia Moro 61
Doug Corrance 224T
Courtesy of Instituto Geografico Nacional 16/17
J D Dallet 56, 130, 148, 162T, 171, 173, 178, 184, 188/187, 195, 223, 226, 232/233, 235, 237, 242T&B, 245T, 287, 294T, 317, 319, 320, 324
Courtesy of Pedro Domecq 222
Andrew Eames 35, 44
Annabel Elston 251, 252, 252T, 253, 255L&R, 255T, 260, 261, 261T, 262, 263, 263T, back cover centre, back flap top
Europa Press Reportajes 53
Expo Tenerife 333, 337
Muriel Feiner 78, 82, 83, back cover bottom
Albert Fortuny 174
Wolfgang Fritz 140T
Jaume Gual 127
Glyn Genin 109, 342, 343, 345, 347, 348T, back flap bottom
Blaine Harrington 71, 72, 79, 80, 120, 165, 180, 302
Dallas & John Heaton 197
Dave G Houser 14
Imagen 3 22, 28, 29, 32, 59, 62, 327
Imagen MAS 149, 150, 152T, 156, 161, 172, 175, 176, 181, 182, 183,

185, 234, 246, 247, 282T&B, 283, 301, 313, 314, 315
Nick Inman 238L&R, 239, 244, 245
Index 116/117, 339
Veronica Janssen 1, 326
Michael Jenner 134
Jean Kugler 122/123, 162, 205, 211, front flap top
Rita Kummel 81, 269, 298
Antonio Lafuente 107
Lyle Lawson 65, 158T&B, 160T, 288T, 292T, 300T, 303, 304T, 308T, 310, 313T, 314T, 316, 322T&B
Alain Le Garsmeur 95, 219
Jose Lucas 190, 352
M+W Fine Arts/New York/José Martin 24, 37, 40
Fiona MacGregor 131, 133
José Martin 23, 25, 30, 38, 41, 43, 45, 46/47, 48, 49, 54, 55, 84/85, 86, 90, 91, 93, 129T, 134, 134T, 143L&R, 145, 145T, 147, 149T, 159, 279T, 321
Mike Mockler 96, 98, 99
Robert Mort 106, 108
Museu d'Art Modern 92
National Maritime Museum 39
Gary John Norman 334T, 336T
Richard Nowitz 164
Oronoz Archivo Fotografico 34, 58
Patronat de Catalunya 276
Andrea Pistolesi 146, 169, 279
Jens Poulsen 57
Carl Purcell 26, 100, 128, 129, 140, 155
Mark Read 8/9, 76, 114/115, 194T, 196T, 199T, 200T, 204B&T, 206T, 207T, 211T, 212T, 214T, 222T, 225, 227T, 229B&T, 230T, spine bottom
Jörg Reuther 336, 338
Martin Rosefeldt 137T, 138T
Servei Fotografic M.A.C 88
Jeroen Snijders 268T, 270T, 272B&T, 274B&T, 275B&T **Spectrum** 330/331
Martinez Tajadura 154L&R, 163, 271, 346
Roger Tidman 97
Klaus Thiele 195T
Topham Picturepoint 64, 135, 290T, 302T
Robin Townsend 21, 256R

Bill Wassman 2/3, 10/11, 12/13, 20, 27, 66/67, 73, 112/113, 126, 132, 134L, 136, 137, 138, 139, 140, 141, 147T, 170, 191, 193, 194, 199, 201, 203, 205, 207, 209, 218, 221, 227, 230, 231, 254, 256T, 266, 273, 323, 328, 332, 348, 349, 351, front flap bottom, back cover right
Roger Williams 50, 258
George Wright 207, 212

Picture Spreads

Pages 110/111: Top row left to right: J D Dallet, Gonzalo M Azumendi, M Angeles Sanchez, Ellen Rooney; Centre row: AISA, M Angeles Sanchez, Imagen MAS; Bottom row: Imagen MAS, AISA
Pages 186/187: Top row: Imagen MAS, AISA, Andrea Pistolesi, Imagen MAS; Centre row: J D Dallet, Imagen MAS; Bottom row: Imagen MAS, Imagen MAS, AISA
Pages 216/217: Top row: Mark Read, AISA, Jose Lucas, Jose Lucas; Centre row: Jose Lucas; Bottom row: Jose Lucas, Jose Lucas, Mark Read, Jose Lucas, Mark Read
Pages 264/265: Top row: AR/Gau, AISA, J D Dallet, AR/Gau; Centre row: J D Dallet; Bottom row: AR/Gau, J D Dallet, AR/Gau, Ellen Rooney
Pages 296/297: Top row: Inaki Andres, Guggenheim Bilbao/Erika Barahona Ede, Mitxi-Miguel Calvo, Roger Williams; Centre row: Inaki Andres; Bottom row: Carlos Garcia, Mitxi-Miguel Calvo, Inaki Andres
Maps Colourmap Scanning Ltd
© 2006 Apa Publications GmbH & Co. Verlag KG (Singapore branch)

INSIGHT GUIDE
Spain

Cartographic Editor **Zoë Goodwin**
Design Consultants
Carlotta Junger, Graham Mitchener
Picture Research **Hilary Genin, Monica Allende**

A
B
C
D
E
F
G
H
I
J
a
b
c
d
e
f
g
h
i
j
k
l

※ INSIGHT GUIDES

The world's largest collection of visual travel guides & maps

A range of guides and maps to meet every travel need

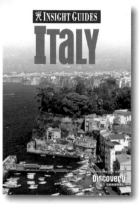

Insight Guides

This classic series gives you the complete picture of a destination through expert, well written and informative text and stunning photography. Each book is an ideal background information and travel planner, serves as an on-the-spot companion – and is a superb visual souvenir of a trip. **Nearly 200 titles**.

Insight Pocket Guides

focus on the best choices for places to see and things to do, picked by our local correspondents. They are ideal for visitors new to a destination. To help readers follow the routes easily, the books contain full-size pull-out maps. **125 titles.**

Insight Maps

are designed to complement the guides. They provide full mapping of major cities, regions and countries, and their laminated finish makes them easy to fold and gives them durability. **133 titles.**

Insight Compact Guides

are convenient, comprehensive reference books, modestly priced. The text, photographs and maps are all carefully cross-referenced, making the books ideal for on-the-spot use when in a destination. **133 titles.**

Different travellers have different needs. Since 1970, Insight Guides has been meeting these needs with a range of practical and stimulating guidebooks and maps

INSIGHT GUIDES

The classic series that puts you in the picture

※ INSIGHT GUIDES

The world's largest collection of visual travel guides & maps